For additional copies of Ohio Arrest, Search 1-800-328-9352 or fill out and return this postage-paid card.

✓ Yes!

Please send me ___ additional copy(ies) of the 1996 Edition of *Ohio Arrest, Search & Seizure.*

Also, please provide information on:

___ *Ohio Criminal Justice*

___ *Ohio Driving Under the Influence Law*

___ *Schroeder-Katz, Ohio Criminal Law and Practice*

___ *Ohio Rules of Court, State and Federal*

___ *Ohio Appellate Practice*

___ *Baldwin's Ohio Practice, Evidence, by Giannelli and Snyder*

___ *Ohio Juvenile Law*

___ *Drug Laws of Ohio, Official Edition*

Name_____ Date _____

Address _____

City_____ State_____ Zip_____

Phone _____

Affiliation _____

BANKS BALDWIN
LAW PUBLISHING COMPANY
A West Publishing Affiliated Company

© 1996 Banks-Baldwin Law Publishing Company 6-9469-6/2-96 608318
West products available through Banks-Baldwin in Ohio and Kentucky.
1-220-577-5

For information on related books from Banks-Baldwin, call 1-800-328-9352 or fill out and return this postage-paid card.

Please contact me regarding:

___ *Ohio Criminal Justice*

___ *Ohio Driving Under the Influence Law*

___ *Schroeder-Katz,Ohio Criminal Law and Practice*

___ *Ohio Rules of Court, State and Federal*

___ *Ohio Appellate Practice*

___ *Baldwin's Ohio Practice, Evidence, by Giannelli and Snyder*

___ *Ohio Juvenile Law*

___ *Drug Laws of Ohio, Official Edition*

Name_____ Date _____

Address _____

City_____ State_____ Zip_____

Phone _____

Affiliation _____

BANKS BALDWIN
LAW PUBLISHING COMPANY
A West Publishing Affiliated Company

© 1996 Banks-Baldwin Law Publishing Company 6-9469-6/2-96 608318
West products available through Banks-Baldwin in Ohio and Kentucky.
1-220-577-5

BUSINESS REPLY MAIL
FIRST CLASS MAIL   PERMIT NO. 545   CLEVELAND, OH

POSTAGE WILL BE PAID BY ADDRESSEE

BANKS-BALDWIN LAW PUBLISHING COMPANY
ATTN: MARKETING DEPARTMENT
6111 OAK TREE BLVD
PO BOX 318063
CLEVELAND OH 44131-9747

BUSINESS REPLY MAIL
FIRST CLASS MAIL   PERMIT NO. 545   CLEVELAND, OH

POSTAGE WILL BE PAID BY ADDRESSEE

BANKS-BALDWIN LAW PUBLISHING COMPANY
ATTN: MARKETING DEPARTMENT
6111 OAK TREE BLVD
PO BOX 318063
CLEVELAND OH 44131-9747

OHIO ARREST, SEARCH AND SEIZURE

Baldwin's
OHIO
HANDBOOK
SERIES

by
Lewis R.
Katz

1996 Edition

Banks-Baldwin Law Publishing Company
A West Publishing Affiliated Company

For information, please call or write:

Banks-Baldwin Law Publishing Company
6111 Oak Tree Boulevard
P.O. Box 318063
Cleveland, Ohio 44131

800/362-4500

WEST'S COMMITMENT TO THE ENVIRONMENT
In 1906, West Publishing Company began recycling materials left over from the production of books. This began a tradition of efficient and responsible use of resources. Today, 100% of our legal bound volumes are printed on acid-free, recycled paper consisting of 50% new paper pulp and 50% paper that has undergone a de-inking process. We also use vegetable-based inks to print all of our books. West recycles nearly 22,650,000 pounds of scrap paper annually—the equivalent of 187,500 trees. Since the 1960s, West has devised ways to capture and recycle waste inks, solvents, oils, and vapors created in the printing process. We also recycle plastics of all kinds, wood, glass, corrugated cardboard, and batteries, and have eliminated the use of polystyrene book packaging. We at West are proud of the longevity and the scope of our commitment to the environment.

West pocket parts and advance sheets are printed on recyclable paper and can be collected and recycled with the newspapers. Staples do not have to be removed. Bound volumes can be recycled after removing the cover.

ISBN 0-8322-0629-6

1995 Edition: Copyright 1994, by Banks-Baldwin Law Publishing Company, a West Publishing Affiliated Company.
Third Edition: Copyright 1992, by Banks-Baldwin Law Publishing Company.
Second Edition: Copyright 1987, by Banks-Baldwin Law Publishing Company.
First Edition: Copyright 1984, by Banks-Baldwin Law Publishing Company.

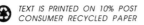 *TEXT IS PRINTED ON 10% POST CONSUMER RECYCLED PAPER*  Printed with Printwise Environmentally Advanced Water Washable Ink

OHIO ARREST, SEARCH AND SEIZURE

Baldwin's
OHIO
HANDBOOK
SERIES

by
Lewis R.
Katz

1996 Edition

Banks-Baldwin Law Publishing Company
A West Publishing Affiliated Company

For information, please call or write:

Banks-Baldwin Law Publishing Company
6111 Oak Tree Boulevard
P.O. Box 318063
Cleveland, Ohio 44131

800/362-4500

WEST'S COMMITMENT TO THE ENVIRONMENT

In 1906, West Publishing Company began recycling materials left over from the production of books. This began a tradition of efficient and responsible use of resources. Today, 100% of our legal bound volumes are printed on acid-free, recycled paper consisting of 50% new paper pulp and 50% paper that has undergone a de-inking process. We also use vegetable-based inks to print all of our books. West recycles nearly 22,650,000 pounds of scrap paper annually—the equivalent of 187,500 trees. Since the 1960s, West has devised ways to capture and recycle waste inks, solvents, oils, and vapors created in the printing process. We also recycle plastics of all kinds, wood, glass, corrugated cardboard, and batteries, and have eliminated the use of polystyrene book packaging. We at West are proud of the longevity and the scope of our commitment to the environment.

West pocket parts and advance sheets are printed on recyclable paper and can be collected and recycled with the newspapers. Staples do not have to be removed. Bound volumes can be recycled after removing the cover.

ISBN 0-8322-0629-6

1995 Edition: Copyright 1994, by Banks-Baldwin Law Publishing Company,
    a West Publishing Affiliated Company.
Third Edition: Copyright 1992, by Banks-Baldwin Law Publishing Company.
Second Edition: Copyright 1987, by Banks-Baldwin Law Publishing Company.
First Edition: Copyright 1984, by Banks-Baldwin Law Publishing Company.

 *TEXT IS PRINTED ON 10% POST CONSUMER RECYCLED PAPER*  Printed with Printwise Environmentally Advanced Water Washable Ink

Dedication

To my Mother and Father

Preface

I continue to be the beneficiary of valuable correspondence from judges, lawyers, police officers, and students who call cases and trends to my attention. I am very grateful to them and to those who have let me know when they have disagreed with my analysis or conclusions in previous editions of this book. I hope that you will continue to write to me. This correspondence has helped to broaden my understanding of this area of the law which I consider to be the most important in shaping American freedom and our society's response to the serious problems of crime and violence.

Since I began work on the first edition of this book over a decade ago, I have been blessed with able and hard-working research assistants who have given me some of their scarce time during their student years at Case Western Reserve University School of Law. I want to thank Andrew Agati ('95) for his assistance in the preparation of this edition.

L. R. Katz

Cleveland, Ohio
February 1996

Foreword

In this 1996 Edition, Professor Lewis R. Katz, Professor of Law at Case Western Reserve University and a nationally known expert on the Fourth Amendment, updates and revises his thorough and practical guide to the law of search and seizure, interrogation and confession, and pretrial identification as defined by the United States Supreme Court, the Ohio criminal rules, the Ohio criminal statutes, and state case law, including unreported appellate decisions.

Focusing on questions and issues that routinely confront judges, prosecutors, defense attorneys, law enforcement officials, teachers, and students, this book has become a basic reference on Ohio criminal procedure. Complete through the 1994-95 term of the U.S. Supreme Court, it explains new trends and developments, while dealing with the facts and holdings of nearly 800 cases.

In addition, for this 1996 Edition, Professor Katz has written a new chapter (Chapter 15) on "Traffic Stops and Their Aftermath," detailing the struggle of Ohio courts to create standards that protect Fourth Amendment rights while also accommodating legitimate law enforcement needs. Topics include vehicle stops, traffic offenses, expansion to other offenses, searches incident to non-custodial traffic arrest, license, safety and registration checks, and highway sobriety checkpoint stops.

Other areas of new or expanded coverage in the 1996 Edition include:

- An overview of the Ohio Courts' recent ventures into Fourth Amendment jurisprudence, T 1.01

- U.S. Supreme Court limitations on habeas corpus in relation to claims arising out of *Miranda* violations, T 2.04

- Expansion of the good faith exception to the exclusionary rule, per *Arizona v Evans*, T 2.05

- Causal connection with a constitutional violation required for suppression of derivative evidence, T 2.07(B), (C)

- Federal constitutional requirements and Ohio statutory guidelines for forced entry of a residence, T 7.02

- An alternative to a pretextual challenge of a traffic stop, T 11.05

- Investigative stops in high crime areas, per *State v Carter*, T 14.03(B)

- Further delineation of guidelines for a pat-down weapons search, T 14.04

- Limitations on a warrantless regulatory search of a business in a pervasively regulated industry, T 16.04

- Drug testing of school children, per *Veronia School District v Acton*, T 16.05(B)(4)

- Probationer and parolee searches, per *Griffin v Wisconsin*, T 16.05(E), and

- Validity of a *Miranda* waiver for a mentally unstable defendant, T 19.09(C).

A Table of Cases, Table of Laws and Rules, and a detailed Subject Index provide easy access to the Text; a Bibliography cites law review articles and other sources for further research; and Checklists offer quick access to arrest, search, and seizure requirements.

We acknowledge with appreciation the contributions of our editorial, indexing, and production staffs—especially Susan Adams, Deborah Burns, Shano Cica-Mraz, L. John Matthews, Paulette Simonetta, and Kelly Weissfeld—in preparing this edition for publication.

Please contact us with your comments and suggestions for future improvements to the publication.

The Publisher

Cleveland, Ohio
February 1996

Table of Contents

APPENDICES

INDEX

Abbreviations

A	Atlantic Reporter
A(2d)	Atlantic Reporter, Second Series
ABF Res J	American Bar Foundation Research Journal
Abs	Ohio Law Abstract
aff	affirmed by or affirming
Akron L Rev	Akron Law Review
Alb L Rev	Albany Law Review
ALI	American Law Institute
ALR	American Law Reports Annotated
ALR2d	American Law Reports Annotated, Second Series
ALR3d	American Law Reports Annotated, Third Series
ALR4th	American Law Reports Annotated, Fourth Series
ALR Fed	American Law Reports Annotated, Federal
Am	Amended
Am Bar Assn Jour	American Bar Association Journal
Am Crim L Rev	American Criminal Law Review
Am Dec	American Decisions
Am J Crim L	American Journal of Criminal Law
Am Jur	American Jurisprudence
Am Jur 2d	American Jurisprudence, Second Series
Am Rep	American Reports
Annot	Annotation
App	Appellate Court
App	Ohio Appellate Reports
App(2d)	Ohio Appellate Reports, Second Series
App(3d)	Ohio Appellate Reports, Third Series
App R	Rules of Appellate Procedure
Ark	Arkansas Reports
Ariz	Arizona Reports
Ariz L Rev	Arizona Law Review
Army Law	Army Lawyer
Assn	Association
B	Weekly Law Bulletin
Bankr	Bankruptcy Reporter
BCL Rev	Boston College Law Review
Bd	Board
Bldg	Building
Bull	Ohio Law Bulletin
BUL Rev	Boston University Law Review
Cal(2d)	California Reports, Second Series
Cal(3d)	California Reports, Third Series
Cal App(3d)	California Appellate Reports, Third Series
Cal Rptr	West's California Reporter
Cal W L Rev	California Western Law Review
Canada USLJ	Canada—United States Law Journal

Capital U Law Rev	Capital University Law Review
Case WRU Law Rev	Case Western Reserve Law Review
CC	Ohio Circuit Court Reports
CC(NS)	Ohio Circuit Court Reports, New Series
CCA	United States Circuit Court of Appeals
CCR	Ohio Court of Claims Rules
CD	Ohio Circuit Decisions
cert	Certiorari
Cf	Compare
Ch	Chapter
Chi L Rev	Chicago Law Review
Cin L Rev	Cincinnati Law Review
Cir	Circuit Court
Civ R	Rules of Civil Procedure
CJS	Corpus Juris Secundum
Clev Bar Jour	Cleveland Bar Journal
Clev L Rec	Cleveland Law Record
Clev L Reg	Cleveland Law Register
Clev L Rep	Cleveland Law Reporter
Clev Mar L R	Cleveland-Marshall Law Review
Clev St L Rev	Cleveland State Law Review
Co	Company
Colo	Colorado Reports
Colo L Rev	Colorado Law Review
Colum L Rev	Columbia Law Review
Comm	Commission
Commr	Commissioner
Conn Bar J	Connecticut Bar Journal
Const	Constitution
Cornell L Rev	Cornell Law Review
Corp	Corporation
CP	Common Pleas Court
CP Sup R	Rules of Superintendence for Court of Common Pleas
Creighton L Rev	Creighton Law Review
Crim Just Ethics	Criminal Justice Ethics
Crim L Bull	Criminal Law Bulletin
Crim L Q	Criminal Law Quarterly
Crim L Rev	Criminal Law Review
Crim R	Rules of Criminal Procedure
CrL	Criminal Law Reporter
Ct	Court
D	Ohio Decisions
DC	District Court
DC Cir	United States Court of Appeals for the District of Columbia
DEA	Drug Enforcement Agency
Den LJ	Denver Law Journal
De Paul L Rev	De Paul Law Review
Dept	Department

Det J Urb L	Detroit Journal of Urban Law
Dick L Rev	Dickinson Law Review
Dist	District
Div	Division
D Repr	Ohio Decisions, Reprint
Duke LJ	Duke Law Journal
DUI	Driving under the influence
DWI	Driving while intoxicated
ED	Eastern District
Ed	Education
eff.	effective
Evid R	Ohio Rules of Evidence
F(2d)	Federal Reporter, Second Series
FAA	Federal Aviation Administration
FBI	Federal Bureau of Investigation
Fed	Federal Reporter
Fed R Serv	Federal Rules Service
Fla Bar J	Florida Bar Journal
FLR	Federal Law Reports
FRD	Federal Rules Decisions
FSupp	Federal Supplement
Ga	Georgia Reports
Ga L Rev	Georgia Law Review
Ga St Bar J	Georgia State Bar Journal
GC	General Code of Ohio
Geo LJ	Georgetown Law Journal
Geo Wash L Rev	George Washington Law Review
H	House Bill
Harv L Rev	Harvard Law Review
Hastings LJ	Hastings Law Journal
How LJ	Howard Law Journal
HR	House Resolution
Idaho	Idaho Reports
Ill	Illinois Reports
Ill Ann Stat	Illinois Annotated Statutes
Ill Bar J	Illinois Bar Journal
Ill L F	Illinois Law Forum
Inc	Incorporated
Ind Legal F	Indiana Legal Forum
Ind LJ	Indiana Law Journal
Iowa	Iowa Reports
Iowa L Rev	Iowa Law Review
IRC	Internal Revenue Code
IRS	Internal Revenue Service
J Crim L	Journal of Criminal Law and Criminology
J Crim L C & P S	Journal of Criminal Law, Criminology and Police Science
J Leg Studies	Journal of Legal Studies
J Natl Dist Atty Assn	Journal of the National District Attorney Association

Jour of Law & Education	Journal of Law & Education
J Police Sci & Ad	Journal of Police Science and Administration
Juv	Juvenile Court
Juv R	Rules of Juvenile Procedure
Ky	Kentucky Reports
Ky LJ	Kentucky Law Journal
LAPD	Los Angeles Police Department
La	Louisiana Reports
Law & Contemp Probs	Law and Contemporary Problems
LEd	Lawyers' Edition, United States Supreme Court Reports
LEd(2d)	Lawyers' Edition, United States Supreme Court Reports, Second Series
Ltd	Limited
Marq L Rev	Marquette Law Review
Mass	Massachusetts Reports
MC Sup R	Rules of Superintendence for Municipal Courts and County Courts
Md App	Maryland Appellate Reports
Mental & Physical Disability L Rep	Mental and Physical Disability Law Reporter
Mercer L Rev	Mercer Law Review
Mfg	Manufacturing
Mich	Michigan Reports
Mich J L Ref	Michigan Journal of Legal Reference
Mich L Rev	Michigan Law Review
Minn	Minnesota Reports
Minn L Rev	Minnesota Law Review
Misc	Ohio Miscellaneous Reports
Misc(2d)	Ohio Miscellaneous Reports, Second Series
Mo	Missouri Reports
Mo KC L Rev	University of Missouri—Kansas City Law Review
Mo L Rev	Missouri Law Review
Muni	Municipal Court
NCL Rev	North Carolina Law Review
ND	Northern District
NE	Northeastern Reporter
NE(2d)	Northeastern Reporter, Second Series
Neb L Rev	Nebraska Law Review
NM	New Mexico Reports
NM L Rev	New Mexico Law Review
Nor Ky L Rev	Northern Kentucky Law Review
Notre Dame Law	Notre Dame Lawyer
NP	Ohio Nisi Prius Reports
NP(NS)	Ohio Nisi Prius Reports, New Series
NW	Northwestern Reporter

NW(2d)	Northwestern Reporter, Second Series
NW L Rev	Northwestern Law Review
NY	New York Reports
NY(2d)	New York Reports, Second Series
NYS(2d)	West's New York Supplement, Second Series
NYU L Rev	New York University Law Review
O	Ohio Reports
OAC	Ohio Administrative Code
OAG	Opinions of the Ohio Attorney General
OBR	Ohio Bar Reports
OCA	Ohio Courts of Appeals Reports
O Const	Ohio Constitution
ODH	Ohio Department of Health
OFD	Ohio Federal Decisions
Ohio Bar	Ohio State Bar Association Reports
Ohio North L Rev	Ohio Northern University Law Review
Ohio St LJ	Ohio State Law Journal
OJur	Ohio Jurisprudence
OJur 2d	Ohio Jurisprudence, Second Series
OJur 3d	Ohio Jurisprudence, Third Series
OLR	Ohio Law Reporter
OO	Ohio Opinions
OO(2d)	Ohio Opinions, Second Series
OO(3d)	Ohio Opinions, Third Series
Or L Rev	Oregon Law Review
OS	Ohio State Reports
OS(2d)	Ohio State Reports, Second Series
OS(3d)	Ohio State Reports, Third Series
OSCt	Ohio Supreme Court
OS Unrep	Ohio State Unreported
OSupp	Ohio Supplement
P(2d)	Pacific Reporter, Second Series
Pa L Rev	Pennsylvania Law Review
Prob	Probate Court
RC	Revised Code of Ohio
Rich L Rev	Richmond Law Review
S	Senate Bill
Santa Clara L Rev	Santa Clara Law Review
S Cal L Rev	Southern California Law Review
SCL Rev	South Carolina Law Review
SCt	United States Supreme Court Reporter
SD	Southern District
SE	Southeastern Reporter
SE(2d)	Southeastern Reporter, Second Series
Search & Seizure L Rep	Search & Seizure Law Report
S Ill LJ	Southern Illinois University Law Journal
SJR	Senate Joint Resolution
So	Southern Reporter

So(2d)	Southern Reporter, Second Series
SR	Senate Resolution
Stan L Rev	Stanford Law Review
Stat	Statutes
S Tex LJ	South Texas Law Journal
St Louis ULJ	Saint Louis University Law Journal
Sup Ct Rev	Supreme Court Review
Sup R	Rules of Superintendence of the Ohio Supreme Court
SW	Southwestern Reporter
SW(2d)	Southwestern Reporter, Second Series
SW LJ	Southwestern Law Journal
Syracuse L Rev	Syracuse Law Review
Temp L Q	Temple Law Quarterly
Tenn	Tennessee Reports
Tenn L Rev	Tennessee Law Review
Tex	Texas Reports
Tex Tech L Rev	Texas Tech Law Review
Trial L Q	Trial Lawyers Quarterly
Tulsa LJ	Tulsa Law Journal
Twp	Township
UC Davis L Rev	University of California—Davis Law Review
UCLA L Rev	UCLA Law Review
U Dayton L Rev	University of Dayton Law Review
U Miami L Rev	University of Miami Law Review
U Pitt L Rev	University of Pittsburgh Law Review
U Rich L Rev	University of Richmond Law Review
US	United States Supreme Court Reports
USC	United States Code
USCA	United States Code Annotated
USCS	United States Code Service
USLW	US Law Week
Utah L Rev	Utah Law Review
U Tol L Rev	University of Toledo Law Review
v	versus
v	volume, Ohio Laws
Va	Virginia Reports
Va L Rev	Virginia Law Review
Vand L Rev	Vanderbilt Law Review
Vill L Rev	Villanova Law Review
Vt L Rev	Vermont Law Review
Wash App	Washington Appellate Reports
Wash & Lee L Rev	Washington & Lee Law Review
Wash L Rev	Washington Law Review
Wayne L Rev	Wayne Law Review
WL	Westlaw
WLR	Weekly Law Reports
Wm & Mary L Rev	William & Mary Law Review
WRU Law Rev	Western Reserve Law Review
Yale LJ	Yale Law Journal

TEXT

Text Outline

Chapter 1
The Fourth Amendment and the Protection of Privacy

Chapter 2
The Exclusionary Rule

Chapter 3
Probable Cause

Chapter 4
Arrest

Chapter 9
Search Warrant Requirement

Chapter 10
Exigent Circumstances

Chapter 11
Search Incident to Arrest

Chapter 12
Automobile Exception to the Warrant Requirement

Chapter 13
Plain View

Chapter 14
Stop and Frisk

Chapter 15
Traffic Stops and Their Aftermath

Chapter 19
Interrogation and Confessions

Chapter 20
Lineups and Pretrial Identification

Chapter 1

The Fourth Amendment and the Protection of Privacy

1.01   The Fourth Amendment today: a personal view

To the dismay of at least some readers, in the past few years this section of the book has become a personal statement. I would be less than true to my principles and not serving you well, however, if all I did was report on the cases handed down the previous twelve months. It is in this section that I take the liberty of expressing opinions related to fourth amendment issues and not tied to the specific case analyses. I welcome your comments about this section, as I do about all parts of the book.

I firmly believe that the strength of American freedom is in some measure, at least, reflected in the relationship between citizens and their law enforcement officers. Equally important is how judges strike the critical balance, protecting legitimate law enforcement needs and individual rights as they are required to do by the fourth amendment. I believe that a book whose audience is composed of judges, prosecutors, criminal defense attorneys and police is a proper vehicle to discuss these issues.

1995 heightened the crisis atmosphere that exists in the relationship between police and at least some Americans. Major police scandals involving that relationship have played across the front pages, whether it was the issue of police and race starkly revealed in the Fuhrman tapes or the admissions about planted evidence in the Philadelphia police prosecutions. In Ohio we have not been plagued by such stark examples, but few people familiar with the relationship between police and persons stopped on the street or in cars would seriously deny that a dangerous level of tension exists. I have been told by police command officers in several Ohio cities that they are increasingly troubled by younger officers who boastfully claim that they can find a dozen reasons to stop any car whose occupants they would like to question and whose car they hope to search. These issues go to the essence of the fourth amendment guarantees and prohibitions.

The United States Supreme Court continues to exercise a diminishing role in this area.

It is a quarter of a century since the end of the Warren Court.[1] By 1968, that Court's decisions on the Fourth Amendment rights of defendants in

---

[1] Earl Warren retired as Chief Justice of the United States in 1969. Other members of the Warren Court majority left the Court within the next eight years: Abe Fortas in 1970, Hugo Black in 1971, and William O. Douglas in 1975. Although not a member of the Warren majority, Justice Harlan, the conservative voice whose

criminal cases had become critical issues in the presidential election. Fourth Amendment expansion had been part and parcel of the Warren Court's due process revolution, which changed the landscape of criminal procedure by applying most of the specific guarantees of the Bill of Rights to the states.[2] With very few deviations,[3] retrenchment and the narrowing of Fourth Amendment rights, especially in the context of criminal litigation, have been important pursuits of the successor Burger and Rehnquist Courts.

The Warren Court's Due Process revolution was powered in large part by a conviction that criminal proceedings in state courts often were unfair and did not adequately protect the rights of criminal defendants. Whether that perception has been drastically revised in the past quarter century is not altogether clear. What is clear, however, is upon whom the task now falls to ensure the protection of constitutional rights in state criminal courts. The void left by the demise of the Warren Court has been filled, if at all, largely by State Supreme Courts expanding the rights of the citizens of their states to be free from unreasonable searches and seizures under the provisions of state constitutions. Where once parties looked only to the United States Constitution to define the rights of Americans when confronted by police, in many states the protection afforded under state constitutions has become far greater than that recognized by the United States Supreme Court under the Bill of Rights.[4]

The movement to turn to state constitutions has grown over the past two decades. The United States Supreme Court has not always greeted this movement magnanimously.[5] In fact, Chief Justice Burger encouraged the

---

concurring and dissenting opinions helped shape and limit the substance of the Fourth Amendment that emerged from the Warren Court, also retired in 1971.

[2]See e.g., Mapp v Ohio, 367 US 643, 81 SCt 1684, 6 LEd(2d) 1081 (1961) (applying the Fourth Amendment exclusionary rule to the states); Gideon v Wainwright, 372 US 335, 83 SCt 792, 9 LEd(2d) 799 (1963) (applying the Sixth Amendment right to counsel in all felony cases to the states); Malloy v Hogan, 378 US 1, 84 SCt 1489, 12 LEd(2d) 653 (1964) (applying the Fifth Amendment privilege against self-incrimination to the states); Duncan v Louisiana, 391 US 145, 88 SCt 1444, 20 LEd(2d) 491 (1968) (applying the Sixth Amendment right to a jury trial to the states), and Benton v Maryland, 395 US 784, 89 SCt 2056, 23 LEd(2d) 707 (1969), the last decision of the Warren Court, overruling Palko v Connecticut, 302 US 319, 58 SCt 149, 82 LEd 288 (1937), superseded by statute as stated in Condemarin v University Hosp, 775 P(2d) 348, 54 ED Law Rptr 669 (Utah 5-1-89), and applying the Fifth Amendment guarantee against double jeopardy to the states).

[3]See e.g., Payton v New York, 445 US 573, 100 SCt 1371, 63 LEd(2d) 639 (1980) (holding that absent consent or exigent circumstances, a warrant is required to enter a residence to make an arrest); and Minnesota v Olson, 495 US 91, 110 SCt 1684, 109 LEd(2d) 85 (1990) (recognizing standing of an overnight guest to challenge an illegal search).

[4]See e.g., People v Oates, 698 P(2d) 811 (Colo 1985), rejecting United States v Karo, 468 US 705, 104 SCt 3296, 82 LEd(2d) 530 (1984), by holding that under the Oregon state Constitution, attachment of a beeper to a car bumper to enable police to monitor the movements of a suspect is a search; People v Griminger, 71 NY(2d) 635, 529 NYS(2d) 55, 524 NE(2d) 409 (1988) and State v Jackson, 102 Wash(2d) 432, 688 P(2d) 136 (1984), rejecting the watering down of the probable cause standard in Illinois v Gates, 462 US 213, 103 SCt 2317, 76 LEd(2d) 527 (1983).

[5]See Michigan v Long, 463 US 1032, 103 SCt 3469, 77 LEd(2d) 1201 (1983) (warning that state reliance upon the adequate state ground of its own constitution

people of the various states to take action when State Supreme Courts extend Fourth Amendment protections beyond that required by the federal constitution:

> when state courts interpret state law to require more than the Federal Constitution requires, the citizens of the state must be aware that they have the power to amend state law to ensure rational law enforcement.[6]

Apparently, not unlike many of us, Chief Justice Burger viewed rational law enforcement as that which coincides with his views.

The Ohio Supreme Court was not in the forefront of expanding individual rights under the state Constitution beyond that which was required by the United States Supreme Court's interpretation of the Federal Constitution. However, in 1992, the Ohio Supreme Court took a tentative step in that direction by ostensibly rejecting a U.S. Supreme Court decision of a decade earlier, *New York v Belton*,[7] which seemed firmly entrenched in Ohio. The Court held that if *Belton* allows police to search the interior of a car anytime an occupant is arrested, regardless of the nature of the offense or the circumstances, "we decline to adopt its rule."[8]

The second major trend, noted in the last edition of this book, is that significant numbers of trial and appellate judges in this state are taking their responsibilities to protect Fourth Amendment rights very seriously. This is not a matter of these judges being liberal or conservative, or pro or anti police. Rather, these judges are taking their oaths and responsibilities seriously. Obviously, not all judges are doing so. Some judges are noted for never granting a motion to suppress or never voting to reverse and remand a case because of the failure of the trial court to suppress evidence. Consequently, the outcome of such motions, in some instances, depends upon which judge or appellate court panel drew a particular case.

The federal Constitution sets the minimum level of Fourth Amendment protection permissible in state courts. The emphasis in the United States Supreme Court has been, for some time, upon setting only a minimum level. The actual protection given to the Fourth Amendment rights of Americans, now more than ever, is determined by how those rights are interpreted and enforced in state courts at every level.

This past year, the Supreme Court's only ventures into fourth amendment jurisprudence were 1) to expand the good faith exception to the exclusionary rule by holding that the computer record errors made by court personnel resulting in an unconstitutional arrest do not trigger the amendment's exclusionary rule,[9] and 2) to uphold a school district's authority to

---

as the basis for greater protection of constitutional rights must be explicit and clear on its face or risk United States Supreme Court reversal.

[6]Florida v Casal, 462 US 637, 639, 103 SCt 3100, 77 LEd(2d) 277 (1983).

[7]New York v Belton, 453 US 454, 101 SCt 2860, 69 LEd(2d) 768 (1981).

[8]State v Brown, 63 OS(3d) 349, 588 NE(2d) 113 (1992), cert denied ___ US ___, 113 SCt 182, 121 LEd(2d) 127 (1992).

[9]See Arizona v Evans, 115 SCt 1185, 131 LEd(2d) 34 (1995); see case discussion Text Chapter 2, Exclusionary Rule.

conduct suspicionless, random drug tests of junior high school athletes.[10] On the other side of the leger, the Court reaffirmed that the "knock and announce" requirement when entering a residence is a part of the fourth amendment standard of reasonableness.[11]

By and large the task of deciding where law enforcement authority ends and fourth amendment rights begin rests today, as it always has, in state courts. The difference now is that the guidance for state trial courts is for the most part coming from state appellate courts construing the fourth amendment and state constitutional provisions rather than the United States Supreme Court.

Ohio courts have become increasingly active among state courts in this debate especially in that area where most Americans come in contact with police, in their cars. The Ohio Supreme Court took the first tentative steps in this direction in 1992 by holding that the State Constitution imposed more stringent requirements upon police searching cars incident to arrest than does the fourth amendment.[12] That activity has become heightened, and Ohio has taken a position in the forefront of the states in determining when, and under what circumstances and in what manner, a police officer may expand a traffic stop to inquire about other offenses.[13] That is an issue which is increasing in importance as law enforcement officers engage in aggressive traffic enforcement as a tool for investigating other offenses. The U.S. Supreme Court has not spoken to this issue since 1973.[14]

This past year also indicated, to me at least, the difficult job trial courts face when deciding motions to suppress. There must be so many pressures on the judge: the obligation to decide the issue according to law, the need to support police, as well as a concern for crime. Without otherwise discussing the O.J. Simpson murder case, the result may be instructive in helping us to sort out how a suppression hearing judge should approach these issues. If the judge had granted the motion to suppress the evidence found at the Simpson estate, thereby rejecting as implausible the claims of the police that they entered because they thought O.J. Simpson might be in danger from the same person who murdered his former wife and her friend, the evidence from the Simpson estate as well as the testimony of Detective Mark Fuhrman would not have been presented to the jury, and Detective Furman likely would not have become the focal issue of the trial. If there is a lesson to be learned from that aspect of the case, it is that decisions on

---

[10]Veronia School Dist 47J v Acton, 115 SCt 2386, 132 LEd(2d) 564 (1995), affirmed by 66 F(3d) 217 (1995); see case discussion in Chapter 16, Administrative Searches.

[11]See Wilson v Arkansas, 115 SCt 1914, 131 LEd(2d) 976 (1995); see case discussion in Text Chapter 8, Issuance and Execution of Search Warrants.

[12]See State v Brown, 63 OS(3d) 349, 588 NE(2d) 113 (1992), cert denied ___ US ___, 113 SCt 182, 121 LEd(2d) 127 (1992); see case discussion Text Chapter 11, Search Incident to Arrest.

[13]See State v Robinette, 73 OS(3d) 650, 653 NE(2d) 695 (1995); see case discussion Text Chapter 15, Traffic Stops and Their Aftermath, as well as a discussion of other cases that would impose even stricter requirements.

[14]See Schneckloth v Bustamonte, 412 US 218, 93 SCt 2041, 36 LEd(2d) 854 (1973).

motions to suppress should be based solely upon the applicable law and should not be swayed by other factors.

1.02   Sources of law and coverage

The law governing arrest, search, and seizure in Ohio is derived from the Fourth Amendment to the United States Constitution and Article I, Section 14 of the Ohio Constitution. This area is also governed by statute and the Ohio Rules of Criminal Procedure.

The United States Supreme Court held that the Fourth Amendment is applicable to the states through the Fourteenth Amendment in *Wolf v Colorado*,[15] and applied the exclusionary rule to the states twelve years later in *Mapp v Ohio*.[16] The Fourth Amendment provides:

> The right of the people to be secure in their persons, houses, papers, and effects, against unreasonable searches and seizures, shall not be violated, and no Warrants shall issue, but upon probable cause, supported by oath or affirmation, and particularly describing the place to be searched, and the persons or things to be seized.

Ohio Constitution, Article I, Section 14 is virtually identical to the Fourth Amendment and provides:

> The right of the people to be secure in their persons, houses, papers, and possessions, against unreasonable searches and seizures shall not be violated; and no warrant shall issue, but upon probable cause, supported by oath or affirmation, particularly describing the place to be searched, and the person and things to be seized.

The similarity in language does not mean that the two texts will be construed identically.[17]

Traditionally, the role of the United States Supreme Court in overseeing state criminal procedure is to impose the minimally acceptable standard below which a state may not venture.[18] Those minimal standards need not be the last word. All that is required is that the states accord their citizens *at least* as much protection as is provided under the Bill of Rights provision.[19] The state has the ultimate responsibility for administering its own system of criminal justice, so long as it does not dip below the minimal standards of fairness imposed under the Federal Constitution. The state constitution is a document of independent force. Above and beyond the minimal federal due process standard, the states are free to offer greater protection under their own constitutions by imposing stricter standards upon state criminal

---

[15]Wolf v Colorado, 338 US 25, 69 SCt 1359, 93 LEd 1782 (1949), overruled by Mapp v Ohio, 367 US 643, 81 SCt 1684, 6 LEd(2d) 1081 (1961).

[16]Mapp v Ohio, 367 US 643, 81 SCt 1684, 6 LEd(2d) 1081 (1961).

[17]See e.g., State v Brown, 63 OS(3d) 349, 588 NE(2d) 113 (1992), cert denied ___ US ___, 113 SCt 182, 121 LEd(2d) 127 (1992).

[18]Adamson v People of State California, 332 US 46, 67 SCt 1672, 91 LEd 1903 (1947).

[19]See Curry v Superior Court of San Francisco, 2 Cal(3d) 707, 470 P(2d) 345, 350, 87 Cal Rptr 361 (1970).

justice agencies.[20] The state may do so by interpreting its own law as supplementing or expanding federal constitutional rights.[21]

The Fourth Amendment, a product of the American Revolution, resulted from what the colonists perceived as wholesale violations of their common-law rights as Englishmen by colonial representatives of the English crown. Specifically, these violations occurred through the use of general search warrants employed to enforce the trade laws and preserve the American market for British merchants. These warrants authorized officials holding Writs of Assistance to "go into any house, shop, cellar, warehouse or room, or other place, and in case of resistance, to break open doors, chests, trunks and other packages" to search for and seize "prohibited and uncustomed" goods. The Writs permitted unlimited intrusion into every aspect of the colonists' lives by vesting absolute powers of discretion in the enforcing customs officials. A search conducted under a Writ of Assistance was as insidious as a warrantless search undertaken by a police officer acting solely upon his own judgment without statutorily or judicially imposed limitations. Customs officials were free to enter a residence or business and search at will. No factual basis was required to justify the intrusion; the Writ provided all of the necessary justification. No return of execution was required.[22]

The complaints of the colonists which the drafters of the Fourth Amendment sought to redress focused on (1) the wholesale violations of the colonists' right of privacy in their homes and other establishments, and (2) the unlimited discretion granted under the Writs of Assistance which were general warrants permitting a government official to act any time that he believed there was adequate cause. Consequently, the Fourth Amendment provided that the security of the person, his home, papers, and effects should not be violated by unreasonable searches and seizures. A violation of that privacy is reasonable when sanctioned by a warrant (warrantless searches and seizures were virtually unknown in England and in colonial America, except incident to arrest) supported by probable cause and specifically describing the place to be searched and the thing to be seized.

The same standards of reasonableness and probable cause govern in federal and state criminal cases.[23] These governing federal standards provide the minimum acceptable protection consonant with American notions of due process. The states may not violate these minimal standards, and evidence obtained in violation of the Fourth Amendment must be excluded in state as well as federal criminal trials.[24] During the halcyon days of Fourth Amendment development before and during the Warren Court era, attention focused upon the Supreme Court's expansion of individual rights

[20]Michigan v Long, 463 US 1032, 103 SCt 3469, 77 LEd(2d) 1201 (1983); Cooper v California, 386 US 58, 87 SCt 788, 17 LEd(2d) 730 (1967).

[21]PruneYard Shopping Center v Robins, 447 US 74, 100 SCt 2035, 64 LEd(2d) 741 (1980).

[22]See generally Katz, *Reflections on Search and Seizure and Illegally Seized Evidence in Canada and the United States*, 3 Canada-US LJ 103 (1980).

[23]Ker v California, 374 US 23, 83 SCt 1623, 10 LEd(2d) 726 (1963); Aguilar v Texas, 378 US 108, 84 SCt 1509, 12 LEd(2d) 723 (1964), overruled by Illinois v Gates, 462 US 213, 103 SCt 2317, 76 LEd(2d) 527 (1983).

[24]Mapp v Ohio, 367 US 643, 81 SCt 1684, 6 LEd(2d) 1081 (1961).

and its demanding interpretations of reasonableness and probable cause. The focus was upon the drive to force state criminal justice systems to meet the minimal standards imposed under the Fourteenth Amendment due process guarantee.

A new realization of the significance of the Court's statement that the United States Constitution imposes only minimal standards below which the states may not tread dawned with the beginning of the Rehnquist era. As the United States Supreme Court limited the reach of the Fourth Amendment protections,[25] the application of the exclusionary rule,[26] and the new limited meaning of the reasonableness guarantee[27] and the probable cause requirement,[28] some state supreme courts have rejected some of the US Supreme Court's narrowing rules and interpretations and imposed higher standards under state constitutions.[29]

The Ohio Supreme Court was not an early participant in the movement to find greater protection against unreasonable searches and seizures under the Ohio state Constitution. In fact, as late as 1990, the US Supreme Court continued to prod the Ohio Supreme Court to enforce even the newer, more minimal federal standard, when it summarily disposed of an appeal from the Ohio Supreme Court in favor of a defendant's Fourth Amendment claim,[30] an almost unheard of result in the past two decades. Generally, the protection under the Ohio Constitution has tracked the guarantees and protections under the Fourth Amendment.[31] Consequently, as federal Fourth Amendment guarantees and protections have diminished, they have diminished in Ohio as well.

That is no longer necessarily so. As a result of the Ohio Supreme Court's decision in *State v Brown*,[32] the Ohio Constitution must be considered a player on this issue. Both prosecutors and defense attorneys should consider the possible implications of each Fourth Amendment issue under the state Constitution.

---

[25]See, e.g., California v Hodari D., 499 US 621, 111 SCt 1547, 113 LEd(2d) 690 (1991); California v Greenwood, 486 US 35, 108 SCt 1625, 100 LEd(2d) 30 (1988); California v Ciraolo, 476 US 207, 106 SCt 1809, 90 LEd(2d) 210 (1986); Smith v Maryland, 442 US 735, 99 SCt 2577, 61 LEd(2d) 220 (1979).

[26]See, e.g., United States v Leon, 468 US 897, 104 SCt 3405, 82 LEd(2d) 677 (1984); Massachusetts v Sheppard, 468 US 981, 104 SCt 3424, 82 LEd(2d) 737 (1984).

[27]See, e.g., California v Acevedo, 500 US 565, 111 SCt 1982, 114 LEd(2d) 619 (1991) (Scalia, J. concurring).

[28]See, e.g., Illinois v Gates, 462 US 213, 103 SCt 2317, 76 LEd(2d) 527 (1983).

[29]See, e.g., State v Novembrino, 105 NJ 95, 519 A(2d) 820 (1987) (rejecting under New Jersey Constitution good faith exception to the exclusionary rule adopted in United States v Leon, 468 US 897, 104 SCt 3405, 82 LEd(2d) 677 (1984)); and People v Griminger, 71 NY(2d) 635, 529 NYS(2d) 55, 524 NE(2d) 409 (1988) and Com v Upton, 394 Mass 363, 476 NE(2d) 548 (1985) (rejecting under New York and Massachusetts Constitutions the modified probable cause standard adopted in Illinois v Gates, 462 US 213, 103 SCt 2317, 76 LEd(2d) 527 (1983)).

[30]Smith v Ohio, 494 US 541, 110 SCt 1288, 108 LEd(2d) 464 (1990).

[31]See State v Thierbach, 92 App(3d) 365, 635 NE(2d) 1276 (Hamilton 1993); State v Bauer, 99 App(3d) 505, 651 NE(2d) 46 (Franklin 1994).

[32]State v Brown, 63 OS(3d) 349, 588 NE(2d) 113 (1992), cert denied ___ US ___, 113 SCt 182, 121 LEd(2d) 127 (1992).

1.03   Applicability of the reasonableness standard

The Constitution only protects against unreasonable intrusions, whether it is a search or a seizure. Police conduct which is neither a search nor a seizure is not subject to review under the Fourth Amendment. A seizure involves the physical taking of any tangible item, and has been extended to include intangibles, such as conversations.[33] An arrest is a seizure of the person and, therefore, subject to the Fourth Amendment command of reasonableness. The protection, however, is not limited to arrests. In *Terry v Ohio*,[34] the US Supreme Court declared that the protection applies any time "an officer, by means of physical force or show of authority, has in some way restrained the liberty of a citizen."[35] Absent at least a show of authority, an intrusion upon a person does not involve a seizure and is unreviewable as to its reasonableness.

The Supreme Court continues to quarrel about when a seizure of a person takes place. In 1990, the Court indicated some readiness to revert to the old arrest standard[36] which would raise questions about the applicability of the Fourth Amendment standard to investigatory stops. If so, the Court seems intent upon creating the same uncertainty in the area of seizures of the person that it has when attempting to define the term "search." The intent here appears to be to diminish the coverage of the Fourth Amendment and to relieve the police from the Amendment's reasonableness standard in more and more encounters with citizens.

The question of exactly what activity constitutes a search, thus triggering Fourth Amendment protection, has long been a matter of controversy. The Court has not defined the term "search" in this century, but instead has been constantly defining it with reference to what is not included within the term, and thus is not subject to the reasonableness command of the Fourth Amendment.

Prior to 1967, the Supreme Court limited the scope of review to physical intrusions into constitutionally protected areas.[37] Consequently, the reasonableness standard applies where there has been a physical invasion of an interest enumerated in the Fourth Amendment—either the person or his house, papers, or effects. The key to the application of this standard lies in the physical intrusion and, aside from the person, a property or proprietary interest in the place searched. Even then, however, the existence of both a physical intrusion and a property interest was not necessarily decisive. A trespass upon private land which led to the discovery of an illegal still was held not to be covered under the Fourth Amendment because the "special protection accorded by the Fourth Amendment to the people in their 'persons, houses, papers, and effects' is not extended to open fields."[38] In

---

[33]Berger v New York, 388 US 41, 87 SCt 1873, 18 LEd(2d) 1040 (1967).

[34]Terry v Ohio, 392 US 1, 88 SCt 1868, 20 LEd(2d) 889 (1968).

[35]Terry v Ohio, 392 US 1, at 19 n.16, 88 SCt 1868, 20 LEd(2d) 889 (1968); see also Michigan v Chesternut, 486 US 567, 108 SCt 1975, 100 LEd(2d) 565 (1988).

[36]California v Hodari D., 499 US 621, 111 SCt 1547, 113 LEd(2d) 690 (1991).

[37]Silverman v United States, 365 US 505, 81 SCt 679, 5 LEd(2d) 734 (1961).

[38]Hester v United States, 265 US 57, 59, 44 SCt 445, 68 LEd 898 (1924).

1967, in *Katz v United States*,[39] the Supreme Court shifted from property interests to privacy interests as the crucial factor in determining the Fourth Amendment's scope.

1.04   Right of privacy

The shift to privacy as the threshold test for determining the applicability of the Fourth Amendment reasonableness standard has not been smooth. In fact, the privacy analysis employed by the Supreme Court today does not resemble the one offered in 1967. That Court intended the privacy analysis to expand Fourth Amendment coverage to more police-citizen encounters; the privacy standard utilized by the present Court seeks to free the police entirely from Fourth Amendment restraints.[40] Of course, the privacy issue is only the preliminary inquiry, but often it is the crucial one because a negative answer forecloses further review. When the threshold inquiry is answered affirmatively, the fact that Fourth Amendment coverage attaches does not, itself, prohibit the police intrusion or deny the government agency the sought-after information. It merely means that the police conduct is subject to the amendment's reasonableness command.

In *Katz*,[41] the defendant was convicted of transmitting wagering information from a public telephone. At his trial, the government introduced evidence of his end of a telephone conversation, obtained by FBI agents who had attached an electronic listening device to the outside of the public telephone booth from which he had placed the calls. The eavesdropping was accomplished without a warrant, but the government contended that the police conduct was neither a search nor covered by the Fourth Amendment because there was no physical penetration of a constitutionally protected area.

Justice Stewart, for the majority, rejected the government's formulation of the issue, maintaining that the focus on whether a given area is constitutionally protected deflects attention from the critical problem. He set forth the following Fourth Amendment principle which has since guided the development of the law in this area:

> For the Fourth Amendment protects people, not places. What a person knowingly exposes to the public, even in his own home or office, is not a subject of Fourth Amendment protection. ... But what he seeks to preserve as private, even in an area accessible to the public may be constitutionally protected.[42]

Applying the principle to the *Katz* case, the Court reasoned that once the defendant entered the telephone booth and closed the door, he had taken steps to protect against being overheard. Although he could be seen through closed doors, Justice Stewart reasoned that Katz was concerned not

---

[39]Katz v United States, 389 US 347, 88 SCt 507, 19 LEd(2d) 576 (1967).
[40]Cf. California v Acevedo, 500 US 565, 111 SCt 1982, 114 LEd(2d) 619 (1991) (Scalia, J. concurring).
[41]Katz v United States, 389 US 347, 88 SCt 507, 19 LEd(2d) 576 (1967).
[42]Katz v United States, 389 US 347, 351-52, 88 SCt 507, 19 LEd(2d) 576 (1967).

with the "intruding eye," but with the "uninvited ear."[43] The Court concluded, "The Government's activities in electronically listening to and recording the petitioner's words violated the privacy upon which he justifiably relied while using the telephone booth and thus constituted a 'search and seizure' within the meaning of the Fourth Amendment."[44]

The Stewart privacy formulation worked well in the context of the facts in the *Katz* case and expanded the coverage of the Fourth Amendment's protection. It was also easy to understand in that context. If the FBI agents had stood outside the closed telephone booth and overheard the conversations, the defendant would have had no valid contention. He would have been aware of their presence, whether or not he knew they were law enforcement officers, and would have run the risk attendant upon talking within the hearing of another. One need not always know of the presence of the "uninvited ear" to be denied the privacy protection. For instance, eavesdropping, without the use of special listening devices, by government officials in an adjoining room of a motel is not an unconstitutional infringement upon the rights protected by the Fourth Amendment.[45]

The reason for this result is that a person in a hotel or motel room knows that the same privacy that exists in a detached single home is unavailable. The "walls have ears" is an old American shibboleth. Nosey persons may make use of common walls in such facilities to eavesdrop. Of course, there is another side to this issue which has not been fully debated. In all of these cases, the standard of constitutional protection is reduced because police are allowed to engage in conduct, here snooping on an adjacent bedroom, that is reprehensible. The implications are limited because presumably a court would be reluctant to extend this immunity from constitutional supervision if the eavesdropping was done from one apartment into a permanent residence, such as the marital bedroom of an apartment. Actually, however, there is no justifiably logical distinction between an apartment bedroom and a hotel or motel room.

The premise upon which *Katz* rested, which also powers most of the later cases, is that what one exposes to others is not protected, regardless of where the exposure takes place. Even curtilage and areas around the home, where the Court recognizes the greatest protection of privacy, that protection is limited or non- existent if the home owner or lease holder exposes private information to public view. For example, police observation of marijuana plants growing in a back yard which are clearly visible from the street involves no invasion of a protected privacy interest.[46] Presumably the same result would obtain even if the police observed the plants from the defendant's front walk or driveway. The courts are likely to conclude that driveways and sidewalks to front doors offer an open invitation and are not protected so long as police remain on these paths.

---

[43]Katz v United States, 389 US 347, 352, 88 SCt 507, 19 LEd(2d) 576 (1967).
[44]Katz v United States, 389 US 347, 353, 88 SCt 507, 19 LEd(2d) 576 (1967).
[45]State v Day, 50 App(2d) 315, 362 NE(2d) 1253 (Hamilton 1976).
[46]State v Curto, 73 App(3d) 16, 595 NE(2d) 1038 (Summit 1991).

Cases involving misplaced confidences are another context where the *Katz* test has been easy to apply. If a person confides in another, the courts have held that he has no expectation of privacy that the confidant will not tell others, including the police, and may in fact be a police agent.[47] Moreover, a conversation is not protected by the Fourth Amendment even when the confidant is wired and transmitting the conversation directly to law enforcement officers.[48] When a defendant admits an acquaintance to his house knowing that he is a police officer, the defendant has no expectation of privacy in items visible within the house.[49] Similarly, a government agent may accept an invitation to do business and may enter the premises for the very purposes contemplated by the occupant.[50]

The Supreme Court has consistently refused to distinguish between a planted police agent and a confidant who spontaneously betrays a confidence by going to the police. It is a distinction that should be made. The planted police agent gains entrance by misrepresentation and should be treated similarly to a search or a planted listening device. It is one thing where defendants are aware that their guest is a police officer or prosecuting attorney, as in *State v VanNewhouse*,[51] and operate on a mistaken belief that their friend would not reveal their wrongdoing. The author does not quarrel with the result in *VanNewhouse* even though the assistant prosecuting attorney went to the house under the guise of a social visit but was really there to see if the defendants had a stolen object. The defendants were aware of the prosecutor's official capacity. It is an altogether different matter where a defendant is not aware that the person he admits to his home has any official capacity.

It is a closer case where a police officer enters a business establishment, where a private meeting is being held, without being stopped or asked for identification or the purpose of his visit. In *State v Taub*,[52] the court held that the police officer's "silent" misrepresentation that he was invited to the business meeting and that his purpose in attending was to become involved in an illegal pyramid sales scheme was permissible provided that he did not attempt to conceal his presence or expressly misrepresent his true purpose in attending. The Ohio Supreme Court, in *State v Pi Kappa Alpha Fraternity*,[53] a case where liquor agents obtained entry to a college fraternity house to check on illegal sales of liquor by misrepresenting themselves, seemed to have taken a stronger stance:

> [G]overnment officers are not privileged to deceptively gain entry into the private home or office of another without a warrant, where such home or office is not a commercial center of criminal activity, and where the invitation to enter the private home or office was not

---

[47]Hoffa v United States, 385 US 293, 87 SCt 408, 17 LEd(2d) 374 (1966).

[48]United States v White, 401 US 745, 91 SCt 1122, 28 LEd(2d) 453 (1971), cert denied 406 US 962, 92 SCt 2070, 32 LEd(2d) 350 (1972).

[49]State v VanNewhouse, 41 App(3d) 191, 534 NE(2d) 1223 (Wood 1987).

[50]Lewis v United States, 385 US 206, 87 SCt 424, 17 LEd(2d) 312 (1966).

[51]State v VanNewhouse, 41 App(3d) 191, 534 NE(2d) 1223 (Wood 1987).

[52]State v Taub, 47 App(3d) 5, 547 NE(2d) 360 (Lucas 1988).

[53]State v Pi Kappa Alpha Fraternity, 23 OS(3d) 141, 23 OBR 295, 491 NE(2d) 1129 (1986), cert denied 479 US 827, 107 SCt 104, 93 LEd(2d) 54 (1986).

extended by the occupant for the purpose of conducting illegal activities.[54]

That position departs from United States Supreme Court pronouncements pertaining to misplaced confidence. The Ohio Supreme Court stated that the state conduct violated both the United States and Ohio Constitutions. If it is to prevail in Ohio over US Supreme Court statements pertaining to planted agents and misplaced confidence, the Ohio Supreme Court will have to clearly state that its decision is an interpretation of the state constitutional guarantee against illegal searches and seizures and not an interpretation under the Fourth Amendment.[55] Another approach would be to reconcile the decision with the holding in *Taub* and to focus upon the difference between silent and overt misrepresentations. The Ohio Supreme Court syllabus, however, states the position which is most consistent with a constitutional provision dedicated to protecting reasonable expectations of privacy.

It should be clear, then, that while *Katz* represented some broadening of the scope of the protection of the Fourth Amendment, it has not proven to be an unlimited expansion. Some police conduct remained immune from review under the reasonableness standard even under the privacy formulation advocated by the authors of the *Katz* opinions, and a great deal more remains immune under the standards imposed by the Burger and Rehnquist Courts.

It has not always been easy to predict whether the Court would find that certain police behavior invades a protected privacy interest. One reason for this involves the shifting grounds upon which the privacy test has stood. Justice Harlan, concurring separately in *Katz*, attempted to explain the Court's standard. He contended that the privacy test contains two parts: (1) whether a person has exhibited an actual or subjective expectation of privacy, and (2) whether that expectation is one that society is prepared to recognize as reasonable. Although it is the basis for many lower court decisions, the Harlan formulation poses significant risks. If the government conditions its citizens to expect little privacy, the scope of the Amendment's protection could fall significantly below that which is tolerable in a free society.

The Hamilton County Court of Appeals has said, "The determining factor is whether the area searched is one in which there is a reasonable anticipation of freedom from governmental intrusion."[56] This emphasis upon the location of the surveillance may appear to be a distortion of the Supreme Court's attempt to shift the focus from places to people, but in some cases it provides the only meaningful context for inquiry.[57] The Ham-

---

[54]State v Pi Kappa Alpha Fraternity, 23 OS(3d) 141, 145, 23 OBR 295, 491 NE(2d) 1129 (1986), cert denied 479 US 827, 107 SCt 104, 93 LEd(2d) 54 (1986).

[55]Cf. Michigan v Long, 463 US 1032, 103 SCt 3469, 77 LEd(2d) 1201 (1983).

[56]State v Hoover, 69 OO(2d) 156, 157 (App, Hamilton 1974), citing Mancusi v DeForte, 392 US 364, 88 SCt 2120, 20 LEd(2d) 1154 (1968).

[57]See also State v McCarthy, 26 OS(2d) 87, 89-90, 269 NE(2d) 424 (1971) ("[A] search ordinarily implies a quest by an officer of the law, a prying into hidden places for that which is concealed.").

ilton County Appeals Court's approach appeared prescient some years later when the US Supreme Court in 1984 reaffirmed a sixty-year-old doctrine which denied the Amendment's protection to open fields.

Applying the privacy formula, the Court affirmed this denial of protection as consistent with the modern formula for testing the scope of Fourth Amendment coverage. Justice Powell, writing for the majority, held that an open field does "not provide the setting for those intimate activities that the Amendment is intended to shelter from government interference or surveillance." Therefore, the defendants' expectation of privacy in the fields in which they had planted marijuana was not one society recognizes as reasonable, and the police entrance onto fenced and posted private property without a warrant was not an unreasonable search under the Fourth Amendment.[58]

Three years later the Court held that a visual inspection of a barn with an open door that is located adjacent to a house but is not within the curtilage of the house did not intrude on a protected privacy interest. In *United States v Dunn*,[59] Justice White for the majority developed four factors for determining whether an area is within the protected curtilage of the house: (1) the proximity of the area claimed to be curtilage to the home; (2) whether the area is included within an enclosure surrounding the home; (3) the nature of the uses to which the area is put; and (4) the steps taken by the resident to protect the area from observation by people passing by. In *Dunn*, the Court found it conclusive that the federal agents had information indicating that the barn was not used for the intimate activities associated with home life but was instead the site of a drug lab. Based on the decision that the barn in *Dunn* was not within the zone of privacy protected by the Fourth Amendment, a court may not review the absence of the warrant or even the basis for the agents' decision that the barn was used as a drug lab which led to the intrusion and visual inspection.

In *Smith v Maryland*,[60] the United States Supreme Court appears to have adopted a formulation which tests whether there was a legitimate expectation of privacy. However, the application of the legitimacy standard prompted Justice Stewart, the author of the *Katz* opinion, to dissent in *Smith* and complain that the majority had forgotten the purpose and teaching of *Katz*. In *Smith*, police obtained telephone numbers dialed from the defendant's home. The majority held that since the defendant had to communicate the number to the telephone company in order to complete the call, he assumed the risk that the company would reveal the numbers he dialed to the police. Consequently, the Court held that there had been no search because the defendant had no legitimate expectation of privacy in that information. A shift from reasonable expectation to legitimate expectation is not insignificant and marks a distinct change in attitude on the part of the Court. Rather than requiring inquiry into how reasonable persons in a democratic society would view the individual's privacy expectation in a

---

[58]Oliver v United States, 466 US 170, 104 SCt 1735, 80 LEd(2d) 214 (1984).
[59]United States v Dunn, 480 US 294, 107 SCt 1134, 94 LEd(2d) 326 (1987).
[60]Smith v Maryland, 442 US 735, 99 SCt 2577, 61 LEd(2d) 220 (1979).

given case, the new standard allows the Court to introduce policy considerations as to whether society is prepared to acknowledge the legitimacy of the individual's privacy expectation. If the Court is result oriented, the label is immaterial. If, however, these tests do provide an analytical framework for decisions, then the tests allow for substantial analytical differences.

Justice Stewart believed that *Katz* required a different result because the numbers dialed revealed the most intimate details of a person's life to a slightly lesser degree than the conversations themselves. Just because the telephone company accumulates that information for a limited purpose, Justice Stewart contended, should not mean that the police may, without any cause whatsoever and for whatever purposes they choose, uncover private relationships with impunity.

The significance of these cases, of course, is that the police behavior is not subject to review under the Fourth Amendment to determine whether it is reasonable or unreasonable.[61] The cases have resulted in a narrowing of the privacy protection by holding that what one reveals for a limited purpose, such as one's presence on the highway or bank records or telephone numbers dialed, appears to be exposed for any governmental purpose. Moreover, limited exposure may open the door to additional exposure. The Supreme Court has said, "It is ... beyond dispute that [the police officer's] shining his flashlight to illuminate the interior of [defendant's] car trenched upon no right secured ... by the Fourth Amendment."[62]

A new test to determine the scope of the Fourth Amendment's protection of privacy emerged in *Minnesota v Olson*,[63] which could have a very healthy effect upon Fourth Amendment litigation and provide a predictable standard, the application of which would not have torturous results. *Olson* raised the question of whether an overnight visitor has a sufficient privacy interest in his host's home to have standing to challenge the legitimacy of a police entry of that home, which was incidentally to arrest the guest. Justice White, writing for the majority, said that the guest did have adequate standing because this conclusion fit the expectation of the American people. There is no better way to determine the reasonableness or legitimacy of a person's privacy expectation than to measure it according to the common expectations that exist in this society. Justice White has since retired, and the Supreme Court subsequently has not had a case which requires application of the privacy test, so it is altogether uncertain whether the Court will shift to the *Olson* standard permanently or will instead use the *ad hoc* standards, which are non-analytical and not anchored to the American experience.

The privacy test's application has caused a curious result in cases involving warrantless field tests of legally seized substances. The Supreme Court

---

[61]See also United States v Miller, 425 US 435, 96 SCt 1619, 48 LEd(2d) 71 (1976) (there is no expectation of privacy in checks and deposit slips conveyed to the banks and exposed to their employees).

[62]Texas v Brown, 460 US 730, 103 SCt 1535, 1541, 75 LEd(2d) 502 (1983), citing a pre-*Katz* decision, United States v Lee, 274 US 559, 47 SCt 746, 71 LEd 1202 (1927).

[63]Minnesota v Olson, 495 US 91, 110 SCt 1684, 109 LEd(2d) 85 (1990).

has held that a chemical test that merely discloses "whether a substance is cocaine, and no other arguably 'private' fact, compromises no legitimate privacy interest."[64] A negative result merely discloses that the substance is not cocaine, revealing "nothing of special interest." Since Congress has chosen to treat possession of cocaine as illegitimate, the Court held that government conduct which could reveal only whether the substance was, in fact, cocaine "compromises no legitimate privacy interest."[65] The uniqueness of Justice Stevens' rationale in *United States v Jacobsen* is that one can infer that because the substance was illegal, the defendant could have had no Fourth Amendment interest to be free from an unreasonable search, provided that the government intrusion revealed nothing about the substance other than whether it was contraband.

The implications of Justice Stevens' rationale cannot be overstated. No one has ever suggested that the Fourth Amendment insulates contraband from detection. The Fourth Amendment, however, by focusing on privacy, limits the means police may use to detect contraband. Justice Stevens turns that inquiry on its head. This century is replete with technological advances that appear unlimited. The Stevens rationale would allow an almost unlimited use of future technology to detect contraband provided that technology discloses nothing else about the subject it is focused on. Imagine some futuristic device which could detect the presence of contraband in a home without requiring the detective to enter the home. It is unlikely that the Supreme Court would sanction the wholesale use of such an instrument, for example, on an apartment house to detect in which apartments illicit drugs or other specified contraband is hidden, but the Stevens analysis would do just that. The damage done by this type of rationale is that it insulates the police conduct from the review of the reasonableness standard of the Fourth Amendment.

The United States Supreme Court's approach results in a continued loss of protected privacy, hence a loss of Fourth Amendment protection, as a result of modern technology. Consequently, surveillance aided by the attachment of a beeper to an automobile bumper does not invade any

---

[64]United States v Jacobsen, 466 US 109, 104 SCt 1652, 1662, 80 LEd(2d) 85 (1984).

[65]United States v Jacobsen, 466 US 109, 104 SCt 1652, 1662, 80 LEd(2d) 85 (1984). Accord United States v Place, 462 US 696, 103 SCt 2637, 77 LEd(2d) 110 (1983) (subjecting luggage to a sniff test by a trained narcotics detection dog was not a search within the Fourth Amendment); State v Riley, 88 App(3d) 468, 624 NE(2d) 302 (Wood 1993) (no search where the information revealed by means of a canine sniff is limited to contraband items); State v Waldroup, 100 App(3d) 508, 654 NE(2d) 390 (Preble 1995) (allowing a drug sniffing dog to indicate location of drugs within a car is not a search; dog alerted to the dash area; it is not clear from the opinion whether the dog was placed in the car; Editor's note: it would be a search if the dog were placed inside the car); State v Palicki, 97 App(3d) 175, 646 (2d) 494 (Wood 1994).

Note however that after State v Robinette, 73 OS(3d) 650, 653 NE(2d) 695 (1995), it is certainly appropriate to question any delay beyond the normal time it would take to write up a traffic ticket involved in bringing the drug sniffing dog to the scene absent reasonable suspicion to justify a further investigatory intrusion. See discussion, Text 15.05 Expanding the inquiry of a traffic offense to other offenses.

legitimate expectation of privacy and is not a search within the contemplation of the Fourth Amendment.[66] Once, however, the object carrying the beeper enters an area which police could not observe from a lawful vantage point, continued monitoring is a search and intrudes upon protected privacy interests because it reveals information which could not have been obtained through visual surveillance.[67]

Advanced technology is being used to erode Fourth Amendment protection. One can erect high fences to keep out the unwanted eye, but the government may thwart such efforts by prying from the sky. The notion of modern technology merely enhancing the senses of law enforcement officers who are legally present at the time of the observation has led to the sanctioning of aerial surveillance[68] as well as photographic magnification from the air.[69] The air space over any property is a public vantage point, and an officer viewing a target's property or activities from that vantage point does not intrude upon a legitimate expectation of privacy. The reasoning behind these decisions is that any member of the public flying in an airplane could have seen and filmed everything below, and consequently police do not need a warrant to observe what is visible to the public. The issue that is overlooked in these decisions is that the chance that a person flying in a commercial airplane may observe activities below is not nearly the same as when officers obtain a plane purposely to observe the defendant's property. They could not legally have done so by scaling a fence which was intended for the very purpose of maintaining privacy. The thrust here is that one takes a risk that someone flying overhead may observe and recognize people and activities below, and the existence of that risk eliminates all protected privacy from the air. The Court has even sanctioned police hovering a helicopter at 400 feet to observe inside a greenhouse.[70]

Allegedly, there are limits to the Court's tolerance of modern technology eliminating all Fourth Amendment concerns. In *Florida v Riley*,[71] two members of the majority split over the standard for determining that limit. Justice White wrote for the majority that the limit would be reached if flying at the particular altitude was illegal or contrary to regulation. In a separate concurring opinion, Justice O'Connor said the limit should not be determined by whether the altitude was in compliance with FAA regulation, whose purpose is to protect safety not Fourth Amendment rights, but whether a helicopter flying at that altitude was "sufficiently rare that police surveillance from such altitudes would violate reasonable expectations of privacy, despite compliance with FAA air safety regulations."[72] Similarly, in

---

[66]United States v Knotts, 460 US 276, 103 SCt 1081, 75 LEd(2d) 55 (1983).

[67]United States v Karo, 468 US 705, 104 SCt 3296, 82 LEd(2d) 530 (1984).

[68]California v Ciraolo, 476 US 207, 106 SCt 1809, 90 LEd(2d) 210 (1986).

[69]Dow Chemical Co v United States, 476 US 227, 106 SCt 1819, 90 LEd(2d) 226 (1986).

[70]Florida v Riley, 488 US 445, 109 SCt 693, 102 LEd(2d) 835 (1989).

[71]Florida v Riley, 488 US 445, 109 SCt 693, 102 LEd(2d) 835 (1989).

[72]Florida v Riley, 488 US 445, 455, 109 SCt 693, 102 LEd(2d) 835 (1989) (O'Connor, J. concurring).

Dow Chemical Co v United States,[73] the Court indicated that the limit might be reached by "surveillance of private property by using highly sophisticated surveillance equipment not generally available to the public, such as satellite technology." These limits are relatively specious. The dissenters in *Dow Chemical* pointed out that the photographs revealed details as small as 1/2 inch in diameter taken by cameras costing in excess of $20,000. Until a Supreme Court majority agrees that a limit has been reached, the case results stand for the proposition that there are no limits upon the government's ability to use advanced technology to sidestep Fourth Amendment protections. Instead, the focus appears firmly planted upon risk measurement which is not an appropriate measurement for the type of individual security which the Fourth Amendment was to secure.

In all it is difficult to treat the Supreme Court's pronouncements on the privacy issue seriously rather than consider these cases result-oriented as part of a greater agenda. In *California v Acevedo*,[74] Justice Scalia said that this body of decisions has been "developed largely as a means of creating ... exceptions ... to the general warrant requirement." The result has been a denial of all Fourth Amendment protection in the majority's effort to eliminate the judicial preference for a warrant rather than the alternative means which would have recognized the need for Fourth Amendment protection but would have imposed a lesser standard than is imposed upon traditional searches.[75]

In Ohio, the issue has been risk rather than technology and more often than not the battleground has been public rest rooms:

(1) *State v Tanner*.[76] A police officer on special duty at a theater entered a crowded restroom and saw two pairs of legs facing the toilet in the stall. There was open space between the stall door and both the floor and the ceiling. The feet of the occupants were visible and the door could be peered over. Nothing was seen that indicated that either party was handicapped. After the officer heard snorting noises, he peered over the top of the stall door and observed the defendant snorting a substance, later identified as cocaine.

(2) *State v Johnson*.[77] State highway patrol officers stopped to check a rest area in accord with policy initiated in response to complaints about homosexual activity in that rest area. The officers saw two unoccupied automobiles in the rest area and went to inspect the two outhouse-type facilities which had no locks. One officer opened the first pit toilet stall and found the defendants engaging in sexual conduct.

(3) *State v Hunter*.[78] Police officers at a concert believed that patrons would use toilet stalls as a hiding place for drug activity. During a routine

---

[73]Dow Chemical Co v United States, 476 US 227, 106 SCt 1819, 90 LEd(2d) 226 (1986).

[74]California v Acevedo, 500 US 565, 111 SCt 1982, 114 LEd(2d) 619 (1991) (Scalia, J. concurring).

[75]See, e.g., Terry v Ohio, 392 US 1, 88 SCt 1868, 20 LEd(2d) 889 (1968).

[76]State v Tanner, 42 App(3d) 196, 537 NE(2d) 702 (Franklin 1988).

[77]State v Johnson, 42 App(3d) 81, 536 NE(2d) 648 (Tuscarawas 1987).

[78]State v Hunter, 48 App(3d) 170, 548 NE(2d) 1321 (Cuyahoga 1988).

patrol of the restroom facility, an officer noticed defendant's feet positioned in a manner that suggested the toilet was not being used for its intended purpose. The defendant's trousers were not gathered around his ankles, leading the officer to believe that he was not using the toilet.

(4) *State v Thurman*.[79] In a public restroom, police climbed a ten- or fifteen-foot scaffold above the restroom floor behind a partition where they could peer into toilet stalls through ventilator screens. The defendant was observed in the toilet stall; he was also observed by another patron of the restroom because the stalls had no doors.

In *Johnson*, the Fifth District Court of Appeals concluded that "society is not prepared to recognize as reasonable an expectation of privacy of people engaging in sexual acts in a public outhouse with no lock on the door."[80] If the court is stating that the defendants had no protected right of privacy because they were engaged in sexual acts in the public outhouse, but that others using the facility for its intended purpose would have a protected right of privacy, notwithstanding the absence of locks, then the court is applying the wrong test. It is determining the scope of Fourth Amendment protection by the nature of the wrongdoing.

The issue is whether the police had the right to observe the wrongdoing. The court, doubtless consistent with Supreme Court thinking, could hold as the First District Court of Appeals held in *Thurman* that because there were no locks on the outhouse door, and no doors on the facility in *Thurman*, that no one using the facility had a legitimate expectation of privacy in the facility regardless of whether or not they were using the facility for its intended legal purpose.[81] In *Johnson*, anyone for any reason might have opened the unlocked doors; in *Thurman*, anyone coming into the facility would have observed the stall with no doors. The emphasis cannot be placed upon the defendants' conduct within the facility because the Fourth Amendment either embraces all who use the facility or it embraces no one. Perhaps a proper inquiry in *Thurman* is whether society is prepared to have police clandestinely observe inside toilet stalls from hidden locations without requiring them to justify such intrusions? There is a difference between people using a facility for legitimate or improper purposes being observed by people who walk into that facility and observations by police officials hiding behind screens and the like. After all, they are observing everyone using the facility. But that is not what the risk test requires and likely is not what the Supreme Court would require under such circumstances.

The analyses in *Hunter* and *Tanner* seem so much more consistent with protecting personal security. In both cases, the courts found a protected privacy interest in the toilet stalls but concluded that the police officers' conduct was reasonable based upon their observations. The burden these

---

[79]State v Thurman, No. C-790398 (1st Dist Ct App, Hamilton, 4-30-80).

[80]State v Johnson, 42 App(3d) 81, 83, 536 NE(2d) 648 (Tuscarawas 1987).

[81]See also State v McClung, No. C-810299, 1982 WL 4678 (1st Dist Ct App, Hamilton, 3-3-82) (defendants had no reasonable expectation of privacy in toilet stalls where they could be observed through openings between the stall doors and the frames).

cases place on law enforcement is minimal, but even then it may exceed that which the United States Supreme Court would require.

The issue of risk is rarely entertained where the observation is into a residence. In *State v Scott*,[82] a police officer who stood on her partner's shoulders to observe illegal gambling through a space in the curtains was held to violate the reasonable expectation of privacy of the occupier of the premises and his guests.[83]

The narrowness of Fourth Amendment coverage now requires consideration of other violations when evaluating a police intrusion. Sometimes a police intrusion may not violate a protected expectation of privacy but may be an interference with other rights. For example, there is no reasonable expectation of privacy in a jail or prison setting,[84] but that does not mean that a prisoner has no rights comparable to those protected under the rubric of privacy. That issue arose in *State v Milligan*,[85] where the defendant was permitted to talk by telephone with his attorney. Unknown to the defendant, a jail official stood nearby and secretly recorded the defendant's side of the telephone conversation. A copy of that tape was provided to the sheriff. The defendant moved to dismiss because the state had purposefully, intentionally, and deliberately violated his right to counsel. The state not only appealed from the granting of the motion to dismiss but also argued that the evidence should not be suppressed.

The Ohio Supreme Court agreed with the state's initial argument that the defendant had no reasonable expectation of privacy within the county jail but disagreed with the state's conclusion that the absence of a privacy right meant that the defendant's right to counsel was not violated. The Court held that the state had violated the defendant's federal and state constitutional rights to counsel. The remedy for violation of the state constitutional right required, at the least, suppression of the unauthorized interception of the private conversation between the defendant and his attorney. The Court was sympathetic to the defendant's claim that suppression is an inadequate remedy because the motivation for the violation, knowing that the evidence would be suppressed, would be to obtain a tactical advantage at trial or to secure other evidence. Yet the Court was unwilling to accept the defendant's advocacy of a rule of automatic dismissal.

Consequently, to strike the proper balance and determine whether the charges should be dismissed, the court adopted the test devised by the United States Supreme Court in *Weatherford v Bursey*,[86] which requires a case-by-case analysis based on the following factors:

(1) Whether the government deliberately intruded in order to obtain confidential and privileged information;

---

[82]State v Scott, 27 Misc(2d) 38, 27 OBR 423, 500 NE(2d) 939 (Muni, Hamilton 1986).

[83]See also State v Person, 34 Misc 97, 298 NE(2d) 922 (Muni, Toledo 1973) (holding that officer who peered through keyhole and listened to sounds coming from an adjoining room engaged in a search).

[84]Hudson v Palmer, 468 US 517, 104 SCt 3194, 82 LEd(2d) 393 (1984).

[85]State v Milligan, 40 OS(3d) 341, 533 NE(2d) 724 (1988).

[86]Weatherford v Bursey, 429 US 545, 97 SCt 837, 51 LEd(2d) 30 (1977).

(2) Whether the government obtained directly or indirectly any evidence which was or could be used at trial as a result of the intrusion;

(3) Whether any information obtained was or could be used in any manner detrimental to the defendant; and

(4) Whether details about trial preparation were learned by the government.[87]

Review by the trial court is to be accomplished through an in camera inspection of the communication in order to protect its confidentiality. Here, a tape was made. When the only evidence will be the testimony of the eavesdropping officer, that testimony should be taken in camera subject to transcription under seal. The defendant is obliged to make a prima facie showing of prejudice, but the government which has exclusive control of the evidence of the transgression bears the burden of showing no prejudice.

A different situation arises when a conversation between an attorney and his client takes place in a room where others are present. The presence of others has been deemed to indicate that the conversations were never intended to be confidential and defeats the claim of attorney-client privilege.[88]

1.05   Probable cause

(A) Introduction

The Fourth Amendment prescribes that no warrant shall issue but upon probable cause.[89] While the Amendment makes no mention of warrantless arrests or searches, the Supreme Court has applied the probable cause requirement to warrantless arrest and searches, as well.[90] In fact, the Court has indicated that a stricter probable cause standard may apply when there is no warrant: "[I]n a doubtful or marginal case a search under a warrant may be sustainable where without one it would fail."[91] Additionally, evidence which is seized with a warrant may be admissible notwithstanding the subsequent determination that the warrant was invalid where the police reasonably relied upon the warrant.[92]

The review of probable cause at a suppression hearing considering the validity of an arrest or search undertaken with authority of a warrant questions whether the affidavit contained sufficient facts and circumstances to allow the judge or magistrate to draw his own reasonable and fair inferences to believe that a crime had been committed. In the case of an arrest warrant, the question includes inquiry into the facts implicating the

---

[87]State v Milligan, 40 OS(3d) 341, 344, 533 NE(2d) 724 (1988).

[88]State v Jurek, 52 App(3d) 30, 556 NE(2d) 1191 (Cuyahoga 1989), appeal dismissed by 47 OS 711, 548 NE(2d) 241 (1989).

[89]For a full discussion of the probable cause requirement see Text Chapter 3, Probable Cause.

[90]Wong Sun v United States, 371 US 471, 83 SCt 407, 9 LEd(2d) 441 (1963).

[91]United States v Ventresca, 380 US 102, 106, 85 SCt 741, 13 LEd(2d) 684 (1965).

[92]United States v Leon, 468 US 897, 104 SCt 3405, 82 LEd(2d) 677 (1984); Massachusetts v Sheppard, 468 US 981, 104 SCt 3424, 82 LEd(2d) 737 (1984).

person whose arrest is sought and, in the case of a search warrant, that evidence of a crime is to be found at the place to be searched.[93] Where the review is of an arrest or search without a warrant, its constitutional validity depends on whether, at the moment the arrest or search took place, the facts and circumstances within the officers' knowledge and of which they had reasonably trustworthy information were sufficient to warrant a prudent man in believing that (1) the person to be arrested had committed or was committing an offense, or (2) evidence was linked to a crime and was presently at the place to be searched.[94]

Probable cause for an arrest is not the same as probable cause for a search. The existence of one does not necessarily give rise to the other. For an arrest, there must be sufficient facts and circumstances giving rise to a belief that a crime has been committed and that the person to be arrested committed it. In *Dixon v Maxwell*,[95] the Ohio Supreme Court upheld a warrantless arrest and said that it is not necessary for an arresting officer to know specifically what crime has been committed, so long as the officer had reasonable grounds to believe some felony had been committed. The Ohio Supreme Court misstated the requirement. Certainly no warrant could issue without a showing of probable cause that a specific offense has been committed. Similarly, a warrantless arrest should be invalid without probable cause to believe a specific crime has been committed. In *Dixon*, officers responded to a report that an apartment was being used for prostitution. When they arrived at the building, the officers saw three men removing a large quantity of clothing from the trunk of an automobile. The police arrested the three men after following them into the apartment building. Clearly, the officers had a reasonable suspicion that some illegality was being committed, but nothing more. Probable cause to arrest, whether with or without a warrant, requires probable cause to believe that a specific offense has been committed.

The inquiry differs when the intrusion is a search. There must be probable cause to believe that evidence of a crime is *presently* at the location to be searched. Consequently, it must be determined that the object sought is evidence of a crime and that it is likely to be at the location to be searched. Therefore, the probable cause for a search may become stale, which is never a problem when the intrusion is an arrest. The contraband which was observed on the premises may no longer be there just a few days later. Staleness does not become an issue when the items are stationary or are likely to remain permanently at one location, such as business records.[96]

It is impossible to reduce to a percentage how probable the cause must be to justify issuance of a warrant or a warrantless intrusion. With good reason, the Supreme Court has avoided a mathematical definition. Nonetheless, the Court has provided some guidance for testing each factual situation, and probable cause will differ depending upon minor factual

---

[93]United States v Ventresca, 380 US 102, 106, 85 SCt 741, 13 LEd(2d) 684 (1965).
[94]Beck v Ohio, 379 US 89, 85 SCt 223, 13 LEd(2d) 142 (1964).
[95]Dixon v Maxwell, 177 OS 20, 201 NE(2d) 592 (1964).
[96]Andresen v Maryland, 427 US 463, 96 SCt 2737, 49 LEd(2d) 627 (1976).

variations. No hard and fast rules are possible because it depends upon a case-by-case analysis.

In the early days of the republic, Chief Justice Marshall said that probable cause exists where the facts warrant suspicion.[97] Probable cause based upon mere suspicion will not suffice today; the standard falls somewhere between suspicion and reasonable doubt necessary to convict. The Court has equated probable cause with reasonable grounds to believe and has used the phrases interchangeably.[98]

The message that the Court has attempted to convey is that probable cause is a "flexible, common-sense standard."[99] "The rule of probable cause is a practical, nontechnical conception."[100] In *Brinegar v United States*,[101] the Court set forth the standard which has been cited most often with approval: "In dealing with probable cause, however, as the very name implies, we deal with probabilities. These are not technical; they are the factual and practical considerations of everyday life on which reasonable and prudent men, not legal technicians, act."[102]

Currently, probable cause is determined on the totality of the circumstances. The magistrate must make a practical, common sense decision whether, given all the circumstances set forth in the affidavit, there is a fair probability that contraband or evidence of a crime will be found in a particular place.[103]

Moreover, judges determining whether probable cause exists in order to issue a warrant or police officers assessing whether they have probable cause in situations where they may act without a warrant are entitled to draw common sense conclusions about human behavior.[104] The evidence is to be evaluated in terms understood by those versed in the field of law enforcement.[105]

The purpose of the warrant requirement is to interpose a neutral and detached magistrate between the police and invasions of a citizen's privacy. That purpose is served only if the issuing authority reviews the facts and circumstances and draws his own inferences as to whether probable cause exists. Therefore, an affidavit couched only in conclusions, i.e., that probable cause exists to believe that evidence of a crime will be found, denies the judge the opportunity to draw those conclusions and robs the Fourth Amendment of its essence. The affidavit must set forth sufficient underlying circumstances to support the inference of probable cause.[106] A judge may

[97]Locke v United States, 11 US 339, 3 LEd 364 (1813).
[98]Zurcher v Stanford Daily, 436 US 547, 98 SCt 1970, 56 LEd(2d) 525 (1978).
[99]Texas v Brown, 460 US 730, 103 SCt 1535, 1543, 75 LEd(2d) 502 (1983).
[100]Brinegar v United States, 338 US 160, 176, 69 SCt 1302, 93 LEd 1879 (1949).
[101]Brinegar v United States, 338 US 160, 176, 69 SCt 1302, 93 LEd 1879 (1949).
[102]Brinegar v United States, 338 US 160, 175, 69 SCt 1302, 93 LEd 1879 (1949).
[103]Illinois v Gates, 462 US 213, 103 SCt 2317, 76 LEd(2d) 527 (1983); see also State v Brown, 20 App(3d) 36, 20 OBR 38, 484 NE(2d) 215 (Hamilton 1984).
[104]Texas v Brown, 460 US 730, 103 SCt 1535, 75 LEd(2d) 502 (1983).
[105]United States v Cortez, 449 US 411, 101 SCt 690, 66 LEd(2d) 621 (1981), cert denied 455 US 923, 102 SCt 1281, 71 LEd(2d) 464 (1982).
[106]Johnson v United States, 333 US 10, 68 SCt 367, 92 LEd 436 (1948).

draw reasonable, common sense inferences, "but those inferences are valid only when drawn from facts actually alleged in the affidavit."[107] The alternative is for the judge issuing a warrant to be a rubber stamp for the police. Where an affidavit for a search alleges only that the affiant believes and has good cause to believe that the things to be searched for are concealed in a house or place, but does not state the facts upon which such belief is based, the warrant issued upon such conclusions is illegal and void.[108]

(B) Hearsay as a basis for issuance of warrant

An affidavit for an arrest or search warrant may be based upon hearsay information rather than the personal observation of the affiant.[109] Moreover, the source of the hearsay may be a confidential informant whose identity need not be disclosed to the judge issuing a warrant or to the court reviewing probable cause on a motion to suppress.[110] If the judge does not believe the informant exists, he may refuse to issue the warrant. The only time an informant's identity need be disclosed is if his testimony is critical to the issue of guilt or innocence at trial.[111]

When probable cause is based upon the hearsay statements of an informant, certain precautions must be taken to ensure that the warrant does not issue upon unsubstantiated rumor. More is needed than merely the conclusion of the informant that criminal evidence is located at the place to be searched. A process has developed over two decades to test the information provided by the informant so that the judge may draw his own conclusions about the probable truthfulness of the information and the likelihood that the evidence will be found if a search is authorized. That process was significantly watered down in 1983 in *Illinois v Gates*,[112] when a majority of the Court overruled *Aguilar v Texas*[113] and *Spinelli v United States*,[114] which had set the standards for testing an informant's tip.

Aguilar required that the informant set forth the underlying circumstances which provided the basis for his conclusion that evidence of a crime was located at the place to be searched. This requirement is self-explanatory: an affiant must present his own basis for believing probable cause exists and cannot avoid that requirement merely by crediting the conclusion to another source. *Aguilar* further required that the affidavit provide a basis for the judge to conclude that the informant is a credible person. *Spinelli* explained that the latter requirement is necessary for the judge to determine whether the informant is trustworthy and should be believed. The

---

[107]State v Bean, 13 App(3d) 69, 72, 13 OBR 83, 468 NE(2d) 146 (Lucas 1983).

[108]Nicholas v Cleveland, 125 OS 474, 182 NE 26 (1932), overruled by State v Lindway, 131 OS 166, 2 NE(2d) 490 (1936), cert denied 299 US 506, 57 SCt 36, 81 LEd 375 (1936).

[109]Aguilar v Texas, 378 US 108, 84 SCt 1509, 12 LEd(2d) 723 (1964), overruled by Illinois v Gates, 462 US 213, 103 SCt 2317, 76 LEd(2d) 527 (1983).

[110]McCray v Illinois, 386 US 300, 87 SCt 1056, 18 LEd(2d) 62 (1967).

[111]Roviaro v United States, 353 US 53, 77 SCt 623, 1 LEd(2d) 639 (1957).

[112]Illinois v Gates, 462 US 213, 103 SCt 2317, 76 LEd(2d) 527 (1983).

[113]Aguilar v Texas, 378 US 108, 84 SCt 1509, 12 LEd(2d) 723 (1964), overruled by Illinois v Gates, 462 US 213, 103 SCt 2317, 76 LEd(2d) 527 (1983).

[114]Spinelli v United States, 393 US 410, 89 SCt 584, 21 LEd(2d) 637 (1969), overruled by Illinois v Gates, 462 US 213, 103 SCt 2317, 76 LEd(2d) 527 (1983).

credibility of an informant may be established if he has provided correct information in the past.[115] Similarly, credibility can be established if the informant acknowledges his participation in the illegal enterprise and makes an admission against penal interest.[116] Finally, the *Spinelli* Court indicated that where an informant's credibility is established but the reliability of his information is not adequately demonstrated, the gap could be filled if the information contains great detail which is corroborated and is sufficient to infer that the informant knew what he was talking about and gained his information in a reliable manner.[117]

In *Gates*, the Supreme Court rejected the formal analysis required by *Aguilar* and *Spinelli*. The information about drug trafficking in *Gates* came to police through an anonymous tip which provided no underlying circumstances, nor any way to test the informant's credibility or the reliability of his information. Illinois police and federal narcotics agents were able to corroborate some of the details contained in the anonymous tip, but these facts, while sufficient to raise suspicions about the defendants' activities, involved noncriminal behavior. The corroboration, in itself, did not provide probable cause. Three Illinois courts held that the tip plus the affidavit failed both prongs of the *Aguilar-Spinelli* test because they failed to reveal the informant's basis of knowledge *and* failed to establish either the informant's credibility or the reliability of his information.

Justice Rehnquist, for a majority of the Supreme Court, rejected this analysis as well as the *Aguilar-Spinelli* test. The Court substituted a "totality of the circumstances" approach in which the elements of the two-pronged test, the basis of knowledge *and* credibility or reliability, are just issues to be considered by a judge in determining whether probable cause exists to believe that evidence will be found in a particular place. The Court stressed that probable cause is a practical, common sense decision, requiring only a "fair probability" that contraband will be found, and held that the *Aguilar-Spinelli* tests were inconsistent with this type of analysis. Applying the totality of the circumstances approach to the facts in *Gates*, the Court ruled that the police corroboration of the defendants' travels, which suggested involvement in narcotics trafficking, was sufficient, together with the anonymous tip, to provide probable cause. The weakness of the *Gates* analysis lies not so much in its renunciation of the *Aguillar-Spinelli* test but in its application of the substituted formula to the facts of the case. The police corroboration of the tip was limited to innocuous facts which did not point to criminality but related only the defendants' travels. Actually, the corroboration pointed up some errors in the anonymous tip. The decision to issue the search warrant, consequently, and the ultimate ratification of that decision by the Supreme Court majority rested on very little other than the anonymous tip.

One year later, the Court reaffirmed its intent to reject the old tests when it summarily reversed a Massachusetts decision that failed to read

[115]McCray v Illinois, 386 US 300, 87 SCt 1056, 18 LEd(2d) 62 (1967).
[116]United States v Harris, 403 US 573, 91 SCt 2075, 29 LEd(2d) 723 (1971).
[117]Compare Draper v United States, 358 US 307, 79 SCt 329, 3 LEd(2d) 327 (1959).

Gates as "a significant change in the appropriate Fourth Amendment treatment of applications for search warrants." In a per curiam decision, the Court said that the *Gates* decision involved a rejection of the two-pronged test, not merely its refinement. The Court also chided the state appellate court for failing to give deference to the magistrate's initial review and decision.[118]

The *Gates* decision in 1983 has been attributed with doing far more mischief than it actually does. True, the decision eliminates the two-prong test for assessing the reliability and veracity of an informant's tip, thereby making it easier for police to secure a warrant on the basis of a tip. But the test itself, as opposed to its application in that case, reaffirmed the basic probable cause standard. A bare-bones affidavit, containing only conclusions—whether an informant's or a police officer's—will not suffice to establish probable cause. Justice Rehnquist wrote, "Sufficient information must be presented to the magistrate to allow that official to determine probable cause; his action cannot be a mere ratification of the bare conclusions of others."[119] The *Gates* majority admonished that "courts must continue to conscientiously review the sufficiency of affidavits on which warrants are issued."[120]

(C) Actions of the suspect and probable cause

Occasionally, noncriminal activity of the defendant in the presence of an officer may give rise to probable cause. However, mere questionable associations and furtive movements are insufficient to provide the basis for probable cause. In *State v Hill*,[121] a police officer entered a bar while his partner was writing a traffic ticket on the street. The area was known as one in which drugs were sold. In fact, the officer had made four arrests in the bar during the past three weeks. The defendant was seated in the bar with two female impersonators. The officer recognized the defendant as having been in the company of others who had been arrested for possession of narcotics. The officer had no information about the defendant's past record. One of the female impersonators saw the police officer and said something to the defendant and both of the female impersonators then left the table. The defendant then leaned forward and placed his hands and arms under the table near his legs and the officer could not see the defendant's hands. As the officer approached the defendant's table, the defendant started to leave, but the officer stopped him and asked for identification. After the defendant gave the officer some identification, the officer frisked him. In the rolled-up cuff of his jeans the officer found a glassine envelope of heroin and he then arrested the defendant. The defendant contended the arrest was unlawful because the officer did not have probable cause; therefore, the search was not incident to a lawful arrest.

---

[118]Massachusetts v Upton, 466 US 727, 104 SCt 2085, 80 LEd(2d) 721 (1984) (per curiam).

[119]Illinois v Gates, 462 US 213, 239, 103 SCt 2317, 76 LEd(2d) 527 (1983).

[120]Illinois v Gates, 462 US 213, 239, 103 SCt 2317, 76 LEd(2d) 527 (1983).

[121]State v Hill, 52 App(2d) 393, 370 NE(2d) 775 (Hamilton 1977).

The Court ruled that the defendant's behavior did not give the officer probable cause to arrest. To have probable cause to arrest or search, the officer had to have sufficient evidence to warrant a prudent man's believing that a felony had been or was being committed by the accused. In this case, the officer had reason to be suspicious, but not probable cause to search or arrest. Before placing a hand on the accused, the officer must have had probable cause. Questionable associations and furtive movements are insufficient to satisfy that requirement.

While furtive movement may not equal probable cause, flight from authority can be added to other factors in order to give probable cause to arrest. This was the issue in *United States v Pope*,[122] where two special agents of the Drug Enforcement Administration (DEA), who were on duty in the Cleveland airport monitoring flights to and from cities known to be drug distribution centers, observed the defendant, Pope, getting off a flight from Los Angeles. A month before, the agents had seen defendant purchase a one-way ticket to Los Angeles using cash from a large roll of bills. The agents followed the defendant through the airport. Pope appeared nervous, looking back repeatedly at the agents following him. Outside the terminal, one agent approached Pope and displayed his credentials. Pope broke into a run and the agent followed, shouting to Pope that he was a federal agent. As the agent gained on Pope, Pope threw his briefcase at him, and the agent drew his revolver. Pope then removed a bag from his jacket and stuffed it down a storm sewer in full view of both agents. Pope was detained and the bag was retrieved and found to contain two plastic bags of heroin. In addition, inside the briefcase was a bottle of methadone and Pope was arrested. The defense moved to suppress the evidence on the ground that the defendant's meeting a "drug courier profile" used by the DEA agents does not give the agents probable cause to arrest.

The court agreed that the satisfaction of drug courier profiles does not, standing alone, give rise to probable cause but may be taken into account. At the time the agent approached Pope outside the terminal, there was no probable cause to arrest. However, Pope's flight in the face of lawful authority gave the agent grounds to reasonably suspect that Pope was engaged in unlawful activity. Flight invites pursuit. Flight itself is not grounds for probable cause but can be taken into account. When Pope threw his briefcase at the agent, the agent had probable cause to arrest him for assaulting a federal officer. After the bag was found to contain heroin, the officers arrested Pope. The arrest was supported by probable cause.

CROSS REFERENCES

Text 6.02

1 Giannelli & Snyder, Baldwin's Ohio Practice, *Evidence* § 101.12

---

[122]United States v Pope, 561 F(2d) 663 (6th Cir Ohio 1977).

1.06   Fourth Amendment Protection of Property Interest

In *Katz*, the majority made it clear that they did not intend to limit Fourth Amendment rights to those that fit within the new privacy test. Justice Stewart wrote that Fourth Amendment "protections go further [than privacy], and often have nothing to do with privacy at all."[123] For example, the Fourth Amendment also protects liberty interests.[124]

In *Soldal v Cook County, Illinois*,[125] a civil suit which arose out of an unlawful eviction, the Court reaffirmed that the Fourth Amendment protects property interests even in situations which do not affect privacy or liberty interests. The Court wrote that the Fourth Amendment protects "the people's security from governmental interference" regardless of the reasons, or lack thereof, for the intrusion.

---

[123]Katz v United States, 389 US 347, 350, 88 SCt 507, 19 LEd(2d) 576 (1967).
[124]Cf. Terry v Ohio, 392 US 1, 88 SCt 1868, 20 LEd(2d) 889 (1968).
[125]Soldal v Cook County, Illinois, 506 US 56, 113 SCt 538, 547, 121 LEd(2d) 450 (1992).

Chapter 2

The Exclusionary Rule

2.01 Introduction

The principal remedy for violation of Fourth Amendment rights is the exclusion of evidence from the criminal trial of the person whose rights have been violated. The Supreme Court adopted the rule for federal criminal trials in 1914,[1] and extended its applicability to state criminal trials in 1961.[2] No principle of American constitutional law has provoked such prolonged and sustained controversy. The exclusionary rule has remained a convenient political target even though it and Fourth Amendment protections, generally, have been diminished. Nearly three quarters of a century after the exclusionary rule's initial adoption and nearly a quarter of a century after it was made applicable to the states, the Supreme Court adopted a broad so-called good faith exception to the exclusionary rule. So far the exception is applicable only to searches with warrants; its greatest impact and harm will occur if it is extended to warrantless searches.

The exclusionary rule is unique to the United States, virtually unknown in the legal systems of other common-law countries or other systems of law.[3] Although there are isolated examples of similar evidentiary rules found in other countries, e.g., West Germany's response to the repression of its previous regime, it must be viewed as a peculiarly American institution. This should not be surprising since Americans possess what has normally been considered a healthy distrust of government, born during colonial times and nurtured by subsequent examples of official misconduct. The exclusionary rule rests on two principles: (1) that while enforcing the law, the police must obey the law; and (2) that the government shall not profit by the illegal acts of its agents. The opponents of the exclusionary rule do not contest these two principles, but focus instead on the high cost to society and the irrationality of a guilty person going free while the government official who committed the illegal act is not punished.

The real key to understanding the present approach to the exclusionary rule is to be found in the Supreme Court's frequent reminder that exclusion for a Fourth Amendment violation is not a constitutional right. Unlike a Fifth Amendment violation that occurs when a defendant's involuntary statement is offered in evidence at trial, the Fourth Amendment violation

---

[1]Weeks v United States, 232 US 383, 34 SCt 341, 58 LEd 652 (1914).

[2]Mapp v Ohio, 367 US 643, 81 SCt 1684, 6 LEd(2d) 1081 (1961).

[3]Bivens v Six Unknown Named Agents of Federal Bureau of Narcotics, 403 US 388, 415, 91 SCt 1999, 29 LEd(2d) 619 (1971).

occurs at the time of illegal arrest, search or seizure, not when evidence is sought to be used at trial.[4]

CROSS REFERENCES

Text Ch 18

2.02   Development of the exclusionary rule

The underpinnings for all later decisions protecting the individual right of privacy appear in the 1886 United States Supreme Court decision *Boyd v United States.*[5] *Boyd* was decided under both the Fourth and Fifth Amendments to the United States Constitution, but the Court's reasoning relied most heavily on the Fifth Amendment's explicit exclusion of compelled self-incrimination. A glimmer of the exclusionary rule appeared in federal and state decisions at the end of the nineteenth and beginning of the twentieth century with statements such as "These constitutional safeguards would be deprived of a large part of their value if they could be invoked only for preventing the obtaining of such evidence, and not for the protection against its use"[6] and "[not to exclude] is to emasculate the constitutional guaranty, and deprive it of all beneficial force or effect in preventing unreasonable searches and seizures."[7] There are decisions during this period rejecting the exclusionary rule,[8] but the impetus for its full evolution and development existed in *Boyd* and other nineteenth century decisions.

In 1914, the Court formally adopted the exclusionary rule in *Weeks v United States,*[9] holding that evidence secured by federal law enforcement officers in violation of an accused's Fourth Amendment rights could not be used in a federal criminal prosecution against him. The *Weeks* opinion did not adopt the exclusionary rule as a deterrent to illegal police behavior. Rather, the Court simply treated the exclusionary rule as a logical corollary to the language of the Fourth Amendment and its guarantee of individual privacy. The Court discussed the importance of the Fourth Amendment and developed a charter setting forth the role of the courts in enforcing it:

> The effect of the Fourth Amendment is to put the courts of the United States and Federal officials, in the exercise of their power and authority, under limitations and restraints as to the exercise of such power and authority, and to forever secure the people, their persons, houses, papers and effects against all unreasonable searches and seizures under the guise of law. This protection reaches all alike, whether accused of crime or not, and the duty of giving to it force and effect is obligatory upon all entrusted under our Federal system with the enforcement of the laws. The tendency of those who execute the criminal laws of the country to obtain conviction by means of unlawful seizures and enforced confessions, the latter often obtained after subjecting accused persons to unwarranted practices destructive of rights secured by the

---

[4]United States v Verdugo-Urquidez, 494 US 259, 110 SCt 1056, 108 LEd(2d) 222 (1990).

[5]Boyd v United States, 116 US 616, 6 SCt 524, 29 LEd 746 (1886).

[6]United States v Wong Quong Wong, 94 Fed 832, 834 (2d Cir Vt 1899).

[7]State v Sheridan, 121 Iowa 164, 168, 96 NW 730 (1903).

[8]Adams v New York, 192 US 585, 24 SCt 372, 48 LEd 575 (1904).

[9]Weeks v United States, 232 US 383, 34 SCt 341, 58 LEd 652 (1914).

federal Constitution, should find no sanction in the judgments of the courts which are charged at all times with the support of the Constitution and to which people of all conditions have a right to appeal for the maintenance of such fundamental rights.[10]

Furthermore, the Court said that while efforts to bring the guilty to punishment are praiseworthy, those efforts "are not to be aided by the sacrifice of those great principles established by years of endeavor and suffering which have resulted in their embodiment in the fundamental law of the land."[11]

The Supreme Court, then, did not adopt the exclusionary rule principally to deter illegal police behavior, although it is fair to infer an expectation on the part of the Court that it would have that effect. The Court's primary reason appears to be a belief that if a trial court looks the other way and ignores the unconstitutional manner in which the evidence in question is secured, then the courts would be sanctioning "a manifest neglect if not an open defiance of the prohibitions of the Constitution."[12] The belief was that through such silence the courts would become a party to the illegality and help to make the Fourth Amendment a fundamental right without a remedy.

The applicability of the *Weeks* rule was limited to federal criminal trials. For thirty-four years thereafter there was no decision applying the general principles of the Fourth Amendment to the states through the due process clause of the Fourteenth Amendment. When such a decision was finally rendered in 1949 in *Wolf v Colorado,*[13] only the principle of freedom from unreasonable intrusions was made applicable to the states through the due process clause of the Fourteenth Amendment, not the federal remedy, the exclusionary rule. In the face of the most egregious violations of that right, the states remained free to choose remedies to protect or not protect it. The Court reasoned that the exclusionary rule was not an explicit requirement of the Fourth Amendment, but was a matter of judicial implication and thus not constitutionally mandated.[14]

Even during this hands-off period, the Supreme Court fashioned an exclusionary rule, albeit a very limited one, which was applied to the states for certain extraordinarily unreasonable intrusions committed by state and local law enforcement officers. A unanimous Supreme Court in *Rochin v California*[15] held that the conditions surrounding certain unreasonable searches and seizures required the suppression of the fruits of those intrusions in state criminal proceedings notwithstanding the general inapplicability of the exclusionary rule to the states. Justice Frankfurter, who wrote the majority opinion in *Wolf,* also wrote for the five members of the *Rochin* Court and stated that a conviction based on the fruits of illegal police

---

[10]Weeks v United States, 232 US 383, 391-92, 34 SCt 341, 58 LEd 652 (1914).

[11]Weeks v United States, 232 US 383, 393, 34 SCt 341, 58 LEd 652 (1914).

[12]Weeks v United States, 232 US 383, 394, 34 SCt 341, 58 LEd 652 (1914).

[13]Wolf v Colorado, 338 US 25, 69 SCt 1359, 93 LEd 1782 (1949), overruled by Mapp v Ohio, 367 US 643, 81 SCt 1684, 6 LEd(2d) 1081 (1961).

[14]Wolf v Colorado, 338 US 25, 69 SCt 1359, 93 LEd 1782 (1949), overruled by Mapp v Ohio, 367 US 643, 81 SCt 1684, 6 LEd(2d) 1081 (1961).

[15]Rochin v California, 342 US 165, 72 SCt 205, 96 LEd 183 (1952).

behavior violated due process when the conduct of the police "shock[ed] the conscience" of the Court and offended its sense of justice.[16]

In *Rochin,* police officers, without authority, entered the accused's home and jumped on him in an unsuccessful attempt to extract two morphine capsules which he deliberately had swallowed to prevent their seizure. A subsequent stomach pumping by a doctor, against the accused's will, produced the morphine capsules. While not overruling *Wolf,* the Court acknowledged that notions of due process, and thus the Constitution itself, required an exclusionary rule to protect the rights of citizens against some forms of illegal police behavior. The inherent subjectivity of the *Rochin* test became readily apparent when Justice Frankfurter broke from the majority of the Court in a later case. The majority's conscience in that case was not "shocked" by illegal police behavior, which involved the planting of hidden microphones in a suspect's marital bedroom,[17] as an atrocious invasion of the accused's person.

The Supreme Court finally reversed *Wolf* in 1961, in *Mapp v Ohio.*[18] Forty-seven years after the Court applied the exclusionary rule to federal criminal proceedings, it extended the exclusionary rule for Fourth Amendment violations to state criminal proceedings. By 1961, the atmosphere in the Supreme Court was definitely changing; gone was the Court's reluctance to find a broad and distinctive meaning in the Fourteenth Amendment's guarantee against state violations of due process. The Court rejected the assertion in *Wolf* that the exclusionary rule was merely a creature of judicial implication and reasserted its earlier position, developed in *Weeks,* affirming the exclusionary rule's constitutional origins and justifications. The Supreme Court also pointed out that the factual considerations stressed in the *Wolf* opinion no longer existed.

By 1961, a majority of states had applied the exclusionary rule on their own because, as the Court stressed, the other remedies failed to secure compliance with the constitutional provision.[19] The Court said that failure to apply the exclusionary rule was to make the right of privacy meaningless and amounted to a withholding of its privilege and enjoyment. Perhaps most profound in light of later criticism of the decision was the Court's insistence that permitting the introduction of illegally seized evidence served to encourage disobedience to the federal Constitution.[20]

The years since *Mapp* have hardly been tranquil. *Mapp* resolved one issue and opened the door to many others. Search and seizure questions have predominated in criminal litigation just as the prosecution of crimes has dominated all areas of litigation and preoccupied the courts.[21]

---

[16]Rochin v California, 342 US 165, 172-73, 72 SCt 205, 96 LEd 183 (1952).

[17]Irvine v California, 347 US 128, 74 SCt 381, 98 LEd 561 (1954).

[18]Mapp v Ohio, 367 US 643, 81 SCt 1684, 6 LEd(2d) 1081 (1961).

[19]Mapp v Ohio, 367 US 643, 81 SCt 1684, 6 LEd(2d) 1081 (1961).

[20]Mapp v Ohio, 367 US 643, 81 SCt 1684, 6 LEd(2d) 1081 (1961).

[21]Bacigal, *Some Observations and Proposals on the Nature of the Fourth Amendment,* 46 Geo Wash L Rev 529 (1978); Nedrud & Oberto, *The Supreme Court and the Criminal Law* (1979).

As a result of *Mapp*, courts at every level have been compelled to spend considerable time on search and seizure issues and have had to expend considerable thought on the meaning of the Fourth Amendment guarantee. The legal community, particularly, and the lay community as well have focused on the limits of permissible police behavior and, by necessity, on the meaning and parameters of the Fourth Amendment assurance of individual privacy and freedom from unreasonable searches and seizures.

Perhaps the most noteworthy, yet frequently the most overlooked, effect of the exclusionary rule has been the spotlight it has focused on the greater issue involving the relationship between citizens and police in a free society. Unlike any other approach to the consideration of these issues, the exclusionary rule provides a forum in which their consideration is unavoidable. Motions to suppress evidence are filed in courts throughout this country every day, and within that context the issues must be faced. Along with issues of freedom and individual integrity, society is also forced to face up to the cost of this freedom: that either through blunder or intent, relevant and reliable evidence of guilt is excluded as a direct result of police error, and a potentially guilty person may go free. It is healthy for a society to be continually faced with such basic issues of freedom and its costs. The exclusionary rule demands that society constantly reaffirm its commitment to individual freedom, as it daily reconsiders the basic questions as to when and under what circumstances police intrusions into individual privacy satisfy the constitutional test of reasonableness.

2.03   Exclusion for violation of state law

Exclusion is mandated under *Mapp v Ohio*[22] when evidence is derived from an illegal arrest, search, or seizure that violates the Fourth Amendment of the United States Constitution. Prior to *Mapp*, almost half of the states adopted the exclusionary rule even though the Supreme Court had not yet held that violations of the Fourth Amendment required that evidence be suppressed in state criminal prosecutions. These states did so under a variety of theories, most often determining that their own state constitutions, which contained provisions virtually identical to the Fourth Amendment, required such a result. Although the Ohio Constitution includes a similar provision, Ohio did not follow suit.

Consequently, until *Mapp*, violations of either the federal or state constitutional or statutory provisions prohibiting unreasonable searches and seizures did not result in exclusion. Moreover, the United States Supreme Court has held that the federal Constitution requires the exclusion of evidence only when a particular arrest, search, or seizure violates the Fourth Amendment.[23] States remain free to fashion their own remedies when a particular procedure violates only state law. They may choose to exclude evidence in such cases, but exclusion flows from the state law and is not mandated under the United States Constitution.

---

[22]Mapp v Ohio, 367 US 643, 81 SCt 1684, 6 LEd(2d) 1081 (1961).
[23]Ker v California, 374 US 23, 83 SCt 1623, 10 LEd(2d) 726 (1963).

When a state court elects in such situations to impose a higher standard on government officials than that required by the United States Supreme Court under the Fourth Amendment, the state court must clearly indicate that the result flows from state constitutional or statutory law rather than from the Fourth Amendment. If the state court does not so clearly indicate, it runs the risk that the Supreme Court will conclude that the state court misinterpreted Fourth Amendment requirements.[24] On the other hand, when a police practice violates state law, but state law imposes a standard higher than that required by the Fourth Amendment, the state courts are not compelled to exclude evidence derived from that violation.

The Ohio Supreme Court has consistently held that the exclusionary rule will not be applied to evidence secured in violation of state law, but not in violation of constitutional rights.[25] Presumably, this position is based on the principle that the Ohio Constitution, similar to the Fourth Amendment, imposes no higher standard than those demanded by the federal provision, and consequently state statutes that impose a higher standard on police do not rise to violations of the state constitution. One court of appeals has simplified this discussion by suggesting that the Ohio Supreme Court "has not even imposed an exclusionary rule for violations of the provisions of the Ohio Constitution."[26] The state court will require exclusion only when the legislature mandates such a result.[27] Yet the clarity of Ohio's position has become unsettled as a result of the Supreme Court's exclusion of certain evidence in DUI prosecutions.[28]

In *State v Thompson*,[29] the Ohio Supreme Court held that the failure of the police to confine the defendant in the county in which he was arrested, in violation of RC 2967.15, did not rise to a constitutional level and thus did

---

[24]Michigan v Long, 463 US 1032, 103 SCt 3469, 77 LEd(2d) 1201 (1983).

[25]See State v Thompson, 33 OS(3d) 1, 514 NE(2d) 407 (1987) ("We do not, however, believe that such a technical violation of the statute is sufficient to justify an application of the exclusionary rule to either appellant's statements or the evidence obtained at the time of his arrest. This violation is simply not one of constitutional magnitude."). See also State v Wilmoth, 22 OS(3d) 251, 262-63, 22 OBR 427, 490 NE(2d) 1236 (1986), cert denied 501 US 1238, 111 SCt 2871, 115 LEd(2d) 1037 (1991); State v Unger, 67 OS(2d) 65, 41, 423 NE(2d) 1078 (1981). But see Fairborn v Mattachione, 72 OS(3d) 345, 650 NE(2d) 426 (1995) (even though there is no constitutional right to counsel prior to taking a breathalyzer, violation of an accused's statutory right to counsel under RC 2935.20 constitutes a violation of due process requiring suppression of breathalyzer results); City of Lakewood v Waselenchuk, 94 App(3d) 684, 641 NE(2d) 767 (Cuyahoga 1994).

[26]Columbus v Harris, No. 86AP-792, at 3, 1987 WL 9490 (10th Dist Ct App, Franklin, 3-31-87).

[27]Kettering v Hollen, 64 OS(2d) 232, 416 NE(2d) 598 (1980); State v Myers, 26 OS(2d) 190, 271 NE(2d) 245 (1971).

[28]See Defiance v Kretz, 60 OS(3d) 1, 573 NE(2d) 32 (1991).

[29]State v Thompson, 33 OS(3d) 1, 514 NE(2d) 407 (1987); see also State v Filler, No. 2442-M, 1995 WL 599031 (9th Dist Ct App, Medina, 11-11-95) (a traffic stop by a township police outside their jurisdiction does not rise to the level of a constitutional violation invoking the exclusionary rule where reasonable suspicion existed for the stop).

not merit application of the exclusionary rule. Similarly, in *State v Klemm*,[30] the court found suppression improper where it was based on execution of a warrant outside the jurisdiction of the officers because the violation did not rise to a constitutional level. Most significantly, the Hamilton County Court of Appeals, in *State v Allen*,[31] said the reason that DUI arrests based on probable cause, where the offense is not committed in the officer's presence, do not lead to exclusion is because such a violation does not rise to a constitutional level. That doctrine was invoked in *State v Barshick*,[32] where a decision to admit evidence secured during a strip search, which did not conform to the requirements set forth in RC 2933.32, was upheld on the grounds that the violation of the Revised Code section was not one of constitutional magnitude. The Medina County Court of Appeals pointed out that there was probable cause in *Barshick* but did not otherwise analyze the strip search to ascertain whether it was reasonable under the circumstances, nor did the court indicate what aspect of the Revised Code section was violated. Strip searches raise sensitive issues, and the argument could be made that the provisions of RC 2933.32 were enacted by the General Assembly to ensure that strip searches in Ohio meet the reasonableness standard of the Fourth Amendment.

A good example of this proposition may be found in *State v Holmes*,[33] where a police officer on a stake-out observed two males smoking a marijuana cigarette pull away in a vehicle. He radioed two officers participating in the operation who intercepted the vehicle, arrested one of the men, and charged him with the minor misdemeanor of possession of marijuana. The trial court suppressed the evidence seized at the time of the arrest because of two violations of state law. First, RC 2935.03 prohibits a warrantless misdemeanor arrest for an offense not committed in the arresting officer's presence. There are exceptions to this statutory provision that are not applicable to possession of marijuana. The arresting officer did not see the individual smoking the marijuana cigarette at the time of the stop and arrest. Second, RC 2935.26 generally requires issuance of a citation for a minor misdemeanor, rather than a custodial arrest. The evidence was seized as a result of these violations. The Hamilton County Court of Appeals reversed the trial judge's suppression of the evidence because, while it was seized in violation of two statutory provisions, the police conduct in the case did not violate constitutional rights.

The United States Supreme Court has generally held that rules governing arrests, except for the probable cause requirement[34] and issues pertaining to warrantless arrests in homes,[35] are not governed by the Fourth

---

[30]State v Klemm, 41 App(3d) 382, 536 NE(2d) 14 (Hamilton 1987); City of Stow v Riggenbach, 97 App(3d) 661, 647 NE(2d) 246 (Summit 1994) (evidence seized by officers was admissible because arrest by officers outside their jurisdiction in violation of state law did not give rise to a violation of defendant's constitutional rights).
[31]State v Allen, 2 App(3d) 441, 2 OBR 536, 442 NE(2d) 784 (Hamilton 1981).
[32]State v Barshick, No. 1908, 1991 WL 6150 (9th Dist Ct App, Medina, 1-16-91).
[33]State v Holmes, 28 App(3d) 12, 28 OBR 21, 501 NE(2d) 629 (Hamilton 1985).
[34]Beck v Ohio, 379 US 89, 85 SCt 223, 13 LEd(2d) 142 (1964).
[35]Payton v New York, 445 US 573, 100 SCt 1371, 63 LEd(2d) 639 (1980); Steagald v United States, 451 US 204, 101 SCt 1642, 68 LEd(2d) 38 (1981).

Amendment but are determined by state law. However, even though state law pertaining to when police may make warrantless arrests for misdemeanors will prevail, and the state will determine whether to suppress evidence when there is a violation of state law, basic Fourth Amendment standards governing reasonableness also come into play. Consequently, in *State v Reymann*,[36] where the officer made a warrantless arrest for a misdemeanor in violation of a state statute, the arrest was held unreasonable under the Fourth Amendment because it was without probable cause.[37]

The Ohio Supreme Court enunciated tests for determining whether evidence seized in violation of Criminal Rule 41 should be suppressed in *State v Wilmoth*.[38] Suppression is not required in all cases where the issuance of a search warrant is a violation of Criminal Rule 41. Only where a fundamental violation occurs will suppression be required. A fundamental violation is one that, in effect, renders the search unconstitutional under traditional Fourth Amendment standards. Violations that do not rise to the constitutional level are classified as "nonfundamental." Nonfundamental errors require suppression only where (1) the error results in prejudice because the search might not have occurred or would not have been so "abrasive" if the rule had been followed; or (2) there is evidence of an intentional or deliberate disregard of a provision of the rule.[39] Generally, appellate courts have found Criminal Rule 41 violations not to require suppression. A motion to suppress was denied in *State v Applebury*,[40] where the officer's name on the affidavit differed from the name of the affiant sworn by the magistrate. Likewise, in *State v Ulrich*,[41] the failure of the police department to store evidence in accordance with the requirements of Criminal Rule 41(D) was held not to require suppression.

The Supreme Court appeared to abandon its own standards in *Defiance v Kretz*[42] by suppressing a breathalyzer result because of the failure to substantially comply with Ohio Department of Health (ODH) regulations, even though the violation did not rise to a constitutional one nor was the result mandated by statute. The Court said admissibility turned on substantial compliance with ODH regulations. Dissenting Justice Resnick seemed to have the better of the argument when she said, "The issue of whether the test was reasonably reliable clearly goes to the weight of the evidence sought to be excluded, rather than admissibility based upon the constitutionality of the means by which it was obtained."[43] Obviously, the majority

---

[36]State v Reymann, 55 App(3d) 222, 563 NE(2d) 749 (Summit 1989), appeal dismissed by 42 OS(3d) 702, 536 NE(2d) 1171 (1989).

[37]State v Peay, 62 Misc(2d) 92, 592 NE(2d) 926 (CP, Lucas 1991).

[38]State v Wilmoth, 22 OS(3d) 251, 22 OBR 427, 490 NE(2d) 1236 (1986), cert denied 501 US 1238, 111 SCt 2871, 115 LEd(2d) 1037 (1991).

[39]State v Wilmoth, 22 OS(3d) 251, 263-64, 22 OBR 427, 490 NE(2d) 1236 (1986), cert denied 501 US 1238, 111 SCt 2871, 115 LEd(2d) 1037 (1991).

[40]State v Applebury, 34 App(3d) 376, 518 NE(2d) 977 (Hamilton 1987).

[41]State v Ulrich, 41 App(3d) 384, 536 NE(2d) 17 (Franklin 1987).

[42]Defiance v Kretz, 60 OS(3d) 1, 573 NE(2d) 32 (1991); see also State v Plummer, 22 OS(3d) 292, 22 OBR 461, 490 NE(2d) 902 (1986); Upper Arlington v Kimball, 95 App(3d) 630, 643 NE(2d) 177 (Franklin 1994).

[43]Defiance v Kretz, 60 OS(3d) 1, 5, 573 NE(2d) 32 (1991) (Resnick, J., dissenting).

felt that the legislative requirement demanded suppression as the result of failure to meet state imposed standards. Moreover, the state has the burden of proof and persuasion that it has met the statutory and administrative standards.[44]

2.04 Limitations on the exclusionary rule

Ever since the decision in *Mapp v Ohio*,[45] the Supreme Court has been limiting the reach of the exclusionary rule in several different directions. The Court has been redefining the Fourth Amendment command of reasonableness, thereby relaxing restrictions on police behavior.[46] There has also been a marked growth in the scope of exceptions to the warrant requirement. These exceptions have developed into general rules, exempting most searches from the general principle that "warrantless searches are per se unreasonable."[47] Additionally, the past decade ushered in the growth of "special circumstances" searches that excuse both the warrant and probable cause requirements of the warrant clause,[48] and in some instances allow intrusions without any individualized cause.[49] These cases all turn on the Supreme Court's exercise of its traditional and proper role, the interpretation of the amendment's ultimate test, reasonableness. The Court, however, has had equal impact by limiting the exclusionary rule.

The Supreme Court's approach to the exclusionary rule is currently powered by the belief that the only reason to exclude evidence is to deter illegal police behavior. The other philosophical underpinnings that led to the adoption of the rule have been rejected. This singular reliance on deterrence as the sole criterion allows for a very limited exclusionary rule. If the application of the rule in a specific proceeding is not likely to deter the police, according to this approach, the rule should not be applied and evidence should not be excluded. Accordingly, the Court held, in *United States v Calandra*,[50] that a grand jury witness may not refuse to answer questions on the ground that they are based on evidence obtained from him in an earlier unlawful search. There the Court reasoned that the exclusion-

---

[44]State v Gasser, 5 App(3d) 217, 5 OBR 501, 451 NE(2d) 249 (Paulding 1980); State v Mays, 83 App(3d) 610, 615 NE(2d) 641 (Pike 1992) (failure to show substantial compliance results in suppression where, as here, the state failed to prove that the needle which drew blood from the defendant was not sterilized in an alcohol solution which would affect the BAC test).

[45]Mapp v Ohio, 367 US 643, 81 SCt 1684, 6 LEd(2d) 1081 (1961).

[46]See Terry v Ohio, 392 US 1, 88 SCt 1868, 20 LEd(2d) 889 (1968).

[47]See United States v Ross, 456 US 798, 102 SCt 2157, 72 LEd(2d) 572 (1982); New York v Belton, 453 US 454, 101 SCt 2860, 69 LEd(2d) 768 (1981); Chambers v Maroney, 399 US 42, 90 SCt 1975, 26 LEd(2d) 419 (1970).

[48]See New Jersey v T.L.O., 469 US 325, 105 SCt 733, 83 LEd(2d) 720 (1985); O'Connor v Ortega, 480 US 709, 107 SCt 1492, 94 LEd(2d) 714 (1987); see also O'Connor v Ortega, 50 F(3d) 778, 31 Fed R Serv(3d) 984 (1995).

[49]See Delaware v Prouse, 440 US 648, 99 SCt 1391, 59 LEd(2d) 660 (1979); Michigan Dept of State Police v Stitz, 496 US 444, 110 SCt 2481, 110 LEd(2d) 412 (1990), affirmed by 443 Mich 744, 506 NW(2d) 209 (1993); National Treasury Employees Union v Von Raab, 489 US 656, 109 SCt 1384, 103 LEd(2d) 685 (1989), affirmed sub nom National Treasury Employees Union v Bush, 891 F(2d) 99 (1989).

[50]United States v Calandra, 414 US 338, 94 SCt 613, 38 LEd(2d) 561 (1974).

ary rule is a judicially created remedy designed to safeguard Fourth Amendment rights generally through its deterrent effect, and the application of the rule should be restricted to those areas where its remedial objectives are most effectively served. The Court exempted grand jury investigations from the sweep of the rule because such an extension would deter only police investigation consciously directed toward the discovery of evidence solely for use in a grand jury investigation. Any incentive to disregard the requirements of the Fourth Amendment solely to obtain an indictment from a grand jury, the Court reasoned, is substantially negated by the inadmissibility of the illegally seized evidence in a subsequent criminal prosecution.[51]

The broadest and most significant of this line of cases, *Stone v Powell*,[52] held that a prisoner, in a habeas corpus petition, could not raise the claim that his conviction was based on evidence obtained by an unconstitutional search where he had previously been afforded an opportunity for full and fair litigation of his claim in state courts. The Court concluded that the additional deterrent effect, if any, of applying the exclusionary rule through collateral attack was far outweighed by the costs involved. The effect of *Stone v Powell* is to ensure that state rulings on Fourth Amendment issues, except for the handful of cases heard in the Supreme Court on certiorari, will not be reviewed by federal courts. Consequently, erroneous applications of Fourth Amendment principles made by trial courts and not corrected in state appellate courts will be left intact. Until *Stone* the potential for collateral attack was the most potent weapon for ensuring the enforcement and protection of constitutional rights at criminal trials.

The limitation on habeas review, however, is not applicable when the petition asserts a Sixth Amendment claim of ineffective assistance of counsel even though that claim is premised on the attorney's failure to raise a Fourth Amendment violation at trial. The Supreme Court asserted that even though the Fourth Amendment claim is one element of proof of the Sixth Amendment claim, the two claims have separate identities and reflect different constitutional values. The petitioner must prove that his Fourth Amendment claim is meritorious and that there is a reasonable probability that the verdict would have been different absent the excludable evidence in order to demonstrate actual prejudice.[53] The limitation upon habeas claims has similarly not been extended to claims arising out of *Miranda* violations. In *Withrow v Williams*,[54] the Supreme Court held that the reasoning behind

[51]See also United States v Janis, 428 US 433, 96 SCt 3021, 49 LEd(2d) 1046 (1976) (exclusionary rule inapplicable in civil proceeding against a different sovereign from the one committing the Fourth Amendment violation); United States v Peltier, 422 US 531, 95 SCt 2313, 45 LEd(2d) 374 (1975) (Fourth Amendment decision prohibiting moving border stops need not be given retroactive application because it would not enhance deterrent effect). But see State v Burkholder, 12 OS(3d) 205, 12 OBR 269, 466 NE(2d) 176 (1984), cert denied 469 US 1062, 105 SCt 545, 83 LEd(2d) 432 (1984) (Ohio Supreme Court imposed higher standard under Ohio Constitution and held exclusionary rule applicable to probation proceedings).

[52]Stone v Powell, 428 US 465, 96 SCt 3037, 49 LEd(2d) 1067 (1976).

[53]Kimmelman v Morrison, 477 US 365, 106 SCt 2574, 91 LEd(2d) 305 (1986).

[54]Withrow v Williams, 507 US 680, 113 SCt 1745, 123 LEd(2d) 407 (1993), cert denied 114 SCt 882, 127 LEd(2d) 77 (1994).

Stone v Powell would not support such a limitation upon habeas claims arising out of *Miranda* violations because such claims stand on an entirely different footing. Justice Souter wrote that even if *Miranda* is merely prophylactic, it safeguards a fundamental trial right: the right not to be compelled to incriminate oneself. Also, he recognized, little would be gained in reducing federal courts' workload because *Miranda* claims would simply be recast as due process/involuntariness claims.

2.05   Good faith exception to the exclusionary rule

A decade ago, the Supreme Court was poised to adopt a good faith exception to the exclusionary rule. First, they ordered *Illinois v Gates*[55] restored to the docket for reargument and directed the parties to brief and argue the question of whether the exclusionary rule should be modified. It was only after both parties argued that any modification would be irrelevant to their case that the Court, "with apologies to all," relented and reserved the issue for another day.[56] One week after deciding *Gates*, the majority indicated that it would not be thwarted for long and docketed three cases for the 1983-84 term in which the proposed modification had been urged at trial and argued on appeal.[57] *United States v Leon* and *Massachusetts v Sheppard* were decided by the Court and involved searches conducted with warrants. *Colorado v Quintero* involved a warrantless search, and the defendant died before the case was argued. The decisions handed down did not determine the very important question of the applicability of the modification to searches conducted without warrants, an issue that the court has not yet revisited.

A decade passed without the Court expanding the good faith exception, but it did so in *Arizona v Evans*,[58] extending the exception to evidence seized in violation of the Fourth Amendment as a result of clerical errors committed by court employees. In *Evans*, an Arizona police officer stopped a motorist for a traffic violation and discovered an outstanding arrest warrant when he did a computer check on the driver. However, the warrant had been quashed seventeen days earlier, although a court clerk failed to notify the sheriff's office of that fact and the warrant was not removed from computer records. The U.S. Supreme Court held that there was a considerable distinction between errors made by police personnel and those made by court employees. The Court seemed to be saying that the exclusionary rule cannot deter negligent errors, although dissenting Justice Ginsburg pointed out that this reasoning runs counter the premise underlying negligence law that liability creates an incentive to act with greater care.[59] The rule is based on the cornerstone of the conservative majority's philosophy,

[55]Illinois v Gates, 462 US 213, 103 SCt 2317, 76 LEd(2d) 527 (1983).
[56]Illinois v Gates, 462 US 213, 217, 103 SCt 2317, 76 LEd(2d) 527 (1983).
[57]United States v Leon, 468 US 897, 104 SCt 3405, 82 LEd(2d) 677 (1984); Massachusetts v Sheppard, 468 US 981, 104 SCt 3424, 82 LEd(2d) 737 (1984); Colorado v Quintero, 464 US 1014, 104 SCt 543, 78 LEd(2d) 719 (1983).
[58]Arizona v Evans, 115 SCt 1185, 131 LEd(2d) 34 (1995).
[59]Massachusetts v Sheppard, 468 US 981, 987-88, 104 SCt 3424, 82 LEd(2d) 737 (1984).

which is that the Fourth Amendment does not expressly preclude the use of evidence obtained in violation of its commands, and that the exclusionary rule is not a personal constitutional right, but a judicially created remedy designed to safeguard Fourth Amendment rights generally. Once that proposition is accepted, the Court is free to decide whether to apply the exclusionary rule in a particular context.

In *Leon*, the majority reaffirmed its adherence to the test adopted in *United States v Calandra*,[60] which denied application of the exclusionary rule to grand jury proceedings, and in *United States v Janis*,[61] which permitted the use of evidence illegally seized by state officials in a federal civil proceeding. That test is twofold: first, determine the deterrent value of excluding evidence toward achievement of Fourth Amendment aims. The majority operates from the position that the only purpose of the exclusionary rule is to deter illegal police behavior. Second, assuming the presence of some deterrent value, weigh the social costs of exclusion. Thus, the test ends up as a cost-benefit analysis.

Applying this test, the majority concluded that an exclusionary rule cannot deter officers who believe that their conduct is lawful under the Constitution. This conclusion is based on a narrow view of deterrence, which looks only to the effect of the rule upon individual police officers, rather than taking a broader view of institutional deterrence aimed at departmental decision-making, leadership, and training. Moreover, the majority argued that even if some deterrent value is achieved by excluding evidence where the police misconduct is not willful, the gain is negligible and, therefore, is outweighed by the social cost involved in excluding tangible, reliable evidence of guilt.

As a result of its view of the limited purpose of the exclusionary rule, the majority concluded that the rule operates only upon the behavior of the police officer; it does not serve as a check upon the judge or magistrate who issued the search warrant. First, the majority contended that the rule was designed to deter police misconduct, not judicial or magisterial misconduct. Of course, when the Supreme Court adopted the exclusionary rule some seventy years ago, it never discussed deterrence; it discussed only the Constitution's proscription against unreasonable searches and seizures.[62] Second, the majority found no need for a rule to deter judges and magistrates, concluding that there is no evidence that judges are inclined to ignore or subvert the Fourth Amendment. Third, Justice White's majority opinion argued that exclusion would not deter judges anyway, since they are not part of law enforcement and have no stake in the outcome of a criminal case. Finally, the majority could not conclude that

> admitting evidence pursuant to a warrant while at the same time declaring that the warrant was somehow defective will in any way reduce judicial officers' professional incentives to comply with the Fourth

---

[60]United States v Calandra, 414 US 338, 94 SCt 613, 38 LEd(2d) 561 (1974).
[61]United States v Janis, 428 US 433, 96 SCt 3021, 49 LEd(2d) 1046 (1976).
[62]Weeks v United States, 232 US 383, 34 SCt 341, 58 LEd 652 (1914).

Amendment, encourage them to repeat their mistakes, or lead to the granting of all colorable warrant requests.[63]

Under the good faith exception to the exclusionary rule, the critical determination is whether the officer's reliance on the legitimacy of the search warrant was objectively reasonable. The inquiry is confined to the objectively ascertainable question of whether a reasonably well-trained officer would have known that the search was illegal despite the magistrate's authorization. All factors may be considered in making this determination, including whether the warrant application was previously rejected by a different magistrate.[64] The Court rejected inquiry into an officer's subjective belief or motivation, which, in some cases, might be easier to establish than the absence of reasonable good faith. According to the Court, the only time subjective belief is relevant is when inquiry is made into the knowing or reckless falsity of information contained in the affidavit.[65]

The Court's emphasis on the objective test of reasonableness must have resulted from self-consciousness at the criticism leveled, even before the decisions, that the expected modification would focus only on the subjective belief of the officer. The risk of such a test is self-apparent: if the officer testified to a belief in the legality of the warrant, absent actual evidence that the officer knew that the warrant was improper, a motion to suppress would be denied regardless of the unreasonableness of the belief. Consequently, the Court focused on and emphasized the test of reasonable reliance. However, such emphasis should not eliminate concern with and inquiry into the officer's good faith. Moreover, such an inquiry is totally consistent with the Court's explicit limitation of the good faith exception when the warrant is the result of perjured affidavits.

Reasonableness is predicated on a finding that a reasonable law enforcement officer would have been entitled to rely on the warrant. That determination requires that the reasonable law enforcement officer have the same knowledge of the facts as the officer had who secured or executed the warrant. A reasonableness inquiry is not conducted in a vacuum; it is premised on those facts that the actor knew and should have known. Consequently, when an officer is in possession of information that casts doubt on the validity of a warrant, reliance on that warrant is improper and unreasonable. A good faith exception requires no less.

When determining whether an officer acted in reasonable good faith, one should not confine inquiry to the officer who executes the search warrant. The good faith of the police officers who provided information material to the probable cause determination and who executed the warrant is to be evaluated as well. Anything else, of course, would encourage police officers acting in bad faith to simply substitute an officer not previously involved in the investigation to execute the search warrant.

---

[63]United States v Leon, 468 US 897, 104 SCt 3405, 82 LEd(2d) 677 (1984).

[64]United States v Leon, 468 US 897, 922 n.23, 104 SCt 3405, 82 LEd(2d) 677 (1984).

[65]United States v Leon, 468 US 897, 923, 104 SCt 3405, 82 LEd(2d) 677 (1984), citing Franks v Delaware, 438 US 154, 98 SCt 2674, 57 LEd(2d) 667 (1978).

All of these factors are to be considered in determining whether the officer executing the search warrant acted in good faith reliance on the issuing magistrate's decision. The illustrations provided by the Supreme Court indicate how infrequently evidence is to be excluded. A police officer may not rely on "a warrant based on an affidavit 'so lacking in indicia of probable cause as to render official belief in its existence entirely unreasonable.' "[66] Moreover, "a warrant may be so facially deficient—i.e. in failing to particularize the place to be searched or the things to be seized—that the executing officers cannot reasonably presume it to be valid."[67]

The Supreme Court applied these two limitations on the good faith exception to the two cases before it. In *Leon*, there was insufficient probable cause. The Court concluded, however, that the application for a warrant was supported by much more than a "bare bones" affidavit; it related the results of an intensive investigation sufficient to create disagreement among the judges of the court of appeals as to the existence of probable cause. Under these circumstances, Justice White concluded that "the officers' reliance on the magistrate's determination of probable cause was objectively reasonable, and application of the extreme sanction of exclusion is inappropriate."

In *Massachusetts v Sheppard*,[68] a murder case, there was sufficient probable cause. The deficiency was in the form of the search warrant, a form used to search for controlled substances, which was not altered although controlled substances were not in issue in the case. The warrant was sought on a Sunday, and the form was the only one the officer could find. He called the magistrate's attention to the need for corrections. The judge made some corrections but not the critical one, returned the warrant to the officer, and assured him that he could rely on it. Obviously, neither the judge nor the officer read the warrant as issued. Nonetheless, Justice White concluded that "the police conduct in this case clearly was objectively reasonable and largely error free. An error of constitutional dimensions may have been committed ... but it was the judge, not the police officers, who made the critical mistake,"[69] and thus the deterrent purpose of the exclusionary rule would not be furthered by suppressing the evidence.

The outcome of the analyses in both *Leon* and *Sheppard* is critical to courts reviewing searches with warrants. It results in a judge's issuance of a warrant insulating police from the consequences of their own failure to provide adequate information and frees police from having to double-check the correctness of a warrant issued by a judge. Except in the most egregious cases, the Supreme Court expects that evidence secured with a search warrant is admissible in the prosecution's case-in-chief in a criminal case.

---

[66]United States v Leon, 468 US 897, 923, 104 SCt 3405, 82 LEd(2d) 677 (1984), quoting Brown v Illinois, 422 US 590, 610-11, 95 SCt 2254, 45 LEd(2d) 416 (1975).

[67]United States v Leon, 468 US 897, 923, 104 SCt 3405, 82 LEd(2d) 677 (1984), quoting Brown v Illinois, 422 US 590, 610-11, 95 SCt 2254, 45 LEd(2d) 416 (1975).

[68]Massachusetts v Sheppard, 468 US 981, 104 SCt 3424, 82 LEd(2d) 737 (1984).

[69]Massachusetts v Sheppard, 468 US 981, 990, 104 SCt 3424, 82 LEd(2d) 737 (1984).

The third and final limitation on the scope of the good faith exception is the narrowest. The exception does not apply where the magistrate abandons his neutral and detached role and, rather than supervising the police, acts as though he is part of the law enforcement team. The example Justice White provided of this limitation demonstrates its narrowness. He cited to *Lo-Ji Sales, Inc v New York*,[70] where the Court condemned a magistrate who, except for two items, failed to specify the items to be seized during a search. Instead, the magistrate accompanied police during the search and determined on the spot whether additional items fell within the purview of the search warrant.

Of the six justices in the majority, only Justice Blackmun expressed some reservations about the assumptions underlying the rules announced in *Leon*[71] and *Sheppard*. He indicated that the decisions were unavoidably provisional and warned:

> If it should emerge from experience that, contrary to our expectations, the good faith exception to the exclusionary rule results in a material change in police compliance with the Fourth Amendment, we shall have to reconsider what we have undertaken here. The logic of a decision that rests on untested predictions about police conduct demands no less.[72]

Philosophical differences aside, there are considerable problems with the rule announced in *Leon*. The limitations on the exception, both as defined and as applied, are so narrow that the Court signaled its intention that the exclusionary rule simply is no longer to play a major role, at least where the search is authorized by a warrant. Any recitation of facts going beyond mere conclusory statements, which is used as the basis for a probable cause finding, likely will be sufficient to allow police to rely on a search warrant. Moreover, sloppy search warrants providing little guidance and less control over police discretion may be found adequate for purposes of avoiding suppression. A process that is subject, at best, to minimal review is not likely to be taken very seriously by the participants, and police and magistrates are hardly going to exert much effort in complying with the Fourth Amendment's dictates when the Supreme Court has so drastically minimized the Amendment's role in criminal litigation.

The majority chose to leave to the discretion of reviewing courts the question of whether to consider the constitutionality of the search before determining the good faith of the police officers. The Supreme Court left that critical issue solely in the hands of reviewing courts, which are free to determine the constitutional issue if they believe guidance is necessary; otherwise, the reviewing court need only decide the good faith issue. One effect of this procedure will be to stultify the growth of Fourth Amendment law: unresolved Fourth Amendment issues need never be resolved if the courts can simply decide the case on the good faith of the police. Moreover, courts are unlikely to offer guidance that will not be enforced, nor will

---

[70]Lo-Ji Sales, Inc v New York, 442 US 319, 99 SCt 2319, 60 LEd(2d) 920 (1979).

[71]United States v Leon, 468 US 897, 104 SCt 3405, 82 LEd(2d) 677 (1984) (Blackmun, J., concurring; Justices Brennan, Marshall, and Stevens, dissenting).

[72]United States v Leon, 468 US 897, 928, 104 SCt 3405, 82 LEd(2d) 677 (1984).

defendants litigate Fourth Amendment issues that will not affect the outcome of their cases. Fourth Amendment jurisprudence, at least that part of the law concerning warrants and probable cause, could remain as it was on July 5, 1984, the date the Court decided *Leon* and *Sheppard*.

Finally, it remains unclear whether the rule in *Leon* and *Sheppard* will be applied to warrantless searches. On the one hand, the *Leon* majority stressed the importance of the warrant process in both cases, the need for deferring to the magistrate's judgment, and the fact that the police officers in each case sought prior approval for the search. These factors support a limitation of the good faith exception to search warrant cases, rather than an expansion to warrantless searches where the officer decides for himself whether to conduct the search. On the other hand, the philosophical basis for the exception is that the deterrent purpose of the exclusionary rule is not furthered when the officer believes he is acting constitutionally. Arguably the officer is no more deterred when searching without a warrant, if he believes his conduct is sanctioned by the Constitution, than he would be when searching with a warrant. A warrant in hand, however, lends greater credence to the argument that one's belief is reasonable and held in good faith.

That almost a decade has passed without the expansion of the exception to warrantless searches indicates a reluctance of a majority to test the full reach of the exception. The Court has extended a variation of the exception to the reasonable reliance by police on invalid consent to police entry and search by a third person who does not have authority to consent.[73] But that is different in kind from police reliance on their own judgment that a warrantless search is lawful. The Justice Department sought expansion to warrantless searches in the 1991 Crime Bill but was thwarted by Congress. While the United States Supreme Court has yet to speak on this issue, the Tuscarawas County Court of Appeals applied the exception to a warrantless search.[74]

The United States Supreme Court has dealt with the breadth of the exception in only one case. In *Illinois v Krull*,[75] the Court held that the exclusionary rule does not apply to evidence obtained by police who acted in objectively reasonable reliance on a statute authorizing warrantless administrative searches but which is subsequently found to violate the Fourth Amendment. The limitations on this extension of the exception are relatively illusory. The majority said that a law enforcement officer cannot be said to have acted in good faith reliance on a statute if its provisions are such that a reasonable officer should have known that the statute was unconstitutional. Moreover, the statute cannot support objectively reasonable reliance if, in passing the statute, the legislature wholly abandoned its responsibility to enact constitutional laws. Surprisingly, the most apt criticism of this decision was succinctly stated in a dissent by Justice O'Connor, accusing the Court of providing "a grace period for unconstitutional search

---

[73]Illinois v Rodriguez, 497 US 177, 110 SCt 2793, 111 LEd(2d) 148 (1990).
[74]State v Day, 19 App(3d) 252, 19 OBR 405, 483 NE(2d) 1195 (Tuscarawas 1984).
[75]Illinois v Krull, 480 US 340, 107 SCt 1160, 94 LEd(2d) 364 (1987).

and seizure legislation during which the state is permitted to violate constitutional requirements with impunity."[76]

2.06   Good faith exception applied in Ohio

The Ohio Supreme Court has accepted both aspects of the good faith exception. In *State v Wilmoth*,[77] the Court held the rule applicable to defects in the warrant procedure, admitting evidence where the affiants who provided the magistrate with oral testimony testified before they were sworn and then were asked to swear that the testimony they were "about to give" is the truth when in fact they had already testified. The Court, however, in *State v Williams*,[78] held that the exception could not be used where the magistrate fails to sign the warrant. Admittedly, the author is not a supporter of the good faith exception, but even so he fails to see the greater significance of the one error over the other, or more precisely the lesser significance of the one over the other. The Court said that a warrant without a signature is void and cannot be a command because the signature is the only identifiable manifestation of a judge's subjective intent to issue a warrant. Thus, Ohio is prepared to draw the line on some facial deficiencies, even though some other states treat the absence of a signature as a mere oversight.[79]

The greater impact of the good faith exception was its application to the probable cause in *United States v Leon*.[80] The Ohio Supreme Court followed suit in *State v George*,[81] holding the exception applicable to deficiencies in the probable cause supporting a warrant. Here, as in *Leon*, the court stressed that the exclusionary rule should not be applicable to the errors of a magistrate.

Although the Ohio Supreme Court, like the United States Supreme Court, has not ruled on the applicability of the exception to warrantless intrusions, it seemed to address that issue the year before *Leon* and *Massachusetts v Sheppard*[82] were decided. In the 1983 case of *State v Williams*,[83] where the police acted in violation of *Payton v New York*,[84] which required a warrant to enter a residence to make an arrest, the Ohio Supreme Court held that the good faith belief of the officers that they were acting in compliance with the permissible standards of conduct precluded application of the exclusionary rule. Of course, the search in *Williams* significantly differed from most warrantless searches. At the time of the entry, the

[76]Illinois v Krull, 480 US 340, 361, 107 SCt 1160, 94 LEd(2d) 364 (1987).
[77]State v Wilmoth, 22 OS(3d) 251, 22 OBR 427, 490 NE(2d) 1236 (1986), cert denied 501 US 1238, 111 SCt 2871, 115 LEd(2d) 1037 (1991).
[78]State v Williams, 57 OS(3d) 24, 565 NE(2d) 563 (1991), cert denied 501 US 1238, 111 SCt 2871, 115 LEd(2d) 1037 (1991).
[79]See, e.g., State v Spaulding, 239 Kan 439, 720 P(2d) 1047 (1986).
[80]United States v Leon, 468 US 897, 104 SCt 3405, 82 LEd(2d) 677 (1984).
[81]State v George, 45 OS(3d) 325, 544 NE(2d) 640 (1989).
[82]Massachusetts v Sheppard, 468 US 981, 104 SCt 3424, 82 LEd(2d) 737 (1984).
[83]State v Williams, 6 OS(3d) 281, 6 OBR 345, 452 NE(2d) 1323 (1983), cert denied 464 US 1020, 104 SCt 554, 78 LEd(2d) 727 (1983).
[84]Payton v New York, 445 US 573, 100 SCt 1371, 63 LEd(2d) 639 (1980).

officers were acting under authority of a statute that reflected four centuries of Anglo-American law, a situation far different from the scenario involved in an officer's ordinary determination to conduct a warrantless search. Courts of appeals in Ohio have differed on the applicability of the good faith exception to warrantless searches.[85] The Eleventh District Court of Appeals stated that the exception is not applicable to warrantless arrests.[86]

Real guidance must be sought in the courts of appeals on the extent and effect of the good faith exception. There, judgments are made about the nature of errors in the warrant process and the degree to which probable cause was lacking in the issuance of a warrant. In some cases the courts are engaging in a more rigorous analysis than in others. The less rigorous analysis results in a mechanical application of the good faith exception. The more rigorous analysis does not foretell the result, but it assures a more serious consideration of constitutional standards. The standards and guidelines that have emerged in Ohio are a result of courts of appeals decisions that in some way are far more crucial to the dimensions of the good faith exception than are the broad policy statements of the United States and Ohio Supreme Courts. These appellate courts have generally not engaged in a cursory analysis but have made a serious effort.

A police officer's lack of good faith reliance may not be called into question unless it can be established that the warrant is invalid.[87] Once the issue of the good faith exception is pertinent, however, the burden rests on the state, not the defendant, to establish that the exception should apply in the particular case.[88]

Ohio cases have followed the general principle that the exclusionary rule is not intended to deter judges from misconduct, and therefore judicial errors do not require suppression.[89] Consequently, the failure of the judge to note in the warrant that the items to be seized were not used or possessed in violation of a particular statute was a technical error by the judge,

---

[85]See State v Masten, No. 5-88-7, 1989 WL 111983 (3d Dist Ct App, Hancock, 9-29-89) (exception not applied); contra State v Day, 19 App(3d) 252, 19 OBR 405, 483 NE(2d) 1195 (Tuscarawas 1984) (decided same year as *Leon* and *Sheppard* assuming, without discussion, that exception applies to warrantless searches); State v Tuff, No. 10-232, 1985 WL 10227 (11th Dist Ct App, Lake, 6-28-85) (where court ignored trial judge's reliance on good faith exception to uphold warrantless search, but instead upheld on other grounds); State v Wuensch, No. 1772, 1989 WL 69735 (9th Dist Ct App, Medina, 6-21-89) (where dissent accused majority of extending exception to warrantless search; if accusation correct, majority approach is same reasoning adopted by US Supreme Court in Illinois v Rodriguez, 497 US 177, 110 SCt 2793, 111 LEd(2d) 148 (1990), upholding warrantless entry by police when based on consent of third person who police reasonably but erroneously believe possesses common authority over premises).

[86]State v Hill, Nos. 3720, 3745, 1989 WL 142761 (11th Dist Ct App, Trumbull, 11-27-89).

[87]State v Rodriguez, 66 App(3d) 5, 583 NE(2d) 384 (Wood 1990).

[88]State v Navarre, No. WD-88-43, 1989 WL 61669 (6th Dist Ct App, Wood, 6-9-89).

[89]Cleveland v Becvar, 63 App(3d) 163, 578 NE(2d) 489 (Cuyahoga 1989), appeal dismissed by 45 OS(3d) 716, 545 NE(2d) 901 (1989).

and therefore exclusion is inappropriate.[90] The attribution of error to the judge, however, can disguise more serious violations that might require exclusion, or at least a more substantive consideration of whether to apply the exception. For example, in *Columbus v Wright*,[91] there was no affidavit on file with the warrant. The Franklin County Court of Appeals said this was the court's error that occurred after the issuance of the warrant and therefore the police were entitled to reasonably rely on that warrant. All well and good, up to a point. The absence of the affidavit precluded consideration of the sufficiency of the probable cause which made it impossible for the state to establish that the probable cause presentation, even if inadequate, was sufficient to justify a reasonable reliance. The problem may have been created in the assignment of error where the defendant claimed a Criminal Rule 41 defect in the warrant, rather than that the warrant was not supported by probable cause.

Similarly, in *State v Gerace*,[92] the court properly attributed to the judge the error of not recording supplemental testimony offered to establish probable cause to issue a warrant.[93] The court may have been correct in finding that the police relied on the warrant, but that is not the issue. Instead, the issue is whether that reliance was reasonable and therefore justifiable. Clearly, the affidavit was insufficient to provide probable cause, which was why supplemental testimony was required. Without the supplemental testimony, the reviewing court could not, and did not, ascertain whether there was enough evidence of probable cause to justify a reasonable reliance on the warrant. By placing blame for the error, the court failed to consider the more important issue.

A warrant may not be the subject of good faith reasonable reliance where the magistrate fails the tests of neutrality and detachment. In *State v Torres*,[94] the Wood County Court of Appeals held that a police dispatcher who was also deputized as a municipal court clerk was not a neutral and detached magistrate, and therefore a warrant issued by such a magistrate could not be the basis for a good faith reasonable reliance. However, a warrant issued by a judge whose demeanor does not reflect the requirements of neutrality and detachment, such as in *State v Brooks*,[95] where the judge added phrases on his own that greatly and unreasonably increased the scope of the warrant, may still be the subject of good faith reasonable reliance where it is not clear whether the judge's conduct was intentional

---

[90]Cleveland v Becvar, 63 App(3d) 163, 578 NE(2d) 489 (Cuyahoga 1989), appeal dismissed by 45 OS(3d) 716, 545 NE(2d) 901 (1989).

[91]Columbus v Wright, 48 App(3d) 107, 548 NE(2d) 320 (Franklin 1988).

[92]State v Gerace, No. 12177, 1986 WL 2478 (9th Dist Ct App, Summit, 2-19-86).

[93]See also State v Johnson, No. 88-02-002, 1989 WL 6171 (12th Dist Ct App, Clinton, 1-30-89), affirmed by 1996 WL 12877 (1996) (court's failure to record conversation with affiant deemed not relevant because court jumped to good faith reliance issue saying evidence was admissible under exception whether or not the warrant was valid).

[94]State v Torres, No. WD-85-64, 1986 WL 9097 (6th Dist Ct App, Wood 8-22-86).

[95]State v Brooks, No. S-87-64, 1988 WL 134181 (6th Dist Ct App, Sandusky 12-16-88).

and where the misconduct does not rise to the egregious level of the judge's behavior in *Lo-Ji Sales, Inc v New York*.[96] A closer case involved the judge in *State v Adkins*,[97] who issued a search warrant for an inn in which he had a small interest. The judge also transferred calls about drug problems from the manager of the inn to the appropriate law enforcement agency. The Athens County Appellate Court held that those facts did not deprive the judge of his neutral and detached character where he did not participate in the police investigation nor serve as the manager's advisor on the matter.

A court's mode of analysis is significant. Whether error is attributed to the court issuing the warrant or to the police dictates whether exclusion is an issue at all. If the error is the court's, exclusion is not a proper consideration. If the error is attributed to the police, then it is the beginning of the process and of the consideration whether despite the error the evidence should be admissible under the good faith exception. Interesting insight to this issue was provided by the Licking County Court of Appeals in an unreported opinion.[98] There, the defendant was arrested on an improperly issued bench warrant. The court had been notified that the defendant had failed to serve the remainder of a sentence for disorderly conduct, when in fact the defendant had served his time. The defendant's name did not appear on a list of people who had served their time. A search incident to the arrest on the bench warrant turned up LSD, and the defendant was prosecuted.

The state argued at the suppression hearing that the exclusionary rule should not be applied because the arresting officer acted in good faith reliance on the warrant. The court of appeals rejected this argument. Acknowledging that *Leon* and *Sheppard* held that the exclusionary rule should not be applied to a judge's errors, the court, nonetheless, suppressed the evidence because of the need to deter the police conduct involved in the case. While the arresting officer acted in good faith and relied on the warrant, the court correctly read *Leon* and *Sheppard* to require that the exception be applied only when the collective effort of the law enforcement personnel in the case meets the standard of reasonableness. Here, the court found that the error was not the judge's but that of the law enforcement agency, which had communicated inaccurate information to the municipal court. This occurred, according to the court, because at the time the bench warrant was issued, there was no standard procedure by which law enforcement personnel informed the municipal court whether a defendant had properly served his time. Not to suppress, the court said, "would be to encourage careless, perhaps deliberately neglectful, record keeping."[99]

---

[96]Lo-Ji Sales, Inc v New York, 442 US 319, 99 SCt 2319, 60 LEd(2d) 920 (1979).

[97]State v Adkins, 80 App(3d) 211, 608 NE(2d) 1152 (Athens 1992), cert denied 507 US 975, 113 SCt 1423, 122 LEd(2d) 792 (1993) (nor did the judge's limited 0.07% ownership in the inn violate the Ohio Code of Judicial Conduct, Canon 3(C)(1), where the issue in controversy in the search warrant was the drugs, not the inn).

[98]State v Gough, 35 App(3d) 81, 519 NE(2d) 842 (Licking 1986), cert denied 113 SCt 1311, 122 LEd(2d) 699 (1993).

[99]State v Gough, 35 App(3d) 81, 84, 519 NE(2d) 842 (Licking 1986), cert denied 113 SCt 1311, 122 LEd(2d) 699 (1993).

In a concurring opinion, Judge Milligan wrote that the remedy of exclusion is particularly appropriate to the constitutional offense in this case because it was different from a situation where the error was reasonably unavoidable. He pointed out that the same police department that created the clerical inaccuracy had also made the arrest and had the capacity to ameliorate the practice that led to the error.

In determining good faith, all of the police officers engaged in the enterprise, those involved in securing the warrant as well as those involved in its execution, must be considered. The executing officer's good faith will not save an otherwise faulty process where an affiant withholds important information from the court.[100] In establishing good faith, the state must be able to prove the good faith reliance of all of the officers. The state may not go beyond the four corners of the affidavit to show that the affiant had probable cause when the probable cause in the affidavit was so lacking that the executing officer could not reasonably rely on it.[101] The state's claim of good faith reliance was rejected where the affiant also executed the warrant because the officer's knowledge was "no less than equal to that of the magistrate, and being subject to the same deficiencies, he could not acquire any greater authority by any asserted 'good faith' reliance on the warrant issued by the magistrate."[102]

The failure to follow the limits of a warrant cannot be saved by the good faith exception to the exclusionary rule because the good faith reasonable reliance must be on the warrant, and the search must be pursuant to the warrant. An improper search of persons present during the execution of an otherwise valid warrant is not pursuant to the warrant and will not be saved by the good faith exception.[103] Similarly, the seizure of evidence that goes beyond the scope of the warrant's command cannot be considered objectively reasonable.[104] However, in *State v Brock*,[105] the court of appeals remanded to the trial court for a determination of whether the police acted in good faith. In *Brock*, the trial court suppressed evidence found on the defendant and in his car while the police were executing a warrant to search the defendant's residence, which was one-half mile from where the defendant was stopped. The defendant was then taken to his house where the warrant was executed. It is difficult to imagine a finding that the police were operating in good faith reasonable reliance on the warrant to search defendant's residence when he was stopped and searched away from the house.

The process is at its best when Ohio appellate courts evaluate probable cause deficiencies to ascertain whether, despite such deficiencies, a warrant could support a good faith reasonable reliance. If the warrant is so lacking

[100]State v Johnson, 48 App(3d) 256, 549 NE(2d) 550 (Highland 1988).
[101]State v Navarre, No. WD-88-43, 1989 WL 61669 (6th Dist Ct App, Wood, 6-9-89).
[102]State v Carpenter, No. 7-88-1, 10, 1989 WL 22030 (3d Dist Ct App, Henry, 3-9-89), appeal dismissed by 44 OS(3d) 703, 541 NE(2d) 622 (1989).
[103]State v Murphy, No. 13080, 1987 WL 17780 (9th Dist Ct App, Summit, 9-30-87), cert denied 485 US 1040, 108 SCt 1603, 99 LEd(2d) 917 (1988).
[104]State v Hunter, 48 App(3d) 31, 548 NE(2d) 272 (Lorain 1988).
[105]State v Brock, No. 11449, 1989 WL 109303 (2d Dist Ct App, Montgomery, 9-21-89).

in probable cause as to be "bare bones" in nature, such as an affidavit that presents to the magistrate only conclusions, then an officer is not entitled to rely on the warrant. This process may appear to be circuitous if one reviews the issuing magistrate's decision, necessitated by the Supreme Court in *Leon*, that stressed that the exclusionary rule operates only to deter and limit police, not judges.

Consequently, an affidavit that merely concluded that weapons will be found in a house, even though there was ample probable cause presented about other evidence, was not sufficient to allow the executing officer to rely on the warrant in a search for those weapons.[106] However, the Ohio Supreme Court, on appeal by the state in *Harrell*,[107] remanded the case to the appellate court to determine whether the evidence would be admissible under the inevitable discovery exception.[108] It is submitted that the Ohio Supreme Court fell into a trap in *Harrell*. Inevitable discovery is an exception applicable only to derivative evidence where there is no independent constitutional violation and the only reason to exclude depends upon the connection between the derivative evidence and the primary evidence obtained as a result of a constitutional violation. In *Harrell*, the evidence was not derivative but primary and the very subject of the constitutional violation. This is a fine distinction, but one that must be made if the exclusionary rule is to retain any deterrent value.

Information presented in an affidavit may be so stale that it reduces the affidavit to "bare bones" and does not subject the warrant to good faith reasonable reliance.[109] Moreover, the inclusion of facts that just pad an affidavit but do not materially contribute to a finding of probable cause will also fail the good faith reasonable reliance test. In *Toledo v McHugh*,[110] a warrant issued on the tip of an informant, who had given reliable information in the past, that the defendant had leased two phone lines that were being used for a sports betting operation was neither sufficient probable cause nor salvageable under the good faith exception where the prosecution failed to show the link between the noncriminal activity and the crime. A warrant issued on a tip to Crimestoppers from a previously reliable informant, simply stating that the defendant possessed cocaine at his residence but not indicating how the informant knew this or when the cocaine was at the defendant's house, was deemed to be bare bones and so lacking in indicia of probable cause that the officer's reliance on the warrant was not reasonable.[111] And in *State v Rees*,[112] the court held that police surveillance to supplement two insufficient tips that the defendant was dealing drugs from his home was not enough to elevate a warrant above bare bones because the

---

[106]State v Harrell, No. 60888, 1991 WL 95144 (8th Dist Ct App, Cuyahoga, 5-30-91), reversed on other grounds by 65 OS(3d) 37, 599 NE(2d) 695 (1992).

[107]State v Harrell, 65 OS(3d) 37, 599 NE(2d) 695 (1992).

[108]See discussion in Text 2.07(G), Inevitable discovery exception.

[109]State v Jones, 72 App(3d) 522, 595 NE(2d) 485 (Erie 1991).

[110]Toledo v McHugh, No. CA L-87-008, 1987 WL 19971 (6th Dist Ct App, Lucas, 11-13-87).

[111]State v Rodriguez, 64 App(3d) 183, 580 NE(2d) 1127 (Wood 1989).

[112]State v Rees, No. 88-CA-17, 1989 WL 145614 (4th Dist Ct App, Gallia, 10-27-89) (surveillance disclosed that known drug users had entered the residence).

information gained from the surveillance was of little assistance. *State v Jones*,[113] is instructive because it involved a warrant found not to support a reasonable reliance, even though the affidavit was rather lengthy. The court pierced the affidavit and concluded that the information was not timely, failed to establish a pattern of conduct or an ongoing investigation, relied upon an anonymous tip which stood alone, and did not provide adequate information to link the defendant to drug activity.

The Montgomery County Court of Appeals upheld the state's claim of reasonable reliance in *State v Zinkiewicz*[114] even though the issuing magistrate expressed reservations about the sufficiency of the probable cause. The fact that the magistrate issued the warrant despite his expressed reservations was deemed critical by the appellate court in the absence of any evidence that the magistrate abandoned his neutral and detached role. Erroneous information provided to a magistrate on which a finding of probable cause rests will not preclude a finding of good faith reasonable reliance absent evidence that establishes that the error resulted from perjury or reckless disregard of the truth.[115]

The least adequate approach to the good faith exception occurs when a court finds evidence admissible under the good faith exception without determining whether the warrant was valid.[116] Although this approach was sanctioned by the Supreme Court in *Leon* and *Sheppard*, this process really avoids the critical determination of how bad a warrant actually is. The potential for mechanical application of the exception is too great to justify avoidance of the full process in the name of judicial economy.

2.07　Derivative evidence rule

(A) In general

Over a half century ago, the Supreme Court recognized that suppressing the immediate product of a Fourth Amendment violation was not enough. The evidence illegally seized, and excluded at trial on the defendant's motion to suppress, may lead police to secondary evidence, which they may obtain in a seemingly lawful manner but which they learned about because of the original violation of constitutional rights. The secondary evidence is called derivative evidence or the fruit of the poisonous tree, the tree being the initial police illegality.

---

[113]State v Jones, 72 App(3d) 522, 595 NE(2d) 485 (Erie 1991).

[114]State v Zinkiewicz, 67 App(3d) 99, 585 NE(2d) 1007 (Montgomery 1990).

[115]State v Mobley, No. CA88-08-063, 1989 WL 53604 (12th Dist Ct App, Warren, 5-22-89), appeal dismissed by 45 OS(3d) 712, 545 NE(2d) 900 (1989); see also State v Spitler, 75 App(3d) 341, 599 NE(2d) 408 (Franklin 1991), appeal dismissed by 63 OS(3d) 1409, 585 NE(2d) 834 (1992) (where the appellate court ignored defendant's assignment of error claiming that the affidavit omitted evidence known to the police which would tend to prove that probable cause was lacking).

[116]State v Johnson, No. 88-02-002, 1989 WL 6171 (12th Dist Ct App, Clinton, 1-30-89), affirmed by 1996 WL 12877 (1996).

(B) Derivative of a constitutional violation

Before evidence may be excluded, it must be derivative of police illegality that amounts to a constitutional violation. The justification for this abandonment of the general principle that seeks to expose juries to all probative evidence of a crime stems from the need to deter unlawful police conduct that violates constitutional rights.[117] For example, an illegal arrest, search, or seizure, or a coerced confession that leads to additional evidence, will taint the additional evidence unless its discovery fits into one of the exceptions adopted by the Supreme Court. Where information supporting probable cause for a search warrant was illegally obtained, the warrant is irreparably tainted and any evidence obtained pursuant to the warrant should be suppressed.[118] The reason for the rule is the concern that if derivative evidence were not suppressed, police would have an incentive to violate constitutional rights in order to secure admissible derivative evidence even though the primary evidence secured as a result of the constitutional violation would be inadmissible.

However, the Supreme Court has held that the failure to give *Miranda*[119] warnings, alone, is not a violation of the Fifth Amendment.[120] Consequently, an initial statement taken without satisfying the *Miranda* warnings will not serve as a poisonous tree and will not taint the evidence that is discovered as a result of that statement. If the failure to give *Miranda* warnings is accompanied by other coercive tactics amounting to a Fifth Amendment violation, the additional evidence may be tainted.[121]

(C) Causal connection between violation and evidence

There must be a causal connection between the constitutional violation and the derivative evidence for the latter to be suppressed. This stands to reason because the latter is excluded solely because of its connection to the constitutional violation.[122]

The ruling that a *Miranda* violation cannot be a poisonous tree for purposes of excluding derivative evidence may have served as an opening wedge to adopt broad exceptions to the derivative evidence rule. A *Payton v New York*[123] violation, which holds illegal nonconsensual warrantless entries

---

[117]Nix v Williams, 467 US 431, 104 SCt 2501, 81 LEd(2d) 377 (1984), cert denied 471 US 1138, 105 SCt 2681, 86 LEd(2d) 699 (1985).

[118]State v Carter, 69 OS(3d) 57, 630 NE(2d) 355 (1994).

[119]Miranda v Arizona, 384 US 436, 86 SCt 1602, 16 LEd(2d) 694 (1966).

[120]New York v Quarles, 467 US 649, 104 SCt 2626, 81 LEd(2d) 550 (1984); Michigan v Tucker, 417 US 433, 94 SCt 2357, 41 LEd(2d) 182 (1974).

[121]Oregon v Elstad, 470 US 298, 105 SCt 1285, 84 LEd(2d) 222 (1985); see also State v Knuckles, No. CA93-11-222, 1995 WL 22713 (12th Dist Ct App, Butler, 1-23-95), cert denied 116 SCt 421, 133 LEd(2d) 338 (1995) (physical evidence derived from a statement obtained in violation of Miranda and Edwards is admissible).

[122]See State v Sanchez, No. 14904, 1995 WL 126667 (2d Dist Ct App, Montgomery, 3-24-95) (a factual determination is required whether the subsequent stop of a truck in which the defendant is a passenger is derived from the previous unlawful search and whether the police officers would have made the stop independently of the unlawful search of defendant's room).

[123]Payton v New York, 445 US 573, 100 SCt 1371, 63 LEd(2d) 639 (1980).

of residences to effect an arrest absent exigent circumstances, is not a poisonous tree once the arrestee is removed from the residence. In *New York v Harris*,[124] officers, having probable cause to arrest the defendant for murder, arrested the defendant in his home without an arrest warrant. Police entered the defendant's home without consent and without exigent circumstances justifying a warrantless entry. After reading the defendant *Miranda* rights, he made an admission of guilt. The defendant was removed from his home and taken to the police station where he signed a written confession after being advised of *Miranda* rights again. Despite the constitutional violation, the Supreme Court held that the exclusionary rule does not bar the use of the second confession because a *Payton* violation ends once the police have removed the arrestee from the home. Provided there is probable cause to justify the arrest, the detention is lawful once the defendant is taken from the house. *Harris* stands for the proposition that even though a constitutional violation is established, evidence will not be excluded unless it is obtained as a direct consequence of the illegal act.

The real significance of *Harris* is the black-letter rule separating the second confession from the constitutional violation once the violation ends without the attenuation analysis. Under the attenuation doctrine, the second confession, too, would have been excluded because of the bad faith aspect of the police conduct. The Supreme Court majority, however, did not really justify its decision other than to conclude that exclusion would not have served as a deterrent to *Payton* violations, a conclusion with which the dissent disagreed.

(D) What may be suppressed

Both tangible evidence and statements may be suppressed as derivative evidence. However, the person of the defendant may not be suppressed. Even if the defendant is in court as a result of an illegal arrest, he cannot have his face suppressed as the fruit of an illegal arrest to prevent an in-court identification.[125]

Controversy exists over whether the testimony of a live witness can be excluded as the fruit of the poisonous tree. On the one hand, the argument is made that the testimony of a witness discovered as a result of a constitutional violation should be treated identically to tangible evidence or a confession, which are the fruits of a poisonous tree. The other side argues that the testimony of a live witness is not the same as tangible evidence because it is powered by free will, and the witness might have come forward on his own. The Supreme Court in *United States v Ceccolini*[126] refused to accept a bright line rule that would have barred exclusion of live witness testimony but nonetheless adopted a process for consideration of such evidence that is likely to lead to its admission in most cases.

---

[124]New York v Harris, 495 US 14, 110 SCt 1640, 109 LEd(2d) 13 (1990).
[125]United States v Crews, 445 US 463, 100 SCt 1244, 63 LEd(2d) 537 (1980).
[126]United States v Ceccolini, 435 US 268, 98 SCt 1054, 55 LEd(2d) 268 (1978).

(E) Exceptions to the derivative evidence rule

Justice Oliver Wendell Holmes wrote in *Silverthorne Lumber Co v United States*,[127] "The essence of a provision forbidding the acquisition of evidence in a certain way is that not merely evidence so acquired shall not be used before the Court *but that it shall not be used at all.*" Similarly, Justice Frankfurter, in *Nardone v United States*,[128] explained the purposes behind the derivative evidence rule: "[T]o forbid the direct use of methods thus characterized but to put no curb on their full indirect use would only invite the very methods deemed 'inconsistent with ethical standards and destructive of personal liberty.' " Consequently, such evidence is barred from use by the prosecution because it is the fruit of the poisonous tree, unless it falls into one of the exceptions that have been developed to limit the reach of the derivative evidence rule.

Justices Holmes and Frankfurter whose opinions institutionalized the derivative evidence rule recognized that it is not absolute. Thus evidence that is derivative of a constitutional violation need not be excluded if it falls within one of the three exceptions limiting the doctrine's reach. These exceptions are the independent source exception, the inevitable discovery exception, and the attenuation doctrine.

The exceptions to the derivative evidence rule are just that and not exceptions to the exclusionary rule. These exceptions should not be applied where the evidence sought to be suppressed is the very evidence obtained in the illegal search. The exceptions should be applied only where the evidence is obtained in a lawful manner and not, itself, the product of a constitutional violation but only derivative of a constitutional violation.[129]

(F) Independent source exception

Justice Holmes, in *Silverthorne,* allowed that if knowledge of the derivative evidence is gained from an independent source, rather than from the government's own illegality, the derivative evidence may be used. In actuality, the independent source exception is not an exception at all. The secondary evidence is not derivative because it was not obtained as a result of the initial police illegality.

The finding of an independent source is not always as crisp and logical as Justice Holmes indicated it should be; sometimes the only support for a claim of an independent source is a court's unsupported claim. *In re Smalley*[130] involved evidence following an arrest that flowed from an illegal search. The court found an independent source, separating inadmissible from admissible evidence, based on a search incident to a lawful arrest for false identification that took place at the police station where the defendant

---

[127]Silverthorne Lumber Co v United States, 251 US 385, 392, 40 SCt 182, 64 LEd 319 (1920) (emphasis added).

[128]Nardone v United States, 308 US 338, 340, 60 SCt 266, 84 LEd 307 (1939).

[129]Cf. State v Bevan, 80 App(3d) 126, 131, 608 NE(2d) 1099 (Lake 1992) (police officers search and seizure of a cigarette pack were not done independently of the unlawful search of an automobile for open containers of alcohol, but were performed during and as a result of the unlawful search for open containers of alcohol).

[130]In re Smalley, 62 App(3d) 435, 575 NE(2d) 1198 (Cuyahoga 1989).

"volunteered" to be interviewed. The search occurred after police learned of the defendant's true identity. The court's claim of independent source rested on its assertion that the defendant was not already in custody as a result of the earlier illegal search.

The independent source rule has been significantly expanded in the last decade so that the independence of the source is not quite so clear as it once was. In *Segura v United States*,[131] the Supreme Court held admissible items "not discovered during the illegal entry and first discovered ... the day after the entry, under an admittedly valid search warrant" for which there was an independent source. In *State v Davis*,[132] the court relied on *Segura* to uphold a search of an automobile pursuant to a warrant despite the illegal seizure of the automobile. The probable cause supporting the warrant was totally independent of the illegal seizure.

The independence of the independent source exception virtually disappeared in *Murray v United States*,[133] where the Court disregarded the narrowness of *Segura* and held that evidence observed by police during an illegal entry need not be excluded if such evidence is later discovered during the execution of a valid search warrant issued on information wholly unconnected to the prior entry. The Court said the government must establish that (1) no information presented in the affidavit for the warrant was seen during the initial entry; and (2) the agents' decision to seek the warrant was not prompted by what they had seen during the initial entry. Since the same agents who had illegally entered and searched sought the subsequent warrant, it is incredible that their decision to seek the warrant was not influenced by what they observed. At the very least, the initial illegal entry was confirmatory, which destroys the claim of independence. Had the initial entry not confirmed the presence of the contraband would the agents still have sought the warrant? If they would have, they would have been misleading the magistrate when they knew that the evidence sought in the warrant would not be found at the place to be searched. The likely reason for the initial entry was to ensure the presence of the marijuana so as not to expend the effort to obtain a warrant unless the agents were sure to find what they sought when they came back with the warrant. It should be impossible to meet the Court's second condition.

An additional problem with *Murray* is that it does not limit the exception to secondary evidence because the evidence at issue in *Murray* was the identical evidence discovered during the illegal entry. The case eliminates the hard principles on which Justice Holmes's independent source exception rested: the evidence was discovered initially during the constitutional violation, not independent of the violation. At this point the exception becomes indistinguishable from the inevitable discovery exception.

---

[131]Segura v United States, 468 US 796, 104 SCt 3380, 82 LEd(2d) 599 (1984).

[132]State v Davis, No. CA89-03-016, 1989 WL 149413 (12th Dist Ct App, Clermont, 12-11-89), appeal dismissed by 51 OS(3d) 707, 555 NE(2d) 316 (1990).

[133]Murray v United States, 487 US 533, 108 SCt 2529, 101 LEd(2d) 472 (1988).

(G) Inevitable discovery exception

The inevitable discovery exception is the newest limitation on the derivative evidence rule. This exception was explained by the Supreme Court in *Nix v Williams*[134] as putting the prosecution in the same, not a worse, position than it would have been in if no police error or misconduct had occurred. The exception works the same way as the independent source doctrine, and after *Murray* they look very much alike.

In *Nix v Williams*,[135] the Court unanimously agreed on the existence of the exception but split on how it should be applied. Under this exception, evidence that was obtained illegally is admitted, nonetheless, if it would inevitably have been obtained lawfully. The Court held that the purpose of the exclusionary rule is to deter illegal police behavior. The inevitable discovery exception works in the same way as the independent source doctrine: if the evidence would have been discovered by lawful means, then the deterrence rationale has so little basis that the evidence should be received.

A majority of the Supreme Court held that it is sufficient for purposes of obtaining admissibility of the derivative evidence for the prosecution to prove by a preponderance of the evidence that police would have inevitably and lawfully discovered the evidence. Dissenting Justices Brennan and Marshall would have imposed a heightened burden of proof, a clear and convincing standard, before allowing the prosecution to use such evidence.[136] The problem with this exception is that courts frequently apply a test that results in the admission of evidence if police "could" have discovered it rather than if they "would" have discovered it.[137] The standard of proof adopted by the Supreme Court majority may facilitate application of the incorrect standard.

Some courts dealing with the exception prior to *Nix* included a "good faith" component as an additional element, requiring that the officer in good faith must have believed that he had not violated the defendant's rights in discovering the evidence. Those courts held that if the officer acted in bad faith, the fact that the evidence would have been discovered lawfully would not make it admissible.[138] The Supreme Court rejected a good faith component of the test as too costly and as doing more than putting the prosecution in the same position it would have been in without the violation.

---

[134]Nix v Williams, 467 US 431, 104 SCt 2501, 81 LEd(2d) 377 (1984), cert denied 471 US 1138, 105 SCt 2681, 86 LEd(2d) 699 (1985).

[135]Nix v Williams, 467 US 431, 104 SCt 2501, 81 LEd(2d) 377 (1984), cert denied 471 US 1138, 105 SCt 2681, 86 LEd(2d) 699 (1985), followed by State v Perkins, 18 OS(3d) 193, 18 OBR 259, 480 NE(2d) 763 (1985).

[136]Nix v Williams, 467 US 431, 459, 104 SCt 2501, 81 LEd(2d) 377 (1984), cert denied 471 US 1138, 105 SCt 2681, 86 LEd(2d) 699 (1985) (Brennan, J., dissenting).

[137]See, e.g., A.L.I., Model Pre-Arraignment Code § 290.2(5) (1975) (allowing derivative evidence when the prosecution establishes that such evidence would probably have been discovered).

[138]Williams v Nix, 700 F(2d) 1164 (8th Cir Iowa 1983), reversed by 467 US 431, 104 SCt 2501, 81 LEd(2d) 377 (1984).

The inevitable discovery exception was applied by the Ohio Supreme Court in *State v Jackson*,[139] where fingerprints found at a murder scene matched those of the defendant, which were taken when he was arrested on an unrelated charge. The defendant was interviewed, during a possible illegal arrest, by the police as a witness to the murder, rather than as a suspect. As a result of statements he made during the interview, he was arrested for tampering with evidence and fingerprinted, the prints later being found to match the prints at the scene. The Ohio Supreme Court said that even if the interview with the defendant and the prints taken at that time were illegal, the match of the prints at the scene and those taken following the earlier unrelated initial lawful arrest was inevitable and would have provided probable cause to arrest the defendant for murder. *Jackson* provides an almost classic application of the inevitable discovery exception except the court failed to apply the test and instead assumed that a match would have occurred with the initial set of prints on file. Possibly, the court engaged in this shorthand analysis because it did not accept the second set of prints as having been obtained illegally and thought it was engaging only in a hypothetical process. However, the second set of prints was obtained, it appears, as a result of an illegal arrest.

In *State v Perkins*,[140] the Ohio Supreme Court said it is the state's burden to prove within a reasonable probability that the derivative evidence would have been discovered apart from the unlawful search. State claims of inevitable discovery have been rejected following a stop for a traffic violation, which did not allow for an arrest or impoundment of the vehicle, where evidence found during a *Terry* search exceeded permissible scope.[141] Similarly, where a police officer conducted a *Terry*-stop and frisk without an objective basis, the state's claim of inevitable discovery was rejected because if the officer had not made the illegal search, he would not have found the shells that led him to walk to the defendant's truck and look in the window.[142] The same result obtained where police could not prove by a preponderance of the evidence that a license in the defendant's wallet would have been inevitably discovered by lawful means where the cohabitant/victim had no authority to consent to a search of the inside of the defendant's wallet, and police could not establish with reasonable certainty that the wallet would have been secured in an inventory search.[143]

The doctrine was strictly applied in *State v Masten*,[144] where police broke open the defendant's locked file cabinet pursuant to an invalid third party consent. The state invoked inevitable discovery because there was adequate probable cause to secure a search warrant. The Third District Court of Appeals rejected this line of argument, saying that the mere fact that a

---

[139]State v Jackson, 57 OS(3d) 29, 565 NE(2d) 549 (1991), cert denied 502 US 835, 112 SCt 117, 116 LEd(2d) 86 (1991).

[140]State v Perkins, 18 OS(3d) 193, 196, 18 OBR 259, 480 NE(2d) 763 (1985).

[141]State v Dotson, 66 App(3d) 182, 583 NE(2d) 1068 (Franklin 1990).

[142]State v Williams, No. S-88-7, 1988 WL 131439 (6th Dist Ct App, Sandusky, 12-9-88), reversed by 51 OS(3d) 58, 554 NE(2d) 108 (1990).

[143]See also State v Smith, 73 App(3d) 471, 597 NE(2d) 1132 (Wood 1991).

[144]State v Masten, No. 5-88-7, 1989 WL 111983 (3d Dist Ct App, Hancock, 9-29-89).

warrant likely could have been issued on request cannot be considered as the implementation of investigative procedures that would have ultimately led to the inevitable discovery of the evidence. The court pointed out that circumstances justifying application of the rule are not likely to be present if investigative procedures are already in place prior to the discovery by illegal means. The court's point is well taken because to accept the state's argument when alternative legal procedures have not been initiated is to engage in a "could have been discovered" rather than inevitable discovery analysis. Similarly, a claim of inevitable discovery was rejected where after an arrest in a motel room, a police officer picked up the defendant's wallet from the dresser. While the officer testified at the suppression hearing that it was his personal practice to secure the personal property of an arrestee, the Sixth District Court of Appeals rejected a claim of inevitable discovery, saying that the officer's bare assertion was not adequate to meet the state's burden of proving inevitable discovery.[145]

Not all courts have as strictly applied the standards set forth in *Nix* and *Perkins*. In *State v Mosher*,[146] police investigating a homicide were admitted to the defendant's home where they questioned him about whether he had a gun. The court said that if *Miranda* was violated, the gun inevitably would have been discovered because if the defendant had not told them of the gun, the police would have obtained a search warrant and eventually found it. The failure to engage in careful reasoning, here, is doubtless explained by the court's first making a strong argument that no *Miranda* violation took place; consequently, the discussion about inevitable discovery was purely speculative. Other courts, however, have accepted inevitable discovery arguments where an inventory search,[147] consent search,[148] plain view,[149] or

---

[145]State v Smith, 73 App(3d) 471, 597 NE(2d) 1132 (Wood 1991); see also State v Thompson, 72 Misc(2d) 39, 655 NE(2d) 835 (CP, Lucas 1995) (where officers possessed no leads which would have implicated the defendant and were not pursuing any other line of investigation against the defendant, evidence discovered by police officers is not admissible under the inevitable discovery exception).

[146]State v Mosher, 37 App(3d) 50, 523 NE(2d) 527 (Summit 1987).

[147]State v Yuncker, No. 60744, 1991 WL 106054 (8th Dist Ct App, Cuyahoga, 6-13-91) (following search of automobile after DUI arrest, court said record showed that both occupants of car were drunk; therefore, the vehicle had to be towed and would have been inventoried prior to towing); State v Miley, No. 56168, 1989 WL 136352 (8th Dist Ct App, Cuyahoga, 11-9-89) (despite the possibility of investigatory intent, the court admitted weapon found during pretextual search incident to arrest because defendant's purse ultimately would have been subject to an inventory search).

[148]State v Birt, No. 8-86-4, 1987 WL 14998 (3d Dist Ct App, Logan, 7-30-87) (regardless of whether seizure of gun was lawful following arrest, gun would have been inevitably discovered because of subsequent written consent to search by a co-resident).

[149]State v Ford, 64 App(3d) 105, 580 NE(2d) 827 (Licking 1989), appeal dismissed by 47 OS(3d) 715, 549 NE(2d) 170 (1989) (evidence discovered as a result of an illegal *Terry*-stop held admissible as inevitably discovered evidence because the court thought it highly probable that officer would have obtained the contraband because of its plain view).

search incident to arrest[150] might ultimately have occurred. In all but one of these cases, the court believed the grounds offered for the search to be valid and engaged in inevitable discovery discussion arguendo. However, inevitable discovery is not relevant because in all of these cases the doctrine is being considered as a limitation on the exclusionary rule, not of the derivative evidence rule. The Ohio Supreme Court mischaracterized the inevitable discovery exception from the beginning as an exception to the exclusionary rule rather than as a limited exception to the derivative evidence rule.[151] It continues to do so as it did in *State v Harrell*,[152] where the court remanded a case for determination of whether primary evidence barred under the exclusionary rule and not falling within the good faith exception should still come in under the inevitable exception doctrine. Clearly, this is an issue that must be addressed both by the Ohio and United States Supreme Courts.

(H) Attenuation

Over half a century ago, Justice Frankfurter held that even though the secondary evidence is derivative, it may nonetheless be used at trial if the original illegality becomes "so attenuated as to dissipate the taint." The attenuation doctrine was applied in *Wong Sun v United States*,[153] where a defendant who had been illegally arrested and freed on bail returned to the police station several days later after consulting with an attorney and confessed to the crime. The Court said that the police did not obtain the confession by exploiting the illegality. Even though Wong Sun probably would not have confessed had he not been arrested and faced with criminal prosecution, the Court said that the connection between his arrest and his statement had become so attenuated as to dissipate the taint.

Frequently, the issue is raised concerning the admissibility of statements following an illegal arrest, as in *Wong Sun*. Unlike the situation in *Wong Sun*,[154] however, the defendant is typically still in custody. *Miranda* warnings following an illegal arrest are not sufficient by themselves to dissipate the taint of the initial illegality and justify admission into evidence of forthcoming voluntary statements.[155] However, the taint may be purged by lawful warrants or arrests.[156] *Miranda* warnings alone will not purge the taint of an unlawful search. The Eighth District Court of Appeals court, in *In re Smalley*, stated, "The warnings are even less effective in the case of an illegal search since the continued presence of the incriminating evidence is inherently exploitative."[157]

---

[150]State v Johnson, No. 86-CA-0084, 1987 WL 13627 (2d Dist Ct App, Greene, 6-25-87) (even if automobile exception failed, evidence would likely have been discovered incident to arrest and inventory search of vehicle).

[151]State v Perkins, 18 OS(3d) 193, 18 OBR 259, 480 NE(2d) 763 (1985).

[152]State v Harrell, 65 OS(3d) 37, 599 NE(2d) 695 (1992).

[153]Wong Sun v United States, 371 US 471, 83 SCt 407, 9 LEd(2d) 441 (1963).

[154]Wong Sun v United States, 371 US 471, 83 SCt 407, 9 LEd(2d) 441 (1963).

[155]Brown v Illinois, 422 US 590, 95 SCt 2254, 45 LEd(2d) 416 (1975).

[156]In re Smalley, 62 App(3d) 435, 575 NE(2d) 1198 (Cuyahoga 1989).

[157]In re Smalley, 62 App(3d) 435, 443, 575 NE(2d) 1198 (Cuyahoga 1989).

Brown v Illinois[158] presented a set of facts giving rise to other issues that helped set the standards in these cases. The defendant in *Brown*, illegally arrested so that she could be interrogated, made incriminating statements a few hours later. The Supreme Court found the time that had elapsed between the illegal arrest and confession insufficient to purge the taint. Furthermore, the Court held that police good faith is an important factor to be considered under the doctrine of attenuation. In *Brown*, the defendant was arrested for the express purpose of interrogation. Consequently, the statements were the product of the police bad faith and had to be excluded. Thus in testing for attenuation there are two critical issues: (1) the amount of time that elapses between the illegality and the derivative evidence (or the "length of the road"), and (2) whether the police acted in good faith.

The state must also be able to show a break in the causal chain to establish sufficient attenuation. Where the statement or other evidence is derived in one continuous chain of events leading from the illegality, attenuation is insufficient. However, the causal break is not too difficult to establish where the "length of the road" between the initial illegality and the subsequent evidence is long. The critical events in *Wong Sun* were the release from custody and the meeting with counsel. Events other than consultation with counsel may also be sufficient to break the causal connection and prove attenuation. However, in *Taylor v Alabama*,[159] the defendant's short meeting with his girlfriend while in custody was insufficient to purge the taint. However, a defendant's independent act may break the causal chain and purge the taint of an illegal arrest.

The attenuation doctrine need not be applied following a constitutional violation if the evidence was not derived from the violation. In *New York v Harris*,[160] the Supreme Court held that an unlawful, warrantless arrest in a suspect's home does not require suppression of otherwise admissible statements made later at the police station. In *Harris*, the Supreme Court held that the attenuation analysis is not necessary following a *Payton* violation. Instead, the Court held that provided there is adequate probable cause to justify the arrest, once the suspect is removed from the home, the detention is lawful and the statement taken at the police station is not an exploitation of the illegal entry of the home. On the other hand, any statement taken while still at the house must be suppressed.[161] A similar claim was raised in *State v Byrd*,[162] where the Twelfth District Court of Appeals held that following an illegal arrest, where police had read *Miranda* warnings, and all of the accused "were kind of more at ease," a defendant's coming forward and showing police a gun and clip of shells in another room was a voluntary act and not the product of the initial illegality. However, since the gun was turned over while police were searching following the illegal arrest, the

---

[158]Brown v Illinois, 422 US 590, 95 SCt 2254, 45 LEd(2d) 416 (1975).

[159]Taylor v Alabama, 457 US 687, 102 SCt 2664, 73 LEd(2d) 314 (1982).

[160]New York v Harris, 495 US 14, 110 SCt 1640, 109 LEd(2d) 13 (1990).

[161]Cf. Minnesota v Olson, 495 US 91, 110 SCt 1684, 109 LEd(2d) 85 (1990).

[162]State v Byrd, No. 86-08-057, 1987 WL 13699 (12th Dist Ct App, Warren, 6-29-87), cert denied 487 US 1234, 108 SCt 2899, 101 LEd(2d) 932 (1988).

claim that the defendant's act was not a result of the illegal arrest and custody lacks merit.

When the challenged evidence is a live witness' testimony, the test for attenuation is less rigorous than for the defendant's own statement. There is almost a presumption in favor of admitting live witness testimony. The test focuses not on the manner in which the witness was discovered but on whether the witness' testimony ultimately is the product of the witness' own free will.[163] In *United States v Ceccolini*,[164] the Court indicated that the admissibility should be evaluated by the length of the road between the initial illegality and the discovery of the witness, as well as the willingness of the witness to testify. Where the witness becomes a volitional source of testimony, even though the witness is discovered by means of a constitutional violation of a defendant's rights, that witness' testimony likely will be admissible. However, if the witness is coerced into testifying, the claim of free will self-destructs. Note that *Ceccolini* principles are inapplicable to a police agent's testimony about a defendant's inadmissible statement.

CROSS REFERENCES

1 Giannelli & Snyder, Baldwin's Ohio Practice, *Evidence* § 402.6

2.08   Searches by private persons

The Fourth Amendment limits official government behavior; it does not regulate private conduct. Courts have regularly declined to exclude evidence when it is obtained by private persons.[165] The exception applies only to private persons; the Fourth Amendment is applicable to all government officials, not just law enforcement officers.[166] If a private person is acting as an agent of the police, the result is different. Official participation in the planning or implementation of a private person's efforts to secure evidence may taint the operation sufficiently as to require suppression of the evidence. The test of government participation is whether under all of the circumstances the private individual must be regarded as an agent or instrument of the state.[167]

Determining when a private person becomes the agent of the state as a result of official participation in the planning or implementation of an illegal search is the critical inquiry. A police officer's entry of a defendant's apartment at a landlord's request was a strictly private action where the officer was not even aware that he was not in the landlord's apartment.[168]

---

[163]United States v Ceccolini, 435 US 268, 98 SCt 1054, 55 LEd(2d) 268 (1978).

[164]United States v Ceccolini, 435 US 268, 98 SCt 1054, 55 LEd(2d) 268 (1978).

[165]Burdeau v McDowell, 256 US 465, 41 SCt 574, 65 LEd 1048 (1921); see also State v Henry, 1 App(3d) 126, 1 OBR 432, 439 NE(2d) 941 (Franklin 1981) (Fourth Amendment not violated where a maid seizes a gun from a motel room).

[166]Cf. New Jersey v T.L.O., 469 US 325, 105 SCt 733, 83 LEd(2d) 720 (1985) (school officials); State v Polansky, No. 45402, 1983 WL 3012 (8th Dist Ct App, Cuyahoga, 5-19-83) (public hospital security guards).

[167]Coolidge v New Hampshire, 403 US 443, 91 SCt 2022, 29 LEd(2d) 564 (1971); State v Dillon, No. 90-CA-07, 1991 WL 6347 (2d Dist Ct App, Miami, 1-23-91).

[168]State v Dillon, No. 90-CA-07, 1991 WL 6347 (2d Dist Ct App, Miami, 1-23-91).

Also, where a landlord has retaken possession of premises and seized the defendant's property that was left there before a search by a law enforcement officer, any illegality of the search rests on the landlord and not on the officer who was requested by the landlord to enter.[169] However, where hospital personnel, told by a police officer that drugs might be in the defendant's mouth, transmitted the defendant's mother's request that they be removed, the hospital personnel became state agents.[170]

Ordinarily, the inquiry is whether government officials are so involved in a private person's search as to make that person a state agent. In *State v Morris*,[171] the reverse was true when the Ohio Supreme Court said an officer's search of a suitcase was turned into a private search because it was done at the direction of a private person. The suitcase was checked and left at a railroad baggage room under suspicious circumstances. The baggage agent was concerned that the suitcase might contain a bomb but took no action for almost a week. The agent notified police, and in attendance for the opening were several police officers, including one with experience in opening locks, and others from drug units. The suitcase was actually opened by the police lock specialist who testified that he was told that the suitcase was Penn Central property and to open it up.

The Ohio Supreme Court said that when "a warrantless search is not an exclusively private undertaking but involves some degree of police participation,"[172] the court must decide "whether it is an unreasonable police search or an excepted private search."[173] Participation, beyond mere observation, the Court said, does not render it a government search. The determination should be based on examination of all the circumstances surrounding the search with the aim of preventing circuitous and indirect violations of the Fourth Amendment. That analysis led the Court to conclude that the search was instigated solely by the Penn Central baggage agent for Penn Central purposes, i.e., protection of the facilities and persons in the terminal. The involvement of the police officer resulted from difficulty in unlocking the suitcase, which was opened by the Penn Central employee after the officer unlocked it. The Court found that there was no record that the police expected to find contraband (although a suspicious person would wonder about the presence of officers from narcotics units). The Court concluded that the search was a private search and the police presence was pursuant to a legitimate community function, their duty to safeguard the community from harm.

The question of illegal searches and seizures conducted by private security personnel raises issues about governmental involvement, as well, and

---

[169]State v White, No. 9-87-53, 1990 WL 20067 (3d Dist Ct App, Marion, 3-2-90).

[170]State v Curry, Nos. 52766 et al., 1987 WL 14729 (8th Dist Ct App, Cuyahoga, 10-8-87).

[171]State v Morris, 42 OS(2d) 307, 329 NE(2d) 85 (1975), cert denied sub nom McSpadden v Ohio, 423 US 1049, 96 SCt 774, 46 LEd(2d) 637 (1976).

[172]State v Morris, 42 OS(2d) 307, 316, 329 NE(2d) 85 (1975), cert denied sub nom McSpadden v Ohio, 423 US 1049, 96 SCt 774, 46 LEd(2d) 637 (1976).

[173]State v Morris, 42 OS(2d) 307, 316, 329 NE(2d) 85 (1975), cert denied sub nom McSpadden v Ohio, 423 US 1049, 96 SCt 774, 46 LEd(2d) 637 (1976).

issues pertaining to normal governmental duties. The state grants private security guards a measure of authority that allows them to effectively protect store property, normally a duty of the state. Additionally, the state commissions and sets training requirements for private security guards. *State v McDaniel*[174] held that a security guard performing duties solely for the benefit of his employer was not performing public duties. The *McDaniel* court, however, indicated that a different result might be obtained if the guard were exercising power authorized under a statute providing for the commission of private policemen.

That Franklin County Court of Appeals dictum has not been adopted by the Cuyahoga County Court of Appeals. In *State v Hegbar*,[175] that court held that a private security guard was not covered by the Fourth Amendment because the primary function of privately employed security officers is protection of their employer's property. Similarly, in *State v Smith*,[176] the court held that a Cleveland Clinic security guard's conduct was not state action for Fourth Amendment purposes even though the guards were commissioned by the City of Cleveland to carry guns. However, the court reached a different conclusion earlier in *State v Polansky*,[177] concerning security guards at Cleveland Metropolitan Hospital, not because of commissions or function, but rather because the hospital is publicly owned and the security guards are public employees.

In a related matter, the Ohio Supreme Court held that a confession extracted from a suspect by a commissioned security guard lacked the requisite state action requiring *Miranda* warnings prior to interrogation.[178] That decision appears to rest not on the state action issue but rather on the premise that commissioned security guards do not have police powers. On a different confession front, however, the Ohio Supreme Court in *State v Parobek*[179] implied that a store security guard's conduct, regulated by RC 2935.041, is state action for purposes of suppression of involuntary confessions.[180] Admittedly, that may be reading too much into *Parobek*, but if RC

---

[174]State v McDaniel, 44 App(2d) 163, 337 NE(2d) 173 (Franklin 1975).

[175]State v Hegbar, No. 49828, 1985 WL 4219 (8th Dist Ct App, Cuyahoga 12-5-85).

[176]State v Smith, No. 50700, 1986 WL 5955 (8th Dist Ct App, Cuyahoga, 5-22-86).

[177]State v Polansky, No. 45402, 1983 WL 3012 (8th Dist Ct App, Cuyahoga, 5-19-83).

[178]State v Bolan, 27 OS(2d) 15, 271 NE(2d) 839 (1971); see also State v Giallombardo, 29 App(3d) 279, 29 OBR 343, 504 NE(2d) 1202 (Portage 1986); State v Ferrette, 18 OS(3d) 106, 18 OBR 139, 480 NE(2d) 399 (1985) (same result involving security personnel of the State Lottery Commission because, even though they are state employees, the court said *Miranda* inapplicable because the security personnel are not law enforcement officers); State v Stout, 42 App(3d) 38, 536 NE(2d) 42 (Butler 1987) (a volunteer who supervises probation department's substance abuse program is not a "law enforcement officer" within the meaning of *Miranda*).

[179]State v Parobek, 49 OS(3d) 61, 550 NE(2d) 476 (1990).

[180]See Cleveland Heights v Stross, 10 App(3d) 246, 461 NE(2d) 935 (Cuyahoga 1983) (suggesting that involuntary confession is inadmissible only because due process prohibits use of involuntary confessions regardless of state action). For a discussion of the distinction between violation of *Miranda* rights and violation of constitutional rights, see Text Ch 19, Interrogation and Confessions.

2935.041 creates state action for coercive interrogation by employees of retail establishments, museums, and libraries, then there would be state action to implement the exclusionary rule in the case of illegal arrests, searches, and seizures under authority of that statute. What is not clear is whether that statutory authorization creates state action because it sanctions the private exercise of normally a state function, law enforcement. Another approach would be to recognize state action in the commissioning of private security personnel, but RC 2935.041 does not limit authority to detain to commissioned security officers but to any merchant or his employee.

Similar issues existed with regard to the applicability of the exclusionary rule to searches directed at students. That confusion existed because of a misunderstanding about *Burdeau v McDowell*,[181] the seminal United States Supreme Court decision on the subject. *Burdeau* did not intend to limit the exclusionary rule to searches conducted by law enforcement officers[182] but, instead, limited the applicability of the rule to governmental action. The issue is now well settled; the Fourth Amendment and the exclusionary rule are applicable to public school and university students.[183]

Even though evidence is secured illegally by a private person and turned over to the police, possession by the police does not invoke the exclusionary rule.[184] In *State v Hammett*,[185] where a film processor accomplished a search before disclosing the contents to postal inspectors, the search was a private search for purposes of the Fourth Amendment, and revealing to postal inspectors what the processor found was not a new or separate search. Once contents of a package are revealed to law enforcement personnel, they violate no rights by using that information.[186] In *United States v Jacobsen*,[187] the Supreme Court held that it was permissible for police to remove the contents of a container because "the visual inspection of [the] contents enabled the agent to learn nothing that had not previously been learned during the private search."[188] However, a subsequent examination of the evidence by the police without a warrant, which exceeds the scope of the private search, will result in the exclusion of the evidence. A significant

---

[181]Burdeau v McDowell, 256 US 465, 41 SCt 574, 65 LEd 1048 (1921).

[182]See, e.g., State v Wingerd, 40 App(2d) 236, 318 NE(2d) 866 (Athens 1974) (holding exclusionary rule inapplicable to a search of a dormitory room at a state university by a university employee who was not a law enforcement officer); Athens v Wolf, 38 OS(2d) 237, 313 NE(2d) 405 (1974) (Fourth Amendment applicable to search of dormitory room by a police officer).

[183]Cf. New Jersey v T.L.O., 469 US 325, 105 SCt 733, 83 LEd(2d) 720 (1985).

[184]State v Ford, No. L-86-338, 1987 WL 18126 (6th Dist Ct App, Lucas, 10-9-87).

[185]State v Hammett, No. 48675, 1985 WL 6652 (8th Dist Ct App, Cuyahoga, 2-21-85).

[186]State v Hammett, No. 48675, 1985 WL 6652 (8th Dist Ct App, Cuyahoga, 2-21-85). See also Illinois v Andreas, 463 US 765, 103 SCt 3319, 77 LEd(2d) 1003 (1983).

[187]United States v Jacobsen, 466 US 109, 104 SCt 1652, 80 LEd(2d) 85 (1984).

[188]United States v Jacobsen, 466 US 109, 120, 104 SCt 1652, 80 LEd(2d) 85 (1984). *Jacobsen* also upheld the warrantless field testing of the contents of the package. See discussion at Text 1.04, Right of privacy.

expansion by police of the search that had been conducted previously by a private party must be characterized as a separate search.[189]

CROSS REFERENCES

1 Giannelli & Snyder, Baldwin's Ohio Practice, *Evidence* § 402.3, 402.4

---

[189]Walter v United States, 447 US 649, 100 SCt 2395, 65 LEd(2d) 410 (1980) (warrantless screening by FBI agents of obscene films turned over by a private person held a separate search).

Chapter 3

Probable Cause

3.01   Introduction

Probable cause is the level of "certainty" required before a person may be arrested or a place searched. The probable cause requirement balances legitimate law enforcement needs with constitutional guarantees against unreasonable searches and seizures. Arrests and searches do not require proof beyond a reasonable doubt, but they must be based on something more than unfounded suspicions or inarticulable hunches.[1]

Federal and state constitutions prescribe that no warrant shall issue but upon probable cause;[2] neither constitution mentions searches and arrests without warrants. Some commentators ascribe great significance to the silence on warrantless intrusions and suggest that the framers intended to regulate these activities according to the less specific "reasonableness" standard of the first clause of the Fourth Amendment. However, warrantless intrusions per se were rare when the Fourth Amendment was adopted, given the widespread use of general warrants and Writs of Assistance. Therefore, it is unlikely that the framers even considered warrantless searches and arrests when composing the language of the Fourth Amendment. If they had, there is no reason to believe that the framers would have tolerated warrantless intrusions on less than probable cause when they so clearly disfavored the colonial system of searches and seizures with warrants based on mere whim and caprice.

In any event, it is well settled that probable cause is required for *all* arrests and searches.[3] The alternative, general "reasonableness" standard would make it easier to justify warrantless intrusions after the fact than it is to get a warrant before the fact, which is inconsistent with the declared policy of encouraging police to obtain warrants.[4] In fact, the Court has indicated that the probable cause review of a warrantless search might be stricter than in a case where there is a warrant: "[I]n a doubtful or marginal case a search under a warrant may be sustainable where without one it would fall."[5]

---

[1]Beck v Ohio, 379 US 89, 85 SCt 223, 13 LEd(2d) 142 (1964).

[2]US Const Am 4; O Const Art I §14.

[3]Wong Sun v United States, 371 US 471, 83 SCt 407, 9 LEd(2d) 441 (1963). For discussion of administrative and special circumstance searches, which require less than traditional probable cause, see Text Ch 10, Exigent Circumstances.

[4]Wong Sun v United States, 371 US 471, 83 SCt 407, 9 LEd(2d) 441 (1963).

[5]United States v Ventresca, 380 US 102, 106, 85 SCt 741, 13 LEd(2d) 684 (1965); State v George, 45 OS(3d) 325, 544 NE(2d) 640 (1989).

3.02   Definition of probable cause

(A) Quantum of proof

The definition of probable cause flows directly from constitutional guarantees against *unreasonable* search and seizure. Probable cause exists when a *reasonably prudent* person would believe that the person to be arrested has committed a crime or that the place to be searched contains evidence of a crime.[6] It is impossible to precisely quantify how much probability is required to foster such a belief in the reasonable person. In the early days of the republic, Chief Justice Marshall said that probable cause exists where the facts warrant suspicion.[7] Probable cause based on mere suspicion will not suffice today; the standard falls somewhere between suspicion and reasonable doubt necessary to convict.[8] Attempts to narrow the definition usually result in variations of the words already used. Courts have variously described the requisite quantum of certainty as "reasonable cause to believe"[9] or a "fair probability."[10]

The message that the United States Supreme Court has attempted to convey is that probable cause is a "flexible, common-sense standard,"[11] and that the rule of probable cause is a practical, nontechnical concept.[12] In *Brinegar v United States*,[13] the Court set forth the standard which has been cited most often with approval:

> In dealing with probable cause, however, as the very name implies, we deal with probabilities. These are not technical; they are the factual and practical considerations of everyday life on which reasonable and prudent men, not legal technicians, act.[14]

Currently, probable cause determinations are based on the totality of the circumstances. The magistrate must make a practical, common sense decision whether, given all the circumstances set forth in the affidavit, there is a fair probability that contraband or evidence of a crime will be found in a particular place.[15]

Moreover, judges determining whether probable cause exists in order to issue a warrant or police officers assessing whether they have probable cause in situations where they may act without a warrant are entitled to draw common sense conclusions about human behavior.[16] The evidence is

---

[6]State v Timson, 38 OS(2d) 122, 311 NE(2d) 16 (1974) (probable cause for arrest); State v George, 45 OS(3d) 325, 544 NE(2d) 640 (1989) (probable cause for search). See also Brinegar v United States, 338 US 160, 69 SCt 1302, 93 LEd 1879 (1949) (probable cause generally).

[7]Locke v United States, 11 US 339, 3 LEd 364 (1813).

[8]Brinegar v United States, 338 US 160, 69 SCt 1302, 93 LEd 1879 (1949).

[9]Zurcher v Stanford Daily, 436 US 547, 98 SCt 1970, 56 LEd(2d) 525 (1978).

[10]State v George, 45 OS(3d) 325, 329, 544 NE(2d) 640 (1989), quoting Illinois v Gates, 462 US 213, 238-39, 103 SCt 2317, 76 LEd(2d) 527 (1983).

[11]Texas v Brown, 460 US 730, 742, 103 SCt 1535, 75 LEd(2d) 502 (1983).

[12]Brinegar v United States, 338 US 160, 176, 69 SCt 1302, 93 LEd 1879 (1949).

[13]Brinegar v United States, 338 US 160, 176, 69 SCt 1302, 93 LEd 1879 (1949).

[14]Brinegar v United States, 338 US 160, 175, 69 SCt 1302, 93 LEd 1879 (1949).

[15]Illinois v Gates, 462 US 213, 103 SCt 2317, 76 LEd(2d) 527 (1983); see also State v Brown, 20 App(3d) 36, 20 OBR 38, 484 NE(2d) 215 (Hamilton 1984).

[16]Texas v Brown, 460 US 730, 103 SCt 1535, 75 LEd(2d) 502 (1983).

to be evaluated in terms understood by those versed in the field of law enforcement.[17] Nevertheless, no hard and fast rules are possible because determination depends upon a case-by-case analysis.

The review of probable cause at a suppression hearing considering the validity of an arrest or search made under the authority of a warrant questions whether the affidavit contained sufficient facts and circumstances to allow the judge or magistrate to draw his own, detached inferences to believe that a crime had been committed or that evidence was likely to be found at the location to be searched.[18] Where the review is of a warrantless arrest or search, the constitutional validity hinges upon whether, at the moment the arrest or search took place, the facts and circumstances within the officers' knowledge and of which they had reasonably trustworthy information were sufficient to warrant a prudent man in believing that (1) the person to be arrested had committed or was committing an offense, or (2) evidence linked to a crime was presently at the place to be searched.[19]

(B) Probable cause to arrest versus probable cause to search

Probable cause for an arrest is not the same as probable cause for a search. The existence of one does not necessarily give rise to or satisfy the other. Probable cause to arrest focuses on the prior activities of a person, while probable cause to search is concerned with the present location of evidence. These are clearly independent tests, and satisfaction of one test does not necessarily satisfy the other. Probable cause to arrest focuses on the prior activities of a person, whereas probable cause to search is concerned with the present location of evidence. In *Ybarra v Illinois*,[20] the United States Supreme Court held that a valid warrant to search a bar did not establish probable cause to arrest or search all patrons found on the premises. The Court stressed that the requirement of showing probable cause to arrest or search an *individual* "cannot be undercut or avoided by simply pointing to the fact that coincidentally there exists probable cause ... to search the *premises* where the person may happen to be."[21]

On the other hand, in *United States v Savoca*,[22] the United States Court of Appeals agreed that probable cause existed to arrest an armed robbery suspect, but invalidated a search warrant of the defendant's hotel room (2,000 miles from the site of the robberies) where probable cause to search was based on nothing more than the contention that " 'known bank robbers'

---

[17]United States v Cortez, 449 US 411, 101 SCt 690, 66 LEd(2d) 621 (1981), cert denied 455 US 923, 102 SCt 1281, 71 LEd(2d) 464 (1982).

[18]United States v Ventresca, 380 US 102, 106, 85 SCt 741, 13 LEd(2d) 684 (1965).

[19]Beck v Ohio, 379 US 89, 85 SCt 223, 13 LEd(2d) 142 (1964).

[20]Ybarra v Illinois, 444 US 85, 100 SCt 338, 62 LEd(2d) 238 (1979).

[21]Ybarra v Illinois, 444 US 85, 91, 100 SCt 338, 62 LEd(2d) 238 (1979) (emphasis added); see also State v Newell, 68 App(3d) 623, 589 NE(2d) 412 (Lucas 1990). Concerning detention and search of persons on premises during execution of search warrants, see Text 8.05, Detention and search of persons on the premises.

[22]United States v Savoca, 739 F(2d) 220 (6th Cir Ohio 1984), cert denied 474 US 852, 106 SCt 153, 88 LEd(2d) 126 (1985).

tend to conceal fruits and instrumentalities of crime in places which are both accessible and private."[23]

(C) Requirement of knowing what specific crime has been committed

In order for a reasonable person to believe that a person has committed a crime or that a place contains evidence of a crime, it seems obvious that the reasonable person must first believe that a crime has actually been committed. A questionable ruling by the Ohio Supreme Court in *Dixon v Maxwell*[24] suggests otherwise. In *Dixon*, police responding to a complaint of prostitution in an apartment building observed three men removing a large quantity of clothing from an automobile trunk and carrying the clothing into the building. The officers followed the men into the building and arrested them; a search of the apartment revealed allegedly stolen clothing. The Court declared that the arrest was legal:

> It is not necessary that an officer know that a specific crime has been committed in order for him to have probable cause to make an arrest. It is sufficient if he has reasonable grounds to believe from the circumstances that a felony has been committed, and that the accused has committed it.[25]

The above language might be interpreted as allowing probable cause to be based upon a vague feeling that some crime has occurred. However, subsequent Ohio cases have not used *Dixon* in this manner, but instead have focused on the distinction between "know" and "reasonable grounds to believe." For example, in *State v Noe*,[26] the appellate court used *Dixon* to state that the quantum of certainty before an arrest need not rise to the level of absolute knowledge.[27]

There is no such ambiguity in the United States Supreme Court's treatment of the issue. In *Berger v New York*,[28] the Court struck down a vague eavesdropping statute and noted, "The purpose of the probable cause requirement of the Fourth Amendment [is] to keep the state out of constitutionally protected areas until it has reason to believe that a specific crime has been or is being committed."[29]

(D) Present location of evidence

(1) In general

The focus on the *present* is unique to the definition of probable cause to search. Timing is not an issue when considering probable cause to arrest because the focus is properly upon the *past* activities of the defendant. Information that gave rise to probable cause for an arrest warrant will become "stale" only when, after a warrant is issued but before it is executed, police learn facts that refute the earlier information that gave rise to

---

[23]United States v Savoca, 739 F(2d) 220, 225 (6th Cir Ohio 1984), cert denied 474 US 852, 106 SCt 153, 88 LEd(2d) 126 (1985). But see Text Ch 11, Search Incident to Arrest.

[24]Dixon v Maxwell, 177 OS 20, 201 NE(2d) 592 (1964).

[25]Dixon v Maxwell, 177 OS 20, 21, 201 NE(2d) 592 (1964).

[26]State v Noe, No. F-82-3, 1982 WL 6560 (6th Dist Ct App, Fulton, 9-3-82).

[27]State v Noe, No. F-82-3, 1982 WL 6560 (6th Dist Ct App, Fulton, 9-3-82).

[28]Berger v New York, 388 US 41, 87 SCt 1873, 18 LEd(2d) 1040 (1967).

[29]Berger v New York, 388 US 41, 59, 87 SCt 1873, 18 LEd(2d) 1040 (1967).

probable cause. At that point, probable cause no longer exists, and it would be wrong to execute the warrant with that knowledge.

The inquiry is different when considering probable cause to search. There must be probable cause to believe that evidence of a crime is *presently* at the location to be searched.[30] This belief is not as strong if the information is stale or if the evidence may not have arrived yet at the location to be searched.

(2) Staleness

Information that evidence existed in the past may or may not help determine whether the evidence is still present at the same location. The more "stale" the evidence becomes, the less likely it is to support probable cause.

Therefore, a judge must always know approximately when the underlying crime occurred or when the information was obtained in order to evaluate the likelihood that the evidence will be found at the location to be searched. In *United States v Savoca*,[31] the United States Court of Appeals for the Sixth Circuit invalidated a search warrant and suppressed all evidence seized when the hotel room of suspected bank robbers was searched. The court noted that the affidavit failed to state when the robberies occurred, and therefore the issuing magistrate had no basis for concluding that evidence of the robberies was presently located in the hotel room.[32]

Staleness cannot be expressed as a precise amount of time because standards will vary depending on the type of evidence. Quickly disposable stolen property observed on the premises may no longer be there just a few days later, while stationary items such as business records or heavy equipment are likely to remain permanently at one location.[33] Even then, however, there are no blanket rules, and the judge must look at the "totality of the circumstances."[34] In *State v Roe*,[35] for example, police had probable cause to believe that a handgun stolen two years earlier was still at the defendant's home. The same type of handgun had been used during the past year to commit a murder in which the defendant was a suspect, and an informant had seen a similar weapon at the defendant's home three weeks previously.[36] But in *State v Jones*,[37] three-month-old information about a small amount of cocaine located at the defendant's residence was too stale

---

[30]Sgro v United States, 287 US 206, 53 SCt 138, 77 LEd 260 (1932).

[31]United States v Savoca, 739 F(2d) 220 (6th Cir Ohio 1984), cert denied 474 US 852, 106 SCt 153, 88 LEd(2d) 126 (1985).

[32]United States v Savoca, 739 F(2d) 220, 225 (6th Cir Ohio 1984), cert denied 474 US 852, 106 SCt 153, 88 LEd(2d) 126 (1985); see also State v Navarre, No. WD-88-43, 1989 WL 61669 (6th Dist Ct App, Wood, 6-9-89) (search warrant invalidated where affiant failed to state date crime allegedly occurred).

[33]See, e.g., Andresen v Maryland, 427 US 463, 96 SCt 2737, 49 LEd(2d) 627 (1976).

[34]Illinois v Gates, 462 US 213, 103 SCt 2317, 76 LEd(2d) 527 (1983).

[35]State v Roe, 41 OS(3d) 18, 535 NE(2d) 1351 (1989), affirmed by 1992 WL 246023 (1992), appeal dismissed by 66 OS(3d) 1444, 609 NE(2d) 171 (1993).

[36]State v Roe, 41 OS(3d) 18, 24, 535 NE(2d) 1351 (1989), affirmed by 1992 WL 246023 (1992), appeal dismissed by 66 OS(3d) 1444, 609 NE(2d) 171 (1993).

[37]State v Jones, 72 App(3d) 522, 595 NE(2d) 485 (Erie 1991).

to establish present probable cause because there was no evidence that the defendants were engaged in an ongoing drug business.[38]

(3) Anticipatory search warrants

Different probable cause issues arise when the evidence to be seized is not yet at the place to be searched. The difficult question is how a magistrate can make a finding of *present* probable cause which anticipates the *future* arrival of evidence at the place to be searched.

All search warrants must (1) be based on facts that establish probable cause; (2) particularly describe the place to be searched; (3) particularly describe the things to be seized; and (4) be issued by a neutral and detached magistrate.[39]

An anticipatory search warrant must meet two additional criteria. First, an affidavit seeking an anticipatory search warrant must show that the evidence is on a sure and irreversible course to its destination. Additionally, an anticipatory search warrant must provide adequate judicial control of the warrant's execution. The issuing court should list clear, narrowly drawn conditions in the warrant controlling the discretion of the police executing the warrant.

An anticipatory search warrant was upheld in *State v Folk*,[40] where the affidavit provided sufficient information to assure that the evidence was on a sure and irreversible course. The Los Angeles Police Department (LAPD) had intercepted a Federal Express package containing cocaine, which was addressed to the defendant in Dayton. The LAPD instead sent the package to Dayton police, who sought a warrant in anticipation of a controlled delivery. The appellate court found adequate probable cause.[41]

Anticipatory search warrants are allowed in the federal system.[42] The federal rules allow judges to issue search warrants for evidence located outside their judicial districts.

The argument in favor of the validity of anticipatory search warrants is supported by the preference for searches with warrants. Anticipatory search warrants encourage judicial approval before a search, rather than a warrantless search after the object arrives. Furthermore, warrants that anticipate delivery of a specified object are not very different from warrants that authorize the seizure of oral communications through electronic surveillance.[43] In fact, the seizure of the object, especially when its delivery is in

---

[38]State v Jones, 72 App(3d) 522, 595 NE(2d) 485 (Erie 1991); State v Hollis, 98 App(3d) 549, 649 NE(2d) 11 (Lake 1994) (probable cause supporting warrant to search defendant's office based upon 3-½ year old allegations of prostitution and alleged incident of rape five months old was stale).

[39]Berger v New York, 388 US 41, 87 SCt 1873, 18 LEd(2d) 1040 (1967); see also Text Ch 9, Search Warrant Requirement.

[40]State v Folk, 74 App(3d) 468, 599 NE(2d) 334 (Montgomery 1991).

[41]State v Folk, 74 App(3d) 468, 599 NE(2d) 334 (Montgomery 1991).

[42]Federal Rule of Criminal Procedure 41(a).

[43]Cf. Katz v United States, 389 US 347, 88 SCt 507, 19 LEd(2d) 576 (1967); Berger v New York, 388 US 41, 87 SCt 1873, 18 LEd(2d) 1040 (1967).

the control of the police, is more certain than the seizure of incriminating communications in conversations that have not yet taken place.

3.03   Probable cause determination

(A) Need for independent assessment by judiciary

A cornerstone of the probable cause requirement is that judges, and not police officers, determine the existence of probable cause. Little protection against unreasonable search and seizure is afforded when police activities are regulated by the very people caught up "in the often competitive enterprise of ferreting out crime."[44] Instead, the Fourth Amendment demands that a "neutral and detached magistrate"[45] be interposed between the police and invasions of a citizen's privacy.

For judicial participation in the probable cause determination to be meaningful, the judge must serve as more than a rubber stamp for the police. Therefore, those seeking a warrant, or seeking to justify a warrantless intrusion after the fact, must present enough underlying facts and circumstances to allow a judge to draw his or her own inferences about the existence of probable cause. An affidavit couched only in conclusions, i.e., that probable cause exists to believe that evidence of a crime will be found, denies the judge the opportunity to draw those conclusions and robs the Fourth Amendment of its essence.[46] The same is true when probable cause is reviewed following a warrantless arrest or search. The police officer must present more than conclusory statements that probable cause existed.[47] Otherwise, the arrest or search is not based on probable cause and is illegal and void.[48]

(B) Practical approach to probable cause determination

Requiring police to present underlying facts and circumstances does not mean that police must be experts in the minutiae of probable cause theory. Indeed, courts have consistently stressed flexibility and common sense when evaluating the information presented by police.[49] This policy recognizes that decisions to search and arrest are usually initiated by nonlawyers under the extreme time pressure of a criminal investigation.[50] As noted in *United States v Ventresca*,[51] "Technical requirements of elaborate specificity once

---

[44]Johnson v United States, 333 US 10, 14, 68 SCt 367, 92 LEd 436 (1948).

[45]Johnson v United States, 333 US 10, 14, 68 SCt 367, 92 LEd 436 (1948).

[46]Johnson v United States, 333 US 10, 14, 68 SCt 367, 92 LEd 436 (1948).

[47]See, e.g., Beck v Ohio, 379 US 89, 85 SCt 223, 13 LEd(2d) 142 (1964); State v Hollis, 98 App(3d) 549, 649 NE(2d) 11 (Lake 1994) (warrant to search for obscene materials contained conclusory statements about purchased items without facts supporting the obscenity allegations).

[48]Nicholas v Cleveland, 125 OS 474, 182 NE 26 (1932), overruled by State v Lindway, 131 OS 166, 2 NE(2d) 490 (1936), cert denied 299 US 506, 57 SCt 36, 81 LEd 375 (1936).

[49]Texas v Brown, 460 US 730, 103 SCt 1535, 75 LEd(2d) 502 (1983).

[50]Illinois v Gates, 462 US 213, 103 SCt 2317, 76 LEd(2d) 527 (1983).

[51]United States v Ventresca, 380 US 102, 108, 85 SCt 741, 13 LEd(2d) 684 (1965).

exacted under common law pleadings have no proper place in this area."[52] The 1949 characterization of probable cause by the United States Supreme Court in *Brinegar v United States*[53] is still approved and widely quoted today:

> In dealing with probable cause, however, as the very name implies, we deal with probabilities. These are not technical; they are the factual and practical considerations of everyday life on which reasonable and prudent men, not legal technicians, act.[54]

Actually, the term "reasonable and prudent men" from above might be more accurately characterized as "reasonable and prudent law enforcement professionals." Facts and circumstances that seem innocent to the average person might be viewed quite differently by an experienced police officer. While a judge cannot rely solely on an officer's conclusions, a judge evaluating information provided by police should respect an officer's common sense conclusions about human behavior,[55] as well as inferences drawn by someone well versed in the field of law enforcement.[56]

Another practical consideration is that hearsay information may be the evidence upon which an affidavit for an arrest or search warrant may be based.[57] The source of the hearsay may be a confidential informant whose identity need not be disclosed to the judge issuing the warrant or to the court reviewing probable cause on a motion to suppress.[58] The only time an informant's identity must be disclosed is if his testimony is critical to the issue of guilt or innocence at trial.[59] However, a judge may refuse to issue a warrant if he does not believe the informant exists. When that occurs, the state must produce the informant or other evidence of probable cause or do without the warrant.

Furthermore, a simple conclusory allegation that the evidence is located at the place to be searched is not a sufficient indicator of probable cause on its own.[60]

3.04   Subsequent review of probable cause

(A) Antecedent requirement

The initial probable cause determination is reviewable in the trial court, upon a motion to suppress, and again in the appellate courts, initiated by

---

[52]See also State v Karr, 44 OS(2d) 163, 339 NE(2d) 641 (1975), cert denied 426 US 936, 96 SCt 2650, 49 LEd(2d) 52 (1976).

[53]Brinegar v United States, 338 US 160, 69 SCt 1302, 93 LEd 1879 (1949).

[54]Brinegar v United States, 338 US 160, 175, 69 SCt 1302, 93 LEd 1879 (1949).

[55]Texas v Brown, 460 US 730, 103 SCt 1535, 75 LEd(2d) 502 (1983).

[56]United States v Cortez, 449 US 411, 101 SCt 690, 66 LEd(2d) 621 (1981), cert denied 455 US 923, 102 SCt 1281, 71 LEd(2d) 464 (1982).

[57]Aguilar v Texas, 378 US 108, 84 SCt 1509, 12 LEd(2d) 723 (1964), overruled by Illinois v Gates, 462 US 213, 103 SCt 2317, 76 LEd(2d) 527 (1983).

[58]McCray v Illinois, 386 US 300, 87 SCt 1056, 18 LEd(2d) 62 (1967).

[59]Roviaro v United States, 353 US 53, 77 SCt 623, 1 LEd(2d) 639 (1957).

[60]See Aguilar v Texas, 378 US 108, 84 SCt 1509, 12 LEd(2d) 723 (1964), overruled by Illinois v Gates, 462 US 213, 103 SCt 2317, 76 LEd(2d) 527 (1983); Spinelli v United States, 393 US 410, 89 SCt 584, 21 LEd(2d) 637 (1969), overruled by Illinois v Gates, 462 US 213, 103 SCt 2317, 76 LEd(2d) 527 (1983).

the defendant upon conviction or by the state following the granting of a motion to suppress.[61] Whatever the context, probable cause can only be measured by objective facts made known to a magistrate *prior* to the issuance of a warrant, or known to a police officer *prior* to a warrantless arrest or search. When determining the sufficiency of probable cause, it is not material that a search revealed the evidence sought.[62] Evidence gathered as the result of a search or arrest may not be used to retroactively establish probable cause.[63] While the requirement that probable cause must exist prior to the intrusion has been virtually unquestioned for over sixty years, Chief Justice Rehnquist has sent conflicting signals on the subject. In 1979, he suggested that discovery of contraband is compelling evidence that the search was justified and alternatively suggested that the failure to establish probable cause prior to the intrusion was, at most, harmless error.[64] However, in 1990, the Chief Justice joined in a per curiam decision rejecting an attempt to use the fruits of a search-incident-to-arrest to justify the arrest itself, indicating that antecedent probable cause continues to be an important requirement.[65] Either his later vote indicates a change of heart or a realization that his extreme earlier position is unlikely ever to receive support from a majority of the Court.

(B) Function of reviewing courts

The role of reviewing courts has not been seriously questioned in the case of warrantless arrests and searches. When police do not first seek the guidance of a detached and neutral magistrate, the reviewing court must make its own independent assessment of probable cause.[66]

The function of reviewing courts is not altogether clear when the review is of a magistrate's decision to issue a warrant. The confusion stems from *Illinois v Gates*,[67] the seminal probable cause case. According to *Gates*, a reviewing court must pay "great deference" to a magistrate's decision and may not conduct a de novo review of probable cause.[68] On the other hand, *Gates* also stressed that "courts must continue to conscientiously review the sufficiency of affidavits on which warrants are issued."[69]

The Ohio Supreme Court endorsed the *Gates* approach to probable cause, including the language pertaining to the review of warrants, in *State v George*.[70] According to the Court, reviewing courts may not conduct "a *de novo* determination as to whether the affidavit contains sufficient probable

---

[61]Crim R 12(J).

[62]Byars v United States, 273 US 28, 47 SCt 248, 71 LEd 520 (1927).

[63]Smith v Ohio, 494 US 541, 110 SCt 1288, 108 LEd(2d) 464 (1990) (per curiam); Mapp v Ohio, 367 US 643, 81 SCt 1684, 6 LED (2d) 1081 (1961); Akron v Williams, 175 OS 186, 192 NE(2d) 63, 23 OO(2d) 466 (1963).

[64]California v Minjares, 443 US 916, 921, 100 SCt 9, 61 LEd(2d) 892 (1979) (Rehnquist, J., dissenting from denial of stay).

[65]Smith v Ohio, 494 US 541, 110 SCt 1288, 108 LEd(2d) 464 (1990) (per curiam).

[66]See, e.g., Terry v Ohio, 392 US 1, 88 SCt 1868, 20 LEd(2d) 889 (1968).

[67]Illinois v Gates, 462 US 213, 103 SCt 2317, 76 LEd(2d) 527 (1983).

[68]Illinois v Gates, 462 US 213, 235, 103 SCt 2317, 76 LEd(2d) 527 (1983).

[69]Illinois v Gates, 462 US 213, 239, 103 SCt 2317, 76 LEd(2d) 527 (1983).

[70]State v George, 45 OS(3d) 325, 544 NE(2d) 640 (1989).

cause upon which the reviewing court would issue the search warrant."[71] Instead, reviewing courts are merely to determine whether the "affidavit provided a *substantial basis* for the magistrate's conclusion that there was a *fair probability* that [contraband would be found on the premises]."[72]

The admonition to conscientiously review probable cause determinations but not to engage in de novo substitution of the magistrate's judgment has not seemed to preoccupy or confuse Ohio courts.[73] Review of a search warrant has traditionally been limited to the four corners of the affidavit and supplemental recorded testimony taken under oath, and reviewing courts have not interpreted *Gates* and *George* as diminishing their roles when reviewing probable cause determinations. Instead, they seem to have read the high courts' decisions as simply affirming the policy of encouraging police to obtain warrants by suggesting a slight predisposition toward upholding the decisions of magistrates.

3.05 Factors to consider when evaluating probable cause

(A) Totality of the circumstances

The factors discussed below are examples of what is relevant to an evaluation of probable cause. The issues are grouped separately for the sake of clarity, but the factors should not be considered in isolation because probable cause is determined from the totality of the circumstances.[74] Rarely is a single factor dispositive; it is more accurate to think of individual elements as favoring or disfavoring a finding of probable cause. As the United States Supreme Court has cautioned, "There are so many variables in the probable-cause equation that one determination will seldom be a useful 'precedent' for another."[75]

(B) Defendant's conduct

The most important consideration in determining probable cause is, of course, the conduct of the defendant.

(1) Criminal behavior

The strongest showing of probable cause is based on an officer's observation of criminal behavior. There is no question about probable cause when an officer observes a marijuana plant growing in a residential back yard,[76]

---

[71]State v George, 45 OS(3d) 325, 330, 544 NE(2d) 640 (1989).

[72]State v George, 45 OS(3d) 325, 330, 544 NE(2d) 640 (1989) (emphasis in original).

[73]See, e.g., State v Harrell, No. 60888, 1991 WL 95144 (8th Dist Ct App, Cuyahoga, 5-30-91), reversed on other grounds by 65 OS(3d) 37, 599 NE(2d) 695 (1992); State v Lenegar, No. 465, 1991 WL 28322 (4th Dist Ct App, Vinton, 2-25-91); State v White, No. 1-89-30, 1991 WL 1558 (3d Dist Ct App, Allen, 1-4-91); State v Mills, No. C-880581, 1990 WL 203563 (1st Dist Ct App, Hamilton, 12-12-90), affirmed by 70 OS(3d) 1407, 637 NE(2d) 5 (1994).

[74]Illinois v Gates, 462 US 213, 103 SCt 2317, 76 LEd(2d) 527 (1983); see also Text 3.02, Definition of probable cause; Text 3.03, Probable cause determination.

[75]Illinois v Gates, 462 US 213, 238 n.11, 103 SCt 2317, 76 LEd(2d) 527 (1983).

[76]State v George, 45 OS(3d) 325, 544 NE(2d) 640 (1989).

or cocaine in a voluntarily opened suitcase,[77] or when a defendant punches an officer in the face.[78] In these examples, the conclusion is clear and does not depend on inferences. Here, often the only issue is the manner in which the officer discovered the illegal conduct: the criminal activity must be viewed from a lawful vantage point. Police may not use the fruits of an illegal violation of privacy to establish probable cause.[79]

(2) Furtive or suspicious behavior

The analysis is more complicated when a suspect engages in noncriminal furtive or suspicious behavior. Quite often, however, police do not observe actual criminal conduct but infer criminal behavior from a series of acts, innocent in themselves. An officer's suspicions are naturally aroused when his or her presence causes a person to attempt to hide something,[80] act nervously,[81] or duck down below the level of a car window.[82] An officer should not ignore such signals; indeed, *Terry v Ohio*[83] and its progeny give the officer a variety of options under such circumstances, ranging from a simple request for information to a nonconsensual investigatory detention.[84] But conduct that can be attributed to innocent circumstances just as easily as criminal activity cannot form the basis of probable cause.[85]

Even when the probabilities favor a criminal explanation more than an innocent one, the finding should not be stretched too far. In *State v Burkett*,[86] for example, a police officer suspected that occupants of a vehicle were smoking a marijuana cigarette, based on the size of the cigarette, the way it was held, and the fact that the defendant ducked down when he noticed the officer was observing him. Two police cars stopped the subject vehicle, and the suspects immediately exited the car. Before the first officer could ask the suspects any questions, the second officer began searching the car and discovered marijuana. The appellate court held that the initial stop was clearly justified on a "reasonable suspicion" ground, but the court also held that this fact pattern is an example of how " 'furtive movements' alone are insufficient to establish such probable cause."[87]

---

[77]State v Morris, 48 App(3d) 137, 548 NE(2d) 969 (Cuyahoga 1988).

[78]Hoover v Garfield Heights Municipal Court, 802 F(2d) 168 (6th Cir 1986), cert denied 480 US 949, 107 SCt 1610, 94 LEd (2d) 796 (1987).

[79]Byars v United States, 273 US 28, 47 SCt 248, 71 LEd 520 (1927); Wong Sun v United States, 371 US 471, 83 SCt 407, 9 LEd(2d) 441 (1963).

[80]State v Hill, 52 App(2d) 393, 370 NE(2d) 775 (Hamilton 1977).

[81]United States v Savoca, 739 F(2d) 220 (6th Cir Ohio 1984), cert denied 474 US 852, 106 SCt 153, 88 LEd(2d) 126 (1985), on rehearing 761 F(2d) 292 (1985), cert denied 474 US 852, 106 SCt 153, 88 LEd(2d) 126 (1985).

[82]State v Bobo, 37 OS(3d) 177, 524 NE(2d) 489 (1988), cert denied 488 US 910, 109 SCt 264, 102 LEd(2d) 252 (1988).

[83]Terry v Ohio, 392 US 1, 88 SCt 1868, 20 LEd(2d) 889 (1968).

[84]See Text Ch 14, Stop and Frisk.

[85]See, e.g., State v Fahy, 49 App(3d) 160, 551 NE(2d) 1311 (Henry 1988), appeal dismissed by 40 OS(3d) 704, 534 NE(2d) 841 (1988).

[86]State v Burkett, No. L-88-174, 1989 WL 41723 (6th Dist Ct App, Lucas, 4-28-89).

[87]State v Burkett, No. L-88-174, at 2, 1989 WL 41723 (6th Dist Ct App, Lucas, 4-28-89), quoting State v Hill, 52 App(2d) 393, 370 NE(2d) 775 (Hamilton 1977).

This distinction between furtive or suspicious behavior and probable cause was recognized by the Hamilton County Court of Appeals in *State v Hill*.[88] There, the court concluded that police did not have probable cause to search a defendant who tried to conceal his hands and leave a bar when a police officer approached his table. The fact that the officer recognized the defendant as having been in the presence of known drug users was not enough to change the determination, nor was the fact that the bar was notorious for drug sales. The court ruled that the defendant's behavior gave the officer reason to be suspicious, but not probable cause to search or arrest.[89]

The distinction between furtive or suspicious behavior and probable cause was apparently not fully appreciated by the United States Supreme Court in *Illinois v Gates*.[90] There, the defendants' suspicious, but wholly legal, travel behavior was held to constitute probable cause because it partially corroborated a conclusory allegation of drug dealing contained in an anonymous letter.[91] *Gates* mostly receives attention for its holdings on judicial review of search warrants[92] and use of information supplied by informants, but the real problem with *Gates* may be the way in which the Court disregarded the findings of three Illinois state courts by basing probable cause on such tenuous grounds.

(3) Flight from law enforcement officers

Flight from an identified law enforcement officer is a special case of furtive behavior. Although flight alone will not constitute probable cause, flight colors otherwise innocent behavior and is accorded substantial weight in a probable cause determination.[93] In *United States v Pope*,[94] federal narcotics agents followed a suspect fitting a "drug courier profile" as he left an airport. The suspect glanced back nervously at the plainclothes agents as they walked through the concourse and broke into a run when one of the agents showed credentials. The United States Court of Appeals for the Sixth Circuit held that neither the match with the drug courier profile nor the nervous glancing at undercover officers constituted probable cause, as both factors were easily attributable to innocent behavior. However, the flight from an identified law enforcement officer changed the complexion of

---

[88]State v Hill, 52 App(2d) 393, 370 NE(2d) 775 (Hamilton 1977).

[89]State v Hill, 52 App(2d) 393, 370 NE(2d) 775 (Hamilton 1977) (officer recognized defendant in a bar in which multiple drug related arrests had recently been made, and as being in the company of two individuals who had previously been arrested for possession of narcotics); see also State v Nelson, 72 App(3d) 506, 595 NE(2d) 475 (Cuyahoga 1991) (police observation of defendant and others moving their hands but exchanging nothing and defendant's flight at the approach of police does not give rise to probable cause that defendant had committed a drug offense); State v Wells, 68 App(3d) 648, 589 NE(2d) 428 (1990) (where defendant was standing in a specific area—in which defendant also happened to live—where drugs are known to be sold and walked away at a normal pace upon sighting police, probable cause was not established).

[90]Illinois v Gates, 462 US 213, 103 SCt 2317, 76 LEd(2d) 527 (1983).

[91]Illinois v Gates, 462 US 213, 103 SCt 2317, 76 LEd(2d) 527 (1983).

[92]See Text 3.04(B), Function of reviewing courts.

[93]United States v Pope, 561 F(2d) 663 (6th Cir Ohio 1977).

[94]United States v Pope, 561 F(2d) 663 (6th Cir Ohio 1977).

the encounter and, when combined with the other factors, entitled the police officers to reasonably conclude that the defendant was engaged in drug activity. Even so, the court took some comfort that its holding was correct in any event because the defendant's subsequent assault on one of the officers during the chase unquestionably constituted probable cause to arrest.

Similarly, in *State v Klump*,[95] a state appellate court included flight from officers in its evaluation of the totality of the circumstances. The defendant was present at a site being searched pursuant to a search warrant. While this fact did not automatically establish probable cause to arrest the defendant,[96] his attempted flight from officers executing the search warrant tipped the balance in favor of probable cause, and the defendant's warrantless arrest was upheld.[97] Flight invites pursuit. Although flight itself is not grounds for probable cause, it is unquestionably a factor of significant persuasion.

(4) Escalation of reasonable suspicion into probable cause

Even when suspicious circumstances do not establish probable cause, they may provide justification for an investigatory stop.[98] Events during an investigatory stop will often escalate quickly into probable cause. In *State v Morris*,[99] a case very similar to *United States v Pope*,[100] police stationed themselves in an airline terminal and watched passengers arriving from Atlanta. They saw a woman nervously hand her suitcase to a man upon deplaning, and both suspects "furtively" glanced about as they left the airport. Police approached the two people and asked them to answer a few questions. When the answers the woman gave concerning her name and itinerary differed from the information on her ticket, and police noticed that the ticket had been paid for in cash, they then had a reasonable and articulable suspicion that the two were involved in drug activity. Thus, the consensual encounter escalated into an investigatory *Terry*-stop. When the man consented to a search of the suitcase, police observed cocaine, and the situation escalated into probable cause to arrest the subjects.[101] Simple traffic stops may also escalate into probable cause for arrest.[102]

(5) Association with criminals

The First Amendment guarantees freedom of association, and a person's association with known or suspected criminals cannot form the basis of a

---

[95]State v Klump, No. CA88-03-026, 1988 WL 141701 (12th Dist Ct App, Clermont, 12-30-88).

[96]See Text 3.02(B), Probable cause to arrest versus probable cause to search.

[97]State v Klump, No. CA88-03-026, 1988 WL 141701 (12th Dist Ct App, Clermont, 12-30-88).

[98]See Text Ch 14, Stop and Frisk.

[99]State v Morris, 48 App(3d) 137, 548 NE(2d) 969 (Cuyahoga 1988).

[100]United States v Pope, 561 F(2d) 663 (6th Cir Ohio 1977); see also Text 3.05(B)(3), Flight from law enforcement officers.

[101]State v Morris, 48 App(3d) 137, 548 NE(2d) 969 (Cuyahoga 1988).

[102]See State v Price, 80 App(3d) 108, 608 NE(2d) 1088 (Wayne 1992) (police officer smelled alcohol on defendant's breath who was stopped for passing in a "No Pass Zone" and then performed poorly on field sobriety tests).

search or arrest. In *Sibron v New York*,[103] the United States Supreme Court ruled that the arrest of a suspect was illegal because it was based mainly on police observation of the suspect talking to a number of known narcotics addicts over an eight-hour period. Police did not know the content of the conversations, nor did they see anything pass between the defendant and the addicts. The Court pointed out that the police observation over this lengthy period of time in which they did not observe a drug transaction weakened any claim of probable cause.[104]

(C) Location

A person's lawful presence in a public area cannot establish probable cause,[105] but under incriminating circumstances location can contribute to a finding of probable cause. In *United States v Edwards*,[106] police had probable cause to arrest defendants for suspected burglary of a post office for the following reasons:

(1) Police had observed the defendants directly in front of the post office three minutes before police received dispatch of a silent alarm;

(2) It was late on a Sunday night and few people were on the street;

(3) The defendants were the only people observed in the vicinity; and

(4) It appeared to police that the defendants had just turned out of a driveway leading to the post office.

Edwards is especially significant because the location in question was the vicinity of an actual crime. It was not a general, amorphous claim that the defendants were in a "high crime" area.[107]

(D) Sources of probable cause information

(1) In general

An affidavit for an arrest or search warrant may be based on hearsay information.[108] The "totality of the circumstances" approach to probable cause properly includes an analysis of whether to believe the source of information; different sources of information deserve different levels of belief. The fact that information is double hearsay is relevant to an evaluation of its value but does not *per se* invalidate a finding of probable cause.[109] For example, a statement by an undercover narcotics agent attesting to a

---

[103]Sibron v New York, 392 US 40, 88 SCt 1889, 20 LEd(2d) 917 (1968).

[104]Sibron v New York, 392 US 40, 62, 88 SCt 1889, 20 LEd(2d) 917 (1968); see also State v Fahy, 49 App(3d) 160, 551 NE(2d) 1311 (Henry 1988), appeal dismissed by 40 OS(3d) 704, 534 NE(2d) 841 (1988).

[105]See State v Newell, 68 App(3d) 623, 589 NE(2d) 412 (Lucas 1990) (where deputies found sixteen people—three of whom were minors—in a motel room containing alcohol, police lacked probable cause to arrest defendant for contributing to the delinquency of minors based upon mere presence).

[106]United States v Edwards, 474 F(2d) 1206 (6th Cir 1973), reversed on other grounds by 415 US 800, 94 SCt 1234, 39 LEd(2d) 771 (1974).

[107]Cf. State v Bobo, 37 OS(3d) 177, 524 NE(2d) 489 (1988), cert denied 488 US 910, 109 SCt 264, 102 LEd(2d) 252 (1988).

[108]Aguilar v Texas, 378 US 108, 84 SCt 1509, 12 LEd(2d) 723 (1964), overruled by Illinois v Gates, 462 US 213, 103 SCt 2317, 76 LEd(2d) 527 (1983).

[109]State v Taylor, 82 App(3d) 434, 612 NE(2d) 728 (Montgomery 1992).

controlled drug purchase should carry far more weight than the same allegation by someone engaged in narcotics trafficking, which in turn should carry more weight than the conclusory allegation of an anonymous 911 caller.

(2) Police officers

Law enforcement officers who personally observe criminal activity or suspicious circumstances are obviously good sources of information. A police officer's statements are entitled to be taken at face value and, absent evidence to the contrary, are assumed to be truthful. A magistrate may accept a police officer's sworn accounting of facts and circumstances without inquiring into the officer's veracity. Police officers may also reasonably rely on information provided by other officers when proceeding with a warrantless search or arrest.[110] Similarly, information received over the police radio is considered to be trustworthy for the purposes of establishing probable cause.[111] If probable cause is later challenged, the issue would be whether the source of information had probable cause to search or arrest.[112] Dictum in a 1975 state appellate decision[113] suggests that even if the information conveyed to a police officer in person did not constitute probable cause, this same information would withstand subsequent probable cause scrutiny if broadcast over a police radio. This somewhat curious assertion, however, is in direct conflict with the United States Supreme Court's holding in *Whiteley v Warden, Wyoming State Penitentiary*[114] and is apparently not followed in subsequent state decisions.

(3) Informants

Personal observations of police officers are not required to establish probable cause; reliable information obtained from credible informants will suffice. A report of a crime by an identified victim or a disinterested, identified witness may be taken at face value and acted upon without further checking the veracity of the source of information.[115] A spouse who is identified may provide probable cause information against his/her spouse.[116]

Police may also use information obtained from confidential informants. The identity of such informants need not be disclosed to a judge issuing a warrant or to the court subsequently reviewing probable cause,[117] although

---

[110]State v Henderson, 51 OS(3d) 54, 554 NE(2d) 104 (1990); State v Holmes, 28 App(3d) 12, 28 OBR 21, 501 NE(2d) 629 (Hamilton 1985).

[111]State v Fultz, 13 OS(2d) 79, 234 NE(2d) 593 (1968), cert denied 393 US 854, 89 SCt 95, 21 LEd(2d) 123 (1968).

[112]Whiteley v Warden, Wyoming State Penitentiary, 401 US 560, 91 SCt 1031, 28 LEd(2d) 306 (1971).

[113]State v King, 324 NE(2d) 292 (Hamilton 1975).

[114]Whiteley v Warden, Wyoming State Penitentiary, 401 US 560, 91 SCt 1031, 28 LEd(2d) 306 (1971).

[115]United States v Swihart, 554 F(2d) 264 (6th Cir Ohio 1977); State v Walling, No. 82-CA-10, 1983 WL 5024 (2d Dist Ct App, Greene, 1-18-83); State v Boll, No. C-810078, 1981 WL 10161 (1st Dist Ct App, Hamilton, 12-16-81).

[116]State v Jaschik, 85 App(3d) 589, 620 NE(2d) 883 (Trumbull 1993), appeal dismissed by 67 OS(3d) 1450, 619 NE(2d) 419 (1993).

[117]McCray v Illinois, 386 US 300, 87 SCt 1056, 18 LEd(2d) 62 (1967).

a judge who does not believe that the informant exists may refuse to issue the warrant. The only time an informant's identity need be disclosed is if the testimony is critical to the issue of guilt or innocence at trial.[118]

Whether identified or confidential, not all informants are victims or otherwise upstanding citizens. Police must seek and rely on information provided by all types of persons, including some who are paid and others who are involved in the criminal enterprise. When probable cause is based on the hearsay statements of this type of informant, certain precautions must be taken to ensure that the warrant does not issue upon unsubstantiated rumor. More is needed than merely the conclusion of the informant that criminal evidence is located at the place to be searched. A process has developed over two decades to test the information provided by the informant so that the judge may draw independent conclusions about the probable truthfulness of the information and the likelihood that the evidence will be found if a search is authorized. That process was significantly watered down in 1983 in *Illinois v Gates*,[119] when a majority of the United States Supreme Court overruled *Aguilar v Texas*[120] and *Spinelli v United States*,[121] which had set the standards for testing an informant's tip.

Aguilar required the informant to set forth the underlying circumstances providing the basis for the conclusion that evidence of a crime was located at the place to be searched. This requirement is self-explanatory. An affiant must present his or her own basis for believing probable cause exists and cannot avoid that requirement merely by crediting the conclusion to another source. *Aguilar* further required that the affidavit provide a basis for the judge to conclude that the informant was a credible person. *Spinelli* explained that the latter requirement is necessary for the judge to determine whether the informant is trustworthy and should be believed. The credibility of an informant may be established if he or she has provided correct information in the past.[122] Similarly, credibility can be established if the informant acknowledges participation in the illegal enterprise and makes an admission against penal interest.[123] Finally, the *Spinelli* Court indicated that where an informant's credibility is established but the reliability of the information is not adequately demonstrated, the gap could be filled if the information contains great detail that is corroborated and is sufficient to infer that the informant was knowledgeable and gained the information in a reliable manner.[124]

---

[118]Roviaro v United States, 353 US 53, 77 SCt 623, 1 LEd(2d) 639 (1957).

[119]Illinois v Gates, 462 US 213, 103 SCt 2317, 76 LEd(2d) 527 (1983).

[120]Aguilar v Texas, 378 US 108, 84 SCt 1509, 12 LEd(2d) 723 (1964), overruled by Illinois v Gates, 462 US 213, 103 SCt 2317, 76 LEd(2d) 527 (1983).

[121]Spinelli v United States, 393 US 410, 89 SCt 584, 21 LEd(2d) 637 (1969), overruled by Illinois v Gates, 462 US 213, 103 SCt 2317, 76 LEd(2d) 527 (1983).

[122]McCray v Illinois, 386 US 300, 87 SCt 1056, 18 LEd(2d) 62 (1967).

[123]United States v Harris, 403 US 573, 91 SCt 2075, 29 LEd(2d) 723 (1971). But see State v Paladin, 48 App(3d) 16, 548 NE(2d) 263 (Lake 1988) (statement against penal interest insufficient to establish probable cause because strong evidence already existed against informant, and informant held grudge against defendant from adverse testimony in earlier trial).

[124]Cf. Draper v United States, 358 US 307, 79 SCt 329, 3 LEd(2d) 327 (1959).

In *Gates*, the United States Supreme Court rejected the formal analysis required by *Aguilar* and *Spinelli*. The information about drug trafficking in *Gates* came to police through the conclusory allegations of an anonymous letter-writer and gave no underlying circumstances nor any way to test the informant's credibility or the reliability of his information. Illinois police and federal narcotics agents were able to corroborate some of the defendants' travel details contained in the anonymous tip, but these facts, while sufficient to raise suspicions about the defendants' activities, involved non-criminal behavior. A police officer then swore out an affidavit, giving the details of the letter and the fact that some details had been corroborated. Three Illinois courts held that this information failed both prongs of the *Aguilar-Spinelli* test because it failed to reveal the informant's basis of knowledge *and* failed to establish either the informant's credibility or the reliability of his information.

Justice Rehnquist, for a majority of the Supreme Court, rejected this analysis as well as the *Aguilar-Spinelli* test. The Court substituted a "totality of the circumstances" approach in which the elements of the two-pronged test, the basis of knowledge *and* credibility or reliability, are just factors to be considered by a judge in determining whether probable cause exists to believe that evidence will be found in a particular place. The Court stressed that probable cause is a practical, common sense decision, requiring only a "fair probability" that contraband will be found, and held that the *Aguilar-Spinelli* tests were inconsistent with this type of analysis. Applying the totality of the circumstances approach to the facts in *Gates*, the Court ruled that the police corroboration of the defendants' travels was sufficient, together with the anonymous tip, to provide probable cause. The weakness of the *Gates* analysis lies not so much in its renunciation of the *Aguilar-Spinelli* test but in its application of the substituted formula to the facts of the case.

Although the Court itself has since struck down attempts to limit *Gates*,[125] the decision has been attributed with doing far more mischief than it actually does. *Gates* did not say that the *Aguilar-Spinelli* test is irrelevant; it simply said that satisfaction of the two-prong test is not indispensable to a finding of probable cause in every single case. *Gates* did not substitute a new way of evaluating hearsay information, and under the totality of the circumstances approach advanced by *Gates*, the *Aguilar-Spinelli* tests will often be the only common sense approach to treating such information.

Aguilar-Spinelli retains relevance for determining probable cause when information is supplied by an informant. The two-prong test is the easiest way to evaluate information derived from an informant's tip. For example, in *State v Taylor*,[126] probable cause was established based upon the affidavit's claim that the informant had personally seen the items to be searched for within the previous twenty-four hours, and that the police could vouch for the informant's reliability. On the other hand, in *State v Cavanaugh*,[127]

---

[125]Massachusetts v Upton, 466 US 727, 104 SCt 2085, 80 LEd(2d) 721 (1984) (per curiam).

[126]State v Taylor, 82 App(3d) 434, 612 NE(2d) 728 (Montgomery 1992).

[127]State v Cavanaugh, 46 Misc(2d) 2, 545 NE(2d) 1325 (Muni, Akron 1988).

the Akron Municipal Court suppressed evidence seized in a warrantless search of a suspected drug dealer. The chain of events began when police responded to a restaurant owner's complaint of people loitering inside the restaurant. The loitering suspects, under police questioning, provided unsolicited conclusory information that a drug deal was imminent at a certain location. The police located one of the subjects mentioned and immediately searched him, finding drugs. In suppressing the evidence, the court dutifully cited *Gates* and the totality of the circumstances approach. However, the court unhesitatingly cited *Aguilar* and *Spinelli* in noting that the informant had no track record of reliability or credibility with the Akron police. Further, the court expressed skepticism about the information provided by the informants, as it tended to shift attention away from the potential loitering charge.[128]

Moreover, even after *Gates*, a bare-bones affidavit containing only conclusions, whether an informant's or a police officer's, will not suffice to establish probable cause. Justice Rehnquist wrote, "Sufficient information must be presented to the magistrate to allow that official to determine probable cause; his action cannot be a mere ratification of the bare conclusions of others."[129] The *Gates* majority admonished that "courts must continue to conscientiously review the sufficiency of affidavits on which warrants are issued."[130]

3.06   Probable cause established by perjured information

Ordinarily, it does not matter if an affidavit in support of a search warrant contains factual errors. The critical issue is whether the affidavit provided a substantial basis upon which the magistrate could make an independent determination that probable cause existed for the search.[131] Consequently, the defendant is not permitted to pierce the warrant and prove factual inaccuracies.

One narrow exception, however, allows the defendant to focus on misinformation in the affidavit. When misstatements are the result of outright perjury, the integrity of the warrant process is compromised and deviation from ordinary procedures is justified. In *Franks v Delaware*,[132] the United States Supreme Court held that a defendant is entitled to a hearing on a

---

[128]State v Cavanaugh, 46 Misc(2d) 2, 8, 545 NE(2d) 1325 (Muni, Akron 1988); see also State v Navarre, No. WD-88-43, 1989 WL 61669 (6th Dist Ct App, Wood, 6-9-89) (invalidating warrant where affiant failed to present any information about reliability or credibility of informant); State v McIntire, No. 94-CA-33, 1995 WL 137025 (2d Dist Ct App, Miami, 3-31-95) (affidavit lacks sufficient information to conclude that anonymous tip is from a reliable source where the affiant does not indicate whether the informant has provided reliable information in the past or had any basis for providing the information); but see State v Brown, 101 App(3d) 227, 655 NE(2d) 269 (Montgomery 1995) (sufficient probable cause existed where affidavit contained anonymous tip corroborated by detectives).

[129]Illinois v Gates, 462 US 213, 239, 103 SCt 2317, 76 LEd(2d) 527 (1983).

[130]Illinois v Gates, 462 US 213, 239, 103 SCt 2317, 76 LEd(2d) 527 (1983); see also Text 3.04(B), Function of reviewing courts.

[131]Illinois v Gates, 462 US 213, 103 SCt 2317, 76 LEd(2d) 527 (1983).

[132]Franks v Delaware, 438 US 154, 98 SCt 2674, 57 LEd(2d) 667 (1978).

motion to suppress when there is a "substantial preliminary showing"[133] that a false statement was included by the affiant in the warrant affidavit. This substantial preliminary showing must be more than mere identification of the errors in the affidavit.[134] Instead, the defendant must show by a preponderance of the evidence that the misstatements were made knowingly, or with a reckless disregard for the truth.[135]

Even then, establishment of the perjury claim does not automatically lead to suppression of the evidence. The affidavit, after the false portion is excised, must be scrutinized to determine whether there are sufficient facts and circumstances remaining to establish probable cause. The prosecution has the opportunity to demonstrate that the false statement was not material to the probable cause finding. If the remaining content is sufficient to establish probable cause, the motion to suppress will be denied, notwithstanding the allegation and proof of perjury.[136]

If, however, perjured allegations cause evidence to be suppressed, the "good faith" exception to the exclusionary rule[137] will not save the evidence. The United States Supreme Court has said that suppression remains an appropriate remedy in such cases.[138]

Requiring proof of perjury on the part of the affiant creates an almost insurmountable barrier to a defendant seeking suppression. Police can simply claim that any errors in the affidavit occurred inadvertently during the haste of a criminal investigation. While courts are understandably sympathetic to such claims, clearly a court determined to admit evidence can stretch the mens rea requirement to meet that end. A particularly egregious example is *State v Mobley*,[139] where the Twelfth District Court of Appeals simply refused to believe that police were capable of deliberate misstatements in an affidavit. In *Mobley*, a magistrate issued a search warrant based solely on an affidavit that offered only two facts: that police had made a controlled purchase of cocaine from the defendant's residence, and that the entire transaction had been recorded on tape. At trial, it was established that the purchase was actually made at another person's residence and that the contact with the defendant was not recorded. The affiant (police officer) claimed inadvertent error, citing the confusion of several ongoing investigations on the day the affidavit was prepared. However, further

---

[133]Franks v Delaware, 438 US 154, 155-56, 98 SCt 2674, 57 LEd(2d) 667 (1978).

[134]State v Roberts, 62 OS(2d) 170, 405 NE(2d) 247 (1980), cert denied 449 US 879, 101 SCt 227, 66 LEd(2d) 102 (1980).

[135]Franks v Delaware, 438 US 154, 98 SCt 2674, 57 LEd(2d) 667 (1978).

[136]See, e.g., State v Booker, 63 App(3d) 459, 579 NE(2d) 264 (Montgomery 1989) (perjured allegation that confidential informant had previously submitted reliable information not material to probable cause determination); State v Mills, No. CA-85-21, 1986 WL 4621 (5th Dist Ct App, Muskingum, 4-14-86), appeal dismissed sub nom State v McHenry, 53 OS(3d) 703, 558 NE(2d) 57 (1990) (perjured allegations defeated probable cause, but no probable cause necessary where police found contraband in open field).

[137]See Text 2.01, Introduction; Text 2.05, Good faith exception to the exclusionary rule.

[138]United States v Leon, 468 US 897, 104 SCt 3405, 82 LEd(2d) 677 (1984).

[139]State v Mobley, No. CA88-08-063, 1989 WL 53604 (12th Dist Ct App, Warren, 5-22-89), appeal dismissed by 45 OS(3d) 712, 545 NE(2d) 900 (1989).

testimony established that (1) the officer prepared the affidavit only ninety minutes after the events in question; and (2) he was reminded twice by other participants that no recordings were made of the defendant's activities. Accordingly, the trial court concluded that the misstatements were made knowingly or at least with reckless disregard for the truth, and it suppressed evidence seized during execution of the search warrant. Over the strenuous objections of the dissent,[140] the Twelfth District Court reversed this factual finding of the lower court on the basis that it was "entirely possible" that the misstatements were the result of "oversight or confusion."[141]

Mobley also provides an extreme example of the second impediment to a successful invocation of the *Franks* challenge to a warrant: even when perjury is proven, it must be shown that the misstatements were essential to the finding of probable cause. This would appear to be the case in *Mobley*: once the incorrect portions of the one-paragraph affidavit were excised, there literally was nothing left to even form a coherent sentence, let alone establish probable cause. Undeterred, the majority cited *Illinois v Gates*[142] for the proposition that probable cause must be determined from the totality of the circumstances. It then summarily dispensed with the doctrines of antecedent probable cause[143] and judicial determination of probable cause[144] in concluding that "totality of the circumstances" included all information known to at least one member of the investigative team, regardless of whether the team disclosed that information to the magistrate for evaluation.[145] As the dissent incredulously protested, "In going beyond what we know was presented to the magistrate ..., the majority ignores the holding of the very United States Supreme Court decision it cites."[146]

Franks is not completely ineffectual, however. When courts correctly apply the law, *Franks* protects the integrity of the warrant process. This was illustrated only two weeks after the *Mobley* decision by the very same panel of the Twelfth District Court of Appeals. In *State v Murphy*,[147] an affidavit for a search warrant attested to items that were likely to be found in the defendant's home. In fact, the items were already in the possession of the sheriff's department, and the affiant was actually one of the officers present when the defendant's wife delivered the items. Upon executing the search

[140]State v Mobley, No. CA88-08-063, at 4-10, 1989 WL 53604 (12th Dist Ct App, Warren, 5-22-89), appeal dismissed by 45 OS(3d) 712, 545 NE(2d) 900 (1989) (Koehler, J., dissenting).
[141]State v Mobley, No. CA88-08-063, at 2, 1989 WL 53604 (12th Dist Ct App, Warren, 5-22-89), appeal dismissed by 45 OS(3d) 712, 545 NE(2d) 900 (1989) (Koehler, J., dissenting).
[142]Illinois v Gates, 462 US 213, 103 SCt 2317, 76 LEd(2d) 527 (1983).
[143]See Text 3.03(A), Need for independent assessment by judiciary.
[144]See Text 3.04(A), Antecedent requirement.
[145]State v Mobley, No. CA88-08-063, 1989 WL 53604 (12th Dist Ct App, Warren, 5-22-89), appeal dismissed by 45 OS(3d) 712, 545 NE(2d) 900 (1989).
[146]State v Mobley, No. CA88-08-063, at 5, 1989 WL 53604 (12th Dist Ct App, Warren, 5-22-89), appeal dismissed by 45 OS(3d) 712, 545 NE(2d) 900 (1989) (Koehler, J., dissenting).
[147]State v Murphy, No. CA88-08-064, 1989 WL 59028 (12th Dist Ct App, Warren, 6-5-89).

warrant, the officers discovered other contraband in plain view and then obtained a second search warrant to allow seizure of the new contraband. Upon learning of the perjury, the trial court suppressed all evidence seized during execution of the two search warrants. The Twelfth District Court agreed, finding per curiam that the affidavit was "replete with false statements,"[148] that the misstatements were made knowingly, and that they were material to a finding of probable cause.

---

[148]State v Murphy, No. CA88-08-064, at 2, 1989 WL 59028 (12th Dist Ct App, Warren, 6-5-89).

Chapter 4

Arrest

4.01   Introduction

The development of constitutional principles applicable to arrests has generally lagged behind those governing the search and seizure of tangible evidence. Indeed, arrest has only been mentioned in passing in recent United States Supreme Court decisions that have moved various police-citizen encounters outside the purview of the Fourth Amendment.[1] The main reasons for this development are that the state common law on arrest was well settled, and little significance is given in the criminal law to an illegal arrest unaccompanied by a search. Despite the serious impact of illegal arrests upon Fourth Amendment privacy interests, the arrest itself has little impact upon the ensuing criminal proceeding unless it serves as justification for a subsequent search which turns up evidence.

An illegal arrest does not affect the jurisdiction of the court trying the defendant,[2] void a subsequent conviction,[3] nor furnish grounds for release by habeas corpus after conviction.[4] That general proposition may be deemed inconsistent with the due process principles that have evolved in the past two decades requiring that police obey the law while enforcing it. At least one court has suggested that due process requires "a court to divest itself of jurisdiction over the person of a defendant where it has been acquired as the result of the government's deliberate, unnecessary and unreasonable invasion of the accused's constitutional rights."[5] *United States v Toscanino*,[6] however, was a particularly egregious case involving allegations of kidnapping of a non-United States citizen from a foreign country and torture by foreign police, all with the connivance of American officials. The Second Circuit Court narrowed *Toscanino* in a subsequent case where a claim of kidnapping in a foreign country was unaccompanied by allegations of "cruel, inhuman and outrageous treatment."[7]

---

[1] See, e.g., California v Hodari D., 499 US 621, 111 SCt 1547, 113 LEd(2d) 690 (1991) (unsuccessful pursuit of suspect does not implicate Fourth Amendment); Florida v Bostick, 501 US 429, 111 SCt 2382, 115 LEd(2d) 389 (1991) (reversed Florida Supreme Court holding that "working the buses" with accompanying search was per se nonconsensual); see also Text Ch 14, Stop and Frisk.

[2] Frisbie v Collins, 342 US 519, 72 SCt 509, 96 LEd 541 (1952); Ker v Illinois, 119 US 436, 7 SCt 225, 30 LEd 421 (1886); State v Henderson, 51 OS(3d) 54, 554 NE(2d) 104 (1990).

[3] Gerstein v Pugh, 420 US 103, 95 SCt 854, 43 LEd(2d) 54 (1975); State v Delaney, 11 OS(3d) 231, 11 OBR 545, 465 NE(2d) 72 (1984).

[4] Krauter v Maxwell, 3 OS(2d) 142, 209 NE(2d) 571 (1965).

[5] United States v Toscanino, 500 F(2d) 267, 275 (2d Cir NY 1974).

[6] United States v Toscanino, 500 F(2d) 267, 275 (2d Cir NY 1974).

[7] United States ex rel Lujan v Gengler, 510 F(2d) 62, 65 (2d Cir NY 1975), cert denied 421 US 1001, 95 SCt 2400, 44 LEd(2d) 668 (1975).

While cases adhering to *Frisbie v Collins*[8] and *Ker v Illinois*[9] as precedent may appear contrary to due process principles, there has been no movement toward erosion of the rule that an illegal arrest does not affect the continued jurisdiction of the court to try to punish a defendant. The unwillingness to attach greater independent significance to an illegal arrest can be explained by the unsatisfactory consequence of a contrary rule. If jurisdiction was denied as the result of an illegal arrest, a defendant would never have to answer for his criminal behavior. Such a rule would make courts even more reluctant than they are now to consider the validity of an arrest. It can be argued that the same situation follows suppression of tangible evidence of guilt obtained in an illegal search, but the analogy is weak. The suppression of evidence does not a fortiori result in the dismissal of criminal charges. The state is free to try the defendant and attempt to secure a conviction with evidence that is not tainted by unconstitutional practices. While suppression of evidence may result in the dismissal of criminal charges, that result is not automatic.

The state appellate court decision in *Fairborn v Douglas*[10] illustrates the impact of an illegal arrest upon a conviction. Police, responding to a complaint of indecent exposure, received no answer when they knocked at the defendant's apartment door. They then illegally entered the apartment and arrested the defendant for disorderly conduct after he became verbally abusive. At trial, the defendant was convicted of public indecency (for exposing himself) and for disorderly conduct (for his actions after police entered the apartment). On appeal, the court ruled that the arrest was illegal because the police entered the apartment without a warrant in the absence of exigent circumstances.[11] Accordingly, the court reversed the disorderly conduct conviction because it was based on conduct following the illegal entry; because of the illegality, police testimony about the disorderly conduct was inadmissible. However, the illegal arrest was inconsequential for the public indecency charge. No evidence derived as a result of the illegal arrest was necessary to convict the defendant on that charge. The arrest, itself, would not lead to dismissal of the charge.

4.02 Defining arrest

An arrest is the "quintessential" seizure of the person.[12] The governing standard for arrests is found in the Fourth Amendment's warrant clause. Probable cause is the standard dictated in that clause, and the same standard applies to arrests with or without a warrant.[13] The probable cause standard, however, governs only seizures that constitute an arrest.

Since 1968, the law has recognized seizures of the person which are substantially less intrusive than an arrest and are governed by a lesser

---

[8]Frisbie v Collins, 342 US 519, 72 SCt 509, 96 LEd 541 (1952).
[9]Ker v Illinois, 119 US 436, 7 SCt 225, 30 LEd 421 (1886).
[10]Fairborn v Douglas, 49 App(3d) 20, 550 NE(2d) 201 (Greene 1988).
[11]See Text Ch 10, Exigent Circumstances.
[12]California v Hodari D., 499 US 621, 111 SCt 1547, 113 LEd(2d) 690 (1991).
[13]Wong Sun v United States, 371 US 471, 83 SCt 407, 9 LEd(2d) 441 (1963).

standard.[14] Since *Terry v Ohio*,[15] the law has become clouded by the recognition of variations of intrusions upon an individual's liberty interest. Some encounters between a citizen and a police officer in a public place, such as general requests for information, are so informal and unthreatening that they are not subject to constitutional scrutiny at all. Other encounters, such as a brief period of investigation, constitute a temporary seizure of the person and are recognized as less substantial than an arrest. These seizures, frequently referred to as *Terry*-stops, must be supported by distinct facts and circumstances giving rise to a reasonable suspicion that the individual stopped is engaged in criminal activity.[16] Since these seizures are very brief and do not involve substantial movement of the suspect, the standard of review is the general Fourth Amendment reasonableness test, not the more stringent probable cause test. Finally, there are encounters that are so intrusive as to constitute an arrest.

The inquiry as to whether a seizure constitutes an arrest is not an academic one; it is critical in a criminal case. It will determine what type of justification the officer needed prior to the seizure. It will also dictate what may be done with the suspect and the type of search, if any, that might be undertaken during and following the intrusion.

Since the label attached to an intrusion is so significant and because the statutes offer no guidance,[17] various factors must be carefully examined when classifying a police-citizen encounter.[18] Ohio courts have traditionally used a four-part test to determine whether an arrest has occurred:

(1) there must be an intent to arrest;

(2) under real or pretended authority;

(3) accompanied by an actual or constructive seizure or detention; and

(4) which is so understood by the person arrested.[19]

By 1980, the Ohio Supreme Court indicated that a fifth test might be necessary. In *State v Darrah*,[20] the Court said that the detention must be a restraint of freedom in contemplation of the formal charging with a crime. Apparently, the fifth test is a result of the confusion emanating from the

---

[14]See Terry v Ohio, 392 US 1, 88 SCt 1868, 20 LEd(2d) 889 (1968).

[15]Terry v Ohio, 392 US 1, 88 SCt 1868, 20 LEd(2d) 889 (1968).

[16]Cf. Zanesville v Osborne, 73 App(3d) 580, 597 NE(2d) 1200 (Muskingum 1992), appeal dismissed by 64 OS(3d) 1414, 593 NE(2d) 4 (1992) (trial court correctly denied motion to suppress because defendant was not under arrest even though he was asked to remain in shopping mall parking lot for a short period of time while officer drove witnesses from the mall to spot where defendant was being detained).

[17]RC 2935.01, the section defining critical terms used in the Ohio arrest statutes, does not include a definition of the word "arrest."

[18]For a full discussion on seizures less than arrest and the problems that arise in drawing distinctions, see Text Ch 14, Stop and Frisk.

[19]State v Darrah, 64 OS(2d) 22, 412 NE(2d) 1328 (1980); State v Barker, 53 OS(2d) 135, 372 NE(2d) 1324 (1978), cert denied 439 US 913, 99 SCt 285, 58 LEd(2d) 260 (1978); both citing State v Milam, 108 App 254, 156 NE(2d) 840 (Cuyahoga 1959).

[20]State v Darrah, 64 OS(2d) 22, 412 NE(2d) 1328 (1980).

United States Supreme Court's inability to provide clear guidance as to when a *Terry*-stop matures into an arrest. Unfortunately, that fifth test is unlikely to provide the breakthrough that resolves the issue. While a police officer may not contemplate a formal charge resulting from the stop, the nature of the intrusion may be so extensive as to require probable cause rather than reasonable suspicion to justify the officer's behavior.[21] *State v Gaddis*[22] provides an example where the police officers who seized the suspect acted in a manner more consistent with an arrest than a *Terry*-stop. The Butler County Court of Appeals held that the officers' behavior had to be supported by probable cause, which it was not, rather than by reasonable suspicion, which doubtless existed. The officers in *Gaddis* grabbed the suspect's arm, pursued him when he fled, grabbed and held him again, and then searched him instead of performing a limited pat-down for weapons. Similarly, where police handcuffed a defendant upon finding him following a pursuit for suspected drug activity, the defendant had been arrested and not detained during an investigative stop.[23] And asking a defendant to empty his pockets prior to a *Terry* frisk converts an investigatory detention into an unlawful arrest without probable cause.[24]

Dictum in a recent United States Supreme Court decision indicates that Ohio's definition of arrest is similar (though not identical) to that Court's interpretation under the United States Constitution. In *California v Hodari D.*,[25] the majority defined arrest (with the approval of the dissenters)[26] as "an assertion of authority and purpose to arrest followed by submission of the arrestee."[27] Alternatively, the Court said that "an officer effects an arrest of a person whom he has authority to arrest, by laying his hand on him for the purpose of arresting him, though he may not succeed in stopping and holding him."[28] In *State v Franklin*,[29] a defendant was found to have been arrested when he ignored an officer's direction to walk over to a police car, and the officer said "that is far enough" and placed his hand on the defendant, even though the defendant pushed the officer to the ground and ran. During the chase, the defendant lost a firearm which was recovered by the police. The court held that the arrest took place when the

[21]See Davis v Mississippi, 394 US 721, 89 SCt 1394, 22 LEd(2d) 676 (1969), cert denied 409 US 855, 93 SCt 191, 34 LEd(2d) 99 (1972).

[22]State v Gaddis, 35 App(2d) 15, 299 NE(2d) 304 (Butler 1973).

[23]State v Nelson, 72 App(3d) 506, 595 NE(2d) 475 (Cuyahoga 1991).

[24]State v Franklin, 86 App(3d) 101, 619 NE(2d) 1182 (Hamilton 1993), appeal dismissed by 67 OS(3d) 1421, 616 NE(2d) 504 (1993).

[25]California v Hodari D., 499 US 621, 111 SCt 1547, 113 LEd(2d) 690 (1991).

[26]California v Hodari D., 499 US 621, 630, 111 SCt 1547, 113 LEd(2d) 690 (1991) (Stevens, J., dissenting). At the same time, however, the dissenters vigorously disagreed with the majority's conclusions about the lack of constitutional implications of an attempted arrest.

[27]California v Hodari D., 499 US 621, 626, 111 SCt 1547, 113 LEd(2d) 690 (1991), quoting Perkins, *The Law of an Arrest,* 25 Iowa L Rev 201, 206 (1940).

[28]California v Hodari D., 499 US 621, 624, 111 SCt 1547, 113 LEd(2d) 690 (1991), quoting Restatement (First) of Torts, § 41 comment h (1934).

[29]State v Franklin, 86 App(3d) 101, 619 NE(2d) 1182 (Hamilton 1993), appeal dismissed by 67 OS(3d) 1421, 616 NE(2d) 504 (1993).

officer placed a hand on the defendant, and that probable cause had to exist at that time.

Consequently, it becomes necessary in a particular case to carefully scrutinize the restraints imposed by police officers and the extent of the intrusion upon freedom of movement in order to identify the type of seizure that has taken place. There is no difficulty in identifying an arrest when a suspect is handcuffed, detained for a lengthy period of time, and placed in a squad car or removed to the police station. Quite frequently, the restraint imposed on the suspect will not meet all of the indicia: handcuffing, prolonged detention, and removal from the scene. The prosecution will maintain that the seizure was merely a *Terry*-stop while the defense contends it was an arrest. In other circumstances, the roles are switched. Police who performed a warrantless search of a person may subsequently claim that the person was under arrest just before the search and the search was therefore incident to arrest. The defense will assert that the encounter was a *Terry*-stop, and that the warrantless search was improper.[30] There are instances where reviewing courts have concentrated on only one of the indicators and have found the intent of the officers and the understanding of the suspect helpful.

The length of time a suspect is detained for investigation may determine whether an arrest has taken place, but the Supreme Court has steadfastly resisted identifying when an investigatory stop and detention escalates into an arrest in terms of minutes. It seems reasonable to permit police to check a suspect's identification and to determine by radio whether a crime has been reported in the vicinity, but this action should be very brief and last only a few minutes.[31]

The behavior of the police during an encounter will help to determine whether the intrusion amounts to a traditional arrest. Significant for the purpose of this inquiry is whether the suspect is touched by police during the encounter, whether a weapon was displayed, whether the suspect is handcuffed, and the type of words spoken by the police officer. In other words, this test turns upon the degree of physical force and show of authority communicated by police.[32] However, no single factor is dispositive. Police may detain a subject during a *Terry*-stop without converting the encounter into arrest, and police may grab the person by the arm[33] or even draw their guns[34] to prevent the person from escaping. Also, police may use force, including handcuffs, to temporarily secure a person on the premises during the execution of a search warrant.[35] The problem with these lines of

---

[30]See, e.g., State v Scott, 61 App(3d) 391, 572 NE(2d) 819 (Hamilton 1989).

[31]See Text Ch 14, Stop and Frisk.

[32]See Dunaway v New York, 442 US 200, 99 SCt 2248, 60 LEd(2d) 824 (1979).

[33]State v Sbarra, No. 89-P-2132, 1990 WL 208824 (11th Dist Ct App, Portage, 12-14-90).

[34]State v McFarland, 4 App(3d) 158, 4 OBR 252, 446 NE(2d) 1168 (Cuyahoga 1982), citing United States v White, 648 F(2d) 29, 208 US App DC 289 (1981), cert denied 454 US 924, 102 SCt 424, 70 LEd(2d) 233 (1981).

[35]State v Schultz, 23 App(3d) 130, 23 OBR 242, 491 NE(2d) 735 (Franklin 1985) (temporary detention of person on premises during execution of search warrant does not constitute arrest).

inquiry is that they identify only those situations in which a traditional arrest has taken place; they are unhelpful in categorizing an intrusion that does not constitute a classic arrest because the intent of the officers and the perceptions of the suspect may rest upon less tangibly communicated signals.

A trip to the police station is usually the best indication of a traditional arrest because it involves the most significant and prolonged intrusion upon freedom of movement. In *Davis v Mississippi*,[36] the suspect and twenty-four other black youths were detained at a police station for fingerprinting and interrogation during a rape investigation. The victim had given a general description of her assailant, and a set of fingerprints was found around the window through which the assailant entered. According to the Supreme Court, the suspect's prints, which matched those found on the window, should have been excluded as the fruit of an illegal seizure of the suspect. In dictum, Justice Brennan indicated that it might be constitutionally permissible under the Fourth Amendment to obtain the fingerprints of a suspect for whom there is no probable cause to arrest. The Court found it unnecessary to decide that question in *Davis* because no attempt was made to secure a warrant, and the suspect was required to undergo two fingerprinting sessions and was also subjected to interrogation. The Court's dictum stressed the reliability of fingerprints, but seemed to signal that a seizure without probable cause for fingerprinting must be authorized by a warrant issued by a judicial officer to avoid the abuses that took place in *Davis*.

The Court has had several opportunities since *Davis* to explore and consider the dictum which indicates that under some circumstances a trip to the police station may not qualify as a seizure and therefore need not meet the constitutional standard of reasonableness. In *Dunaway v New York*,[37] the Court found it impossible to accept the state's claim that a suspect was not under arrest when he was taken from a neighbor's home to a police car, transported to a police station, and placed in an interrogation room. Not only was the suspect never informed that he was free to go, but as the Court pointed out, "[I]ndeed, he would have been physically restrained if he had refused to accompany the officers or had tried to escape their custody."[38] Finally, the Court concluded that merely because the suspect had not been told he was under arrest and was not, in fact, booked did not make his seizure even roughly analogous to the narrowly defined intrusion involved in the *Terry* case.[39] None of these cases met the criteria considered essential in *Davis*: that the detention be authorized by a warrant and not for interrogation purposes.[40]

---

[36]Davis v Mississippi, 394 US 721, 89 SCt 1394, 22 LEd(2d) 676 (1969), cert denied 409 US 855, 93 SCt 191, 34 LEd(2d) 99 (1972).

[37]Dunaway v New York, 442 US 200, 99 SCt 2248, 60 LEd(2d) 824 (1979).

[38]Dunaway v New York, 442 US 200, 212, 99 SCt 2248, 60 LEd(2d) 824 (1979).

[39]See also Brown v Illinois, 422 US 590, 95 SCt 2254, 45 LEd(2d) 416 (1975); Taylor v Alabama, 457 US 687, 102 SCt 2664, 73 LEd(2d) 314 (1982).

[40]But see Cupp v Murphy, 412 US 291, 93 SCt 2000, 36 LEd(2d) 900 (1973) (where a limited search of the person for highly perishable fingernail scrapings was upheld when the defendant, who was not under arrest, appeared voluntarily at police station for interrogation).

In light of *Cupp v Murphy*,[41] it becomes necessary to closely examine the voluntary nature of a person's presence at a police station. Ohio courts have looked both to the understanding of the suspect and the intent of the police officer to determine whether an appearance at a police station is voluntary or constitutes an arrest. In *State v Barker*,[42] a defendant who was asked to appear at the police station the following day for questioning and on that day called the sheriff's office and requested transportation was held to have voluntarily appeared and not to have been under arrest. On the other hand, a suspect who was asked by the police to accompany them to a police station and who went was found to be under arrest when a police officer testified that if the suspect had not cooperated, he would have been arrested immediately.[43]

Consequently, no single indicator serves to properly categorize the nature of a seizure. It is necessary to look at all of the factors surrounding an intrusion before an encounter may be classified for Fourth Amendment purposes.

CROSS REFERENCES

Text 8.05, Ch 11, Ch 14, 19.05

4.03   Use of deadly force

(A) Introduction

Ohio law on the use of deadly force by a police officer developed along the lines drawn by the common law. A law enforcement officer is never justified in using deadly force to prevent the commission of a misdemeanor or to apprehend a person for committing a misdemeanor.[44] Traditionally, until modified by the United States Supreme Court in 1985, case law held that a law enforcement officer could use deadly force to the extent he had reasonable ground to believe that such force was necessary to prevent a felony or apprehend the offender. Consequently, the use of deadly force was upheld to stop fleeing suspects discovered burglarizing a commercial establishment following warning shots fired over the suspects' heads and repeated orders by a police officer to stop. That principle was justified by the court on two grounds: (1) the officer had a statutory duty to arrest persons found violating the law; and (2) deadly force was necessary under

---

[41]But see Cupp v Murphy, 412 US 291, 93 SCt 2000, 36 LEd(2d) 900 (1973) (where a limited search of the person for highly perishable fingernail scrapings was upheld when the defendant, who was not under arrest, appeared voluntarily at police station for interrogation).

[42]State v Barker, 53 OS(2d) 135, 372 NE(2d) 1324 (1978), cert denied 439 US 913, 99 SCt 285, 58 LEd(2d) 260 (1978).

[43]State v Austin, 52 App(2d) 59, 368 NE(2d) 59 (Franklin 1976); see also Brookville v Louthan, 3 Misc(2d) 1, 3 OBR 64, 441 NE(2d) 308 (County Ct, Montgomery 1982) (defendant was arrested when off-duty police officer witnessed violation, followed defendant home, and "requested" that defendant accompany him to police station).

[44]State v Foster, 60 Misc 46, 396 NE(2d) 246 (CP, Franklin 1979).

the circumstances because the suspects probably would have escaped had deadly force not been used.[45]

Whenever the use of force, deadly or nondeadly, is permissible, only such force as is necessary under the circumstances may be used to prevent an offense or arrest the offender.[46] The amount of force must always be scaled to the circumstances calling for its use in the first place. Thus, using a blackjack on a person arrested for improper parking is excessive force.[47]

(B) Constitutional limitations on the use of deadly force

The United States Supreme Court, in *Tennessee v Garner*,[48] held that apprehension by the use of deadly force is a seizure subject to the reasonableness requirement of the Fourth Amendment. The Court said:

> The use of deadly force to prevent the escape of all felony suspects, whatever the circumstances, is constitutionally unreasonable. It is not better that all felony suspects die than that they escape. Where the suspect poses no immediate threat to others, the harm resulting from failing to apprehend him does not justify the use of deadly force to do so.[49]

The facts in *Garner* are instructive as to how reasonableness is to be determined. Late in the evening two police officers responded to a "prowler inside call." At the scene they were informed by a neighbor that she had heard a break-in taking place at the adjacent house. One of the officers went behind the house and observed someone running across the backyard immediately after a door slammed. The fleeing suspect stopped at a chain-link fence, enabling the officer with the aid of a flashlight to see the suspect's face and hands. The officer did not see a weapon and testified that he was reasonably sure that the suspect was unarmed. The officer thought the suspect was an older teenager and about 5'5" or 5'7" in height. In fact, the suspect was fifteen years old and 5'4" tall. The officer ordered the suspect to halt, but the suspect did not heed the order and began to climb over the chainlink fence. The officer testified that he believed the suspect would have escaped if he succeeded in climbing over the fence. The officer, acting under authority of a Tennessee statute authorizing the use of deadly force to effect an arrest and departmental policy which authorized the use of deadly force to arrest a burglary suspect, shot the suspect who subsequently died.

The Supreme Court adopted a balancing test to determine the reasonableness of using deadly force to stop a fleeing felon. Balancing the nature and quality of the intrusion on the individual's Fourth Amendment interests against the governmental interest alleged to justify the intrusion, a majority

---

[45]Clark v Carney, 71 App 14, 42 NE(2d) 938 (Hamilton 1942); see also State v Foster, 60 Misc 46, 396 NE(2d) 246 (CP, Franklin 1979).

[46]State v Yingling, 36 Abs 436, 44 NE(2d) 361 (Summit 1942).

[47]State v Sells, 30 Abs 355 (Fayette 1939).

[48]Tennessee v Garner, 471 US 1, 105 SCt 1694, 85 LEd(2d) 1 (1985), cert denied sub nom Memphis Police Dept v Garner, 114 SCt 1219, 127 LEd(2d) 565 (1994).

[49]Tennessee v Garner, 471 US 1, 11, 105 SCt 1694, 85 LEd(2d) 1 (1985), cert denied sub nom Memphis Police Dept v Garner, 114 SCt 1219, 127 LEd(2d) 565 (1994).

of the Court held that a police officer may not seize an unarmed, nondangerous suspect by shooting him dead. However, deadly force may be used if the officer has probable cause to believe that a suspect poses a threat of serious physical harm to the officer or others, or that the suspect has committed a violent crime. The majority clarified the rule by limiting violent crimes to those involving *actual or threatened serious physical harm*. Absent a threat by the suspect to the pursuing officer, the burglary of an empty house did not qualify. Further, the majority said that deadly force could be used to prevent escape only where, when feasible, some warning has been given. The dissenting Justices argued that the majority ignored the dangerous nature of burglary and related crimes.

The effect of *Garner* is to limit the former Ohio rule exemplified in *Clark v Carney*,[50] where there was no evidence that the suspects were armed or otherwise posed a threat to anyone. Moreover, the subject of the burglary in *Carney* was an unoccupied bakery which the *Garner* Court would characterize as the scene of a nonviolent crime.

Garner dealt only with the use of deadly force to effect an arrest. The Court did not speak to the alternative issue of using deadly force to prevent the commission of a felony. Different issues might tip the balance when the force is used to prevent the felony rather than to apprehend the suspect after completion of the felony. The societal interest might be somewhat greater where the police officer acts to prevent loss rather than to redress it. Moreover, the possibility of danger to the officer and to others might be greater or at least unknown when the suspect is interrupted in the commission of the felony.

(C) Use of deadly force to disperse a riot

RC 2917.05 is the only Ohio statute governing the use of force generally and deadly force specifically in law enforcement. That statute provides that a law enforcement officer or firefighter is justified in using force when and to the extent he has probable cause to believe such force is necessary to disperse or apprehend rioters.[51] The statute authorizes deadly force *only* when the rioter's conduct is creating a substantial risk of serious physical harm to persons. This statutory authorization of deadly force is likely to be consistent with the principle set forth in *Garner* because both require a threat of serious physical harm to others before the use of deadly force is justified.

(D) Use of deadly force in self-defense

A claim of self-defense by a law enforcement officer as justification for the use of deadly force during an arrest always changes the equation. A legitimate claim of self-defense more than satisfies the standard of a "threat of serious physical harm" enunciated by the *Garner* Court. Peace officers have the same right of self-defense as other persons, and a law enforcement officer is entitled to use deadly force to the extent he believes it is necessary to defend himself or another from death or serious injury from an attack,

---

[50]Clark v Carney, 71 App 14, 42 NE(2d) 938 (Hamilton 1942).
[51]See In re Removal of Pickering, 25 App(2d) 58, 266 NE(2d) 248 (Logan 1970).

without regard to whether the offense under which the necessity for self-defense arises is a felony or misdemeanor.[52] Actual necessity is not a requirement. Rather, the test of whether deadly force in self-defense is justified is whether the actor has reasonable cause to believe, and does believe in good faith, that deadly force is necessary to prevent death or serious injury to himself or another, under the circumstances as he sees them at the time.[53] In Ohio, self-defense is an affirmative defense which the defendant in a criminal action must prove by a preponderance of the evidence.[54] The United States Supreme Court has upheld Ohio's allocation of the burden of proving self-defense on the defendant.[55]

CROSS REFERENCES

Text Ch 7, 8.03

---

[52]Graham v State, 98 OS 77, 120 NE 232 (1918).

[53]Marts v State, 26 OS 162 (1875).

[54]State v Jackson, 22 OS(3d) 281, 22 OBR 452, 490 NE(2d) 893 (1986), cert denied 480 US 917, 107 SCt 1370, 94 LEd(2d) 686 (1987).

[55]Martin v Ohio, 480 US 228, 107 SCt 1098, 94 LEd(2d) 267 (1987).

Chapter 5

Need for an Arrest Warrant

5.01   Introduction

Although constitutional principles affect the determination of whether a warrant is necessary for an arrest, the Constitution plays less of a role in this issue than in any other Fourth Amendment question. Common-law principles, reflected and revised in Ohio statutes, continue to play a significant role. Whether a warrant is necessary prior to an arrest is governed by two major factors: (1) the nature of the offense and (2) where an arrest takes place.

5.02   Nature of the offense

(A) Felonies

State law governs the determination of the type of offense for which an arrest may be made without a warrant. Ohio law provides that any person may be arrested for a felony without a warrant upon reasonable cause to believe that a felony has been committed and reasonable cause to believe that the person arrested is guilty of the offense. The person making the arrest is authorized to detain until a warrant can be obtained.[1] A police officer making a warrantless arrest upon probable cause must identify himself as a police officer and advise the arrestee of the cause of the arrest.[2] An officer's failure to advise an arrestee of the cause of his arrest, however, does not render the arrest illegal.[3] If the arrest occurs during the commission of a felony, the officer need not advise the arrestee of the cause of the arrest. On the other hand, RC 2935.07 provides that when an arrest is made by a private person, he shall, before the arrest, inform the arrestee of his intention to arrest and the cause of the arrest. The notice provision, required when a private person makes a felony arrest on probable cause, is a mandatory standard for a lawful citizen's arrest.[4] In *State v Rogers*,[5] a murder conviction was upheld and the defendant's claim that he was using reasonable force to effect a citizen's arrest failed because the defendant did not provide the proper notice required when the cause for the arrest is not contemporaneous with the arrest.

---

[1]RC 2935.04.
[2]RC 2935.07.
[3]State v Fairbanks, 32 OS(2d) 34, 289 NE(2d) 352 (1972).
[4]State v Rogers, 43 OS(2d) 28, 330 NE(2d) 674 (1975), cert denied 423 US 1061, 96 SCt 801, 46 LEd(2d) 653 (1976).
[5]State v Rogers, 43 OS(2d) 28, 330 NE(2d) 674 (1975), cert denied 423 US 1061, 96 SCt 801, 46 LEd(2d) 653 (1976).

(B) Misdemeanors

(1) In general

Warrantless arrests for misdemeanors have traditionally been limited by statute and common law. RC 2935.03 provides that warrantless misdemeanor arrests may be made only by a police officer,[6] acting within his own jurisdiction,[7] and only if the misdemeanor is committed in the officer's presence.[8] All three prongs of this general rule, however, have been modified by common law and statute.

(2) Private misdemeanor arrests

RC 2935.041 creates a narrow exception to the general rule that only police officers may make warrantless misdemeanor arrests. Under the statute, merchants and their employees may, upon probable cause,[9] temporarily detain suspected shoplifters. Similar authority is granted to employees of libraries and museums to detain persons suspected of theft or defacement.

The private detention statute is not meant to remove public authorities from the arrest process. Indeed, if private authorities intend to detain a suspect longer than is necessary to recover the unlawfully taken property, they must either summon a police officer or promptly deliver the suspect to a judicial authority to obtain an arrest warrant.[10] Nor is the private detention authority as comprehensive as police arrest powers. Private authorities may not search a suspect without consent; they may not use undue restraint in detaining the suspect, and the detention may only be for a reasonable amount of time.[11] Also, there is no authority to detain others who try to interfere with the lawful detention of a suspected thief or vandal.[12] Private authorities, however, may interrogate suspects without first giving *Miranda* warnings,[13] and statements obtained during such interrogation are admissible notwithstanding the absence of *Miranda* warnings.[14]

(3) Exceptions to the "in presence" requirement

RC 2935.03(A) authorizes warrantless arrests of persons "found violating" the laws of the state. In 1893, the Ohio Supreme Court in *State v Lewis*[15] limited those words[16] to mean "committed in [the officer's] view" when the law in question was a misdemeanor.[17] According to the Court,

---

[6]See also Jackson v Gossard, 48 App(3d) 309, 310, 549 NE(2d) 1234(Allen 1989) ("It cannot be disputed that a citizen's arrest may not be lawfully made for the commission of a misdemeanor.").

[7]Cincinnati v Alexander, 54 OS(2d) 248, 375 NE(2d) 1241 (1978).

[8]State v Lewis, 19 LRA 449, 50 OS 179, 33 NE 405 (1893).

[9]See Text Ch 3, Probable Cause.

[10]See also RC 2935.06 (duty of private person making arrest).

[11]RC 2935.041.

[12]State v Griffin, 54 Misc 52, 376 NE(2d) 1364 (Muni, Akron 1977).

[13]See Text Ch 19, Interrogation and Confessions.

[14]State v Bolan, 27 OS(2d) 15, 271 NE(2d) 839 (1971); State v Giallombardo, 29 App(3d) 279, 29 OBR 343, 504 NE(2d) 1202 (Portage 1986).

[15]State v Lewis, 19 LRA 449, 50 OS 179, 33 NE 405 (1893).

[16]Contained in the analogous statutes of the day, RS Ch 1849, RS Ch 7129.

[17]State v Lewis, 19 LRA 449, 50 OS 179, 180, 33 NE 405 (1893).

warrantless arrest authority existed solely to "maintain the public peace."[18] If the offense was already an accomplished fact, the public peace had already been breached and there was no need to make a warrantless arrest.

The Ohio legislature has long recognized exceptions to the "in presence" requirement for misdemeanors involving acts of violence or the potential for violent recriminations.[19] Officers may arrest without a warrant when there is "reasonable ground to believe"[20] that a person has committed offenses such as assault, criminal child enticement, public indecency, domestic violence, or theft.[21]

In 1925, the United States Supreme Court relaxed the "in presence" requirement somewhat by holding that the offense may be detected by any of the senses, not just sight.[22] A 1972 Ohio Supreme Court decision appeared to abolish the in-presence requirement. In *Oregon v Szakovits*,[23] the Court went beyond the letter of the misdemeanor arrest statute and ruled that an officer need not witness the actual operation of a vehicle in order to make a warrantless arrest for driving while intoxicated (DWI). In the two cases decided in *Szakovits*, the defendants were involved in traffic accidents and had exited their vehicles by the time police arrived. Both defendants admitted to the investigating officers that they had been driving, and both were found to be under the influence of alcohol. The Court held that the arrests were proper because "[a]fter viewing the scene of the accident, and hearing appellants' admissions on a first-hand basis, the officers could reasonably conclude that each had been operating his vehicle shortly before the officers arrived."[24] It should be noted that even though an officer need not observe a defendant driving, an arrest for drunk driving must be based on something more than the defendant's appearance, such as field sobriety tests or some other indication that the defendant's motor coordination is adversely affected.[25]

Szakovits had a certain practical appeal: it helped maintain the public order (the original intent of *Lewis*) by preventing impaired drivers from getting back into their cars. Unfortunately, the *Szakovits* majority did not carefully articulate a legal basis for its holding, and Ohio appellate courts have not agreed on how to interpret the decision. One court implied in dictum that "found violating" should be construed to include an officer's reasonable conclusions from surrounding circumstances, seemingly extending *Szakovits* to all misdemeanor arrests.[26] At the other extreme, a

---

[18]State v Lewis, 19 LRA 449, 50 OS 179, 187, 33 NE 405 (1893).

[19]RC 2935.03(B).

[20]RC 2935.03(B). The functional equivalent of probable cause. Concerning definition of probable cause, see Text 3.02, Definition of probable cause.

[21]In addition to warrantless theft arrests, police may make warrantless arrests of people who they reasonably believe have defaced the property of a library or museum. See RC 2935.041(E); Text 5.02(B)(2), Private misdemeanor arrests.

[22]Carroll v United States, 267 US 132, 45 SCt 280, 69 LEd 543 (1925).

[23]Oregon v Szakovits, 32 OS(2d) 271, 291 NE(2d) 742 (1972).

[24]Oregon v Szakovits, 32 OS(2d) 271, 274, 291 NE(2d) 742 (1972).

[25]State v Cloud, 61 Misc(2d) 87, 573 NE(2d) 1244 (1991).

[26]State v Stacy, 9 App(3d) 55, 9 OBR 74, 458 NE(2d) 403 (Lorain 1983); see also 2 LaFave, *Search and Seizure* § 5.1(C) (1978).

different court characterized DWI as an offense of violence and read *Szakovits* as merely adding one narrowly defined exception to the misdemeanor arrest statute.[27] Another court has suggested that the in presence requirement is not applicable if there has been an automobile accident.[28] Yet another court suggested that the arrests in *Szakovits* were illegal but went on to rule that the statutory violations did not implicate constitutional guarantees against unreasonable search and seizure.[29]

Notwithstanding the broad language in *Szakovits*, the in presence requirement still exists in Ohio unless there is a statutory or court-made exception.[30] One court of appeals, however, has indicated that the requirement is modified so that the officer need not actually observe the criminal conduct to make a warrantless misdemeanor arrest so long as the officer is able to conclude by his own senses from the surrounding circumstances that an offense has been committed.[31]

(4) Extraterritorial misdemeanor arrests

Law enforcement officers have long been prohibited by common law from making warrantless misdemeanor arrests outside their duly constituted territories.[32] Even then, however, the common law recognized exceptions to the general rule. For example, an officer witnessing a misdemeanor violation in his own jurisdiction was authorized to pursue the suspect into another jurisdiction to make an arrest.[33]

Today, both the rule and the exceptions are codified in some detail. The sections of RC 2935.03 granting warrantless arrest authority limit the exercise of this authority to "the limits of the political subdivision, metropolitan housing authority housing project, college, university, or Ohio veterans' home in which the peace officer is appointed, employed, or elected ... ."[34] Similarly, the arrest authority of a constable is confined to the "limits of the township in which the constable is appointed or elected."[35]

Recent statutory revisions retain and expand on the common-law exceptions. Officers may now make extraterritorial arrests following pursuit provided (1) the pursuit occurs reasonably soon after the commission of the offense; (2) the pursuit is initiated within the officer's jurisdictional area;

---

[27]State v Ferguson, 5 OO(3d) 416 (App, Licking 1977).

[28]Middleton v McGuire, No. CA94-11-202, 1995 WL 591238 (12th Dist Ct App, Butler, 10-9-95.

[29]State v Allen, 2 App(3d) 441, 2 OBR 536, 442 NE(2d) 784 (Hamilton 1981). The Ohio legislature has finally addressed the discrepancy between statutory and common law. Ohio police officers are now authorized by statute to make warrantless arrests for DUI in cases involving vehicles regulated by PUCO where the officer has "reasonable cause to believe ... after investigating the circumstances surrounding the operation of the vehicle" that the DUI laws were violated. RC 2935.03.

[30]State v Miller, 70 App(3d) 727, 591 NE(2d) 1355 (Highland 1990); Columbus v Lenear, 16 App(3d) 466, 16 OBR 548, 476 NE(2d) 1085 (Franklin 1984).

[31]State v Reymann, 55 App(3d) 222, 563 NE(2d) 749 (Summit 1989), appeal dismissed by 42 OS(3d) 702, 536 NE(2d) 1171 (1989).

[32]See, e.g., State v Zdovc, 106 App 481, 151 NE(2d) 672 (Cuyahoga 1958).

[33]See, e.g., State v Zdovc, 106 App 481, 151 NE(2d) 672 (Cuyahoga 1958).

[34]RC 2935.03(A), (B).

[35]RC 2935.03(D).

and (3) the offense is at least a second-degree misdemeanor (or the municipal code equivalent) or a traffic offense for which points may be assessed.[36] Additionally, police may make arrests on streets and highways immediately adjacent to their jurisdictional boundaries for certain traffic code violations.[37] This last provision recognizes that many municipal boundaries run down the middle of principal roads and highways in the state, and the legislature wished to end litigation over the legality of traffic arrests occurring on one side of the street rather than the other.[38]

Most litigation over extraterritorial arrests, however, is limited to civil actions for false arrest. In *Kettering v Hollen*,[39] the Ohio Supreme Court declared unequivocally that a statutory violation of RC 2935.03 does not implicate constitutional protections and does not merit use of the exclusionary rule.[40] Lower courts, of course, adhere to this binding limitation concerning the exclusionary rule.[41] In *State v Tennison*,[42] the court held that the exclusionary rule is inapplicable to an unauthorized extra-territorial arrest made by a police officer, outside of his or her jurisdiction, who observes the commission of numerous misdemeanors by the driver of a motor vehicle, who is obviously endangering the lives of others.

One enterprising court has found another way to deal with the issue. In *State v Schmidt*,[43] the Twelfth District Court of Appeals affirmed dismissal of a case by the Clermont County Court of Common Pleas where the defendant was arrested in violation of the extraterritorial provisions of RC 2935.03. As the appellate court noted, "To hold otherwise would render RC 2935.03 powerless and grant constables arrest authority which the General Assembly expressly prohibited."[44] However, most courts adhere to the general rule that an unlawful arrest is no bar to prosecution.[45]

---

[36]RC 2935.03(D).

[37]RC 2935.03(E).

[38]See, e.g., State v Zdovc, 106 App 481, 151 NE(2d) 672 (Cuyahoga 1958) (Parma police officer made drunk driving arrest on Brooklyn side of Brookpark Road).

[39]Kettering v Hollen, 64 OS(2d) 232, 416 NE(2d) 598 (1980).

[40]Kettering v Hollen, 64 OS(2d) 232, 416 NE(2d) 598 (1980).

[41]See, e.g., State v Collart, No. 90CA004947, 1991 WL 149708 (9th Dist Ct App, Lorain, 7-31-91); State v James, No. WD-90-12, 1991 WL 53766 (6th Dist Ct App, Wood, 4-12-91); State v Curry, No. CA89-02-032, 1989 WL 101652 (12th Dist Ct App, Butler, 9-5-89); State v Vance, No. 2246, 1987 WL 11035 (2d Dist Ct App, Clark, 5-11-87); State v Hyka, No. 46285, 1983 WL 5626 (8th Dist Ct App, Cuyahoga, 8-4-83).

[42]State v Tennison, No. WD-88-41, 1989 WL 35534 (6th Dist Ct App, Wood, 4-14-89).

[43]State v Schmidt, No. CA90-02-016, 1990 WL 183505 (12th Dist Ct App, Clermont, 11-26-90).

[44]State v Schmidt, No. CA90-02-016, at 1, 1990 WL 183505 (12th Dist Ct App, Clermont, 11-26-90). But see State v Curry, No. CA89-02-032, 1989 WL 101652 (12th Dist Ct App, Butler, 9-5-89) (affirming trial court's strict application of *Kettering v Hollen*).

[45]See, e.g., State v Vance, No. 2246, 1987 WL 11035 (2d Dist Ct App, Clark, 5-11-87).

(C) Minor misdemeanors

RC 2935.26 prohibits arrest for one class of misdemeanors even if the misdemeanor is committed in the presence of an officer. A police officer must issue a citation, rather than arrest a person committing a minor misdemeanor. RC 2935.26 creates a substantive right of freedom from arrest for one accused of the commission of a minor misdemeanor[46] unless one of the statutory exemptions exists.[47] There are exceptions to the Code section, permitting an arrest for a minor misdemeanor, when the offender (1) requires medical aid or is unable to provide for his own safety; (2) does not offer satisfactory evidence of his identity or refuses to sign the citation; or (3) has previously disregarded a citation for that offense. Even when an officer violates RC 2935.26 and arrests a person for a minor misdemeanor, evidence seized incident to that illegal arrest will not be suppressed because the arrest violates a statutory right, not a constitutional right.[48]

Although Ohio requires citation in lieu of arrest for minor misdemeanors, the Constitution could require citations in lieu of arrest for more offenses. An arrest is sometimes unnecessary when the offense is not serious and is likely to invoke only a minor penalty. When a person stopped for such an offense satisfactorily identifies himself, is a resident of the community, and has not previously sought to avoid the jurisdiction of the court, a custodial arrest may be deemed unreasonable under the Fourth Amendment as totally unnecessary. When an offender is arrested under those circumstances, possibly the arrest is a pretext to justify a search of the offender and his vehicle if he is driving at the time he is stopped. Justice Stewart recognized, in *Gustafson v Florida*,[49] that a persuasive claim might be made that a custodial arrest for a minor traffic offense violates the Fourth Amendment. The United States Supreme Court has not addressed this issue. Absent these exceptional developments, the narrow rule remains that a search following an illegal arrest for a minor misdemeanor is also illegal.[50]

CROSS REFERENCES

Text Ch 9

5.03   Warrantless arrests in public places

Provided that the statutory requirements pertaining to probable cause or "in presence" are satisfied, no warrant is necessary to make an arrest in a public place. Notwithstanding the judicial preference for warrants, that preference has never developed into a warrant requirement when the arrest takes place in public, even if there was ample time to secure a warrant. No necessity must be demonstrated for bypassing the warrant process. This common-law rule was based on the general necessity of protecting the

---

[46]A minor misdemeanor is defined in Crim R 4.1(B) as an offense for which the potential penalty does not exceed a fine of $100.

[47]State v Slatter, 66 OS(2d) 452, 423 NE(2d) 100 (1981).

[48]State v Holmes, 28 App(3d) 12, 28 OBR 21, 501 NE(2d) 629 (Hamilton 1985).

[49]Gustafson v Florida, 414 US 260, 94 SCt 488, 38 LEd(2d) 456 (1973).

[50]State v Peay, 62 Misc(2d) 92, 592 NE(2d) 926 (CP, Lucas 1991).

public from further crimes or violence, thus preventing a criminal from escaping or secreting away stolen property or other fruits or evidence of a crime.

In 1976, the United States Supreme Court, in *United States v Watson*,[51] ratified the common-law rule that no immediate necessity must be shown in a particular case to justify waiver of a warrant when an arrest is made in public.[52] In *Watson*, Justice White traced the history of the common-law rule and its acceptance in federal and state statutes. While acknowledging that law enforcement officers may find it wise to seek arrest warrants where practicable to do so, the Court refused to transform the judicial preference into a constitutional rule. Moreover, the Court expressed reluctance to encumber criminal prosecutions with endless litigation with respect to the existence of exigent circumstances.

5.04   Warrant necessary to enter a dwelling to make an arrest

(A) Arrest warrants

The Supreme Court did not show the same reluctance when it transformed the judicial preference for a warrant when entry is made into a residence to make an arrest into a constitutional requirement. In *Payton v New York*,[53] the Court held that the Constitution distinguishes between arrests that take place in public and those in a home. The Court overturned statutes in twenty states, including Ohio, which authorized warrantless entries for the purpose of making an arrest.

The Court reasoned in *Payton* that an individual's interest in the privacy of his own home is violated both when there is a warrantless entry for the purpose of arresting a resident of the house and a warrantless entry to search for weapons or contraband. The same privacy interests are implicated whether the entry is to arrest or search, and, therefore, the same level of constitutional protection is justified. Consequently, the Court held that an arrest warrant is necessary, absent exigent circumstances to justify a warrantless, unconsented[54] entry, to enter a private dwelling and arrest a resident.

Previously, in *United States v Santana*,[55] the Court upheld a warrantless entry to arrest where the arrest, which was initiated when the defendant was standing in the doorway of her residence, was completed in the inside vestibule where the defendant retreated to avoid the police officers. The Court said in *Santana* that the defendant could not thwart a lawful arrest by retreating from a public to a private place. Moreover, the Court found that the police officers were in hot pursuit when they followed the defendant

---

[51]United States v Watson, 423 US 411, 96 SCt 820, 46 LEd(2d) 598 (1976).

[52]See also State v Torres, No. WD-85-64, 1986 WL 9097 (6th Dist Ct App, Wood, 8-22-86) (warrantless public arrests are valid absent exigent circumstances where warrantless arrests are permitted by statute and the statutory requirement for probable cause is satisfied).

[53]Payton v New York, 445 US 573, 100 SCt 1371, 63 LEd(2d) 639 (1980).

[54]State v Thompson, 33 OS(3d) 1, 514 NE(2d) 407 (1987).

[55]United States v Santana, 427 US 38, 96 SCt 2406, 49 LEd(2d) 300 (1976).

into her house. However, the Hamilton County Court of Appeals held that an officer who enters an apartment in pursuit of a defendant, whose arrest for a misdemeanor was initiated in the hallway, is not in "hot pursuit" when the officer waits several minutes for back-up assistance. The court held that the period of time waiting for help terminated the "hot pursuit."[56] Courts have continued to require that the hot pursuit be actual.[57]

One court, in *United States v Minick*,[58] has held that in order to justify a warrantless entry to arrest, the government must meet a "heavy burden of showing 'that there was a need that could not brook the delay incident to obtaining a warrant.' " *Minick* was reversed in an en banc rehearing, which applied the same standard but found the entry to arrest constitutional. The court rejected its panel's determination that the "warrant clock" begins to run at the point when police obtain the minimally necessary probable cause; instead, the court said the warrant clock begins to run when police "reasonably conclude they should move against a suspect."[59]

The United States Supreme Court has been reluctant to affirmatively define the types of exigent circumstances that justify a warrantless entry into a home. The *Payton* Court did not reach the issue, and lower courts have subsequently fashioned the rules. However, through its treatment of these lower court decisions on appeal, the United States Supreme Court has identified some broad guidelines to use in evaluating whether exigent circumstances exist to enter a home without a warrant.

In *Welsh v Wisconsin*,[60] the Court agreed with the Wisconsin Supreme Court that hot pursuit and imminent destruction of evidence would qualify as exigent circumstances in certain instances.[61] Additionally, in *Minnesota v Olson*,[62] the United States Supreme Court was "not inclined to disagree" with the Minnesota Supreme Court's holding that exigent circumstances also include (1) the possibility that a suspect might escape, and (2) the risk of danger to police or others inside the home.[63] In essence, the Court has recognized that determinations of exigent circumstances are very fact-sensitive,[64] and, thus, the Court is generally unwilling to tamper with findings by lower courts.

However, the Court has added an important caveat: when considering the relevant factors (i.e., danger to others, destruction of evidence, escape of suspect), a court must consider the seriousness of the crime and the

---

[56]State v Hablutzel, Nos. C-870789 et al., 1988 WL 125019 (1st Dist Ct App, Hamilton, 11-23-88).

[57]See, Blanchester v Hester, 81 App(3d) 815, 612 NE(2d) 412 (Clinton 1992) (rejecting claim of hot pursuit where neighbors did not see police lights or hear sirens).

[58]United States v Minick, 438 A(2d) 205, 211 (DC Ct App 1981).

[59]United States v Minick, 455 A(2d) 874, 877 (DC Ct App 1983), cert denied 464 US 831, 104 SCt 111, 78 LEd(2d) 112 (1983).

[60]Welsh v Wisconsin, 466 US 740, 104 SCt 2091, 80 LEd(2d) 732 (1984).

[61]Welsh v Wisconsin, 466 US 740, 753, 104 SCt 2091, 80 LEd(2d) 732 (1984).

[62]Minnesota v Olson, 495 US 91, 110 SCt 1684, 109 LEd(2d) 85 (1990).

[63]Minnesota v Olson, 495 US 91, 100, 110 SCt 1684, 109 LEd(2d) 85 (1990).

[64]Minnesota v Olson, 495 US 91, 100, 110 SCt 1684, 109 LEd(2d) 85 (1990).

likelihood that the suspect is armed.[65] The fact patterns in *Welsh* and *Olson* illustrate the distinctions.

In *Welsh*, a witness told police that a car had been driven erratically and that the driver had stopped the car without incident in a field and walked away. Police examined the vehicle and obtained the owner's address from the registration. They went to the home, entered without a warrant, found the defendant asleep in bed, and arrested the defendant for driving while intoxicated. The United States Supreme Court noted that according to Wisconsin statute the drunk driving violation was a civil offense with a maximum $200 fine.[66] Even though evidence of drunkenness might have disappeared if police had taken the time to obtain a warrant, the Court held that "it is difficult to conceive of a warrantless home arrest that would not be unreasonable under the Fourth Amendment when the underlying offense is extremely minor."[67]

In *Olson*, the crime was serious: the defendant was suspected of driving a getaway car used in a murder. However, police had surrounded the home where the defendant was staying; the murder weapon had already been recovered; and police had no reason to believe there was any danger in taking the time to secure a warrant. Therefore, the Supreme Court accepted the state court's finding that there was insufficient justification to enter the home without a warrant to arrest the defendant.[68]

Ohio courts have followed the broad outlines of *Welsh* and *Olson* when considering warrantless home arrests that do not fall within the typical emergency situations such as hot pursuit or destruction of evidence. In *State v Bragg*,[69] an appellate court upheld the warrantless arrest of a murder suspect, citing the serious nature of the underlying crime and the fact that the suspect was alerted to the police investigation and might try to escape.[70] In *State v Constant*,[71] another Ohio appellate court applied a four-point set of factors first suggested by the United States Court of Appeals for the District of Columbia:[72]

(1) The underlying crimes of rape and robbery were serious;

(2) The victim had positively identified the suspect in two separate photograph arrays;

(3) The suspect had a known history of flight from law enforcement agencies; and

---

[65]Minnesota v Olson, 495 US 91, 100, 110 SCt 1684, 109 LEd(2d) 85 (1990).

[66]The offense occurred in 1978 and was evaluated according to the more lenient standards of the day.

[67]Welsh v Wisconsin, 466 US 740, 753, 104 SCt 2091, 80 LEd(2d) 732 (1984).

[68]Minnesota v Olson, 495 US 91, 110 SCt 1684, 109 LEd(2d) 85 (1990).

[69]State v Bragg, No. 58859, 1991 WL 127135 (8th Dist Ct App, Cuyahoga, 6-27-91), appeal dismissed by 62 OS(3d) 1475, 581 NE(2d) 1097 (1991).

[70]State v Bragg, No. 58859, 1991 WL 127135 (8th Dist Ct App, Cuyahoga, 6-27-91), appeal dismissed by 62 OS(3d) 1475, 581 NE(2d) 1097 (1991).

[71]State v Constant, No. 12-082, 1988 WL 38828 (11th Dist Ct App, Lake, 4-22-88).

[72]Dorman v United States, 435 F(2d) 385 (DC Cir 1970).

(4) It was after midnight and there would be substantial delays in obtaining a warrant.[73]

Actually only two of the factors were legitimate considerations, the seriousness of the crimes and the suspect's history of flight, but they alone may have been sufficient to justify a warrantless entry. The last factor mentioned by the court, the lateness of the hour and the likelihood of delay in obtaining a warrant, is worthy of comment. This factor no longer justifies avoiding compliance with Fourth Amendment requirements: criminal justice agencies—police, but especially prosecutors and courts—share the responsibility for ensuring the availability of a judge to issue a warrant at all times. This is but one of the reasons for amending Criminal Rule 41 to authorize issuance of telephonic arrest and search warrants.

The Summit County Court of Appeals in *State v Bowe*[74] engaged in an interesting analysis. First, the court rejected the state's claim of emergency, pointing out that allowing civilian passers-by to enter with the police to identify the defendants destroyed any argument that this was a situation threatening life or limb. Then the court reviewed the six-point test applied by the trial court in this case, "six factors that constitute an immediate major crisis"[75] justifying a warrantless entry of a home:

(1) The offense is a crime of violence;

(2) The suspect is perceived to be armed;

(3) Probable cause exists to arrest the suspect for the offense;

(4) The suspect is believed to be on the premises;

(5) The suspect will likely escape if not swiftly apprehended; and

(6) The entry is made peaceably.

Factors one, two, four, and five go to the heart of establishing exigent circumstances. Since this is an after-the-fact review, whether the entry is made peaceably should not be a critical factor in determining whether exigent circumstances existed to justify the decision to enter without a warrant or consent. The court said elements three, four and six existed but were not enough. The critical factors according to the court were that there was no evidence of violence or that the suspects were armed, and since the police had all exits secured, the defendants could not have escaped.

---

[73]State v Constant, No. 12-082, 1988 WL 38828 (11th Dist Ct App, Lake, 4-22-88).

[74]State v Bowe, 52 App(3d) 112, 557 NE(2d) 139 (Summit 1988), cert denied 489 US 1090, 109 SCt 1557, 103 LEd(2d) 860 (1989), appeal dismissed by 53 OS(3d) 703, 558 NE(2d) 57 (1990).

[75]State v Bowe, 52 App(3d) 112, 114, 557 NE(2d) 139 (Summit 1988), cert denied 489 US 1090, 109 SCt 1557, 103 LEd(2d) 860 (1989), appeal dismissed by 53 OS(3d) 703, 558 NE(2d) 57 (1990).

State courts also continue to follow the specific *Welsh v Wisconsin*[76] holding on drunk driving. Ohio courts are divided as to whether drunk driving is sufficiently serious to justify a warrantless home arrest.[77]

What an arrestee may do to thwart an illegal entry into a home to effect an arrest was dealt with by the Cuyahoga County Court of Appeals in *Middleburg Heights v Theiss*.[78] There, police responding to a noise complaint attempted to enter a home and were resisted and assaulted. The court acknowledged that under *Welsh*, warrantless arrests in the home for minor offenses are presumptively unreasonable, and that the presumption is difficult to rebut. Further, the court recognized that an individual has a limited right to resist entrance. The individual is privileged to refuse entry, may close and lock the door, and may even place himself in the officer's way. The court did not determine the extent of permissible resistance, noting only that passive resistance is more likely to be privileged than a physical attack on the officer. However, the court ruled that once an officer has gained access to the residence, even though unlawfully, violence with the purpose to injure the officer rather than to resist entry is not privileged.

Since *Theiss*, state courts have placed additional restrictions on a person's lawful responses to an illegal arrest. In *State v Kattman*,[79] a case with facts very similar to those in *Theiss*, an appellate court ruled that a person may resist an unlawful arrest only when the arresting officer uses "excessive or unnecessary" force. Judicial reluctance to endorse any sort of resistance to police officers was also expressed in *Akron v Recklaw*,[80] where the court held that "[f]urther criminal acts—including assault and resisting arrest— are not legitimatized by Fourth Amendment transgressions."[81]

The Pike County Court of Appeals provided a different approach to this issue. In *State v Howard*,[82] a home owner resisted a police attempt to illegally enter his house without a search warrant to arrest a visitor, allowing the visitor to escape arrest. The court reversed the home owner's conviction for obstruction of justice, disapproving the imposition of penalties for exercising constitutional rights.

---

[76]Welsh v Wisconsin, 466 US 740, 104 SCt 2091, 80 LEd(2d) 732 (1984).

[77]See, e.g., State v Petrosky, Nos. C-900264, C-900265, 1991 WL 40550 (1st Dist Ct App, Hamilton, 3-27-91), appeal dismissed by 61 OS(3d) 1428, 575 NE(2d) 216 (1991); State v Zimmerman, No. 88AP020019, 1988 WL 83510 (5th Dist Ct App, Tuscarawas, 8-2-88) (all disallowing a warrantless entry of a residence to arrest for drunk driving). But see State v Rouse, 53 App(3d) 48, 557 NE(2d) 1227 (Franklin 1988) (where court of appeals characterized DWI as serious offense and upheld as not unreasonable sheriff's kicking in door in "hot pursuit" of DWI defendant); Beachwood v Sims, 98 App(3d) 9, 647 NE(2d) 821 (Cuyahoga 1994) (drunk driving arrest in defendant's home on probable cause upheld).

[78]Middleburg Heights v Theiss, 28 App(3d) 1, 28 OBR 9, 501 NE(2d) 1226 (Cuyahoga 1985).

[79]State v Kattman, No. CA-8412, 1991 WL 123724 (5th Dist Ct App, Stark, 7-1-91).

[80]Akron v Recklaw, No. 14671, 1991 WL 11392 (9th Dist Ct App, Summit, 1-30-91).

[81]Akron v Recklaw, No. 14671, at 3, 1991 WL 11392 (9th Dist Ct App, Summit, 1-30-91).

[82]State v Howard, 75 App(3d) 760, 600 NE(2d) 809 (Pike 1991).

(B) Search warrants

An arrest warrant, while adequately protecting the Fourth Amendment interests of the person to be arrested, does absolutely nothing to protect the privacy interest involved when it is used as the legal authority to enter the residence of a third person in order to arrest a nonresident who police believe is there. The third person's Fourth Amendment interest involved is his right to be free from an unreasonable invasion and search of his home for the person named in the arrest warrant. The Supreme Court, in *Steagald v United States*,[83] held that, absent exigent circumstances, the only way to protect the third person's privacy interest in his home was to require a search warrant to enter a residence to effect the arrest of a nonresident.[84] The Court saw no reason to depart from the settled doctrine that a search warrant is required to enter a residence when the search of a home is for a person (a nonresident) rather than an object. The Court saw too great a potential for abuse if an arrest warrant was deemed sufficient justification for searching a residence for a nonresident.

The facts in *Steagald* fully displayed the conflicts involved and the potential for abuse. Police went to the defendant's home to execute an arrest warrant for Ricky Lyons, a nonresident who police believed was present. While searching the home for Lyons, who was not there, police discovered evidence of a crime and charged the defendant. The Court found it unreasonable that police could enter a third person's home to search for another without a judicial evaluation of the facts that led them to believe that the nonresident would be found at that home. The majority pointed out the danger of a contrary result, raising the possibility that police might have conducted entries without search warrants of homes of all of Lyons' friends.

The Ohio Supreme Court has concluded that *Steagald* "is equally persuasive" concerning the entry of a private business premises as it is a private home.[85] However, the Court has held that "absent bad faith on the part of the law enforcement officer, an occupant of business premises cannot obstruct the officer in the discharge of his duty, whether or not the officer's actions are lawful under the circumstances."[86]

CROSS REFERENCES

Text Ch 14

5.05   Post-arrest warrants

The United States Constitution requires a determination of probable cause as a condition for any significant pretrial restraint on liberty. This determination must be made by a judicial officer either before or promptly

---

[83]Steagald v United States, 451 US 204, 101 SCt 1642, 68 LEd(2d) 38 (1981).

[84]See also State v Wilson, 2 App(3d) 151, 440 NE(2d) 1373 (Lucas 1981); see also State v Howard, 75 App(3d) 760, 600 NE(2d) 809 (Pike 1991).

[85]State v Pembaur, 9 OS(3d) 136, 9 OBR 385, 459 NE(2d) 217 (1984), cert denied 467 US 1219, 104 SCt 2668, 81 LEd(2d) 373 (1984).

[86]State v Pembaur, 9 OS(3d) 136, 138, 9 OBR 385, 459 NE(2d) 217 (1984), cert denied 467 US 1219, 104 SCt 2668, 81 LEd(2d) 373 (1984).

after arrest.[87] The constitutional requirement following a warrantless arrest is applicable only to those who suffer restraints on liberty other than the requirement to appear for trial. Consequently, this protection applies only to defendants held while awaiting trial. The United States Supreme Court has watered down the promptness requirement, holding that federal constitutional principles do not require an immediate determination of probable cause upon completion of the administrative steps incident to arrest. Rather, federal constitutional requirements are satisfied if the neutral determination of probable cause takes place within forty-eight hours of arrest.[88] This requirement may be satisfied by a warrant issued by a magistrate in a nonadversary proceeding on hearsay and written testimony; it is also satisfied by a preliminary hearing or grand jury determination.

In Ohio, Criminal Rule 4(E)(2) provides that following a warrantless arrest, the arresting officer is obligated to bring the arrestee promptly before a court having jurisdiction and to file or cause to be filed a complaint describing the offense, except when a person is arrested on a misdemeanor charge and then released upon the issuance of a summons. Satisfaction of the *Gerstein v Pugh*[89] requirement, however, is to be found in RC 2935.08, which authorizes the issuance of a warrant by a judge, clerk, or magistrate following the filing of the complaint. Subsequent detention of the arrestee is pursuant to the complaint and warrant.

The post-arrest warrant was eliminated from the adopted draft of Criminal Rule 4 on the theory that a cursory probable cause determination based on the complaint after an arrest serves little purpose and an arrestee's interests are better served at a promptly held adversarial preliminary hearing. The procedure set forth in Criminal Rule 4 does not, however, fully satisfy the *Gerstein* requirements. First, a preliminary hearing is not available in misdemeanor cases. In felony cases where a preliminary hearing is available, a delay of a week does not seem to satisfy the prompt probable cause review required by the Supreme Court. Compliance with these requirements has been achieved by adherence to the post-arrest warrant procedure contained in RC 2935.08, even though the adoption of the rules was intended to supersede such procedures. Failure to comply with these procedures, however, does not have any effect on an otherwise proper conviction.[90] Its benefit is only as a preventive measure against oppressive pretrial incarceration without a review of the legitimacy of the arrest.

CROSS REFERENCES

Schroeder-Katz, Ohio Criminal Law, Text 3.02

---

[87]Gerstein v Pugh, 420 US 103, 95 SCt 854, 43 LEd(2d) 54 (1975).

[88]County of Riverside v McLaughlin, 500 US 44, 111 SCt 1661, 114 LEd(2d) 49 (1991).

[89]Gerstein v Pugh, 420 US 103, 95 SCt 854, 43 LEd(2d) 54 (1975).

[90]Cato v Alvis, 288 F(2d) 530 (6th Cir Ohio 1961).

Chapter 6

Arrest Warrants and Summons

6.01   Introduction

An arrest warrant or summons is the orderly way to notify an accused that criminal charges have been initiated. In Ohio, a warrant may issue either before or after arrest. Although the criminal rules did not incorporate the statutory provision for post-arrest warrants, the practice has generally been continued in this state and in some cases may be constitutionally required.[1] A warrant issued prior to an arrest orders that the named individual be seized and brought before the court to submit to its jurisdiction and respond to the criminal charges.

6.02   Issuance of arrest warrants

Criminal Rule 4(A)(1) provides for the issuance of an arrest warrant following the filing of a complaint. The warrant shall issue if the complaint or affidavits filed with the complaint show that probable cause exists to believe that a crime has been committed and that the defendant committed the crime. A complaint in the form of a statutory charge does not provide sufficient information upon which an arrest warrant may be properly issued. It would have to be accompanied by an affidavit setting forth the facts and circumstances which would establish probable cause.[2] However, courts have occasionally upheld arrest warrants where the affidavit stated little or nothing more than the complaint itself. In *State v Miller*,[3] for example, a police officer prepared a document stating only that the defendant was observed in a state of "public intoxication." Another unidentified member of the police department filled in the requisite statutory language and sections of the Revised Code. The appellate court concluded that this document "was

---

[1] See Text 4.01, Introduction (Arrest).

[2] See, e.g., State v Ezell, No. H-86-31, 1987 WL 7792 (6th Dist Ct App, Huron, 3-13-87) (complaint that only stated that defendant "fail[ed] to abide by an order of the zoning inspector" was insufficient because it was devoid of any facts concerning crime charged); State v Carroll, No. 55611, 1989 WL 85128 (8th Dist Ct App, Cuyahoga, 7-27-89) (citation issued pursuant to Ohio Uniform Traffic Rules charging that defendant disobeyed red traffic light adequately described offense charged). But see Norwalk v Hoffman, 64 App(3d) 34, 580 NE(2d) 511 (Huron 1989) (traffic ticket with check mark next to box—"operated without regard to safety"—and with only description, "driving without due regard for safety," did not inform defendant of his acts or omissions which constituted the offense).

[3] State v Miller, No. 8-89-3 et al., 1990 WL 113542 (3d Dist Ct App, Logan, 7-26-90).

sufficient to inform the accused of the crimes of which he was charged and to cause his arrest."[4]

In addition to the complaint and affidavit, the issuing authority may rely upon the complainant's testimony in making a determination whether probable cause exists.[5] The additional testimony must be given under oath and is admissible at a hearing on a motion to suppress.[6] Its admissibility, on review of the probable cause determination at a suppression hearing, is dependent upon the testimony having been recorded at the time it was given. The recording requirement is essential because the reviewing court must have access to the same evidence relied upon by the issuing authority when the finding was made that probable cause existed to justify issuance of a warrant.

RC 2935.09 provides the requirements for accusation by affidavit sufficient to enable arrest. That section requires that in cases where the arrest warrant issues prior to arrest, a peace officer or private citizen with knowledge of the offense or offenses alleged must file an affidavit. The affiant has a choice of two procedures: (1) file an affidavit charging the offense with the judge, clerk of a court of record, or magistrate; or (2) file the affidavit with the prosecuting attorney for the purpose of having the prosecuting attorney file a complaint.[7]

The statute specifies that the affidavit be filed by a peace officer or private citizen with knowledge of the facts. The courts have interpreted this section as not requiring "personal knowledge" on the part of the affiant. In *Sopko v Maxwell*,[8] the court, in a per curiam opinion, stated, "It is not necessary that the affidavit be executed by one who observed the commission of the offense. It is sufficient if such person has reasonable grounds to believe that the accused has committed the crime."

The Hamilton County Court of Appeals offered additional guidance as to the type of knowledge required by an affiant. In *State v Biedenharn*,[9] the defendant exposed himself to two fifteen-year-old girls. The affidavits were signed by the mother of one girl and the father of the other. The defendant was arrested on a warrant issued on these affidavits. The defendant moved to quash on the grounds that the affidavits were made by persons without personal knowledge. The court denied the motion, stating that the purpose of the affidavit is to cause the arrest and prosecution of the defendant and to advise him of the charges against him. Its effect, according to the court, is to place the burden of proving the allegations on the prosecution. As the

---

[4]State v Miller, No. 8-89-3 et al., at 2, 1990 WL 113542 (3d Dist Ct App, Logan, 7-26-90).

[5]Crim R 4(A)(1).

[6]See, e.g., State v Green, 48 App(3d) 121, 548 NE(2d) 334 (Portage 1988); South Euclid v Samartini, 5 Misc 38, 204 NE(2d) 425 (Muni, South Euclid 1965); see also State v Green, 48 App(3d) 121, 548 NE(2d) 334 (Portage 1988) (charging officer must sign both complaint and jurat).

[7]State v Maynard, 1 OS(2d) 57, 203 NE(2d) 332 (1964), cert denied 382 US 871, 86 SCt 105, 15 LEd(2d) 110 (1965).

[8]Sopko v Maxwell, 3 OS(2d) 123, 124, 209 NE(2d) 201 (1965).

[9]State v Biedenharn, 19 App(2d) 204, 250 NE(2d) 778 (Hamilton 1969).

statute itself does not set out a requirement for personal knowledge, no such knowledge is necessary in order to file an affidavit. In addition, there is sufficient remedy at law for the filing of a false affidavit. This ruling was held to comport with the Ohio Rules of Criminal Procedure in *State v Villagomez.*[10] When a victim of an offense files an affidavit or complaint, the fact that the victim does not state that the accused's identity was provided by an unidentified witness is immaterial.[11]

Other statutory provisions for the affidavit/complaint process are found in RC 2935.17, which contains the forms for affidavits and complaints, and Criminal Rule 3, which states the requirements for a complaint. Criminal Rule 3 provides that the complaint state the essential facts of the offense charged, the numerical designation of the statute or ordinance violated, and be made upon oath before a person authorized to administer oaths.

CROSS REFERENCES

Text 1.04, 8.03

1 Giannelli & Snyder, Baldwin's Ohio Practice, *Evidence* § 101.12

6.03   Who may issue arrest warrants

Arrest warrants may be issued by a judge, clerk of court, or officer of the court designated by the judge.[12] This provision contrasts with Criminal Rule 41(A), which only permits a judge of a court of record to issue a search warrant. Since 1932, a judge or magistrate has been established as the sole authority for the issuance of a search warrant.[13] Language in the *Nicholas v Cleveland* opinion, however, bears upon the propriety of permitting clerks or officers of a court to issue arrest warrants without a probable cause determination first being made by a grand jury in an indictment.[14] In *Nicholas,* the Ohio Supreme Court indicated that the issuance of a warrant (albeit a search warrant in that case) is a judicial and not a ministerial act because it involves the determination of whether sufficient probable cause has been demonstrated to justify issuance of a warrant. The court indicated that a clerk of court was incompetent to make judicial determinations because "[t]he clerk is merely a ministerial officer; his function is to carry out the orders of the judge."

The United States Supreme Court, in *Shadwick v Tampa,*[15] has upheld a provision similar to the Ohio rule when it found that a city charter provision authorizing municipal court clerks to issue arrest warrants for the breach of municipal ordinances did not violate the Fourth and Fourteenth Amend-

---

[10]State v Villagomez, 44 App(2d) 209, 337 NE(2d) 167 (Defiance 1974).
[11]State v Moore, 28 App(3d) 10, 28 OBR 19, 501 NE(2d) 1209 (Summit 1985).
[12]Crim R 4(A)(1).
[13]See Nicholas v Cleveland, 125 OS 474, 182 NE 26 (1932), overruled by State v Lindway, 131 OS 166, 2 NE(2d) 490 (1936), cert denied 299 US 506, 57 SCt 36, 81 LEd 375 (1936), reversed on other grounds by State v Lindway, 131 OS 166, 2 NE(2d) 490 (1936), appeal dismissed by 299 US 506, 57 SCt 36, 81 LEd 375 (1936).
[14]See Crim R 9(A).
[15]Shadwick v Tampa, 407 US 345, 92 SCt 2119, 32 LEd(2d) 783 (1972).

ments.[16] The Court held that the clerks, though not judges or lawyers, qualified as neutral and detached magistrates. Several factors in *Shadwick* were stressed as the basis of the decision. There was no showing of partiality since the clerks were divorced from law enforcement activity which might distort their independent judgment. The clerks in the case were employees of the judicial branch and under the supervision of the court. There was no showing that the clerks lacked the capacity to determine probable cause or that the task was too difficult for them to accomplish. The authority extended only to the issuing of arrest warrants for violation of municipal ordinances. Note that the Eleventh District Court of Appeals held that a police dispatcher could not qualify as a neutral and detached magistrate for purposes of issuing an arrest warrant.[17]

The Ohio provision is not limited to violations of municipal ordinances but extends to arrest warrants for all offenses. While the decision raises no question about the propriety of a clerk or other judicial officer authorizing the arrest of an individual charged with a misdemeanor, different issues might arise with respect to arrest warrants for felonies. Misdemeanor arrests do not generally carry the likelihood of any detention prior to release on bail, but a felony arrest may involve detention for a day or two before a bail determination is made by a judge. Nonetheless, the factors relied upon by the Supreme Court in *Shadwick* did not turn upon the severity of the offense but the capacity of a clerk to make a neutral and detached judgment. Therefore, the *Shadwick* decision would govern situations involving arrest warrants for all types of offenses. Still, one might legitimately question the Court's assumption of sufficient independence on the clerk's part to refuse to comply with an officer's request for a warrant.

The Hamilton County Court of Appeals, in *State v Fairbanks*,[18] has ruled on this issue and found no error in the issuance of a post-arrest warrant by the clerk of a municipal court in a first degree murder case.[19] That court, however, held that the issuance of a warrant is a ministerial act, a holding which is incompatible with the decision in *Shadwick*. The issuance of a warrant, except following the return of an indictment, is not ministerial but involves the exercise of judicial discretion. *Fairbanks* was decided prior to adoption of the Criminal Rules. The Rules superseded RC 2935.10, requiring issuance of a warrant unless there was reason to believe "that it was not filed in good faith, or the claim is not meritorious." It can be argued that the language was sufficiently broad to encompass probable cause which was

---

[16]See also State v Townsend, No. 1618, 1990 WL 138472 (4th Dist Ct App, Ross, 9-14-90).

[17]State v Torres, No. WD-85-64, 1986 WL 9097 (6th Dist Ct App, Wood, 8-22-86). But see State v Palider, No. 12557, 1987 WL 6964 (9th Dist Ct App, Summit, 2-18-87) (complaint, however, may be sworn to before a police dispatcher who is also deputy clerk of court because the swearing of a complaint does not require a finding of probable cause but is merely a charging instrument designed to give notice).

[18]State v Fairbanks, 33 App(2d) 39, 292 NE(2d) 325 (Hamilton 1971), modified by 32 OS(2d) 34, 289 NE(2d) 352 (1972).

[19]For a discussion of post-arrest warrants, see Text 6.05, Form of the warrant and summons.

already applicable in state court proceedings[20] and which since has been specifically incorporated into the language of the Rules.

A city mayor may also issue arrest warrants under RC 1905.20. The mayor's authority to issue arrest warrants is limited to the municipal corporation's territorial boundaries. In order to be valid, the statute requires the mayor to subscribe his name and affix his seal. In keeping with the judicial tendency to disregard minor variations from formal requirements, the Coshocton County Court of Appeals, in *State v Elson*,[21] refused to invalidate an arrest warrant in which the mayor had neglected to affix his official seal. The court held that the error was clerical, "one of form and not of substance." The defendant was not prejudiced by the omission of the seal, and the proceedings were still valid.

6.04   Summons in lieu of arrest

Where authorized by law, a summons may issue in lieu of an arrest warrant.[22] Neither is necessary, however, to commence prosecution, which begins with the filing of the complaint, provided that the defendant has notice of the charges against him.[23]

On a showing of probable cause, the judge, clerk of court, or officer of the court may issue a summons when requested to do so by the prosecuting attorney. They may also do so when it appears that a summons is likely to assure the accused's appearance in court.[24] Criminal Rule 4(A)(1) makes no distinction between felonies and misdemeanors, allowing a summons for both. Prior Ohio law limited summons in lieu of arrest warrants for misdemeanor charges.[25]

Law enforcement officers, as well, are authorized to issue a summons instead of executing an arrest warrant in misdemeanor cases or in those cases where the officer is authorized by law to arrest without a warrant.[26] Criminal Rule 4(F) also authorizes the issuance of a summons in misdemeanor cases following an arrest with or without a warrant by the arresting officer, the officer in charge of the detention facility to which the defendant is brought, or the superior of either officer. In either case, the same standard applies: whether a summons is reasonably likely to assure the accused's presence. When an officer issues a summons instead of executing an arrest warrant, he is to note on the warrant and return that the warrant was executed by issuance of a summons. An officer who issues a summons instead of arresting without a warrant is directed to file, or cause to be filed, a complaint describing the offense. In these cases, a recent revision to

---

[20]Aguilar v Texas, 378 US 108, 84 SCt 1509, 12 LEd(2d) 723 (1964), overruled by Illinois v Gates, 462 US 213, 103 SCt 2317, 76 LEd(2d) 527 (1983); United States v Ventresca, 380 US 102, 85 SCt 741, 13 LEd(2d) 684 (1965).

[21]State v Elson, 16 App 184, 189 (Coshocton 1922).

[22]State v Hooper, 10 App(2d) 229, 227 NE(2d) 414 (Monroe 1966), cert denied 389 US 928, 88 SCt 292, 19 LEd(2d) 281 (1967).

[23]State v Hooper, 25 OS(2d) 59, 267 NE(2d) 285 (1971).

[24]Crim R 4(A)(1).

[25]RC 2935.10.

[26]Crim R 4(A)(2), (3).

Criminal Rule 4(A)(2) provides that "[n]o alias warrant shall be issued unless the defendant fails to appear in response to the summons, or unless subsequent to the issuance of summons it appears improbable that the defendant will appear in response thereto."

Criminal Rule 4(F), providing for the issuance of a summons following an arrest, is an attempt to make the arrest procedures in misdemeanor cases less harsh. It is consistent with Criminal Rule 46(D), which was intended to facilitate the prompt release of persons charged with misdemeanors, and seeks to minimize wherever possible any pretrial incarceration for those defendants. A summons, where appropriate, is less complicated and will facilitate an earlier release than the other conditions set forth in Criminal Rule 46.

If a defendant fails to appear in response to a summons, an arrest warrant will issue.[27] Similarly, if at any time it appears likely that a defendant will not respond to a summons, an arrest warrant may be issued. A defendant charged with a misdemeanor who fails to respond to a summons without just cause may be found guilty of contempt of court and fined no more than \$20.[28] This contempt provision was adopted when summons were only available for persons charged with misdemeanor offenses; there is no comparable provision for felony defendants who fail to respond to a summons.

6.05   Form of the warrant and summons

An arrest warrant must contain the following:

(1) The name of the defendant, if known, or any name or description by which he can be identified with reasonable certainty;

(2) A description of the offense charged;

(3) The numerical designation of the offense charged; and

(4) A command that the defendant be arrested and brought before the issuing court without delay.

A copy of the complaint must be attached to the warrant.[29]

The summons repeats the form of the warrant except that instead of ordering the arrest of the defendant, the defendant is commanded to appear before the court at a designated time. A defendant is also advised in the summons that if he so does not appear, he is subject to arrest. A copy of the complaint must be attached to the summons except where the summons is issued before a complaint is filed.

A warrant is used to limit the discretion of the police officer who executes it. Consequently, the warrant should identify the person who is to be arrested, preferably by his correct name, as the best way of indicating to the officer exactly whom he may seize under authority of the court. This infor-

---

[27]Crim R 4(B).
[28]RC 2935.11.
[29]Crim R 4(C)(1).

mation, however, is not always known at the time a warrant is sought. John Doe warrants, when issued in bulk, are no better than blank warrants issued to a police officer permitting that officer to fill in a name as needed. They fail constitutional tests on two counts: probable cause and particularization. A warrant may issue only upon a showing of probable cause to believe that a crime has been committed and that a specific person has committed that crime. If the warrant does not specify which person is to be arrested, that part of the probable cause test fails. Similarly, warrants should specify the person or item to be seized. The absence of a sufficient description of the person to be arrested is inadequate under this test because the warrant will not sufficiently limit the discretion of the officer as he attempts to execute the warrant.

John Doe warrants, "although not [a] recommended practice,"[30] will not necessarily prove fatal if the person to be arrested is otherwise identified so as to sufficiently limit the exercise of discretion by the arresting officer. The subject of a John Doe warrant may be properly identified by place of residence, occupation, appearance, or any combination of characteristics which provide reasonable certainty as to the identity of the subject of the warrant.

---

[30]State v Young, 91 Abs 21, 24, 185 NE(2d) 33 (Cuyahoga 1962), appeal dismissed by 174 OS 329, 189 NE(2d) 151 (1963).

Chapter 7

Execution of Arrest Warrants

7.01   Introduction

Criminal Rule 4(D) permits execution of an arrest warrant by any officer authorized by law and in any place in the state. At the time of arrest, the officer need not have the warrant in his possession, but he must inform the defendant of the charges and the fact that a warrant has been issued. A copy of the warrant must be provided to the defendant as soon as possible.

The Revised Code also permits execution of a teletype copy of an arrest warrant. RC 2935.24 provides that a teletype copy of a warrant is effective in the hands of any law enforcement officer.

RC 2901.13(E) provides that a criminal prosecution commences upon the return of an indictment, filing of an information, or the date process issues if reasonable diligence is exercised to execute the process. The purpose of the reasonable diligence requirement of the statute is to avoid dilatory law enforcement. The court ordered warrants quashed and cases dismissed where an arrest warrant was not served for nearly three years, defendant was in jail for forty-five days of that period, and there was no effort to serve the warrants nor reason offered for the failure.[1] Constitutional speedy trial rights begin when an accused has been indicted or arrested.[2] The Portage County Court of Appeals has held that a person is not "accused" for speedy trial purposes until the indictment is actually served upon him.[3] Inordinate delay in the period before a person is accused, however, can still result in dismissal of charges if the delay results in actual prejudice to the defendant.[4]

7.02   Forced entry

Entry of a residence to make an arrest is controlled by federal constitutional requirements and RC 2935.12. The United States Supreme Court has

---

[1]State v Crow, 28 Misc(2d) 1, 501 NE(2d) 1250 (Muni, Ashtabula 1986).

[2]United States v McDonald, 456 US 1, 102 SCt 1497, 71 LEd(2d) 696 (1982), appeal dismissed by 459 US 1103, 103 SCt 726, 74 LEd(2d) 951 (1983).

[3]State v Burrell, No. 1948, 1989 WL 42980 (11th Dist Ct App, Portage, 4-28-89).

[4]State v Luck, 15 OS(3d) 150, 15 OBR 296, 472 NE(2d) 1097 (1984), cert denied 470 US 1084, 105 SCt 1845, 85 LEd(2d) 144 (1985); see also State v Burrell, No. 1948, 1989 WL 42980 (11th Dist Ct App, Portage, 4-28-89) (even though court rejected speedy trial claim where defendant not served with indictment for nineteen months, court upheld trial court's dismissal for inordinate (nineteen-month) "charging" delay between return of indictment and execution of warrant where defendant showed actual prejudice caused by delay in presenting a defense).

held that, in the absence of exigent circumstances, an arrest may be made at home only with a warrant, and there must be reason to believe the suspect is inside the home.[5]

A unanimous Supreme Court interpreted the Fourth Amendment to incorporate the common law principle of "knock-and-announce" prior to entering a residence.[6] However, the Court concluded that the framers "intended" whether or not officers should announce their presence in a particular situation is just a factor to be considered in assessing the reasonableness of a search or seizure. Therefore, the issue is to be determined on a case-by-case basis. State law is likely to be more instructive and in most cases state law will determine the lawfulness of the way police enter to execute an arrest warrant.[7] It only requires that the officers act reasonably. RC 2935.12 restricts forcible entry to execute an arrest or search warrant. That section provides that an officer may break down an outer or inner door or window if, after notice of intent to arrest, he is refused admittance. The statute only limits violent, forcible entry; it applies only if an officer breaks down a door to enter.[8]

The statute places an obligation to knock and announce before entering without consent.[9] The police must identify themselves[10] and state their purpose for seeking admittance.[11] The requirement is a common sense approach intended to protect individual privacy and to reduce the likelihood that occupants will resist with force if they do not know who is attempting to enter.

A forced entry is not reasonable when police do not afford the occupants an opportunity to respond to the police announcement of their purpose.[12] Thre is an exigent circumstances exception to the requirement that police give the occupants of a house an opportunity to respond.[13] Entry without waiting for a response is reasonable under the statute if the police act because they reasonably believe it is necessary to protect themselves from danger, to prevent the destruction of evidence, or to prevent the escape of the occupants.[14] Where there are exigent circumstances, police may enter without being refused admittance.[15] A mere general knowledge that evidence can be destroyed will not provide the exigency required to avoid the knock and announce rule.[16]

---

[5]See Text Ch 5, Need for an Arrest Warrant.

[6]Wilson v Arkansas, 115 SCt 1914, 131 LEd(2d) 976 (1995).

[7]Ker v California, 374 US 23, 37-8, 83 SCt 1623, 10 LEd(2d) 726 (1963).

[8]State v Baker, 87 App(3d) 186, 621 NE(2d) 1347 (Hamilton 1993).

[9]State v Hall, No. CA L-85-03, 1995 WL 7373 (6th Dist Ct App, Lucas, 6-30-86).

[10]State v Early, 7 OO(3d) 227 (App, Cuyahoga 1977).

[11]State v Furry, 31 App(2d) 107, 286 NE(2d) 301 (Wood 1971).

[12]State v Davies, Nos. C-850112, et al., 1986 WL 657 (1st Dist Ct App, Hamilton, 1-8-86) (here, entry was for purpose of executing search warrant).

[13]State v Boya, No. CA 13425 (2d Dist Ct App, Montgomery, 5-21-93).

[14]State v Davies, Nos. C-850112, et al., 1986 WL 657 (1st Dist Ct App, Hamilton, 1-8-86).

[15]State v Boya, No. CA 13425 (2d Dist Ct App, Montgomery, 5-21-93).

[16]State v Snyder, No. WD-94-098, 1995 WL 504758 (6th Dist Ct App, Wood, 8-25-95).

Absent the existence of exigent circumstances, a forced entry is illegal before police have been actually or constructively denied admittance.[17] Repeated responses of "just a minute"[18] and noises from within[19] have been held to be adequate refusals of admittance justifying a forcible entry.

The validity of a forced entry was the issue in *State v Clark*,[20] where officers with arrest warrants went to the headquarters of the Black Panthers and National Committee to Prevent Fascism. The officers knocked on the door, identified themselves as police officers, and stated that they had arrest warrants for Clark and Johnson. The occupants made no response, but the officers heard noises inside. The officers broke down the door and the defendants started shooting. The defendants claimed that the officers' forced entry was illegal. The court rejected this contention, holding that RC 2935.12 permits an officer, acting pursuant to an arrest warrant, to break down a door if refused admission after giving notice of intent to make an arrest. Since the officers identified themselves and announced their purpose to arrest, the court found the defendants' failure to admit the officers made a forcible entry lawful.

A different result was reached in *State v Early*,[21] where the court determined that the officers did not have the right to make a forced entry. In *Early*, the officers had an arrest warrant for Chris Canant. The warrant did not specify an address. The officers mistakenly believed that apartment number five at a certain address was rented to "Karen Canant." In fact, it was occupied by Karen Cran, and Chris Canant occupied apartment number seven. The officers went to apartment five. At the time, the defendant was visiting apartment five. When the officers knocked on the door, they asked to speak to Karen. The defendant slammed the door shut. The officers broke open the door, found Karen Cran, the defendant, and others in possession of drugs. After ascertaining that Chris Canant was not there, all of the occupants were arrested for illegal possession. The defendant moved to suppress on the ground that the forced entry was illegal. The court agreed, holding that the officers would be entitled to break down the door only after giving notice of intent to arrest and being refused admission. As the officers never told the occupants that they were there to arrest Chris Canant, they could not lawfully force entry.

CROSS REFERENCES

Text 8.03(E)

---

[17]State v DeFiore, 64 App(2d) 115, 411 NE(2d) 837 (Hamilton 1979) (executing search warrant, entry illegal).

[18]State v Morgan, 55 App(3d) 182, 563 NE(2d) 307 (Mercer 1988).

[19]State v Clark, 40 App(2d) 365, 319 NE(2d) 605 (Cuyahoga 1974).

[20]State v Clark, 40 App(2d) 365, 319 NE(2d) 605 (Cuyahoga 1974).

[21]State v Early, 7 OO(3d) 227 (App, Cuyahoga 1977).

7.03 Resisting arrest

At common law, one had a privilege to resist an unlawful arrest. That privilege was purportedly abrogated by the Ohio Supreme Court in *Columbus v Fraley*.[22] In rejecting the common-law rule, the court stated:

> [I]n the absence of excessive or unnecessary force by an arresting officer, a private citizen may not use force to resist arrest by one he knows, or has good reason to believe, is an authorized police officer engaged in the performance of his duties, whether or not the arrest is illegal under the circumstances.[23]

The court has similarly limited the privilege to resist unlawful entry onto business premises. In *State v Pembaur*,[24] police sought access to a doctor's private office in an attempt to serve capiases. The defendant resisted and the deputies had to break through the office door with an ax. The Ohio Supreme Court upheld the defendant's conviction of obstructing official business under RC 2921.31(A), stating that absent bad faith on the part of a law enforcement officer, an occupant of business premises may not obstruct the officer in the discharge of his duty, whether or not the officer's actions are lawful under the circumstances.[25]

The *Pembaur* decision was extended to residential premises. In *State v Pitts*,[26] the defendant, who was visiting his sister at her residence, was charged with obstructing official business when police officers forced their way through the front door past the defendant as they attempted to find his sister who had shouted obscenities at officers through an upstairs window. Despite being a warrantless entry on what appeared to be unreasonable grounds, the court held that the defendant had no right to resist the officer's entrance into the home. Relying on *Fraley* and *Pembaur*, the municipal court said, "Though the *Pembaur* case is limited to 'business premises,' surely a visitor, not the lessee, of residential premises could have no greater rights than a lessee of business premises."[27]

This principle was extended to a residential setting, again, in a case involving violation of a city ordinance. In *Middleburg Heights v Theiss*,[28] officers made an unlawful, warrantless entry into a home to arrest one of the defendants for a minor offense. The defendants resisted the officers' entry into their home and the arrest of one of the defendants. The court acknowledged the right of individuals to resist a warrantless and illegal entry into their home, but said once the officers were in the home, the defendants no longer had the right to resist: "[V]iolence against an officer

---

[22]Columbus v Fraley, 41 OS(2d) 173, 324 NE(2d) 735 (1975), cert denied 423 US 872, 96 SCt 138, 46 LEd(2d) 102 (1975).

[23]Columbus v Fraley, 41 OS(2d) 173, 180, 324 NE(2d) 735 (1975), cert denied 423 US 872, 96 SCt 138, 46 LEd(2d) 102 (1975).

[24]State v Pembaur, 9 OS(3d) 136, 9 OBR 385, 459 NE(2d) 217 (1984), cert denied 467 US 1219, 104 SCt 2668, 81 LEd(2d) 373 (1984).

[25]State v Pembaur, 9 OS(3d) 136, 9 OBR 385, 459 NE(2d) 217 (1984), cert denied 467 US 1219, 104 SCt 2668, 81 LEd(2d) 373 (1984).

[26]State v Pitts, 31 Misc(2d) 10, 509 NE(2d) 1284 (Muni, Hamilton 1986).

[27]State v Pitts, 31 Misc(2d) 10, 13, 509 NE(2d) 1284 (Muni, Hamilton 1986).

[28]Middleburg Heights v Theiss, 28 App(3d) 1, 28 OBR 9, 501 NE(2d) 1226 (Cuyahoga 1985).

after he has gained entrance into the residence, albeit unlawfully, with a purpose to cause injury rather than to resist entry, is not privileged conduct."[29]

The *Fraley* principle, however, has not been applied in prosecutions brought under the state statute prohibiting resisting arrest. RC 2921.33(A) defines resisting arrest as follows: "No person, recklessly or by force, shall resist or interfere with a *lawful arrest* of himself or another" [emphasis added].

RC 2921.33(A) clearly makes "lawful arrest" an element that the state must prove to establish the crime of resisting arrest. In *State v Johnson*,[30] the defendant was arrested on charges that were later found unlawful. The defendant contested the charge of resisting, brought under the state statute, on the grounds that a lawful arrest was necessary to validate a companion charge of resisting arrest. The court found that the *Fraley* decision was based on an alleged violation of a Columbus ordinance, which provided that no person shall assault or offer violence against a police officer engaged in the execution of his office. The ordinance was, thus, dissimilar to the Revised Code section. Because lawful arrest is an element of RC 2921.33, the court found the *Fraley* decision not binding on the charge of resisting arrest brought under the state statute. Although the court in *Fraley* may have set forth social policy for the state of Ohio, it did not change the specific elements of the legislation that defines the crime of resisting arrest.[31] This position has been succinctly stated by the Franklin County Court of Appeals: "The arrest being unlawful, there could be no offense of resisting arrest."[32]

Similarly, the court in *Elyria v Tress*[33] found that because a warrantless entry had occurred, the defendant had been unlawfully arrested and thus was privileged to resist arrest. Here, police responded to a drunk driving incident where the defendant had driven into a neighbor's mobile home and then went into his own residence. Police confronted the defendant at the door of his residence. They then stepped into the open doorway and arrested the defendant inside his home. Because the court found the warrantless entry to be a violation of the Fourth Amendment, the arrest was unlawful; thus, the state could not meet the lawful arrest element of RC 2921.33.

The Cuyahoga County Court of Appeals concurred in *Strongsville v Waiwood*,[34] pointing out that despite the broad language in *Fraley*, clearly

[29]Middleburg Heights v Theiss, 28 App(3d) 1, 5, 28 OBR 9, 501 NE(2d) 1226 (Cuyahoga 1985).
[30]State v Johnson, 6 App(3d) 56, 6 OBR 268, 453 NE(2d) 1101 (Clinton 1982).
[31]See, e.g., Strongsville v Waiwood, 62 App(3d) 521, 577 NE(2d) 63 (Cuyahoga 1989) (where defendant was arrested pursuant to an illegal warrant for failure to pay court costs, court held that resisting arrest charges could not be sustained against either of the defendants).
[32]Columbus v DePaso, No. 89AP-268, 1989 WL 111001 (10th Dist Ct App, Franklin, 9-26-89).
[33]Elyria v Tress, 73 App(3d) 5, 595 NE(2d) 1031 (Lorain 1991).
[34]Strongsville v Waiwood, 62 App(3d) 521, 577 NE(2d) 63 (Cuyahoga 1989).

disapproving of resisting regardless of the legality of the arrest, that language is not binding because the Supreme Court was not interpreting a resisting arrest statute. Consequently, in *Waiwood*, where the municipal court lacked authority to punish the defendant for failure to attend the hearing, it had no power to issue an arrest warrant. The court of appeals concluded that as a matter of law the prosecution could not prove all of the elements of resisting arrest.

Thus, because lawful arrest is an element of RC 2921.33, the state must meet this element to establish the crime of resisting arrest. Various appellate courts have recognized this element.[35] Because the *Fraley* decision interpreted a Columbus ordinance, which prohibited a broader scope of activity than resisting arrest, it will not be applicable to RC 2921.33: "[I]nsofar as the Ohio Supreme Court in *Fraley* purported to abandon the common law rule allowing a person to resist an unlawful arrest ... it is inconsistent with the plain statutory language of sec. 2921.33."[36] Neither should *Fraley* be applied to unlawful arrests by private citizens where the standard of resistance is the use of force as may be necessary to prevent the arrest.[37]

That the person arrested is never formally charged with a criminal offense other than resisting arrest bears no relevance to the lawfulness of the person's arrest.[38] In determining the lawfulness of an arrest, the elements of the underlying charge need not be proven. No law requires that the accused be convicted of the offense for which he is arrested.[39] However, a reasonable basis for the arrest must exist.[40] In *State v McCrone*,[41] police were called to a residence at approximately 2 a.m. on a report of an "aggravated burglary in progress." The officers confronted the defendant

---

[35]See e.g., State v Miller, 70 App(3d) 727, 591 NE(2d) 1355 (Highland 1990); State v Clay, 43 Misc(2d) 5, 539 NE(2d) 1168 (Muni, Hamilton 1988); State v Hill, No. CA85-12, 1986 WL 1766 (5th Dist Ct App, Morgan, 1-30-86); Chillicothe v Jobe, No. 1115, 1985 WL 8287 (4th Dist Ct App, Ross, 7-1-85); State v Lamm, 80 App(3d) 510, 609 NE(2d) 1286 (Gallia 1992); State v Miller, 70 App(3d) 727, 591 NE(2d) 1355 (Highland 1990); Columbus v Henry, No. 95APC02-159, 1995 WL 507453 (10th Dist Ct App, Franklin, 8-29-95).

[36]Hoover v Garfield Heights Municipal Court, 802 F(2d) 168 (6th Cir 1986), cert denied 480 US 949, 107 SCt 1610, 94 LEd(2d) 796 (1987).

[37]Jackson v Gossard, 48 App(3d) 309, 549 NE(2d) 1234 (Allen 1989).

[38]State v Johnson, No. 11417, 1990 WL 7945 (2d Dist Ct App, Montgomery, 1-30-90); State v Clay, 43 Misc(2d) 5, 539 NE(2d) 1168 (Muni, Hamilton 1988).

[39]Columbus v Griffith, No. 87AP-656, 1988 WL 41163 (10th Dist Ct App, Franklin, 4-28-88) (defendant's conviction on resisting arrest was affirmed because arresting officer had probable cause to arrest where defendant was charged with two counts of assault, resisting arrest, obstructing official business, and disorderly conduct but only convicted on resisting arrest charge). Cf. State v Mann, 19 OS(3d) 34, 19 OBR 28, 482 NE(2d) 592 (1985).

[40]State v Johnson, 6 App(3d) 56, 6 OBR 268, 453 NE(2d) 1101 (Clinton 1982); State v Keyes, No. 89-A-1443, 1990 WL 36560 (11th Dist Ct App, Ashtabula, 3-30-90); City of Garfield Heights v Simpson, 82 App(3d) 286, 611 NE(2d) 892 (Cuyahoga 1992) (where no rational basis for arresting defendant for obstructing justice or disorderly conduct exists, the lawful arrest element of resisting arrest cannot be established).

[41]State v McCrone, 63 App(3d) 831, 580 NE(2d) 468 (Lorain 1989), appeal dismissed by 48 OS(3d) 704, 549 NE(2d) 1190 (1990).

and two others with him at the address of the reported burglary and asked the defendant for identification. The defendant refused to show identification whereupon a struggle ensued and the defendant was arrested for resisting arrest and obstructing official business. Even though the court of appeals reversed the conviction on obstructing official business (producing identification was not an affirmative act required by RC 2921.31), the court affirmed the resisting arrest conviction. The rationale for upholding the resisting conviction is questionable. Even though the defendant could not be guilty of obstructing, the court said that the defendant was properly the subject of a *Terry*-stop and his failure to cooperate with the officer and produce identification constituted resisting a lawful detainment.

Where excessive or unnecessary force is used in the arrest, the defendant may claim a defense to the charge of resisting arrest.[42] In *State v Logsdon*,[43] the court held that a claim of unnecessary or excessive force must be regarded as an affirmative defense to a charge of resisting arrest, with the burden of going forward and the burden of proof, by a preponderance of the evidence, resting on the defendant. The court based this decision on the fact that the defendant who claims this defense must first admit that the arrest was resisted, if only to show that it was necessary in order to protect himself from the officer's excessive force.

7.04   Execution of summons

A summons may be executed by the same officers and within the same territorial restrictions as an arrest warrant. The manner of execution, however, is different. Criminal Rule 4(D)(3) sets the procedure for execution of a summons. That Rule provides that any summons may be served by personal service upon the defendant, or by leaving the summons at the defendant's residence with some person of reasonable age. Except where a summons is issued by an officer with a warrant in lieu of arrest, the summons may also be served by mailing it to the last known address of the defendant by certified mail, return receipt requested.

7.05   Return

Criminal Rule 4(D)(4) prescribes the return procedure for both warrants and summons. A warrant is returned to the issuing court before whom the defendant is brought. Unexecuted warrants returned to the court, upon the

---

[42]State v Steusloff, No. F-85-6, 1986 WL 2956 (6th Dist Ct App, Fulton, 3-7-86); see also State v Mullis, No. CA 85-07-051, 1986 WL 908 (12th Dist Ct App, Clermont, 1-21-86) (court found excessive force where, after questioning appellant, officer hit appellant in mouth and forced him to the ground, constraining appellant by placing his knee on back of his neck and later using foot bindings to transport appellant). But see State v Holaday, No. 1210, 1987 WL 15485 (4th Dist Ct App, Ross, 8-11-87) (no excessive force found where officer attempted to apprehend defendant after a scuffle and then defendant was chased and later apprehended by other officers).

[43]State v Logsdon, No. 13-89-10, 1990 WL 197883 (3d Dist Ct App, Seneca, 12-4-90), appeal dismissed by 58 OS(3d) 717, 570 NE(2d) 1129 (1991).

recommendation of the prosecuting attorney, may be cancelled by the judge. An unexecuted, uncancelled warrant may be redelivered by the court to an authorized officer for re-execution.

When a summons is served, the officer performing service endorses the summons and returns it to the clerk of court. When service cannot be accomplished within twenty-eight days of issuance, that fact should be endorsed on the summons and the summons returned to the clerk of court.

7.06   Post-arrest procedures

Post-arrest procedure is set forth in RC 2935.13 and Criminal Rule 4. RC 2935.13 provides that following an arrest, a defendant must be taken before the court issuing the arrest warrant, if the court is in session. If the court is not in session, and the offense charged is a misdemeanor or municipal ordinance violation, the defendant is to be taken before a clerk or deputy clerk and let to bail if a magistrate is unavailable. If the defendant was arrested in a county other than the one issuing the warrant, and the violation charged is a misdemeanor or ordinance violation, he must be taken before the most convenient magistrate, clerk, or deputy clerk, and let to bail.

Criminal Rule 4(E)(1) states that if a defendant is arrested in the issuing county or an adjoining county, the arresting officer must bring the defendant before the issuing court without unnecessary delay. In the respect that the Ohio Criminal Rules require persons arrested in adjoining counties to be brought before the issuing court, the Rules supersede the statutory provision. The Rules also provide that if the defendant is arrested in a county other than that issuing the warrant or an adjoining county, the defendant must be brought before a court of record in the county of arrest having jurisdiction over that type of offense. If the defendant is not released on bail, he must have an opportunity to consult an attorney or person of his choice before being removed to the jurisdiction of the issuing court. If a defendant is not to be released because of a hold order from another jurisdiction, the provisions of Criminal Rule 4(E) apply to the hold order, and the defendant must be taken before the court ordering the hold without unnecessary delay.[44] Violation of the rule requiring that a defendant be brought before a court without unnecessary delay will not result in the invalidation of an otherwise valid conviction.[45]

Criminal Rule 4(F) provides for release after arrest. That Rule states that if the arresting officer, or the officer in charge of the detention facility to which the defendant is brought, or either's superior, determines that a summons is reasonably calculated to ensure appearance, he may issue a summons and release the defendant.

---

[44]State v Keyse, No. 12-122, 1988 WL 94383 (11th Dist Ct App, Lake, 9-9-88).

[45]State v Bragg, No. 58859, 1991 WL 127135 (8th Dist Ct App, Cuyahoga, 6-27-91), appeal dismissed by 62 OS(3d) 1475, 581 NE(2d) 1097 (1991); State v Pettry, Nos. 617, 618, 1990 WL 119162 (4th Dist Ct App, Jackson, 8-9-90), appeal dismissed by 56 OS(3d) 707, 565 NE(2d) 602 (1990); State v Wright, No. 1189-CA, 1988 WL 25910 (2d Dist Ct App, Darke, 2-22-88).

Chapter 8

Issuance and Execution of Search Warrants

8.01   Introduction

Although the issuance and execution of search warrants are subject to the constitutional standard of reasonableness and the requirements of probable cause and specificity of the place to be searched and the item to be seized, the mechanics are governed by state statutes and Rules of Criminal Procedure. RC Chapter 2933 and Criminal Rule 41 set forth the specifics regarding the issuance and execution of search warrants.

8.02   Filing of an affidavit

For a prosecuting attorney or law enforcement officer to obtain a search warrant, RC 2933.23 and Criminal Rule 41(C) require that an affidavit describing the place to be searched, the things to be searched for and seized, the offense believed to be committed, and the facts giving rise to probable cause[1] be filed with the judge or magistrate requested to issue the warrant. The affidavit must set forth in particular all facts that led the affiant to believe that the property for which the warrant would be issued is at the address listed. Otherwise the warrant issued on that affidavit will be invalid.[2] In *Akron v Williams*,[3] the affidavit contained merely a statement that the affiant had "personal knowledge or knowledge from a reliable source." As the affidavit contained no facts upon which this knowledge was based, it was held to be insufficient. Without this information, the judge cannot make an independent determination that the item will be found. The judge would instead be relying on the officer's unsubstantiated assertion.

Criminal Rule 41(C) requires that the affidavit be sworn to before a judge. In *State v Kuykendall*,[4] the affidavit was acknowledged by a clerk of court in the presence of a judge. Noting that the procedure was technically incorrect, the court stated that the error was not prejudicial since the affiant was sworn in and testified in open court before the judge as to the facts enumerated in the affidavit.

Technical errors in the affidavit are not deemed constitutional violations and will not result in exclusion.[5] Moreover, even errors that result in consti-

---

[1]See Text Ch 3, Probable Cause.
[2]Akron v Williams, 175 OS 186, 192 NE(2d) 63, 23 OO(2d) 466 (1963).
[3]Akron v Williams, 175 OS 186, 188, 192 NE(2d) 63, 23 OO(2d) 466 (1963).
[4]State v Kuykendall, 51 App(2d) 215, 367 NE(2d) 905 (Wayne 1977).
[5]State v Wilmoth, 22 OS(3d) 251, 22 OBR 427, 490 NE(2d) 1236 (1986), cert denied 501 US 1238, 111 SCt 2871, 115 LEd(2d) 1037 (1991) (failure to file written affidavit and failure to administer oath prior to officer's testimony were not constitu-

tutional violations may not result in suppression of evidence if police reliance on the issuing warrant is deemed reasonable.[6] A discrepancy on the face of the affidavit between the affiant named on the first line and the officer who swore to and signed it on the last line is a technical violation.[7] Similarly, a warrant that does not have the affidavit attached will not require exclusion.[8] How such a warrant could be the subject of reasonable reliance in the event probable cause is lacking, however, is questionable.[9] Failure to specify the offense to which the evidence is related is "not constitutionally significant."[10] Errors pertaining to probable cause are constitutional and will require suppression[11] unless saved by the good faith exception to the exclusionary rule.[12] Similarly, where an affidavit listed the wrong apartment number, a search of the right apartment resulted in suppression where there were no exigent circumstances and the error could be corrected before execution.[13] Some courts considering the same issue have upheld searches of the right address provided the warrant sufficiently limited the officers' discretion.

8.03   Issuance of the search warrant and execution

(A) In general

The affidavit must be filed with a judge or magistrate with authority to issue the warrant.[14] Criminal Rule 41(A) requires the warrant to be issued by a judge of a court of record with jurisdiction over the place to be searched. Prior to the codification of criminal procedure in 1929, clerks of

---

tional errors); Columbus v Wright, 48 App(3d) 107, 548 NE(2d) 320 (Franklin 1988) (absence of affidavit on file with the clerk as required by Crim R 41 is an absence of records, rather than a demonstration that such an affidavit does not exist).

[6]State v Wilmoth, 22 OS(3d) 251, 22 OBR 427, 490 NE(2d) 1236 (1986), cert denied 501 US 1238, 111 SCt 2871, 115 LEd(2d) 1037 (1991) (failure to file written affidavit and failure to administer oath prior to officer's testimony were not constitutional errors); Columbus v Wright, 48 App(3d) 107, 548 NE(2d) 320 (Franklin 1988) (absence of affidavit on file with the clerk as required by Crim R 41 is an absence of records, rather than a demonstration that such an affidavit does not exist).

[7]State v Applebury, 34 App(3d) 376, 518 NE(2d) 977 (Hamilton 1987); State v Waddy, Nos. 87AP-1159, 87AP-1160, 1989 WL 133508 (10th Dist Ct App, Franklin, 11-2-89) (affidavit signed by two officers not indicating who had what personal knowledge is not deficient).

[8]State v McDonald, No. 9-87-30, 1988 WL 63955 (3d Dist Ct App, Marion, 6-14-88); State v Brooks, No. S-87-64, 1988 WL 134181 (6th Dist Ct App, Sandusky, 12-16-88).

[9]But see State v Wilmoth, 22 OS(3d) 251, 22 OBR 427, 490 NE(2d) 1236 (1986), cert denied 501 US 1238, 111 SCt 2871, 115 LEd(2d) 1037 (1991).

[10]Cleveland v Becvar, 63 App(3d) 163, 578 NE(2d) 489 (Cuyahoga 1989), appeal dismissed by 45 OS(3d) 716, 545 NE(2d) 901 (1989).

[11]See, e.g., State v Boggs, No. WD-88-73, 1989 WL 61715 (6th Dist Ct App, Wood, 6-9-89).

[12]State v George, 45 OS(3d) 325, 544 NE(2d) 640 (1989); State v Zinkiewicz, 67 App(3d) 99, 585 NE(2d) 1007 (Montgomery 1990); see also Text Ch 2, The Exclusionary Rule.

[13]State v Henderson, 66 App(3d) 447, 585 NE(2d) 539 (Montgomery 1990), appeal dismissed by 53 OS(3d) 703, 558 NE(2d) 57 (1990).

[14]RC 2933.23.

court were permitted to issue search warrants. RC 2933.23 has limited the authority to issue search warrants to judges or magistrates. In 1932, the Ohio Supreme Court, in *Nicholas v Cleveland*,[15] recognized that issuance of a search warrant is judicial rather than ministerial in nature and not within the authority of a court clerk.

If the judge or magistrate determines that the facts in the affidavit show probable cause that the items named are at the location listed, he or she will issue a search warrant. The standard form for a search warrant is provided by RC 2933.25. The search warrant must, as follows:

(1) Be directed to a law enforcement officer;

(2) Name the persons or places to be searched and items to be seized;

(3) Be signed by the issuing judge;

(4) State whether the search is to take place during daytime or night-time; and

(5) Be executed within three days and returned to the specified judge.[16]

(B) Law enforcement officer to direct search

Although the law requires that the search warrant be directed to "a law enforcement officer," the court need not name the individual officer to conduct the search. In *State v Prince*,[17] the defendant moved to suppress the evidence on the ground that the search warrant was directed to "[a]ny police officer of authority," rather than to a specific officer. The court ruled:

> The defendant could not possibly have any interest in the precise person who serves the warrant, so long as he is a "police officer of authority." Reason demands that the language of Crim R 41(C) be construed to mean ... *to no one other than* a law enforcement officer.[18]

The definition of "law enforcement officer" is limited, though, for purposes of executing a search warrant. In *State v Martins Ferry Eagles*,[19] the search warrant was executed by a secret service agent appointed by the prosecuting attorney. The court ruled that the agent had no authority to execute the warrant as Criminal Rule 2 defines "law enforcement officer" as "a sheriff, deputy sheriff, constable, municipal police officer, marshal, deputy marshal, or state highway patrolman, ... and any officer, agent, or employee of the state or any of its agencies, instrumentalities, or political subdivisions, upon whom, by statute, the authority to arrest violators is conferred." A secret service officer appointed by a prosecuting attorney has

---

[15]Nicholas v Cleveland, 125 OS 474, 182 NE 26 (1932), overruled by State v Lindway, 131 OS 166, 2 NE(2d) 490 (1936), cert denied 299 US 506, 57 SCt 36, 81 LEd 375 (1936).

[16]Crim R 41(C); RC 2933.24.

[17]State v Prince, 52 Misc 93, 369 NE(2d) 823 (CP, Fulton 1977).

[18]State v Prince, 52 Misc 93, 97 (emphasis in original), 369 NE(2d) 823 (CP, Fulton 1977).

[19]State v Martins Ferry Eagles, 62 Misc 3, 404 NE(2d) 177 (County Ct, Belmont 1979).

no statutory authority to arrest; therefore, he was not authorized to execute the search warrant.

Authority to execute the warrant is further restricted to the territorial jurisdiction in which the officer has authority. However, execution of a warrant by a police officer outside of his jurisdiction will not result in suppression because the error does not affect constitutional rights.[20]

(C) Description of persons and places to be searched and things to be seized

Criminal Rule 41(B) permits a warrant to be issued to search for (1) evidence of the commission of a crime; (2) contraband, the fruits of a crime, or things criminally possessed; and (3) weapons or other instruments used to commit a crime. Actually, the first classification encompasses all; the other two are redundant. The Rule provision is broader than its statutory predecessor, which limited searches to contraband, the fruits of a crime, and the tools used to commit the crime. The Rule reflects the current constitutional standard that searches may be conducted for what was previously labeled mere evidence. The mere evidence rule was repudiated in *Warden, Maryland Penitentiary v Hayden*,[21] where the Court stressed that the purpose of the Fourth Amendment is to protect privacy not property. The demise of the mere evidence rule opened the possibility of obtaining a warrant to search the home or business of a person not suspected of involvement in the criminal activity but who is merely in possession, whether knowingly or unknowingly, of evidence of criminal activity. No other stringent standards have been developed to support such third-party search warrants. The criterion is the same as where the search warrant is for the office or residence of a person suspected of criminal activity.[22]

Matters pertaining to the particularization of the place to be searched and the items to be seized raise constitutional issues. A warrant must specify the premises to be searched. Where the search involves a multiunit building, the warrant must describe the specific unit.[23] The listing on a warrant of an entire house (a single dwelling unit) will not be overly broad if

---

[20]State v Leadingham, No. CA-1753, 1990 WL 9963 (4th Dist Ct App, Scioto, 2-6-90); State v Klemm, 41 App(3d) 382, 536 NE(2d) 14 (Hamilton 1987). Cf. Kettering v Hollen, 64 OS(2d) 232, 416 NE(2d) 598 (1980) (arrest occurring outside a police officer's jurisdiction is not a violation of the arrestee's constitutional rights if the arrest is supported by probable cause) and State v Harrison, 20 Misc 282, 251 NE(2d) 521 (CP, Montgomery 1969) (suppressing evidence seized by Dayton police executing warrant issued by Dayton municipal judge in Jefferson township, which is outside Dayton city limits; although decision focused upon execution, judge lacked authority to order search out of court's jurisdiction).

[21]Warden, Maryland Penitentiary v Hayden, 387 US 294, 87 SCt 1642, 18 LEd(2d) 782 (1967).

[22]Zurcher v Stanford Daily, 436 US 547, 98 SCt 1970, 56 LEd(2d) 525 (1978).

[23]State v Scott, No. L-88-323, 1989 WL 100995 (6th Dist Ct App, Lucas, 9-1-89), affirmed by 67 OS(3d) 1509, 622 NE(2d) 656 (1993) (must describe the targeted unit with sufficient specificity to prevent a search of all units; multiunit rule does not apply if defendant in control of entire premises); State v Wright, No. 89-CA-55, 1990 WL 205106 (2d Dist Ct App, Miami, 12-11-90); State v Stokes, No. 56645, 1989 WL 65599 (8th Dist Ct App, Cuyahoga, 6-15-89) (command to search house extends to garage because if a house is being used as a drug storage and distribution center, it is logical to conclude that evidence may be stored in garage).

the item or items to be seized may be anywhere in the house.[24] A requirement of greater specificity would exceed the constitutional standard of reasonableness. Police officers are not expected to know where within a house or apartment evidence sought will be found. A more stringent requirement, moreover, would encourage police to surreptitiously and illegally enter the premises to discover the specific location of the item sought, defeating the whole purpose of requiring a search warrant. The principle of particularity also applies to warrants to search cars[25] as well as persons.[26]

The description of the place and items must appear in the command portion of the warrant for the search to be valid. A search based on any other portion is unlawful. This issue was addressed in *State v Simpson,*[27] where the affidavit attached to the search warrant listed the place to be searched as apartment numbers 204 and 304. In the command portion of the warrant, apartment 304 was inadvertently omitted. The officers executing the warrant searched both apartments. The defendant lived in 304. He moved to suppress the evidence on the ground of an unlawful search. The state contended that the affidavit and warrant should be read together. The court disagreed, holding that "the search warrant must stand on its own." As the warrant did not list apartment 304 in the command portion, the search of that apartment was unlawful.

The federal constitutional requirement that warrants specify the place to be searched is satisfied "if the description is such that an officer with a search warrant can, with reasonable effort, ascertain and identify the place searched."[28] The purpose of the specificity requirement is to limit the discretion of the officers executing the warrant and to ensure that the search is limited to the place ordered by the court where probable cause existed to believe that evidence would be found. Even a minor error in the number of the house or apartment will not necessarily be fatal to the search, if the place to be searched is otherwise sufficiently described in the warrant and readily identifiable. The Fourth Amendment standard is reasonable-

---

[24]State v Johnston, No. 412, 1986 WL 8799 (4th Dist Ct App, Hocking, 8-6-86).

[25]State v Johnson, No. L-88-085, 1989 WL 18137 (6th Dist Ct App, Lucas, 3-3-89).

[26]State v Bailey, No. 55938, 1989 WL 117414 (8th Dist Ct App, Cuyahoga, 10-5-89) (warrant issued to search a person should describe that person, or give his name, if known; the validity of a warrant is not affected by the use of the name, John Doe, provided that police discretion is otherwise properly limited); see also State v Brock, No. 11449, 1989 WL 109303 (2d Dist Ct App, Montgomery, 9-21-89) (search of defendant substantial distance away from his home was illegal based on warrant issued to search residence and defendant because affidavit failed to support a conclusion that defendant would likely have evidence on his person while away from that location); State v Tucker, 98 App(3d) 308, 648 NE(2d) 557 (Sandusky 1994), appeal dismissed by 71 OS(3d) 1499, 646 NE(2d) 1124 (1995) (search warrant authorizing search of all persons in suspected "crack" house was overly broad and invalid).

[27]State v Simpson, 64 Misc 42, 412 NE(2d) 956 (CP, Lake 1980).

[28]Steele v United States, 267 US 498, 503, 45 SCt 414, 69 LEd 757 (1925); State v Pruitt, 97 App(3d) 258, 646 NE(2d) 547 (Trumbull 1994) (where street number contained was correct as was description of the residence, warrant adequately described defendant's residence even though the street name was improperly listed and the description of a dog house in front of the residence was incorrect).

ness. A mistake in the identification of the premises to be searched will not necessarily invalidate the warrant so long as the mistake is reasonable. Where an investigation led police to believe that the entire third floor of a house was one apartment and this belief continued during execution of the warrant until they discovered incriminating evidence in a second apartment, not occupied by the original suspect, the mistake was held to be reasonable and the search upheld.[29]

Similarly, the Fourth Amendment requirement that the warrant describe the things to be seized with particularity is designed to prevent general searches.[30] Only items listed in the warrant may be seized. But even so, there is some flexibility in the Rule. In *State v Fields,*[31] the court ruled that items closely related to those listed in the search warrant may also be seized. In *Fields*, police officers were issued a warrant to search the defendant's home in connection with a robbery and murder. The warrant ordered police to seize a .38 calibre revolver and a woman's purse. During the search, the officers failed to find those items, but did find a spent .38 calibre shell. The defendant moved to suppress on the ground that the shell was not listed on the warrant and therefore illegally seized. The court held that the shell had a reasonable relationship to the purpose of the search and was a component part of the weapon for which the officers were searching. The search was lawful.[32]

The key to particularization is whether the officer can identify the item to be seized. Absent clear guidance from the warrant, an officer is improperly vested with unbounded discretion.[33] An exception to this rule provides that a generic description will be sufficient if greater particularity is impossible, provided that the warrant instructs the police officer which items are not to be seized. Consequently, a warrant that directed the executing officer to seize "winches" (among other items) was deemed inadequate because (1) a "winch" could be any number of devices; and (2) the officer's testimony clearly indicated that he "was unable to distinguish, based upon the description provided in the warrant, which winches or hoists were to be seized."[34]

A clause in a search warrant directing seizure of "other fruits, instrumentalities and evidence of crime at this [time] unknown" did not transform an otherwise valid search warrant into a general warrant. It did not properly authorize a search for evidence of any crime but only evidence that fit within the context of the crimes and items enumerated in the warrant.[35] An affidavit authorizing a search for marijuana "and any other fruits and instrumentalities" was read to authorize a search for evidence of traffick-

---

[29]Maryland v Garrison, 480 US 79, 107 SCt 1013, 94 LEd(2d) 72 (1987).

[30]Go-Bart Importing Co v United States, 282 US 344, 51 SCt 153, 75 LEd 374 (1931).

[31]State v Fields, 29 App(2d) 154, 279 NE(2d) 616 (Union 1971).

[32]See also Text Ch 13, Plain View.

[33]Marron v United States, 275 US 192, 48 SCt 74, 72 LEd 231 (1927).

[34]State v Strzesynski, No. WD-85-68, at 5, 1986 WL 4660 (6th Dist Ct App, Wood, 4-18-86).

[35]Andresen v Maryland, 427 US 463, 96 SCt 2737, 49 LEd(2d) 627 (1976).

ing.[36] Generally, the catch-all afterthought, "and fruits of any other crimes," provides no additional authority for officers executing the warrant. The parts of a warrant are severable, however, and such overly broad language will not result in suppression of items properly specified or found in plain view while searching for items properly specified.

Items not listed in the warrant may be seized if the items are closely related to the crime being investigated or the officer has reason to believe the items were instrumentalities of the crime,[37] or the items are evidence of other crimes and fall within the plain view doctrine.[38]

(D) Signature

A valid search warrant must be signed by the issuing judge. The Ohio Supreme Court has said that a warrant without a signature is a command without a known commander and thus cannot be a command.[39] The Court held that the signature requirement is the best procedural means of insuring the validity of a warrant and thus of protecting individual rights because the signature is the only objectively identifiable manifestation of a judge's subjective intent to actually issue a warrant. Further, the good faith exception to the exclusionary rule will not save a search executed with an unsigned warrant because police may not act in reasonable reliance on a search warrant issued without a judge's signature.[40]

(E) Nighttime searches

Searches authorized by warrant are to be executed during the daytime, between 7:00 a.m. and 8:00 p.m. A search is an extraordinary invasion of privacy, and that invasion becomes greater if conducted during the night. On a showing of reasonable cause demonstrating a need for a nighttime search, the judge may authorize a night search in the warrant.[41] The reasonable cause standard for night searches contained in Criminal Rule 41 is less stringent than the statutory standard that it supersedes, RC 2933.24, which authorizes night searches only on a showing of "urgent necessity." Apparently there is no federal constitutional requirement for the execution of search warrants during daytime hours, absent some special showing.[42]

The judge or magistrate's decision to order a nighttime search is within his or her discretion. The burden rests with the defendant to show an abuse

---

[36]State v Stebner, 46 App(3d) 145, 546 NE(2d) 428 (Portage 1988).

[37]State v Miley, No. 56168, 1989 WL 136352 (8th Dist Ct App, Cuyahoga, 11-9-89) (money orders found to be related to the discrepancies in auditing records); State v Cooey, 46 OS(3d) 20, 544 NE(2d) 895 (1989), affirmed by 1994 WL 201009 (1994) (police seizure of "trace evidence" proper because they were believed to be recently worn by the defendant); State v Benner, 40 OS(3d) 301, 533 NE(2d) 701 (1988), cert denied 494 US 1090, 110 SCt 1834, 108 LEd(2d) 962 (1990) (items were properly seized as potential sources of hair, fibers and other trace evidence).

[38]See Text Ch 13, Plain View.

[39]State v Williams, 57 OS(3d) 24, 565 NE(2d) 563 (1991), cert denied 501 US 1238, 111 SCt 2871, 115 LEd(2d) 1037 (1991).

[40]State v Williams, 57 OS(3d) 24, 565 NE(2d) 563 (1991), cert denied 501 US 1238, 111 SCt 2871, 115 LEd(2d) 1037 (1991); see also State v Spaw, 18 App(3d) 77, 480 NE(2d) 1138 (Defiance 1984).

[41]Crim R 41(F).

[42]See Gooding v United States, 416 US 430, 94 SCt 1780, 40 LEd(2d) 250 (1974).

of discretion.[43] Even where a warrant fails to specifically authorize a night-time search, a nighttime search will be upheld if it appears that the issuing judge intended to authorize it and failed to fill in the blank.[44] In *State v Marko*,[45] the search warrant was for stolen watches and jewelry. Even though the affidavit contained no information relating to the necessity for a night search, the judge did so authorize. The defendant moved to suppress the evidence, claiming that the night search was unjustified. The appellate court found the night search reasonable, citing "[t]he proclivity of small stolen articles to disappear when the news of an arrest circulates, as it does quite quickly in the criminal world."[46]

A nighttime search warrant issued on the assertion that the evidence could easily be destroyed was upheld as not an abuse of discretion even though the defendant was in custody.[47] Requests for authority to conduct searches for drugs at night are routinely granted and upheld. A simple assertion in the affidavit for a warrant to search for drugs, stating that a nighttime search was needed for the officers' safety and the preservation of evidence, was characterized as conclusory but upheld given the nature of the evidence sought.[48] A nighttime search of a bar did not involve an abuse of discretion because the appellate court said it is common knowledge that bars tend to be frequented more at night.[49]

(F) Execution of search warrants

(1) Reasonableness standard

Criminal Rule 41(C) requires execution of a search warrant within three days of its issuance, thus insuring that probable cause still exists that the evidence will be found at the place searched. Substantial delay in the execution of a warrant increases the possibility that the information will be stale and lessens the likelihood that the evidence will be found there. The time period for satisfaction of the rule requiring execution of a search

---

[43]State v Eichhorn, 47 App(2d) 227, 353 NE(2d) 861 (Franklin 1975); State v Lenegar, No. 465, 1991 WL 28322 (4th Dist Ct App, Vinton, 2-25-91); State v Heaton, Nos. 4069, 4070, 1987 WL 6171 (9th Dist Ct App, Lorain, 2-4-87).

[44]State v Coburn, No. 1744, 1990 WL 85151 (4th Dist Ct App, Scioto, 5-31-90), appeal dismissed by 55 OS(3d) 707, 563 NE(2d) 297 (1990) (affidavit presented to judge during the night contained allegation that nighttime search was a necessity).

[45]State v Marko, 36 App(2d) 114, 303 NE(2d) 94 (Franklin 1973).

[46]State v Marko, 36 App(2d) 114, 124, 303 NE(2d) 94 (Franklin 1973); see also State v Kuykendall, 51 App(2d) 215, 367 NE(2d) 905 (Wayne 1977) (nighttime search justified to recover marked money and drugs); State v Eichhorn, 47 App(2d) 227, 353 NE(2d) 861 (Franklin 1975) (night search justified because of the possibility that the stolen items would be sold or moved by the "fence").

[47]State v Weatherford, No. WD-87-67, 1988 WL 128280 (4th Dist Ct App, Wood, 12-2-88) (court said evidence could easily have been destroyed by friend or relative of defendant).

[48]State v Gordon, No. 12036, 1990 WL 131874 (2d Dist Ct App, Montgomery, 9-12-90); see also State v Tschudy, No. CA-3187, 1986 WL 7459 (5th Dist Ct App, Licking, 6-24-86); State v Warny, No. 52866, 1987 WL 19859 (8th Dist Ct App, Cuyahoga, 11-12-87) (where affidavit stated that most of the drug activity occurred in the late afternoon or at night).

[49]Columbus v Wright, 48 App(3d) 107, 548 NE(2d) 320 (Franklin 1988).

warrant within three days of issuance has been held not to include Saturdays and Sundays.[50]

Execution of search warrants is governed by the overarching constitutional standard of reasonableness as well as state common law and statutory provisions. Violation of the constitutional command may result in exclusion. However, not every error made by police while executing a search warrant is unreasonable. For example, in *Maryland v Garrison*,[51] police executing a search warrant for a third floor apartment searched the entire third floor before, they claimed, they realized there were two apartments on the third floor. Evidence was found in the other apartment. The warrant authorized search of the "third floor apartment" and was issued without the court's knowledge that there were two apartments on the third floor. The Supreme Court found the execution valid because the police "failure to realize the overbreadth of the warrant was objectively understandable and reasonable."[52]

The force used to execute a search warrant is regulated by RC 2935.12, which lists the procedures for an officer to follow when executing a warrant and being refused entry, and RC 2933.231, which allows a court to waive the knock and notify rule.

(2) Knock and notify rule and the use of force

In most instances, the knock and notify rule applies. Initially, of course, the officer must have the right to enter to conduct a search, either with a warrant or under authority provided by an exception to the warrant requirement.[53] An officer must make clear his intentions.[54] It is not sufficient for the officer to merely identify himself as a police officer.[55] However, this requirement has not always been strictly construed. In *State v Brooks*,[56] the defendant complained that the police gained entry without complying with the "knock and announce" rule. The court said that "police need not show that they knocked where they forced entry, so long as they gave the occupants a reasonable opportunity to respond."[57]

Refusal to admit an officer need not be actual; constructive refusal enables the officer to use force. In *State v DeFiore*,[58] the court held that ten to thirty seconds is not a sufficient time period from which an officer could

---

[50]State v Hudson, No. 54274, 1987 WL 20467 (8th Dist Ct App, Cuyahoga, 11-25-87). Cf. United States v Richmond, 694 FSupp 1310 (SD Ohio 1988).

[51]Maryland v Garrison, 480 US 79, 107 SCt 1013, 94 LEd(2d) 72 (1987).

[52]Maryland v Garrison, 480 US 79, 88, 107 SCt 1013, 94 LEd(2d) 72 (1987).

[53]Middleburg Heights v Theiss, 28 App(3d) 1, 28 OBR 9, 501 NE(2d) 1226 (Cuyahoga 1985).

[54]State v Early, 7 OO(3d) 227 (App, Cuyahoga 1977) (the officers' failure to state their intent violated the knock and announce statute).

[55]State v Valentine, 74 App(3d) 110, 598 NE(2d) 82 (Lawrence 1991); see also State v Furry, 31 App(2d) 107, 286 NE(2d) 301 (Wood 1971); State v Early, 7 OO(3d) 227 (App, Cuyahoga 1977).

[56]State v Brooks, No. 50384, 1986 WL 2677 (8th Dist Ct App, Cuyahoga, 2-27-86).

[57]State v Brooks, No. 50384, at 2, 1986 WL 2677 (8th Dist Ct App, Cuyahoga, 2-27-86).

[58]State v DeFiore, 64 App(2d) 115, 411 NE(2d) 837 (Hamilton 1979).

determine that a constructive refusal had occurred. However, in *State v Morgan*,[59] the officer testified that he knocked on the door on three separate occasions. On the first occasion, he made two or three raps on the door but did not announce his purpose. He heard no response. Several seconds later, he knocked again, two or three times, and announced his purpose in a loud voice, saying that he had a search warrant. He heard a response, stating, "Just a minute." Right after this, the officer knocked again, telling the appellant to open the door. At this point, he entered. In considering the totality of the circumstances, the court of appeals found that, because the appellant had been served a warrant in the past and because the officer was experienced and recognized the possibility of evidence being disposed, telling the officer to wait was a constructive if not actual refusal to admit.

While RC 2935.12 requires that an officer be refused entry before he may force entry, the requirement, of course, will give way if exigent circumstances exist that require otherwise.[60] In *Ker v California*,[61] Justice Brennan stated three exceptions to the general rule that unannounced police intrusions are violative of the Fourth Amendment: (1) where the persons within already know the officers' authority to enter, (2) where the officers are justified in the belief that persons within are in imminent peril of bodily harm, or (3) where those within are engaged in the destruction of evidence. Thus, if it appears that the evidence sought can and will be destroyed on short notice, or that compliance could place the officers in peril of great bodily harm, then officers need not comply with the knock and announce rule.[62] While there is no dispute that exigencies may excuse strict compliance with the statute, there has been disagreement as to what must be shown to prove exigent circumstances. Some courts have held that the mere fact evidence is easily destroyed is sufficient to meet the burden.[63] Others have required that articulable facts must be introduced that prove that in the particular case there is a strong probability that evidence will be destroyed.[64] As the court stated in *DeFiore*, "A reasonable apprehension of

---

[59]State v Morgan, 55 App(3d) 182, 563 NE(2d) 307 (Mercer 1988).

[60]State v DeFiore, 64 App(2d) 115, 411 NE(2d) 837 (Hamilton 1979); see also State v Roper, 27 App(3d) 212, 500 NE(2d) 353 (Summit 1985).

[61]Ker v California, 374 US 23, 83 SCt 1623, 10 LEd(2d) 726 (1963) (Brennan, J., dissenting).

[62]Ker v California, 374 US 23, 83 SCt 1623, 10 LEd(2d) 726 (1963) (Brennan, J., dissenting); see also State v Turner, No. CA-7865, 1989 WL 154621 (5th Dist Ct App, Stark, 12-11-89) (exigent circumstances justified use of battering ram on suspected cocaine and crack operation).

[63]State v Roper, 27 App(3d) 212, 500 NE(2d) 353 (Summit 1985); see also State v Castillo, No. WD-87-44, 1988 WL 62988 (6th Dist Ct App, Wood, 6-17-88) (where the court held that because there were drugs that could have been easily and quickly destroyed and because the police believed themselves to be in peril because the appellant was suspected of being involved in a prior assault of an officer, exigent circumstances existed justifying no announcement of their intent to search and absence of refusal of entry).

[64]See State v Valentine, 74 App(3d) 110, 598 NE(2d) 82 (Lawrence 1991) (reasonable cause to believe that notice would endanger the successful execution of the warrant); State v Davies, Nos. C-850112 et al., 1986 WL 657 (1st Dist Ct App, Hamilton, 1-8-86); see also Model Code of Pre-Arraignment Procedure §SS 220.3(3) (1975).

the existence of illegal ... activities does not, without more, give rise to a sufficient warranty of an exigent circumstance which will validate an otherwise unreasonable search and seizure."[65]

There is an exception to the "refusal rule." In *State v Wilson*,[66] the officers knocked on the door but no one was home. They then entered through a window and began their search. When the defendant returned home, the officers immediately identified themselves and their purpose. The defendant moved to suppress the evidence seized on the ground that the officers entered forcibly when there was no refusal to admit. The Montgomery County Court of Appeals upheld the search, stating that the fact that no one was home to refuse did not mean the officers could not force entry. The court said absence of the occupant cannot be used to thwart a search.

(3) Judicial waiver of the knock and notify rule

RC 2933.231 allows waiver of the statutory preconditions for nonconsensual entry during the execution of search warrants. A request for a waiver must be contained in the affidavit for a search warrant and must (1) allege that law enforcement officials risk serious physical harm if they comply with the knock and announce rules; (2) set forth the facts on which the belief is based, including the names of persons who pose the risk of harm; and (3) verify that the place to be searched is the correct address of the location related to the underlying criminal offense.[67] The issuing judge may waive the statutory preconditions for entry if there is probable cause to believe the allegations in the affidavit.[68] Such a waiver does not authorize entry of any building other than the one described in the warrant.[69] The state or political subdivision associated with an officer executing a warrant that waives the statutory preconditions for entry is liable in tort for damages proximately caused by execution of the warrant in accordance with the waiver.[70]

(G) Obligations of subject of search warrant during execution

A person whose premises are being searched pursuant to a valid search warrant is under no obligation to cooperate with police. That person need not provide information which would shorten the search nor lead police to the objects of the search warrant. Neither the failure to cooperate nor the making of misleading statements is sufficient to amount to obstructing official business.[71]

CROSS REFERENCES

Text Ch 6, Ch 7

---

[65]State v DeFiore, 64 App(2d) 115, 118-19, 411 NE(2d) 837 (Hamilton 1979).
[66]State v Wilson, 41 App(2d) 240, 325 NE(2d) 249 (Montgomery 1974).
[67]RC 2933.231(B).
[68]RC 2933.231(C).
[69]RC 2933.231(D)(1).
[70]RC 2933.231(D)(2).
[71]Cleveland v Corrai, 70 App(3d) 679, 591 NE(2d) 1325 (Cuyahoga 1990); cf., Dayton v Rodgers, 60 OS(2d) 162, 398 NE(2d) 781 (1979). Presumably, however, overt physical conduct which hinders the police in execution of a valid search warrant would have a different result.

1 Giannelli & Snyder, Baldwin's Ohio Practice, *Evidence* § 101.12

8.04   Inventory and return

During the execution of a search warrant, the officer must inventory the items seized in the presence of the person whose home or business is searched. A receipt for the items seized must be given to that person. If the householder is absent, the inventory must be made and the receipt left with another "credible person." Following the search, the officer must return the warrant promptly to the issuing authority with a copy of the inventory.[72]

The requirements of inventory and return are not of such constitutional magnitude that violations result in the exclusion of evidence.[73] The failure of officers to make a prompt inventory and return does not affect the validity of an otherwise valid warrant.[74] Failure to prepare an inventory will not result in exclusion.[75] In *State v Downs*,[76] the defendant moved to suppress the evidence because the warrant and inventory were returned to the clerk of court rather than the judge. The court held that return of the warrant was a ministerial act and that the administrative error was not of "constitutional magnitude." The defendant had no interest in the person to whom the warrant was returned. There was therefore no prejudice to the defendant nor invalidation of the search. The failure to include an item seized in the inventory filed with the court does not give rise to a motion to suppress such items, provided that the officer executing the warrant testifies at the trial that the items presented in court were, in fact, the items seized in execution of the warrant.[77]

If the person in possession of the seized articles is not present at the search, the officer may substitute another credible person to witness the inventory. The inventory need not state on its face that the defendant was not present and that a credible person was substituted.[78] Another law enforcement officer present for the search qualifies as a substitute credible person.[79] In *State v Gordon*, the court held that there is no statutory requirement that such information appear on the face of the return, and classified the preparation of the inventory and return as a ministerial act that can be cured without prejudice.

---

[72]Crim R 41(D); RC 2933.241.

[73]State v Downs, 51 OS(2d) 47, 364 NE(2d) 1140 (1977), vacated by 438 US 909, 98 SCt 3133, 57 LEd(2d) 1153 (1978).

[74]State v Watson, No. 8-89-6, 1990 WL 131948 (3d Dist Ct App, Logan, 8-27-90); State v Ward, 44 App(2d) 85, 335 NE(2d) 727 (Medina 1974).

[75]State v Brooks, No. S-87-64, 1988 WL 134181 (6th Dist Ct App, Sandusky, 12-16-88); State v Miley, No. 56168, 1989 WL 136352 (8th Dist Ct App, Cuyahoga, 11-9-89) (failure to make an inventory or return does not render evidence inadmissible absent a showing of prejudice).

[76]State v Downs, 51 OS(2d) 47, 364 NE(2d) 1140 (1977), vacated by 438 US 909, 98 SCt 3133, 57 LEd(2d) 1153 (1978).

[77]State v Givens, 14 App(3d) 2, 14 OBR 5, 469 NE(2d) 1332 (Summit 1983).

[78]State v Weichowski, 49 App(2d) 151, 359 NE(2d) 1008 (Medina 1975).

[79]State v Gordon, No. 12036, 1990 WL 131874 (2d Dist Ct App, Montgomery, 9-12-90).

Moreover, the failure of the officer with a warrant to search in the presence of even one credible person will not invalidate the search. The officer in *State v Ward*[80] searched the defendant's automobile after the car was impounded. The defendant moved to suppress the evidence discovered during the search on the ground that the search was without the presence of an additional credible person. The court held the search was valid because the "failure of officers executing a validly issued search warrant to comply with Criminal Rule 41(D) absolutely does not affect the validity of the search, where it is otherwise reasonable."[81]

8.05   Detention and search of persons on the premises

(A) In general

As in other Fourth Amendment areas, the authority of police to detain, and sometimes to search, persons found on the premises during execution of a search warrant has expanded. That expansion, however, in no way equals or ever would equal the view formerly held by many law enforcement personnel that the right existed to detain and search everyone found on the premises during a lawful search.

(B) Detention during execution of a search warrant

The law in Ohio has developed and expanded upon the authority first granted by the United States Supreme Court, in *Michigan v Summers*,[82] to detain the occupant of a house that is the subject of a valid search warrant. In *Summers*, upon arriving at the address named in the search warrant, police saw the defendant leave by the front door of the house. When the defendant was asked to open the door, he replied that he had left his keys inside but that he could ring someone over the intercom. Another occupant came to the door but would not admit the police officers, who obtained entrance by forcing open the front door. Once they had gained entry, the officers detained the defendant and the seven other occupants of the house while they conducted a search. After finding narcotics in the basement and ascertaining that the defendant owned the house, the officers arrested the defendant, searched him, and found heroin in his jacket pocket. The defendant moved to suppress the heroin found on his person on the ground that the initial detention constituted an arrest without probable cause.

The Court focused on the defendant's initial detention. Holding that such detention constituted a seizure within the meaning of the Fourth Amendment because the defendant was not free to leave, the Court nonetheless upheld the seizure on less than probable cause because it did not amount to a formal arrest. The court relied on the line of cases beginning with *Terry v Ohio*,[83] which have upheld, under the reasonableness standard embodied in the Fourth Amendment, some seizures that are significantly less intrusive than an arrest.

---

[80]State v Ward, 44 App(2d) 85, 335 NE(2d) 727 (Medina 1974).
[81]State v Ward, 44 App(2d) 85, 88, 335 NE(2d) 727 (Medina 1974).
[82]Michigan v Summers, 452 US 692, 101 SCt 2587, 69 LEd(2d) 340 (1981).
[83]Terry v Ohio, 392 US 1, 88 SCt 1868, 20 LEd(2d) 889 (1968).

These cases recognize that some seizures admittedly covered by the
Fourth Amendment constitute such limited intrusions on the personal
security of those detained and are justified by such substantial law
enforcement interests that they may be made on less than probable
cause, so long as police have an articulable basis for suspecting criminal
activity. ... [T]hey demonstrate that the exception for limited intrusions
that may be justified by special law enforcement interests is not confined to the momentary, on-the-street detention accompanied by a frisk
for weapons.[84]

The majority was impressed by the fact that a neutral and detached
magistrate had found probable cause to believe that the law was being
violated in that house and had authorized a substantial invasion of the
privacy of the persons residing there. Although the Court acknowledged
that the detention of the residents while the premises were searched constituted a significant restraint on their liberty, the majority concluded that the
detention (1) was less intrusive than the search itself, (2) was not likely to be
exploited by the officer or unduly prolonged to gain more information, and
(3) involved only a minimal increment in the inconvenience or public stigma
associated with the search itself.

On the other hand, the majority found the substantial law enforcement
interests to be overwhelming: (1) preventing flight in the event that incriminating evidence is found, and (2) minimizing the risk of harm to the police
officers since the search for narcotics may give rise to sudden violence or
frantic efforts to conceal or destroy evidence. Consequently, the Court
concluded that a warrant to search for contraband founded on probable
cause implicitly carries with it the limited authority to detain the occupants
of the premises while a proper search is conducted. *Summers* was relied on
in *State v Schultz*,[85] where the court, in defining occupant, said the "issue
[is] whether there is such a relationship between the premises and the
detained individual that the police may make a reasonable connection
between the person and his property within the house."

While *Schultz* closely followed *Summers* in requiring a relationship and
connection between the premises and the detained person, later decisions
have discussed connection but focused mostly on presence. This shift is
most noticeable in searches of suspected "drug houses." The Cuyahoga
County Court of Appeals said that a search warrant carries with it the
limited authority to detain occupants inside while a proper search is executed.[86] A person who is not in the residence but merely on the premises or
near the house where the warrant is executed may be detained if there is
reasonable suspicion to believe that the person may be connected to subject
matter of the offense underlying the search warrant. Consequently, that
court upheld the detention of a person who was leaving a known drug house

---

[84]Michigan v Summers, 452 US 692, 699, 101 SCt 2587, 69 LEd(2d) 340 (1981).

[85]State v Schultz, 23 App(3d) 130, 133, 23 OBR 242, 491 NE(2d) 735 (Franklin 1985).

[86]State v Bobo, 65 App(3d) 685, 585 NE(2d) 429 (Cuyahoga 1989), appeal dismissed by 50 OS(3d) 714, 553 NE(2d) 1363 (1990) (nothing in the court of appeals opinion leads to the conclusion that defendant was a resident of the place searched rather than a visitor).

when police arrived to execute a search warrant.[87] The same court upheld the detention of a person walking quickly from an automobile toward (or within five feet of) an apartment as police were converging on the building to execute a warrant.[88] That court again upheld the detention of a person who was standing outside a suspected drug house while police executed a search warrant. The police had been informed that a dealer sold drugs in front of the house.[89] A detention is not permissible if the person is not within the immediate vicinity of the place to be searched even if there is a connection between that person and the place searched. Accordingly, the Hamilton County Court of Appeals held the detention of a person four or five miles away from a place to be searched was illegal even though he was seen leaving the residence just before the warrant was executed.[90]

(C) Search of person found on premises during execution of a search warrant

The same emphasis as that on the control of drugs is shaping the outcome of issues raised by searches of persons found on premises during execution of a search warrant. A search warrant gives police authority to search the premises and persons specified in the warrant. A search warrant authorizing the search of a specific person[91] in addition to the location that is the subject of the warrant may restrict the search of that person to when he or she is present in the place to be searched.[92] Even where the warrant does not specify the person to be searched but instead generally directs the search of persons found on the premises[93] or persons in control of the

---

[87]State v Bridges, No. 55954, 1989 WL 117339 (8th Dist Ct App, Cuyahoga, 10-5-89), appeal dismissed by 51 OS(3d) 703, 555 NE(2d) 315 (1990) (where police information identified the defendant as a suspect in the drug house's activity).

[88]State v Cancel, No. 56727, 1990 WL 88743 (8th Dist Ct App, Cuyahoga, 6-28-90).

[89]State v Seigers, No. 54675, 1988 WL 121039 (8th Dist Ct App, Cuyahoga, 11-10-88).

[90]State v Donohue, No. C-860458, 1987 WL 12741 (1st Dist Ct App, Hamilton, 6-17-87) (search warrant did not authorize the detention of the defendant away from the residence covered by the warrant).

[91]State v Bailey, No. 55938, 1989 WL 117414 (8th Dist Ct App, Cuyahoga, 10-5-89) (search warrant issued for the purpose of searching a person should describe that person or give his name, if known; however, validity of the warrant was not affected by use of name, "John Doe").

[92]State v Brock, No. 11449, 1989 WL 109303 (2d Dist Ct App, Montgomery, 9-21-89) (court suppressed evidence found on defendant searched away from his house even though the search warrant authorized search of him and his house because the facts failed to connect the defendant with criminal activity other than at his residence).

[93]Cf. State v Murphy, No. 13080, 1987 WL 17780 (9th Dist Ct App, Summit, 9-30-87), cert denied 485 US 1040, 108 SCt 1603, 99 LEd(2d) 917 (1988) (although the police alleged that the house was a drug house, they made no effort to obtain a warrant for the search of all persons in the home, but rather the warrant was for the home and its resident; court indicates that a warrant could have been issued for all persons found in a drug house); but see State v Tucker, 98 App(3d) 308, 648 NE(2d) 557 (Sandusky 1994), appeal dismissed by 71 OS(3d) 1499, 646 NE(2d) 1124 (1995) (search warrant authorizing search of all persons found on premises of suspected "crack" house was broad and invalid because defendant was not specifically named or described in the warrant).

premises, the search will be upheld and the evidence admitted.[94] Absent a specific direction in a search warrant, the search of persons found on the premises during execution of a warrant is not constitutionally permissible without a reasonable belief that the person is involved in some criminal activity or is armed and dangerous.[95]

Consequently, this discussion involves two different kinds of searches requiring different levels of cause. First, a search for evidence of a person found on the premises must be supported by probable cause to believe that the person is involved in the criminal activity. Second, a *Terry* type, limited pat-down search may be conducted if there is reasonable suspicion to believe that the subject is armed and/or dangerous. Sometimes the line between a search for evidence and a limited search for weapons is not altogether clear. A limited pat-down search may lead to evidence of a crime rather than to a weapon,[96] but there is a distinct need to separate legitimate pat-downs to protect the officer's safety from those that are pretextual searches for evidence.

In *Ybarra v Illinois,*[97] police entered a tavern with a search warrant authorizing the search of the tavern and the bartender for drugs and evidence of drug trafficking. On entering the tavern, the police advised all those present that they intended to conduct a cursory weapons search. The defendant, a customer, was lined up along with the other patrons. While patting down the defendant, an officer felt "a cigarette pack with objects in it." The officer did not remove the pack but patted down the remainder of the customers and then returned to the defendant, removed the cigarette pack from his pocket, and found six tinfoil packets containing heroin. The search was authorized under Illinois Revised Statute Chapter 38, § 108-09, which permits a police officer executing a search warrant to detain and search any person found on the premises to protect himself or to prevent the disposal or concealment of items described in the warrant.

The Court reversed the conviction and held that "a person's mere propinquity to others independently suspected of criminal activity does not, without more, give rise to probable cause to search that person."[98] Justice Stewart's use of the word "propinquity" probably was not accidental. The word means "nearness of place or kinship," and the ruling is broad enough to cover those persons who happen to be present during a search as well as those who are present and related to the person suspected of criminal activity. Blood relationship should not, in itself, give rise to probable cause

---

[94]State v Bailey, No. 55938, 1989 WL 117414 (8th Dist Ct App, Cuyahoga, 10-5-89) (the warrant did not order the search of all those present but "persons in control of such premises").

[95]Ybarra v Illinois, 444 US 85, 100 SCt 338, 62 LEd(2d) 238 (1979).

[96]State v Klump, No. CA88-03-026, 1988 WL 141701 (12th Dist Ct App, Clermont, 12-30-88) (defendant found in hotel room by police executing a search warrant was observed to have a bulge in his pocket that turned out to be an aspirin bottle containing drugs that was removed following a pat-down frisk; although officer testified that the items sought could easily have been in defendant's pocket, the court held that the bulge could easily have been a weapon).

[97]Ybarra v Illinois, 444 US 85, 100 SCt 338, 62 LEd(2d) 238 (1979).

[98]Ybarra v Illinois, 444 US 85, 91, 100 SCt 338, 62 LEd(2d) 238 (1979).

to justify a search when no independent grounds exist. Illinois attempted to justify the intrusion as the result of an initial limited frisk for weapons. Justice Stewart, writing for the majority, rejected this attempt to expand police search powers. The Court pointed out that the police failed to articulate any specific fact that would have justified a police officer at the scene even suspecting that Ybarra was armed and dangerous. They therefore refused to expand the exception to the probable cause requirement crafted in *Terry v Ohio,*[99] "whose 'narrow scope' this Court 'has been careful to maintain.' "[100]

However, where an officer has articulable facts and circumstances that give rise to a reasonable belief that the person may be armed and dangerous, a limited pat-down frisk for weapons is permissible.[101] There appears to be a growing general belief accepted by courts that probable cause to believe that drug activity is occurring is sufficient to create a reasonable suspicion that persons found at the site are likely to be armed and/or dangerous; however, police must articulate their fear as the justification for the pat-down frisk. Any indication that the search was more intensive than a pat-down frisk or that the pat-down frisk was for a reason other than to determine if the defendant was armed should result in suppression of evidence found.[102]

The state offered an alternative justification for this type of intrusion, suggesting that the government interest in controlling drug trafficking is so great and the drugs themselves are so mobile that a *Terry* reasonable belief or suspicion standard should be employed to aid the evidence-gathering function of the search warrant. In rejecting this proposal, the Court said:

> The "long prevailing" constitutional standard of probable cause embodies "the best compromise that has been found for accommodating [the] often opposing interests in 'safeguard[ing] citizens from rash and unreasonable interferences with privacy' and in 'seek[ing] to give fair leeway for enforcing the law in the community's protection.' "[103]

In *Michigan v Summers,*[104] the Court specifically avoided deciding whether the *Ybarra* ban on searches of persons found at the scene of a public place that is to be searched would apply to a search of a private dwelling where the person may have some special connection. In *Ybarra,* the defendant was a patron in the bar. The state offered no evidence of any connection between the defendant and the criminal activity. In a private residence, persons found on the scene are likely to have some connection with the occupants. However, as the Supreme Court in *Ybarra* pointed out, "mere propinquity" is not sufficient to justify either a pat-down frisk or a search. Police may have probable cause to search a residence for criminal

---

[99]Terry v Ohio, 392 US 1, 88 SCt 1868, 20 LEd(2d) 889 (1968).

[100]Ybarra v Illinois, 444 US 85, 93, 100 SCt 338, 62 LEd(2d) 238 (1979).

[101]State v Moody, 30 App(3d) 44, 30 OBR 99, 506 NE(2d) 256 (Hamilton 1985).

[102]See State v Murphy, No. 13080, 1987 WL 17780 (9th Dist Ct App, Summit, 9-30-87), cert denied 485 US 1040, 108 SCt 1603, 99 LEd(2d) 917 (1988) (state's claim of *Terry* justification where only reason stated for search of persons was the fear of losing marked money).

[103]Ybarra v Illinois, 444 US 85, 100 SCt 338, 62 LEd(2d) 238 (1979).

[104]Michigan v Summers, 452 US 692, 101 SCt 2587, 69 LEd(2d) 340 (1981).

evidence, but other nonillegal activities may take place in that residence by the occupant, who is suspected of criminal activity, and others. That presumption would not apply where the only purpose served by the residence is for illegal activity, such as a drug house, except that phrase should be used cautiously and not indiscriminately.[105] In that situation mere propinquity may suffice. Where a location that is the subject of a search warrant serves only as a drug house, it would be reasonable to search all persons found on the premises; but if that fact is known prior to entry, it should be included in the request for a search warrant that encompasses both a search of the premises and a search of all persons found on the premises. However, in *State v Tucker*,[106] that very issue was raised where a warrant ordering the search of a suspected "crack" house contained an authorization to search all persons found on the premises. The Court of Appeals found the warrant to be invalid and suppressed the evidence found on the defendant because he was not specifically named or described in the warrant.

CROSS REFERENCES

Text Ch 14

---

[105]State v Taylor, 82 App(3d) 434, 612 NE(2d) 728 (Montgomery 1992).
[106]State v Tucker, 98 App(3d) 308, 648 NE(2d) 557 (Sandusky 1994), appeal dismissed by 71 OS(3d) 1499, 646 NE(2d) 1124 (1995).

Chapter 9

Search Warrant Requirement

9.01   Introduction

The excesses of British colonial authorities prior to the American Revolution continue to have a profound effect upon the law of the United States governing searches and seizures. In response to and in order to break the resistance given by colonists to what they considered unfair taxes imposed upon them by the English crown, colonial authorities engaged in wholesale violations of the colonists' privacy. The primary tool used by those authorities was the Writ of Assistance.

The Writ of Assistance was a general warrant issued to a sheriff or other specified law enforcement officer entitling the bearer to enter, by force if necessary, any establishment or dwelling and search for contraband or merchandise upon which colonial import taxes had not been paid. No factual basis was required to justify the intrusion, and return of execution was unnecessary if no contraband was found. The Writ provided all of the necessary justification; the only requirement was that the officer holding the Writ believe that cause existed to justify the entry and search. Resistance to the Writs was credited by John Adams as the spark which generated the movement for independence. In contrast, Writs of Assistance remain one of the primary tools used by Canadian law enforcement authorities to combat illegal narcotics trafficking.

The Fourth Amendment, as originally proposed by James Madison, was directed only to general warrant searches. By the time the Bill of Rights was voted on in Congress and submitted for ratification to the states, the language had been transformed into its present form prohibiting all unreasonable searches and seizures.

The Fourth Amendment is silent on the critical issue of when a warrant is required. Two competing views of the Supreme Court have vied for the support of a majority of the justices for the past fifty years. The judicial preference for a search warrant no longer commands a majority of the Supreme Court. This acknowledgment of reality is long overdue and reflects the steady growth of new exceptions to the warrant requirement as well as the expansion of existing exceptions.

9.02   Judicial preference for a warrant

The judicial preference for a warrant, which has held sway for most of the century, adheres to the proposition that "searches conducted outside the judicial process, without prior approval by judge or magistrate, are *per se* unreasonable."[1] The rule, stated in *Katz v United States,*[2] takes the position that the *reasonableness,* the Fourth Amendment litmus test, of a search and seizure is not to be considered in the abstract. Instead, reasonableness is to be determined by measuring the police officer's conduct with the commands of the Amendment's warrant clause. Consequently, the reviewing court is to determine the validity of the search and seizure by testing whether, under the facts and circumstances of the particular case, it was reasonable for the police officers to forego securing a warrant prior to conducting the search and/or seizure.

According to this view, which finds intrinsic value in the warrant process, warrantless searches are to be the exception, not the rule. For one to be upheld, there must be conditions that necessitate avoiding the delay inherent in procuring a search warrant. Additionally, to meet constitutional standards, a warrantless search must fit within "a few specifically established and well-delineated exceptions."[3] Satisfaction of the probable cause standard of the warrant clause is not an adequate substitute for a warrant, and the Court has declared warrantless searches unconstitutional "notwithstanding facts unquestionably showing probable cause."[4]

The value of a search warrant is seen as threefold. The warrant process interposes the impartial judgment of a judicial officer between the citizen and police.[5] This requirement evolved from the "basic constitutional doctrine that individual freedoms will best be preserved through a separation of powers and division of functions among the different branches and levels of Government."[6]

Reliance upon a judicial review prior to the intrusion ensures that the inferences which give rise to reasonable cause are drawn by a disinterested official "instead of being judged by the officer engaged in the often competitive enterprise of ferreting out crime."[7] The Supreme Court has argued that without judicial determinations, police officers would be able to decide when there is probable cause which "would reduce the Amendment to a nullity and leave the people's homes secure only in the discretion of police officers."[8] Consequently, the search warrant is used to control police discretion in determining when to conduct a search and, equally important, in setting limitations upon the scope of the search.[9]

A search warrant is valued so highly because the alternative process is an after-the-fact determination on a motion to suppress, a procedure the Supreme Court has labeled as less reliable because it is "too likely to be

---

[1]Katz v United States, 389 US 347, 357, 88 SCt 507, 19 LEd(2d) 576 (1967).

[2]Katz v United States, 389 US 347, 357, 88 SCt 507, 19 LEd(2d) 576 (1967).

[3]Katz v United States, 389 US 347, 357, 88 SCt 507, 19 LEd(2d) 576 (1967).

[4]Agnello v United States, 269 US 20, 33, 46 SCt 4, 70 LEd 145 (1925).

[5]Wong Sun v United States, 371 US 471, 83 SCt 407, 9 LEd(2d) 441 (1963).

[6]United States v United States Dist Court for Eastern Dist of Michigan, 407 US 297, 317, 92 SCt 2125, 32 LEd(2d) 752 (1972).

[7]Johnson v United States, 333 US 10, 14, 68 SCt 367, 92 LEd 436 (1948).

[8]Johnson v United States, 333 US 10, 14, 68 SCt 367, 92 LEd 436 (1948).

[9]Trupiano v United States, 334 US 699, 68 SCt 1229, 92 LEd 1663 (1948), overruled on other grounds by United States v Rabinowitz, 339 US 56, 70 SCt 430, 94 LEd(2d) 653 (1950).

subtly influenced by the familiar shortcomings of hindsight judgment."[10] The Court has stressed that "we cannot accept the view that Fourth Amendment interests are vindicated so long as 'the rights of the criminal' are 'protect[ed] … against introduction of evidence seized without probable cause.' The Amendment is designed to prevent, not simply to redress, unlawful police action."[11] Moreover, the suppression process and the exclusionary rule have been criticized extensively because they only protect the rights of the guilty—those who are discovered with reliable evidence of guilt. Rigorous enforcement of the warrant requirement provides protection for the innocent as well as the guilty prior to the intrusion.

Staunch advocates of the warrant requirement would limit its exceptions only to those instances which are "justified by absolute necessity."[12] Necessity is established when the "societal costs of obtaining a warrant, such as danger to law enforcement officers or the risk of loss or destruction of evidence, outweigh the reasons for prior recourse to a neutral magistrate."[13] The normal inconvenience and slight delay associated with securing a warrant "are never very convincing reasons and … certainly are not enough to bypass the constitutional requirement."[14]

The Supreme Court has claimed that the preference for a warrant is so great that it will affect a court's review of whether probable cause existed to justify the search. "[I]n a doubtful or marginal case a search under a warrant may be sustainable where without one it would fall."[15] This difference is based on the view that a search with a warrant is the orderly process required by the Constitution and warrantless searches constitute an extraordinary intrusion upon Fourth Amendment protected interests. On a motion to suppress, a court reviewing the existence of probable cause will have the complaint and affidavits, and any recorded, supplemental testimony taken under oath, relied on by the magistrate in finding sufficient probable cause to issue the search warrant. In reviewing a claim that probable cause existed to justify a warrantless search, the court must rely upon the officer's testimony recounting the facts and circumstances known to him on which he relied when making the decision to conduct the search. This after-the-fact reconstruction may be aided, at least subtly, by facts and circumstances discovered during and after the search.

9.03   Contrary view

Opponents of the preference for a warrant stress that "[t]he Fourth Amendment does not by its terms require a prior warrant for searches and

---

[10]Beck v Ohio, 379 US 89, 96, 85 SCt 223, 13 LEd(2d) 142 (1964).

[11]Chimel v California, 395 US 752, 766 n.12, 89 SCt 2034, 23 LEd(2d) 685 (1969).

[12]United States v Rabinowitz, 339 US 56, 70, 70 SCt 430, 94 LEd(2d) 653 (1950), overruled by Chimel v California, 395 US 752, 89 SCt 2034, 23 LEd(2d) 685 (1969).

[13]Arkansas v Sanders, 442 US 753, 759, 99 SCt 2586, 61 LEd(2d) 235 (1979), overruled by California v Acevedo, 500 US 565, 111 SCt 1982, 114 LEd(2d) 619 (1991).

[14]Johnson v United States, 333 US 10, 15, 68 SCt 367, 92 LEd 436 (1948).

[15]United States v Ventresca, 380 US 102, 106, 85 SCt 741, 13 LEd(2d) 684 (1965).

seizures."[16] This view rejects the theory that the warrant requirement is central to the protection of the Fourth Amendment. Rather than focusing attention upon conformity with the requirements of the warrant clause, the constitutionality of a particular intrusion is to be determined in the abstract by asking whether the police determination to search was reasonable under the circumstances of the particular case.

The theory rests on the charge that the warrant requirement is nothing more than a judicially created rule. It finds that the Amendment did not intend to adopt a warrant requirement because it has no basis in common law.[17] "[N]othing in the Fourth Amendment itself requires that searches be conducted pursuant to warrants."[18] Chief Justice Rehnquist has stressed that the Amendment only requires "that any warrant which *may* issue shall only issue upon probable cause."[19] Justice Scalia has suggested that a search is reasonable if supported by a warrant only in those instances where the common law would have required a warrant.[20] However, the warrant requirement's constitutional roots are far deeper than Justices Rehnquist and Scalia claim. While seeming factually acceptable, their criticism ignores the fact that at common-law warrantless searches were virtually nonexistent except for searches incident to arrest.[21] Consequently, if the framers intended to adopt the existing common law system and to redress the crown's abuse of that system, the Amendment, then, reflects a tradition where a warrant virtually was always required. Moreover, it is highly unlikely that the framers intended to eliminate general warrants in favor of a system of no warrants at all.

Justice Rehnquist has been the most forceful advocate of this position on the Court. He argues that nothing in the Fourth Amendment requires that searches be conducted pursuant to warrants, and that in emphasizing the warrant requirement over the reasonableness of a search, the Court has "stood the Fourth Amendment on its head."[22] Justice Rehnquist's argument not only is based on the language of the Fourth Amendment but also is linked to his view of the effect of the warrant requirement upon law enforcement. He contends that the preference for a warrant substantially frustrates law enforcement officers in their efforts to apprehend those

---

[16]California v Acevedo, 500 US 565, 111 SCt 1982, 1992, 114 LEd(2d) 619 (1991) (Scalia, J., concurring).

[17]California v Acevedo, 500 US 565, 111 SCt 1982, 1992, 114 LEd(2d) 619 (1991) (Scalia, J., concurring).

[18]Robbins v California, 453 US 420, 101 SCt 2841, 69 LEd(2d) 744 (1981), overruled by United States v Ross, 456 US 798, 102 SCt 2157, 72 LEd(2d) 572 (1982) (Rehnquist, J., dissenting).

[19]Robbins v California, 453 US 420, 101 SCt 2841, 69 LEd(2d) 744 (1981), overruled by United States v Ross, 456 US 798, 102 SCt 2157, 72 LEd(2d) 572 (1982) (Rehnquist, J., dissenting).

[20]California v Acevedo, 500 US 565, 111 SCt 1982, 114 LEd(2d) 619 (1991) (Scalia, J., concurring).

[21]Cf. Grano, *Rethinking the Fourth Amendment Warrant Requirement,* 19 Am Crim L Rev 603 (1982).

[22]Robbins v California, 453 US 420, 438, 101 SCt 2841, 69 LEd(2d) 744 (1981), overruled by United States v Ross, 456 US 798, 102 SCt 2157, 72 LEd(2d) 572 (1982).

whom they have probable cause to arrest or to gather evidence of a crime when they have probable cause to search. "In emphasizing the warrant requirement the Court has therefore not only erected an edifice without solid foundation but also one with little substance."[23]

9.04 Judicial preference for warrantless searches

(A) In general

The judicial preference for a warrant is now a matter of historical curiosity. Although the Court persists in paying homage to the principle enunciated in *Katz v United States*[24] that warrantless searches are "*per se* unreasonable," it is generally paid in the context of Supreme Court decisions expanding the permissible scope of warrantless searches.[25] Subtly, even this homage has slowed to a stop as the Court's preference for warrantless searches becomes clearer.[26] Meanwhile, Chief Justice Rehnquist and Justice Scalia have continued but so far failed to persuade the Court to embrace their general theory and announce that reasonableness should be determined wholly in the abstract rather than within the context of the warrant clause requirements.[27] While the Court has yet to adopt their rhetoric, their approach is prevailing.

The Court continues to maintain that the number of warrantless search categories is few and well defined. For example, the Court rejects a "murder scene exception" to the warrant requirement.[28] More significantly, the Court rejected the government's argument in *United States v Chadwick*[29] that the warrant requirement be confined to intrusions into the core interests of the Fourth Amendment, such as homes, offices, and private communications. However, some recent decisions have been written as though a "public place" exception to the warrant requirement exists, creating irreconcilable anomalies. For example, if a police officer has probable cause to believe that a container in a public place contains contraband, the officer may seize the container[30] but may not search it without a warrant.[31] If,

---

[23]Robbins v California, 453 US 420, 439, 101 SCt 2841, 69 LEd(2d) 744 (1981), overruled by United States v Ross, 456 US 798, 102 SCt 2157, 72 LEd(2d) 572 (1982).

[24]Katz v United States, 389 US 347, 88 SCt 507, 19 LEd(2d) 576 (1967).

[25]See, e.g., California v Acevedo, 500 US 565, 111 SCt 1982, 114 LEd(2d) 619 (1991); New York v Belton, 453 US 454, 101 SCt 2860, 69 LEd(2d) 768 (1981).

[26]See, e.g., California v Acevedo, 500 US 565, 111 SCt 1982, 114 LEd(2d) 619 (1991); California v Carney, 471 US 386, 105 SCt 2066, 85 LEd(2d) 406 (1985); United States v Ross, 456 US 798, 102 SCt 2157, 72 LEd(2d) 572 (1982).

[27]See Michigan v Tyler, 436 US 499, 98 SCt 1942, 56 LEd(2d) 486 (1978) (Rehnquist, J., dissenting).

[28]See Thompson v Louisiana, 469 US 17, 105 SCt 409, 83 LEd(2d) 246 (1984); Mincey v Arizona, 437 US 385, 98 SCt 2408, 57 LEd(2d) 290 (1978), cert denied 469 US 1040, 105 SCt 521, 83 LEd(2d) 409 (1984), modified sub nom Arizona v Hicks, 480 US 321, 107 SCt 1149, 94 LEd(2d) 347 (1987).

[29]United States v Chadwick, 433 US 1, 97 SCt 2476, 53 LEd(2d) 538 (1977).

[30]United States v Chadwick, 433 US 1, 97 SCt 2476, 53 LEd(2d) 538 (1977); United States v Place, 462 US 696, 103 SCt 2637, 77 LEd(2d) 110 (1983).

[31]United States v Chadwick, 433 US 1, 97 SCt 2476, 53 LEd(2d) 538 (1977).

however, the officer observes someone place the container in an automobile, the officer may seize the container and search it without a warrant.[32] The different treatment accorded containers found in public and found in an automobile raises questions about the continuing viability of the *Chadwick* doctrine. That doctrine has been plagued by questioning footsteps since its announcement, but those footsteps grew much louder when Justice Blackmun for the majority in *California v Acevedo* said, "To the extent that the *Chadwick-Sanders* rule protects privacy, its protection is minimal."[33]

On the other hand, the preference for a warrant has been retained and in some respects even strengthened when the place to be searched is a home. The Court has overturned centuries-old precedent, now requiring a warrant when entering a house to make an arrest.[34] The Court has continued to protect the privacy interest in residences against warrantless encroachments.[35]

The Supreme Court appears to be straining unnaturally to expand existing exceptions to the warrant requirement in an effort to avoid contradicting another often-cited reference that a warrantless search must fit within "a few specifically established and well-delineated exceptions."[36] However, Justice Scalia says that the Court is no longer rejecting the creation of new exceptions, suggesting that there might now be as many as twenty-two exceptions to the warrant requirement.[37] Whether Scalia's count is correct or not, the Court's course of conduct is serious because it indicates a disregard for several other established Fourth Amendment principles.

Additionally, the number of "special needs" or "special circumstances" searches, in which the warrant is dispensed with and a standard less than probable cause is imposed, has grown.[38] The explosive expansion of these searches is a clear avoidance of traditional warrant clause requirements. Often they rest on the claim that the purposes of the search are unrelated to traditional searches for evidence of crimes, although criminal prosecution may be the result of such searches.[39] There has even been pressure at the margins of these searches to eliminate the requirement that some level of particularized cause or suspicion justify the intrusion so long as the use made of the evidence discovered is limited to non-criminal purposes.[40] Of course, the Fourth Amendment has never been limited to searches made by

---

[32]California v Acevedo, 500 US 565, 111 SCt 1982, 114 LEd(2d) 619 (1991), reversing Arkansas v Sanders, 442 US 753, 99 SCt 2586, 61 LEd(2d) 235 (1979).

[33]California v Acevedo, 500 US 565, 111 SCt 1982, 1987, 114 LEd(2d) 619 (1991).

[34]Payton v New York, 445 US 573, 100 SCt 1371, 63 LEd(2d) 639 (1980); Steagald v United States, 451 US 204, 101 SCt 1642, 68 LEd(2d) 38 (1981); Welsh v Wisconsin, 466 US 740, 104 SCt 2091, 80 LEd(2d) 732 (1984).

[35]Minnesota v Olson, 495 US 91, 110 SCt 1684, 109 LEd(2d) 85 (1990).

[36]Katz v United States, 389 US 347, 357, 88 SCt 507, 19 LEd(2d) 576 (1967).

[37]California v Acevedo, 500 US 565, 111 SCt 1982, 1992, 114 LEd(2d) 619 (1991).

[38]See e.g., New Jersey v T.L.O., 469 US 325, 105 SCt 733, 83 LEd(2d) 720 (1985).

[39]See e.g., New Jersey v T.L.O., 469 US 325, 105 SCt 733, 83 LEd(2d) 720 (1985).

[40]See e.g., National Treasury Employees Union v Von Raab, 489 US 656, 109 SCt 1384, 103 LEd(2d) 685 (1989), affirmed sub nom National Treasury Employees Union v Bush, 891 F(2d) 99 (1989).

criminal justice agencies in search of convictions but, rather, covers intrusions by all government agencies.

(B) Fact-specific adjudication versus bright-line rules

A marked change in Fourth Amendment adjudication has been the trend over the past two decades for the Court to adopt expansive "bright-line" rules which grant broad exemptions from the warrant requirement. A bright-line or general rule covers countless situations and signals an abandonment of "the central teaching of [the Supreme] Court's Fourth Amendment jurisprudence,"[41] "which has ordinarily required individualized inquiry into the particular facts justifying every police intrusion."[42] Bright-line authorizations of warrantless searches have, for example, replaced inquiry in each case of "whether or not there was present one of the reasons supporting the authority for a search of the person incident to arrest,"[43] supplanted the exigency inquiry in the automobile exception,[44] and superseded the control test for searches of automobiles incident to arrest.[45]

The purpose of the bright-line rules is to produce certainty on Fourth Amendment issues and clear guidance for police officers in the field rather than the uncertainty which follows the fact-specific inquiry used to determine the reasonableness of police conduct in each case. The bright-line rules function on the understanding that "[a] single familiar standard is essential to guide police officers, who have only limited time and expertise to reflect on and balance the social and individual interests involved in the specific circumstances."[46] These rules are premised upon generalizations which are assumed to apply to an entire class of cases. The weakness of this approach is that often the generalization upon which the bright-line rule supposedly rests is not supported by the facts of the case in which the rule was adopted.[47]

(C) Shifting of burdens

A less than subtle shift in the burden of persuasion has occurred in Supreme Court litigation pertaining to exemptions from the warrant requirement. Traditionally, the government agency seeking an exemption from the warrant requirement carried the burden of justifying its failure to obtain a warrant.[48] That burden involved more than simply demonstrating

---

[41]Terry v Ohio, 392 US 1, 88 SCt 1868, 20 LEd(2d) 889 (1968).

[42]Pennsylvania v Mimms, 434 US 106, 98 SCt 330, 54 LEd(2d) 331 (1977) (Stevens, J., dissenting).

[43]United States v Robinson, 414 US 218, 94 SCt 467, 38 LEd(2d) 427 (1973).

[44]Michigan v Thomas, 458 US 259, 102 SCt 3079, 73 LEd(2d) 750 (1982) (per curiam finding of error in state appellate court holding "that the absence of 'exigent circumstances' precluded a warrantless search").

[45]New York v Belton, 453 US 454, 101 SCt 2860, 69 LEd(2d) 768 (1981).

[46]New York v Belton, 453 US 454, 458, 101 SCt 2860, 69 LEd(2d) 768 (1981), quoting Dunaway v New York, 442 US 200, 99 SCt 2248, 60 LEd(2d) 824 (1979).

[47]See, e.g., Washington v Chrisman, 455 US 1, 102 SCt 812, 70 LEd(2d) 778 (1982) (where the Court held it permissible as a matter of routine to monitor the movements of an arrested person even though the officer had testified that he acted as he did in order to get a look at evidence rather than for the underlying reasons which justify a search incident to arrest).

[48]United States v Jeffers, 342 US 48, 72 SCt 93, 96 LEd(2d) 59 (1951).

that the facts of the case fell within a broad parameter. Instead, it involved a demonstration of "need,"[49] "exceptional circumstances,"[50] "a grave emergency,"[51] "exigencies of the situation [which] made that course imperative,"[52] or "absolute necessity."[53]

Presently, the Court has turned the Amendment on its head by demanding that the party questioning a warrantless search demonstrate how requiring a warrant will further Fourth Amendment interests. This shift makes warrantless searches the general rule, resulting in broad grants of authority to law enforcement officers to conduct warrantless searches on purely convenience grounds. For example, Justice Stevens, in *United States v Ross*,[54] attributed the growth of the automobile exception in large measure to "a realistic appraisal of the relatively minor protection that a contrary rule [requiring a search warrant] would provide for privacy interests."[55] Similarly, Justice O'Connor, in *United States v Johns*,[56] allowed a warrantless search of packages three days after they had been taken from the vehicle and stored in a government warehouse because the defendants had failed to allege and prove that the delay in the search of packages adversely affected legitimate interests protected by the Fourth Amendment. In 1991, Justice Blackmun, in *California v Acevedo*,[57] eliminated one of the last limitations upon an absolute automobile exception theorizing that "[t]o the extent that the [existing] rule protects privacy, its protection is minimal." Equally important was the burden imposed upon the state to demonstrate that the search fell within one of the recognized categories of exceptions to the warrant requirement created by necessity.[58]

(D) Growth in the scope of warrantless searches

One of the values attributed to requiring search warrants was that in addition to governing the initial intrusion, a search warrant also fixes reasonable limitations upon the scope of that intrusion. When warrantless searches were treated as extraordinary and subject to strict control, the law enforcement authority seeking exemption from the warrant requirement was obligated to justify the scope of the warrantless search as well as the initial intrusion. Consequently, the scope of a warrantless search was limited to satisfaction of the important societal interests which justified the initial intrusion that occurred without prior judicial approval. Consequently,

---

[49]United States v Jeffers, 342 US 48, 51, 72 SCt 93, 96 LEd(2d) 59 (1951).
[50]Johnson v United States, 333 US 10, 68 SCt 367, 92 LEd 436 (1948).
[51]McDonald v United States, 335 US 451, 455, 69 SCt 191, 93 LEd(2d) 153 (1948).
[52]McDonald v United States, 335 US 451, 456, 69 SCt 191, 93 LEd(2d) 153 (1948).
[53]United States v Rabinowitz, 339 US 56, 70 SCt 430, 94 LEd(2d) 653 (1950) overruled by Chimel v California, 395 US 752, 89 SCt 2034, 23 LEd(2d) 685 (1969) (Frankfurter, J., dissenting).
[54]United States v Ross, 456 US 798, 102 SCt 2157, 72 LEd(2d) 572 (1982).
[55]United States v Ross, 456 US 798, 807 n.9, 102 SCt 2157, 72 LEd(2d) 572 (1982).
[56]United States v Johns, 469 US 478, 105 SCt 881, 83 LEd(2d) 890 (1985).
[57]California v Acevedo, 500 US 565, 111 SCt 1982, 1989, 114 LEd(2d) 619 (1991).
[58]State v Penn, 61 OS(3d) 720, 576 NE(2d) 790 (1991).

authority to engage in Fourth Amendment intrusions without prior judicial authority should extend only to the time and area relevant to the exigency which justifies the exemption[59] and should terminate the instant that emergency is neutralized.[60]

This was the policy behind the development of the "control" test in *Chimel v California*,[61] which allowed an officer to search the area within the control—the reaching or grabbing distance—of the arrestee, without either a warrant or probable cause, to protect the officer against an undetected weapon or the destruction of evidence. Beyond the area of the arrestee's control, *Chimel* required a search warrant, thus demonstrating that the intrusion should be limited to the emergency which originally justified the warrantless intrusion.

This principle was abandoned in *United States v Ross*,[62] where Justice Stevens said that the scope of a warrantless search authorized by the automobile exception is as broad as a search conducted with a warrant. This shift was not at all surprising since by the time of *Ross*, the Court had lost track of the exigency which had given rise to the automobile exception; thus, there was no longer an emergency by which to measure either the initial intrusion or its scope.[63]

(E) Other ramifications of the demise of the judicial preference for a warrant

The Rehnquist majority's zeal to eliminate the warrant requirement may have broader implications for Fourth Amendment protections. In *California v Acevedo*,[64] Justice Scalia said:

> Our intricate body of law regarding "reasonable expectations of privacy" has been developed largely as a means of creating these exceptions [to the warrant requirement], enabling a search to be denominated not a Fourth Amendment "search" and therefore not subject to the general warrant requirement.

Consequently, in order to thwart the search warrant requirement, this Supreme Court denies all Fourth Amendment protection, including the general test of reasonableness advocated by the Chief Justice and Justice Scalia, to vast aspects of modern American life.[65]

CROSS REFERENCES

Text Ch 5

---

[59]See Chimel v California, 395 US 752, 89 SCt 2034, 23 LEd(2d) 685 (1969).

[60]See Michigan v Tyler, 436 US 499, 98 SCt 1942, 56 LEd(2d) 486 (1978) (government officials may enter building to fight fire and determine its causes, but additional entries are authorized only pursuant to warrant process).

[61]Chimel v California, 395 US 752, 89 SCt 2034, 23 LEd(2d) 685 (1969).

[62]United States v Ross, 456 US 798, 102 SCt 2157, 72 LEd(2d) 572 (1982).

[63]See New York v Belton, 453 US 454, 101 SCt 2860, 69 LEd(2d) 768 (1981) (where search incident to arrest extended to interior of vehicle which might have actually endangered the officer's life when he searched the car for evidence without back-up assistance).

[64]California v Acevedo, 500 US 565, 111 SCt 1982, 1993, 114 LEd(2d) 619 (1991).

[65]See Text Ch 1, The Fourth Amendment and the Protection of Privacy.

Chapter 10

Exigent Circumstances

10.01   Introduction

The development of general exemptions to the warrant requirement, called bright-line rules, disassociated from the exigent circumstances, which originally gave rise to the warrant exceptions, masks the continued importance of exigency in other contexts. The Supreme Court's unwillingness to create wholly new exceptions to the warrant requirement means that exigent circumstances remain the basis for other warrant exceptions. In this context, the term exigent circumstances means an actual and on-going emergency. Consequently, the search warrant requirement has been excused because of the existence of exigent circumstances, which means generally that the delay associated with securing a warrant would result in endangering police officers or other individuals or would result in the concealment or loss of evidence. The "bright-line" rules adopted for searches incident to arrest in *United States v Edwards*,[1] allowing a delayed search of the defendant's clothing after he had been jailed for ten hours, and in *New York v Belton*,[2] allowing a search of the interior compartment of the vehicle following an arrest even though the arrestee was no longer in reaching or grabbing distance of the compartment, have discounted the exigencies which gave rise to the exception. Similar treatment has been accorded under the automobile exception, where under *United States v Ross*,[3] a search of a vehicle and all containers found therein is permitted, notwithstanding the fact that the automobile is no longer mobile and is safely in the exclusive control of the police.

Outside of these general exceptions, the United States Supreme Court has tended to maintain the requirement that warrantless searches must be supported by an emergency. The type of entry supported by emergency was described very well by the Shaker Heights Municipal Court in *University Heights v Seibert*:[4]

> [W]here by the use of the ordinary senses of smell, hearing or sight, an individual believes that reasonable cause exists to enter private premises for the purpose of averting personal injury to the occupants or damage to property, discovery of criminal acts or presence of contraband may be the subject of prosecution and such discovery is not violative of the Fourth Amendment for lack of a search warrant.

---

[1]United States v Edwards, 415 US 800, 94 SCt 1234, 39 LEd(2d) 771 (1974); see also United States v Edwards, 497 F(2d) 925 (1974).

[2]New York v Belton, 453 US 454, 101 SCt 2860, 69 LEd(2d) 768 (1981).

[3]United States v Ross, 456 US 798, 102 SCt 2157, 72 LEd(2d) 572 (1982).

[4]University Heights v Seibert, 26 Misc 234, 238, 270 NE(2d) 381 (Muni, Shaker Hts 1971).

The emergency justifies the warrantless entry, and while lawfully present, police may seize evidence in plain view.[5] However, police may remain on the premises only so long as is necessary to quell the emergency; a warrantless emergency entry may not be used as an evidence-gathering expedition.[6]

10.02   Nature of the exigency

Generally, a warrantless entry, even to make an arrest, violates the Fourth Amendment.[7] Similarly, entry of a residence to conduct a search, even for a person, must be conducted with a warrant, absent exigent circumstances.[8] The factors to be considered as to whether there is an emergency that will permit a warrantless police intrusion into a home to effect an arrest are as follows:

(1) The offense is a crime of violence;

(2) It is reasonably believed that the suspect is armed;

(3) There is strong reason to believe that the suspect is on the premises; and

(4) It is likely that the suspect will escape if not swiftly apprehended.[9]

Society expects police officers to respond to emergency situations. Conflicts arise when police seize evidence "in plain view" while responding to the emergency, leading to a claim that the emergency was contrived. Unquestionably, police officers may enter and investigate in an emergency without the accompanying intent to either search or arrest.[10] Chief Justice Burger, then on the Court of Appeals for the District of Columbia, described in *Wayne v United States*[11] the balancing of interests that may result in the warrantless entry of a home being reasonable:

> But a warrant is not required to break down a door to enter a burning home to rescue occupants or extinguish a fire, to prevent a shooting or to bring emergency aid to an injured person. The need to protect or preserve life or avoid serious injury is justification for what would be otherwise illegal absent an exigency or emergency. Fires or dead bodies are reported to police by cranks where no fires or bodies are to be found. Acting in response to reports of "dead bodies," the police may find the "bodies" to be common drunks, diabetics in shock, or distressed cardiac patients. But the business of policemen and firemen is *to*

---

[5]Thompson v Louisiana, 469 US 17, 105 SCt 409, 83 LEd(2d) 246 (1984).

[6]State v Garrett, 76 App(3d) 57, 600 NE(2d) 1130 (Portage 1991).

[7]Payton v New York, 445 US 573, 100 SCt 1371, 63 LEd(2d) 639 (1980).

[8]Steagald v United States, 451 US 204, 101 SCt 1642, 68 LEd(2d) 38 (1981).

[9]Minnesota v Olson, 495 US 91, 110 SCt 1684, 109 LEd(2d) 85 (1990); State v Bowe, 52 App(3d) 112, 557 NE(2d) 139 (Summit 1988), cert denied 489 US 1090, 109 SCt 1557, 103 LEd(2d) 860 (1989), appeal dismissed by 53 OS(3d) 703, 558 NE(2d) 57 (1990) (these courts also suggest that there must be probable cause to believe that the suspect committed the crime and the entry can be made peaceably; however, the greater the emergency, the less likely and less important it is that the entry can be made peaceably).

[10]See United States v Barone, 330 F(2d) 543 (2d Cir NY 1964), cert denied 377 US 1004, 84 SCt 1940, 12 LEd(2d) 1053 (1964).

[11]Wayne v United States, 318 F(2d) 205, 212 (DC Cir 1963), cert denied 375 US 860, 84 SCt 125, 11 LEd(2d) 86 (1963).

act, not to speculate or meditate on whether the report is correct. People could well die in emergencies if police tried to act with the calm deliberation associated with the judicial process. Even the apparently dead often are saved by swift police response. A myriad of circumstances could fall within the terms "exigent circumstances" ..., e.g., smoke coming out a window or under a door, the sound of gunfire in a house, threats from the inside to shoot through the door at police, reasonable grounds to believe an injured or seriously ill person is being held within.

This position is illustrated in an opinion by the Summit County Court of Appeals, *State v Hyde,*[12] where police officers, responding to an hysterical phone call, arrived at a residence where there had been family violence the previous night, and were met at the porch of the house by a young girl who was crying and told the officers, "Get inside, there is trouble in there." The defendant sought to suppress the officers' testimony as to what they had observed in the house on the ground that, lacking an arrest or search warrant, they had no lawful right to enter the dwelling. The court held that the officers' entry was reasonable under the Fourth Amendment as they were discharging their statutory duty to prevent crime, preserve the peace, and protect persons and property. The court reasoned that the officers had reasonable ground to believe that there was an emergency in the house and it was their duty to enter and investigate. Similarly, exigent circumstances justifying a warrantless entry exist where police are responding to a domestic violence call and hear sounds from inside which are indicative of violence.[13] On the other hand, courts will make their own determination concerning the existence of an emergency situation[14] and will not accept the exigency justification when the emergency is created by the police acting without a warrant.[15]

A classic emergency situation was presented in *State v Morris,*[16] where an officer entered without a warrant to find an abducted fourteen-year-old child. The court said the appropriate standard for determining the propriety of such an entry is based on the totality of the circumstances, i.e., whether it was reasonable for the officer to believe that someone inside was in grave danger. Here, the fourteen-year-old's brother told police that the defendant had murdered their mother and had abducted the girl. Additional evidence pointed to the defendant's apartment, and noises coming from inside the apartment led the officers to believe that the defendant was lying when he told them through the door that he was alone. The court also noted that there was evidence that the emergency was real, not a pretext to search. The search lasted no longer than was necessary to rescue the child and arrest the defendant, and then the police left the premises to secure a search warrant.

Similarly, an emergency claim was upheld in *State v Love,*[17] where police reasonably believed that a rape had taken place on the premises and that

---

[12]State v Hyde, 26 App(2d) 32, 268 NE(2d) 820 (Summit 1971).

[13]State v Applegate, 68 OS(3d) 348, 626 NE(2d) 942 (1994).

[14]See State v Keeling, 182 NE(2d) 60 (CP, Cuyahoga 1962).

[15]See Vale v Louisiana, 399 US 30, 90 SCt 1969, 26 LEd(2d) 409 (1970).

[16]State v Morris, No. 10992, 1989 WL 145175 (2d Dist Ct App, Montgomery, 11-29-89).

[17]State v Love, 49 App(3d) 88, 550 NE(2d) 951 (Hamilton 1988).

the victim might be present and in need of immediate aid. Not quite as strong or classic a case was *State v Roach*,[18] where the court, stating that police had reasonable cause to believe that an emergency situation existed because the occupant was in need of immediate aid to protect his life, upheld a warrantless intrusion into a locked restroom at a gas station. Evidence of the "immediate need" was provided by the gas station attendant who thought the defendant was drunk as he drove into the station and struck a soft drink machine and then stumbled into the restroom where he remained for twenty-five minutes, thus prompting the attendant to call police.

A weak claim of emergency in *State v Blevins*[19] was upheld where police were called on behalf of the defendant's companion who was concerned about her car keys and the defendant's health. The woman was locked out of a motel room by her male companion, the defendant. She was upset because her keys were inside and she could not go home. She was concerned that the defendant, who was drinking earlier, did not respond to her calls. When the police arrived, the defendant opened the door in response to their knock. Nonetheless, the court said that the exigency was not dissipated when the defendant unlocked the door, and the officers had the right to enter the room where they observed contraband in plain view. Once the defendant answered the door, it was clear that he was not in need of emergency medical care. Whether he would let his companion into the room to retrieve her keys was not clear, but even if he would not, this situation doubtless would not rise to exigent circumstances.

Another weak claim was accepted in *Parma v Jackson*,[20] where four uninvited police officers followed a civilian into the defendant's home because of a reasonable belief that the defendant was in need of emergency assistance. They found him on the telephone and refused to leave even though the defendant ordered them to do so. The dissenting judge argued that evidence seen and seized after the officers had no right to remain—as soon as they determined that no emergency existed and were ordered to leave—should have been rejected.

The presence of evidence in a dwelling does not create an emergency. Probable cause, no matter how well founded, that an article sought is concealed in a dwelling does not constitute exigent circumstances and does not furnish justification for a warrantless search.[21] The same, of course, applies to a situation where police spot a wanted suspect in a residence.

---

[18]State v Roach, 8 App(3d) 42, 8 OBR 44, 455 NE(2d) 1328 (Warren 1982); State v Oliver, 91 App(3d) 607, 632 NE(2d) 1382 (Wayne 1993) (police had reasonable cause to believe that an emergency situation existed and were justified in stopping defendant's vehicle to determine if defendant was in need of immediate aid or help where they were informed that the defendant was threatening suicide, was distraught and intoxicated, and owned two handguns that he had said were "ready to go").

[19]State v Blevins, No. 57231, 1990 WL 118706 (8th Dist Ct App, Cuyahoga, 8-16-90).

[20]Parma v Jackson, 58 App(3d) 17, 568 NE(2d) 702 (Cuyahoga 1989).

[21]Agnello v United States, 269 US 20, 46 SCt 4, 70 LEd 145 (1925); State v Jenkins, No. C-940840, 1995 WL 366344 (1st Dist Ct App, Hamilton, 6-21-95) (the

They may not enter without a warrant absent real exigency, nor may they create the exigency by making their presence known.[22] Similarly, a claim of emergency was rejected where police entered an apartment without a warrant following a complaint that the defendant was indecently exposing himself at the window.[23] Since the defendant was not engaged in the conduct when police arrived, the entry presumably was simply to investigate. The claim of exigency might have been accepted if the defendant was still in the window when the police arrived on the scene.

In order to justify a warrantless entry to seize evidence under the rubric of exigency, the state must, in addition to demonstrating probable cause, establish that there is a real likelihood that the evidence is in danger of being moved or destroyed in the amount of time it would take police officers to secure a warrant.[24] Additionally, attention should be paid to the nature of the crime involved. A claim of exigency could not justify a warrantless entry and search for evidence of a minor misdemeanor[25] and may even be justifiable only if the offense is a felony.

10.03   Scope of an emergency search

It has not been unusual for an exception to the warrant requirement originally justified by exigent circumstances to lose its emergency characteristic as the exception develops. A prime example of this development has been the automobile exception, which no longer can be linked fairly to any concept of exigency. In the course of the automobile exception's development, moreover, the scope of the search has expanded as well. Presently, the automobile exception allows for a search of the entire vehicle of the same scope as would be permitted if authorized by a warrant.[26]

That same expansive growth has not marked the development of searches justified by emergency situations. The scope of these searches has remained linked to the nature and scope of the emergency; the search has not been allowed to become a fishing expedition. Once the actual emergency is alleviated, and the danger associated with it has been relieved, the authority to search without a warrant terminates. There is a line of cases begun in 1978 and strengthened in 1985 in which the Supreme Court has insisted on maintaining reasonable controls on warrantless searches justified by exigent circumstances. In these cases, the Court has required law enforcement authorities to comply with the warrant requirement once the exigency that justified the initial intrusion has passed. This treatment is

---

mere presence of firearms or destructible contraband does not create exigent circumstances).

[22]Cf., State v Howard, 75 App(3d) 760, 600 NE(2d) 809 (Pike 1991); State v Jenkins, No. C-940840, 1995 WL 366344 (1st Dist Ct App, Hamilton, 6-21-95) (the government cannot justify a warrantless search on the basis of exigent circumstances of its own making).

[23]Fairborn v Douglas, 49 App(3d) 20, 550 NE(2d) 201 (Greene 1988).

[24]State v Hickson, 69 App(3d) 278, 590 NE(2d) 779 (Cuyahoga 1990).

[25]Cf., Welsh v Wisconsin, 466 US 740, 104 SCt 2091, 80 LEd(2d) 732 (1984).

[26]See Text Ch 12, Automobile Exception to the Warrant Requirement.

peculiarly unique in light of the Court's willingness to expand other exceptions to the warrant requirement.

The emergency concept was defined in *Michigan v Tyler*,[27] which involved the search of a burned building. The fire had raged through most of the night and was not brought under control until the early hours of the morning. A brief search conducted at the time the fire was extinguished turned up evidence of arson, but smoke and darkness prevented a thorough search at that time. The search was resumed later that morning, and more evidence of arson was found. There were no further searches for three weeks, at which time officers returned to the scene, again without a search warrant, and found additional evidence of arson. The defendant contended that all three warrantless searches were unlawful. The Supreme Court drew careful distinctions in ruling on the three searches, upholding the first two searches but striking down the third.

The Court held that the original entry into the building was justified by the exigency of the fire. Justice Stewart wrote:

> Indeed, it would defy reason to suppose that firemen must secure a warrant or consent before entering a burning structure to put out a blaze. And once in the building for that purpose, firefighters may seize evidence of arson that is in plain view.[28]

Moreover, the Court held that no warrant was needed for the second entry of the building later that morning, finding it a continuation of the initial entry. The Stewart opinion's reasoning focused on the additional duty of public officials to determine the cause of a fire's occurrence as concomitant to their duty to extinguish the blaze. Stewart contended that finding a fire's cause will help to prevent its recurrence. The intrusion for this purpose must be limited to a "reasonable time."

The third entry, three weeks later, was unlawful because, while there obviously was a causal relationship to the fire, the Court rejected the argument that the delayed entry was related to the exigency caused by the fire. Consequently, the third search conducted without a warrant was not justified by the emergency exception and, therefore, was unlawful.

In *Michigan v Clifford*,[29] the Court clarified the need for a warrant, as well as the type of warrant required, following a fire in a residence, indicating that the authority to enter the home without a warrant ends with the emergency. The Court said:

> The constitutionality of warrantless and nonconsensual entries onto fire-damaged premises, therefore, normally turns on several factors: whether there are legitimate privacy interests in the fire-damaged property that are protected by the Fourth Amendment; whether exigent circumstances justify the government intrusion regardless of any reasonable expectations of privacy; and whether the object of the search is to determine the cause of the fire or to gather evidence of criminal activity.[30] the

---

[27]Michigan v Tyler, 436 US 499, 98 SCt 1942, 56 LEd(2d) 486 (1978).
[28]Michigan v Tyler, 436 US 499, 509, 98 SCt 1942, 56 LEd(2d) 486 (1978).
[29]Michigan v Clifford, 464 US 287, 104 SCt 641, 78 LEd(2d) 477 (1984).
[30]Michigan v Clifford, 464 US 287, 292, 104 SCt 641, 78 LEd(2d) 477 (1984).

When this standard is applied, a burning building creates an exigency that justifies a warrantless entry by fire officials to fight the blaze. Further, the Court held in *Tyler* that once in the building, fire officials need no warrant to remain for a reasonable time in order to investigate the cause of the blaze after it has been extinguished. While firefighters are present at the scene, investigators need no warrant to enter and conduct an investigation.[31] However, if reasonable privacy expectations remain in the building or are restored, further entries for investigation purposes, once fire officials have left the scene, must be made pursuant to a warrant or identification of a new exigency. *Tyler* held that an analysis of remaining expectations of privacy do not commence until after firefighters have left the scene.

However, it was implied in *State v Newcome*[32] that a better analysis focuses on a totality of the circumstances, rather than solely on reentry. In *Newcome*, where firefighters had never left the scene and were seeking remaining hot spots and the cause of the fire, illegal drugs, money, and weapons found in plain view by firefighters were admissible. When a warrant is required, the object of the search determines the type of warrant required. If the primary purpose is to identify the cause and origin of a fire, an administrative warrant will suffice. An administrative warrant may be obtained merely upon a showing that a fire of undetermined origin recently occurred on the premises. If, however, the primary object of the search is to gather evidence of criminal activity, a criminal search warrant is required and may be obtained only on a showing of probable cause.[33] These distinctions may seem pedantic and hypertechnical, but they actually serve as a practical balance accommodating legitimate law enforcement needs and individual privacy interests. Consequently, when a search to discover the cause of a fire, whether immediately after the fire without a warrant or with benefit of an administrative warrant, uncovers evidence of arson, the investigators must withdraw and obtain a conventional search warrant, after securing the premises, in order to continue the criminal investigation.

The rejection of a murder scene exception to the warrant, requirement, which would permit police responding to a report of a homicide to remain on the scene and conduct a full search of the premises for evidence, remains the strongest evidence of the Supreme Court's unwillingness to carve a broad, general exception out of the emergency doctrine. In *Mincey v Arizona*[34] and *Thompson v Louisiana*,[35] state officials attempted to create a "murder scene" exception under the rubric of exigent circumstances. In *Mincey*, a police officer was shot and killed during a police raid. The police then conducted a search of the apartment that lasted for four days. In the later *Thompson* case, police responded to a call for help and, at the scene, found the defendant unconscious apparently from a drug overdose and her

---

[31]State v Coomer, 20 App(3d) 264, 20 OBR 326, 485 NE(2d) 808 (Warren 1984).

[32]State v Newcome, 41 App(3d) 51, 534 NE(2d) 370 (Crawford 1987).

[33]Michigan v Clifford, 464 US 287, 294, 104 SCt 641, 78 LEd(2d) 477 (1984).

[34]Mincey v Arizona, 437 US 385, 98 SCt 2408, 57 LEd(2d) 290 (1978), cert denied 469 US 1040, 105 SCt 521, 83 LEd(2d) 409 (1984), modified sub nom Arizona v Hicks, 480 US 321, 107 SCt 1149, 94 LEd(2d) 347 (1987).

[35]Thompson v Louisiana, 469 US 17, 105 SCt 409, 83 LEd(2d) 246 (1984).

husband dead in another room. Homicide detectives arrived at the scene and conducted a two-hour search.

In both cases, the Supreme Court agreed that murder creates an emergency situation but rejected the contention that the emergency continues beyond the dissipation of any danger. The Court insisted that the right of the police to conduct a warrantless search "must be strictly circumscribed by the exigencies which justify its initiation."[36] While police may make a warrantless entry onto a murder scene to render immediate aid to victims and may also conduct a warrantless search for suspects, any further search must be conducted by warrant or fall within one of the established exceptions to the warrant requirement. In *Thompson*, the Court acknowledged that the two-hour search on the same day as the murder was not nearly as broad as the four-day search in *Mincey*. Nonetheless, the Court said such a search "remains a significant intrusion on petitioner's privacy and therefore may only be conducted subject to the restraints ... of the Fourth Amendment."[37] In *Thompson*, the defendant had called for help. The Court said the defendant's call did not constitute a consent other than for the initial entry, nor did it convert her home into the type of public place for which no warrant would be necessary.

The Franklin County Court of Appeals attempted to distinguish *Thompson* in *State v Sage*[38] but in reality rejected the Supreme Court's limiting principles on the scope of searches accomplished under the exigent circumstances exception. In *Sage*, rescue units found the defendant wounded, lying in bed in his apartment next to a dead woman. On the way to the hospital, the defendant told the rescue squad of a suicide pact. At a suppression hearing, the defendant moved to suppress all evidence found at the scene on the ground that the evidence was discovered after the police were no longer assisting anyone at the scene. The items were discovered during a search of the area by the Columbus Police Department Crime Scene Search Unit "over the course of several hours after police initially responded to the scene."[39] The trial court granted the motion regarding bullets found lodged in the wall behind the bed and in the mattress. The trial court, however, admitted other evidence found in and around the bed and the chest of drawers in the bedroom.

The court of appeals sought to distinguish *Thompson* and *Sage*: in *Thompson*, the police had to look into a chest of drawers and remove a letter from a wastebasket, take it out of an envelope, and read it; in *Sage*, the evidence found was in plain view even though it was collected hours after the police had stopped rendering emergency assistance and the defendant had been removed and transported to the hospital. To hold otherwise,

---

[36]Mincey v Arizona, 437 US 385, 393, 98 SCt 2408, 57 LEd(2d) 290 (1978), cert denied 469 US 1040, 105 SCt 521, 83 LEd(2d) 409 (1984), modified sub nom Arizona v Hicks, 480 US 321, 107 SCt 1149, 94 LEd(2d) 347 (1987).

[37]Thompson v Louisiana, 469 US 17, 21, 105 SCt 409, 83 LEd(2d) 246 (1984).

[38]State v Sage, No. 85AP-596, 1986 WL 5419 (10th Dist Ct App, Franklin, 5-6-86).

[39]State v Sage, No. 85AP-596, at 21, 1986 WL 5419 (10th Dist Ct App, Franklin, 5-6-86).

the court said, "would cause law enforcement officials to focus their primary attention on the collection of incriminating evidence rather than attending to the need of victims at the scene"[40] and would result in "possible improper collection of evidence by those inadequately trained [i.e. EMS attendants?] for such purpose, to the detriment of both the state and the accused."[41] The problem with the offered rationale is that it stretches the rule to avoid police misconduct, assuming that the police will violate the rule if not accommodated.

This approach underestimates the professionalism of police engaged in emergency care situations by assuming that they will disregard their primary obligation, to secure care for victims, in favor of maximizing the windfall opportunity to gather criminal evidence. Moreover, the facts in *Sage* fell clearly within the *Thompson* rule. Granted the search in *Thompson* was more intrusive; however, the case did not turn on that fact. The rule enunciated in *Thompson* precludes the continued warrantless presence of the police under the aegis of the exigent circumstances exception once the emergency is dissipated, regardless of whether it is to collect evidence that was seen during the emergency or to examine evidence for the first time even if it was in plain view during the emergency. In *Sage* as in *Thompson,* the police should have secured the premises and obtained a search warrant, which would have been readily forthcoming. The fact that a warrant is readily obtainable does not excuse searching the premises or seizing the evidence without it.

Some general principles about the emergency doctrine can be extrapolated from *Tyler* and *Mincey.* Exigent circumstances create justification for limited warrantless searches. The duration of the intrusion and the scope of the search are governed by the constitutional command of reasonableness, which will be evaluated in terms of the emergency.[42] Once the emergency conditions have been alleviated, further intrusion must be sanctioned by a warrant. Any other interpretation of the emergency exception would create another general exception that would swallow the Fourth Amendment principle that warrantless intrusions are per se unreasonable. Furthermore, searches that extend beyond the scope of the actual emergency lead to an inference that the emergency is serving as a pretext to conduct a warrantless search.[43]

---

[40]State v Sage, No. 85AP-596, at 24, 1986 WL 5419 (10th Dist Ct App, Franklin, 5-6-86).

[41]State v Sage, No. 85AP-596, at 24, 1986 WL 5419 (10th Dist Ct App, Franklin, 5-6-86).

[42]State v Oliver, 91 App(3d) 607, 632 NE(2d) 1382 (Wayne 1993) (search of defendant's vehicle for weapons was justified where police had received a report that defendant was contemplating suicide and that defendant had two weapons with him in the car).

[43]See, e.g., State v Jemison, 9 App(2d) 227, 223 NE(2d) 904 (Franklin 1967), reversed by 14 OS(2d) 47, 236 NE(2d) 538 (1968), cert denied 393 US 943, 89 SCt 312, 21 LEd(2d) 280 (1968).

10.04 Hot pursuit

The most common example of exigent circumstances justifying a warrantless intrusion occurs when police are chasing a suspect and that pursuit leads them into a building. In *Warden, Maryland Penitentiary v Hayden*,[44] police were summoned by two taxi drivers who claimed that they had followed a suspect who had robbed their company. The police were admitted to the house by the wife of the suspect, and in the course of their search for the suspect, the officers found clothing in a washing machine, linked to the robber, and weapons in a bathroom. The Supreme Court held that police may seize weapons as well as evidence that they discover while in hot pursuit of a suspected criminal.

Even though the officers did not witness the crime or observe the suspect enter the house, the Court felt that the doctrine was broad enough to cover a situation where police have probable cause to believe that the house contains a suspect whom they are hotly pursuing for a recently committed crime. Hot pursuit commonly involves a chase but it need not be an extended hue and cry in and about public streets.[45] It involves immediate and continuous pursuit from the moment probable cause arose to arrest.[46] At any time the pursuit is discontinued, even for a few minutes while the pursuing officer awaits back-up assistance, the authority to enter in hot pursuit is terminated.[47]

A person may not thwart an arrest by fleeing into a private place. In *United States v Santana*,[48] as police approached a woman standing in a doorway whom they had probable cause to arrest, she retreated into the vestibule. Police followed and made the arrest. The Supreme Court held that a suspect could not thwart a lawful arrest by retreating from a public to a private place to evade police. In both *Hayden* and *Santana*, there was actual pursuit, which would satisfy the exigent circumstance requirement for a warrantless entry of a dwelling to effect an arrest.[49] Exigent circumstances do not exist to avoid the warrant requirement in the absence of actual pursuit. In *State v Howard*,[50] police entered the defendant's trailer without a warrant after receiving a tip that a fugitive was visiting the defendant and after observing the fugitive through the trailer window. The Pike County Court of Appeals rejected the state's claim that the entry was in hot pursuit

---

[44]Warden, Maryland Penitentiary v Hayden, 387 US 294, 87 SCt 1642, 18 LEd(2d) 782 (1967).

[45]United States v Santana, 427 US 38, 96 SCt 2406, 49 LEd(2d) 300 (1976).

[46]State v Rouse, 53 App(3d) 48, 557 NE(2d) 1227 (Franklin 1988).

[47]State v Hablutzel, Nos. C-870789 et al., 1988 WL 125019 (1st Dist Ct App, Hamilton, 11-23-88).

[48]United States v Santana, 427 US 38, 96 SCt 2406, 49 LEd(2d) 300 (1976).

[49]See Payton v New York, 445 US 573, 100 SCt 1371, 63 LEd(2d) 639 (1980) (arrest warrant needed to enter dwelling absent exigent circumstances); Steagald v United States, 451 US 204, 101 SCt 1642, 68 LEd(2d) 38 (1981) (search warrant needed to enter residence to arrest nonresident absent exigent circumstances); State v Thompson, 72 Misc(2d) 39, 655 NE(2d) 835 (CP, Lucas 1995) (officers are not validly in hot pursuit of a defendant after they approach a house seeking consent to enter and search and the defendant fled from the porch into the house); see also Text 5.04, Warrant necessary to enter a dwelling to make an arrest.

[50]State v Howard, 75 App(3d) 760, 600 NE(2d) 809 (Pike 1991).

because the fugitive was not in a public place when first observed, nor was the arrest set in motion in a public place. Nor may police enter an apartment in order to prevent destruction of evidence by a defendant whom they have probable cause to arrest where police made no effort to prevent him from entering the apartment.[51]

CROSS REFERENCES

Text 19.03

---

[51]State v Brooks, No. 94APA03-386, 1995 WL 390935 (10th Dist Ct App, Franklin, 6-27-95).

Chapter 11

Search Incident to Arrest

11.01   Introduction

Except for searches conducted with a warrant, the only other type of search known in colonial America was incident to arrest.[1] The Fourth Amendment contains no mention of warrantless searches because the attention of the framers focused on the abuses of the warrant prior to the Revolution.

Most searches in the United States are conducted without benefit of a search warrant and are incident to an arrest. The Supreme Court, in a long line of cases, has upheld warrantless searches incident to arrest and made them subject to Fourth Amendment requirements.[2] The two principal issues affecting the constitutionality of a search incident to arrest are (1) the legality of the arrest and (2) the scope of the search.

11.02   Validity of the arrest

A search incident to arrest need not be supported by independent proba- ble cause to believe that the arrestee has a weapon or evidence of a crime on his person. The right to conduct the search flows automatically from the arrest; consequently, the critical issue is the legality of the arrest. Since most arrests also take place without a warrant, significant judicial review of the facts and circumstances that gave rise to probable cause for the arrest will not occur until there is a motion to suppress the evidence found during the incidental search. The reviewing court, then, should carefully examine the claim of preexisting probable cause to ensure that justification for the search existed before its inception and that the fruit of the search is not subtly offered as the justification for the arrest and the search itself. In *State v Block*,[3] the Clermont County Court of Appeals carefully reviewed the state's claim that an informant's tip provided probable cause, justifying the arrest and subsequent search. The court concluded that the tip was insuffi- ciently verified and said, "Any red-haired female in the vicinity would have

---

[1]See generally Grano, *Rethinking the Fourth Amendment Warrant Requirement,* 19 Am Crim L Rev 603 (1982).

[2]Draper v United States, 358 US 307, 79 SCt 329, 3 LEd(2d) 327 (1959).

[3]State v Block, 67 App(3d) 497, 587 NE(2d) 858 (Clermont 1990).

been subject to a search that night."[4] The court's conclusion was strengthened by the arresting officer's testimony at the suppression hearing when he admitted that if no cocaine had been found in the defendant's purse, she would not have been arrested.

The general proposition is that the arrest must precede the search[5] to ensure the valid basis for the initial intrusion. Probable cause to arrest must exist prior to the search and not be predicated on evidence that is found during the search. A search prior to arrest may not then justify the arrest.[6] Otherwise, the arrest would become incident to the search as occurred in *Smith v Ohio*,[7] prompting the United States Supreme Court to lecture the Ohio Supreme Court and to rule in favor of a defendant arguing that his Fourth Amendment rights were violated. The Ohio Supreme Court said that the search of the paper bag in that case was "contemporaneous with [the defendant's] arrest [and] was justified by the need to prevent the destruction of evidence of the crime."[8] In the abstract that argument would have found a sympathetic ear other than the fact, which the US Supreme Court pointed out, that no probable cause to arrest existed until the officer looked into the paper bag and saw that it contained contraband. *Smith* can be distinguished from two Ohio appellate court cases where the courts upheld searches but did not make the fatal mistake made in *Smith*.

In *State v Ector*,[9] the Franklin County Court of Appeals rejected a defendant's claim that the search incident to arrest preceded his arrest and served as justification for the arrest. The court pointed out that the officer had probable cause to arrest prior to the search because the defendant had thrown an object onto the ground and identified it to the officer as a rock of cocaine. Similarly, in *State v Rainey*,[10] the defendant claimed that the search could not be incident to arrest since he was ordered to remove the crack from his pocket prior to the arrest. The Montgomery County Court of Appeals rejected the argument, concluding that if probable cause to arrest without a warrant exists prior to the search, it is immaterial that the search incident to arrest actually precedes the arrest. The key is the prior existence of probable cause and that the fruit of the search not provide the justification for the arrest.

The requirements have been relaxed somewhat, provided that the purpose of the rule is satisfied. A search of a person undertaken prior to arrest

---

[4]State v Block, 67 App(3d) 497, 501, 587 NE(2d) 858 (Clermont 1990).

[5]Sibron v New York, 392 US 40, 88 SCt 1889, 20 LEd(2d) 917 (1968); State v Younts, 92 App(3d) 708, 637 NE(2d) 64 (Madison 1993), appeal dismissed 69 OS(3d) 1436, 632 NE(2d) 520 (1994) (search incident to arrest invalid where arrest occurred after a search of defendant's person and after the officer had decided to search the vehicle).

[6]State v Gaddis, 35 App(2d) 15, 299 NE(2d) 304 (Butler 1973).

[7]Smith v Ohio, 494 US 541, 110 SCt 1288, 108 LEd(2d) 464 (1990) (per curiam).

[8]State v Smith, 45 OS(3d) 255, 544 NE(2d) 239 (1989), reversed by 494 US 541, 110 SCt 1288, 108 LEd(2d) 464 (1990).

[9]State v Ector, No. 90AP-1093, 1991 WL 82046 (10th Dist Ct App, Franklin, 5-16-91).

[10]State v Rainey, No. 11380, 1989 WL 73985 (2d Dist Ct App, Montgomery, 7-6-89).

qualifies as a search incident to arrest if the formal arrest follows immediately and is not grounded on evidence uncovered during the search.[11]

In *Cupp v Murphy*,[12] a limited search of a person was upheld without an arrest preceding or immediately following the search. The Court found that the warrantless taking of fingernail scrapings from a suspect who had appeared voluntarily at the police station for questioning concerning the strangulation of his wife was constitutionally permissible. The holding was based on the very limited nature of the search and its necessity "to preserve the highly evanescent evidence they found under [defendant's] fingernails."[13] Emphasizing the limited nature of the search and the exigencies involved, the Court stressed that it was not opening the door to full searches. The exigency that justified the warrantless search in *Cupp* is likely to be strictly enforced when the defendant is not arrested immediately after the search. In other instances, the search may precede the arrest provided probable cause already exists and the arrest follows immediately thereafter. So long as the court carefully reviews the probable cause on the facts known prior to the search, the relaxation of the rule does not seriously threaten Fourth Amendment protection.

The legitimacy of the arrest is critical to ensure that the arrest was justified and not a pretext to conduct a search. Pretext arrests are illegal, and the fruits of searches incident to pretextual arrests must be suppressed.[14]

11.03 Purposes and scope of a search incident to arrest

As an exception to the warrant requirement, a search incident to arrest is permissible because societal needs are sufficient to outweigh the reasons for requiring pre-approval of searches by a neutral magistrate.[15] Although all of the exemptions from the warrant requirement fall under the heading of exigent circumstances, the rationale and permissible scope of warrantless intrusions differ depending on the underlying societal needs justifying the exception.

The initial intrusion and the scope of an incidental search should be governed and limited by its legitimate purposes. An unlimited incidental search is no longer uncommon and threatens to swallow the rule requiring a warrant to conduct a search. The purposes governing incidental searches were set forth in the landmark decision of *Chimel v California*.[16] In *Chimel,* following the arrest of the defendant in his home, police proceeded to

---

[11]Rawlings v Kentucky, 448 US 98, 100 SCt 2556, 65 LEd(2d) 633 (1980); see also State v Fahy, 49 App(3d) 160, 551 NE(2d) 1311 (Henry 1988), appeal dismissed by 40 OS(3d) 704, 534 NE(2d) 841 (1988); State v Farndon, 22 App(3d) 31, 22 OBR 107, 488 NE(2d) 894 (Cuyahoga 1984).

[12]Cupp v Murphy, 412 US 291, 93 SCt 2000, 36 LEd(2d) 900 (1973).

[13]Cupp v Murphy, 412 US 291, 296, 93 SCt 2000, 36 LEd(2d) 900 (1973).

[14]For a discussion of legal standards applicable to proving pretext arrests, see Text 11.05, Pretext arrests.

[15]Arkansas v Sanders, 442 US 753, 99 SCt 2586, 61 LEd(2d) 235 (1979), overruled by California v Acevedo, 500 US 565, 111 SCt 1982, 114 LEd(2d) 619 (1991).

[16]Chimel v California, 395 US 752, 89 SCt 2034, 23 LEd(2d) 685 (1969).

search the entire three-bedroom house, attic, garage, and a small workshop. The Supreme Court rejected the authorities relied on by the state of California and proceeded to analyze the justifications for searches incident to arrest and limit their scope to the satisfaction of those purposes. Justice Stewart wrote the majority opinion, creating an analytical framework that works in application and is easily understood, although not always accepted by courts and police. Its premise is that warrantless searches incident to arrest are allowed only because of important societal reasons that justify bypassing the warrant process, and the permissible scope of the warrantless search should be just broad enough to satisfy those purposes and no broader.

The primary justification for a search incident to arrest, according to the *Chimel* Court, is to remove any weapons that an arrestee might use to resist arrest or effect his escape. Otherwise, the arrestee might endanger the police officer and thwart the arrest. Consequently, exemptions to the warrant requirement are most often necessary (1) to avoid the possibility of harm to the police officer, and (2) to ensure that the arrestee is taken into custody. Also, the Court deemed it eminently reasonable to permit the search to extend to evidence that the arrestee might seek to destroy. Extending incidental searches to evidence of the crime for which the defendant is arrested, or for that matter other crimes, does not open the door to an investigatory search for evidence. It allows a search only to deprive the defendant of the opportunity to destroy evidence.

Having defined the purposes underlying the exception, the Court set forth its limits. Under its definition of the purposes of the rule, the Court found it axiomatic that a search of the person is permissible.

For a search beyond the person, the subject of controversy in *Chimel,* the Court set forth the following standard:

> And the area into which an arrestee might reach in order to grab a weapon or evidentiary item must, of course, be governed by a like rule. A gun on a table or in a drawer in front of one who is arrested can be as dangerous to the arresting officer as one concealed in the clothing of the person arrested. There is ample justification, therefore, for a search of the arrestee's person and the area "within his immediate control"—construing that phrase to mean the area from within which he might gain possession of a weapon or destructible evidence.[17]

This standard, setting temporal and spacial limitations, is necessary in order to maintain the distinction between a search for evidence requiring a warrant and a permissible warrantless search incident to arrest.

The brilliance of the *Chimel* test rested in its simplicity. It affirmed the need for warrantless searches incident to arrest, identified the historical and legitimate reasons for the exception, and then drew limitations that fulfilled its purposes consistent with the traditional Fourth Amendment jurisprudence, which requires that exceptions to the warrant clause be limited and well delineated. To guarantee that the scope of an incidental search be less broad than a search with a warrant, which is supported by independent

---

[17]Chimel v California, 395 US 752, 763, 89 SCt 2034, 23 LEd(2d) 685 (1969).

probable cause and has the benefit of being reviewed by a judge prior to the intrusion, *Chimel* set temporal and spacial limitations, which can be applied to the facts in each case.

Despite its simplicity, the *Chimel* test ran into difficulty in the lower courts. While the Supreme Court was not explicit as to when the "control" of an arrestee should be measured, it seemed abundantly clear that the measurement should be taken immediately before the search, rather than immediately preceding the arrest. If the control test was set forth to limit the scope of incidental searches to those purposes that gave rise to the exception, it became incumbent upon the courts to determine what is necessary to search to protect the police officer and prevent the arrestee from having access to evidence. The arrestee's control might expand or contract depending on the facts of the particular arrest at the moment of the search. If an arrestee wishes to retrieve a coat or purse before accompanying the arresting officers, control will extend to those items and the area where the arrestee must secure the items, even though it was not within grabbing or reaching distance at the moment of arrest.

Similarly, the scope of a search should be narrower a few moments after an arrest than it would have been immediately upon arrest once the arrestee has been neutralized and unable to reach for evidence. Lower courts, however, were reluctant to apply the narrowing test, permitting incidental searches to extend to areas outside the reaching or grabbing distance of an accused. One court said that "it is not at all clear that the 'grabbing distance' authorized in the *Chimel* case is conditioned upon the arrested person's continued capacity 'to grab.' "[18] The reluctance of lower courts to apply the *Chimel* standards resulted in distortions of the control test. The Supreme Court added fuel to the fire in 1981, in an opinion by Justice Stewart, the author of the *Chimel* opinion. There, the Court redefined the control test for searches of automobiles incident to the arrest of a recent occupant.[19]

The Supreme Court's penchant for "bright-line" rules in the last decade also has had the effect of diminishing the importance of the *Chimel* standard. Following an arrest, the police may conduct an incidental search whether there is any cause to fear for the officers' safety or whether evidence of the crime for which the arrest was made could possibly exist.[20]

11.04   Search of the person incident to arrest

(A) In general

Search of the defendant was not raised as an issue in *Chimel v California*,[21] but the Court considered it a foregone conclusion because it met the purposes underlying the incidental search exception. They found it neces-

---

[18]People v Floyd, 26 NY(2d) 558, 563, 312 NYS(2d) 193, 260 NE(2d) 815 (1970).
[19]New York v Belton, 453 US 454, 101 SCt 2860, 69 LEd(2d) 768 (1981); see also Text 11.10, Search of an automobile incident to arrest.
[20]See United States v Robinson, 414 US 218, 94 SCt 467, 38 LEd(2d) 427 (1973); Gustafson v Florida, 414 US 260, 94 SCt 488, 38 LEd(2d) 456 (1973).
[21]Chimel v California, 395 US 752, 89 SCt 2034, 23 LEd(2d) 685 (1969).

sary for police to protect their safety by disarming an arrestee, and any evidence on the person of the arrestee definitely remains in his control. Several years later, the Supreme Court addressed the remaining issues: (1) whether a full search of the person may occur for any arrestable offense, and (2) whether an officer may conduct a full search for evidence following an arrest for an offense for which no evidence could conceivably exist. Left untreated by the Court was the issue of how to protect against pretext arrests.

(B) The offense

In *United States v Robinson*,[22] a police officer stopped a vehicle whose driver, the officer had cause to believe, was operating the vehicle after the revocation of his operator's permit. Under the law of the jurisdiction, the offense carried a mandatory minimum jail sentence. The jurisdiction's written police procedures required that the offender be taken into custody for the offense and the officer conduct a full field-type search including an examination of the contents of all pockets. Pursuant to these regulations, the arresting officer searched the defendant and found a crumpled-up cigarette package in the left breast pocket of the defendant's coat. The officer opened the pack and found gelatin capsules containing a white powder that the officer believed, and analysis confirmed, to be heroin.

The Court of Appeals for the District of Columbia reversed the conviction for possession on the ground that the evidence had been obtained in violation of defendant's Fourth Amendment rights. The court reasoned that since no further evidence of driving with a revoked license could be found during a search of the arrestee, only a limited pat-down search for weapons could be justified.

A majority of the Supreme Court disagreed. In an opinion by Justice Rehnquist, the majority traced the history of the exception and found that the authorities tended to support a broad interpretation of the power to search incident to arrest. The Court labeled the assumption that persons arrested for the offense of driving while their licenses have been revoked are less likely to be possessed of dangerous weapons than are those arrested for other crimes as "speculative." The potential for danger following the taking of a suspect into custody and transporting him to the police station is an adequate basis, the Court found, for treating all custodial arrests alike for purposes of search justification. In Ohio, a full search incident to arrest is permissible following a lawful custodial arrest for a traffic offense.[23]

Further, the Court recognized no merit in requiring an officer to justify his action in a particular case: "A custodial arrest of a suspect based on probable cause is a reasonable intrusion under the Fourth Amendment; that intrusion being lawful, a search incident to the arrest requires no additional justification."[24] Given the fact of the custodial arrest, the Court deemed it insignificant that the officer did not indicate any subjective fear of the defendant, nor suspect that the defendant was armed.

---

[22]United States v Robinson, 414 US 218, 94 SCt 467, 38 LEd(2d) 427 (1973).
[23]State v Ferman, 58 OS(2d) 216, 389 NE(2d) 843 (1979).
[24]United States v Robinson, 414 US 218, 235, 94 SCt 467, 38 LEd(2d) 427 (1973).

(C) Search for evidence

Robinson, of course, involved a search that went beyond looking for weapons. First, no evidence of driving while one's license is revoked could exist. Second, once the officer had seized the cigarette package from the defendant's pocket, it was out of the defendant's "control."

The improbable existence of evidence of the crime for which the defendant was arrested did not affect the Court's judgment: the authority to search incident to a lawful arrest is not affected "by the absence of probable fruits or further evidence of the particular crime for which the arrest is made."[25] Consequently, any "custodial arrest" provides all of the justification necessary to conduct a full search of the person of the arrestee.

Even though the only rationale available for a search in a case like *Robinson,* where no evidence of the crime could exist, is the removal of weapons that the arrestee might use to effect his escape or harm the officer, Justice Rehnquist acknowledged no need to limit the search even though the officer is assured that the arrestee is unarmed. This unwillingness extended the scope of the exception beyond fulfillment of the limited purposes that justify incidental searches as an exception to the warrant requirement. Justice Rehnquist addressed this issue obliquely when he said that a full search of the person not only is an exception to the warrant requirement, but also is a "reasonable" search under the Fourth Amendment. By invoking *reasonableness* outside the context of exceptions to the warrant requirement, he was applying his philosophy that the reasonableness of a search should be considered in the abstract and not limited by the warrant requirement. That view was the position explicitly rejected by the *Chimel* majority.

The dissent in *Robinson* also raised the issue involved in the officer's opening of the cigarette pack after it was removed from the defendant's control. That problem was faced in *United States v Edwards,*[26] where the defendant's clothing was taken from him ten hours after he had been arrested and paint chips on the clothing were found to match paint chips from a window at the scene of the crime. The *Edwards* Court found the search of defendant's clothing to be within the penumbra of a search incident to arrest. Again applying an abstract test to determine the reasonableness of the delayed search, the Court set forth the following rule:

> [O]nce the accused is lawfully arrested and is in custody, the effects in his possession at the place of detention that were subject to search at the time and place of his arrest may lawfully be searched and seized without a warrant even though a substantial period of time has elapsed between the arrest and subsequent administrative processing, on the one hand, and the taking of property for use as evidence, on the other. This is true where the clothing or effects are immediately seized upon arrival at the jail, held under the defendant's name in the "property room" of the jail, and at a later time searched and taken for use at the subsequent criminal trial. The result is the same where the property is

---

[25]United States v Robinson, 414 US 218, 234, 94 SCt 467, 38 LEd(2d) 427 (1973).
[26]United States v Edwards, 415 US 800, 94 SCt 1234, 39 LEd(2d) 771 (1974); see also United States v Edwards, 497 F(2d) 925 (1974).

not physically taken from the defendant until sometime after his incarceration.[27]

The "bright-line" rules set forth in *Robinson* and *Edwards* together create an enormous exception to the *Chimel* standard. The search of a person and his effects incident to a lawful arrest is not confined to fulfillment of the justifications that gave rise to the exception to the warrant requirement, nor is it limited in time, nor is it subject to the control test. While fitting these searches within the rubric created by a search incident to arrest, the Supreme Court was creating, in fact, a new exception. The full breadth of the new rule, however, remains clouded. Although *Edwards* extended the authority to "effects in [the defendant's] immediate possession," the Supreme Court has been troubled and sent conflicting signals when those effects are packages or luggage.[28] Whatever categories are assigned to other containers, purses have generally been included automatically as part of a search incident to arrest.[29]

Edwards does make it clear, however, that a delayed search of the arrestee and his effects at the booking or pursuant to an inventory (either to safeguard the arrestee's property or prevent contraband from being introduced into the jail) is not limited in scope to those purposes. The *Robinson-Edwards* rationales seem equally applicable to physical examinations conducted at the police station such as strip searches, internal examinations, and other tests involving routine bodily functions. Naturally, the manner in which the particular intrusion is conducted and the regularity of the procedure will determine the reasonableness of the search in each case. An arrestee at the police station is subject to a full search of his person incident to arrest as well as of objects associated with his person under *Edwards*, and an inventory of any other items that somehow fall outside of the broad search authorized under *Edwards*. The inventory may not be a pretext for an investigatory search and must be conducted according to written guidelines.[30] A routine station house inventory is permissible even following custodial arrest for offenses as minor as disorderly intoxication.[31] The degree of permissible intrusion is illustrated in *State v Bush*,[32] where the court held that a strip search as part of an inventory was not unreasonable prior to placing the defendant in a holding cell where he had the opportunity to turn over items and refused and where a frisk, prior to the strip search, revealed objects on the defendant's person.

(D) Use of force to retrieve evidence

Rarely discussed is what a police officer may do when an arrestee tries to secret evidence upon his person at the moment of arrest. The issue was addressed by the United States Supreme Court nearly half a century ago

---

[27]United States v Edwards, 415 US 800, 807-808, 94 SCt 1234, 39 LEd(2d) 771 (1974).

[28]See Text 11.11, Search of packages and other receptacles incident to arrest.

[29]State v Mathews, 46 OS(2d) 72, 346 NE(2d) 151 (1976).

[30]Illinois v Lafayette, 462 US 640, 103 SCt 2605, 77 LEd(2d) 65 (1983); Florida v Wells, 495 US 1, 110 SCt 1632, 109 LEd(2d) 1 (1990).

[31]State v Raines, No. 1426, 1988 WL 125031 (4th Dist Ct App, Ross, 11-16-88).

[32]State v Bush, 65 App(3d) 560, 584 NE(2d) 1253 (Cuyahoga 1989).

prior to imposition of the Fourth Amendment exclusionary rule on the states under the Fourteenth Amendment. In *Rochin v California*,[33] the notorious "stomach pumping" case, the Supreme Court found the state's attempts to retrieve evidence swallowed by the arrestee to shock the conscience of the Court and violate the Due Process guarantee of the Fourteenth Amendment. In *Rochin*, police officers jumped upon the defendant and unsuccessfully attempted to extract the drug evidence. When that effort failed, the officers handcuffed the defendant, took him to a hospital, where a doctor forced an emetic solution into the defendant's stomach against his will extracting two capsules containing morphine.

Since *Rochin*, it takes a great deal more to shock the Supreme Court's and other courts' consciences.[34] In a case remarkably like *Rochin*, the Cuyahoga County Court of Appeals upheld the actions of Cleveland police officers who applied a choke hold to a suspect in order to forcibly search the suspect's mouth and retrieve suspected drugs which he was attempting to swallow. The appellate court reversed the trial court's granting of a motion to suppress, notwithstanding the trial court's findings that the methods were life threatening, that there were less intrusive means available to obtain the evidence, and that the police acted without first giving the suspect the opportunity to open his mouth.[35]

(E) Medical intrusions into the body

Medical intrusions into the body are far more serious and will normally require a warrant, except where the procedure is not uncommon, is performed in a reasonable manner, *and* where the delay associated with securing a warrant threatens the destruction of the evidence.[36] Consequently, routine physical tests following an arrest are permissible without a warrant. If the test is not routine and involves a serious intrusion of the arrestee's body, a warrant might be required. Some physical and medical procedures, however, involve such extraordinary intrusions that they are per se unreasonable under the Fourth Amendment and are barred even if authorized by a warrant if they endanger the life or health of the suspect.

In *Winston v Lee*,[37] the US Supreme Court held that a surgical removal of a bullet from a defendant's chest was unreasonable because it would require a general anesthetic, and significant health threats resulting from

---

[33]Rochin v California, 342 US 165, 72 SCt 205, 96 LEd 183 (1952).

[34]See e.g., United States ex rel Guy v McCauley, 385 FSupp 193 (ED Wis 1974) (upholding two inspections of a pregnant woman's vagina by untrained police personnel).

[35]State v Victor, 76 App(3d) 372, 601 NE(2d) 648 (1991), cert denied 113 SCt 292, 121 LEd(2d) 217 (1992).

[36]See Schmerber v California, 384 US 757, 86 SCt 1826, 16 LEd(2d) 908 (1966) (upholding the taking by a physician, at police direction, of a blood sample over the defendant's objection); South Dakota v Neville, 459 US 553, 103 SCt 916, 74 LEd(2d) 748 (1983); United States v Crowder, 543 F(2d) 312 (DC Cir 1976) (holding that the Fourth Amendment rights of the defendant were not violated when the trial court ordered surgical removal of a bullet from the defendant's arm and allowed its admission into evidence), cert denied 429 US 1062, 97 SCt 788, 50 LEd(2d) 779 (1977); see also 2 LaFave, *Search and Seizure* § 4.1(d) (1978).

[37]Winston v Lee, 470 US 753, 105 SCt 1611, 84 LEd(2d) 662 (1985).

the anesthetic were a possibility. The Court further stated that surgical intrusions beneath the skin would have to be analyzed on a case-by-case basis in which the individual's privacy and security are weighed against society's interest in obtaining the evidence. Consequently, even when a warrant is supported by probable cause, a search for evidence may be unjustifiable if it endangers the life and health of the suspect.

In *Winston*, the Court balanced the interests and found for the defendant because the possibility of a health threat was not overcome by the state's interest, which demonstrated little need for the invasion. The state had the victim's account and identification of the defendant as well as additional forensic evidence. Consequently, the Court concluded that a compelled surgical intrusion into the suspect's body was unreasonable under the Fourth Amendment where the surgery would require a general anesthetic, where medical risks were in dispute, and where there is no compelling societal need to obtain evidence in such a manner.

11.05   Pretext arrests

Robinson presented a fact situation where the officer's conduct was controlled by departmental regulations. The arresting officer was required to effect a full custody arrest of a driver whose license had been revoked and to conduct a full search of the person following the arrest. Whether to take the arrestee into custody or issue a summons was not left to the discretion of the police officer. More often, discretion is granted to the police officer to issue a summons when stopping a motorist for an arrest-able offense. In those instances, the search of the person is unlikely for the reasons sanctioned in *Robinson,* i.e., to protect the police officer while transporting the offender to the police station, but is instead a fishing expedition for evidence of other crimes without the benefit of a warrant or probable cause to believe that evidence will be found. When a search is conducted under those circumstances and evidence of another offense is found, the decision to arrest and take the defendant into custody is actually incident to the search rather than the search being incident to the arrest.

The *Robinson* Court emphasized "custodial arrest," but it is virtually impossible to distinguish a custodial arrest from another arrest. Criminal Rule 4(F) authorizes a police officer to issue a summons following an arrest for a misdemeanor. That provision and the rule in *Robinson* work together to permit the officer to search the arrestee and then decide whether to take the arrestee into custody, creating the possibility of a pretextual arrest in order to conduct a search.

In *Robinson's* companion case, *Gustafson v Florida,*[38] that possibility arose when the defendant was arrested for failing to have a driver's license, and no statutory or police regulation required that the arrestee be taken into custody or searched. Nonetheless, the officer conducted a search and found a cigarette box containing marijuana cigarettes on the person of the arrestee. Justice Rehnquist, for the majority, upheld the search and did not

---

[38]Gustafson v Florida, 414 US 260, 94 SCt 488, 38 LEd(2d) 456 (1973).

detect the crucial distinction between the *Gustafson* and *Robinson* facts that is determinative of the constitutional issue. In *Gustafson*, the officer could have issued a summons in lieu of making an arrest and was therefore not compelled to conduct a search. Yet, in creating a general rule, rather than requiring a case-by-case adjudication of the facts to determine the reasons for both the custodial arrest and the search, the Court has made it virtually impossible to make a persuasive claim that there was, in fact, a pretextual arrest for the purpose of conducting a search. Although the Supreme Court has said often, including in *Robinson,* that pretextual arrests are unconstitutional, the unlimited authority recognized in *Robinson-Gustafson* makes it virtually impossible to challenge a pretextual arrest.

The difficulty, of course, lies in proving the pretext unless it is an absolute sham. In *Gustafson*, Justice Stewart acknowledged the almost insurmountable burden on the defense in attempting to prove that an arrest is pretextual. Rather than focus on whether an arrest is pretextual, Justice Stewart suggested that an alternative argument might be made that a custodial arrest that gives rise to the authority to conduct an incidental search for a minor offense is a per se violation of the Fourth Amendment, i.e., unreasonable because there is no need for such an extensive intrusion on a violator's liberty interest. The Stewart suggestion, however, has never been pursued by a litigator in the Supreme Court.

Moreover, the Supreme Court subsequently compounded the difficulty of proving that an arrest was pretextual. In *Scott v United States*,[39] the Supreme Court held that the constitutionality of a search is to be determined by "a standard of objective reasonableness without regard to the underlying intent or motivation of the officers involved." Although *Scott* did not relate directly to the issue of pretextual arrests, the holding appears to render it impossible to prove improper motivation on the part of an officer, absent an admission by the officer, when the custodial arrest is authorized by statute.

There are three different standards to determine whether an arrest is pretextual: (1) a focus on the subjective intent of the officers, (2) a focus on whether the initial seizure was legal (objectively reasonable) regardless of the intent of the officers, and (3) the so-called "reasonable officer" test.[40] There is no clear guidance from state or federal high courts on which standard to use, and conflicting approaches can be found even within the same state appellate districts. Unless and until the Ohio or United States Supreme Court clarifies the situation and adopts a particular standard, a practitioner must carefully research the precedents within the appellate district and be prepared to make arguments according to all three standards.

---

[39]Scott v United States, 436 US 128, 98 SCt 1717, 56 LEd(2d) 168 (1978).

[40]For a full explanation of these categories and an analysis of relevant case law, see State v Whitsell, 69 App(3d) 512, 591 NE(2d) 265 (Ashtabula 1990), appeal dismissed by 60 OS(3d) 718, 574 NE(2d) 1079 (1991) (evaluating state law). Joseph, *Pretextual Searches and Seizures: Going, Going, Gone?*, 18 Search and Seizure L Rep 129 (June 1991) (evaluating federal law).

(A) Subjective test

The subjective test focuses on whether the police officer had an improper intent, i.e., evasion of the Fourth Amendment requirements in making the initial arrest or stop. This test has been criticized as doing nothing more than encouraging police perjury, on the theory that officers would never admit to improper motives for their actions. While this somewhat cynical view might often be justified, it certainly is not universally true. For example, in *Cleveland v Tedar*,[41] undercover narcotics officers had received a tip that the defendant was carrying a weapon and intended to kill the first police officer who tried to confront him. At trial, the officers candidly admitted that they were not at all interested in the defendant's illegal lane change but merely used the traffic violation to justify a stop of the defendant's vehicle. Similarly, in *State v Whitsell*,[42] officers wishing to inspect a murder suspect's vehicle kept the vehicle under surveillance for a short time before making an arrest for driving with a suspended license. During cross-examination, the officers acknowledged that they were primarily interested in the continuing murder investigation, although it was certainly a routine procedure to arrest people who were found driving with suspended driver's licenses.

A more significant criticism of the subjective test is that most Fourth Amendment questions are evaluated according to an objective standard. The United States Supreme Court, in *Scott v United States*,[43] explicitly refused to consider an officer's subjective motivation when considering the propriety of a wiretap. The Court also struck down the subjective test when considering the plain view doctrine in *Horton v California*,[44] holding that "evenhanded law enforcement is best achieved by the application of objective standards of conduct, rather than standards that depend upon the subjective state of mind of the officer."[45] Given the Court's repeated assertions that the exclusionary rule is intended to deter police misconduct, it is difficult to understand how a proven improper subjective intent could be considered irrelevant. Still, if the Court ever squarely confronts the pretextual issue, it is not likely to be receptive to a subjective standard.

In any event, the subjective test still has its adherents. The Second District Court of Appeals applied a subjective test in early 1991 when considering the case of a driver who was stopped for failure to stop in a driveway before crossing a sidewalk, and who was subsequently arrested for failure to show a driver's license and to wear a seat belt.[46] The court agreed with the defendant that the proper inquiry was whether the police really wanted to act on a tip that the vehicle contained automatic weapons,

---

[41]Cleveland v Tedar, No. 34622 (8th Dist Ct App, Cuyahoga, 3-4-76).

[42]State v Whitsell, 69 App(3d) 512, 591 NE(2d) 265 (Ashtabula 1990), appeal dismissed by 60 OS(3d) 718, 574 NE(2d) 1079 (1991).

[43]Scott v United States, 436 US 128, 138, 98 SCt 1717, 56 LEd(2d) 168 (1978).

[44]Horton v California, 496 US 128, 110 SCt 2301, 110 LEd(2d) 112 (1990).

[45]Horton v California, 496 US 128, 138, 110 SCt 2301, 110 LEd(2d) 112 (1990), as quoted in Joseph, *Pretextual Searches and Seizures: Going, Going, Gone?*, 18 Search and Seizure L Rep 129, 133 (June 1991).

[46]State v Lenker, No. 12083, 1991 WL 26683 (2d Dist Ct App, Montgomery, 2-25-91).

although the court upheld the trial court's finding that the officers had a proper intent in making the stop. Similarly, in *State v Bishop*,[47] the court found the stop pretextual where the officer decided to stop the motorist before she observed the motorist commit a minor traffic offense. The court said: "A stop is pretextual when a police officer uses a minor traffic violation as a justification to investigate a vague suspicion that a motorist might be engaging in illegal activity."[48]

(B) Objective test

According to the objective standard for determining a pretextual search or seizure, the admissibility of evidence seized during a police-citizen encounter depends only on whether there was a lawful basis for the initial arrest or stop. Such a standard is more accurately characterized as a complete rejection of the pretext issue because if there is a lawful basis for the officer's conduct, his motivation is irrelevant. Again, refusal to consider an officer's subjective intent seems contrary to the deterrent goal of the exclusionary rule. However, this approach is powered by the Supreme Court's opinion in *Scott*, and some Ohio courts have elected the objective test when considering claims of pretextual searches and seizures.

In *State v Jackson*,[49] the defendant admitted to police that he had located and tampered with evidence sought by police in a murder investigation. Police arrested the defendant for evidence tampering, and during the course of several jail house interrogations eventually secured inculpatory statements from the defendant as to the murder. The defendant was convicted of murder and on appeal contended that the initial arrest was a pretext used by police to be able to repeatedly interrogate him. The Ohio Supreme Court dismissed this argument simply by noting that the evidence-tampering arrest was amply supported by probable cause. Thus, while the court did not say it was applying the objective test, it stopped its inquiry after determining that the arrest was legal.

The Eighth District Court of Appeals has also used the objective test on occasion. In *State v Sammour*,[50] the court approvingly quoted *Scott v United States*[51] as justification for applying the objective test in a case where the defendant claimed that his arrest for receiving a stolen car was a pretext to search the car for narcotics and weapons. The Ninth District Court of Appeals has rejected the reasonable officer test and held that "all challenges to the validity of a traffic stop are subject to the same Terry standard

---

[47]State v Bishop, 95 App(3d) 619, 643 NE(2d) 170 (Warren 1994).

[48]State v Bishop, 95 App(3d) 619, 622, 643 NE(2d) 170 (Warren 1994).

[49]State v Jackson, 57 OS(3d) 29, 565 NE(2d) 549 (1991), cert denied 502 US 835, 112 SCt 117, 116 LEd(2d) 86 (1991).

[50]State v Sammour, No. 51584, 1987 WL 9851 (8th Dist Ct App, Cuyahoga, 4-16-87).

[51]Scott v United States, 436 US 128, 138, 98 SCt 1717, 56 LEd(2d) 168 (1978); see also Crittenden v State, 899 SW(2d) 668 (Texas Ct Crim App 1995) (an objectively valid traffic stop is not invalid because the detaining officer had an ulterior motive for making the stop).

of review, regardless of whether the defendant raises allegations of pretext.[52]

(C) "Reasonable officer" test

The *Robinson* doctrine allowing a full search of the person is dependant upon there being a custodial arrest. Absent a custodial arrest, such as when a summons in lieu of arrest is required or standard procedure, a search of the person is not permitted. This most commonly occurs during traffic stops where a motorist is detained while a citation is prepared and issued. The "reasonable officer" test, as the name suggests, focuses on whether a reasonable officer, considering all the circumstances, would have made the initial arrest or stop. This standard is consistent with the US Supreme Court's apparent desire to apply some sort of objective test when considering Fourth Amendment questions, yet it still preserves the ability to deter improper police conduct.

The first Ohio case to propose the reasonable officer test was *State v Whitsell*.[53] There, the Eleventh District Court of Appeals held that a reasonable police officer who found a car parked at a bar and who knew the owner's driver's license was suspended might well keep the car under surveillance for a short time. In *State v Spencer*,[54] the defendant's vehicle was stopped by two police sergeants who were returning to the police station from a restaurant. The reason for the stop was an unsignalled left turn; the defendant claimed that the officers had stared at him and formed arbitrary suspicions of narcotics activity before making the stop. The Second District Court of Appeals remanded the case to the trial court for a finding on whether the stop was pretextual, with instructions to use the reasonable officer test.

The Hamilton County Court of Appeals also endorsed the "reasonable officer" test in *State v Richardson*,[55] that court, in an opinion by Judge Gorman, reasoned that adoption of a straight objective test for determining pretext, the same test held to govern investigatory stops or arrests in general, would deprive pretext

> of any constitutional significance whenever a stop or an arrest meets the ordinarily accepted standard, no matter how egregious or illegal an

---

[52]State v Carlson, 102 App(3d) 585, 657 NE(2d) 591 (Medina 1995).

[53]State v Whitsell, 69 App(3d) 512, 591 NE(2d) 265 (Ashtabula 1990), appeal dismissed by 60 OS(3d) 718, 574 NE(2d) 1079 (1991); see also State v Medlar, 93 App(3d) 483, 638 NE(2d) 1105 (Cuyahoga 1994) (officer's practice to wait for driver of illegally parked vehicle to return to vehicle in order to personally issue a parking citation was unreasonable and was an unlawful pretext to effect a DUI arrest; officer simply should have issued the citation and placed it on the windshield).

[54]State v Spencer, 75 App(3d) 581, 600 NE(2d) 335 (Montgomery 1991); State v Richardson, 94 App(3d) 501, 641 NE(2d) 216 (Hamilton 1994), appeal dismissed by 70 OS(3d) 1446, 639 NE(2d) 114 (1994) (however, the fact that drugs were found in an ensuing search after defendant's vehicle was stopped for a traffic offense is insufficient by itself to prove that the stop was pretextual, given that the officer was not looking for drug offenders, and had no knowledge of the history or personal characteristics of the driver).

[55]State v Richardson, 94 App(3d) 501, 641 NE(2d) 216 (Hamilton 1994), appeal dismissed by 70 OS(3d) 1446, 639 NE(2d) 114 (1994).

officer's actions may be when viewed from the perspective of the actual goal of the investigation.[56]

The court went on to conclude that the straight objective test, which would reject a pretext claim anytime there is probable cause or reasonable suspicion, grants

> such broad latitude to the police in all minor traffic cases, including those that qualify factually as pretexts, [that it] is at odds with a foundational purpose of the exclusionary rule, which is to deter police misconduct.[57]

The "reasonable officer" test commends itself for several reasons. It monitors flagrant misconduct, a safeguard which completely disappears if the objective standard becomes the sole criterion for evaluating police conduct. Meanwhile, this test does not bestow an undesirable windfall on a wrongdoer who would have been intercepted by a police officer who was acting without improper motives.

(D) Alternatives to pretext challenges

Since challenging a stop on the basis of pretext is so problematic, it is important to note that Ohio has established an alternative route which, although not establishing a defense to the primary traffic offense, limits the expansion of such stops to other offenses which might be the actual reason for the initial stop.[58]

11.06   Absent a custodial arrest

Where a police officer stops a vehicle for a nonarrestable offense, the Robinson-Gustafson rule does not permit a search of the person. The Supreme Court, in Pennsylvania v Mimms,[59] upheld a procedure whereby a driver, who is not under arrest, may be ordered from the vehicle while the officer issues a traffic summons. The Court reasoned that encounters of this nature pose a threat to police safety, absent any particularized suspicion that the driver is dangerous. On the other hand, the Court believed that the additional intrusion involved in requiring a motorist to exit his vehicle is de minimis and struck a balance in favor of police safety. That same balance strikes in favor of allowing a police officer to order passengers out of the car as well.[60] The authority to order the driver of a vehicle out of the car was extended in Ohio to drivers of cars involved in accidents even though no decision had yet been made whether to cite for a traffic offense.[61]

---

[56]State v Richardson, 94 App(3d) 501, 641 NE(2d) 216 (Hamilton 1994), appeal dismissed by 70 OS(3d) 1446, 639 NE(2d) 114 (1994).
[57]State v Richardson, 94 App(3d) 501, 641 NE(2d) 216 (Hamilton 1994), appeal dismissed by 70 OS(3d) 1446, 639 NE(2d) 114 (1994).
[58]See State v Robinette, 73 OS(3d) 650, 653 NE(2d) 695 (1995) (a police officer may not ask a person stopped for a traffic offense about other offenses, absent reasonable suspicion, unless the officer has clearly indicated that the motorist is free to leave and not answer the additional inquiries); see discussion of Robinette in Text Chapter 15, Traffic Stops and Their Aftermath.
[59]Pennsylvania v Mimms, 434 US 106, 98 SCt 330, 54 LEd(2d) 331 (1977).
[60]Cf. State v Townsend, 77 App(3d) 651, 603 NE(2d) 261 (Lake 1991).
[61]State v Darrington, 54 OS(2d) 321, 376 NE(2d) 954 (1978).

Once the motorist has alighted from the vehicle, any further intrusion must be supported by a particularized suspicion, the standard set forth in *Terry v Ohio*.[62] For example, once the motorist in *Mimms* was out of his car, the officer observed a large bulge under his pocket, prompting a frisk and discovery of a gun.[63]

A frisk may not be conducted absent satisfaction of the *Terry* standard. In *State v Townsend*,[64] the police officer frisked a passenger ordered out of the vehicle who was to be driven in the police car to a nearby telephone for the passenger's own convenience. The frisk was unconstitutional, the appellate court concluded, notwithstanding the state's contention that the frisk, which led to the discovery of evidence of a crime, was "a matter of routine department procedure."

11.07   Strip searches

Most jails provide as part of the administrative booking procedure that any arrestee introduced into the jail population undergo a strip search and in some instances a body cavity inspection. The purposes of such a search are to ensure that the arrestee does not have a hidden weapon to use upon himself or someone else, and to ensure that contraband is not introduced into the facility. As a matter of course, today these searches are conducted by jailers of the same sex as the arrestee. Reports of abuses in the decision to conduct a strip search or in the manner that it was done have resulted in the focus of attention on this practice.

The value of a standardized policy applicable to all incoming inmates is self-apparent. One of the purposes of the Fourth Amendment is to control the exercise of unbridled police discretion. If the policy requires that everyone be searched prior to introduction into the jail population, there can be no claim that officers have singled out certain arrestees and subjected them to discriminatory treatment. The problem with the policy is equally apparent and, at least in some cases, clearly outweighs its value. Primarily, the Fourth Amendment seeks to protect against unreasonable invasions of privacy, and the deprivation of a right does not become reasonable simply from the fact that all members of the population are equally affected.

The claim has been made that subjecting persons who are arrested for minor traffic offenses to the humiliation of a strip search involves an unreasonable invasion of privacy. These persons are rarely introduced into the general jail population but, instead, are detained often for a very short period of time while bail is arranged. An arrestee who knows that he will be released within a short period is not likely to be desperate and represents

---

[62]*Terry v Ohio*, 392 US 1, 88 SCt 1868, 20 LEd(2d) 889 (1968).

[63]See also *United States v Green*, 465 F(2d) 620 (DC Cir 1972) (police officer stopped a vehicle for a traffic offense and observed the defendant engage in furtive movements in the vehicle, causing the officer to become fearful of danger; the court held that once the defendant was out of the car, the officer could search under the driver's seat where the defendant had been reaching and to which the driver will return).

[64]*State v Townsend*, 77 App(3d) 651, 603 NE(2d) 261 (Lake 1991).

no threat of violence to himself or others. Moreover, that person is unlikely to have secreted contraband on or within his person or to possess a weapon that is not discoverable through a routine search. He did not expect to be apprehended, since the arrest is for a minor traffic offense.

For example, California has adopted this reasoning with respect to routine searches, not even strip searches, following arrests for routine traffic violations. California courts, applying the state constitution, rejected the *Robinson-Gustafson* rule. The California Supreme Court has held that when arresting for a routine traffic violation, if the officer cannot reasonably expect to find contraband or a weapon and if the offense has no fruits or instrumentalities, he cannot justify a routine search as incident to the arrest.[65] Moreover, a defendant arrested on a bench warrant for failure to appear for a traffic offense may not be booked or searched until he has been given an opportunity to post bail.[66] The reasoning underlying the California rule applies even more strongly to strip searches of persons arrested for minor traffic offenses or on bench warrants for failure to appear for a traffic offense.

In a civil suit brought under 42 USCA 1983, the United States Court of Appeals for the Fourth Circuit held that the strip search of a woman arrested for DWI violated due process standards because it bore no discernible relationship to security needs at the jail where she was detained.[67] The Fourth Circuit arrived at that conclusion by balancing the need for the particular search against the invasion that the search entails. The court found that at no time would the defendant or similar detainees be intermingled with the general population. Her offense, though not a minor traffic offense, was nevertheless one not commonly associated by its very nature with the possession of weapons or contraband. There was no cause in her specific case to believe that she might possess either, and when strip-searched, the defendant, an attorney, had been at the detention center for one and one-half hours without even a pat-down search. The court said that an indiscriminate strip search policy cannot be constitutionally justified on the basis of administrative ease in attending to security considerations. The United States Supreme Court refused to hear an appeal from this decision.[68]

In a civil suit arising out of the strip search of a speeder taken into custody because of an outstanding drunk driving capias, where the evidence shows the arrestee was cooperative and presented no problem, the Ohio Supreme Court held that the state must demonstrate an institutional justification for the strip search.[69]

Strip searches are regulated in Ohio by RC 2933.32, which limits the scope of a search incident to arrest for persons detained or arrested for

---

[65]See People v Superior Court of Yolo County, 3 Cal(3d) 807, 478 P(2d) 449, 91 Cal Rptr 729 (1970).

[66]People v Collin, 35 Cal App(3d) 416, 110 Cal Rptr 869 (1973).

[67]Logan v Shealy, 660 F(2d) 1007 (4th Cir Va 1981), cert denied sub nom Clements v Logan, 455 US 942, 102 SCt 1435, 71 LEd(2d) 653 (1982).

[68]Clements v Logan, 455 US 942, 102 SCt 1435, 71 LEd(2d) 653 (1982).

[69]Fricker v Stokes, 22 OS(3d) 202, 22 OBR 354, 490 NE(2d) 577 (1986).

misdemeanors or traffic offenses. Such persons are subject to strip searches and body cavity searches only if there is probable cause to believe that the person is concealing evidence of a crime "that could not otherwise be discovered." This limitation increases the risk that contraband may be smuggled into local jails. Its adoption signals a legislative determination that the risk is not great from this class of arrestees, but in any event the state mandates that the risk be taken to avoid the abuses. A strip search that violates RC 2933.32 has been held not to be of constitutional magnitude and does not require suppression of the evidence found during the search.[70]

CROSS REFERENCES

Text Ch 14

11.08   Search of a residence incident to arrest

(A) Control test

The *Chimel v California*[71] "control" test was devised to put an end to the free-wheeling warrantless searches of entire homes and business establishments that accompanied arrests. *Chimel* overturned precedent which permitted that practice.[72] The pre-existing practice resulted in delayed arrests until the arrestee arrived at the location that police wished to search. *Harris v United States*[73] involved a warrantless search of a four-room house; *United States v Rabinowitz*[74] a warrantless search incident to a lawful arrest of the desk, safe, and file cabinets in the arrestee's one-room office.

In *Chimel,* the Supreme Court could have adopted a rule rejecting *Harris* and limiting *Rabinowitz* to its facts, thus permitting a warrantless search of the room in which the arrest occurs. Such a rule, however, would not have had the desired effect: to encourage police to obtain search warrants. Furthermore, a *Rabinowitz* rule was inconsistent with the Court's philosophy that warrantless searches are strictly circumscribed and only for a limited purpose. The purpose of a search incident to arrest, consequently, is not a search for evidence, but a limited search permitted only to deny the arrestee access to a weapon or evidence. Consequently, the Court opted to overrule *Rabinowitz* and adopt the "control" test. When making a lawful arrest in the home, police may search only those areas within the immediate control of the arrestee—"meaning the area from which he might gain possession of a weapon or destructible evidence."[75]

---

[70]State v Barshick, No. 1908, 1991 WL 6150 (9th Dist Ct App, Medina, 1-16-91).
[71]Chimel v California, 395 US 752, 89 SCt 2034, 23 LEd(2d) 685 (1969).
[72]United States v Rabinowitz, 339 US 56, 70 SCt 430, 94 LEd(2d) 653 (1950), overruled by Chimel v California, 395 US 752, 89 SCt 2034, 23 LEd(2d) 685 (1969); Harris v United States, 331 US 145, 67 SCt 1098, 91 LEd 1399 (1947), overruled by Chimel v California, 395 US 752, 89 SCt 2034, 23 LEd(2d) 685 (1969).
[73]Harris v United States, 331 US 145, 67 SCt 1098, 91 LEd 1399 (1947), overruled by Chimel v California, 395 US 752, 89 SCt 2034, 23 LEd(2d) 685 (1969).
[74]United States v Rabinowitz, 339 US 56, 70 SCt 430, 94 LEd(2d) 653 (1950), overruled by Chimel v California, 395 US 752, 89 SCt 2034, 23 LEd(2d) 685 (1969).
[75]Chimel v California, 395 US 752, 763, 89 SCt 2034, 23 LEd(2d) 685 (1969); State v Koren, 100 App(3d) 358, 654 NE(2d) 131 (Lake 1995) (while arrest of defendant in his home on an outstanding federal warrant was lawful, seizure of a

Control, then, is to be determined by the continuing ability of the arrestee to maintain control and to reach weapons or evidence. Once police officers have neutralized an arrestee, the authority to search without a warrant, except on his person, ceases. That principle is basic to the *Chimel* decision but is not always applied by lower courts.

(B) Arrestee's control of the house

Clearly police may not arrest outside a home and then move the arrestee into the house for the purpose of conducting a search.[76] The same principle should be applicable to movements within a house. *Chimel* dictates that law enforcement officers cannot create a fiction of control. For example, police may not move an arrestee from room to room or even within a room, such as to place him within reach of a desk or dresser, to create the fiction of control for the purpose of conducting a warrantless search. The natural order of events, however, may result in an extension of control, thus permitting a broader search incident to arrest. If it is necessary for the arrestee to dress prior to being transported to the station house, police may search the closet or dresser from which the arrestee intends to secure clothing, and that search may take place even if the closet or dresser is in a different room from the one where the arrest takes place. The search is consistent with the *Chimel* test because the arrestee's control has extended to areas beyond his reaching or grabbing distance at the time of the arrest.[77] Recognition that control may be extended for legitimate reasons permitting a wider incidental search should not be misconstrued as a license to defeat the intent of the Supreme Court in adopting the *Chimel* test.

More often, an arrestee's control will diminish. An arrestee who is neutralized by police officers, especially one in handcuffs, is deprived of the ability to reach into a desk, dresser, or cupboard drawers. Although an area may have been under the control of an arrestee upon his arrest, control over that area diminishes within moments as the police dominate the situation. That principle was recognized by the Montgomery County Court of Appeals in *Centerville v Smith*.[78] In *Smith,* the defendant was arrested in a bathroom and removed to the living room. After the defendant was in the living room, police searched the bathroom and an adjoining bedroom. The court held, "It cannot reasonably be argued that the element of the officer's self-protection was involved in order to justify the warrantless search. Also, it cannot be reasonably argued that such search and seizure was with the aim of preventing the concealment or destruction of evidence in the closet."[79] The same approach led the Wood County Court of Appeals to disallow as incident to arrest a search of a wallet lying on a dresser while the defendant was lying on the bed. The court said that the defendant's position

---

gun in another room was unjustified because it was not in the immediate reach of the defendant).

[76]Shipley v California, 395 US 818, 89 SCt 2053, 23 LEd(2d) 732 (1969); State v Green, 36 Misc 140, 303 NE(2d) 917 (CP, Montgomery 1973).

[77]Giacalone v Lucas, 445 F(2d) 1238 (6th Cir Mich 1971), cert denied 405 US 922, 92 SCt 960, 30 LEd(2d) 793 (1972).

[78]Centerville v Smith, 43 App(2d) 3, 332 NE(2d) 69 (Montgomery 1973).

[79]Centerville v Smith, 43 App(2d) 3, 7-8, 332 NE(2d) 69 (Montgomery 1973).

was non-threatening when the search was made, and that neither weapons nor evidence of the crime for which the defendant was arrested would likely be contained in the wallet.[80]

Despite the United States Supreme Court's revisionist definition of an arrestee's control in other contexts,[81] it is not likely to allow the same leeway when the search is of a home. The Court has, heretofore, refused to limit the requirements of the warrant clause to the core interests of the Fourth Amendment—homes, offices, and private communication[82]—and has been least inclined to relax the Amendment's protection of privacy interests when the intrusion involves a home.[83] A 1982 decision, *Washington v Chrisman*,[84] may be seen as the beginning of a contrary trend and the harbinger of a relaxation of restrictions on the scope of permissible warrantless searches within the home.[85] More likely, however, *Chrisman* represents a narrow position, which does not affect the scope of incidental searches within a home. The decision is probably restricted to recognizing the unlimited and unfettered right of an arresting officer to remain at the side of an arrestee even if the officer does so for reasons other than self-protection or denying the arrestee the opportunity to conceal or destroy evidence.

11.09   Protective sweeps and securing a house

(A) Protective sweeps

Situations may arise when a police officer's authority incident to an arrest may extend within a house, even where the arrest takes place immediately outside, or to rooms in a house other than the one in which the arrest takes place. A substantial danger to the safety of arresting officers will justify a protective sweep through the entire house, and may even justify entry of the house for a protective sweep when the arrest takes place outside.

In *Maryland v Buie*,[86] the U.S. Supreme Court recognized two types of protective sweeps following an arrest in a home. The Court reasoned that an arrest in a home is dangerous because the officer is on his adversary's home turf. Consequently, as a precautionary matter, without probable cause or reasonable suspicion, a police officer may, incident to arrest, look in closets and other spaces immediately adjacent to the place of arrest, from which an attack could be launched. This is not a search for evidence, but solely a means of protection from attack for the officers. Nonetheless, evidence that is in plain view in those locations will be admissible at a

---

[80]State v Smith, 73 App(3d) 471, 597 NE(2d) 1132 (Wood 1991).

[81]See New York v Belton, 453 US 454, 101 SCt 2860, 69 LEd(2d) 768 (1981). See also Text 11.10, Search of an automobile incident to arrest.

[82]United States v Chadwick, 433 US 1, 97 SCt 2476, 53 LEd(2d) 538 (1977).

[83]See Payton v New York, 445 US 573, 100 SCt 1371, 63 LEd(2d) 639 (1980); Steagald v United States, 451 US 204, 101 SCt 1642, 68 LEd(2d) 38 (1981).

[84]Washington v Chrisman, 455 US 1, 102 SCt 812, 70 LEd(2d) 778 (1982).

[85]See also Text Ch 13, Plain View.

[86]Maryland v Buie, 494 US 325, 110 SCt 1093, 108 LEd(2d) 276 (1990), cert denied 498 US 1106, 111 SCt 1011, 112 LEd(2d) 1094 (1991).

subsequent trial. This authority naturally extends the scope of a search incident to an arrest.

Beyond that, however, *Buie* allows a police officer to conduct a limited protective sweep of the **entire** dwelling in conjunction with an in-home arrest if there are "articulable facts which, taken together with the rational inferences from those facts, would warrant a reasonably prudent officer in believing that the area to be swept harbors an individual posing a danger to those on the arrest scene."[87] The Supreme Court cautioned, though, that it was not sanctioning a "top to bottom search,"[88] and stressed that the authority to conduct a protective sweep of the entire house is not automatic, but only available when there is reasonable suspicion to believe that the "house is harboring a person posing a danger."[89] Moreover, a sweep is only to be a cursory inspection of those places where a person may be found. And the authority lasts no longer than it takes to complete the arrest and leave the house. That danger may exist when the officer has reason to believe that accomplices may be on the premises,[90] but not if accomplices are already in custody.[91] One United States Court of Appeals has upheld a protective sweep of an apartment after arresting the defendant in the hallway outside the apartment on the basis of an informant's statement that defendant's confederates might be inside the apartment.[92]

(B) Securing a house incident to arrest while awaiting a search warrant

Law enforcement officers should be permitted to take reasonable steps to secure the premises while waiting for a search warrant. What actions are reasonable under the circumstances, however, is perplexing, for the problem is delay. Telephonic search warrants would minimize the delay but are not provided for in Ohio law. Both Criminal Rule 41 and RC 2933.23 require that a search warrant shall not be issued until an affidavit is filed.[93] Courts have differed over what action police officers may take to secure a house in which they have reasonable cause to believe contraband or other evidence may be found.[94]

---

[87]Maryland v Buie, 494 US 325, 334, 110 SCt 1093, 108 LEd(2d) 276 (1990), cert denied 498 US 1106, 111 SCt 1011, 112 LEd(2d) 1094 (1991).

[88]Maryland v Buie, 494 US 325, 336, 110 SCt 1093, 108 LEd(2d) 276 (1990), cert denied 498 US 1106, 111 SCt 1011, 112 LEd(2d) 1094 (1991).

[89]Maryland v Buie, 494 US 325, 336, 110 SCt 1093, 108 LEd(2d) 276 (1990), cert denied 498 US 1106, 111 SCt 1011, 112 LEd(2d) 1094 (1991).

[90]Cf. State v Lyons, 83 App(3d) 525, 615 NE(2d) 310 (Darke 1992), appeal dismissed by 66 OS(3d) 1455, 610 NE(2d) 420 (1993) (upholding a sweep for accomplices of an arrestee's home, who was indicted along with 21 others, some of whom were described by the appellate court as violent and still known to be in the area, which led to the discovery of other evidence); United States v Weber, 518 F(2d) 987 (8th Cir Mo 1975), cert denied Rich v United States, 427 US 907, 96 SCt 3193, 49 LEd(2d) 1200 (1976).

[91]Cf. United States v Gamble, 473 F(2d) 1274 (7th Cir Ill 1973).

[92]United States v Henry, 48 F(3d) 1282 (CA, DC 1995) (conflicting information from defendant's girlfriend that he was alone did not have to be credited by the police).

[93]See contra Fed Crim R 41(c)(2).

[94]See United States v Grummel, 542 F(2d) 789 (9th Cir Wash 1976) (proper where mother of the defendant at home to secure the premises to the extent

Partial guidance as to what police may do when they develop probable cause to search a residence was finally forthcoming in *Segura v United States*.[95] The Court has been extremely reluctant to allow a warrantless search of a home, maintaining at least in that one area its purported preference for a warrant. When a police officer makes an arrest in a home or is otherwise lawfully present and acquires probable cause to search the home, absent real exigent circumstances, the officer may not search the home without a warrant. The presence of another member of the household, as in *Chimel v California*[96] and *Vale v Louisiana*,[97] will not ordinarily provide the exigency to justify a warrantless search. Presumably, the officer may secure the home, which in effect is a seizure, and protect the premises while a warrant is sought.[98] A seizure of the premises, which interferes with possessory interest while a warrant is sought, is deemed preferable to a warrantless search, which eliminates the privacy interest. But the seizure must be reasonable and for a reasonable duration.

The problem with *Segura* was that the initial entry into the apartment was illegal—the arrest was conducted in the hallway, and the officers occupied the apartment for nineteen hours before the warrant was obtained. Because the probable cause that supported the warrant was formed independently of the illegal entry, it did not invalidate the subsequent search with a warrant. But *Segura* raises additional problems. There was no need for the officers to remain in the apartment while they awaited the warrant; the occupants had been arrested and removed. They could have secured the apartment from outside. The Court was unconcerned. Secondly, if the occupants of the apartment had been present during the nineteen-hour period, the seizure and restraint on those occupants for nineteen hours likely would have been unreasonable. The lawful presence of others will result in a reviewing court taking a closer look at the reasonableness of the nature and duration of the intrusion.

11.10   Search of an automobile incident to arrest[99]

(A) The law prior to Chimel

The most significant change in Ohio law since the last edition of this Text affects the authority of police to search a car incident to the arrest of a

---

necessary to prevent destruction of the evidence until a warrant could be obtained), cert denied 429 US 1051, 97 SCt 763, 50 LEd(2d) 767 (1977); contra State v Dorson, 62 Hawaii 377, 615 P(2d) 740 (1980) (illegal for police to impound a defendant's home and curtail the occupants' freedom of movement absent specific facts pointing to the likelihood that contraband will be removed or destroyed).

[95]Segura v United States, 468 US 796, 104 SCt 3380, 82 LEd(2d) 599 (1984).

[96]Chimel v California, 395 US 752, 89 SCt 2034, 23 LEd(2d) 685 (1969).

[97]Vale v Louisiana, 399 US 30, 90 SCt 1969, 26 LEd(2d) 409 (1970).

[98]But see State v Brooks, No. 94APA03-386, 1995 WL 390935 (10th Dist Ct App, Franklin, 6-27-95) (police may not enter apartment to secure and prevent destruction of evidence where they could have prevented the defendant and others from entering the apartment to begin with).

[99]See also Text 14.06(C), Search of an automobile incident to a non-custodial traffic arrest.

recent occupant. *State v Brown*[100] is significant for several reasons: For the first time, employing the Ohio State Constitution, the Ohio Supreme Court rejected a US Supreme Court decision which narrowed Fourth Amendment rights of citizens and expanded police authority. However, the Court rejected a case and its doctrine which already was a decade old and which seemed firmly entrenched in Ohio. Finally, the Ohio Supreme Court was not at all clear how much of the federal doctrine was no longer acceptable under the State Constitution, and, likely most important, in what types of cases the federal law no longer prevails. In order to fully understand *Brown*, and its significance, it is necessary to understand the *Belton*[101] doctrine and the law it displaced.

Prior to *Chimel v California*,[102] there was very little need for an automobile exception because then, as now, most car searches followed an arrest, and the scope of a search incident to arrest extended to the entire premises where the arrest occurred. Courts naturally assumed that if a search incident to arrest in a house extended to the entire house, it would also extend to incidental searches of automobiles contemporaneous with a lawful arrest.[103] That authority extended to searches following arrests for minor offenses.[104] Most states, however, did not go so far as to extend the authority to search a vehicle incident to an arrest for a minor traffic offense.[105]

(B) Impact of Chimel

The impact of the *Chimel* control test should have been the end of vehicular searches incident to arrest once an arrestee is removed from the vehicle and deprived of the opportunity to reach or grab for weapons or evidence inside the automobile.[106] That, however, was not the immediate effect of the decision. Initially, *Chimel* resulted in a revival of the automobile exception to the warrant requirement, which permits a police officer to search an automobile without a warrant if he has probable cause to believe that evidence of a crime is contained therein. But that separate and discrete exception, which has undergone remarkable growth, requires independent probable cause and is not automatically triggered every time an arrest, especially one for a traffic offense, occurs. Consequently, the second trend resulting from *Chimel* was a movement by lower courts to deny its application to vehicles or demonstrate why the interior compartment of an auto-

---

[100]State v Brown, 63 OS(3d) 349, 588 NE(2d) 113 (1992), cert denied 506 US 862, 113 SCt 182, 121 LEd(2d) 127 (1992).

[101]New York v Belton, 453 US 454, 101 SCt 2860, 69 LEd(2d) 768 (1981).

[102]Chimel v California, 395 US 752, 89 SCt 2034, 23 LEd(2d) 685 (1969).

[103]Preston v United States, 376 US 364, 84 SCt 881, 11 LEd(2d) 777 (1964); State v Call, 8 App(2d) 277, 220 NE(2d) 130 (Montgomery 1965).

[104]See South Euclid v Palladino, 93 Abs 24, 193 NE(2d) 560 (Muni, South Euclid 1963) (search of a car upheld following arrest under suspicious persons ordinance).

[105]Amador-Gonzalez v United States, 391 F(2d) 308 (5th Cir Tex 1968), overruled on other grounds by United States v Causey, 834 F(2d) 1179 (5th Cir La 1987). Annot, 10 ALR3d 314 (1966). Contra State v Coles, 20 Misc 12, 249 NE(2d) 553 (CP, Montgomery 1969). For a discussion of *State v Coles* see Text 11.10, Search of an automobile incident to arrest.

[106]Contra State v Bradley, 26 App(2d) 229, 270 NE(2d) 654 (Scioto 1971).

mobile remained under the "control" of an arrestee who had been removed from the automobile.

The reluctance to apply *Chimel* standards was manifested in extreme distortions of the control test. "Control" was interpreted to mean at the moment preceding or contemporaneous with the arrest.[107] Other courts blurred the distinction between incidental searches and searches under the automobile exception or boldly ignored basic physical limitations in order to conclude that an item within the interior of an automobile remained in the arrestee's control.[108] In a whole line of cases avoiding application of the *Chimel* test, the search incident to arrest was not to protect the arresting officers or to deny the arrestee access to the evidence; the officers were exclusively searching for evidence, which is not one of the recognized and legitimate purposes of a search incident to arrest.[109]

The lengths to which some courts would go to uphold a warrantless search of a vehicle incident to arrest are demonstrated in a very thoughtful opinion from the Montgomery County Court of Common Pleas, in *State v Coles*.[110] The court admittedly was motivated because "the cemeteries and police stations contain living epitaphs of those dedicated traffic officers who failed to take reasonable precautions for their own protection."[111] The decision was handed down one week after the Supreme Court offered the *Chimel* test. Nonetheless, in upholding the search, the court used a control test. The defendant was stopped for speeding and left his vehicle, closing the door to the automobile. While surrounded by the two officers, the defendant made a movement for the door handle and was told by the officers not to get back into the car. Then, one of the two officers opened the door of the vehicle, searched the area around the driver's seat, and found a gun under the seat.

The court rejected the defense contention that since the door of the vehicle was closed and defendant was outside, weapons on the inside were thereby rendered inaccessible. The court said, "This would be the case had the officers handcuffed [the defendant] and removed him from the close proximity to his vehicle."[112] Instead, the court accepted the officers' claim that the search of the vehicle incident to a speeding arrest was for the purpose of finding weapons and a means of escape, and said no circumstances in addition to the arrest should be necessary to justify a search of a vehicle for weapons. The court said that it was unwilling to limit police authority in such instances because it was impossible to predict whether the defendant would have gone for his gun while the officers routinely went

---

[107]See People v Floyd, 26 NY(2d) 558, 312 NYS(2d) 193, 260 NE(2d) 815 (1970) ("not at all clear that the 'grabbing distance' authorized in the *Chimel* case is conditioned upon the arrested person's continued capacity 'to grab' ").

[108]See United States v Frick, 490 F(2d) 666 (5th Cir La 1973), cert denied sub nom Peterson v United States, 419 US 831, 95 SCt 55, 42 LEd(2d) 57 (1974).

[109]See generally Katz, *Automobile Searches and Diminished Expectations in the Warrant Clause,* 19 Am Crim L Rev 558, 585-90 (1982).

[110]State v Coles, 20 Misc 12, 249 NE(2d) 553 (CP, Montgomery 1969).

[111]State v Coles, 20 Misc 12, 20, 249 NE(2d) 553 (CP, Montgomery 1969).

[112]State v Coles, 20 Misc 12, 23, 249 NE(2d) 553 (CP, Montgomery 1969).

about their business or whether, having received the ticket for the offense, he would have turned the gun on the officers on reentering the vehicle.

While ostensibly applying a control test, the *Coles* court actually balanced interests and found in favor of the police. It is difficult to argue that the defendant remained in control of objects that were inside the vehicle when he was outside and the door to the automobile was closed. Rather, the court was formulating a general rule that the interior of a vehicle could be searched following the arrest of the driver for *any* offense; the court was certainly not applying the *Chimel* test even though the opinion is framed in the language of control.

(C) Supreme Court redefines "control"

In *New York v Belton,*[113] the United States Supreme Court acknowledged the inability or unwillingness of lower courts to apply *Chimel* standards to searches of automobiles incident to arrests. Rather than instruct these courts to apply *Chimel,* the Court redefined control in the context of searches of automobiles incident to arrest and developed a "bright-line" rule that is even more expansive than the one set forth by the Ohio court in *Coles.*

The search in *Belton* occurred after a lone police officer, patrolling the New York State Thruway, ordered an automobile that had been speeding over to the side of the road. He found four men in the car and, after checking the driver's license and automobile registration, learned that none of the four either owned the car or were related to its owner. The defendant, Belton, was one of the passengers. While talking to the driver and passengers, the officer smelled marijuana coming from the car and also noticed an envelope on the floor marked "Supergold," which he recognized as a name and packaging commonly used to sell marijuana. He ordered the men out of the vehicle, patted them down, and directed them to separate areas on the highway beyond touching distance of each other. He retrieved the package from the car, opened it, and ascertained that it contained marijuana. He then advised the four men of their *Miranda* rights and searched each of them. The officer returned to the automobile a second time to conduct a full search of the passenger compartment, and found marijuana butts in the ashtray. He then looked through five jackets which were left on the rear seat and, in the closed-zipper pockets of one of the jackets, discovered cocaine and identification linking the jacket to Belton. Throughout the proceedings in this case, the state maintained that the search was incident to the arrest of the occupants of the vehicle. At no time did the state offer the automobile exception as the legal justification for the search.

Justice Stewart, the author of the *Chimel* opinion, also wrote for the majority in *Belton.* The bright-line rule established in *Belton* permits a search of the passenger compartment of the vehicle and all containers found within that compartment as incident to the "custodial arrest" of a recent occupant of the automobile. The Court found a mechanical rule

---

[113]New York v Belton, 453 US 454, 101 SCt 2860, 69 LEd(2d) 768 (1981).

necessary because of lower courts' difficulties interpreting *Chimel* in the automobile context. More likely, the lower courts were not having difficulty applying *Chimel;* they were unwilling to do so. The rule fashioned by the *Belton* majority assumes the existence, in the context of a search of a vehicle following an arrest, of exigent circumstances. It permits the rule's application to situations where exigency is nonexistent and, thus, severs the scope of incidental searches from the possibility of exigent circumstances that gave rise to the limited exception to the warrant requirement in the first place.

The Court fashioned its rule around "the generalization that articles inside the relatively narrow compass of the passenger compartment are in fact generally, even if not inevitably, within 'the area into which an arrestee might reach in order to grab a weapon or evidentiary item.' "[114] Consequently, a search of the passenger compartment automatically becomes incident to an arrest, whether the facts of the case even remotely fit within the generality on which the rule is based. The Court created a second fiction when Justice Stewart said that "it followed" that containers within the passenger compartment, whether open or closed, are also within the reach of the arrestee and subject to incidental search. In developing the rule, the Court relied on the *Robinson-Gustafson*[115] line of cases, which permit a search of the person following a custodial arrest. Yet once an arrestee is deprived of access to the interior compartment or its contents, as when he has been removed from the vehicle, any search of the automobile is severed from the reasoning underlying the *Robinson-Gustafson* rule.

In *Belton,* Justice Stewart warned that this rule "in no way alters the fundamental principles established in the *Chimel* case regarding the basic scope of searches incident to lawful custodial arrests."[116] The Court was attempting to confine the effects of *Belton* to automobile searches following arrests and to prevent *Belton's* new concept of control from seeping into the context of searches incident to arrest not involving an automobile. Following *Belton,* however, the case was cited by lower courts to justify extended searches incident to arrest not involving automobiles.[117] It would be difficult to confine *Belton's* definition of control to searches of automobiles following an arrest because its redefinition of control is applicable in all contexts. *Chimel* dictated that once an object was out of the control of an arrestee and in the control of a police officer the search incident to arrest be ended and any further search be authorized by a warrant issued by a judge. However, *Belton's* impact will affect the determination of when a police officer establishes exclusive control over an object.

---

[114]New York v Belton, 453 US 454, 460, 101 SCt 2860, 69 LEd(2d) 768 (1981).

[115]United States v Robinson, 414 US 218, 94 SCt 467, 38 LEd(2d) 427 (1973); Gustafson v Florida, 414 US 260, 94 SCt 488, 38 LEd(2d) 456 (1973).

[116]New York v Belton, 453 US 454, 460 n.3, 101 SCt 2860, 69 LEd(2d) 768 (1981).

[117]See United States v Sierra, No. 81 Cr 0522 (SD NY 9-15-81) (affirming search of paper bag in room where arrest occurred); People v Gomez, 632 P(2d) 586 (Colo 1981) (affirming search of motel room after arrest), cert denied 455 US 943, 102 SCt 1439, 71 LEd(2d) 655 (1982).

Belton's logic requires a broad interpretation of the area within the arrestee's control and a correspondingly narrow interpretation of when an officer has achieved exclusive control over the same package. This is demonstrated by the fact that a container that is physically unattainable to an arrestee may be legally attainable to him under *Belton*. The *Belton* rule is important because a legally attainable container may be searched, without probable cause to believe that it contains a weapon or evidence, even though the actual purpose of the search can no longer be to protect the police officer or the evidence.

Essentially, *Belton* encourages a distinction between "prudent" control and "exclusive" control. Prudence dictates that an object be placed out of the lunging distance of an arrestee. Exclusivity, on the other hand, involves a disposition of the object in a manner that would not permit any circumstance in which an arrestee might regain access to the object. Later decisions may hold that the *Belton* reasoning dictates that a suitcase or other container is not reduced to an officer's exclusive control until it is safely locked away from an arrestee.

(D) Ohio charts its own course and rejects Belton

Belton vastly expanded police power by allowing a search of the interior compartment of a vehicle even after the removal of the societal purposes which gave rise to the exemption from the warrant requirement for warrantless searches incident to arrest. After all, once the occupants of the vehicle are removed from the vehicle, there is no longer any opportunity for them to secure a weapon or evidence left in the car. Moreover, any transitory argument for the authority granted in *Belton*, which may have existed at the time the case was decided, no longer existed a year later when the automobile exception to the warrant requirement was extended to containers found within the vehicle. Some state courts rejected *Belton* immediately;[118] while, for eleven years, Ohio appeared to accept the *Belton* doctrine's expansion of police powers.

In *Brown*, the defendant was arrested for driving under the influence of alcohol. After the defendant was placed in the police patrol car, the officer, while searching the interior compartment of the defendant's vehicle, searched an unlocked wooden box containing LSD, which he found in the locked glove compartment. The search was clearly lawful under the *Belton* standards. The Ohio Supreme Court distinguished the facts in *Brown* from those in *Belton*, where the officer had probable cause to believe that evidence of the crime for which he had arrested the occupants would be found in the vehicle. The officer in Ohio did not have probable cause, but under *Belton* he did not need it. Further, the Ohio Supreme Court pointed out that there was no need to search the car for weapons because the arrestee

---

[118]See e.g., People v Belton, 55 NY(2d) 49, 447 NYS(2d) 873, 432 NE(2d) 745 (1982) (rejecting the rule that police may search the interior of the vehicle following every custodial arrest and requiring, instead, that police search the vehicle only when they have reason to believe that the car may contain evidence related to the crime for which the occupant was arrested or that a weapon may be discovered or a means of escape thwarted).

was already in the back of the police car. These points traditionally have been the foundation of criticism leveled at the *Belton* doctrine.

After distinguishing the facts from those in *Belton*, Justice Wright, the author of the unanimous *Brown* opinion, cut to the chase. Recognizing that *Belton* may stand for the broader proposition (which it clearly does), Justice Wright wrote:

> If *Belton* does stand for the proposition that a police officer may conduct a detailed search of an automobile *solely* because he has arrested one of its occupants, *on any charge*, we decline to adopt its rule.[119]

Justice Wright then dropped a footnote indicating clearly that the Court recognized that it was invoking the State Constitution to arrive at this result.[120] Finally, the Court concluded:

> A police officer may not open a small, closed container found inside an automobile's glove compartment *solely* as a search incident to the driver's arrest for a traffic violation, after the officer has the suspect— and sole occupant of the vehicle—under control in the police cruiser.[121]

The broad language in the opinion seems to indicate that the Court totally rejected the *Belton* rationale and, therefore, would not allow a search incident to arrest for any offense once the arrestee is out of the car, absent cause to believe that evidence or a weapon will be found in the car. This language would allow for a search if the offense is a violent one or if the police have cause to believe that the arrestee may have been armed. Similarly, a search for evidence would not be allowed except under the broad parameters of the automobile exception, which allows for a search of the entire vehicle if there is probable cause to believe that evidence will be found somewhere in the car, or under the inventory exception. On the other hand, the narrower language of the concluding sentence would seem to reject *Belton* under the Ohio Constitution only where the arrest is for a traffic offense.[122] Clearly, the issue is not finally resolved.

Brown was applied by the Franklin County Court of Appeals in *State v Hines*,[123] where police stopped a motorist for failure to use a turn signal and then arrested the motorist when they discovered that he had no license and two outstanding warrants. As the officer approached the vehicle, she noticed the defendant make motions in the vehicle which made her concerned for her safety. The officer ordered the motorist out of the car, patted him down for weapons, and placed him in the police car. Once backup arrived on the scene, the arresting officer searched under the front seats in the car and found a semi- automatic handgun. On the authority of *Brown*,

---

[119]State v Brown, 63 OS(3d) 349, at 352, 588 NE(2d) 113 (1992), cert denied 506 US 862, 113 SCt 182, 121 LEd(2d) 127 (1992).

[120]State v Brown, 63 OS(3d) 349, at 352 n.3, 588 NE(2d) 113 (1992), cert denied 506 US 862, 113 SCt 182, 121 LEd(2d) 127 (1992).

[121]State v Brown, 63 OS(3d) 349, at 353, 588 NE(2d) 113 (1992), cert denied ___ US ___, 113 SCt 182, 121 LEd(2d) 127 (1992).

[122]See State v Davidson, 82 App(3d) 282, 611 NE(2d) 889 (Darke 1992) (police may not search absent any furtive gesture or suspicious behavior by DUI defendant who is handcuffed and in the back of a police cruiser).

[123]State v Hines, 92 App(3d) 163, 634 NE(2d) 654 (Franklin 1993), appeal dismissed by 68 OS(3d) 1449, 626 NE(2d) 690 (1994).

the appellate court reversed the conviction and held that the motion to suppress the gun should have been granted.

> Here, as in *Brown*, defendant had been removed from the vehicle, frisked and placed in the police wagon, where he remained until arrested and handcuffed. It is apparent from the record that defendant was under close supervision in the police wagon from the time he was removed from the automobile. The record also reveals that the police wagon was approximately ten feet away from defendant's vehicle. Therefore, it cannot be reasonably maintained that the contents of the vehicle remained within defendant's "immediate control" so that defendant would have access to the contents of the vehicle. Defendant had no opportunity to obtain a weapon or anything else from the vehicle at this point and, consequently, [the officer] was not justified in searching the vehicle.[124] Nor in *Hines* could the police officer have impounded the vehicle and conducted an inventory search. The owner of the car, who was the defendant's sister, was on (or arrived at) the scene and was given custody of the vehicle.

CROSS REFERENCES

Text Ch 12

11.11   Search of packages and other receptacles incident to arrest

(A) Introduction

Whether packages, containers, or other receptacles seized from an arrestee may be searched without a warrant is uncertain. Seemingly irreconcilable lines of authority govern this issue. Guidance must be gleaned from related issues, and the only pointed discussion on this question to be found in Supreme Court decisions comes from dissenting and concurring opinions.

The issues are (1) whether a container, once out of the hands of an arrestee, may be searched contemporaneous with the arrest; and (2) whether a container that may be searched at the scene of an arrest may be searched without a warrant later at the police station.

(B) Conflicting precedent

A rigid application of the *Chimel v California*[125] control test, which limits incidental searches to the area from which an arrestee might gain possession of a weapon or destructible evidence, would dictate that once a container is out of the reach of an arrestee, the authority to conduct a warrantless search terminates. *Chimel*, however, has been modified in several instances by succeeding cases. Specifically, the bright-line rule established in *New York v Belton*,[126] authorizing the search of the interior compartment of a vehicle following the arrest of an occupant, presents just such a modification. There, the search of the automobile and the jackets found therein occurred after the arrestees were ordered from the vehicle and directed by the officer to stay out of reach of each other and the vehicle.

---

[124]State v Hines, 92 App(3d) 163, 167, 634 NE(2d) 654 (Franklin 1993), appeal dismissed by 68 OS(3d) 1449, 626 NE(2d) 690 (1994).

[125]Chimel v California, 395 US 752, 89 SCt 2034, 23 LEd(2d) 685 (1969).

[126]New York v Belton, 453 US 454, 101 SCt 2860, 69 LEd(2d) 768 (1981).

While the Court attempted to limit *Belton* to the context of automobiles, it does provide a general definition of control. Similarly, *Robinson-Gustafson*[127] did not question the right of the police officers to open the cigarette packages seized from the arrestees and investigate the contents of those packages. When the officers looked inside the packets and discovered the contraband, the packets were no longer in the arrestees' control, being in the hands of the officers. Consequently, the immediate control of the packets did not dictate the results in those two cases.

Moreover, support for a sweeping rule is to be found in the broad language used by the Supreme Court majority in *United States v Edwards,*[128] authorizing a warrantless search at the scene or later at the police station of property or effects in an arrestee's immediate possession. Although *Edwards* involved a delayed taking and search of the clothing worn by the defendant, the Court included within the scope of its rule items stored in the property room of the jail. Consequently, the cases following *Chimel* appear to modify the control test in two possible ways. First, the cases seem to permit the search of objects incident to arrest even though those objects are no longer technically in the control of the arrestee. This sweeping modification, however, is evolved from *Belton,* which is unreliable precedent in light of the peculiar approach this Court takes when dealing with automobiles. The second modification, more likely to be generally applicable, fashions a rule that eliminates the control test when the search involves items taken from the person of an arrestee even when the search is not temporally proximate to the arrest. Either analysis, though, extends the parameters of a search incident to arrest beyond that which is necessary to deprive an arrestee of access to weapons or evidence.

A different signal, however, was conveyed in *United States v Chadwick,*[129] where the Supreme Court disallowed the search of a footlocker one and one-half hours after the defendants had been arrested, the footlocker seized, and the search conducted at a federal detention center out of the defendant's presence. Although the issue in the case was entwined with other exceptions to the warrant clause, the Supreme Court also discussed the scope of searches incident to arrest. The Court said:

> [W]arrantless searches of luggage or other property seized at the time of an arrest cannot be justified as incident to that arrest either if the "search is remote in time or place from the arrest," ... or no exigency exists. Once law enforcement officers have reduced luggage or other personal property not immediately associated with the person of the arrestee to their exclusive control, and there is no longer any danger that the arrestee might gain access to the property to seize a weapon or destroy evidence, a search of that property is no longer an incident of the arrest.[130]

As guidance, *Chadwick* left much to be desired. The Court failed to clarify the meaning of its discussion pertaining to searches incident to arrest

---

[127]United States v Robinson, 414 US 218, 94 SCt 467, 38 LEd(2d) 427 (1973); Gustafson v Florida, 414 US 260, 94 SCt 488, 38 LEd(2d) 456 (1973).

[128]United States v Edwards, 415 US 800, 94 SCt 1234, 39 LEd(2d) 771 (1974).

[129]United States v Chadwick, 433 US 1, 97 SCt 2476, 53 LEd(2d) 538 (1977).

[130]United States v Chadwick, 433 US 1, 15, 97 SCt 2476, 53 LEd(2d) 538 (1977).

when it did not determine whether the footlocker would have been subject to a warrantless search if it had been opened at the scene of the arrest even after the defendants were subdued, instead of as it had been, later and out of their presence.

The text of the opinion quoted above appears to go both ways on the subject. It can be read to permit a warrantless search incident to arrest of such items provided that the search takes place at the point of arrest. On the other hand, the Court also said that once property is reduced to the *exclusive* control of the officers "and there is no longer any danger that the arrestee might gain access to the property,"[131] the authority to conduct a warrantless search disappears. It is unclear whether *"exclusive* control" is different from "control," and whether the authority to search persists so long as the object is in the presence of the arrestee or whether that authority terminates once the arrestee is subdued even though the object is still in his presence. Consequently, the Court provided inadequate guidance as to whether control is tested by the ability of the arrestee to reach and grab at the time of the arrest provided the search is "substantially contemporaneous" with the arrest, or whether control is to be determined at the moment of the search.

(C) Search of containers contemporaneous with the arrest

The natural tendency of courts is to uphold the search of containers in the hands of an arrestee contemporaneous with the arrest. In *State v Mathews,*[132] the court upheld the search of defendant's purse after it had been reluctantly given to the police officer immediately following the arrest. The court held that the search of the purse clutched by the defendant "and under her immediate control" was a reasonable search incident to her arrest. Application of *Chimel,* however, would indicate that once the purse was in the police officer's hands, it was no longer clutched by the defendant and "under her control." Nonetheless, the facts are almost identical to *Robinson-Gustafson* except that the receptacle here was a purse and not a cigarette package removed from the defendant's pocket. Similarly, *Chadwick* indicated that the authority to search extends until the object is within the *exclusive control* of the police officer.

Arguably so long as the item is in the defendant's presence at the scene of the arrest, the possibility exists that the arrestee can still lunge, reach, or grab for a weapon or evidence in the container. This analysis requires a reading of the *Chadwick* term, exclusive control, to put the emphasis solely on the word exclusive and to virtually ignore control. Surely consideration should be given to whether the arrestee is handcuffed and other issues such as the arrestee's proximity to the container and the number of police officers surrounding an arrestee. The validity of the search in any case should turn on the particular facts surrounding the arrest and the moments immediately following. The present Supreme Court, however, has a penchant for bright-line rules, arguing that such rules provide greater gui-

---

[131]United States v Chadwick, 433 US 1, 15, 97 SCt 2476, 53 LEd(2d) 538 (1977).
[132]State v Mathews, 46 OS(2d) 72, 346 NE(2d) 151 (1976).

dance despite the absence of factors leading to the creation of the rule in a great number of cases.

Justice Blackmun, dissenting in *Chadwick,* asserted, "It is well established that an immediate search of packages or luggage carried by an arrested person is proper"[133] even if the arrestee is handcuffed. However, the law pertaining to the warrantless search of packages and containers, even at the scene of an arrest, is not nearly as clear-cut as Justice Blackmun suggests. The Court of Appeals for the Sixth Circuit, in a case decided prior to *Chadwick, United States v Kaye,*[134] certainly thought the rule advocated later by Justice Blackmun was clearly established. The court upheld the search of a suitcase after the defendant was arrested and the suitcase seized. The court assumed that the suitcase could have been searched at the point of arrest.

On the other hand, Justice Brennan, concurring in *Chadwick,* disagreed, saying that "it is not at all obvious" that a package may be searched at the time and place of an arrest. According to Brennan, the decision will turn on the actual control of the arrestee. In *Chadwick,* he would not have allowed a search of the footlocker at the moment of arrest because it was heavy and locked and the defendants could not gain access to weapons or destructible evidence.

Obviously, this area is in need of clarification. The outcome will depend upon which philosophy governing the nature of exceptions to the warrant clause holds sway. Justice Blackmun advocates adoption of "a clear-cut rule permitting property seized in conjunction with a valid arrest in a public place to be searched without a warrant."[135] Retired Justice Brennan insisted on application of the strict *Chimel* standards. In light of *Belton,* the Blackmun position appears to be prevailing.[136]

(D) Delayed search of containers incident to arrest

Although there is more guidance as to whether a warrantless, delayed search of a receptacle may be conducted away from the scene of and after an arrest, there remains some uncertainty. *Edwards,* although involving a search of clothing, indicated that other property in the possession of an arrestee may be searched later at the police station. The broad language in *Edwards* was later limited, however, in *Chadwick,* where the Court invalidated a delayed warrantless search of a footlocker. Thus, some items seized from an arrestee may be searched later at the police station and others may not; the difficulty is in drawing the line.

Following *Chadwick,* in *United States v Schleis,*[137] a delayed stationhouse search of a locked briefcase was not allowed as it was no longer incident to

---

[133]United States v Chadwick, 433 US 1, 23 n.5, 97 SCt 2476, 53 LEd(2d) 538 (1977).

[134]United States v Kaye, 492 F(2d) 744 (6th Cir Ohio 1974), cert denied 444 US 991, 100 SCt 522, 62 LEd(2d) 420 (1979).

[135]United States v Chadwick, 433 US 1, 21, 97 SCt 2476, 53 LEd(2d) 538 (1977).

[136]See United States v Brown, 671 F(2d) 585 (DC Cir 1982) (upholding search of a zippered pouch at time of arrest).

[137]United States v Schleis, 582 F(2d) 1166 (8th Cir Minn 1978).

arrest. On the other hand, courts have generally upheld, on *Edwards* grounds, the delayed search of a wallet at the stationhouse.[138]

Some objects do not fit neatly into categories distinguishing between briefcases and wallets. A purse, for instance, shares the characteristics of both. In *United States v Monclavo-Cruz,*[139] the search of a purse at the stationhouse an hour after it was seized was held unlawful. In *Monclavo-Cruz,* the Ninth Circuit Court said that *Edwards* was limited to the person and clothing. By contrast, the Alaska Supreme Court held that a purse is "immediately associated" with the person and thus exempted from the *Chadwick* limitation.[140] Some courts have found reason to exempt even luggage from the *Chadwick* rule if the delayed search is not as far removed from the scene of the arrest as the police station.[141]

The question of the scope of a search of containers seized from an arrestee must now be considered under the inventory search exception. In *Illinois v Lafayette,*[142] Justice Burger said:

> [A]t the stationhouse, it is entirely proper for police to remove and list or inventory property found on the person or in the possession of an arrested person who is to be jailed. A range of governmental interests support an inventory process. ... In short, every consideration of orderly police administration benefitting both police and the public points to the appropriateness of the examination.

In the concurring opinion, Justices Marshall and Brennan agreed that "[t]he practical necessities of securing persons and property in a jailhouse setting justify an inventory search as part of the standard procedure incident to incarceration."[143] However, the two Justices caution:

> A very different case would be presented if the State had relied solely on the fact of arrest to justify the search of respondent's shoulder bag. A warrantless search incident to arrest must be justified by a need to remove weapons or prevent the destruction of evidence.[144]

While the extent to which arresting officers may search luggage and other containers without a warrant at the scene of an arrest remains unclear, if the officers are patient and delay the search until the arrestee is taken to the police station and the search is part of a routine booking procedure, the search may be conducted. It is a round-about procedure that on its face appears irrational. Nonetheless, the Court is willing to permit

---

[138]See United States v Ziller, 623 F(2d) 562 (9th Cir Cal 1980), cert denied 449 US 877, 101 SCt 221, 66 LEd(2d) 99 (1980); United States v Passaro, 624 F(2d) 938 (9th Cir Cal 1980) (a wallet is an element of an arrestee's clothing), cert denied 449 US 1113, 101 SCt 925, 66 LEd(2d) 842 (1981).

[139]United States v Monclavo-Cruz, 662 F(2d) 1285 (9th Cir Ariz 1981).

[140]See Hinkel v Anchorage, 618 P(2d) 1069 (Alaska 1980), cert denied 450 US 1032, 101 SCt 1744, 68 LEd(2d) 228 (1981).

[141]See United States v Garcia, 605 F(2d) 349 (7th Cir Ill 1979), cert denied 446 US 984, 100 SCt 2966, 64 LEd(2d) 841 (1980); United States v Kaye, 492 F(2d) 744 (6th Cir Ohio 1974) (search of suitcase permissible after the arrestee and suitcase taken to the airport security office where the search took place; pre-*Chadwick*), cert denied 444 US 991, 100 SCt 522, 62 LEd(2d) 420 (1979).

[142]Illinois v Lafayette, 462 US 640, 646-47, 103 SCt 2605, 77 LEd(2d) 65 (1983).

[143]Illinois v Lafayette, 462 US 640, 648, 103 SCt 2605, 77 LEd(2d) 65 (1983).

[144]Illinois v Lafayette, 462 US 640, 648, 103 SCt 2605, 77 LEd(2d) 65 (1983).

warrantless intrusions under the rubric of an inventory search, which appears to be part of a routine administrative procedure, which the justices would be unable to agree is within the scope of a search incident to arrest.

Chapter 12

Automobile Exception to the Warrant Requirement

12.01   Introduction

(A) In general

Students of the Fourth Amendment are wise to study automobile searches. The word "automobile" has become "a talisman in whose presence the Fourth Amendment fades away and disappears,"[1] precisely what Justice Stewart warned against. The automobile search provides the best example of the weakening of the Fourth Amendment warrant requirement and the incredible expansions of the exceptions to the requirement.

The following three types of permissible searches have rendered the Constitution's protections virtually inapplicable to automobiles:

(1) Searches incident to arrest;

(2) Searches that come within the expanding "automobile exception"; and

(3) Inventory searches.

The Ohio Constitution imposes some limitations upon the broad authority granted to police under the federal Constitution to conduct expansive searches of automobiles incident to arrest.[2] Note that the limited authority to conduct a search of the interior of an automobile incident to arrest may give rise to probable cause to search the entire vehicle.[3] Searches of automobiles, as a result of the authority established under the three exceptions, rarely require a warrant to satisfy Fourth Amendment standards.

(B) Automobile exception, generally

The automobile exception to the Fourth Amendment warrant requirement provides that an officer having probable cause to believe that evidence of a crime will be found in a vehicle may stop the car and conduct a

---

[1]Coolidge v New Hampshire, 403 US 443, 461, 91 SCt 2022, 29 LEd(2d) 564 (1971) (Stewart, J., plurality opinion).

[2]The automobile exception generally applies to any private vehicle, such as an airplane or boat. One Ohio Court of Appeals has also said that "an analogy to automobiles is appropriate" when considering a search of a passenger's belongings on a public bus. See State v Bradley, 101 App(3d) 752, 656 NE(2d) 721 (Cuyahoga 1995) (however, note, the court never said that the automobile exception applies to a warrantless search of bus passenger's belongings). For an in-depth discussion, see Text Chapter 11, Search Incident to Arrest.

[3]See, e.g., State v Ingledue, No. 15-90-15, 1991 WL 104344 (3d Dist Ct App, Van Wert, 6-12-91).

warrantless search of the entire vehicle and all containers located within the vehicle that may hold the item sought.[4] The requirements and authority granted under this exception must be differentiated from the authority to search a vehicle incident to arrest developed one year earlier in *New York v Belton*.[5] To fit within the automobile exception, there must be independent probable cause to believe that evidence will be found in the vehicle. Once established, the authority granted under the automobile exception exceeds the authority that flows incident to an arrest. Operating together, however, the two exceptions vest enormous discretion in police officers and virtually eliminate the warrant requirement when the subject of a search is a vehicle.

The automobile exception is the best example of how the narrow exemptions from the warrant requirement, originally developed in response to manifested law enforcement needs, have outstripped those needs and become general rules.

12.02   Development of the automobile exception

Since 1925, the Supreme Court has recognized that Fourth Amendment considerations are different when a search involves an automobile rather than a home or office. That year, in *Carroll v United States*,[6] the Court held that a warrantless search of an automobile, supported by probable cause, was valid because the Fourth Amendment's requirements were amply satisfied by the exigent circumstances created by the mobility of the vehicle and society's legitimate interest in not losing the contraband pending issuance of a search warrant. Mobility created the exigency for the particular vehicle in *Carroll*, a prohibition enforcement case, because the occupants of the automobile were not under arrest and could have driven the car away while police sought a search warrant. Failure to conduct an immediate search, then, would have resulted in a permanent loss of the evidence. Consequently, the exemption recognized in *Carroll* rested upon (1) the existence of probable cause and (2) the mobility of the particular vehicle.

The Burger Court has eliminated the exigency requirement as the basis for the automobile exception. Although the Court continues to describe the exception in terms of exigency, the warrant exemption has been extended to cases where the occupants of the automobile were under arrest and their car effectively immobilized.[7] Moreover, a car that may be searched without a warrant on the highway where it has been stopped by police may be searched later at the police station, also without a warrant, notwithstanding the absence of any exigency justifying the failure to search the car at the scene or secure a warrant prior to the delayed search once the vehicle was securely in the custody of the police.[8]

---

[4]United States v Ross, 456 US 798, 102 SCt 2157, 72 LEd(2d) 572 (1982).

[5]New York v Belton, 453 US 454, 101 SCt 2860, 69 LEd(2d) 768 (1981). For discussion of the *Belton* rule, see Text 11.10, Search of an automobile incident to arrest.

[6]Carroll v United States, 267 US 132, 45 SCt 280, 69 LEd 543 (1925).

[7]See Chambers v Maroney, 399 US 42, 90 SCt 1975, 26 LEd(2d) 419 (1970).

[8]Texas v White, 423 US 67, 96 SCt 304, 46 LEd(2d) 209 (1975).

Consequently, the automobile exception has been transformed in just under six decades. Originally, it was a limited exception based on the mobility of a particular automobile and the impracticability of securing that automobile, in an era when police did not have the facilities to tow and secure vehicles. Today, it is a general exemption that extends to automobiles "in which the possibilities of the vehicle's being removed or evidence in it destroyed [are] remote, if not non-existent."[9]

The growth of the automobile exception has rested on various theories. It began in *Carroll,* wherein it was justified on the mobility of the particular vehicle and the impracticability in 1925 of securing the vehicle on an open highway. However, the impracticability dissipated as each police and sheriff's department acquired the ability to secure and tow vehicles, and the exception was extended to vehicles that were securely immobilized, having been removed to police facilities and later searched. The Court then developed alternative theories to justify bypassing the warrant process before searching. According to the Supreme Court, that justification existed because there is a diminished expectation of privacy associated with a car. A vehicle, under this theory, is simply a means of transport for its occupants and contents which, by virtue of being in a vehicle, are exposed to public view. Moreover, an automobile is not typically a repository for personal effects.[10]

Logical inconsistencies did not matter to the Court as it continued to apply the exception to areas of vehicles, such as a locked trunk, where the diminished expectation of privacy was patently inapplicable. Further, the Court sought to buttress the theory that an automobile is the subject of a diminished privacy expectation by pointing out that it is subject to a high degree of government regulation.[11] These theories were used by the Court to extend the warrant exemption to cases in which securing a warrant prior to a search was not impractical and merely involved inconvenience of the sort intended by the Fourth Amendment. Despite the development of theories that supplanted exigent circumstances as the basis for the automobile exception, the Supreme Court's decisions were not altogether clear, and they continued to refer to exigent circumstances as supporting the exemption.

This confusion resulted in different applications of the automobile exception by lower courts. Some read the Supreme Court opinions as creating a general exemption for vehicles. Others, however, read the Court's continuing reference to exigent circumstances as a limitation on the automobile exception and disallowed vehicular searches where there was no

---

[9]Cady v Dombrowski, 413 US 433, 441-42, 93 SCt 2523, 37 LEd(2d) 706 (1973).

[10]Cardwell v Lewis, 417 US 583, 94 SCt 2464, 41 LEd(2d) 325 (1974).

[11]Robbins v California, 453 US 420, 101 SCt 2841, 69 LEd(2d) 744 (1981), overruled by United States v Ross, 456 US 798, 102 SCt 2157, 72 LEd(2d) 572 (1982); Arkansas v Sanders, 442 US 753, 99 SCt 2586, 61 LEd(2d) 235 (1979), overruled by California v Acevedo, 500 US 565, 111 SCt 1982, 114 LEd(2d) 619 (1991).

exigency.[12] The Ohio Supreme Court, in *State v Kessler*,[13] required a finding of exigent circumstances which the court said was satisfied when the car was stopped on a public highway, and the passenger, who was not immediately arrested, could have removed the car from the scene and, thus, the evidence "from official grasp."

The general rule was produced by the Supreme Court in *United States v Ross*,[14] which clarified the dimensions of the exception and reworked the theory on which it rested. First, the automobile exception applies any time a police officer stops a vehicle, where objective facts exist that give rise to probable cause that would justify the issuance of a search warrant by a magistrate.[15] An argument that probable cause supports a warrantless search of an automobile will not be successful where the facts are insufficient to justify issuing a warrant.[16] For example, while the odor of marijuana may be sufficient to create probable cause, a police officer observing a defendant smoking what appeared to be a marijuana cigarette was insufficient.[17] However, a police officer who found in "plain view" a marijuana cigarette on the front seat of a vehicle was deemed to have sufficient probable cause to search the entire vehicle.[18] Similarly, a limited *Terry* search for weapons within a vehicle[19] led to probable cause to search the entire vehicle when the officer found a "roach" in plain view, the strong odor of deodorizer permeated the interior compartment, the door panels appeared to be displaced, the passengers were found to be in possession of marijuana and pagers, and the car was traveling upon a known "drug pipeline."[20] In such a situation, defense counsel can only focus upon the facts which gave rise to the original *Terry* stop, the claim that the officers

---

[12]See State v Marcum, 24 Wash App 441, 601 P(2d) 975 (1979) (where a police officer had the car keys, removing the mobility factor, no exigent circumstances existed to justify a warrantless search of the trunk of car under the automobile exception); Burkett v State, 271 Ark 150, 607 SW(2d) 399 (1980) (automobile exception inapplicable where exigency vitiated by arrest of the automobile occupants and call for a tow truck).

[13]State v Kessler, 53 OS(2d) 204, 373 NE(2d) 1252 (1978).

[14]United States v Ross, 456 US 798, 102 SCt 2157, 72 LEd(2d) 572 (1982).

[15]See State v Ford, No. 90 CA004801, 1990 WL 178075 (9th Dist Ct App, Lorain, 11-14-90), affirmed by 1993 WL 145835 (1993), appeal dismissed by 67 OS(3d) 1479, 620 NE(2d) 852 (1993).

[16]State v Hughes, No. 1554, 1986 WL 3839 (11th Dist Ct App, Portage, 3-28-86) (assertion that probable cause justified warrantless search of vehicle rejected where officers tried to obtain a warrant prior to the search but were unable to do so).

[17]State v Burkett, No. L-88-174, 1989 WL 41723 (6th Dist Ct App, Lucas, 4-28-89).

[18]State v Fadenholz, Nos. 60865, 60866, 1991 WL 106055 (8th Dist Ct App, Cuyahoga, 6-13-91); State v VanScoder, 92 App(3d) 853, 637 NE(2d) 374 (Wayne 1994) (police justified in searching entire automobile and containers given that the officer lawfully stopped the vehicle, smelled the odor of marijuana, and saw a roach clip in an ashtray).

[19]See Michigan v Long, 463 US 1032, 103 SCt 3469, 77 LEd(2d) 1201 (1983) (allowing a limited search for weapons of a vehicle's interior when justified by an officer's reasonable concern that the occupants may be armed).

[20]State v Chapman, 73 App(3d) 132, 596 NE(2d) 612 (Allen 1992).

believed that the occupants may have been armed, and the manner in which a *Terry* frisk led to discovery of marijuana on the occupants' persons.[21]

Second, where probable cause exists, a police officer may search the entire vehicle. Third, the warrantless search need not be supported by exigent circumstances; the fact that the search is of an automobile brings it within the exemption. Fourth, the search may be conducted on the highway where the car is stopped, or later at the police station; no additional justification is needed for a delayed search. Fifth, the authority to conduct a warrantless search extends to all containers and receptacles, found any-where in the vehicle, that may contain the item sought by police. Obviously, *Ross* states the law of the land and is the law in Ohio absent a radical decision by the Ohio Supreme Court to abandon practice and find broader protection of individual rights in the Ohio Constitution.

Nonetheless, a somewhat different approach from *Ross* was advanced in *State v Bocook*[22] by the Montgomery County Court of Appeals on an issue seemingly decided in *Ross* but sufficiently different from the facts in *Ross* to support a theory distinguishing the two cases. There, police had probable cause to search a suspected stolen van that police checked on periodically for eight months. When the van was being moved, police stopped it and searched it without a warrant. The court of appeals stated that although the exigent circumstances requirement of the automobile exception had declined in importance, it had not disappeared altogether. Consequently, the court held that where police had eight months to obtain a warrant, the warrantless search was invalid absent some exigency.

The *Ross* opinion, written by Justice Stevens, peremptorily abandoned the privacy rationale as the theoretical linchpin of the expanded automobile exception. Instead, Justice Stevens returned to *Carroll* and argued that the exception has always rested on the impracticability of requiring a warrant for the search of automobiles. In *Carroll,* delaying the search was demon-strably impracticable; in *Ross,* as well as other cases in between, securing a search warrant was not at all impracticable. Nonetheless, using the vague rubric of "impracticability," the court has created a general exemption. No impracticability, nor even inconvenience, need be demonstrated to justify the warrantless search of an immobilized vehicle or its contents. The Supreme Court has upheld a delayed warrantless search conducted eight hours after the car was impounded. The Court reaffirmed that "the justifi-cation to conduct such a warrantless search does not vanish once the car has been immobilized."[23]

The Supreme Court's peculiar attitude toward automobile searches and its contrasting protection of privacy in the home clashed in *California v Carney.*[24] The warrantless search involved a mobile home, which was parked

---

[21]See Text Ch 14, Stop and Frisk.

[22]State v Bocook, No. CA-9629, 1986 WL 9091 (2d Dist Ct App, Montgomery, 8-19-86).

[23]Florida v Meyers, 466 US 380, 382, 104 SCt 1852, 80 LEd(2d) 381 (1984), quoting Michigan v Thomas, 458 US 259, 261, 102 SCt 3079, 73 LEd(2d) 750 (1982).

[24]California v Carney, 471 US 386, 105 SCt 2066, 85 LEd(2d) 406 (1985); State v Ratcliff, 95 App(3d) 199, 642 NE(2d) 31 (Ashland 1994) (police had probable cause

in a public lot. The mobile home was searched at the time it was seized and again after it was removed by the police to the police station. The Court held that a mobile home operated on a public street is subject to a warrantless search under the automobile exception. Chief Justice Burger wrote for the majority that a mobile home on a public street is to be treated no differently from any other vehicle and all that need be shown to justify a warrantless search is probable cause to believe evidence of a crime will be found in the mobile home.

The automobile exception, as defined in *Ross,* should be considered, along with the authority granted in *New York v Belton,*[25] to permit the search of the interior compartment of a vehicle incident to the lawful arrest. The two rules rest on different theories and are brought into play under different circumstances. The two rules overlap, however, and when considered together will permit warrantless searches in an overwhelming number of cases. The *Belton* rule permits a search of the interior compartment of the vehicle only, and all containers found within that compartment, following any "custodial arrest" of an occupant of the vehicle. There need not be independent probable cause to believe that weapons or evidence will be found in the compartment. Consequently, anytime a motorist is stopped for an offense that under the Code permits an arrest, rather than mandates issuance of a summons, the officer may conduct a search of the interior compartment or any container in that compartment that arouses his curiosity. Presumably, a *Belton*-type search must be done somewhat contemporaneously with the arrest. If, however, the officer, when he stops the vehicle, has probable cause to believe that the car contains evidence of a crime, or if that belief is created as a result of what is found during a *Belton* search of the interior compartment, the officer may search the entire vehicle for evidence. That search, under the automobile exception, need not be contemporaneous with the stopping or arrest and may be conducted later at the police station.

12.03   Extension of the automobile exception to containers in the vehicle

None of the justifications offered in support of the warrantless search of automobiles supported extension of the warrant exemption to opaque containers found in a vehicle during a search. Mobility that gave rise to the warrant exemption certainly would not support a warrantless search of a container found in the vehicle that could just as easily be seized and secured until a warrant issued without the impairments attributed to seizing a vehicle. The cost of towing vehicles long distance as well as the specious argument that not all communities had towing and storage capabilities certainly offered no support to extension of the exemption to packages and contain-

---

to conduct warrantless search of entire motor home that was lawfully stopped where driver, who smelled of alcohol, admitted that he had been smoking marijuana and had been drinking, and drug sniffing dog reacted positively when approaching the outside of the motor home).

[25]New York v Belton, 453 US 454, 101 SCt 2860, 69 LEd(2d) 768 (1981). See Text 11.10, Search of an automobile incident to arrest.

ers that could be securely placed in the trunk of the police car and easily safeguarded and stored at the police station while a warrant was sought. Moreover, the spill-over argument that an automobile is entitled to a lesser expectation of privacy because an automobile is, by its nature, out and about in public and is subject to a high degree of regulation in the interest of safety could not be extended to containers placed out of view, under a seat or in the trunk to enhance and ensure the owner's privacy. But, of course, logical consistency has never been the hallmark of the automobile exception nor of the Supreme Court justices who have nurtured its expansive growth over the past two decades. It, then, was no surprise when the exception was extended to the contents of an automobile.

In *United States v Ross*,[26] the United States Supreme Court extended the automobile exception to all containers located in a vehicle that might hold the object police are seeking. In extending authority to containers and receptacles, the Court overruled precedent that had been reaffirmed only a year earlier in *Robbins v California*.[27] Before *Ross*, the Court held that the automobile exception did not extend to containers whose contents were not open to plain view or whose contents were undisclosed by the packaging. Rather, the Court sought to find an independent justification for extending the automobile exception to such containers. Finding none, the Court said that while the entire automobile might be searched, a container found therein could only be seized without a warrant and held while a warrant was sought.

Justice Stevens rejected the approach requiring independent justification for the warrantless search of containers discovered in a vehicle and, in so doing, redefined the scope of warrantless searches. In *Ross*, he said that a search under the automobile exception has the same breadth as a search conducted pursuant to a warrant. Therefore, just as a search with a warrant extends to everything within the place searched, a warrantless search under the automobile exception applies to everything found in the car that may contain the object police are seeking. Equating the scope of a search under the automobile exception with a search authorized by a warrant epitomizes the modern Court's approach to warrantless searches. Their scope is usually not limited to neutralizing the exigency that justified the initial warrantless intrusion. Exceptions to the warrant requirement are equivalent to a judicially authorized warrant. Searches conducted under an exception are not limited in scope to the societal need that gave rise to the creation of the exception. A set of facts that triggers a search under the automobile exception allows as broad a search as though a judge had issued a warrant and ordered the search.[28]

The same rules pertaining to delayed searches of automobiles apply to delayed searches of containers found in the automobile. In *Ross*, the Court

[26]United States v Ross, 456 US 798, 102 SCt 2157, 72 LEd(2d) 572 (1982).

[27]Robbins v California, 453 US 420, 101 SCt 2841, 69 LEd(2d) 744 (1981), overruled by United States v Ross, 456 US 798, 102 SCt 2157, 72 LEd(2d) 572 (1982).

[28]State v Welch, 18 OS(3d) 88, 18 OBR 124, 480 NE(2d) 384 (1985), cert denied 474 US 1010, 106 SCt 537, 88 LEd(2d) 468 (1985) (*United States v Ross* followed).

approved the warrantless search of the paper bag and the leather pouch at the police station after they had been separated from the car. Three years following *Ross*, the Court again upheld a warrantless delayed search of containers seized from an automobile. What is significant about *United States v Johns*[29] is the application of the automobile exception to a search of containers conducted three days after the containers were seized and securely stored in a government warehouse, and where the government attempted no justification for the delay or for its failure to secure a warrant other than the right to conduct the search flowed directly from the automobile exception.

In *Johns*, the Court indicated its declining allegiance to the warrant requirement when Justice O'Connor concluded for the majority that it would not further Fourth Amendment interests to require a warrant in this instance because it would merely compel police to conduct warrantless searches earlier. While her factual prediction was likely correct, Justice O'Connor's analysis turns the Fourth Amendment on its head. Formerly, the party seeking dispensation from the constitutionally required and pre-ferred procedure—searching with a warrant—was required to justify the failure to follow that route. Now, the party seeking adherence to Fourth Amendment procedures must demonstrate how compliance with those pro-cedures would further Fourth Amendment values and interests. It is diffi-cult to imagine that this attitude will be confined to the Court's considera-tion of the automobile exception.

In the 1991 case, *California v Acevedo*,[30] the United States Supreme Court abandoned the narrow limitation on the search of containers allowed under the automobile exception, which it had retained in *United States v Ross*.[31] *Ross* expanded the automobile exception to containers found in the automobile but exempted from the broad authorization to search without a warrant those situations where probable cause did not focus on the car, generally, but on a specific container before it was placed in the automobile. That limitation on the automobile exception arose in *Arkansas v Sanders*,[32] where probable cause arose from the activities of the defendant in an airport terminal. Police officers, seeking to bring the case within the auto-mobile exception, did not intervene until the defendant hailed a taxicab and placed the suitcase in the trunk of the cab. The cab then pulled away from the terminal. At that point, the officers stopped the cab, arrested the defendant, seized the suitcase from the trunk, and proceeded to search it without a warrant.

Instead of expanding the automobile exception, the *Sanders* Court applied the *United States v Chadwick*[33] rationale and invalidated the search, contending that a suitcase seized from a vehicle could no more be searched without a warrant than a suitcase seized from any other location. The decision in *Sanders* made abundant sense. If *Chadwick* stated a viable

---

[29]United States v Johns, 469 US 478, 105 SCt 881, 83 LEd(2d) 890 (1985).
[30]California v Acevedo, 500 US 565, 111 SCt 1982, 114 LEd(2d) 619 (1991).
[31]United States v Ross, 456 US 798, 102 SCt 2157, 72 LEd(2d) 572 (1982).
[32]Arkansas v Sanders, 442 US 753, 99 SCt 2586, 61 LEd(2d) 235 (1979).
[33]United States v Chadwick, 433 US 1, 97 SCt 2476, 53 LEd(2d) 538 (1977).

principle, it had to extend to containers found in a vehicle. *Ross* rejected that broad rule but retained the narrow holding of *Sanders* refusing to extend the automobile exception to the warrant requirement to those situations where the probable cause focused upon the container before it was placed in the vehicle. To hold otherwise would be to encourage police to exploit the automobile exception and further erode the already damaged judicial preference for a warrant. *Sanders* was strictly enforced in *State v Tincher*[34] to exclude a plastic baggy of marijuana on probable cause focused before it was tossed into an automobile. The court said that the relationship between the bag and the automobile was fortuitous. The court did not pay heed to the fact that the officers had hidden behind the automobile exception to avoid obtaining a warrant.

The broad parameters of the automobile exception made the limitation appear illogical, although the limitation was impeccably logical and consistent with the Court's stated preference for warrants as well as its often-stated shibboleth that "warrantless searches are per se unreasonable." Moreover, narrowing the limitation from all containers to just those where the probable cause existed prior to their being placed in the automobile further weakened the logic and further eroded the sound analysis on which the *Chadwick* rule rests. Nonetheless, the distinction could be justified because it served to prevent police abuse and exploitation of the automobile exception.

Finally, in *California v Acevedo*,[35] the Court abandoned the narrow *Sanders* limitation it had retained. In *Acevedo*, police searched only a container that they saw the defendant place in an automobile. They observed the defendant leaving an apartment, known to contain marijuana, with a brown paper bag "the size of one of the wrapped marijuana packages they had seen earlier"[36] taken into the apartment. The defendant placed the bag in the trunk of the vehicle and drove away. The police stopped the car, opened the trunk, and opened the bag in which they found marijuana.

The Supreme Court held that police may search a container seized from a vehicle where they have probable cause to believe it contains contraband, even though the probable cause focuses on the container before it was placed in the vehicle. No limitation was suggested by the majority regarding the expansion of the warrant exemption to those cases where police do not have a prior opportunity to secure a warrant. Such a limitation would not have affected the outcome in *Acevedo*, but the truth is this Court is unconcerned about police exploitation of the warrant exemption in order to avoid a judge's making the probable cause determination.

Justice Blackmun, for the *Acevedo* majority, argued that there is no principled distinction between the containers searched under the automobile exception and those that were beyond its scope because probable cause focused on the container before it was placed in the vehicle. The weakness in this argument is that it presupposes that the automobile exception, itself,

---

[34]State v Tincher, 47 App(3d) 188, 548 NE(2d) 251 (Preble 1988).
[35]California v Acevedo, 500 US 565, 111 SCt 1982, 114 LEd(2d) 619 (1991).
[36]California v Acevedo, 500 US 565, 111 SCt 1982, 114 LEd(2d) 619 (1991).

is based on principle when in fact its continuous expansion reflects a rejection of all of the principles that guided and limited the growth of exceptions to the warrant requirement. The illogic is in the automobile exception and its extension to containers, not in the single rule that rejected expansion. However, the tables were turned: the single rule that reflected application of traditional Fourth Amendment principle appeared illogical alongside the myriad of rules established not in conformity with the principle. The automobile exception has outstripped all of the societal needs that gave rise to this particular exemption from the warrant requirement. Its continued growth is the result of this Court's rejection of the value of search warrants. It has already spilled over into other exceptions, and the expansion in *Acevedo* will continue that trend. The issue remaining at the federal level is whether anything is left of *United States v Chadwick*[37] that does not allow for the warrantless search of containers seized on probable cause in places other than automobiles, or whether its illogic alongside all of these rules spells its doom.

12.04   Limits on the automobile exception

Once *California v Acevedo*[38] eliminated the major limitation on the search of containers retained in *Ross*,[39] the general rule is that a warrant is unnecessary to search an automobile and all its contents once a police officer has probable cause to believe that evidence of a crime is contained within that automobile. Nonetheless, despite the automobile exception's apparent capability to expand to meet every law enforcement request, there remains a tenuous limitation on the scope of the exception.

In *Coolidge v New Hampshire*,[40] the Court refused to extend the automobile exception to an automobile that was seized while parked on the suspect's driveway and later searched at a police facility. The fact that the car in *Coolidge* was parked rather than moving no longer provides an arguable basis for a limitation on the automobile exception. The Supreme Court has subsequently upheld the warrantless search of a parked vehicle.[41] The second *Coolidge* limitation has never been reviewed by the Supreme Court. Not only was the automobile parked and not moving, but also it was parked on the defendant's own property. Subsequent Supreme Court decisions have affirmed the applicability of the automobile exception to parked vehicles removed from public parking lots[42] but have never considered whether different considerations would prevail if the car was removed from the

---

[37]United States v Chadwick, 433 US 1, 97 SCt 2476, 53 LEd(2d) 538 (1977).

[38]California v Acevedo, 500 US 565, 111 SCt 1982, 114 LEd(2d) 619 (1991).

[39]United States v Ross, 456 US 798, 102 SCt 2157, 72 LEd(2d) 572 (1982).

[40]Coolidge v New Hampshire, 403 US 443, 91 SCt 2022, 29 LEd(2d) 564 (1971).

[41]United States v Johns, 469 US 478, 105 SCt 881, 83 LEd(2d) 890 (1985) (although the pickup truck was attended); Texas v White, 423 US 67, 96 SCt 304, 46 LEd(2d) 209 (1975) (upholding the warrantless seizure from a city street and subsequent warrantless search of an unattended parked car).

[42]California v Carney, 471 US 386, 105 SCt 2066, 85 LEd(2d) 406 (1985); Cardwell v Lewis, 417 US 583, 94 SCt 2464, 41 LEd(2d) 325 (1974).

defendant's property. Relying on *Coolidge*, the court in *State v Sprague*[43] refused to extend the exception to a search of the defendant's automobile at the defendant's residence, especially since the officers delayed the search until the car was at the residence, affording the defendant ample time to destroy any incriminating evidence. The outcome of this issue may hinge on the circumstances surrounding the search or seizure of an automobile from private property. If police ignore a pre-existing opportunity to secure a warrant, the total absence of exigent circumstances coupled with the automobile's being located on private property may prevail. Of course, clinging to vestiges of exigent circumstances as a basis for limiting the automobile exception, which seems limitless, may be unrealistic.

Acevedo imposed a limitation at the same time that it eliminated the meaningful limitations imposed by *Chadwick* and *Sanders*. The Court said that when probable cause focuses upon a container prior to its placement within a vehicle, the permissible scope of the warrantless search extends only to that container and not to the vehicle as a whole. Naturally, if the suspect container is searched and evidence found, the state can always argue that the discovery of the evidence sought gave rise to probable cause to search the entire vehicle.

Note also that a search of a vehicle may not be conducted during field sobriety testing. Searches conducted during such a procedure which result in the only charges being filed arising from what the search turns up[44] are particularly suspect and vulnerable to challenge.[45]

12.05   Inventory searches of vehicles

(A) In general

Another source of authority for a warrantless search of a vehicle arises under the recognized power of police officers to inventory the contents of a lawfully impounded vehicle.[46] In *South Dakota v Opperman*,[47] the Supreme Court held that automobile inventory searches are reasonable, and therefore lawful, under the Fourth Amendment. Consequently, a routine inventory of a lawfully impounded vehicle is reasonable when performed pursuant to standardized policy, and "when the evidence does not demonstrate that the procedure involved is merely a pretext for an evidentiary search of the impounded automobile."[48]

---

[43]State v Sprague, Nos. CA88-05-037, CA88-06-049, 1989 WL 36301 (12th Dist Ct App, Clermont, 4-17-89).

[44]Cf. Smith v Ohio, 494 US 541, 110 SCt 1288, 108 LEd(2d) 464 (1990) (probable cause must exist prior to the search; what is found cannot provide the probable cause to justify the search).

[45]Cf. State v Lewis, 69 App(3d) 318, 590 NE(2d) 805 (Geauga 1990).

[46]South Dakota v Opperman, 428 US 364, 96 SCt 3092, 49 LEd(2d) 1000 (1976).

[47]South Dakota v Opperman, 428 US 364, 96 SCt 3092, 49 LEd(2d) 1000 (1976).

[48]State v Robinson, 58 OS(2d) 478, 391 NE(2d) 317 (1979), cert denied 444 US 942, 100 SCt 297, 62 LEd(2d) 309 (1979); State v Gordon, 95 App(3d) 334, 642 NE(2d) 440 (Cuyahoga 1994) (inventory upheld where officers followed standardized regulations by refusing to allow uninvolved individual to drive the vehicle home and where the officers performed the inventory search in "good faith."

The car in *Opperman* was towed to the city impoundment lot after police officers had issued two citations for illegal parking in a restricted zone and the car had not been removed. At the lot, police observed a watch on the dashboard and other personal items in the back of the car. An officer unlocked the car to inventory the property and found marijuana in an unlocked glove compartment.

The Supreme Court indicated that routine police inventories are justified to protect the owner's property, to protect the police against claims of lost or stolen property, and to protect the police from potential danger. Chief Justice Burger, for the Supreme Court majority, indicated that reasonableness in each case would depend on the particular facts of the case. The factors in *Opperman* that tipped the balance in favor of the state's position were (1) the automobile was lawfully impounded; (2) the inventory was conducted after impoundment; (3) the owner was not present to make other arrangements for the safekeeping of the vehicle; (4) the inventory was prompted by valuables in plain view and was pursuant to standard police procedure; and (5) the inventory was not a pretext to conceal an investigatory search.

Implicit in Chief Justice Burger's approach to inventories was the rationale that the impounding of the illegally parked vehicle was lawful because the owner was not present to make other arrangements for the automobile. That theory has not been pursued in subsequent litigation and merits clarification. It is one way of ensuring that the impoundment is not a pretext to conduct a search.

(B) Lawful impoundment

In determining the lawfulness of the impoundment, authority to impound should never be assumed. A car may be impounded if it is evidence in a criminal case, used to commit a crime, obtained with funds derived from criminal activities,[49] or unlawfully parked or obstructing traffic;[50] or if the occupant of the vehicle is arrested; or when impoundment is otherwise authorized by statute or municipal ordinance.[51] A legally parked automobile may not be impounded simply because the owner or driver is arrested while away from the car.[52] In *State v Collura*,[53] the defendant went to the police station on a Saturday and parked his car legally in the police

---

[49]Cleveland v Becvar, 55 App(3d) 11, 561 NE(2d) 1036 (Cuyahoga 1988).

[50]State v Gordon, 95 App(3d) 334, 642 NE(2d) 440 (Cuyahoga 1994).

[51]State v Dotson, 66 App(3d) 182, 583 NE(2d) 1068 (Franklin 1990) (impoundment illegal because driver was not arrested nor do Columbus ordinances authorize impoundment for expired tags).

[52]State v Tabasso, No. 34031 (8th Dist Ct App, Cuyahoga, 5-29-75).

[53]State v Collura, 72 App(3d) 364, 594 NE(2d) 975 (Cuyahoga 1991), appeal dismissed by 60 OS(3d) 718, 574 NE(2d) 1079 (1991); State v Cole, 93 App(3d) 712, 639 NE(2d) 859 (Summit 1994) (defendant's vehicle was unlawfully impounded where the officer testified that an inventory is conducted whenever someone is placed under arrest; the testimony failed to establish existence of any valid or standard criteria for determining when a car should be impounded, and defendant was not arrested for traffic offense, nor in his car, which was lawfully parked, and officer made no effort to find a third party to secure the contents of the vehicle or drive the car if needed be).

lot. Inside, he found that charges had been filed against him. The charge required a court appearance, and the defendant was arrested until he could appear in court on Monday. His car, though legally parked, was immediately impounded because overnight parking was not allowed. An inventory search turned up contraband. The court held the impounding to be illegal because the car was not abandoned, the defendant was not arrested on the highway, the car was legally parked when searched, and the defendant's companion could have removed the car to avoid the overnight parking restriction.

An impoundment implies some public policy purposes being served; a legitimate purpose should not be assumed. Removal from a lawful parking spot makes the impoundment especially suspect and justifies an inference that the impoundment is a pretext to allow an inventory search.[54]

The Cuyahoga County Court of Appeals held that a car is lawfully impounded once it is in the security of the station house, not when the vehicle is attached to a police tow.[55] While such a rule would help to control and limit pretextual impoundments, it is not necessarily a wise rule. First, the physical attributes of an impoundment actually occur at the scene when police take custody of the vehicle. Second, the underlying purposes for allowing inventorying of such vehicles—protection of the owner's property and insulation of the police from false claims of loss—are better served by an early inventory before the vehicle is removed. Finally, impounded cars are not always removed to a police station. Frequently, they are removed by a private towing agency to a contracted private lot. Undoubtedly, requiring inventories to be delayed until the car is at the police station would greatly ensure that the impoundment is not for devious purposes. Too many conditions, however, intervene to make that goal pragmatic or desirable.

(C) Lawful inventory

Following a lawful impoundment, a vehicle may be inventoried. However, not every search contemporaneous with or following an impoundment is an inventory. To provide a useful way to distinguish between inventory searches and pretextual inventories, which are disguised investigatory searches, courts inquire as to what devices exist to control police discretion. Underlying this quest is the belief that standardization will prevent pretextual inventory searches.[56] It does not quite work that way; however, under this approach the unique situation stands out as a pretext.

A police officer's own testimony may support an inference that a search was conducted with an investigatory intent and was not a valid inventory

[54]Cf. State v Collura, 72 App(3d) 364, 594 NE(2d) 975 (Cuyahoga 1991), appeal dismissed by 60 OS(3d) 718, 574 NE(2d) 1079 (1991) (impoundment especially pretextual where a friend of the defendant's was available to drive the vehicle).
[55]State v Smith, 80 App(3d) 337, 609 NE(2d) 212 (Cuyahoga 1992), appeal dismissed by 65 OS(3d) 1417, 598 NE(2d) 1169 (1992).
[56]State v Fettro, No. 612, 1986 WL 12406 (4th Dist Ct App, Highland, 11-4-86) (search of lawfully impounded truck that following arrest was blocking traffic illegally because there was no evidence that the search was performed pursuant to standardized police practice).

search. In *State v Bailey*,[57] the state contended that an inventory of a vehicle was undertaken solely because the officer believed that it might be stolen. That assertion, however, was undercut by the officer's own testimony that he was looking for drugs. Consequently, the court of appeals reversed the conviction based on evidence seized during the search. Similarly, in *State v Rutherford*,[58] an appellate court would not reverse the trial court's granting of a motion to suppress where the arresting officer intercepted the defendant, who had been arrested for DUI, after the defendant was released and did an inventory of his vehicle. The officer testified that he might have suspected that contraband was in the car based on the defendant's past history. The trial and appellate courts' decisions appeared premised on the total absence of a need to impound and inventory when the search was undertaken. The same result was reached in *State v Himmelhaver*,[59] where the state's assertion that a search was an inventory was rejected by the court of appeals because standard inventory forms were not completed and retained for future reference; the two officers conducting the search testified differently as to where they found the evidence in question; and the record did not demonstrate that a tow truck had been called prior to the search.

Opperman provided no general rule, relying instead on the particular facts in the case. However, since the court upheld the admissibility of the marijuana found in the glove compartment, the case clearly advises that the Fourth Amendment does not restrict the scope of an inventory search to items in plain view. Prior to *Opperman,* an Ohio court, in *State v Bradshaw*,[60] had taken the position that the police duty to safeguard an owner's property while it is in custody does not justify a detailed inventory search but is limited to items in plain view. The *Bradshaw* limitation, following *Opperman,* is not compelled by the federal Constitution. Some states, including South Dakota, reviewed and rejected the breadth of the inventory search sanctioned by the Supreme Court on state constitutional grounds.[61] The Ohio Supreme Court, however, has held that "a standard inventory search of the trunk of a lawfully impounded automobile" is permissible.[62]

In *State v Carder*,[63] the court took seriously the Supreme Court's concern that an inventory search not mask and serve as a pretext for an investigatory search for evidence. The *Carder* court held that once an inventory search uncovers evidence giving rise to probable cause, the inventory search must cease and a warrant must be sought to continue the search. The court, however, did not realize that the partial inventory, which gave rise to probable cause, then would be transformed into a search under the automo-

---

[57]State v Bailey, No. WD-89-15, 1989 WL 130855 (6th Dist Ct App, Wood, 11-3-89).

[58]State v Rutherford, No. 609, 1987 WL 7003 (4th Dist Ct App, Highland, 2-24-87).

[59]State v Himmelhaver, 39 App(3d) 42, 528 NE(2d) 1320 (Clermont 1987).

[60]State v Bradshaw, 41 App(2d) 48, 322 NE(2d) 311 (Wood 1974).

[61]See State v Opperman, 247 NW(2d) 673 (SD 1976).

[62]State v Robinson, 58 OS(2d) 478, 391 NE(2d) 317 (1979), cert denied 444 US 942, 100 SCt 297, 62 LEd(2d) 309 (1979).

[63]State v Carder, 9 OO(3d) 356 (CP, Lucas 1978).

bile exception. But this is the way the various exceptions operate virtually to eliminate the possibility of requiring a warrant when the object to be searched is an automobile.

The Supreme Court has not retained the same concern for avoiding pretextual inventory searches evidenced in the standards set forth in Chief Justice Burger's *Opperman* decision. The *Opperman* Court focused on control of police discretion as the way to curtail abuse. Chief Justice Rehnquist penned the Court's latest look at this subject in *Colorado v Bertine*[64] and indicated this Court's approach to the problem. In *Bertine*, the defendant was arrested for drunk driving, and police inventoried the contents of his van. Unlike the regulation that controlled the inventory in *Opperman*, the search was not conducted according to standardized procedures. The Boulder, Colorado police department regulation left it to the police officer to determine whether (1) to allow a third person to take custody of an arrestee's vehicle, (2) to park and lock the vehicle, or (3) to inventory its contents and impound the vehicle. These options provided the type of unbridled discretion that the *Opperman* Court frowned on. Moreover, the municipal regulation provided no guidance as to which areas of the car should be searched and what sort of items to inventory.

Chief Justice Rehnquist, for the majority, wrote that there was no showing that the officers acted in bad faith or for the sole purpose of investigation. Rather than impose the prophylactic standards developed in *Opperman*, the *Bertine* Court applied a test that countenances total discretion and applied an alternative standard to prevent abuse that requires an impossible showing. In so doing, the Supreme Court has taken another step toward virtual elimination of the Fourth Amendment from automobile searches. However, it is clear that a search conducted with an investigatory intent, and that is not conducted in the manner of an inventory search, does not constitute an inventory search.[65]

The court in *State v Williams*[66] was convinced that a van was searched with investigatory intent and concluded that the inventory was a pretext where an officer asserted safety violations in the vehicle after the defendant refused permission to search. The vehicle had been under surveillance for three hours when a warrant could have been obtained, and nothing in the facts could lead to a conclusion that an inventory was necessary or undertaken to protect the vehicle or its contents. On the other hand, some courts disregard the prosecution claim that a search was an inventory and avoid the issue of pretext altogether when the facts disclose an alternative justification for a search.[67]

Opperman did not resolve how extensive an inventory search could be. Since the contraband in that case was found in the unlocked glove compart-

---

[64]Colorado v Bertine, 479 US 367, 107 SCt 738, 93 LEd(2d) 739 (1987).

[65]State v Caponi, 12 OS(3d) 302, 12 OBR 375, 466 NE(2d) 551 (1984), cert denied 469 US 1209, 105 SCt 1174, 84 LEd(2d) 324 (1985).

[66]State v Williams, 54 App(3d) 117, 561 NE(2d) 1038 (Ross 1988).

[67]See, e.g., State v Crickon, 43 App(3d) 171, 540 NE(2d) 287 (Sandusky 1988). For a discussion on pretext arrests and the standards used, see Text Ch 11, Search Incident to Arrest.

ment, it was clear that the Court was not limiting inventories to items in plain view. The Ohio Supreme Court upheld a standardized inventory search of a truck.[68] Clearly, the federal Constitution does not bar an inventory search of a vehicle that extends to closed containers if there is a written standard policy governing such inspections, and limiting police discretion.[69] Absent a specific police policy authorizing the opening of closed containers during an inventory, evidence seized will be suppressed.[70] The Ohio Supreme Court held it improper for a Highway Patrol officer to search a closed opaque plastic bag lodged beneath the spare tire of a lawfully impounded vehicle where the patrol had no policy or practice with respect to closed containers.[71] The Patrol's written policy directing the officer to inventory "everything accessible" was not deemed specific enough to cover the requirement imposed in *Wells*.

CROSS REFERENCES

Text 14.06

---

[68]State v Robinson, 58 OS(2d) 478, 391 NE(2d) 317 (1979), cert denied 444 US 942, 100 SCt 297, 62 LEd(2d) 309 (1979).
[69]Florida v Wells, 495 US 1, 110 SCt 1632, 109 LEd(2d) 1 (1990).
[70]State v Brown, No. CA-8392, 1991 WL 123714 (5th Dist Ct App, Stark, 6-28-91), reversed by 65 OS(3d) 483, 605 NE(2d) 46 (1992).
[71]State v Hathman, 65 OS(3d) 403, 604 NE(2d) 743 (1992).

Chapter 13

Plain View

13.01   Introduction

In *Harris v United States*,[1] the United States Supreme Court stated that "it has long been settled that objects falling in the plain view of an officer who has a right to be in the position to have that view are subject to seizure and may be introduced in evidence." Three years later, a plurality of the Supreme Court developed additional standards governing the seizure of items in plain view and indicated that the "plain view" exception to the warrant requirement must meet those additional legal tests because its usage in the context of the Fourth Amendment is not identical to the common meaning of the phrase "plain view."[2] The requirements surrounding the plain view doctrine come into play when a police officer discovers evidence while in the course of a search for other evidence. Plain view is to be distinguished from "open view," when a police officer not engaged in a search or other intrusion upon privacy spots evidence of a crime. Thus, the plain view standards are not limitations on "open view" sightings. The distinction referred to here was described by then Justice Rehnquist in *Texas v Brown*.[3]

> "[O]bjects such as weapons or contraband found in a public place may be seized by the police without a warrant. The seizure of property in plain view involves no invasion of privacy and is presumptively reasonable, assuming there is probable cause to associate the property with criminal activity." A different situation is presented, however, when the property in open view is " 'situated on private premises to which access is not otherwise available for the seizing officer.' " ... "[P]lain view" provides grounds for seizure of an item when an officer's access to an object has some prior justification under the Fourth Amendment.[4]

For the last two decades, the Supreme Court has focused on the governing limitations applicable to plain view seizures. This scrutiny was based, during the early part of those decades, on the Court's concern that, if not carefully circumscribed, the doctrine could be expanded to obliterate both the warrant requirement itself and the historical policy reasons that underlie the Fourth Amendment's particularity requirement as a defense against general warrants. In *Coolidge v New Hampshire*,[5] the plurality opinion, authored by Justice Stewart, focused on the requirements to limit the plain view doctrine from becoming the vehicle for general searches. In a subse-

---

[1]Harris v United States, 390 US 234, 236, 88 SCt 992, 19 LEd(2d) 1067 (1968).
[2]Coolidge v New Hampshire, 403 US 443, 91 SCt 2022, 29 LEd(2d) 564 (1971).
[3]Texas v Brown, 460 US 730, 103 SCt 1535, 75 LEd(2d) 502 (1983) (plurality).
[4]Texas v Brown, 460 US 730, 738, 103 SCt 1535, 75 LEd(2d) 502 (1983) (citation omitted).
[5]Coolidge v New Hampshire, 403 US 443, 91 SCt 2022, 29 LEd(2d) 564 (1971).

quent series of opinions,[6] the Ohio Supreme Court closely adhered to the *Coolidge* plurality's requirements in setting forth the three tests that must be met to justify a plain view search and seizure:

(1) The *intrusion* affording the plain view must be lawful;

(2) The discovery of the evidence must be *inadvertent*;[7] and

(3) The incriminating nature of the evidence must be *immediately apparent* to the seizing authority.

The standards enunciated for the plain view doctrine in *Coolidge* pertained to the requirements for *seizing* objects in plain view. In most instances, an object in plain view is just that, visible. It is not in an opaque container. If it were, it is not likely that the criminal nature of the object would be obvious. But in those instances where the unusual occurs and an object is not totally visible, yet where there is probable cause to believe that the object in the container comprises criminal evidence, the plain view doctrine authorizes its seizure. The current approach assumes that satisfaction of the plain view requirements authorizes the search of objects that are lawfully seized.[8] The transformation of the plain view doctrine from authorization to seize to authorization to seize and search without a warrant is significant and has never been fully addressed by the Supreme Court. Initially, the Court authorized a search of a balloon filled with a powdery substance in *Brown*, with a plurality assuming that the plain view doctrine authorized search, and with two justices joining to uphold the search only because of the unique packaging of the contraband that disclosed its content. *Arizona v Hicks*,[9] without even discussing the issue, seemed to indicate that an object in plain view that is seized may be searched. The issue may not be finally resolved since the *Hicks* language is obtuse and since this inference was not relevant to the disposition of the case.

Additionally, the Rehnquist Court has weakened the plain view standards in the course of time. In 1990, the Court eliminated the inadvertency requirement.[10] Consequently, police who are lawfully present may seize evidence that is in plain view if the incriminating nature of the evidence is immediately apparent to the officer. Further, photographs taken at the scene of the execution of a search warrant are admissible because they depict no more than was in plain view.[11]

---

[6]State v Wilmoth, 1 OS(3d) 118, 1 OBR 157, 438 NE(2d) 105 (1982), cert denied 460 US 1081, 103 SCt 1769, 76 LEd(2d) 343 (1983); State v Williams, 55 OS(2d) 82, 377 NE(2d) 1013 (1978); State v Benner, 40 OS(3d) 301, 533 NE(2d) 701 (1988), cert denied 494 US 1090, 110 SCt 1834, 108 LEd(2d) 962 (1990).

[7]For a discussion of the demise of the inadvertency requirement following the United States Supreme Court's decision in Horton v California, 496 US 128, 110 SCt 2301, 110 LEd(2d) 112 (1990), see Text 13.04, Inadvertence.

[8]Cf. Arizona v Hicks, 480 US 321, 107 SCt 1149, 94 LEd(2d) 347 (1987).

[9]Cf. Arizona v Hicks, 480 US 321, 107 SCt 1149, 94 LEd(2d) 347 (1987).

[10]Horton v California, 496 US 128, 110 SCt 2301, 110 LEd(2d) 112 (1990).

[11]State v Cruise, No. 85-CA-28, 1987 WL 7009 (4th Dist Ct App, Washington, 2-24-87).

13.02   Lawful intrusion

(A) General

For the plain view doctrine to apply, a police officer must be lawfully present at the time of both the search and the seizure.[12] A police officer who observes a large quantity of marijuana plants sitting in a window, visible from the sidewalk where he has a right to be, may not enter the premises to seize the plants without a warrant. Observation of the plants was certainly lawful, but the observation itself will not justify entry of the premises to effect a seizure absent a warrant or exigent circumstances. The Court in *Coolidge v New Hampshire*[13] recognized that the seizure, as well as the search, is governed by the warrant requirement when it said, "Incontrovertible testimony of the senses that an incriminating object is on the premises belonging to a criminal suspect may establish the fullest possible measure of probable cause. But even where the object is contraband, ... the police may not enter and make a warrantless seizure." Probable cause is not a substitute for a warrant; probable cause must exist before the warrant may be issued. Similarly, where a police officer observed a fugitive sitting, in someone else's trailer, that observation in plain view did not authorize a warrantless entry absent consent or exigent circumstances.[14]

The lawfulness of an officer's presence at the time evidence is viewed or seized must be considered in three contexts: whether the presence is authorized by a warrant, whether the presence falls within an exception to the warrant requirement, and whether the situation is one where the warrant requirement is inapplicable.

(B) Presence authorized by warrant

Police officers, authorized by a valid warrant to search for specific items, may seize unanticipated evidence and contraband that they discover during the search for the object specified in the warrant. No new warrant need be obtained to seize the additional evidence. A judge has already passed on the probable cause that justified the intrusion, and the doctrine of exigency provides justification for not securing a new warrant because the delay might result in the destruction of the evidence. Naturally, however, the additional evidence uncovered during the search is governed by the reasonable scope of the search for the items specified in the warrant.

The scope of a search pursuant to a warrant is limited by the nature of the items sought. The specificity required in a search warrant, demanding the particular description of the items to be searched for and the area to be searched based on probable cause determines the limits of the search. Moreover, the plain view doctrine is not intended to transform a search warrant into a general warrant. Officers may not look for evidence in places where the object specified in the search warrant could not be found. If the object sought is a stolen television set, officers executing the warrant may not look in dresser drawers or in a medicine cabinet because the television

---

[12]State v Howard, 75 App(3d) 760, 600 NE(2d) 809 (Pike 1991).

[13]Coolidge v New Hampshire, 403 US 443, 468, 91 SCt 2022, 29 LEd(2d) 564 (1971).

[14]State v Howard, 75 App(3d) 760, 600 NE(2d) 809 (Pike 1991).

set could not be secreted there. They may look inside a closet, however, because the television set could be hidden there, and contraband observed in the closet during such a search is in plain view and may be seized. When the object specified in the warrant is found, the search must end; finding the object or other contraband does not authorize a further search. The search must also end when the object sought does not turn up after a reasonable time. Thus, evidence found during the lawful execution of the search warrant is admissible; evidence found beyond the reasonable scope of the warrant is inadmissible. Contrary rules would result in the transformation of a search warrant into a general warrant and subvert the values protected by the Fourth Amendment.

These principles were illustrated in *Athens v Wolf*,[15] where the Supreme Court held that an officer's entry into an area through an open door and the sighting of contraband in plain view once in that area did not fall within the doctrine because the warrant did not authorize entry or search of that area. The police had a valid warrant to search a dormitory room at Ohio University. The officer went into the connecting bathroom and through the open doorway into the adjacent dorm room. The officer could not observe the evidence from the bathroom, in which he was lawfully present. The court held that the search warrant did not specify the adjacent room and that, therefore, his entry was unauthorized, even though the door was open.

(C) Presence under exceptions to the warrant requirement

Evidence in plain view may be seized and used in a subsequent criminal proceeding when an officer's presence is justified under an exception to the warrant requirement. Thus, when a claim is made that evidence was in plain view during a search incident to arrest or other exception, the test is whether the police activity that led to the discovery of the evidence in plain view fell within the proper scope permissible under the exception to the warrant requirement.

In *Coolidge*, the Supreme Court said that an object "that comes into view during a search incident to arrest that is appropriately limited in scope under existing law may be seized without a warrant."[16] The Court redefined the scope of an officer's authority incident to arrest in *Washington v Chrisman*[17] and stated that on monitoring an arrestee, a police officer has the right to remain at an arrestee's "elbow" at all times. Consequently, wherever an arrestee goes, or is permitted to go, the officer is empowered to accompany him.

On the face of it, the rule in *Chrisman* makes great sense. As applied, however, the rule expands police authority incident to arrest and especially police access to evidence that may then be in plain view. If an arrestee must go to another room to dress or secure some item to take with him to the police station, there can be no dispute that the officer may follow to ensure that the arrestee does not secure a weapon or destroy evidence, the very

---

[15] Athens v Wolf, 38 OS(2d) 237, 313 NE(2d) 405 (1974).

[16] Coolidge v New Hampshire, 403 US 443, 465, 91 SCt 2022, 29 LEd(2d) 564 (1971).

[17] Washington v Chrisman, 455 US 1, 102 SCt 812, 70 LEd(2d) 778 (1982).

justifications for searches incident to arrest. However, in *Chrisman*, the officer remained in the doorway where he could observe the arrestee. When he entered the dormitory room, it was not to control the arrestee or protect himself; the officer entered the room solely because evidence that he saw on a table top piqued his curiosity, and he wanted to ascertain whether it was marijuana paraphernalia. The Supreme Court was unconcerned that his reasons for entering the room were different from the purposes that justify a search incident to arrest. Chief Justice Burger said that a police officer may monitor an arrestee "as his judgment dictates," and the officer may assert that authority at any time, and presumably for any purposes, that he deems essential. Police authority to monitor the movement of an arrestee is not dependent on any indication that the arrested person might have a weapon available or might attempt to escape, nor is the officer's authority altered by the nature of the offense for which the arrest was made.

On the other hand, a police officer may not artificially expand the scope of a search incident to arrest in order to bring additional evidence within plain view. For example, where an officer effects an arrest on the porch of a home, he may not direct the arrestee into the house in order to make a quick inspection of the house to see what may be in plain view.[18]

Where police officers are admitted into a house, however, evidence in plain view that they observe while lawfully on the premises may be seized.[19] Similarly, when an individual consents to a search for specific objects, other evidence in plain view may be seized. The authority offering the evidence at a criminal trial need only establish that the consent was voluntarily given.[20] Nevertheless, when police rely on a third person's consent to enter that leads to plain view seizures, the officers must be able to reasonably rely on that person's authority to grant entry.[21] The Wayne County Court of Appeals provided necessary guidance on a distinction in this area when it upheld the consent of two minor children to police entering their home to investigate domestic violence, while recognizing that the consent of minor children to a search of their parents' home would probably not be allowed.[22]

Often evidence will be seen in plain view in the course of an investigatory stop. The critical issues then become the lawfulness of the stop and the scope of the intrusion that led to the observation of evidence in plain view. Similarly, police lawfully investigating either reports of crime or other circumstances that arise during patrol may be in a position to lawfully observe

---

[18]See Vale v Louisiana, 399 US 30, 90 SCt 1969, 26 LEd(2d) 409 (1970) (finding no exigency to justify ordering an arrestee into a house where contraband was found in plain view).

[19]See State v Clark, Nos. C-900245, C-900246, 1991 WL 155213 (1st Dist Ct App, Hamilton, 8-14-91); State v Christian, No. 58660, 1991 WL 106041 (8th Dist Ct App, Cuyahoga, 6-13-91); State v Skinner, No. 11704, 1990 WL 140897 (2d Dist Ct App, Montgomery, 9-26-90).

[20]State v Glover, 60 App(2d) 283, 396 NE(2d) 1064 (Hamilton 1978).

[21]See State v Penn, 61 OS(3d) 720, 576 NE(2d) 790 (1991) (police and pharmaceutical enforcement agents had no reasonable basis for relying on consent of person authorizing entry).

[22]State v Pamer, 70 App(3d) 540, 591 NE(2d) 801 (Wayne 1990).

evidentiary objects in plain view. Where a police officer reasonably perceives that an emergency situation exists, the officer may enter and conduct a reasonable, limited search of the premises to ascertain the nature of the emergency. Concurrently, even lesser conditions will justify an intrusion on the street, for example when an officer investigates a vehicle that is parked in a manner obstructing traffic. However, courts should scrutinize carefully the justification for stopping a vehicle and gaining an observation of the interior of the vehicle.[23] In all of these situations, the exigency may not be contrived and must be continuing when the officer makes plain view observations.

(D) Presence in other situations

In other situations where the warrant requirement is inapplicable, as long as the police officer's presence is for any lawful purpose, evidence that is in plain view may be seized. Open fields and other places in open or plain view are not constitutionally protected areas.[24] Land that, though privately owned, is left open to the community to view, travel, or use fits within this same category. Similarly, the walk leading to a house is not constitutionally protected, and evidence visible from the walk is in plain view.

13.03   Incriminating nature immediately apparent

The Court in *Coolidge v New Hampshire*[25] also held that the incriminating nature of evidence found in plain view must be "immediately apparent." In 1983, another Supreme Court plurality called the use of this phrase "an unhappy choice of words, since it can be taken to imply that an unduly high degree of certainty as to the incriminatory character of evidence is necessary for application of the 'plain view' doctrine."[26] The *Coolidge* plurality, however, was attempting only to prevent an authorized search for specified items from being turned into a general inspection of all items found on the

---

[23]See State v Thornton, 51 App(3d) 97, 554 NE(2d) 955 (Cuyahoga 1989) (rejecting police claim that a syringe found protruding from a woman's purse was discovered in plain view while the police inquired into the welfare of the woman); State v Bird, 49 App(3d) 156, 551 NE(2d) 622 (Lake 1988) (rejecting claim of investigatory stop that provided justification for initial questioning that led to observation of evidence); State v Howell, No. 1679, 1991 WL 87289 (4th Dist Ct App, Ross, 4-23-91).

[24]But see State v Jedrick, No. 60276, 1991 WL 76108 (8th Dist Ct App, Cuyahoga, 5-9-91) (claim that entry into open field led to plain view sighting was rejected where entry was onto curtilage of a dwelling where there is a reasonable expectation of privacy).

[25]Coolidge v New Hampshire, 403 US 443, 91 SCt 2022, 29 LEd(2d) 564 (1971).

[26]Texas v Brown, 460 US 730, 103 SCt 1535, 1542, 75 LEd(2d) 502 (1983); see also, State v Harvey, No. 14919, 1995 WL 418731 (2d Dist Ct App, Montgomery, 7-12-95) (a search of a wallet containing cocaine located on the floor of a car stopped for running a stop sign does not fall within the plain view exception to the search warrant requirement because the officer did not have probable cause to believe that evidence of a crime would be found in the wallet just because the officer felt it "seemed strange" that the passenger who owned the wallet could not produce identification as requested by the officer when there was a wallet on the floor in front of his seat).

premises in order to determine whether those additional items might possibly be incriminating in nature.

In *Texas v Brown*,[27] a police officer, conducting "a routine driver's license checkpoint," stopped the defendant's car and observed in the defendant's hand an opaque, green party balloon, knotted about one-half inch from the tip. The officer then shifted his position so that he could see in the open glove compartment and noticed several plastic vials, quantities of a white powder, and an open bag of party balloons. The officer seized the balloon, which the defendant had dropped to the floor of the car, and noticed a powdery substance within the tied-off portion of the balloon. The officer testified at the suppression hearing that, based on his previous experience in arrests for drug offenses, he was aware that narcotics were frequently packaged in balloons. The Texas Court of Criminal Appeals reversed the conviction, finding that it was not immediately apparent to the officer that the balloon contained narcotics. Justice Rehnquist, for the plurality, characterized the Texas court's standard to mean that the officer must be possessed of near certainty as to the seizable nature of the items. All nine of the justices rejected near certainty as too demanding.

Instead, the Court found that the police officer need not know that the items in plain view are contraband or evidence of a crime. It is sufficient, according to the Supreme Court, that probable cause exist to associate the property with criminal activity. In reaching the conclusion that the officer had probable cause to believe that the balloon contained narcotics, the Court relied on *United States v Cortez*[28] and held that the facts are to be reviewed in a manner allowing for all of the inferences that would be drawn by one versed in the field of law enforcement.

Because the Supreme Court produced no majority opinion in *Brown*, as so often happens in Fourth Amendment cases, the significance of a key issue may be lost. The Rehnquist opinion, written for a plurality of four, considers the existence of probable cause dispositive of the entire case. The plurality felt its work complete when it substituted probable cause for the "near certainty" standard used by the Texas court. Further, Justice Rehnquist made no distinction between the seizure of the balloon and the examination of its contents.

A majority of the Court, however, in two separate opinions, viewed *Brown* as a container case and saw the necessity to distinguish between the seizure of the balloon and its search. That majority obviously believes that a police officer may seize a container when, in the course of a lawful intrusion, he inadvertently finds in plain view a container that he has probable cause to believe contains contraband or evidence of a crime. Opening the container and searching its contents, however, is a different matter. The officer may seize and safeguard the container until a warrant is obtained authorizing its search, or the container may be opened without a warrant if its nature and construction or the place where it is found fit within one of

[27]Texas v Brown, 460 US 730, 103 SCt 1535, 1542, 75 LEd(2d) 502 (1983).

[28]United States v Cortez, 449 US 411, 101 SCt 690, 66 LEd(2d) 621 (1981), cert denied 455 US 923, 102 SCt 1281, 71 LEd(2d) 464 (1982).

the other exceptions to the warrant clause. Justice Powell, joined by Justice Blackmun, relied on his earlier opinion in *Arkansas v Sanders*[29] in believing that the content of the balloon was known to the officer from its outward appearance because innocent items are not commonly carried in uninflated, tied-off balloons. Consequently, the balloon would not support any reasonable expectation of privacy and could be legitimately opened without a warrant. Justice Stevens, for Justices Brennan and Marshall, argued that a warrantless search might be permissible under the *Sanders* theory offered by Justice Powell or under the automobile exception that extends to containers found in lawfully searched vehicles, but he believed the case should be remanded to the Texas court for findings of fact and a determination of which, if either, exception applied.

Brown hardly provided the guidance that the Rehnquist Court frequently claims is necessary for Fourth Amendment issues. It merely clarified that probable cause, not near certainty, is sufficient for seizure of an item found in plain view. *Arizona v Hicks*[30] provided the missing guidance. First, the Court said that probable cause that an item in plain view justifies a search of that object. The Court did not treat this issue very seriously; it simply assumed that probable cause justifies a search, not only a seizure. The Court did focus, however, on what type of and how much scrutiny may be directed at an object in plain view to determine whether its criminal nature is readily apparent.

Ohio courts have grappled with the "immediately apparent" issue without total consistency. Prior to *Brown*, the Ohio Supreme Court correctly assumed that probable cause was the proper standard, but in keeping with the *Coolidge* spirit, properly indicated that probable cause must exist when the object in plain view is first sighted, not after an extensive examination, which in effect is a search. The Court held that the plain view doctrine did not apply when the incriminating nature of the object became apparent after "an extensive, systematic search."[31]

A different standard was applied by the Hamilton County Court of Appeals in *State v Glover*,[32] where police officers, with the defendant's consent, searched his apartment for a stolen coat. While ostensibly looking for the coat, the officers saw, in plain view, marijuana, cocaine, and drug paraphernalia on a table. During a search of the closet, where the stolen coat was actually found, the officers copied down the serial number of a camera that later turned out to be stolen. The defendant was arrested, and the officers returned later with a warrant to seize the stolen camera. The Hamilton County court admitted the camera into evidence, stating that (1)

[29]Arkansas v Sanders, 442 US 753, 99 SCt 2586, 61 LEd(2d) 235 (1979), overruled by California v Acevedo, 500 US 565, 111 SCt 1982, 114 LEd(2d) 619 (1991).

[30]Arizona v Hicks, 480 US 321, 107 SCt 1149, 94 LEd(2d) 347 (1987).

[31]See State v Wilmoth, 1 OS(3d) 118, 1 OBR 157, 438 NE(2d) 105 (1982), cert denied 460 US 1081, 103 SCt 1769, 76 LEd(2d) 343 (1983); State v Williams, 55 OS(2d) 82, 377 NE(2d) 1013 (1978); State v Younts, 92 App(3d) 708, 637 NE(2d) 64 (Madison 1993), appeal dismissed 69 OS(3d) 1436, 632 NE(2d) 520 (1994) (smell of raw marijuana was not sufficient in and of itself to provide probable cause justifying search of defendant's vehicle).

[32]State v Glover, 60 App(2d) 283, 396 NE(2d) 1064 (Hamilton 1978).

it is well known that persons who traffic in drugs often receive stolen goods, and (2) the copying down of a serial number is not a constructive seizure. The inspection for a serial number may not be a constructive seizure, but it is difficult to maintain that it was not a search. The serial numbers were not in plain view and the inspection of the camera went beyond the consent to search requested by the officers and granted by the defendant. It was the same type of "systematic inspection" condemned by the Ohio Supreme Court in *State v Wilmoth* and *State v Williams* and involved behavior that turns the plain view doctrine into a license for a general search. A different result, in almost identical circumstances, was reached by the United States Court of Appeals for the Sixth Circuit.[33]

The issue was decisively resolved by the United States Supreme Court in 1987. Justice Scalia, in *Arizona v Hicks*,[34] stated that the mere recording of the serial numbers did not constitute a seizure since it did not meaningfully interfere with defendant's possessory interest in the item or the numbers. However, moving the item so that police could inspect it and gain access to the serial numbers constituted a search separate and apart from the search that was the lawful objective of entering the apartment.

The lesson is clear. The object's incriminating nature must be readily apparent from a visible observation only. It may not be handled in any way or turned over to ascertain whether it is criminal evidence. Once there is probable cause that the object in plain view is criminal evidence, then presumably it is subject to a thorough warrantless search. It is important to note, however, that an object sometimes must be moved during a lawful search in order to search for the object specified in a warrant, such as when a radio or turntable blocks the view of part of a shelf where the object sought may be secreted. This type of movement may provide a different view or incidental inspection of the object and also may lead to probable cause to believe that the object moved constitutes criminal evidence.

Hicks was seemingly ignored in *State v Sautter*,[35] however. In this case, where a warranted search of a safety deposit box for "U.S. currency, being the proceeds from drug transactions" led to the finding of an incriminating, three page handwritten memorandum that was seized after it was read, the warrant was upheld. Without reference or citation to *Hicks*, the *Sautter* court said that "the majority of the courts who have considered this issue have held that documents in plain view may be read before a determination is made to seize the documents."[36] In *State v Mitchell*,[37] while police were executing a search warrant for "controlled substances and illegally possessed dangerous ordinances," and "any other items criminally possessed," they discovered unlabeled films that the police inventoried and viewed and that led to sexual pandering charges. The Ross County Court of Appeals

[33]See United States v Gray, 484 F(2d) 352 (6th Cir Ky 1973), cert denied 414 US 1158, 94 SCt 916, 39 LEd(2d) 110 (1974).

[34]Arizona v Hicks, 480 US 321, 107 SCt 1149, 94 LEd(2d) 347 (1987).

[35]State v Sautter, No. L-88-324, 1989 WL 90630 (6th Dist Ct App, Ross, 8-11-89).

[36]State v Sautter, No. L-88-324, at 6, 1989 WL 90630 (6th Dist Ct App, Ross, 8-11-89).

[37]State v Mitchell, No. 1480, 1988 WL 125021 (4th Dist Ct App, Ross, 11-23-88).

affirmed the trial court's granting of the motion to suppress because it was not immediately apparent that the unmarked video tapes were associated with criminal activity; "[i]n order to determine the incriminating nature of those tapes, the officers had to seize and then view them."[38] Hunting guns that were seized from a defendant who was under disability because of a prior felony of violence were suppressed because the incriminating nature of the evidence was not readily apparent to the officer, who testified that he was aware that the defendant had a prior felony conviction but was not aware that the prior conviction was for a felony of violence.[39]

The facts in *Hicks* were remarkably similar to the facts in *Glover*. In both cases, police were lawfully present and became suspicious when they saw an expensive item that was inconsistent with the remainder of the contents of the apartment. To get at the serial numbers, police had to move the suspect item. This, Justice Scalia held, constituted a search because, while the items were in plain view, the serial numbers were not accessible without handling and moving those items. The Court rejected the state's argument that the search should be upheld because it was not a "full-blown search" but only a "cursory inspection" that could be justified by reasonable suspicion. The Court said that a truly cursory inspection, which involves merely looking at what is exposed to view without disturbing it, is not a search for Fourth Amendment purposes and does not even require reasonable suspicion. But when the cursory inspection involves any movement of the item, which was not necessary to get to those items for which the officer was lawfully present and searching, then that movement constituted a search and must be supported by probable cause. Only probable cause, not reasonable suspicion, would support such a search.

The reasoning in *Hicks* decisively rejected the position taken by the Ohio Supreme Court a year earlier in *State v Halczyszak*,[40] where the Court held that officers executing a valid search warrant discovered circumstances "so strongly suggestive" of further dishonesty that they were entitled to make a close inspection and move items around to find vehicle identification and other serial numbers necessary to make computer checks to determine whether the automobiles and parts were stolen. This was contrary to *Hicks* where the Supreme Court limited plain view to those items that did not have to be disturbed. The difference between the two approaches is clear. *Hicks* provides limits to the plain view exception to the warrant requirement, whereas *Halczyszak* would allow for exploratory searches once police were lawfully present. The latter approach disregards one of the traditional purposes of a search warrant, which was to set limits on the scope of the intrusion. As dissenting Justice Sweeney observed in *Halczyszak*, the majority was turning a search warrant into "an admission ticket."

---

[38]State v Mitchell, No. 1480, at 6, 1988 WL 125021 (4th Dist Ct App, Ross, 11-23-88). But see State v Mowbray, 72 App(3d) 243, 594 NE(2d) 626 (Ross 1991) (where same appellate court found that probable cause existed where police found one radio with mounting brackets in defendant's car and another partially installed under dash, and defendant was a suspect in theft of radios).

[39]State v Stebner, 46 App(3d) 145, 546 NE(2d) 428 (Portage 1988).

[40]State v Halczyszak, 25 OS(3d) 301, 25 OBR 360, 496 NE(2d) 925 (1986), cert denied 480 US 919, 107 SCt 1376, 94 LEd(2d) 691 (1987).

13.04 Inadvertence

In *Horton v California*,[41] the United States Supreme Court rejected two decades of precedent requiring that the discovery of evidence in plain view be inadvertent. The purpose behind plurality imposition of this requirement in *Coolidge v New Hampshire*[42] was to ensure that search warrants not turn into general warrants. Inadvertency did not require complete surprise, only that the discovery not exceed a general expectation or suspicion. Police were permitted to seize evidence found during execution of a valid search warrant even though they strongly suspected that other stolen property would be found on the premises. An expectation or hope that additional evidence would be found did not preclude seizure.[43] The inadvertency requirement precluded seizure only when the expectation that other evidence found amounted to probable cause.[44] Police officers who have a valid warrant in hand and who anticipate finding other evidence on the premises are subjected to no extra inconvenience by the demand that the search for the additional evidence be authorized in the warrant. A Supreme Court majority has never fully subscribed to the inadvertence requirement set forth by the *Coolidge* plurality, which Justice White, a *Coolidge* dissenter, has frequently noted.[45]

Despite the absence of a clear majority of the US Supreme Court ratifying inadvertence as an element of the plain view doctrine, most courts, including the Ohio Supreme Court, followed the *Coolidge* plurality's lead. The Ohio Supreme Court, in *State v Wilmoth*,[46] struck down a search where officers seized cars not named in the search warrant but claimed that the cars were in plain view. The US Supreme Court held that the discovery could hardly be termed inadvertent because the officers brought along an expert, indicating their intent to search more than the four cars listed in the warrant. Similarly, a claim of inadvertence failed where the record demonstrated that officers executing a search warrant were accompanied by employees of the company seeking to recover its stolen property. This fact, the court noted, suggested that the officers intended a more extensive search than that authorized by the warrant, and under such circumstances the discovery of evidence could hardly be called inadvertent.[47]

In *Horton*, the Supreme Court held that the discovery of evidence in plain view need not be inadvertent to be admissible. The Court held that inadvertency is not essential to avoid violating the Fourth Amendment requirement that a valid warrant particularly describe the things to be seized. Simply because an officer expects to find an item, the majority

---

[41]Horton v California, 496 US 128, 110 SCt 2301, 110 LEd(2d) 112 (1990).

[42]Coolidge v New Hampshire, 403 US 443, 91 SCt 2022, 29 LEd(2d) 564 (1971).

[43]State v Waddy, Nos. 87AP-1159, 87AP-1160, 1989 WL 133508 (10th Dist Ct App, Franklin, 11-2-89).

[44]State v Halczyszak, 25 OS(3d) 301, 25 OBR 360, 496 NE(2d) 925 (1986), cert denied 480 US 919, 107 SCt 1376, 94 LEd(2d) 691 (1987).

[45]See Texas v Brown, 460 US 730, 103 SCt 1535, 75 LEd(2d) 502 (1983).

[46]State v Wilmoth, 1 OS(3d) 118, 1 OBR 157, 438 NE(2d) 105 (1982), cert denied 460 US 1081, 103 SCt 1769, 76 LEd(2d) 343 (1983).

[47]State v Strzesynski, No. WD-85-68, 1986 WL 4660 (6th Dist Ct App, Wood, 4-18-86).

argued, should not invalidate its seizure if the search is confined in area and duration by a warrant's terms, or by an exception to the warrant requirement. In *Horton*, the warrant authorized a search for jewelry, even though the executing officer hoped also to find weapons used in the crime. The Court concluded that concerns for the protection of privacy are not implicated when a police officer with a lawful right of access to an item in plain view seizes it without a warrant.

Horton was a unique situation because the object specified in the warrant was not found while objects sought, but not specified in the warrant, were seized. The inadvertency requirement ensured that the scope of the search be limited by the warrant and not distorted or rearranged to accommodate the search for other evidence.

13.05   Plain feel

Relying upon the same rationale that underlies the plain view doctrine, the United States Supreme Court in *Minnesota v Dickerson*,[48] held that a "plain feel" corollary to the plain view exception should be recognized. Specifically, the Court held that the seizure of nonthreatening contraband, detected through the sense of touch during a *Terry* protective pat-down search, is permitted, so long as the search stays within the bounds prescribed by *Terry*.

The pat-down in *Dickerson* did not stay within those bounds. The frisking officer felt a small lump in the suspect's front pocket and then, upon further tactile examination, concluded that the object was a lump of crack cocaine in a plastic or cellophane bag, which the officer removed from the suspect's pocket. The Court ruled that the seizure of drugs was unlawful because the officer exceeded the bounds of *Terry* by squeezing, sliding, and manipulating the object. The officer's authority was limited to running his hands over the outer clothing of the suspect to determine if he had a weapon. Once he concluded that there was no weapon, the officer had no further authority to run his hands over the suspect's body. While the lump may have made the officer suspicious, he could not continue to feel the object to confirm those suspicions.

Plain feel is a rational extension of plain view. However, it must be noted that, as described and applied by the Supreme Court, it is strictly circumscribed. Consequently, if fairly applied by reviewing courts, it will not amount to a significant extension of police authority. Rarely, if ever, will an officer's initial feel of an object disclose what it is with adequate certainty to amount to probable cause.

Prior to the decision in *Dickerson*, the Montgomery County Appellate Court allowed precisely what the US Supreme Court did not, when the court said that the officer performed many pat-down searches and knew the "bumpy, gritty material was cocaine."[49] *Dickerson* teaches that an officer

---

[48]Minnesota v Dickerson, 508 US 366, 113 SCt 2130, 124 LEd(2d) 334 (1993).
[49]State v Taylor, 82 App(3d) 434, 612 NE(2d) 728 (Montgomery 1992); State v Cloud, 91 App(3d) 366, 632 NE(2d) 932 (Cuyahoga 1993) (plain feel not applicable

should not be allowed to tarry long enough when making a *Terry* pat-down to identify some indeterminate material as bumpy and gritty. A fair application of *Dickerson* would not allow this result. On the other hand, it has been held that a court errs in suppressing evidence solely on the basis that the officer determined that what she felt was not a weapon without determining whether it was immediately apparent to the officer upon feeling the hard chuncky-like substance that it was crack cocaine.[50]

where officer testified that he did not know what the object in defendant's pocket was during the frisk); see also State v Hunter, 98 App(3d) 632, 649 NE(2d) 289 (8th Dist Ct App, Cuyahoga 11-14-94) (finding that officers' seized "wadded up bag" under plain feel following pat-down search which the defendant put inside his pocket and which police previously observed.

[50]State v Stargell, No. 14780, 1995 WL 141468 (2d Dist Ct App, Montgomery, 3-29-95).

Chapter 14

Stop and Frisk

14.01   Introduction

Long before the Supreme Court gave the practice its imprimatur, police in the United States engaged citizens in on-the-street questioning on less evidence than is necessary to justify an arrest. It is axiomatic that police who are assigned the function of crime prevention, as well as the apprehension of persons who have already committed crimes, must have the ability to intercede prior to the time a crime is committed. Often, however, there is a fine line separating police conduct aimed at crime prevention, which must be sanctioned under the Fourth Amendment, and police conduct that is merely harassment, intrusions that run afoul of the Fourth Amendment's protection of privacy.

In *Terry v Ohio*,[1] the United States Supreme Court upheld the constitutionality of the stop and frisk practice and attempted to set firm standards for its operation. After a period when the Supreme Court's guidance on these issues was diluted by its inability to muster clear majorities, its message is now loud and clear. The Court intends to extend the freedom from Fourth Amendment restraint to encounters that originally would have been governed under *Terry* standards.

The principle issues that must be addressed in this area are (1) the nature of the stop permissible under *Terry*; (2) the nature and characteristics of a consensual encounter that is free of the *Terry* standards; (3) the standards governing the frisk and the admissibility of evidence discovered as a result of that limited search; and (4) the scope of the detention permissible under an investigatory stop. Additionally, checkpoint inspection of licenses, automobile registration, vehicle safety, and driving under the influence (DUI) roadblocks will be discussed.

14.02   The stop

(A) In general

The type of stop recognized in *Terry v Ohio*[2] falls between police-citizen encounters that are not governed by Fourth Amendment standards and arrests that must be supported by probable cause. A police officer, like any other citizen, may approach an individual in a public place, engage that individual in conversation, and request information and assistance. So long as the person is free not to respond and to walk away, no Fourth Amend-

---

[1]Terry v Ohio, 392 US 1, 88 SCt 1868, 20 LEd(2d) 889 (1968).
[2]Terry v Ohio, 392 US 1, 88 SCt 1868, 20 LEd(2d) 889 (1968).

ment interest is engaged and the Amendment's reasonableness standard need not be met. It is not at all clear that encounters that fall into this category are in fact so devoid of the threat of the use of force that the individual engaged by a police officer is aware that he is free not to respond and to ignore the officer's request for information.[3] The Supreme Court is attempting to expand the types of citizen-police encounters that are not subject to the *Terry* standards and, thus, need not conform to the reasonableness command of the Fourth Amendment.

Almost a quarter of a century later, it is hard to imagine the revolutionary character of the *Terry* decision. *Terry* recognized police authority to forcibly stop a person without the probable cause necessary for arrest. It involved recognition of radically expanded police authority. At the same time, the Supreme Court in *Terry* sought to impose constitutional oversight on this expanded power. The thrust of the Supreme Court since *Terry* has been to reduce the impact of the constitutional oversight, generally in the name of the "war on drugs," by continuously redefining those situations that are subject to the reasonableness requirement.[4] The effect has been to eliminate the Constitution from some very coercive police-citizen encounters and to free the police on these occasions from all outside restraint.

(B) Terry v Ohio

Terry v Ohio[5] arose when a Cleveland plainclothes detective with thirty-nine years of police experience observed Terry and another man engaged in suspicious behavior. The detective observed the two men for approximately ten minutes, as they alternately left the corner on which the other was stationed, walked several hundred feet up the block, peered into the windows of a jewelry store and airline office, and returned to the corner to converse with each other. This procedure was repeated several times by each man. During this period, a third man spoke with the original two and then departed. The two men left the corner and proceeded to the front of the jewelry store where they again met the third man, and the three engaged in discussion.

The detective, who had observed all of this activity, suspected that the three men were planning a robbery. With this belief in mind, he approached the three men, identified himself, and asked for their names. When all he received was a mumbled response, the detective spun the defendant, Terry, around, patted down the outside of his clothing, and feeling a hard object in the pocket of the topcoat, removed a loaded handgun. He patted down the other two as well and recovered another loaded revolver; the third man was unarmed. Terry and the second man were charged with carrying concealed weapons.

---

[3]See United States v Mendenhall, 446 US 544, 100 SCt 1870, 64 LEd(2d) 497 (1980).

[4]United States v Mendenhall, 446 US 544, 100 SCt 1870, 64 LEd(2d) 497 (1980); see also California v Hodari D., 499 US 621, 111 SCt 1547, 113 LEd(2d) 690 (1991).

[5]Terry v Ohio, 392 US 1, 88 SCt 1868, 20 LEd(2d) 889 (1968).

The Court held that the officer's encounter with the defendant was a seizure within the Fourth Amendment meaning of seizure and was constitutionally permissible notwithstanding the absence of probable cause. The investigative stop sanctioned in *Terry* on less than probable cause is an important weapon in the law enforcement arsenal. The Supreme Court intended to make it possible for police officers to intervene and prevent a crime prior to its completion. In a rational society, police must be as concerned with crime prevention as with crime solution. The risk, of course, is that the authority may be misused and become a tool of harassment. Consequently, in *Terry*, the Court decreed that an investigative stop must meet the constitutional standard of reasonableness. It does not provide blanket authority to intrude on the individual's right to be left alone, nor does it allow such intrusion based on a police officer's inarticulate hunch that a crime is about to occur or is in progress. Rather, a police officer may use the authority recognized in *Terry* when "articulable facts and circumstances" give rise to reasonable suspicion.

A *Terry*-stop was authorized to prevent crime by permitting a limited detention based on present suspicious behavior. The authority has been extended to situations where there is reasonable suspicion to believe that a suspect is wanted for a past crime.[6]

(C) Subsequent development of the stop

The refinement of the *Terry* rule has been in the definition of the term "stop." Incredibly, the Supreme Court thrust has been to narrow the definition, not to limit police authority but to expand it. The term stop has evolved to exclude police-citizen encounters from its governing standard. *Terry* recognized that not all police-citizen encounters are seizures. Absent force or the threat of force, a police officer, like any other citizen, may seek information and assistance of any citizen. Of course, civilians do not perceive law enforcement officers as they do other citizens. There is an element of coercion in any police request for information, but the Court, probably rightfully, chose to ignore that coercion and distinguish such general requests from demands for cooperation. Nonetheless, the subsequent distinctions developed by the Supreme Court have gone far beyond excluding from Fourth Amendment coverage simple, general exchanges and, instead, have categorized some police-citizen exchanges where there is, in fact, significant coercion as "consensual encounters" free from even the lesser reasonableness standard imposed in *Terry*. This conclusion rests on a fiction that a reasonable person so encountered by a police officer would feel free to "thumb his nose" and disregard the request. While this development may facilitate the "war" on drugs, it places great stress on the fundamental values that the Fourth Amendment protects.

Even before considering the analysis that determines the nature of an encounter, the Supreme Court has drawn another line. The distinction between a *Terry*-stop and a consensual encounter, the Court tells us, only comes into play when a person stops in response to an officer's request or demand. Until a person heeds a police officer's request or demand there is

---

[6]United States v Hensley, 469 US 221, 105 SCt 675, 83 LEd(2d) 604 (1985).

no seizure under the Fourth Amendment, and therefore there is no Fourth Amendment oversight of the reasonableness of the grounds on which the officer makes the demand or the means used to enforce the demand.[7]

This line of cases developed largely in airports, and now bus terminals, beginning with *United States v Mendenhall*,[8] where the US Supreme Court could not agree whether a seizure had taken place that would have activated the reasonableness test. *Mendenhall* arose when a woman disembarking from an airplane in Detroit aroused the suspicions of Drug Enforcement Agency (DEA) agents present at the airport for the purpose of detecting unlawful traffic in narcotics. The agents approached the woman because it appeared to them that her conduct was characteristic of persons unlawfully carrying narcotics, i.e., she arrived on a plane from Los Angeles, she disembarked from the plane last and appeared nervous as she scanned the airport, she claimed no luggage, and she changed airlines for her flight out of Detroit. The agents approached her and asked to see her identification and airline ticket. The names on the ticket and driver's license were different, and Ms. Mendenhall indicated that she had been in California just two days. When the officers identified themselves as federal narcotics agents, Ms. Mendenhall appeared shaken and nervous. The agents returned her ticket and license. Then they asked her if she would accompany them to the airport DEA office for further questioning. Eventually, at the airport security office, Mendenhall turned over the narcotics she was carrying in her underclothing. The admissibility of that evidence ultimately hinged on the nature of her presence in the security office. If Mendenhall's encounter with the DEA agents in the airport concourse and her trip to the security office was a forcible stop, it would have to meet the *Terry* standards for a lawful seizure. The factors that aroused the agents' suspicion turned on the "drug courier profile," an informal compilation of characteristics believed to be typical of persons unlawfully carrying narcotics, which in the same term as *Mendenhall* was described by the Court as "too slender a reed" on which to support a seizure.[9] If, on the other hand, there was no forcible stop and seizure of Ms. Mendenhall, the reasonableness of the agents' conduct would not be open to question. The Supreme Court could not agree.

Two justices, Stewart and Rehnquist, took the position that no seizure occurred because a reasonable person would have believed that she was free to ignore the agents' questions and requests and walk away. The two justices explained that a seizure could be recognized, even when the person does not attempt to leave, by the threatening presence of several officers, the display of a weapon by an officer, some physical touching of the person, or the use of language or tone of voice indicating that compliance with the

---

[7]California v Hodari D., 499 US 621, 111 SCt 1547, 113 LEd(2d) 690 (1991); *compare* State v Fincher, 76 App(3d) 721, 603 NE(2d) 329 (Cuyahoga 1991), appeal dismissed by 63 OS(3d) 1428, 588 NE(2d) 129 (1992) (approach of police constituted a seizure implicating Fourth Amendment) with State v Barnwell, 87 App(3d) 637, 622 NE(2d) 1109 (Cuyahoga 1993) (plain clothes officers' approach of defendant leaning into car with hands clenched in high crime area is not a seizure).

[8]United States v Mendenhall, 446 US 544, 100 SCt 1870, 64 LEd(2d) 497 (1980).

[9]See Reid v Georgia, 448 US 438, 100 SCt 2752, 65 LEd(2d) 890 (1980), cert denied 454 US 883, 102 SCt 369, 70 LEd(2d) 195 (1981).

officer's request might be compelled. Absent these indicia, the two justices contended, "inoffensive conduct" between an individual and the police cannot, as a matter of law, amount to a seizure. Justice Stewart was impressed by the fact that the agents returned Mendenhall's driver's license and airline ticket before requesting that she accompany them to the security office. Consequently, even though Mendenhall may not have believed that she was free to ignore the agents, Stewart and Rehnquist concluded that she had no objective reason to believe that she could not end the conversation in the concourse and proceed on her way.

Acceptance of the Stewart-Rehnquist formulation would have drastic consequences because it labels as consensual the vast majority of police-citizen encounters and places them outside the purview of the Fourth Amendment, immune from review. It states that, as a matter of law, most encounters between citizens and police are consensual and purports to adopt objective criteria to reach this issue, even though most individuals would believe they are not free to ignore the officer's requests for information. Absent some hesitation on the part of individuals in Mendenhall's situation, we are not likely to see police react in a way that would have indicated to Justices Stewart and Rehnquist that Mendenhall was not free to ignore the agents' requests.[10] In *Mendenhall*, Justice Stewart maintained that no Fourth Amendment interest would be served by inquiring into the reasonableness of the agents' behavior, provoking the question of whether any legitimate interest is served by not evaluating police conduct of this sort by the reasonableness-balancing test devised in *Terry*.

The Stewart-Rehnquist approach is dependent on a population that is unaware of its rights. This was highlighted in 1984, in *Immigration & Naturalization Service v Delgado*,[11] where immigration agents conducted two surveys of citizenship in factories suspected of hiring illegal aliens. While agents moved through the factories questioning each employee, other agents were stationed at the exits to ensure that no employee could exit without being questioned. Justice Rehnquist, for the majority, held that the questioning did not constitute a seizure for purposes of Fourth Amendment review because "the circumstances of the encounter [were not] so intimidating as to demonstrate that a reasonable person would have believed he was not free to leave if he had not responded."[12] The philosophy that undergirds *Mendenhall* and *Delgado* avoids basic Fourth Amendment concerns by freeing this type of law enforcement behavior from review. So long as individuals respond to these inquiries, the encounters are deemed "consen-

---

[10]See Brown v Texas, 443 US 47, 99 SCt 2637, 61 LEd(2d) 357 (1979) (defendant approached in an alley refused to identify himself, asserted that police had no right to stop him, whereupon officers frisked defendant. Justice Stewart contended no *Terry* type seizure took place until frisk).

[11]Immigration & Naturalization Service v Delgado, 466 US 210, 104 SCt 1758, 80 LEd(2d) 247 (1984); see also State v Daniel, 81 App(3d) 325, 610 NE(2d) 1099 (Summit 1992) (police officer may ask a person sitting on church steps at night in a high crime area where he lives, why he is in the area, and whether he has identification without creating an intimidating environment that would constitute a seizure).

[12]Immigration & Naturalization Service v Delgado, 466 US 210, 216, 104 SCt 1758, 80 LEd(2d) 247 (1984).

sual" regardless of the pressures operating on the respondees. It is only when the individual questioned is aware that he need not answer, and when the police take additional steps to obtain an answer, that "the Fourth Amendment imposes some minimal level of objective justification to validate the detention or seizure."[13]

The other six justices disagreed with the Stewart-Rehnquist analysis and concluded that a *Terry* seizure had taken place. Even so, they split down the middle: three, Berger, Powell, and Blackmun, concurred with Stewart and Rehnquist on the ground that the seizure was justified by reasonable and articulable suspicion of criminal activity and the other three, Brennan, White, and Marshall, dissented on the ground that Ms. Mendenhall's conduct was insufficient to provide reasonable suspicion that she was engaged in criminal activity and that the agents' treatment of her was indistinguishable from a traditional arrest. The majority forged in *Mendenhall* results from the joining of two justices who did not believe that the defendant had been seized, and three justices who did believe that she was seized but that the seizure was reasonable. While this type of fragmentation offers little guidance, it is a clear indication that a narrow majority of the Court was prepared to allow the police substantial latitude when dealing with persons on the street, in the absence of physical contact or removal to the police station.[14]

In 1983, again in a case involving the stopping of a suspected drug courier, the Court attempted to clarify the position advanced in *Mendenhall*. While the Court in *Florida v Royer*[15] remained unable to put together a majority opinion, by combining the plurality's positions with some of those offered by Justice Brennan (who provided the fifth vote) and still others put forward by the four dissenters, several propositions emerge that are supported by a majority of the Supreme Court. Eight justices were in agreement that the police who approached a suspected drug courier at an airport concourse did not violate the Fourth Amendment by that approach and request for identification because it was not a seizure activating the *Terry* reasonableness test requiring objective justification for the intrusion. Four of those justices, however, along with Justice Brennan, took the position that the consensual aspects of the encounter evaporated when the suspect was removed to the police interrogation room at the airport while the officers retained his ticket and identification, had already removed his luggage to the interrogation room, and had not informed him that he was free to leave. The justices concluded that "[a]s a practical matter, Royer was under arrest"[16] and that it was reasonable for him to believe that he was being detained. The plurality asserted that when the officers requested Royer to accompany them to the interrogation room, a seizure took place that was based on reasonable suspicion.

---

[13]Immigration & Naturalization Service v Delgado, 466 US 210, 216-17, 104 SCt 1758, 80 LEd(2d) 247 (1984).

[14]See, e.g., Dunaway v New York, 442 US 200, 99 SCt 2248, 60 LEd(2d) 824 (1979).

[15]Florida v Royer, 460 US 491, 103 SCt 1319, 75 LEd(2d) 229 (1983).

[16]Florida v Royer, 460 US 491, 503, 103 SCt 1319, 75 LEd(2d) 229 (1983).

The critical difference between *Mendenhall* and *Royer* was that the officers in *Royer* kept the defendant's ticket and identification. According to the plurality, *Royer* quickly changed into an illegal arrest because the officers had possession of his ticket and identification as well as his luggage and, as a practical matter, the suspect could not leave the airport without them. Moreover, the suspect was not informed that he need not consent to a search of his luggage, which the plurality felt was very significant even though that type of warning is not generally a prerequisite to a valid consent search. Obviously, the retention of the travel documents in *Royer* was essential to the plurality's conclusion that a consensual encounter had been transformed into a *Terry* type seizure. That type of show of authority is sufficient to justify a reasonable belief that the individual who is stopped is not free to leave.

The line between consensual encounters that raise no Fourth Amendment reasonableness inquiries and *Terry*-stops that must be supported by reasonable suspicion remains undrawn. Following *Mendenhall* and *Royer*, the Court, in *Florida v Rodriguez*,[17] was faced with yet another case involving an airport encounter between police officers and suspected drug couriers. Three travellers who aroused police suspicion specifically tried to avoid contact with the police officers, and the defendant, when unable to avoid confronting the officers, directed profanity at them. The officer suggested that the defendant step aside about fifteen feet, which he did. The officer then requested and was granted permission to search the defendant's suitcase. Three bags of cocaine were found during the search. The officer testified at the suppression hearing that until the cocaine was found, the three were free to leave.

The Supreme Court held that the initial encounter between the defendant and the police officers, "where they simply asked if he would step aside and talk with them, was clearly the sort of consensual encounter that implicates no Fourth Amendment interests."[18] Apart from one's belief as to whether police conduct of this sort is appropriate and should be encouraged, the Court's analysis is disingenuous. A consensual encounter is one that implies that the individual is free to avoid the encounter altogether or to terminate it at will. In each of the three airport encounter cases, the defendants complied with the police requests only after unsuccessfully attempting to evade police. In *Rodriguez*, the defendant's behavior clearly indicated an intention to avoid the police. It is difficult to conclude that anyone in the defendant's position, after manifesting his intent to avoid the confrontation, would reasonably believe that he need not step aside and talk with police officers. Moreover, the Court refused to characterize the additional intrusion when the defendant was asked to move fifteen feet out of the traffic on the concourse as a *Terry*-stop, but nonetheless held that if this was a *Terry*-stop, it was justified by articulable suspicion.

The attempt to detect drug couriers and other traffickers has been extended to bus terminals where the encounters are taking place not only in

---

[17]Florida v Rodriguez, 469 US 1, 105 SCt 308, 83 LEd(2d) 165 (1984).
[18]Florida v Rodriguez, 469 US 1, 5-6, 105 SCt 308, 83 LEd(2d) 165 (1984).

the terminal but also on the buses. In *Florida v Bostick*,[19] police engaged in a practice called "sweeping the buses," where they boarded stopped passenger buses and approached seated passengers to ask them questions and request consent to search their luggage. The practice involved getting on the bus shortly before it was due to depart and asking some or all of the passengers without individualized suspicion for information about themselves and their destination and for permission to search their luggage for drugs. The Florida Supreme Court found the encounter to be fraught with coercion because the officers would stand over the individual questioned and block the aisle, and because the situation confronted the individual with embarrassment in front of fellow passengers if he refused to consent. Consequently, despite the trial court's finding of fact that the officers informed the defendant that he did not have to consent to a search, the Florida high court characterized the encounter as a seizure that was rendered unconstitutional because of the lack of individualized suspicion.

The United States Supreme Court disagreed and emphasized that a seizure does not take place every time an officer approaches a citizen in public and questions that person. The Court said that the fact that the encounter takes place in the cramped confines of a bus does not render the situation qualitatively different. The Court found error in the Florida court's conclusion that a seizure took place because the passenger aboard a bus that is about to leave does not feel free to leave the bus. Feeling free to leave the bus is the wrong inquiry in this setting, the Court said, because it is not the police but the situation that makes the individual not feel free to leave. The compulsion to remain rather than depart was the result of something other than the conduct of the law enforcement officers. Instead, the right question, according to the Court, is whether the reasonable person would feel free to decline the police request to search and otherwise terminate the encounter. The Supreme Court completely disregarded consideration that the class of persons likely to be riding interstate buses are less likely to feel free to refuse a police request and are likely to believe that a police request is an order, regardless of the actual words used to make the request, an impression that is heightened by the physical dominance assumed by the officer in blocking the aisle and standing over the seated passenger.

More significant in blurring the federal constitutional definition of a Fourth Amendment seizure was the decision in *California v Hodari D.*[20] The Supreme Court indicated that a police officer's conduct and a reasonable person's perception of that conduct are not the only measurements of whether a seizure has occurred. Rather, the suspect's response to the police conduct is highly relevant. Until the police officer's attempt to affect an investigatory stop succeeds, no seizure takes place and, therefore, no Fourth Amendment review of the reasonableness of the officer's decision to intrude on the suspect's privacy may occur. In *Hodari*, the defendant took

---

[19]*Florida v Bostick*, 501 US 429, 111 SCt 2382, 115 LEd(2d) 389 (1991).

[20]*California v Hodari D.*, 499 US 621, 111 SCt 1547, 113 LEd(2d) 690 (1991), followed, *State v Brown*, No. 16683, 1994 WL 716234 (9th Dist Ct App, Summit, 12-28-94).

flight on seeing the police car. An officer left the car to give chase, running on a parallel street. The defendant, while running, was looking behind him for the officer and did not see the officer chasing him until they were almost face-to-face. When the defendant saw the officer, he threw away a "small rock" and then was tackled by the officer.

The state conceded that the police did not have reasonable suspicion or probable cause to seize the defendant. If the chase constituted a "seizure" under the Constitution and was without reasonable suspicion, then the discarded evidence was tainted by the illegal seizure. If the chase was not a "seizure," then the rock was abandoned and therefore admissible.

The Supreme Court redefined "seizure" holding that the *Mendenhall* test "states a necessary but not a sufficient condition for seizure."[21] Notwithstanding the language in *Mendenhall* and subsequent cases, the Court held in *Hodari* that a Fourth Amendment seizure requires more than a determination of whether a reasonable person felt free to leave as a result of a show of authority. That test is sufficient only when the suspect submits.

Looking beyond *Mendenhall* to the common-law definition of arrest, the Supreme Court added that the Fourth Amendment is implicated when there is a touching or a submission to authority. The issuance of a command to "Halt" when not complied with is not a Fourth Amendment seizure.

The inclusion of this additional inquiry adds a Catch-22 quality to the test. In summary, though, it results in relieving the state from having to justify police behavior under federal constitutional standards in additional situations. Thus, if the suspect resists a police demand to stop for investigative questioning by running away, the Court says there is no seizure until the suspect is forced to pay heed to the police command. The potential for disaster is great; the rule relieves the police from satisfying the reasonable suspicion standard, in the extreme situation when the officer draws a gun and shoots while pursuing a fleeing suspect, until the suspect halts or until the bullet strikes the suspect and forces him to halt. However, once a police officer lays hands upon a suspect, whether he is successful in detaining that suspect, a seizure has taken place.[22]

The alternative, when the suspect complies with the officer's request or demand for information, activates Fourth Amendment standards if a reasonable person under the circumstances would have felt free to disregard the request or demand and walk away. Obviously, the use of the alternative phrase "request or demand" is technically incorrect. If the officer made a demand on the suspect, presumably the reasonable person would not feel free to disregard the demand. However, the two can be used together because the Supreme Court has labeled consensual some encounters where it is highly questionable that anyone would have felt free to ignore the request.

---

[21]California v Hodari D., 499 US 621, 628, 111 SCt 1547, 113 LEd(2d) 690 (1991).

[22]State v Franklin, 86 App(3d) 101, 619 NE(2d) 1182 (Hamilton 1993), appeal dismissed by 67 OS(3d) 1421, 616 NE(2d) 504 (1993).

(D) Ohio decisions defining a Terry-stop

While the United States Supreme Court was splitting hairs over whether a police-citizen exchange was a "consensual encounter" or a seizure requiring objective justification, Ohio courts tended to avoid the issue by applying *Terry* standards. Nevertheless, the Ohio Supreme Court became enmeshed in that debate, in *State v Smith*,[23] a case that bears the unseemly distinction of being the only or one of very, very few cases in the last two decades where a state court was unanimously reversed by the US Supreme Court in a defendant's favor on Fourth Amendment grounds (albeit grounds other than those discussed here).

In *Smith*, two police officers on their way to conduct a gambling raid observed two men leave a house about which police had received unsubstantiated reports of drug sales. The officers knew neither man. The defendant was described by one of the officers as "gingerly" carrying a brown paper bag of the type commonly used to carry groceries, which was folded at the top. The officers drove into the parking lot and pulled up behind an automobile that the defendant and his companion were approaching. One officer exited the unmarked police car and started to approach the defendant. He said to the defendant, "Come here a minute." The defendant did not respond and kept walking, at which time the officer identified himself as a police officer and approached the defendant. The ensuing events took place alongside the driver's side door of the automobile that the defendant was presumably about to enter.

The Ohio Supreme Court, relying on *Mendenhall*, concluded that the defendant was not seized within the meaning of the Fourth Amendment because, in view of the circumstances surrounding the incident, a reasonable person would have believed that he was free to ignore the police officer. Had the defendant elected to run and then been physically seized, a contrary answer would be apparent. But how could he run since, presumably, he was headed towards the vehicle where the encounter took place? Moreover, the defendant, at first, ignored the officer's request or demand that he "Come here a minute." Only when the officer identified himself and continued towards the defendant did he respond. It seems foolish to assert that a reasonable person would have felt free to ignore the police officer after first having ignored a request or command. Clearly the defendant did not choose to accommodate the officer's initial request or demand and only did so when the officer persisted.

Nonetheless, the Ohio Supreme Court built on the fiction established in the *Mendenhall* line of cases and concluded that no seizure occurred. The Court noted that the police did not display weapons, physically touch the defendant, or use a threatening tone of voice. Nonetheless, if the US Supreme Court had decided the case on this issue, it likely would have been bound by one of its prior rulings and disagreed with the Ohio Supreme

---

[23]State v Smith, 45 OS(3d) 255, 544 NE(2d) 239 (1989), reversed by 494 US 541, 110 SCt 1288, 1289, 108 LEd(2d) 464 (1990) (per curiam) (issue decided by US Supreme Court as follows: "[A] warrantless search that provides probable cause for an arrest can [not] be justified as an incident of that arrest.")

Court's conclusion. In *Michigan v Chesternut*,[24] the US Supreme Court indicated that an order to a pedestrian to stop constitutes a sufficient show of authority to demonstrate a Fourth Amendment seizure. Here, the request or demand to "Come here a minute," coupled with further attention, probably would constitute such a show of authority.

The Ohio Supreme Court did not have to strain so in *State v Williams*,[25] where the Court also found that no seizure had occurred when an investigating officer asked a suspect what he was doing in the vicinity of an abandoned house. The Court concluded that the questioning did not restrain the suspect's liberty because there was no command or implicit threat of force at the time of the initial questions. Perhaps the foolishness of this entire endeavor is illustrated by the facts of these two cases. The different words used in *Williams* tend to set it apart from *Smith*, although another significant factor is that the defendant in *Williams* answered and cooperated from the outset while the defendant in *Smith* attempted to ignore the officer and did not respond until the officer persisted. These factors do not seem sufficiently significant to warrant a different constitutional outcome, but are the very factors that the US Supreme Court has chosen to use to distinguish those police-citizen exchanges that are free of constitutional oversight from those that must meet the constitutional demand that a seizure take place only on reasonable suspicion.

Lower courts faced with clearer fact situations than that in *Smith* did not have the same difficulty. Consequently, a patron in a bar ordered not to move was found not to be free to leave,[26] and armed officers in uniform who approach a defendant sitting on the steps of an open porch on private property and stand within four feet of the suspect blocking his exit to the street have seized the suspect.[27] On the other hand, a defendant who sought to avoid the police by hiding behind a tree was not seized when officers approached him and asked his name,[28] nor were defendants in an airport

[24]Michigan v Chesternut, 486 US 567, 108 SCt 1975, 100 LEd(2d) 565 (1988). But see State v Gardner, 88 App(3d) 354, 623 NE(2d) 1310 (Hardin 1993) (officer's act of following and observing motorist for four blocks and then approaching motorist after he parked is not a seizure).
[25]State v Williams, 51 OS(3d) 58, 554 NE(2d) 108 (1990), cert denied 498 US 961, 111 SCt 394, 112 LEd(2d) 404 (1990); State v Frost, 77 App(3d) 644, 603 NE(2d) 270 (Franklin 1991), cert denied 506 US 844, 113 SCt 133, 121 LEd(2d) 87 (1992) (same result on facts similar to those in *Mendenhall*); State v McDaniel, 91 App(3d) 189, 631 NE(2d) 1140 (Cuyahoga 1993) (no seizure occurred where defendant, who was standing in the hallway of housing project that was the subject of many drug activity complaints, was approached by three detectives and asked whether he was carrying drugs or weapons given that he was free to decline to respond and could have terminated the encounter). But see State v Robinette, 73 OS(3d) 650, 653 NE(2d) 695 (1995) (motorist stopped for traffic offense is not free to leave unless officer makes it clear that the driver is free to leave and refuse to answer questions about other offenses).
[26]State v Dancer, 52 Misc(2d) 9, 557 NE(2d) 178 (Muni, Hamilton 1989); State v Grayson, 72 App(3d) 283, 594 NE(2d) 651 (Greene 1991) (where police require defendant to stand against a wall at a gas station for a photograph to be taken, a *Terry* seizure has taken place).
[27]State v Ingram, 82 App(3d) 341, 612 NE(2d) 454 (Clark 1992).
[28]State v Johnson, 34 App(3d) 94, 517 NE(2d) 262 (Cuyahoga 1986).

seized when police quickly caught up with them and asked them questions even though the defendants were hurrying towards the exit,[29] nor were defendants stopped who were walking on the sidewalk and were asked by an officer in a marked patrol car how they were doing and if they lived in the area.[30]

The conclusion in *Smith* was premised on the initial unwillingness of the defendant to cooperate and the persistence of the police officer. In other cases, the immediate cooperation of the defendants argues forcefully that they consented to the questioning except where the cooperation follows on a direct command.

14.03   Reasonable suspicion

(A) Federal constitutional standard

The Supreme Court in *Terry v Ohio*[31] acknowledged that a stop involving a restraint on a citizen's freedom to walk away is a "seizure" to be governed by the Fourth Amendment's reasonableness standard. As this type of seizure is not subject to the requirements of the warrant clause, however, the Court held that the probable cause standard that governs arrests is inapplicable. Instead, the conduct must be tested by the Fourth Amendment's general proscription against unreasonable searches and seizures.

Reasonableness, according to the Court, could only be determined by balancing the need to search (or seize) against the invasion that the search (or seizure) entails. Justification for a particular seizure must be based on "specific and articulable facts which, taken together with rational inferences from those facts, reasonably warrant that intrusion."[32] A reviewing court must be able to weigh the facts offered by the officer against an objective standard and decide that the facts available to the officer warranted a man of reasonable caution in believing that the action taken was appropriate. Anything less, the Court said, would invite intrusions on constitutionally guaranteed rights on nothing more substantial than inarticulate hunches.

A companion case to *Terry* clarified that a police officer is not entitled to seize every person he sees or questions on the street. Before exerting force to restrain the individual, the officer must have constitutionally adequate, reasonable grounds for doing so.[33]

Terry involved reliance on a police officer's judgment based on experience on the street. That judgment must withstand an objective evaluation, but by necessity it represented a vote of confidence in a police officer's ability to discern impending criminal behavior even though the facts are

---

[29]State v Morris, 48 App(3d) 137, 548 NE(2d) 969 (Cuyahoga 1988).

[30]State v Hurt, No. 14882, 1995 WL 259176 (2d Dist Ct App, Montgomery, 5-5-95) (nor were they seized when the defendant stopped to respond to one of the officers who exited the cruiser and asked the defendant his name).

[31]Terry v Ohio, 392 US 1, 88 SCt 1868, 20 LEd(2d) 889 (1968).

[32]Terry v Ohio, 392 US 1, at 21, 88 SCt 1868, 20 LEd(2d) 889 (1968); see also State v Bishop, 95 App(3d) 619, 643 NE(2d) 170 (Warren 1994) (stop illegal where officer based it upon suspicion unsupported by any specific or articulable facts).

[33]Sibron v New York, 392 US 40, 88 SCt 1889, 20 LEd(2d) 917 (1968).

insufficient to form the probable cause necessary for an arrest. When reviewing the police officer's conclusion of impending criminal activity, a court must review the evidence along with inferences and deductions drawn by a trained law enforcement officer, "inferences and deductions that might well elude an untrained person."[34] Those facts and circumstances, along with the inferences and deductions "understood by those versed in the field of law enforcement ... must raise a suspicion that the particular individual being stopped is engaged in wrongdoing."[35]

In *Terry*, the officer personally observed the suspects and determined on the basis of those observations that a crime was in progress or about to be committed. *Adams v Williams*[36] held that the reasonable cause for a stop need not be based solely on the officer's personal observations. In *Adams*, the officer relied on a tip from a known informant. While the Court acknowledged that the tip was insufficient to justify an arrest, the Court held that it was sufficient to justify an investigatory stop.

The prejudice against anonymous tips has also given way even though the Supreme Court has acknowledged that the tip provides no way to conclude that the caller is honest or the information reliable, and provides no indication of the basis for the predictions about a suspect's criminal activities. Nonetheless, the Court has held that an anonymous tip may be sufficiently corroborated to furnish reasonable suspicion to justify an investigative stop.[37] The corroboration need not be as complete as would be required to build probable cause for an arrest from an anonymous tip.[38]

A police officer may rely on the collective knowledge of other police departments. A lawful stop may be predicated on a radio report or a

---

[34]United States v Cortez, 449 US 411, 101 SCt 690, 66 LEd(2d) 621 (1981), cert denied 455 US 923, 102 SCt 1281, 71 LEd(2d) 464 (1982).

[35]United States v Cortez, 449 US 411, 418, 101 SCt 690, 66 LEd(2d) 621 (1981), cert denied 455 US 923, 102 SCt 1281, 71 LEd(2d) 464 (1982).

[36]Adams v Williams, 407 US 143, 92 SCt 1921, 32 LEd(2d) 612 (1972).

[37]Alabama v White, 496 US 325, 110 SCt 2412, 110 LEd(2d) 301 (1990); State v English, 85 App(3d) 471, 620 NE(2d) 125 (Montgomery 1993), appeal dismissed by 67 OS(3d) 1434, 617 NE(2d) 685 (1993) (police may properly stop defendant based solely upon anonymous tip where police have informant's address through caller identification and informant verifies that address is her home); State v Franklin, 86 App(3d) 101, 619 NE(2d) 1182 (Hamilton 1993), appeal dismissed by 67 OS(3d) 1421, 616 NE(2d) 504 (1993) (anonymous tip sufficiently corroborated by police discovery, matching the tip, of a group of persons standing next to a green car); State v Lenoir, No. 14663, 1995 WL 558791 (2d Dist Ct App, Montgomery, 9-20-95) (the presence of three individuals in a parked car with tinted windows at 1:30 am, while not in itself sufficiently suspicious to justify intrusion, provides adequate corroboration for a brief investigative stop along with unidentified informant's call that "a bunch of black males" are tampering with a car); Beachwood v Sims, 98 App(3d) 9, 647 NE(2d) 821 (Cuyahoga 1994) (citizen-informant's tip was sufficiently corroborated by defendant's own statements and the positive identification of the defendant by the informant); but see Hamilton v Reasch, 98 App(3d) 814, 649 NE(2d) 922 (Butler 1994) (anonymous tip that defendant was driving without a license was insufficient to support reasonable suspicion); Wise v Dept of Rehabilitation and Correction, 97 App(3d) 741, 647 NE(2d) 538 (Franklin 1994) (strip search of prison visitor based upon uncorroborated anonymous tip was improper).

[38]See Illinois v Gates, 462 US 213, 103 SCt 2317, 76 LEd(2d) 527 (1983).

"wanted flyer" issued by other departments. In those instances the inquiry focuses on whether the department issuing the radio report or flyer had articulable facts supporting a reasonable suspicion that the wanted person committed an offense. If the reviewing court concludes that there was reasonable suspicion to believe that the suspect named in the report or flyer had committed an offense, the report or flyer justifies a stop to investigate and briefly detain the suspect.[39]

Even a match with characteristics contained within a "profile," such as the Drug Enforcement Agency's (DEA's) drug courier profile, may help to form the basis for reasonable suspicion.[40] However, a bald assertion that a defendant's appearance and conduct conformed to a "profile" will not satisfy the state's burden of demonstrating the existence of reasonable suspicion. The police witness must be able to articulate specific factors about a suspect, leading to the conclusion that his behavior was consistent with the profile. Moreover, the department offering such a profile must demonstrate how they arrived at the characteristics that make up the profile. In short, police may be aided by existence of an offender profile, but the profile is no substitution for the state proving the specific and articulable facts that justified the intrusion.

(B) Application of the reasonable suspicion standard in Ohio

It is impossible to read any of the state cases added for this edition and inserted in the notes in Section 14.03(B) and not conclude that often the same facts would lead to a contrary result in a Court of Appeals in a different district. Even more problematic is the conclusion that often the same facts would lead to a contrary result if heard by a different panel in the same district Court of Appeals.

The federal constitutional requirement that investigatory stops be supported by articulable facts and circumstances giving rise to reasonable suspicion has not fared well in the Ohio Supreme Court. While the United States Supreme Court, when weighing the sufficiency of an officer's claim of reasonable suspicion, allows those inferences that would be drawn by an experienced police officer, it did not intend to substitute the police officer's conclusions for an objective assessment of reasonable suspicion. Rather, it intended imposition of the objective standard on the facts and circumstances observed by the police officer, aided by the inferences that a reasonable, experienced officer would draw from such a factual combination. That is an appropriate analysis because it does not impose a reasonableness standard in a vacuum, such as from the safety and security of a courtroom or law school. It takes into consideration the streets. However, this analysis

---

[39]United States v Hensley, 469 US 221, 105 SCt 675, 83 LEd(2d) 604 (1985).

[40]United States v Sokolow, 490 US 1, 109 SCt 1581, 104 LEd(2d) 1 (1989); State v Rojas, 92 App(3d) 336, 635 NE(2d) 66 (Cuyahoga 1993), appeal dismissed by 69 OS(3d) 1415, 630 NE(2d) 376 (1994) (police justified in stopping defendant where he arrived from "source" city, appeared nervous, was dressed inappropriately for winter weather, made furtive movements in placing suitcase in front of car, attempted to throw off suspicion by not acknowledging the people who came to pick him up, and there was a discrepancy in the response as to whether defendant was the friend or relative of the couple who picked him up).

is not meant to be a rubber stamp for the police officer on the street; reasonableness is still an objective standard determined through the analysis of a neutral and detached judge. The Ohio Supreme Court, however, has diluted the federal standard. Rather than objectively viewing the facts along with the inferences that a trained police officer would draw, the Court seemed to abdicate by assessing the "totality of the circumstances"[41] "through the eyes of a reasonable and cautious police officer on the scene, guided by his experience and training,"[42] ready to "react as the events unfold."[43] This is not an insignificant shift. Rather than evaluating police conduct by objective Fourth Amendment standards, it conforms Fourth Amendment standards to police instinct and intuition.

The pattern begun in *State v Freeman* has continued. The Supreme Court purports to evaluate the facts and circumstances allegedly giving rise to reasonable suspicion based on the totality of the circumstances. That totality must be evaluated "through the eyes of a reasonable and cautious police officer on the scene, guided by his experience and training."[44] But the police and the court should not view the facts through the same eyes. The conditions are, by necessity, different; more importantly, their functions are different. The police officer is determining how to react to a street situation, and his reactions may be entirely appropriate to that situation. The court's role, however, is to determine whether those reactions met the constitutional test of reasonableness. The court should not substitute the officer's evaluation for the constitutional determination. However, that is exactly what the Ohio Supreme Court has done. Instead of weighing articulable facts and circumstances, the Court rubber-stamps police intuition and disparages its assigned role. *Terry*, however, required that constitutional adjudication not rely on police instinct or intuition but on articulable facts and circumstances evaluated within the matrix of an objective standard of reasonableness.

That analysis was first adopted over a decade ago in *Freeman*, when the Ohio Supreme Court sanctioned the stop of an automobile leaving a motel parking lot at 3 a.m. where the police officer had previously observed the defendant sitting in his car in the parking lot for fifteen minutes, and where the officer was aware of reports of theft and vandalism in the parking lot.[45]

---

[41]State v Bobo, 37 OS(3d) 177, 177 syl 112, 524 NE(2d) 489 (1988), cert denied 488 US 910, 109 SCt 264, 102 LEd(2d) 252 (1988); State v Smith, 45 OS(3d) 255, 544 NE(2d) 239 (1989), reversed by 494 US 541, 110 SCt 1288, 108 LEd(2d) 464 (1990); State v Andrews, 57 OS(3d) 86, 565 NE(2d) 1271 (1991), cert denied 501 US 1220, 111 SCt 2833, 115 LEd(2d) 1002 (1991).
[42]State v Freeman, 64 OS(2d) 291, 295, 414 NE(2d) 1044 (1980), cert denied 454 US 822, 102 SCt 107, 70 LEd(2d) 94 (1981), quoting United States v Hall, 525 F(2d) 857, 859 (DC Cir 1976).
[43]State v Andrews, 57 OS(3d) 86, 88, 565 NE(2d) 1271 (1991), cert denied 501 US 1220, 111 SCt 2833, 115 LEd(2d) 1002 (1991).
[44]State v Bobo, 37 OS(3d) 177, 179, 524 NE(2d) 489 (1988), cert denied 488 US 910, 109 SCt 264, 102 LEd(2d) 252 (1988), quoting United States v Hall, 525 F(2d) 857, 859 (DC Cir 1976).
[45]State v Freeman, 64 OS(2d) 291, 295, 414 NE(2d) 1044 (1980), cert denied 454 US 822, 102 SCt 107, 70 LEd(2d) 94 (1981), quoting United States v Hall, 525 F(2d) 857, 859 (DC Cir 1976).

The Ohio Supreme Court obviously attached great significance to the hour and locale of the stopping and sanctioned the drawing of inferences from these factors to create reasonable suspicion. The defendant's conduct was innocuous; the stop was upheld only because of where it took place and what had allegedly taken place in the area in the past. The Court accepted the police officer's judgment rather than impose an objective analysis on the facts. Yet reasonableness is a constitutional standard, not measured solely by how a police officer evaluated the facts and circumstances. Whether the fact that the suspect earlier sat in an automobile for fifteen minutes was really significant or critical to the situation is vitally important. If it is not a significant factor, then the Court is sanctioning the stopping of any person driving out of the parking lot late at night, which results in a skewed balance in total disregard of its effect on the private right to be left alone.

Even though a court reviewing the reasonableness of an investigative stop may consider all of the surrounding circumstances, by definition the focus must be on the acts of the defendant. The officer must be able to point to specific articulable facts that would lead a reasonable person to suspect criminal activity is afoot. The officer must independently observe circumstances showing criminal behavior, and the indication of such must be present prior to the detention.[46] The good faith of the police officer will not save an investigatory stop that is not sufficiently supported by adequate facts demonstrating reasonable suspicion.[47] An officer's intuitive feeling

---

[46]State v Johnson, No. 58344, 1990 WL 56775 (8th Dist Ct App, Cuyahoga, 5-3-90).

[47]State v Jackson, No. 9-84-50, 1986 WL 2979 (3d Dist Ct App, Marion, 3-7-86); see also Broadview Heights v Abkemeier, 83 App(3d) 633, 615 NE(2d) 656 (Cuyahoga 1992), appeal dismissed by 66 OS(3d) 1472, 611 NE(2d) 834 (1993) (where a police officer stops defendant for speeding without radar confirmation, the trial court may choose to discount the officer's testimony and find that the officer had no articulable suspicion on which to base a Terry-stop); State v Williams, 86 App(3d) 37, 619 NE(2d) 1141 (Pickaway 1993) (police do not have reasonable suspicion to stop a driver of a pickup truck based upon the motorist moving out of his lane by one tire width two times while executing turns). But see State v Wireman, 86 App(3d) 451, 621 NE(2d) 542 (Defiance 1993) (police have reasonable suspicion to stop motorist who crosses center lane three times); State v Gedeon, 81 App(3d) 617, 611 NE(2d) 972 (Lake 1992) (weaving within one's lane yields sufficient cause for an investigatory stop); State v Drogi, 96 App(3d) 466, 645 NE(2d) 153 (Belmont 1994) (officer's good faith did not save a stop where officer did not have reasonable suspicion to stop defendant's vehicle which crossed the center line by one foot, then went right towards the edge line, and then eventually over the center line, where no one was threatened or endangered, and there was no other evidence of erratic driving); City of Akron v Rowland, 67 OS(3d) 374, 618 NE(2d) 138 (1993) (officer could not rely upon unconstitutional city ordinance which prohibited "loitering in a manner and under circumstances manifesting their purpose to engage in drug activity" which was unconstitutionally vague because it lacked a specific intent requirement and was unconstitutionally and overbroad where the circumstances described in the ordinance as such loitering involved constitutionally protected behavior under the first and fourteenth amendments; City of Cleveland v Stephen, 93 App(3d) 827, 639 NE(2d) 1258 (Cuyahoga 1994) (officer could not rely upon unconstitutional city loitering ordinance, even one which had a mens rea requirement, to save stop where he had inarticulate hunch and not reasonable suspicion that defendant was involved in a drug sale).

that "something was wrong," even though ultimately confirmed, will not provide a sufficient basis for an investigatory stop.[48]

Too often a string of factors is put together, which demonstrates that the stop was made on a hunch. For example, in *State v Dorsey*,[49] one of the factors that made the police officer suspicious was that the suspected drug vehicle was a black Chevrolet Blazer, which the officer's experience led him to believe was a vehicle favored by narcotics traffickers.[50] Nor will general concerns about the possibility of theft or vandalism provide the specific and articulable facts necessary to justify an investigative stop.[51] Racial characteristics rarely, if ever, justify a reasonable suspicion that a person is engaged in criminal activity.[52] However, a suspect's youth was one of several factors relied on for a finding of reasonable suspicion.[53] The infamous reputation of a suspect will not justify an investigatory stop,[54] nor will the suspect's past criminal record.[55] Association with known drug users is not an adequate basis for an investigative detention.[56] An officer's personal

---

[48]State v Ford, 64 App(3d) 105, 580 NE(2d) 827 (Licking 1989), appeal dismissed by 47 OS(3d) 715, 549 NE(2d) 170 (1989); Columbus v Holland, 76 App(3d) 196, 199, 601 NE(2d) 190 (Franklin 1991) (rejects claim of reasonable suspicion from officer who testified that his decision to stop the motorist was based upon his "sixth sense" that driver did not want to have any contact with police, and upon "the kind of intuition that you won't find in a law book").

[49]State v Dorsey, No. 11657, 1989 WL 150806 (2d Dist Ct App, Montgomery, 12-12-89).

[50]State v Dorsey, No. 11657, 1989 WL 150806 (2d Dist Ct App, Montgomery, 12-12-89) (the factor carried no weight because trial judge drove identical vehicle).

[51]State v Heinrichs, 46 App(3d) 63, 545 NE(2d) 1304 (Darke 1988).

[52]State v Thieman, No. 52803, 1987 WL 10592 (8th Dist Ct App, Cuyahoga, 4-30-87) (occupants of defendant's truck who were white stopped and had conversation with pedestrians in almost entirely black neighborhood; even though the neighborhood had a history of drug trafficking, the claim of reasonable suspicion failed); State v Nealen, 84 App(3d) 235, 616 NE(2d) 944 (Cuyahoga 1992), appeal dismissed by 66 OS(3d) 1456, 610 NE(2d) 420 (1993) (an officer's observation of a white defendant walking with his fist clenched in a predominantly black neighborhood known to be an area of high drug activity cannot yield the reasonable suspicion necessary to support a *Terry*-stop).

[53]In re Oliver, No. L-89-118, 1989 WL 155193 (6th Dist Ct App, Lucas, 12-22-89).

[54]State v Fahy, 49 App(3d) 160, 551 NE(2d) 1311 (Henry 1988), appeal dismissed by 40 OS(3d) 704, 534 NE(2d) 841 (1988) (innocuous conduct insufficient to justify stop even though police knew of defendant's reputation for chronic drug abuse and trafficking); State v Bowling, No. CA86-06-038, 1987 WL 6706 (12th Dist Ct App, Warren, 2-17-87). But see State v Metz, 37 Misc(2d) 3, 523 NE(2d) 363 (Muni, Hamilton 1987) (knowledge of defendant's prior arrest for drug trafficking one factor which along with suspicious conduct found to create reasonable suspicion).

[55]State v Linson, 51 App(3d) 49, 554 NE(2d) 146 (Cuyahoga 1988).

[56]See Sibron v New York, 392 US 40, 88 SCt 1889, 20 LEd(2d) 917 (1968) (*Terry* companion case); State v Klein, 73 App(3d) 486, 597 NE(2d) 1141 (Washington 1991) (even though defendant was parked on another's property in an area known for theft and vandalism and left area when police cruiser approached, defendant's conduct was consistent with innocent behavior and did not form an adequate basis for a *Terry*-stop); State v Jones, 70 App(3d) 554, 591 NE(2d) 810 (Montgomery 1990), appeal dismissed by 59 OS(3d) 718, 572 NE(2d) 691 (1991) (detention is not based upon reasonable suspicion where officer observes defendant sitting in legally parked car with known drug abuser, and where several people walk away from the

observations,[57] or current knowledge that a driver's license has been suspended justifies an investigatory stop when the person whose license was suspended is observed driving.[58]

When attempting to articulate facts about a defendant's conduct that created suspicion, police officers often testify about furtive movements. In *State v Bobo*,[59] the defendant's alleged furtive movements were one of seven factors cited by the Ohio Supreme Court to sustain the claim of reasonable suspicion, and the Court instructed that such a movement may in the totality of circumstances justify an investigation. However, some such claims are known to be entirely manufactured. Thus, even an honestly made claim may not be sufficient to constitute reasonable suspicion; a testifying police officer must then proceed to describe in detail the defendant's movement that aroused his suspicion; otherwise, the court is unable to weigh the adequacy of the proffered claim. Also, a court reviewing reasonable suspicion must analyze the facts and not merely accept general claims of "furtive gestures." For example, where police suspicion is triggered merely by movement of a car's occupant, suggesting the concealment of an object under the seat, that alone should not be sufficient because it is also perfectly consistent with innocent behavior.[60] Vague, general claims of movement or "rustling around"[61] or "leaning over"[62] will not provide a satisfactory basis for an investigatory stop. However, stopping a defendant who was seen to make a motion with his shoulder was upheld when coupled with other factors.[63] Also, constant moving back and forth inside a car being followed by a police

---

car upon approach of unmarked police cruiser); State v Crosby, 72 App(3d) 148, 594 NE(2d) 110 (Cuyahoga 1991), appeal dismissed by 60 OS(3d) 711, 573 NE(2d) 667 (1991) (officer's observation of two individuals sitting in a vehicle talking with another who is leaning into the vehicle's window in a high crime area at night is not sufficient to create reasonable suspicion); State v Lockett, 99 App(3d) 81, 649 NE(2d) 1302 (Cuyahoga 1994) (stop invalid where based upon observation of defendant standing in high crime area with two other males who were drinking beer); see also Tallmadge v McCoy, 96 App(3d) 604, 645 NE(2d) 802 (Summit 1994) (stop valid where officer knew that owner of the vehicle had a suspended license and reasonably concluded that the driver was likely the owner).

[57]City of Toledo v Harris, 99 App(3d) 469, 651 NE(2d) 24 (Lucas 1995) (Terry stop valid based upon officer's belief that the weight of the truck and the load it was carrying was illegal based upon observation of bulging tires, straining engine, and the need to shift gears several times while accelerating).

[58]Compare Dayton v Blackburn, No. 11162, 1989 WL 65252 (2d Dist Ct App, Montgomery, 6-8-89) (officer had issued citation to the defendant two weeks earlier) with State v Tackett, 37 Misc(2d) 9, 524 NE(2d) 536 (County Ct, Ashtabula 1987) (information about license suspension which was one and one-half months old did not justify stop).

[59]State v Bobo, 37 OS(3d) 177, 524 NE(2d) 489 (1988), cert denied 488 US 910, 109 SCt 264, 102 LEd(2d) 252 (1988).

[60]State v Bird, 49 App(3d) 156, 551 NE(2d) 622 (Lake 1988).

[61]State v Chandler, 54 App(3d) 92, 560 NE(2d) 832 (Cuyahoga 1989), appeal dismissed by 49 OS(3d) 716, 552 NE(2d) 945 (1990).

[62]State v Jackson, 52 App(3d) 39, 556 NE(2d) 223 (Cuyahoga 1989); State v Dorsey, No. 11657, 1989 WL 150806 (2d Dist Ct App, Montgomery, 12-12-89).

[63]State v Harris, 36 App(3d) 106, 521 NE(2d) 835 (Cuyahoga 1987); see also State v Armstrong, No. 94 CA005992, 1995 WL 283779 (9th Dist Ct App, Lorain, 5-10-95) (while a mere furtive gesture does not establish reasonable suspicion, it was sufficient when coupled with (1) the officer's experience with drug crime, (2) the

officer who did not observe a rear license plate was deemed sufficient for an investigatory detention.[64] Flight, on sighting police officers, is a relevant factor when coupled with other factors.[65]

Obviously, evasive action by a suspect is not and should not provide justification for a stop. Here, like on other issues, however, the sentiment is changing rapidly. Justice Scalia has even suggested that a claim that it is unreasonable "to stop, for brief inquiry, young men who scatter in panic upon the mere sighting of the police is not self-evident, and arguably contradicts proverbial common sense."[66] A police officer need not rely on his own personal knowledge to justify an investigatory stop but may rely on "collective ... knowledge gleaned from other valid sources."[67] A police radio dispatch will provide reasonable cause for an investigative stop[68] provided that the underlying reasonable cause for the radio report or bulletin is established.[69] An enemy's tip, alone, will not support an investigative stop but will when coupled with sufficient independent corroboration.[70] A report of potential violence justifies action on less corroboration than a report not involving violence.[71]

Many courts, when reviewing a claim of reasonable suspicion, place great weight on factors collateral to the suspect's behavior and sanction a forcible stop in a high crime area while disallowing a *Terry*-stop involving the same conduct in a different locale. It is difficult to draw a clear line between inarticulate hunches, which will not support a *Terry*-stop, and reasonable

---

officer's familiarity with the area, (3) the fact that it is night, and (4) recognition of one man in the group as a convicted drug dealer).

[64]State v Shepard, Nos. 88-CA-14, 88-CA-16, 1989 WL 63336 (5th Dist Ct App, Guernsey, 5-15-89).

[65]Cf. State v Ponder, No. 11187, 1989 WL 5803 (2d Dist Ct App, Montgomery, 1-26-89).

[66]California v Hodari D., 499 US 621, 111 SCt 1547, 1549 n.1, 113 LEd(2d) 690 (1991).

[67]State v Thompson, No. 2161, at 4, 1986 WL 9363 (9th Dist Ct App, Wayne, 8-27-86) (citation omitted).

[68]State v Good, 37 App(3d) 174, 525 NE(2d) 527 (Wayne 1987); contra State v Hill, 3 App(3d) 10, 443 NE(2d) 198 (Cuyahoga 1981); City of Hamilton v Jacobs, 100 App(3d) 724, 654 NE(2d) 1057 (Butler 1995) (radio dispatch regarding possible DUI provided sufficient justification to warrant an investigatory stop).

[69]State v Smartt, 61 App(3d) 137, 572 NE(2d) 204 (Cuyahoga 1989).

[70]State v Kuperman, No. 89-L-14-087, 1991 WL 12934 (11th Dist Ct App, Lake, 2-1-91); Vandalia v Huch, No. 11641, 1989 WL 116887 (2d Dist Ct App, Montgomery, 10-2-89).

[71]Cf. State v Antil, 91 App(3d) 589, 632 NE(2d) 1370 (Washington 1993) (police had reasonable suspicion to stop defendant's vehicle based upon defendant's girlfriend's information that defendant was drunk and driving around looking for her, where there was a prior history of domestic problems between the two); Wells v Akron, 42 App(3d) 148, 537 NE(2d) 229 (Summit 1987); State v Turner, No. 91-L-029, 1991 WL 274504 (11th Dist Ct App, Lake, 12-20-91) (a police officer has considerable latitude in initiating an investigative stop where the safety of the public is involved; tip that defendant had shotgun in car was sufficient to raise a reasonable suspicion justifying stop). But see State v Fincher, 76 App(3d) 721, 603 NE(2d) 329 (Cuyahoga 1991), appeal dismissed by 63 OS(3d) 1428, 588 NE(2d) 129 (1992) (approaching an occupied car is not illegal, and even when it occurs in an area of drug activity, it does not justify a seizure, even for investigative purposes).

suspicion, which will. As in all Fourth Amendment issues, the decision should turn on an analysis of the facts surrounding the particular stop. "Bright-line" rules should be avoided because they tend to incorporate fact situations which, when realistically evaluated, would fall outside the scope of the rule. Factors that would support a stop include some which would never be given substantial weight in assessing probable cause for an arrest, but it must be understood that reasonable suspicion and probable cause differ more than quantitatively.

One collateral factor that is given great weight in Ohio is the location where the police officer observed the suspect, notwithstanding that a very sympathetic United States Supreme Court has said that "[appellant's being] in a neighborhood frequented by drug users, standing alone, is not a basis for concluding that appellant himself was engaged in criminal activity."[72] "High crime area" has become a centerpiece that, when coupled with a few other often innocuous factors, justifies a forcible stop. It has become a talismanic signal to justify investigative stops in Ohio.

The real problem with this approach is that most people living in so-called high crime areas are not engaged in illegal behavior but are, nonetheless, subject to investigatory stops. Even though race would not be tolerated as the basis for a stop, location may in fact be a euphemism for race. The cases, of course, only involve those situations where the stops result in the discovery of contraband; there are no data available to ascertain how many people in high crime areas are the subjects of investigatory stops that do not mature into criminal prosecutions because the stop does not result in the discovery of drugs or weapons.

The bright-line quality of the phrase "high crime area" became apparent in *State v Bobo*,[73] where the collateral factor of location became all-important. In *Bobo*, officers from the Cleveland narcotics unit were investigating an area known for heavy drug activity. They saw two occupants in an illegally parked car by an open field. The officers circled the block and, on their return, could see only one occupant. At this time, the second occupant was seen "popping up" in the passenger's side of the front seat, looking at the officers, and then bending forward. The officers approached the vehicle, ordered the suspect out, and then found a gun under the front seat on the passenger side.

The Ohio Supreme Court found the investigative stop justified by seven factors offered by the prosecution:[74]

(1) The area in which the action occurred was an area of very heavy drug activity in which weapons were prevalent;

---

[72]Brown v Texas, 443 US 47, 52, 99 SCt 2637, 61 LEd(2d) 357 (1979).

[73]State v Bobo, 37 OS(3d) 177, 524 NE(2d) 489 (1988), cert denied 488 US 910, 109 SCt 264, 102 LEd(2d) 252 (1988).

[74]But see State v Ball, 72 App(3d) 43, 593 NE(2d) 431 (Cuyahoga 1991), appeal dismissed by 60 OS(3d) 718, 574 NE(2d) 1079 (1991) (court did not find Outhwaite projects located at Woodland Ave. and East 55th St. in Cleveland to be an area where drugs are frequently sold, even though this is the same area where the arrest in *Bobo* took place).

(2) It was nighttime, when weapons could easily be hidden;

(3) One of the officers who approached the vehicle in which Bobo was sitting had about twenty years of experience as a police officer and numerous years in the surveillance of drug and weapon activity; included in this experience were about 500 arrests each for guns or drugs city-wide and over 100 arrests in the area in which Bobo was parked;

(4) The officer had knowledge of how drug transactions occurred in that area;

(5) The officer had observed Bobo disappear from view, reappear when the police car was close, look directly at the officers, and then bend down as if to hide something under the front seat;

(6) The officer had experience in recovering weapons or drugs when an individual would make the type of gesture made by Bobo in ducking under his seat; and

(7) The police officers were out of their vehicle and away from any protection if defendant had been armed.

The Supreme Court majority relied primarily on the area where the stop took place: " 'The reputation of an area for criminal activity is an articulable fact upon which a police officer may legitimately rely' in determining whether an investigative stop is warranted."[75] In fact, the other six factors are window dressing. An evaluation of the Court's analysis might be helped by knowing that the occupants of the vehicle were a man and a woman, and while that does not rule out a drug transaction, it opens the door to consideration of other, innocent behavior (in fact, the officer "testified that when he looked into the car, 'she [the female occupant] was fastening her clothing.' "[76]. Even though an area is known for high drug activity, residents of these areas engage in all of the activities other people engage in in their home neighborhoods. In fact, one could question whether the activity within the car fit the profile of a drug transaction. Ordinarily, a drug transaction in a vehicle is hurried; the parties do not linger in the car as if to socialize. Justice Wright, dissenting, reproduced parts of the suppression hearing transcript to show that the state claims that Bobo was putting something underneath the seat was unsupported and any suspicion resulting from that factor was unwarranted.[77]

The overwhelming effect of a stop in a high drug activity area was evidenced again in State v Andrews,[78] where an officer saw a police cruiser

---

[75]State v Bobo, 37 OS(3d) 177, 179, 524 NE(2d) 489 (1988), cert denied 488 US 910, 109 SCt 264, 102 LEd(2d) 252 (1988), quoting United States v Magda, 547 F(2d) 756 (2d Cir NY 1976), cert denied 434 US 878, 98 SCt 230, 54 LEd(2d) 157 (1977).

[76]State v Bobo, 37 OS(3d) 177, 184 n.3, 524 NE(2d) 489 (1988), cert denied 488 US 910, 109 SCt 264, 102 LEd(2d) 252 (1988) (Wright, J., dissenting).

[77]State v Bobo, 37 OS(3d) 177, 183-84, 524 NE(2d) 489 (1988), cert denied 488 US 910, 109 SCt 264, 102 LEd(2d) 252 (1988).

[78]State v Andrews, 57 OS(3d) 86, 565 NE(2d) 1271 (1991), cert denied 501 US 1220, 111 SCt 2833, 115 LEd(2d) 1002 (1991); distinguished, State v Fincher, 76 App(3d) 721, 603 NE(2d) 329 (Cuyahoga 1991), appeal dismissed by 63 OS(3d) 1428, 588 NE(2d) 129 (1992) (only real factual difference was time of day); State v

drive down the street and then saw the defendant running towards him from the direction of the other police cruiser. The officer shined a light on the defendant, observed the defendant throw down a can of beer, drew his service revolver, and ordered the defendant to put his hands up. Again, as in *Bobo*, the state cited multiple factors that supported its claim of reasonable suspicion: (1) the investigation took place in a high crime area; (2) it took place at night; (3) the officer had many years of experience; (4) he was away from his cruiser at the time of the encounter; and (5) he saw the defendant running away from the direction of the police cruiser. The Court viewed the circumstances through the eyes of the officer and concluded that the officer acted reasonably,[79] reversing the Montgomery County Court of Appeals, which held that merely running in a high crime area, with no other evidence of criminal behavior, is not reasonable suspicion. The Supreme Court said that the case could not be resolved by reference to any single factor, but it is doubtful that the Court would sanction the seizure of a suspect running anywhere but in a high crime area.[80] But mere propinquity to one committing a minor violation of law will not justify a *Terry*-stop of companion.[81]

The effect given by the Ohio Supreme Court to high crime areas impacted on courts of appeals decisions, which also are giving disproportionate weight to the locale where an investigative stop takes place. In *State v Smith*,[82] police officers investigated two men seated in a legally parked automobile because the driver was looking at something in his lap. Even though the officer testified that the driver's conduct "could mean anything,"[83] the Cuyahoga County Court of Appeals concluded that the investi-

---

Davie, 86 App(3d) 460, 621 NE(2d) 548 (Cuyahoga 1993) (no reasonable suspicion based upon observation of defendant who is conversing with driver of a car stopped in an intersection and starts to run at the sight of the police).

[79]State v Andrews, 57 OS(3d) 86, 565 NE(2d) 1271 (1991), cert denied 501 US 1220, 111 SCt 2833, 115 LEd(2d) 1002 (1991); *distinguished*, State v Fincher, 76 App(3d) 721, 603 NE(2d) 329 (Cuyahoga 1991), appeal dismissed by 63 OS(3d) 1428, 588 NE(2d) 129 (1992) (only real factual difference was time of day); State v Davie, 86 App(3d) 460, 621 NE(2d) 548 (Cuyahoga 1993) (no reasonable suspicion based upon observation of defendant who is conversing with driver of a car stopped in an intersection and starts to run at the sight of the police).

[80]But see In re Agosto, 85 App(3d) 188, 619 NE(2d) 475 (Cuyahoga 1993) (where defendant's alleged furtive movements are just as indicative of innocent behavior as criminal behavior, the totality of the circumstances do not support a finding of reasonable suspicion).

[81]State v Brown, 83 App(3d) 673, 615 NE(2d) 682 (Cuyahoga 1992), appeal dismissed by 66 OS(3d) 1444, 609 NE(2d) 170 (1993).

[82]State v Smith, No. 58918, 1991 WL 185720 (8th Dist Ct App, Cuyahoga, 8-29-91); but see State v Ball, 72 App(3d) 43, 593 NE(2d) 431 (Cuyahoga 1991), appeal dismissed by 60 OS(3d) 718, 574 NE(2d) 1079 (1991) (similar facts, different result in same district Court of Appeals); and City of London v Edley, 75 App(3d) 30, 598 NE(2d) 851 (Madison 1991), appeal dismissed by 62 OS(3d) 1475, 581 NE(2d) 1097 (1991) (similar facts, different result).

[83]State v Smith, No. 58918, at 3, 1991 WL 185720 (8th Dist Ct App, Cuyahoga, 8-29-91); State v Morales, 92 App(3d) 580, 636 NE(2d) 404 (Cuyahoa 1993) (court concludes that officer had reasonable suspicion to stop defendant where defendant's vehicle was stopped in the middle of a two-way street, another individual, whom the officer recognized as a drug offender, was leaning into the car window, that individ-

gative stop by experienced officers in a high crime area at night was reasonable, prompting dissenting Judge Harper to complain:

> I find it regrettable that the constitutional guarantees of freedom from unlawful searches and seizures are suspended when four things occur: (1) the police are in a high crime area, which is almost always where blacks, hispanic and poor whites live; (2) it is night time; (3) the officers have years of experience on the police force; and (4) the defendant looks down while seated in a car.[84]

Similarly, in *State v George*,[85] police officers patrolling in a high-crime area in front of a bar "where the officer had made drug arrests in the past"[86] observed three men standing in an alley. The officer did not witness anything pass between the men, but they were standing "with their heads bowed and their backs to the street, *which in the officer's experience indicated that they were conducting a drug transaction.*"[87] When the officers made a U-turn and returned to the alley, only the defendant remained. When he saw the police car, he started to leave the alley in the direction of the car. The Stark County Court of Appeals, relying on *Freeman, Bobo*, and *Andrews*, concluded that the stop was justified because (1) it occurred in a high crime area; (2) it occurred at night "in an alley where drug transactions typically transpire"; (3) the officer was experienced; (4) the officer knew that drug transactions took place in the area; and (5) the officer noted that the way the men were standing with their heads bowed when first observed was "a position typically used to transact in drugs"[88] and that the defendant was later observed walking with something in his hand. The reliance placed on the way the three men were standing is almost absurd, but when police do

---

ual fled after seeing the police, the defendant slowly began to drive away, in an area where there had been "numerous and bitter complaints" of drug trafficking, and the officer had participated in over 700 drug arrests).

[84]State v Smith, No. 58918, at 3, 1991 WL 185720 (8th Dist Ct App, Cuyahoga, 8-29-91). See also State v Ward, 80 App(3d) 701, 705, 610 NE(2d) 579 (Cuyahoga 1992) (Harper J., dissenting) ("The majority of this court today, as has been the recent trend in this court, is actually holding that, as a matter of law, those unfortunate black, Hispanic and poor white citizens who by virtue of their economic and social status live in so-called 'high crime areas' are suspects.").

[85]State v George, No. CA-8519, 1991 WL 207941 (5th Dist Ct App, Stark, 9-30-91); State v Newsome, 71 App(3d) 73, 76, 593 NE(2d) 40 (Cuyahoga 1990), appeal dismissed by 61 OS(3d) 1409, 574 NE(2d) 1073 (1991) ("specific and articulable fact of the co-defendant leaning into the car in a high crime district was enough ..."). But see State v Fanning, 70 App(3d) 648, 591 NE(2d) 869 (Cuyahoga 1990) (different result on similar facts); State v Curry, 95 App(3d) 93, 641 NE(2d) 1172 (Cuyahoga 1994) (reasonable suspicion found to exist where, in a high crime area, defendant was standing on the corner of an intersection in the middle of the night, stopped another man and showed that man an object which defendant immediately placed in his pocket after spotting the detectives and began to run; court also used facts occurring after the stop—that the defendant refused to identify himself after he was detained, refused to take his hands out of his pockets, and he became verbally and physically abusive—as part of the justification for the stop).

[86]State v George, No. CA-8519, at 1, 1991 WL 207941 (5th Dist Ct App, Stark, 9-30-91).

[87]State v George, No. CA-8519, at 1, 1991 WL 207941 (5th Dist Ct App, Stark, 9-30-91) (emphasis added).

[88]State v George, No. CA-8519, at 3, 1991 WL 207941 (5th Dist Ct App, Stark, 9-30-91).

not testify about furtive gestures, the court will recognize the total absence of particular facts other than location.[89]

Both courts of appeals took their lead from the Ohio Supreme Court. Like *Freeman*, *Bobo*, and *Andrews*, these cases were decided solely because of where the stop took place. The guidance given to the police in these cases is clear but should be very unsettling because in most urban areas it negates the rights guaranteed by the Fourth Amendment. The impact of "high crime" and "high drug activity" is apparent. When behavior is innocuous, reasonable suspicion seems to rest on the area where the stop takes place. If it is a high crime area, a stop will be sanctioned that would not otherwise be allowed.[90] In a situation where the "issue is close," appellate courts may cite to the fact that no claim was made that the area is known for heavy drug activity as the basis for rejecting a claim of reasonable suspicion.[91] However, completely innocent behavior that is not subject to multiple interpretations should not justify an investigative stop even in a high crime or drug area.[92] Moreover, in its most recent pronouncement the Ohio Supreme Court has made itself explicitly clear that it does not adhere to the full implications of those earlier statements, when it said, in *State v Carter*,[93] that a high crime area is not sufficient, by itself, to justify an investigative stop.

In other contexts, where reliance is not placed on the high crime urban location, the Supreme Court has focused more on the particular facts and the suspect's behavior in determining the reasonableness of a stop. In *State v Comen*,[94] the critical facts were the nearness of the defendant's automo-

---

[89]See State v Jackson, 52 App(3d) 39, 556 NE(2d) 223 (Cuyahoga 1989) (suspicion that attached to defendant sitting in parked car near location that police arrived to search was unreasonable because officer testified that all he saw was defendant "leaning over"; plus "high crime area" was not sufficient to justify stop). But see Akron v Harris, 36 App(3d) 106, 521 NE(2d) 835 (Cuyahoga 1987) (traffic violation (peeling tires), "furtive gesture" (motion with shoulder), and high crime area made suspicion reasonable).

[90]Compare State v Curry, No. 11138, 1989 WL 35890 (2d Dist Ct App, Montgomery, 4-10-89) (court inferred that since the officers were in a high crime area, twenty people in an apartment warranted reasonable suspicion) and State v Dorsey, No. 11657, 1989 WL 150806 (2d Dist Ct App, Montgomery, 12-12-89) (since area of the stop was not a high crime area, suspicion resulting from observing a man walk away from a car that had a motor running and its lights on, and where the driver of the vehicle was leaning forward, was not reasonable). But see State v Edwards, 80 App(3d) 319, 609 NE(2d) 200 (Cuyahoga 1992), appeal dismissed by 65 OS(3d) 1430, 600 NE(2d) 675 (1992) (police who do not have prior description of persons being searched do not have reasonable suspicion to seize persons standing in their own doorway in high crime area); State v Walker, 90 App(3d) 132, 628 NE(2d) 91 (Cuyahoga 1993) (court holds no reasonable suspicion to justify stop merely because defendant was in high crime area and he fled upon approach of the police).

[91]See, e.g., State v Dorsey, No. 11657, 1989 WL 150806 (2d Dist Ct App, Montgomery, 12-12-89).

[92]State v Dancer, 52 Misc(2d) 9, 557 NE(2d) 178 (Muni, Hamilton 1989) (no constitutional justification for seizing someone who is merely sitting at a bar and having a drink in an area of high crime and drug activity).

[93]State v Carter, 69 OS(3d) 57, 630 NE(2d) 355 (1994).

[94]State v Comen, 50 OS(3d) 206, 553 NE(2d) 640 (1990); see also, State v Norwood, 83 App(3d) 451, 615 NE(2d) 262 (Summit 1992) (being the only car in

bile to the scene of a burglary reported only minutes before and that defendant's car had no frost on the windows. In *State v Williams*,[95] a police officer investigating a report of stolen produce discovered a marijuana field. Reasonable suspicion developed when the defendant, who was at the rear door of an obviously abandoned farmhouse, told the police officer that he was asking permission to hunt squirrel. The officer knew, however, that only a few minutes remained in the day to legally hunt squirrel.

14.04   The frisk

The most common misunderstanding surrounding the area of stop and frisk is the belief that reasonable suspicion justifying a forcible stop automatically authorizes the police officer to conduct a frisk of the suspect for weapons. That general rule was suggested in the Supreme Court by Justice Harlan but rejected by the *Terry v Ohio*[96] majority.

In *Terry*, the Supreme Court acknowledged that a frisk is merely a euphemism for a search and, as such, must be independently supported. The justification for the frisk rests solely on society's need to protect police officers who are engaged in investigative activity. A *Terry* frisk is not a search for evidence; it is only a limited search for weapons. Consequently, when a police officer engages in a lawful investigative stop, he may frisk the suspect if the officer has reasonable grounds to believe that the suspect carries a weapon or otherwise endangers the officer's safety. The *Terry* Court required that lower courts not treat the frisk as flowing automatically from the lawful stopping, but instead as the basis of a separate inquiry. Although the Ohio Supreme Court has said that "[t]he right to frisk is virtually automatic when individuals are suspected of committing a crime, like drug trafficking, for which they are likely to be armed."[97] The author, however, is not aware of any empirical studies which support the supposition that most persons selling drugs are armed.

Ordinarily, a court will accept a claim that an officer was in fear for his safety.[98] However, an officer need not testify that he was personally afraid or scared by the threat of danger.[99] However, the officer is obligated to articulate particular facts from which he reasonably inferred that a suspect

---

vicinity of reported gunfire and attempt by driver of car to evade police creates reasonable suspicion); State v Patterson, 95 App(3d) 255, 642 NE(2d) 390 (Lake 1993), appeal dismissed by 68 OS(3d) 1470, 628 NE(2d) 1389 (1994) (stop valid where defendant, the only person out at the time and appearing to be unfamiliar with the area, was within a quarter of a mile of area where a prowler had just been reported and where there had recently been a series of burglaries).

[95]State v Williams, 51 OS(3d) 58, 554 NE(2d) 108 (1990), cert denied 498 US 961, 111 SCt 394, 112 LEd(2d) 404 (1990).

[96]Terry v Ohio, 392 US 1, 88 SCt 1868, 20 LEd(2d) 889 (1968).

[97]State v Evans, 67 OS(3d) 405, 413, 618 NE(2d) 162 (1993), cert denied ___ US ___, 114 SCt 1195, 127 LEd(2d) 544 (1994).

[98]State v Metz, 37 Misc(2d) 3, 523 NE(2d) 363 (Muni, Hamilton 1987) (officers testified they feared for their safety due to one suspect's "history" and the strange location in which they found the two men).

[99]State v Evans, 67 OS(3d) 405, 413, 618 NE(2d) 162, 170 (1993), cert denied ___ US ___, 114 SCt 1195, 127 LEd(2d) 544 (1994).

was armed and dangerous.[100] Where an officer failed to testify that he feared for his safety, testifying only that in some instances he had found weapons strapped to the legs or ankles of drug users, a court found inadmissible evidence found in the rolled-up portion of the defendant's jeans.[101] Understandably, when issues of a police officer's safety arise, a reviewing court will neither question the claim too closely nor, in a close case, second-guess the officer. However, when no reasons are offered in support of that fear and the facts contradict the claim, the justification for the frisk will be rejected,[102] such as when the evidence that gave rise to the fear for safety occurred many hours before the search.[103]

The frisk described by the *Terry* Court, and conducted by the Cleveland officer in that case, is a limited search for weapons, requiring that the intrusion be limited to a pat-down of the suspect's outer clothing. The pat-down of a suspect's clothing may extend to any area where a weapon may be hidden, including the crotch.[104] If the pat-down reveals an object on the suspect's person, which feels like a gun or other weapon, then the officer is entitled to reach into that area of the suspect's clothing and retrieve the object.[105] The object secured by the officer in this procedure may provide probable cause for an arrest and is admissible in evidence. Its admissibility is not determined by the nature of the object; even if the object retrieved by the officer is not a weapon, but instead turns out to be other contraband, it is lawfully seized and admissible. If, however, the object turns out to be a closed container, the officer may not open it unless probable cause exists prior to its being opened that it contains contraband.[106] The critical inquiries focus first on the stop, second on the existence of reasonable fear for the officer's safety, and third on the reasonableness of the officer's belief that the object he is reaching for is a weapon. However, an officer in Ohio may not remove a soft object from a suspect's pocket which "the officer knows or reasonably should know is not itself a weapon on the grounds that it may contain a small weapon such as a razor blade."[107]

---

[100]Sibron v New York, 392 US 40, 88 SCt 1889, 20 LEd(2d) 917 (1968); State v Marini, 78 App(3d) 279, 604 NE(2d) 769 (Cuyahoga 1992), appeal dismissed by 64 OS(3d) 1413, 593 NE(2d) 4 (1992) (there was nothing to indicate that the defendant or his companion were armed or dangerous; they responded peaceably to the officer's orders, the parking lot was well-lit and not in a known high crime area, and it did not appear that the car they were driving was stolen).

[101]State v Hill, 52 App(2d) 393, 370 NE(2d) 775 (Hamilton 1977).

[102]State v Burkett, No. L-88-174, 1989 WL 41723 (6th Dist Ct App, Lucas, 4-28-89).

[103]State v Isaacs, No. 11167, 1989 WL 13546 (2d Dist Ct App, Montgomery, 2-13-89).

[104]State v Bendett, No. 93CA005655, 1994 WL 479205 (9th Dist Ct App, Lorain, 9-7-94).

[105]See State v Vance, 98 App(3d) 56, 647 NE(2d) 851 (Marion 1994) (officer acted properly in removing package of drugs during pat-down search for weapons where drugs were in hard package and could have felt like a weapon).

[106]State v Oborne, 99 App(3d) 577, 651 NE(2d) 453 (Montgomery 1994).

[107]State v Evans, 67 OS(3d) 405, 416, 618 NE(2d) 162 (1993), cert denied ___ US ___, 114 SCt 1195, 127 LEd(2d) 544 (1994); see also State v Ryan, No. CA94-08-073, 1995 WL 447798 (12th Dist Ct App, Warren, 7-31-95) (where court upheld search of defendant where the officer felt an unidentifiable bulge concealed

During a hearing to determine the admissibility of evidence other than a weapon found during a frisk, the nature of the object is critical. If a reasonable officer concerned for his safety feels an object through clothing that could be a weapon, that object is admissible. At issue is the reasonableness of the belief. Sometimes incredible objects, such as plastic bags containing a leafy, vegetable matter,[108] pass for hard objects at these hearings. All too often, the issue is not properly drawn. The prosecuting and defense attorneys should re-create the situation by placing the evidence inside of clothing similar to that worn by the defendant. A purely verbal description of what took place is not likely to have the same impact on the hearing judge as a demonstration. A judge, even though inclined to support a police claim, may not be able to do so when confronted by a re-creation of the actual situation. Even though a pat-down may be permitted under the circumstances, the seizure may nonetheless be impermissible. A roll of money ($5,000) removed from a suspect's front left pocket was excluded because there was no evidence that the money was concealed in a weapon or that the officer was threatened by its presence.[109] A metal tube and bottle were also suppressed when there was no evidence that the officer believed the objects were weapons.[110] However, a police officer's claim was buttressed when the court determined that he did not reach into pockets that did not contain objects that perhaps might be weapons.[111]

Objects seized in the search of an individual by officers who fail to engage in a preliminary pat-down are inadmissible as evidence because the procedure followed by the police indicates that the search was directed at more than just weapons.[112] Evidence secured when defendants are not frisked but ordered to empty their pockets will not be admissible when the only authority is a search for weapons.[113] Similarly, where a police officer

---

in the passenger's sock and ordered the defendant's sock pulled down exposing several plastic bags filled with marijuana and cocaine; editor's note: issue should be whether at the time the officer felt an unidentifiable bulge, he thought it could have been a weapon).

[108]See e.g., State v Hunter, 98 App(3d) 632, 649 NE(2d) 289 (8th Dist Ct App, Cuyahoga 11-14-94).

[109]State v Bailey, No. WD-89-15, 1989 WL 130855 (6th Dist Ct App, Wood, 11-3-89).

[110]State v Dotson, 66 App(3d) 182, 583 NE(2d) 1068 (Franklin 1990); State v Cartledge, 76 App(3d) 145, 601 NE(2d) 157 (Cuyahoga 1991), appeal dismissed by 63 OS(3d) 1409, 585 NE(2d) 834 (1992) (no reason to believe that glass vial in defendant's pocket was a weapon). But see Minnesota v Dickerson, 508 US 366, 113 SCt 2130, 124 LEd(2d) 334 (1993) (plain feel doctrine), discussed in Text 13.05, Plain feel).

[111]State v Young, No. 51984, 1987 WL 11187 (8th Dist Ct App, Cuyahoga, 5-7-87).

[112]State v Scott, 61 App(3d) 391, 572 NE(2d) 819 (Hamilton 1989); State v Bailey, No. 1725, 1989 WL 74861 (4th Dist Ct App, Scioto, 6-27-89).

[113]State v Linson, 51 App(3d) 49, 554 NE(2d) 146 (Cuyahoga 1988); State v Franklin, 86 App(3d) 101, 619 NE(2d) 1182 (Hamilton 1993), appeal dismissed by 67 OS(3d) 1421, 616 NE(2d) 504 (1993) (request to suspects to empty their pockets during a *Terry*-stop converted stop into an illegal arrest).

reaches into a pocket without first frisking the suspect, evidence retrieved is not admissible under *Terry*.[114]

In *State v Kratzer*, the Franklin County Court of Appeals held inadmissible a bag of marijuana retrieved from a suspect who was not first patted down and who had no hard objects in that pocket. Similarly, the Hamilton County Court of Appeals held a glassine envelope found in the rolled-up portion of a suspect's jeans inadmissible because, aside from the nature of the object seized, the officer failed to testify that he feared for his safety, testifying only that in some instances he had found weapons strapped to the legs or ankles of drug users.[115]

Under certain circumstances, the officer need not conduct the pat-down of outer clothing before retrieving a weapon that he has cause to believe is being carried in a specific spot on the suspect. To require a pat-down under that circumstance would put form over substance and not comport with the reasonableness standard. It might even endanger the officer's safety, the preservation of which is the purpose behind this type of intrusion. In *Adams v Williams*,[116] the Supreme Court upheld the seizure of the gun carried in the suspect's waistband without a prior pat-down because the tip on which the officer relied contained information that the suspect was carrying a gun next to that part of his body, and, moreover, the suspect had failed to respond to the officer's request that he exit his vehicle.

The Ohio Supreme Court has approved a *Terry* type search for weapons of a limited portion of the automobile from which the suspect has been asked to exit. In *State v Smith*,[117] officers pulled over a station wagon which they had observed run a red light. As the officers approached the vehicle to issue a citation, one officer observed the suspect push something under the seat.[118] The officer ordered the defendant out of the vehicle and positioned himself next to the automobile so that he could inspect under the driver's seat, where he observed a weapon. The Ohio Supreme Court upheld the police officer's action as a reasonable search for weapons under the *Terry* standard. The Court held that where a police officer approaches a motor vehicle at night for a traffic violation and sees the driver, while exiting the

---

[114]State v Kratzer, 33 App(2d) 167, 293 NE(2d) 104 (Franklin 1972).

[115]State v Hill, 52 App(2d) 393, 370 NE(2d) 775 (Hamilton 1977).

[116]Adams v Williams, 407 US 143, 92 SCt 1921, 32 LEd(2d) 612 (1972).

[117]State v Smith, 56 OS(2d) 405, 384 NE(2d) 280 (1978); compare State v Chapman, 73 App(3d) 132, 596 NE(2d) 612 (Allen 1992) (protective search of car upheld where tinted windows limit visibility into rear of vehicle and passenger was seen ducking his head when the officer engaged cruiser lights); and State v Green, 75 App(3d) 284, 599 NE(2d) 371 (Cuyahoga 1991), appeal dismissed by 62 OS(3d) 1463, 580 NE(2d) 784 (1991) (protective search of vehicle improper even though officers observed defendant bend over and place something on floor of car, where defendant stopped for driving left of center, and officers have no basis for suspecting defendant of criminal behavior).

[118]See Michigan v Long, 463 US 1032, 103 SCt 3469, 77 LEd(2d) 1201 (1983) (search of passenger compartment of automobile, limited to areas where weapon may be placed or hidden, is permissible if based on "specific and articulable facts which, when taken together with the rational inferences from those facts, reasonably warrant" the officer's belief that suspect is dangerous and may gain immediate control of weapons).

car, furtively conceal something under the seat, a limited search of that area is reasonable for the purpose of the officer's protection. The Court said that the officer had the right to proceed with his business without fear for his safety, and that an accessible weapon presents no less danger to an officer when located in close proximity to, rather than on, a suspect. Presumably, this search could also be supported on the theory that after issuance of the citation, the suspect would have been permitted to reenter the vehicle and a weapon under the seat would have presented a threat to the officers' safety at that time. In *Smith*, there was a limited search of the area where the officers had observed the suspect's furtive conduct, and the officers testified that they acted out of fear for their safety. However, where evidence is insufficient to establish a reasonable fear for the officer's safety, a frisk of the vehicle will not be permitted because it appears to be a search for evidence rather than weapons.[119]

14.05   Scope of permissible inquiry and detention

The totality of any intrusion, even beyond the initial stop, must meet the reasonableness standard. The very purpose of the stop and momentary detention recognized in *Terry v Ohio*[120] is to confirm or dispel the suspicion that the circumstances and the suspect's behavior aroused. A forcible detention is only permissible where reasonable suspicion justifies a *Terry*-stop. A citizen has a right to ignore a police inquiry and walk away when that inquiry is not based on reasonable suspicion justifying a forcible stop,[121] although how a citizen is to ascertain the distinctions that govern his obligations has never been fully explored by the courts. Where a suspect's conduct gives rise to reasonable suspicion, the suspect is obligated to stop when ordered to do so by a police officer, and the officer is justified in grabbing the suspect if he attempts to flee.

Ordinarily one difference between a forcible stop and an arrest is the amount of force used. Most *Terry*-stops will not necessitate the use of force to accomplish the purpose of conducting an inquiry. Comparisons often have been drawn between an arrest situation, where the use of force is expected and automatic, and a *Terry*-stop, where there is rarely a threat of violence and the intrusion is conducted in a polite manner generally devoid of force and humiliation. The amount of force that may accompany a *Terry*-stop is, again, subject to a reasonableness inquiry. The force must be reasonably limited in scope and intensity which will vary depending on the crime investigated and the reasonable risk perceived by the investigating officers.

There has been a measurable escalation of violence in society in the 1980s; consequently there has been a clear escalation of the force that may accompany a *Terry*-stop. The fact that guns were drawn and a suspect

---

[119]See, e.g., State v Burkett, No. L-88-174, 1989 WL 41723 (6th Dist Ct App, Lucas, 4-28-89).

[120]Terry v Ohio, 392 US 1, 88 SCt 1868, 20 LEd(2d) 889 (1968).

[121]United States v Mendenhall, 446 US 544, 100 SCt 1870, 64 LEd(2d) 497 (1980).

ordered to lean against a wall with hands up, once a sure indicium of an arrest, may today be reasonable as part of a *Terry*-stop, depending on the circumstances, because an officer has the right to proceed to make inquiry free from the risk of personal harm.[122] An officer who stopped a motorist and jumped out of the squad car pointing a shotgun at the motorist while yelling "Do as you're told or I'm going to blow your head off" was found to have acted reasonably where the motorist matched the description of a suspect who had just pointed a gun at two juveniles.[123] The use of hand-cuffs, however, would likely still signal the difference between an arrest and a stop.[124]

A police officer may ask questions of a suspect stopped on reasonable suspicion without first issuing *Miranda* warnings; however, the questioning will still be governed by ordinary due process standards prohibiting coercion. A person lawfully subject to a *Terry*-stop has an absolute right to refuse to answer a police officer's questions and need neither produce identification nor otherwise cooperate with the inquiry.[125] Refusal to cooperate with a police officer is not punishable conduct in Ohio.[126] Failure to cooperate by identifying oneself or by answering questions will not justify an arrest absent other circumstances constituting probable cause, although the United States Supreme Court resisted reaffirming the absolute right of a suspect not to cooperate.[127] Even though a suspect may not identify himself or answer an officer's questions about his suspicious behavior, those facts are relevant in a determination of the legitimacy of a subsequent frisk of the suspect[128] and likely will justify a longer detention while the suspicious circumstances are checked out.

Although a stop may be supportable, it does not justify a detention and further inquiry when the suspicion supporting the stop is immediately dissipated by facts readily apparent to the officer. For example, in *State v Chatton*,[129] an officer stopped a vehicle that displayed neither front nor rear

---

[122]See e.g., State v Harrington, No. 14146, 1994 WL 285048 (2d Dist Ct App, Montgomery, 6-1-94).

[123]Wells v Akron, 42 App(3d) 148, 537 NE(2d) 229 (Summit 1987); see also State v Young, No. 51984, 1987 WL 11187 (8th Dist Ct App, Cuyahoga, 5-7-87) (ordering suspect to "freeze" and place his hands on car roof reasonable where officer has reasonable suspicion to believe suspect was armed).

[124]State v Nelson, 72 App(3d) 506, 595 NE(2d) 475 (Cuyahoga 1991).

[125]Terry v Ohio, 392 US 1, 88 SCt 1868, 20 LEd(2d) 889 (1968) (White, J., concurring). See also Kolender v Lawson, 461 US 352, 103 SCt 1855, 75 LEd(2d) 903 (1983) (Brennan, J., concurring).

[126]Columbus v Michel, 55 App(2d) 46, 378 NE(2d) 1077 (Franklin 1978); State v McCrone, 63 App(3d) 831, 580 NE(2d) 468 (Lorain 1989), appeal dismissed by 48 OS(3d) 704, 549 NE(2d) 1190 (1990).

[127]Kolender v Lawson, 461 US 352, 103 SCt 1855, 75 LEd(2d) 903 (1983); Brown v Texas, 443 US 47, 99 SCt 2637, 61 LEd(2d) 357 (1979).

[128]State v Farmer, 21 App(3d) 77, 21 OBR 82, 486 NE(2d) 238 (Lucas 1984).

[129]State v Chatton, 11 OS(3d) 59, 11 OBR 250, 463 NE(2d) 1237 (1984), cert denied 469 US 856, 105 SCt 182, 83 LEd(2d) 116 (1984). But see State v Rose, 1993 WL 211565 (1993); Columbus v Holland, 76 App(3d) 196, 601 NE(2d) 190 (Franklin 1991) (where officer's visual inspection of defendant failed to indicate any suggestion of DUI, officer was not justified in asking for defendant's operator's license); State v Venham, 96 App(3d) 649, 645 NE(2d) 831 (Washington 1994) (detective

license plates. However, when the officer approached the vehicle, he observed a temporary tag in the rear windshield. The court held that the driver of the vehicle could not be detained further for a driver's license check on the original stop. Once the suspicion which gave rise to the stop evaporated, any additional intrusion or detention must be supported by specific articulable facts demonstrating the reasonableness of the continued detention.[130] *Chatton* was distinguished in (1) *State v Shepard*,[131] where, even though the officer after stopping a vehicle saw a temporary tag, the continued detention was upheld because of "behavior and in car activity," which the officer observed; (2) *State v Keathley*,[132] where the continued investigation of a driver who was stopped because of an obscured license validation sticker was upheld, even after the officer verified that the registration was in order, because of an ordinance prohibiting driving with obscured license plates; and (3) *Tallmadge v McCoy*,[133] where the arrest of the defendant was upheld even after the officer verified that the driver of the vehicle was not the owner who had a suspended license after the officer smelled alcohol and observed the defendant's red and watery eyes. Similarly, so long as the driver is genuinely free to leave, a computer check of the defendant's tags, license, or social security number after resolution of the issue behind the initial stop is not improper.[134] However, an officer may not, without additional cause, detain a person stopped for a traffic offense or equipment violation longer than necessary to issue a citation.[135]

The reasonableness of the intrusion undertaken will turn on the facts of each individual case. *Terry* requires the least minimal intrusion possible to investigate the suspicious circumstances. In evaluating the propriety of the intrusion, it is necessary to determine whether the level of the intrusion was reasonably related in scope to the circumstances faced by the police, including the gravity of the suspected crime.

Terry envisioned a brief stop, lasting only a few moments while police investigated suspicious circumstances. The required brevity of the stop has been called into question by the cases involving the interception of travellers at airports where the inquiry lasts more than a few moments. The

---

exceeded the scope of his authority when he demanded to see defendant's driver's license after first verifying that the suspect he thought was in the car, which provided justification for the stop, was not in the defendant's vehicle).

[130]State v Hart, 61 App(3d) 37, 572 NE(2d) 141 (Cuyahoga 1988), appeal dismissed by 42 OS(3d) 702, 536 NE(2d) 1172 (1989); see also Fairborn v Orrick, 49 App(3d) 94, 550 NE(2d) 488 (Greene 1988) (officer had authority to stop motorcycle to warn passenger not wearing required protective eye gear but could not detain the driver to check his driver's license).

[131]State v Shepard, Nos. 88-CA-14, 88-CA-16, 1989 WL 63336 (5th Dist Ct App, Guernsey, 5-15-89).

[132]State v Keathley, 55 App(3d) 130, 562 NE(2d) 932 (Miami 1988).

[133]Tallmadge v McCoy, 96 App(3d) 604, 645 NE(2d) 802 (Summit 1994); see also State v Waldroup, 100 App(3d) 508, 654 NE(2d) 390 (Preble 1995) (reasonable suspicion arose from officer's observations of defendant during lawful traffic stop to further detain defendant until drug sniffing dog arrived on the scene).

[134]State v Vance, 72 App(3d) 589, 595 NE(2d) 528 (Wayne 1991).

[135]State v Foster, 87 App(3d) 32, 621 NE(2d) 843 (Miami 1993).

Supreme Court addressed the issue in *United States v Sharpe*,[136] where the detention on a back road lasted for twenty minutes. In an opinion by Chief Justice Burger, the Court held that a twenty-minute detention based on reasonable and articulable suspicion of criminal activity is not unreasonable where the amount of time is reasonably needed to achieve the purpose of the stop, and where police diligently pursue a means of investigation that is likely to confirm or dispel their suspicion quickly. The reasonableness of the duration of the stop will be determined on a case-by-case basis, and a stop as long as twenty minutes will not necessarily be permissible under the circumstances. The duration of the stop will often be critical in determining whether it is an arrest that must be supported by probable cause.[137]

On the other hand, in a border detention case decided the same year as *Sharpe*, the Court upheld a sixteen-hour incommunicado detention, on reasonable suspicion, of a traveller suspected of smuggling contraband in her alimentary canal, even though the majority admitted the detention was long, uncomfortable, and humiliating.[138] The Court insisted that it had consistently rejected "hard-and-fast" time limits. It must be understood that the Court has also consistently applied different standards to border situations than it has to detentions in other contexts. A similarly intrusive stop in any other context should undoubtedly be called an arrest requiring not reasonable suspicion but probable cause.

Movement of the suspect from the spot where he is stopped will not necessarily turn a stop into an arrest. Whether movement has this effect may depend on where the suspect is taken. In *Florida v Royer*[139] the plurality described the investigation room at the airport in terms that would be applicable to an interrogation room at a police station. But in *United States v Mendenhall*,[140] the fact that the inquiry was moved from the airport concourse to the security room at the airport did not turn it into an arrest. Yet Justice Brennan has indicated that the suspect may not be moved or asked to move more than a short distance.[141] The detention of a suspect for ten minutes in the back of a police cruiser with the suspect directed to place his hands through an opening in the screen between the vehicle's front and back seats was deemed a reasonable detention while the police officer radioed in a warrant check.[142] However, transporting a suspect to a police station, placing him in an interrogation room, and not advising him that he was free to go has been labeled as treatment that must be supported by probable cause whether or not the detention is technically characterized as an arrest.[143]

[136]United States v Sharpe, 470 US 675, 105 SCt 1568, 84 LEd(2d) 605 (1985).
[137]See ALI, Model Code of Pre-Arraignment Procedure § 110.2 (1975).
[138]United States v Montoya de Hernandez, 473 US 531, 105 SCt 3304, 87 LEd(2d) 381 (1985).
[139]Florida v Royer, 460 US 491, 103 SCt 1319, 75 LEd(2d) 229 (1983).
[140]United States v Mendenhall, 446 US 544, 100 SCt 1870, 64 LEd(2d) 497 (1980).
[141]Kolender v Lawson, 461 US 352, 103 SCt 1855, 75 LEd(2d) 903 (1983).
[142]State v McFarland, 4 App(3d) 158, 4 OBR 252, 446 NE(2d) 1168 (Cuyahoga 1982).
[143]Dunaway v New York, 442 US 200, 99 SCt 2248, 60 LEd(2d) 824 (1979).

In the course of a *Terry*-stop, police may be able to fingerprint the suspect provided it is done at the scene. Transportation of the suspect to and detention at the station house without probable cause or judicial authorization even for the limited purpose and duration of fingerprinting is impermissible.[144] If fingerprinting at the scene is permissible during a *Terry*-stop on reasonable suspicion, then other identifying procedures, such as photographing, are also likely permissible. It is another indication of how intrusive *Terry*-stops have become. Fingerprinting that is to be conducted at the police station where there is only reasonable suspicion must be supported by a judicial order.[145]

14.06   Stopping an automobile

(A) In general

Vehicles may no more be randomly stopped without cause than pedestrians. Any time the driver of an automobile is ordered to stop, it is a seizure governed by Fourth Amendment standards. Compliance with an officer's command to stop a vehicle cannot be a consensual encounter.[146] The Supreme Court has stated clearly that the stopping of a vehicle always implicates the Fourth Amendment standards that govern safety checks, DUI checks, traffic arrests, *Terry*-stops, arrests, and searches.[147]

The *Terry* standards for investigative detentions are applicable to automobiles and their occupants. A police officer with reasonable suspicion of criminal activity, based on articulable facts, may stop a vehicle and detain its occupants briefly for purposes of limited questioning.[148] An officer's intuitive feeling that "something was wrong," even though ultimately confirmed, will not provide a sufficient basis for an investigatory stop of a vehicle.[149] Absent suspicious conduct, a police officer may not stop and question the occupants of a vehicle. The stopping of a vehicle constitutes a Fourth Amendment seizure and requires a balancing of the public's privacy interest against legitimate government interests to determine whether the seizure was reasonable.[150]

Initially, the government purpose must be isolated and then the procedure adopted must be weighed in terms of its effectiveness in achieving the government purpose, the degree of intrusion of that procedure on the individual subjected to it, and, finally, the degree of discretion vested in officials charged with implementing the procedure. There are legitimate

---

[144]Hayes v Florida, 470 US 811, 105 SCt 1643, 84 LEd(2d) 705 (1985), cert denied 479 US 831, 107 SCt 119, 93 LEd(2d) 65 (1986); Davis v Mississippi, 394 US 721, 89 SCt 1394, 22 LEd(2d) 676 (1969), cert denied 409 US 855, 93 SCt 191, 34 LEd(2d) 99 (1972).

[145]Cf. In re Order Requiring Fingerprinting of Juvenile, 42 OS(3d) 124, 537 NE(2d) 1286 (1989), cert denied 493 US 857, 110 SCt 165, 107 LEd(2d) 122 (1989).

[146]Michigan v Chesternut, 486 US 567, 108 SCt 1975, 100 LEd(2d) 565 (1988).

[147]Cf. Delaware v Prouse, 440 US 648, 99 SCt 1391, 59 LEd(2d) 660 (1979).

[148]United States v Brignoni-Ponce, 422 US 873, 95 SCt 2574, 45 LEd(2d) 607 (1975).

[149]Columbus v Holland, 76 App(3d) 196, 601 NE(2d) 190 (Franklin 1991).

[150]Delaware v Prouse, 440 US 648, 99 SCt 1391, 59 LEd(2d) 660 (1979).

government interests other than the investigation of apparent criminal conduct that justifies the stopping of an automobile.

In *State v Barrow*,[151] the court construed RC 4507.35, which requires the operator of a motor vehicle to display his license upon demand of a police officer. The *Barrow* court said:

> Although this statute has been cited to allow police to stop motorists on a systematic basis, at regular checkpoints or as part of a truly random selection for the purpose of enforcing motor vehicle laws, this asserted general inspection power may not be used as a pretext for investigating appellant's "suspicious" conduct, where, as here, officers admitted that the purpose for the stop was unrelated to the enforcement of the traffic code.[152]

(B) Stops for traffic offenses

One vital interest that justifies the stopping of a vehicle is enforcement of traffic regulations. Although traffic stops do not significantly curtail the freedom of action of the driver and occupants, they are seizures within the meaning of the Fourth Amendment even where the purpose of the stop is limited to the issuing of a citation and the resulting detention brief. Thus, the underlying traffic stop itself must be proper.[153]

A vehicle stopped for a nonarrestable traffic offense serves as the basis for a greater intrusion on Fourth Amendment interests than would be normally associated with a minor traffic infraction. In the interest of protecting the safety of the officers stopping the vehicle, the driver may be ordered out of his automobile while the citation is being prepared.[154] Requiring the motorist to exit his vehicle was described by the Supreme Court as *"de minimis"* and justified as reducing "the likelihood that the officer will be the victim of an assault."[155] Any further intrusion, however, such as a frisk for weapons, must be supported by articulable facts and circumstances giving rise to a reasonable fear for the officer's safety. If there is a legitimate reason for the officer to require the motorist to sit in the back of the police car, the Ohio Supreme Court has held that a frisk is permissible.[156] The resultant frisk based on a reasonable fear for safety may escalate into a custodial arrest based on a concealed weapon discovered

---

[151]State v Barrow, 60 App(2d) 335, 397 NE(2d) 422 (Hamilton 1978).

[152]State v Barrow, 60 App(2d) 335, 337, 397 NE(2d) 422 (Hamilton 1978).

[153]State v Guysinger, 86 App(3d) 592, 621 NE(2d) 726 (Ross 1993) (driving with one red tail light and one white tail light is not a violation and will not support a stop).

[154]Pennsylvania v Mimms, 434 US 106, 98 SCt 330, 54 LEd(2d) 331 (1977); State v Evans, 67 OS(3d) 405, 618 NE(2d) 162 (1993), cert denied ___ US ___, 114 SCt 1195, 127 LEd(2d) 544 (1994) (ordering a motorist out of the car following a stop for an equipment failure was permissible).

[155]Pennsylvania v Mimms, 434 US 106, 110, 98 SCt 330, 54 LEd(2d) 331 (1977).

[156]State v Evans, 67 OS(3d) 405, 618 NE(2d) 162 (1993), cert denied ___ US ___, 114 SCt 1195, 127 LEd(2d) 544 (1994) (frisk upheld where motorist stopped for equipment failure, did not produce a driver's license, and was required to sit in back of police car).

during the frisk, which may in turn lead to a search of the passenger compartment incident to the custodial arrest.[157]

Police officers may lawfully inspect the vehicle identification number (VIN) following a lawful stop for a traffic violation. The number carries no expectation of privacy, and the authority to check the number flows automatically from the lawful stop. It need not be justified under the automobile exception. If the VIN is visible from the outside of the vehicle, the officer may not enter the vehicle to obtain a dashboard-mounted VIN. If the VIN is not visible from the outside, the officer may open the vehicle door to search for the number, provided that search is no more intrusive than necessary to locate the VIN.[158]

Often during or at the conclusion of a traffic stop, a police officer requests the motorist's consent to search the car. Ordinarily, the legality of a subsequent search depends upon satisfaction of the general standards for voluntariness.[159]

(C) Search of an automobile incident to a non-custodial traffic arrest

Obviously, if a police officer lacks authority to conduct a search or frisk of a driver following a non-custodial traffic arrest, there is no authority to search any part of the vehicle. However, it is not uncommon for officers to request permission to search the car under these circumstances. A sheriff's deputy testified that he had requested motorists to consent to a search of their cars in 789 traffic stops in one year alone and boasted that every car he stops is searched.[160]

The Montgomery County Court of Appeals appraised such requests uniquely. In *Retherford*, the court held that even though the deputy had written a warning ticket, returned the defendant's license, and told the motorist she was free to go, the non-consensual encounter was not transformed "into a 'consensual' encounter in which an officer may 'ask' a citizen, without the slightest articulable suspicion, to relinquish her individual liberties to permit a search of her car and luggage."[161]

The court said that the deputy's freeing of the defendant was a pre-arranged ploy to attempt to end the seizure, but that it did not succeed in converting the seizure into a consensual encounter. The court reached that conclusion because a reasonable person would not feel free to leave, in

---

[157]See, e.g., State v Almalik, 41 App(3d) 101, 534 NE(2d) 898 (Cuyahoga 1987) (traffic stop in high crime area coupled with furtive gestures led to a *Terry* frisk and discovery of handgun which was partially visible when defendant ordered from car); State v Moncrief, 69 App(2d) 51, 431 NE(2d) 336 (Cuyahoga 1980) (traffic offense that led to ordering all occupants out of car at night in high crime area where officers were outnumbered led to frisk and discovery of weapon and subsequent search of interior compartment).

[158]New York v Class, 475 US 106, 106 SCt 960, 89 LEd(2d) 81 (1986).

[159]See Schneckloth v Bustamonte, 412 US 218, 93 SCt 2041, 36 LEd(2d) 854 (1973); Text 17.02, Voluntariness test.

[160]State v Retherford, No. 13987, at p. 9, 1994 WL 459921 (2d Dist Ct App, Montgomery, 3-16-94).

[161]State v Retherford, No. 13987, at 17, 1994 WL 459921 (2d Dist Ct App, Montgomery, 3-16-94).

spite of being told otherwise, when she is asked investigatory questions and faced with a request to search her vehicle for contraband following on the heels of being pulled over. Thus, the seizure never ended, and the officer converted the traffic stop into an expanded investigation based upon pure hunch. The officer's questions and request to search, the court went on to say, "were clearly not the stuff of casual conversation but were in the manner of an investigation"[162] to dispel his inarticulate suspicions. Such an expanded investigation, the court said, must be based at least upon reasonable, articulate suspicion. Under such circumstances, a police officer who has seized a motorist for a traffic offense may not request consent to search the vehicle, absent reasonable suspicion.

This is a significant decision which could affect police and sheriff's departments in many counties within the state. Judge Brogan's reasoning for the Montgomery panel is impeccable. It highlights the illogic of US Supreme Court decisions which categorize coercive street, bus, and airport approaches of travelers by police officers as consensual encounters, when any fair-minded person would conclude that the traveler, even the innocent one, will not feel free to walk away and ignore the officer's requests. *Retherford*, however, can be distinguished from these cases. Every stop of a vehicle is a seizure.[163] Consequently, there is no need to deal with claims that the initial encounter was consensual. Nonetheless, *Retherford* stands out because it demonstrates how all of the US Supreme Court decisions on the subject of consensual encounters are made of whole cloth.

Moreover, the US Supreme Court decision which set the standard for determining the voluntariness of consent searches involved a motorist who gave consent after a stop of his vehicle for equipment failure and was unable to produce a driver's license, and a police officer who made no effort to terminate the seizure prior to requesting permission to search the vehicle.[164] The Supreme Court never directly addressed the issue dealt with by the court in *Retherford*, but obviously this is not the last word on the subject; there will be further litigation on this matter within the state and possibly in the Supreme Court before the issue comes to rest. It would be advisable in any future decisions that proceed along the same lines for the court to make it clear that the result is not only derived from the Fourth Amendment but is also compelled by the Ohio Constitution; this is the only way to insulate this approach from US Supreme Court disapproval.[165]

(D) License, safety and registration checks

Another vital government interest is insuring that drivers are properly licensed and that vehicles are registered and fit for safe operation. Normally, these interests will balance favorably against the minimal intrusion of the public's privacy interest and will be upheld. But document checks and

---

[162]State v Retherford, No. 13987, at 20, 1994 WL 459921 (2d Dist Ct App, Montgomery, 3-16-94).

[163]Delaware v Prouse, 440 US 648, 99 SCt 1391, 59 LEd(2d) 660 (1979).

[164]See Schneckloth v Bustamonte, 412 US 218, 93 SCt 2041, 36 LEd(2d) 854 (1973) and Text 17.02, Voluntariness Test.

[165]See also Text 11.10, Search of an automobile incident to arrest; Ch 17, Consent Searches.

vehicle inspections on a random basis, an unconstrained exercise of police discretion, involve a greater invasion of privacy and violate the Fourth Amendment.[166] In *Delaware v Prouse*,[167] the Supreme Court recognized the need for license and safety checks but disapproved of the police procedure in that case because it involved a random checking of motorists on the whim of the police officers. The Court indicated that the questioning of all oncoming traffic at roadblock-type stops would be permissible. Similarly, the Court had left undisturbed checks that did not involve all vehicles, provided that the officers' discretion was limited and the police behavior did not appear to be a pretext for investigating suspicious behavior on grounds insufficient for a *Terry*-stop.[168] Presumably, the stopping in *United States v Prichard*[169] attracted no attention in the Supreme Court because the decision as to which vehicles were stopped was ostensibly based solely on a stated plan to insure the orderly flow of traffic and to prevent a safety hazard. Similarly, an Ohio court upheld a safety check that involved a calculated pattern of stopping a vehicle, conducting a check, and, after completing an inspection, flagging down the next car.[170]

The principle behind the safety check is that Fourth Amendment interests are adequately furthered provided that the inspection system restrains police discretion. Presumably, there is far less chance of pretextual inspections or harassment where every car or every tenth car is inspected. Absent a check point system that controls and limits police discretion, officers may not stop a vehicle for a safety check without cause.[171] Nevertheless, a reasonable suspicion of a vehicle's unsafe condition provides an adequate basis for a stop and inspection of a particular vehicle.[172]

During the course of a valid license and safety inspection, cause may develop for a further intrusion. Conversation between the driver and the police officer may give rise to reasonable suspicion of criminal activity, thereby validating a *Terry* type intrusion, which may result in ordering the suspect out of the vehicle and conducting a limited frisk for weapons. If this encounter provides probable cause for a custodial arrest, then *Robinson-Gustafson*[173] permits a full search of the person and *New York v Belton*[174] would allow a search of the interior compartment and all containers found in that compartment.

---

[166]See also Text 11.10, Search of an automobile incident to arrest; Ch 17, Consent Searches.

[167]Delaware v Prouse, 440 US 648, 99 SCt 1391, 59 LEd(2d) 660 (1979).

[168]United States v Prichard, 645 F(2d) 854 (10th Cir NM 1981), cert denied 454 US 832, 102 SCt 130, 70 LEd(2d) 110 (1981).

[169]United States v Prichard, 645 F(2d) 854 (10th Cir NM 1981), cert denied 454 US 832, 102 SCt 130, 70 LEd(2d) 110 (1981).

[170]State v Goines, 16 App(3d) 168, 16 OBR 178, 474 NE(2d) 1219 (Clark 1984).

[171]State v Howe, 65 App(3d) 540, 584 NE(2d) 1239 (Logan 1989).

[172]Cleveland v Paltani, No. 60255, 1991 WL 76103 (8th Dist Ct App, Cuyahoga, 5-9-91).

[173]United States v Robinson, 414 US 218, 94 SCt 467, 38 LEd(2d) 427 (1973); Gustafson v Florida, 414 US 260, 94 SCt 488, 38 LEd(2d) 456 (1973).

[174]New York v Belton, 453 US 454, 101 SCt 2860, 69 LEd(2d) 768 (1981).

(E) Highway sobriety checkpoint stops

The same reasoning that led to license and safety checks now permits roadblocks to check for drunk drivers.[175] Although safety concerns are paramount here as they are in safety checks, the immediate result of a violation is a criminal charge. Ordinarily a DUI checkpoint involves police stopping each vehicle in order to observe the driver. In some instances the officer merely shines a light on the driver to determine whether there are visible signs of intoxication or requests the motorist to roll down his window to ascertain whether there is an odor of alcohol or an indication of intoxication that can be ascertained from the driver's speech. There is even an instrument that is able to measure the air quality within a few inches of the driver to ascertain alcoholic content.

Additional sobriety tests may be administered only if particularized suspicion develops from the initial minimal encounter giving rise to a belief that the motorist is inebriated. Obviously, then, these minor intrusions may escalate into probable cause to arrest, and, in some instances, probable cause may develop into a belief that evidence of a crime is located within the automobile, leading to a warrantless search of the vehicle and containers located within the vehicle.[176]

The US Supreme Court used the balancing analysis to uphold DUI roadblocks. The Court said a highway checkpoint stop designed to detect and deter drunken driving does not violate the Fourth Amendment even in the absence of individualized suspicion if it involves an initial stop and brief detention of all motorists.[177] The Court concluded that the public interest in eradicating grave drunk driving problems outweighed the intrusion on the law-abiding motorist's privacy. The Court reached this conclusion even though the Michigan court had found that such roadblocks were not an efficient or effective means of controlling the problem. The choice among reasonable alternatives rests, according to the Court, with law enforcement officials, and not with a court.

The Court emphasized meticulous adherence to established standards. The Michigan sobriety checkpoint program that was upheld had guidelines governing checkpoint operations, site selection, and publicity. No discretion was left to the officers operating the checkpoint. Instead, every vehicle was stopped. The absence of discretion was deemed adequate protection even though these intrusions did violate every motorist's privacy. The scale of the problem, as viewed by the Court, was so great that the invasion of everyone's privacy should be countenanced, provided that no individual's privacy expectation was arbitrarily or discriminatorily violated.

---

[175]State v Alexander, 22 Misc(2d) 34, 22 OBR 342, 489 NE(2d) 1093 (Muni, Hamilton 1985); Michigan Dept of State Police v Stitz, 496 US 444, 110 SCt 2481, 110 LEd(2d) 412 (1990), affirmed by 443 Mich 744, 506 NW(2d) 209 (1993).

[176]Cf. State v Welch, 18 OS(3d) 88, 18 OBR 124, 480 NE(2d) 384 (1985), cert denied 474 US 1010, 106 SCt 537, 88 LEd(2d) 468 (1985).

[177]Michigan Dept of State Police v Stitz, 496 US 444, 110 SCt 2481, 110 LEd(2d) 412 (1990), affirmed by 443 Mich 744, 506 NW(2d) 209 (1993).

Naturally, even the creation of this authority is not the final question. An Indiana court has upheld a stop of a vehicle that made a lawful U-turn to avoid a DUI roadblock.[178] The court held that such evasive action in the face of a DUI roadblock provides reasonable suspicion that the motorist is drunk.

The same reasoning is likely to prevail when the Supreme Court considers the validity of roadblocks set up to check for drunk drivers, although different interests are involved. A DUI roadblock is designed to check for violation of a criminal offense, but the same safety concerns are likely to be viewed as overwhelming, justifying the limited intrusion. Naturally, however, for a police officer to engage in further inquiry of a particular motorist and to request that the motorist take a breathalyzer or other field sobriety tests, articulable facts and circumstances giving rise to reasonable suspicion that the motorist is inebriated must exist.

---

[178]Snyder v State, 538 NE(2d) 961 (Ind App 1989).

Chapter 15

Traffic Stops and Their Aftermath

15.01   Introduction

Special attention need be given to traffic stops for several reasons. First, stops for traffic violations are the area where most Americans come in contact with police. Second, police in Ohio, and probably across America, have been pushing the limits on automobile stops in an aggressive attempt to detect and control other offenses, most notably impaired driving and drug trafficking. Finally, controlling police conduct during such stops is the area of the law where Ohio has been the pioneer state struggling to create new standards to protect rights guaranteed under the Fourth Amendment and the Ohio Constitution while attempting to accommodate legitimate law enforcement needs.[1]

15.02   Stops of vehicles

Vehicles may no more be randomly forcibly stopped without cause than pedestrians. Any time the driver of an automobile is ordered to stop, it is a seizure governed by Fourth Amendment standards. Compliance with an officer's command to stop a vehicle cannot be a consensual encounter.[2] The Supreme Court has stated clearly that the stopping of a vehicle always implicates the Fourth Amendment standards that govern safety checks, DUI checks, traffic arrests, Terry-stops, arrests, and searches.[3] A consensual encounter may occur when a police officer walks over to talk with the occupants of a parked car. Whether or not that encounter is consensual depends upon whether the reasonable person under the circumstances would feel free to leave. Some courts have taken the position that a police officer who walks over to talk to the driver of a vehicle temporarily stopped at a traffic light or stop sign has not necessarily forcibly detained the occupant; rather, whether it is a forcible seizure or a consensual encounter depends upon the facts of the encounter: the number of officers, whether or not their weapons are drawn, and the words used and the tone of the officer's statements, all of which will determine whether the reasonable person would have felt free to refuse to cooperate and leave.[4]

---

[1]See also Text 11.05, Pretext arrests.

[2]Michigan v Chesternut, 486 US 567, 108 SCt 1975, 100 LEd(2d) 565 (1988).

[3]Cf. Delaware v Prouse, 440 US 648, 99 SCt 1391, 59 LEd(2d) 660 (1979).

[4]Cf. People v Ocasio, 85 NY(2d) 982, 629 NYS(2d) 161, 652 NE(2d) 907 (1995) (defendant's progress was halted by a stoplight, not the police; the officers approached on foot, displayed badges and asked for identification; no silence or

The Terry standards for investigative detentions are applicable to automobiles and their occupants. A police officer with reasonable suspicion of criminal activity, based on articulable facts, may stop a vehicle and detain its occupants briefly for purposes of limited questioning.[5] An officer's intuitive feeling that "something was wrong,' even though ultimately confirmed, will not provide a sufficient basis for an investigatory stop of a vehicle.[6] Absent suspicious conduct, a police officer may not stop and question the occupants of a vehicle.[7] The stopping of a vehicle constitutes a Fourth Amend-

---

lights were used to interfere with defendant's transit; no gun was displayed; and at no time was defendant prevented from departing).

[5]See State v Williams, 94 App(3d) 538, 641 NE(2d) 239 (Cuyahoga 1994), appeal dismissed by 70 OS(3d) 1446, 639 NE(2d) 114 (1994) (vehicle may be stopped for impeding the flow of traffic even though it lasts only fifteen seconds). Compare United States v Brignoni-Ponce, 422 US 873, 95 SCt 2574, 45 LEd(2d) 607 (1975); State v Ratcliff, 95 App(3d) 199, 642 NE(2d) 31 (Ashland 1994) (officer had reasonable suspicion that motor home was operated under the influence where officer observed the driver and a companion urinating along an interstate highway and then observed the motor home weave from the center line to the right side of the road three times during a thirty second interval); City of Toledo v Harris, 99 App(3d) 469, 651 NE(2d) 24 (Lucas 1995) (Terry stop of defendant's truck was lawful where the officer believed that weight of the truck and its load were illegal based upon bulging tires, a straining engine, and the fact that the defendant shifted gears several times while accelerating); with City of Maumee v Johnson, 90 App(3d) 169, 628 NE(2d) 115 (Lucas 1993) (police did not have reasonable suspicion to stop vehicle for speeding where they did not use a radar gun or pace clock to determine defendant's speed; the leaning of the vehicle during a turn could have resulted from the condition of the vehicle or the fact that four adults were in the car, and when police caught up to the defendant, the vehicle was not exceeding the speed limit); State v Rhude, 91 App(3d) 623, 632 NE(2d) 1391 (Warren 1993) (officer who did not observe any traffic violations, did not have reasonable suspicion to stop automobile merely because defendant pulled out of one driveway and into another a short distance down the road in an area where several burglaries were reported); State v Medlar, 93 App(3d) 483, 638 NE(2d) 1105 (Cuyahoga 1994) (officer did not have reasonable suspicion to justify stop of defendant's vehicle regarding a parking violation where officer did not issue a citation but waited for defendant to return to car and drive off before stopping car); City of Hamilton v Lawson, 94 App(3d) 462, 640 NE(2d) 1206 (1994) (officer's observation that defendant's vehicle crossed dotted white line once and later crossed an "'imaginary' center line" by one foot did not provide reasonable suspicion that defendant was driving under the influence); Village of New Lebanon v Blankenship, 65 Misc(2d) 1, 640 NE(2d) 271 (Montgomery 1993) (officer did not have reasonable suspicion to stop defendant's vehicle for "weaving within [its] own lane" where there was no center line, no other traffic, no danger or safety problem created by defendant's driving, no facts introduced to indicate how long defendant had been weaving, no testimony of other erratic driving, Revised Code does not prohibit weaving within one's own lane).

[6]Columbus v Holland, 76 App(3d) 196, 601 NE(2d) 190 (Franklin 1991).

[7]See State v Rhude, 91 App(3d) 623, 632 NE(2d) 1391 (Warren 1993) (officer who did not observe traffic violations, did not have reasonable suspicion to stop automobile merely because defendant pulled out of one driveway and into another a short distance down the road in an area where several burglaries had been reported); Maumee v Johnson, 90 App(3d) 169, 628 NE(2d) 115 (Lucas 1993) (police did not have reasonable suspicion to stop defendant's vehicle for speeding where (1) radar nor a pace clock was used to determine defendant's speed, (2) the leaning of the car during a turn could have been due to the condition of the vehicle or the fact that four adults were in the car, and (3) when police caught up to the car it was not speeding); State v Medlar, 93 App(3d) 483, 638 NE(2d) 1105 (Cuyahoga

ment seizure and requires a balancing of the public's privacy interest against legitimate government interests to determine whether the seizure was reasonable.[8]

Even where the stop is permissible, the scope and duration of an investigative stop of an automobile must be limited to effectuate the purpose for the initial stop.[9] Once that purpose is completed and the cause justifying the original stop evaporates, an officer has no authority to detain the motorist any further even to conduct as minimal an operation as a check of the motorist's driver's license.[10] Nor may the officer expand the scope of the inquiry to other offenses absent reasonable suspicion during a simple traffic stop.[11]

Initially, the government purpose must be isolated and then the procedure adopted must be weighed in terms of its effectiveness in achieving the government purpose, the degree of intrusion of that procedure on the individual subjected to it, and, finally, the degree of discretion vested in officials charged with implementing the procedure. There are legitimate government interests other than the investigation of apparent criminal conduct that justify the stopping of an automobile.

In *State v Barrow*,[12] the court construed RC 4507.35, which requires the operator of a motor vehicle to display his license upon demand of a police officer. The Barrow court said:

> Although this statute has been cited to allow police to stop motorists on a systematic basis, at regular check points or as part of a truly random selection for the purpose of enforcing motor vehicle laws, this asserted general inspection power may not be used as a pretext for investigating appellant's "suspicious' conduct, where, as here, officers admitted that the purpose for the stop was unrelated to the enforcement of the traffic code.[13]

1994) (officer did not have reasonable suspicion to stop vehicle regarding a parking violation where officer waited for defendant to return to illegally parked vehicle, permitted the defendant to drive away, and there were no facts indicating that defendant violated any traffic law once leaving the scene).

[8]Delaware v Prouse, 440 US 648, 99 SCt 1391, 59 LEd(2d) 660 (1979).

[9]State v Chatton, 11 OS(3d) 59, 11 OBR 250, 463 NE(2d) 1237 (1984), cert denied 469 US 856, 105 SCt 182, 83 LEd(2d) 116 (1984); see also State v Kelly, No. 94-CA-41, 1995 WL 225442 (2d Dist Ct App, Miami, 4-5-95) (after an initial valid stop for dim taillights, officer was not permitted to prolong detention in order to shine a flashlight into the car and observe contents of back seat).

[10]State v Venham, 96 App(3d) 649, 645 NE(2d) 831 (Washington 1994) (where police officer conducted an investigative stop of an automobile in which a suspect was thought to be, once the officer knew after the stop that the suspect was not in the vehicle the officer had no lawful authority to prolong detention, including check of motorist's driver's license, without reasonable suspicion of some other unlawful activity).

[11]State v Retherford, 93 App(3d) 586, 639 NE(2d) 498 (Montgomery 1994), appeal dismissed by 69 OS(3d) 1488, 635 NE(2d) 43 (1994).

[12]State v Barrow, 60 App(2d) 335, 397 NE(2d) 422 (Hamilton 1978).

[13]State v Barrow, 60 App(2d) 335, 397 NE(2d) 422 (Hamilton 1978).

15.03   General consent decals

In 1994, the Ohio General Assembly authorized creation of "voluntary motor vehicle decal registration programs."[14] Under such a program, the owner of a motor vehicle who elects to enroll is given a decal to affix to his windshield. The decal signifies that the owner of the vehicle has consented in advance to the stopping of his vehicle by any law enforcement officer when it is being driven on the streets between the hours of one a.m. and 5 a.m. A police officer who stops a car with such a decal would not need reasonable suspicion or other cause to legally stop the vehicle. Removal of the decal constitutes withdrawal of the consent. Presumably, an owner who would not expect his car to be lawfully on the highway during those hours might consent so that the car is stopped to determine whether the vehicle is being driven without proper authorization.

15.04   Traffic offenses

One vital interest that justifies the stopping of a vehicle is enforcement of traffic regulations. Traffic stops significantly curtail the freedom of action of the driver and occupants; they are seizures within the meaning of the Fourth Amendment even where the purpose of the stop is limited to the issuing of a citation and the resulting detention brief. Thus, the underlying traffic stop itself must be proper.[15]

Police officers may lawfully inspect the vehicle identification number (VIN) following a lawful stop for a traffic violation. The number carries no expectation of privacy, and the authority to check the number flows automatically from the lawful stop. It need not be justified under the automobile exception. If the VIN is visible from the outside of the vehicle, the officer may not enter the vehicle to obtain a dashboard-mounted VIN. If the VIN is not visible from the outside, the officer may open the vehicle door to search for the number, provided that search is no more intrusive than necessary to locate the VIN.[16]

A vehicle stopped for a nonarrestable traffic offense may serve as the basis for a greater intrusion on Fourth Amendment interests than would be normally associated with a minor traffic infraction. In the interest of protecting the safety of the officers stopping the vehicle, the driver may be ordered out of his automobile while the citation is being prepared.[17] Requiring the motorist to exit his vehicle was described by the Supreme Court as "de minimis' and justified as reducing "the likelihood that the officer will be the victim of an assault."[18] The authority to order the occu-

---

[14]See RC 311.31, 505.67 and 737.40.

[15]State v Guysinger, 86 App(3d) 592, 621 NE(2d) 726 (Ross 1993) (driving with one red tail light and one white tail light is not a violation and will not support a stop).

[16]New York v Class, 475 US 106, 106 SCt 960, 89 LEd(2d) 81 (1986).

[17]Pennsylvania v Mimms, 434 US 106, 98 SCt 330, 54 LEd(2d) 331 (1977); State v Evans, 67 OS(3d) 405, 618 NE(2d) 162 (1993) (ordering a motorist out of the car following a stop for an equipment failure was permissible).

[18]Pennsylvania v Mimms, 434 US 106, 110, 98 SCt 330, 54 LEd(2d) 331 (1977).

pants out of the vehicle is the limit, based solely upon the authority of the traffic offenses, of the permissible intrusion. Any further intrusion, such as a frisk for weapons, must be supported by articulable facts and circumstances giving rise to a reasonable fear for the officer's safety.[19] The authority to order a motorist out of the vehicle does not automatically give rise to authority to frisk the motorist or other occupants.[20]

However, if there is a legitimate reason for the officer to require the motorist to sit in the back of the police car, the Ohio Supreme Court has held that a frisk is permissible.[21] Following up on that decision, the Medina Court of Appeals has held that "in the context of a routine traffic stop, a police officer may ask a detained motorist to sit in the front seat of the patrol car ... if the motorist's detention in the front seat is employed merely as a brief procedure to facilitate the traffic stop."[22] This is an issue likely to be contested and litigated in other districts which have tried to restrict the scope of an intrusion incident to a routine traffic stop. The adoption of general rules makes is easier and likelier for routine traffic stops to escalate.

The resultant frisk based either on a reasonable request that the motorist sit in the police car or on a reasonable fear for safety may escalate into a custodial arrest based on a concealed weapon discovered during the frisk. The discovery of a concealed weapon which leads to a custodial arrest may in turn lead to a search of the passenger compartment incident to the custodial arrest.[23]

15.05   Expanding the inquiry of a traffic offense to other offenses

The United States Supreme Court has never shown any inclination to restrict the subject matter of police discussion with a person stopped for a traffic offense. Ohio courts have taken a completely different tack indicating that police may not question or investigate motorists stopped for a traffic violation about other offenses unless reasonable suspicion arises to warrant further investigation into unrelated matters.[24] However, not all

---

[19]State v Williams, 94 App(3d) 538, 641 NE(2d) 239 (Cuyahoga 1994), appeal dismissed by 70 OS(3d) 1446, 639 NE(2d) 114 (1994) (officer was justified in ordering defendant out of vehicle and conducting a limited search of weapons under the driver's seat given that defendant made "furtive gestures" when the officer approached).

[20]Cf. State v Evans, 67 OS(3d) 405, 618 NE(2d) 162 (1993); State v Potts, No. 93 CA 29, 1994 WL 693916 (4th Dist Ct App, Washington, 12-7-94).

[21]State v Evans, 67 OS(3d) 405, 618 NE(2d) 162 (1993) (frisk upheld where motorist stopped for equipment failure, did not produce a driver's license, and was required to sit in back of police car).

[22]State v Carlson, 102 App(3d) 585, 657 NE(2d) 591 (Medina 1995).

[23]See, e.g., State v Almalik, 41 App(3d) 101, 534 NE(2d) 898 (Cuyahoga 1987) (traffic stop in high crime area coupled with furtive gestures led to a Terry frisk and discovery of handgun which was partially visible when defendant ordered from car); State v Moncrief, 69 App(2d) 51, 431 NE(2d) 336 (Cuyahoga 1980) (traffic offense that led to ordering all occupants out of car at night in high crime area where officers were outnumbered led to frisk and discovery of weapon and subsequent search of interior compartment).

[24]State v Anderson, 100 App(3d) 688, 654 NE(2d) 1034 (Ross 1995).

have taken this position. In *State v Carlson*,[25] the Ninth District Court of Appeals held that "if a vehicle is lawfully detained, an officer does not need a reasonable suspicion of drug-related activity in order to request that a drug-dog be brought to the scene."

Ohio law specifies that the duration of an initial stop may not last longer than is necessary to resolve the issue which led to the original stop.[26] The lawfulness of an initial stop does not justify a "fishing expedition" for evidence of other crimes.[27] Therefore, it has been held that in the absence of articulable facts giving rise to reasonable suspicion, an officer may not ask a motorist, incident to issuing a citation or warning, if he has any drugs, weapons or drug paraphernalia in the car.[28]

However, not uncommonly, in the course of a lawful traffic stop, reasonable suspicion may develop that other criminal activity is afoot. If reasonable suspicion does develop during the course of a legitimate traffic stop, the officer has authority to detain the motorist for a reasonable time beyond the time necessary to process and issue the traffic violation in order to confirm or dispel that suspicion.[29] An extended detention of fourteen minutes while a drug canine was summoned was upheld in *State v Waldroup*.[30] The key, of course, rests upon the legitimacy of the claim of reasonable suspicion justifying detention beyond that which it takes to issue a traffic citation.

The entire issue of the scope of the line of inquiry and the nature of an investigation at the time of a traffic arrest is becoming a contentious and much litigated issue in Ohio and throughout the United States.[31] Often during or at the conclusion of a traffic stop, a police officer requests the motorist's consent to search the car. Ordinarily, the legality of a subsequent search depends upon satisfaction of the general standards for voluntariness.[32] That is no longer the sole inquiry for determining the legality of such searches in Ohio.[33]

15.06   Search of an automobile incident to a non-custodial traffic arrest

Obviously, if a police officer lacks authority to conduct a search or frisk of a driver following a non-custodial traffic arrest, there is no authority to

---

[25]State v Carlson, 102 App(3d) 585, 657 NE(2d) 591 (Medina 1995).

[26]State v Chatton, 11 OS(3d) 59, 11 OBR 250, 463 NE(2d) 1237 (1984), cert denied 469 US 856, 105 SCt 182, 83 LEd(2d) 116 (1984).

[27]State v Bevan, 80 App(3d) 126, 608 NE(2d) 1099 (Lake 1992).

[28]State v Anderson, 100 App(3d) 688, 654 NE(2d) 1034 (Ross 1995).

[29]State v Johnson, No. 13-95-30, 1995 WL 577818 (3d Dist Ct App, Seneca, 9-29-95) (reasonable suspicion justified detention of motorist and companion even though officer's initial justification for the stop—that the motorist's license had expired—proved untrue).

[30]State v Waldroup, 100 App(3d) 508, 654 NE(2d) 390 (Preble 1995).

[31]Cf. State v Carlson, 102 App(3d) 585, 657 NE(2d) 591 (Medina 1995).

[32]See Schneckloth v Bustamonte, 412 US 218, 93 SCt 2041, 36 LEd(2d) 854 (1973); see Text 17.02, Voluntariness test.

[33]See State v Robinette, 73 OS(3d) 650, 653 NE(2d) 695 (1995).

search any part of the vehicle.[34] However, it is increasingly common for officers to request permission to search a car incident to a stop for a traffic offense. Often the very traffic stop is part of an aggressive effort to stop as many traffic offenders as possible in order to inquire about drunk driving or drug trafficking. A sheriff's deputy testified that he had requested motorists to consent to a search of their cars in 789 traffic stops in one year alone and boasted that every car he stops is searched.[35]

The Ohio Supreme Court has adopted a bright-line rule requiring a police officer to make clear that the traffic offense has ended and the motorist is free to leave before any subsequent permission to search may be deemed voluntary.[36] Although the court has adopted a bright-line rule, it is worthwhile to see how this issue developed in Ohio because the standards are still evolving. Initially, the Montgomery County Court of Appeals appraised such requests uniquely. In State v. Retherford, the court held that even though the deputy had written a warning ticket, returned the defendant's license, and told the motorist she was free to go, the non-consensual encounter was not transformed "into a 'consensual' encounter in which an officer may 'ask' a citizen, without the slightest articulable suspicion, to relinquish her individual liberties to permit a search of her car and luggage."[37]

The court said that the deputy's freeing of the defendant was a prearranged ploy to attempt to end the seizure, but that it did not succeed in converting the seizure into a consensual encounter. The court reached that conclusion because a reasonable person would not feel free to leave, in spite of being told otherwise, when she is asked investigatory questions and faced with a request to search her vehicle for contraband following on the heels of being pulled over. Thus, the seizure never ended, and the officer converted the traffic stop into an expanded investigation based upon pure hunch. The officer's questions and request to search, the court went on to say, "were clearly not the stuff of casual conversation but were in the

---

[34]A Terry limited search for weapons may be conducted of the area from which a motorist may obtain a weapon provided that there is a reasonable and articulable basis for a belief that the motorist or a passenger may be armed and dangerous. See State v Smith, 56 OS(2d) 405, 384 NE(2d) 280 (1978); Michigan v Long, 463 US 1032, 103 SCt 3469, 77 LEd(2d) 1201 (1983).

[35]State v Retherford, 93 App(3d) 586, 639 NE(2d) 498 (Montgomery 1994), appeal dismissed by 69 OS(3d) 1488, 635 NE(2d) 43 (1994). The issue of pretext arrests should be considered, as well; see Text 11.05, Pretext arrests.

[36]See State v Robinette, 73 OS(3d) 650, 653 NE(2d) 695 (1995).

[37]State v Retherford, 93 App(3d) 586, 639 NE(2d) 498 (Montgomery 1994), appeal dismissed by 69 OS(3d) 1488, 635 NE(2d) 43 (1994); see also State v Anderson, 100 App(3d) 688, 654 NE(2d) 1034 (Ross 1995) (a mere submission to an officer's request to search a car is not voluntary where (1) the motorist was pulled over and issued a warning ticket for excessive tint; (2) there are two officers, each in a separate car; (3) the officers approached the car, one on each side, accompanied by a dog trained in drug detection; (4) the motorist did not feel free to leave after receiving the ticket; and (5) there was no reasonable suspicion to warrant further investigation). But see United States v Roberson, 6 F(3d) 1088 (5th Cir 1993), cert denied 114 SCt 1322, 127 LEd(2d) 671 (1994).

manner of an investigation"[38] to dispel his inarticulate suspicions. Essentially the court concluded that even telling the motorist following issuance of the ticket cannot transform the stop into a consensual encounter devoid of coercion. Therefore an expanded investigation, the court said, must be based at least upon reasonable, articulate suspicion. Under such circumstances, a police officer who has seized a motorist for a traffic offense may not request consent to search the vehicle, absent reasonable suspicion which would justify such an expanded inquiry.

Retherford is a significant decision which has been followed by several other Ohio Courts of Appeals.[39] Judge Brogan's reasoning for the Second District panel is impeccable. It highlights the illogic of US Supreme Court decisions which categorize coercive street, bus, and airport approaches of travelers by police officers as consensual encounters, when most travelers would not feel free to walk away and ignore the officer's requests. Retherford, however, can be distinguished from these cases. Every stop of a vehicle is a seizure.[40] Consequently, there is no need to deal with claims that the initial encounter was consensual.

The Ohio Supreme Court did not pursue the matter to the same extent as the Second District did in *Retherford*. In *State v Robinette*,[41] the Supreme Court adopted a bright-line rule requiring that "citizens stopped for traffic offenses be clearly informed by the detaining officer when they are free to go after a valid detention, before an officer attempts to engage in a consensual interrogation" or, certainly, attempts secure the motorist's permission to search the car. The court said that any attempt "at consensual interrogation must be preceded by the phrase 'At this time you legally are free to go' or by words of similar import."[42] While the court, obviously, did not share the Second District's belief that it was necessary to superimpose a reasonable suspicion standard as a prerequisite to subsequent questioning, the two courts did share the same abhorrence of the use of such stops for further intrusions under the guise of consent. Although *Robinette* was decided 4 - 3, it is clear that the Ohio Supreme Court majority intends to separate the initial traffic stop from subsequent inquiries, and if it becomes clear that the means the court selected to accomplish that end is not adequate the stricter standard devised in *Retherford* remains an option.

The fact differences in *Retherford* and *Robinette* are significant. In the former case, the sheriff's deputy made a fleeting gesture at telling the motorist she was free to leave but, before allowing the motorist to exercise the option, asked to search the car. In *Robinette* there was not even a fleeting gesture. The Supreme Court's choice of rules should not be misin-

---

[38]State v Retherford, 93 App(3d) 586, 600, 639 NE(2d) 498 (Montgomery 1994), appeal dismissed by 69 OS(3d) 1488, 635 NE(2d) 43 (1994).

[39]See e.g. State v Anderson, 100 App(3d) 688, 654 NE(2d) 1034 (Ross 1995); State v Smotherman, No. 93WD082, 1994 WL 395128 (6th Dist Ct App, Wood, 7-29-94); State v Beaton, No. CA94-03-036, 1994 WL 650048 (12th Dist Ct App, Warren, 11-21-94); State v Robinette, 73 OS(3d) 650, 653 NE(2d) 695 (1995).

[40]Delaware v Prouse, 440 US 648, 99 SCt 1391, 59 LEd(2d) 660 (1979).

[41]State v Robinette, 73 OS(3d) 650, 653 NE(2d) 695 (1995).

[42]State v Robinette, 73 OS(3d) 650, at 655, 653 NE(2d) 695 (1995).

terpreted as an endorsement of the deputy's methods because in *Robinette* the court said quite clearly that the motorist must be made to understand "that he is free to go or that he may answer the question at his option."[43]

Robinette goes far beyond what is required by the United States Supreme Court. That Court's decision which set the standard for determining the voluntariness of consent searches involved a motorist who gave consent after a stop of his vehicle for equipment failure and who was unable to produce a driver's license. The officer made no effort to terminate the seizure prior to requesting permission to search the vehicle.[44] The Supreme Court endorsed the general test for voluntariness in that context and has not since had occasion to revisit the precise same question. Obviously this is not the last word on the subject; there will have to be further litigation on this matter within Ohio and possibly in the United States Supreme Court before the issue comes to rest. It may well be that this line of authority will be developed under the Ohio Constitution to insulate it from the US Supreme Court's different approach.[45]

15.07   License, safety and registration checks

Another vital government interest is insuring that drivers are properly licensed and that vehicles are registered and fit for safe operation. Normally, these interests will balance favorably against the minimal intrusion of the public's privacy interest and will be upheld. But document checks and vehicle inspections, can be an unconstrained exercise of police discretion if not restrained by standards or if not purely random, and then involve a great invasion of privacy and violate the Fourth Amendment.[46]

In *Delaware v Prouse*,[47] the Supreme Court recognized the need for license and safety checks but disapproved of the police procedure in that case because it involved a random checking of motorists on the whim of the police officers. The Court indicated that the questioning of all oncoming traffic at roadblock-type stops would be permissible. Similarly, the Court had left undisturbed checks that did not involve all vehicles, provided that the officers' discretion was limited and the police behavior did not appear to be a pretext for investigating suspicious behavior on grounds insufficient for a Terry-stop.[48] Presumably, the stopping in *United States v Prichard*[49] attracted no attention in the Supreme Court because the decision as to which vehicles were stopped was ostensibly based solely on a stated plan to

---

[43]State v Robinette, 73 OS(3d) 650, at 655, 653 NE(2d) 695 (1995).

[44]See Schneckloth v Bustamonte, 412 US 218, 93 SCt 2041, 36 LEd(2d) 854 (1973) and Text 17.02, Voluntariness test.

[45]See also Text 11.10, Search of an automobile incident to arrest; Ch 17, Consent Searches.

[46]See also Text 11.10, Search of an automobile incident to arrest; Ch 17, Consent Searches.

[47]Delaware v Prouse, 440 US 648, 99 SCt 1391, 59 LEd(2d) 660 (1979).

[48]United States v Prichard, 645 F(2d) 854 (10th Cir NM 1981), cert denied 454 US 832, 102 SCt 130, 70 LEd(2d) 110 (1981).

[49]United States v Prichard, 645 F(2d) 854 (10th Cir NM 1981), cert denied 454 US 832, 102 SCt 130, 70 LEd(2d) 110 (1981).

insure the orderly flow of traffic and to prevent a safety hazard. Similarly, an Ohio court upheld a safety check that involved a calculated pattern of stopping a vehicle, conducting a check, and, after completing an inspection, flagging down the next car.[50]

The principle behind the safety check is that Fourth Amendment interests are adequately protected provided that the inspection system restrains police discretion. Presumably, there is far less chance of pretextual inspections or harassment where every car or every tenth car is inspected. Absent a check point system that controls and limits police discretion, officers may not stop a vehicle for a safety check without cause.[51] Nevertheless, a reasonable suspicion of a vehicle's unsafe condition provides an adequate basis for a stop and inspection of a particular vehicle.[52]

During the course of a valid license and safety inspection, cause may develop for a further intrusion. Conversation between the driver and the police officer may give rise to reasonable suspicion of criminal activity, thereby validating a Terry type intrusion, which may result in ordering the suspect out of the vehicle and conducting a limited frisk for weapons. If this encounter provides probable cause for a custodial arrest, then Robinson-Gustafson[53] permits a full search of the person and *New York v Belton*[54] would allow a search of the interior compartment and all containers found in that compartment.

15.08   Highway sobriety checkpoint stops

The same reasoning that led to license and safety checks now permits roadblocks to check for drunk drivers.[55] Although safety concerns are paramount here as they are in safety checks, the immediate result of a violation is a criminal charge. Ordinarily a DUI checkpoint involves police stopping each vehicle in order to observe the driver. In some instances the officer merely shines a light on the driver to determine whether there are visible signs of intoxication or requests the motorist to roll down his window to ascertain whether there is an odor of alcohol or an indication of intoxication that can be ascertained from the driver's speech. There is even an instrument that is able to measure the air quality within a few inches of the driver to ascertain alcoholic content.[56]

However, once a motorist is diverted from the regular flow of traffic past the checkpoint, the routine standardized stop of all vehicles becomes an investigative stop of a single vehicle for which particularized suspicion is

---

[50]State v Goines, 16 App(3d) 168, 16 OBR 178, 474 NE(2d) 1219 (Clark 1984).

[51]State v Howe, 65 App(3d) 540, 584 NE(2d) 1239 Logan, 1989).

[52]Cleveland v Paltani, No. 60255, 1991 WL 76103 (8th Dist Ct App, Cuyahoga, 5-9-91).

[53]United States v Robinson, 414 US 218, 94 SCt 467, 38 LEd(2d) 427 (1973); Gustafson v Florida, 414 US 260, 94 SCt 488, 38 LEd(2d) 456 (1973).

[54]New York v Belton, 453 US 454, 101 SCt 2860, 69 LEd(2d) 768 (1981).

[55]State v Alexander, 22 Misc(2d) 34, 22 OBR 342, 489 NE(2d) 1093 (Muni, Hamilton 1985); Michigan Dept of State Police v Stitz, 496 US 444, 110 SCt 2481, 110 LEd(2d) 412 (1990), affirmed by 443 Mich 744, 506 NW(2d) 209 (1993).

[56]See State v Bauer, 99 App(3d) 505, 651 NE(2d) 46 (Franklin 1994).

required.[57] Thus additional sobriety tests may be administered only if reasonable suspicion to believe that the motorist is impaired develops from the initial minimal encounter. Obviously, then, these minor intrusions may escalate into probable cause to arrest, and, in some instances, probable cause may develop into a belief that evidence of a crime is located within the automobile, leading to a warrantless search of the vehicle and containers located within the vehicle.[58]

The US Supreme Court used the balancing analysis to uphold DUI roadblocks. The Court said a highway checkpoint stop designed to detect and deter drunken driving does not violate the Fourth Amendment even in the absence of individualized suspicion if it involves an initial stop and brief detention of all motorists.[59] The Court concluded that the public interest in eradicating grave drunk driving problems outweighed the intrusion on the law-abiding motorist's privacy. The Court reached this conclusion even though the Michigan court had found that such roadblocks were not an efficient or effective means of controlling the problem. The choice among reasonable alternatives rests, according to the Court, with law enforcement officials, and not with a court.

The Court emphasized meticulous adherence to established standards. The Michigan sobriety checkpoint program that was upheld had guidelines governing checkpoint operations, site selection, and publicity. No discretion was left to the officers operating the checkpoint. Instead, every vehicle was stopped. The absence of discretion was deemed adequate protection even though these intrusions did violate every motorist's privacy.[60] The scale of the problem, as viewed by the Court, was so great that the invasion of everyone's privacy should be countenanced, provided that no individual's privacy expectation was arbitrarily or discriminatorily violated.

Two Ohio Courts of Appeals have reviewed the constitutionality of the methodology involved in local sobriety checkpoints. In *State v Bauer*,[61] a Franklin county appellate panel upheld the validity of a sobriety checkpoint

---

[57]State v Blackburn, No. 3084, 1994 WL 95224 (2d Dist Ct App, Clark, 3-23-94).

[58]Cf. State v Welch, 18 OS(3d) 88, 18 OBR 124, 480 NE(2d) 384 (1985), cert denied 474 US 1010, 106 SCt 537, 88 LEd(2d) 468 (1985); see also State v Blackburn, No. 3084, 1994 WL 95224 (2d Dist Ct App, Clark, 3-23-94):

> With respect to sobriety checkpoints, it would appear that there are three phases of detention, each requiring somewhat different analysis under the search and seizure provisions of the United States and Ohio constitutions. The first is the initial detection at the checkpoint itself. The second is a continuing investigative stop, resulting in a somewhat longer delay, that may result if the driver, as a result of the initial detention, is reasonably suspected of being under the influence of alcohol. Finally, the third phase is an actual arrest for being under the influence, which would require probable cause.

[59]Michigan Dept of State Police v Stitz, 496 US 444, 110 SCt 2481, 110 LEd(2d) 412 (1990), affirmed by 443 Mich 744, 506 NW(2d) 209 (1993).

[60]See also State v Bauer, 99 App(3d) 505, 651 NE(2d) 46 (Franklin 1994) (the supervising officer did not exercise unbridled discretion even though he personally participated in the stopping of vehicles where they were stopped according to neutral and objective guidelines previously established).

[61]State v Bauer, 99 App(3d) 505, 651 NE(2d) 46 (Franklin, 1994).

which lasted from forty-five seconds to three minutes, and which involved employment of a portable breath analyzer and a horizontal gaze tester to supplement the officer's personal observations of potential intoxication. Additionally, motorists were asked for their driver's license. The court upheld the validity of the methods used even though more extensive than those upheld as constitutional in *Sitz* and even though the duration of the stop was somewhat longer than the twenty-five second average in *Sitz*.

A Ross county appellate panel reached a different conclusion, invalidating a sobriety checkpoint stop under the Ohio Constitution in *State v Blackburn* where the checkpoint stop lasted between two and five minutes, where every driver was required to produce a driver's license and vehicle registration, and where some licenses were subject to computer checks.[62]

Naturally, even the creation of the authority in *Sitz* is not the final question. Methodology, time and intrusiveness of the stop will continue to be litigated. Whether a motorist must be given an opportunity to avoid the checkpoint is, perhaps, the most pressing question. An Indiana court has upheld a stop of a vehicle that made a lawful U-turn to avoid a DUI roadblock.[63] The court held that such evasive action in the face of a DUI roadblock provides reasonable suspicion that the motorist is drunk.

---

[62]State v Blackburn, No. 3084, 1994 WL 95224 (2d Dist Ct App, Clark, 3-23-94).
[63]Snyder v State, 538 NE(2d) 961 (Ind App 1989).

Chapter 16

Administrative Searches

16.01   Introduction

The term administrative search is a broad, general, meaningless term. Originally, it was used to signify a search that was not a conventional search for evidence of a crime and did not implicate the same Fourth Amendment interests implicated in a search by a police officer. The theory on which that distinction rested has been long discredited: the Fourth Amendment protects against all government intrusions, not just those by police officers. Accordingly, an administrative search is an intrusion on basic privacy interests and does implicate Fourth Amendment standards and values.

The term has been applied to regulatory searches prompted by societal needs separate and different from searches for criminal evidence. An example of a traditional regulatory search is a housing inspection. These inspections are carried out under state or municipal codes, generally not pinpointing a specific house but covering neighborhoods at regular intervals. The primary purpose of the inspection is not to gather evidence of violations of the codes but rather to ensure compliance with health and safety standards. However, an inspector who finds conditions not in compliance with the code initiates a court proceeding based on the violations of the particular code and testifies on what he saw. Moreover, inspections in many communities are no longer merely broad general inspections of a neighborhood but may be focused on a particular house or, certainly under other codes, a particular business. Violation of the regulations may result in criminal prosecution.

The methodology that governs administrative searches has been expanded and applied to a whole new set of searches that are called "special circumstances searches." That term has been applied to cover searches of school children by school teachers and administrators, where the euphemism of an inspection has been dropped and where the search is for evidence of a crime or violation of a school regulation.[1] The concept has also been applied to the search of a government employee's work space and possessions for evidence of a work-related violation that likely also involves evidence of a crime.[2] The same concept frequently is being used to sanction employee alcohol and drug testing,[3] sometimes without any individual sus-

---

[1]New Jersey v T.L.O., 469 US 325, 105 SCt 733, 83 LEd(2d) 720 (1985).

[2]O'Connor v Ortega, 480 US 709, 107 SCt 1492, 94 LEd(2d) 714 (1987).

[3]Skinner v Railway Labor Executives' Assn, 489 US 602, 109 SCt 1402, 103 LEd(2d) 639 (1989).

picion,[4] and the airport screening of passengers and their possessions for weapons and explosives. Society has become accustomed to these types of intrusions, accepting limitations on privacy in the name of the greater good. The limit of the "special circumstances search" has not been reached. These issues will be the major policy debates of the future and will involve among other things the general population's willingness to submit to universal drug tests and AIDS testing.

16.02   Administrative search

Administrative searches have traditionally involved government inspection of a private or commercial building for the purpose of ensuring compliance with existing health or safety codes. Because the inspection or search involves an intrusion into privacy interests, Fourth Amendment standards are implicated, however limited the intrusion. But the unique character and purpose of the administrative search, as distinct from the traditional search for evidence of criminal activity, has caused the court to restructure Fourth Amendment analysis. The result has been an emphasis on the reasonableness of the government activity, determined first by balancing the government interest against the extent of the intrusion on the privacy interest, and second by testing the relationship of the inspection system to the purpose of the regulatory scheme.

Administrative searches have expanded to encompass compliance with regulations that have less to do with health or safety and more to do with controlling industries that have a propensity toward unlawful activity. This expansion has introduced new issues to administrative search analysis. Initially, the focus was on the development of a workable standard of reasonableness, both in the immediate facts attending the search as well as in the issuance of the administrative warrant. This focus has given way to the creation of a broad exception to the warrant requirement for so-called pervasively regulated industries, where the courts are more concerned with defining the limits of the search. The result has been twofold: the blurring of the distinction between an administrative search and the conventional criminal search, and the circumvention of the traditional probable cause standard in circumstances where it might otherwise readily apply.

16.03   Determining reasonableness of administrative searches

The Fourth Amendment warrant requirement was imposed on state administrative searches in *Camara v Municipal Court*,[5] where the US Supreme Court held that a warrant must be secured prior to an administrative search, when permission to conduct that search has been refused. The case involved various sections of the San Francisco Housing Code that

---

[4]National Treasury Employees Union v Von Raab, 489 US 656, 109 SCt 1384, 103 LEd(2d) 685 (1989), affirmed sub nom National Treasury Employees Union v Bush, 891 F(2d) 99 (1989).

[5]Camara v Municipal Court of San Francisco, 387 US 523, 87 SCt 1727, 18 LEd(2d) 930 (1967).

authorized warrantless entry by housing officials to conduct periodic inspections. The code also contained provisions penalizing those individuals who violated or impeded the execution of the ordinance. Refusal to admit inspectors was a violation of the municipal ordinance. The defendant was charged with violating the code when he refused to allow a routine inspection by a housing official. The Supreme Court held that a conviction based on such a refusal violated the defendant's Fourth Amendment right against unreasonable search and seizure.

Noting the unique character and purpose of administrative searches, the Supreme Court in *Camara* sought to accommodate the competing public and private interests. The Court did so by formulating a new Fourth Amendment analysis which emphasizes the reasonableness standard as the dispositive factor, a standard that is applied in the abstract without reference to the Amendment's warrant clause. The Court held that the reasonableness of an administrative search is determined by balancing the governmental interest against the nature and extent of the intrusion on the privacy interest. In *Camara*, the Court found a compelling government interest in avoiding dangerous living conditions and maintaining housing stock. Then it weighed the relationship of the regulatory scheme to the stated purposes. The Court concluded that the inspection programs are a reasonable means for enforcing these important societal interests because (1) they are effective in ensuring compliance with minimum health and safety standards; (2) the inspection is limited and noncriminal; and (3) the public has long accepted a similar regulatory scheme.

This reasonableness analysis was substituted for the traditional probable cause analysis in determining the legality of the intrusion. The Supreme Court argued that probable cause "must exist" if reasonable legislative or administrative standards are satisfied. The standards governing the search in *Camara* called for periodic inspection based on the conditions of the general area and the building as well as the passage of time since the last search. Thus, the regulatory statute must specify (1) the purposes justifying the inspection scheme, and (2) the standards for periodic inspections as a means of controlling the discretion of the government agency enforcing the statute.

16.04   Warrant requirement

The Court's extensive reasonableness analysis in *Camara v Municipal Court*[6] for determining the validity of administrative searches conflicts, to some extent, and certainly is much broader than the Supreme Court's narrow holding in the case. The Court was not required to pass on the constitutionality of the inspection scheme in *Camara* because the search had not been conducted; the defendant's refusal resulted in his criminal prosecution. The Court merely held that it is a violation of Fourth Amendment rights to convict an individual who refuses to allow a warrantless administrative inspection. The defendant in *Camara* had refused the inspec-

---

[6]Camara v Municipal Court of San Francisco, 387 US 523, 87 SCt 1727, 18 LEd(2d) 930 (1967).

tor admittance, instead requesting that the inspector obtain a warrant. The Court indicated that warrants for administrative searches, accorded solely on a showing that the regulatory scheme existed and that the inspection followed the natural order of the scheme, would be granted almost automatically. Nonetheless, the Court held that these warrants would serve a valid purpose to indicate to the holder of the premises that (1) the inspection was required by statute or ordinance; (2) the inspector was duly authorized to enter and conduct the inspection; and (3) the inspector's authority was limited.[7] Further, the Court indicated that most people would allow the inspector admittance and that the warrant was not a prerequisite but only necessary as an enforcement tool when admittance is refused.

The administrative warrant requirement is applicable to business establishments.[8] It has been held applicable to an inspection of an apartment house where the building inspector, pursuant to statute, entered and inspected only the common areas on the premises. In *Cincinnati v Morris Investment Co*[9] the Hamilton Municipal Court held, "Whether there are or are not common areas on the premises is really of no great importance for the simple reason that these areas are common only to tenants or their guests, not the public at large."

The warrant requirement is not applicable to that part of a business establishment that is open to the general public. A government inspector is free to enter without a warrant as is any other member of the public.[10] An inspector does not need a warrant to enter the public area of a tavern to check compliance with occupancy limitations.[11]

When a request is for an administrative warrant to inspect a particular structure, such as after a fire when investigators seek the cause of the fire, the existence of the condition will be sufficient to justify issuance of the administrative search warrant. Such warrant, however, does not provide carte blanche to conduct an ongoing, intensive search. In the case of a fire, for example, once arson has been established as the cause of the fire, the authorities must discontinue the search and seek a traditional warrant supported by probable cause to continue the search for evidence of the crime.[12]

Just as with traditional search warrants, the pressure has been on the courts to sanction warrantless administrative searches. The thrust for warrantless inspection systems has focused on regulated businesses. The Supreme Court in *See v Seattle*[13] stated that challenges to such programs

---

[7]Camara v Municipal Court of San Francisco, 387 US 523, 87 SCt 1727, 18 LEd(2d) 930 (1967).

[8]See v Seattle, 387 US 541, 87 SCt 1737, 18 LEd(2d) 943 (1967); State v Penn, 61 OS(3d) 720, 576 NE(2d) 790 (1991).

[9]Cincinnati v Morris Investment Co, Inc, 6 Misc(2d) 1, 3, 6 OBR 80, 451 NE(2d) 259 (Muni, Hamilton 1982).

[10]State v Moody, 30 App(3d) 44, 30 OBR 99, 506 NE(2d) 256 (Hamilton 1985) (routine liquor inspection).

[11]Willoughby Hills v CC Bars, Inc, 18 Misc(2d) 8, 18 OBR 409, 481 NE(2d) 1389 (Muni, Willoughby 1984).

[12]Michigan v Clifford, 464 US 287, 104 SCt 641, 78 LEd(2d) 477 (1984).

[13]See v Seattle, 387 US 541, 87 SCt 1737, 18 LEd(2d) 943 (1967).

could only be resolved on a case-by-case basis under the Fourth Amendment standard of reasonableness.

In *United States v Biswell*,[14] the Court upheld a warrantless administrative search of a gun dealer's premises. The Court recognized the need for an effective inspection system and reasoned that to ensure that inspection served as an effective deterrent, frequent and unannounced inspections were essential. Moreover, the Court asserted that gun dealerships are pervasively regulated businesses, which a dealer operates with knowledge that his business, records, firearms, and ammunition will be subject to effective inspection. Although the need for effective inspection is self-apparent, this type of reasoning is based on the fiction of consent.

A different necessity argument provided the reasoning for the Court's upholding of warrantless inspections under the Mine Safety and Health Act.[15] In *Donovan v Dewey* the Court focused on mining as one of the most hazardous industries in the country. However, the Court rejected as unconstitutional the Occupational Safety and Health Act of 1970 (OSHA) provision that authorized warrantless searches of all work areas for safety hazards.[16]

Ohio courts have interpreted the Supreme Court decisions to authorize warrantless, regulatory searches of businesses that engage in a pervasively regulated industry and where the statutory or code provisions allowing for warrantless inspections set forth procedures that are limited in time, place, and scope. Thus, in *State v Zinmeister*,[17] the Cuyahoga County Court of Appeals upheld a Cleveland ordinance that authorized warrantless inspections of vehicles in public garages, auto sales lots, junkyards, and other vehicle salvage facilities. That court reasoned that the ordinance involved a closely regulated industry and that the inspection is limited to motor vehicles, title registration, vehicle identification numbers, or license plates. The *Zinmeister* court also reasoned that a warrant requirement could easily frustrate inspection because motor vehicles are inherently mobile.

Similarly, the Montgomery County Court of Appeals applied this analysis to Ohio's scheme for warrantless inspections of second-hand dealers. The court found a legitimate state interest because of the concern that these enterprises often become conduits for stolen property. Moreover, the court found that the state procedure for warrantless inspections is carefully limited to inspection of a book listing transactions and does not provide unlimited authority to search the premises of the dealer. On this basis, the court upheld the warrantless inspection system as reasonable.[18]

---

[14]United States v Biswell, 406 US 311, 92 SCt 1593, 32 LEd(2d) 87 (1972).

[15]Donovan v Dewey, 452 US 594, 101 SCt 2534, 69 LEd(2d) 262 (1981).

[16]Marshall v Barlow's Inc, 436 US 307, 98 SCt 1816, 56 LEd(2d) 305 (1978).

[17]State v Zinmeister, 27 App(3d) 313, 27 OBR 370, 501 NE(2d) 59 (Cuyahoga 1985).

[18]State v Norman, 2 App(3d) 159, 2 OBR 175, 441 NE(2d) 292 (Montgomery 1981).

The *Zinmeister* approach prevailed in the United States Supreme Court in *New York v Burger,*[19] where a New York statute authorizing warrantless administrative searches of automobile junkyards was upheld. The Court found that automobile junkyards are pervasively regulated businesses. The *Burger* decision is significant for two reasons. First, it broadened the concept of what constitutes a closely regulated business to the extent that dissenting Justice O'Connor speculated that it would virtually eliminate the warrant requirement for administrative inspections of commercial establishments. Under the majority opinion, a closely regulated business is apparently any business that has a long history of governmental regulation in a substantial number of states. Second, the New York statute is aimed specifically at finding evidence of criminal violations. The whole concept of administrative searches focused on the existence of a critical governmental interest, such as health and safety, which justified excusing traditional Fourth Amendment requirements such as a warrant and probable cause. Thus, historically, even though criminal prosecution may follow upon an administrative search, the primary purpose for the administrative search served a different governmental interest. In *Burger,* the Court upheld a state regulatory inspection scheme that was intended solely to uncover evidence of criminal acts.

Ohio courts have interpreted *Burger* to authorize warrantless, regulatory searches of businesses that engage in a pervasively regulated industry and where the statutory or code provisions allowing for warrantless inspections set forth procedures that are limited in time, place, and scope. The Ohio Supreme Court followed *Burger* and upheld warrantless administrative searches of regulated businesses provided that the search be executed pursuant to statutory standards that limit the scope, time and place of the search.[20] More importantly, *State v VFW Post 3562* established that a warrantless "administrative search may not be used to obtain evidence of general criminality." This proposition was extended by the Franklin Court of Appeals to bar the use of warrantless administrative searches when "forfeiture proceedings are reasonably foreseeable."[21] Thus, an administrative inspection cannot be the basis for a search for evidence of general criminality, and the state may not require, as a condition of doing business, a blanket submission to warrantless searches for any purpose.[22] However, "[t]he fact that police officers are involved in these administrative searches and the fact that those officers have the power to enforce penal laws, does not mean that the 'administrative search' exception is inapplicable."[23] Relying upon *Burger* and the authority recognized in *State v. VFW Post 3562,* the

---

[19]New York v Burger, 482 US 691, 107 SCt 2636, 96 LEd(2d) 601 (1987), appeal dismissed by 70 NY(2d) 828, 518 NE(2d) 1, 523 NYS(2d) 489 (1987).

[20]State v VFW Post 3562, 37 OS(3d) 310, 525 NE(2d) 773 (1988).

[21]Department of Liquor Control v FOE Aerie 0456, 99 App(3d) 380, 650 NE(2d) 940 (Franklin 1994).

[22]See also State v Akron Airport Post No. 8975, 19 OS(3d) 49, 482 NE(2d) 606 (1985), cert denied 474 US 1058, 106 SCt 800, 88 LEd(2d) 777 (1986).

[23]Stone v Stow, 64 OS(3d) 156, 165, 593 NE(2d) 294, ___ (1992).

Ohio Supreme Court upheld the administrative scheme providing for warrantless searches of prescription drugs.[24]

The authority to conduct a warrantless search even of a highly regulated business is not without limits. A warrantless entry and search is illegal if it is for a purpose other than those covered within the regulatory scheme. For example, a search for stolen property is beyond the permissible scope of a warrantless administrative search of a tavern, a highly regulated business.[25] Similarly, the scope of such a search may place it outside the bounds of the regulatory statutes. In *State v Sniezek*,[26] police observed an allegedly underage youth leave a liquor store carrying malt liquor. They entered the store and conducted a thorough search of the premises, finding a sawed-off shotgun on top of a meat cooler. The court of appeals rejected the state's contention that the warrantless search was justified because liquor stores are pervasively regulated businesses:

> The police claimed to be investigating the sale of liquor to a minor, yet they searched the non-public areas, the basement and on top of a meat cooler. They were not searching pursuant to any inspection scheme or procedure. Moreover, the state has failed to show that there existed an authorized inspection procedure for them to follow.[27]

In summary, state law appears to provide more protection than federal constitutional law in this area, by looking to determine whether the scope of the inspection and manner of the intrusion fit within the statutory scheme. Even if the intrusion is into the public area of a business, where the statutory scheme requires notice, it must be given even if the entry is limited to the public area.[28] Moreover, the Ohio Supreme Court has warned that an administrative board cannot act as a surrogate for the police to obviate the constitutional duty of obtaining a search warrant.[29]

---

[24]Stone v Stow, 64 OS(3d) 156, 165, 593 NE(2d) 294, ___ (1992):

> It is clear that the state has a substantial interest in regulating prescription drugs; that the regulatory scheme created by the statutory and administrative provisions at issue serves that interest; and that the inspection scheme provides an adequate substitute for a warrant, because these provisions are "sufficiently comprehensive and defined that the owner of commercial property cannot help but be aware that his property will be subject to periodic inspections undertaken for specific purposes." Finally, the time, place, and scope elements of the scheme are sufficiently limited so that the warrantless search procedure is reasonable. The files must be made available for inspection at reasonable hours only. Access is limited to officials who are "engaged in a specific investigation involving a designated person or drug." Only certain ... drugs alleged to have a high potential for abuse are the objects of these searches.

[25]State v Chapman, No. 1519, 1985 WL 11138 (4th Dist Ct App, Scioto, 5-20-85).

[26]State v Sniezek, 8 App(3d) 147, 8 OBR 204, 456 NE(2d) 542 (Cuyahoga 1982).

[27]State v Sniezek, 8 App(3d) 147, 148, 8 OBR 204, 456 NE(2d) 542 (Cuyahoga 1982).

[28]City of Toledo v Bateson, 83 App(3d) 195, 614 NE(2d) 824 (Lucas 1992).

[29]State v Penn, 61 OS(3d) 720, 576 NE(2d) 790 (1991).

16.05 Special circumstances searches

(A) In general

Limiting the Fourth Amendment rights of school children was the first in a line of "special circumstances searches," following the model of administrative searches by abandoning traditional Fourth Amendment warrant considerations when there are special circumstances caused by a particular societal need. Such circumstances include teacher searches of students, public employee drug testing, postal inspections, and airport and border searches. In these cases, the courts have held that while warrants are not necessary, some level of suspicion or sufficient notification is generally required. The courts consider the context in which the search occurs, its purpose, the compelling government interest, and the general expectation of privacy.

The special circumstances rationale is similar to that used in the exigent circumstances exception but lacks the "urgency" justification. It stems from settings in which the warrant requirement would contravene the government purpose or otherwise be too burdensome. The courts have had to decide when such special circumstances exist and what level of suspicion, if any, should be required to conduct a lawful search. The most recent development is the abandonment of any particularized cause requirement, even the lesser standard of reasonable suspicion, for drug testing for certain government employees.

(B) Searches by school teachers and administrators

(1) Categories in general

Searches by teachers and administrators may be divided into two categories: inspections of students' lockers or possessions and searches of particular students.

(2) Inspections of lockers and student property

There is no dispositive position on this issue from the United States Supreme Court or Ohio courts. Guidance must be sought from the principles that have been developed to govern regulatory or administrative searches. Even here, however, those principles are not altogether on point. The interests involved are different. A municipality's program for regular housing and business inspection is ordinarily related to preventing fire and other safety hazards or maintaining the housing stock within the community. The primary remedy is correction of violations and the dissipation of the hazard. A school administrator's inspection of lockers is for the purpose of finding contraband or evidence of rule infractions, and a finding of that evidence will inevitably result in disciplinary action or possibly referral to juvenile court. Nonetheless, one can hardly argue that the presence of weapons or drugs on school property does not present a hazard to other students and teachers; furthermore, their removal is necessary to maintain the environment that is essential for the school to accomplish its mission. In a case involving a search of a particular student, the Supreme Court recognized the substantial interest in maintaining discipline in the classroom and school grounds.[30]

Notwithstanding, the Court has recognized that the Fourth Amendment is applicable to school children. The reasonableness standard will be applicable to an inspection policy. Consequently, any inspection policy should be set forth so that students and their parents are on notice of its existence, and the procedures set forth in the policy should be adhered to strictly. The policy must be carefully drawn to meet the particular needs that justify the intrusions to prevent the policy from serving as a wholesale abrogation of the students' right to privacy and to prevent abuses in its administration.

Different and more complex considerations prevail with the issue of inspection of dormitory rooms in public colleges. Those rooms are entitled to the same degree of Fourth Amendment privacy that attaches to any residence,[31] but just as residences are subject to administrative searches for health and safety purposes, so are dormitory rooms. A legitimate inspection of a dormitory room under this rubric, however, should be limited to those same health and safety concerns and should not be a pretext for a fishing expedition against a particular student or significant diminution of an individual's privacy interest in his home. Consistency would require an administrative warrant to authorize such inspections.

(3) Search of a particular student

New Jersey v T.L.O.[32] presented issues that the United States Supreme Court did not handle easily or altogether satisfactorily. In fact, it took the Supreme Court two years to decide the case. The student was found smoking in a school lavatory in violation of school rules and was taken to the principal's office. She denied that she had been smoking and claimed that she did not smoke at all. An assistant principal opened T.L.O.'s purse, found a pack of cigarettes, and noticed a package of rolling papers commonly associated with the use of marijuana. The principal then searched the purse thoroughly and found marijuana and marijuana paraphernalia as well as evidence that T.L.O. was selling marijuana to other students.

The state argued three major propositions: (1) the Fourth Amendment is not applicable to children in school; (2) the exclusionary rule should not be applicable to searches conducted by school officials; and (3) the warrantless search of T.L.O.'s purse without probable cause was reasonable. New Jersey lost the first two battles but won the war when the Supreme Court affirmed the reasonableness of the particular search. The Court held that school children are not to be subject to indiscriminate searches, reasoning that the child's person and effects are entitled to the Fourth Amendment's protection of privacy. The Court rejected New Jersey's attempt to equate schools with the Court's pronouncement that a prisoner in a jail or prison has no expectation of privacy, stating, "We are not yet ready to hold that schools

---

[30]New Jersey v T.L.O., 469 US 325, 105 SCt 733, 83 LEd(2d) 720 (1985).
[31]Athens v Wolf, 38 OS(2d) 237, 313 NE(2d) 405 (1974) (a dormitory room is a "home").
[32]New Jersey v T.L.O., 469 US 325, 105 SCt 733, 83 LEd(2d) 720 (1985)

and prisons need be equated for purposes of the Fourth Amendment."[33] Further, the Court was unwilling to agree that school children do not need to bring personal property to school with them or that they have necessarily waived all rights to privacy in such items merely by bringing them on school grounds. Moreover, the Court held that the Fourth Amendment does not prohibit only law enforcement officers from engaging in unreasonable searches and seizures and therefore held that restricting the operation of the exclusionary rule only to illegal searches conducted by law enforcement officers would be unduly restrictive. Public school officials are not exempt from the Amendment's dictates by virtue of the special nature of their authority over school children.

Having disposed of these two arguments, the Court was still required to create a framework for determining the reasonableness of a search of a particular student conducted by a school official. The primary questions for determining reasonableness would turn on the Court's analysis of whether a warrant should be required for such a search and what standard of cause would justify the search.

What is reasonable, the Court said, will turn on all the circumstances surrounding the search or seizure and the nature of the search or seizure itself. Borrowing from the standards devised to govern *Terry*-stops and regulatory searches, the Court held that the reasonableness of a specific search conducted by school personnel must be determined by balancing the need to search against the invasion which the search entails. *T.L.O.* contains extensive discussion pertaining to the need to maintain a safe, orderly, and contraband-free environment in the schools to create a healthy learning environment. Consequently, the Court recognized that to achieve the desired environment "the school setting requires some easing of the restrictions to which searches by public authorities are ordinarily subject."[34]

First, all nine justices agreed that school officials need not obtain a warrant before searching a student who is under their authority. The justices agreed that requiring a warrant would not suit the types of situations that were likely to be recurring in which school searches were desirable. Second, and most important, the seven members of the majority concluded that the school setting requires a modification of the level of suspicion of illicit activity needed to justify a search. Consequently, the Court rejected the probable cause standard in favor of a reasonableness test based on all of the circumstances of the search. Reasonableness, then, is the appropriate test for review of the initial intrusion as well as the scope of the search.

The significance of *T.L.O.* lies in its appropriation of a general reasonableness standard, similar to reasonable suspicion developed in *Terry,* as the test for approving a full search of the student and his effects. Unlike *Terry,* here reasonable suspicion will support a full search, not a limited pat-down or frisk for weapons. T.L.O.'s purse and all its contents were thoroughly examined. Moreover, this lesser standard is applicable whether the school official has reasonable cause to believe that a crime has been committed or

---

[33]New Jersey v T.L.O., 469 US 325, 338-39, 105 SCt 733, 83 LEd(2d) 720 (1985)
[34]New Jersey v T.L.O., 469 US 325, 340, 105 SCt 733, 83 LEd(2d) 720 (1985)

merely a violation of school rules. Thus, a student suspected of violating a school rule is subject to a more intrusive search than a person on the street suspected of committing a crime. *T.L.O.* is the only instance, outside of border-crossing cases,[35] in which the Court has authorized a full search on less than probable cause. With the justices' attention drawn as it has been to strip searches, the Court noted that the scope of the search would be subject to the same reasonableness review. While some infractions may justify a full search of the student, they will be few, and a strip search would not have been deemed reasonable under the facts and circumstances presented in *T.L.O.*

The Court in *T.L.O.* specifically avoided indicating how it would decide the case when a school official is working cooperatively with the police or at the behest of the police. This is a particularly thorny problem. On the one hand, police should not be permitted to avoid Fourth Amendment requirements of a warrant and probable cause by using surrogates to search. Conversely, if police officers bring a school official information that would justify that official taking action if he learned of the information from a teacher or other student, the same societal interests are present that justified the warrantless search on reasonable suspicion in *T.L.O.* The Supreme Court is likely to be persuaded by those interests. The only proper resolution will be a rule that requires consideration of each individual case on its own facts. If the Court opts for a bright-line rule as it has in recent years in so many Fourth Amendment cases, that rule is likely to insulate from review a great many abusive and pretextual searches. Then, notwithstanding its pronouncement in *T.L.O.*, the Court will have effectively eliminated the provisions of the Fourth Amendment from the schools.

(4) Drug testing of school children

In *Veronia School Dist 47J v Acton*,[36] the United States Supreme Court upheld suspicionless, random testing of junior high school athletes. There is no question that such tests would be upheld for high school and college athletes, as well. The question remaining is whether the reasoning which underlies the result would support drug testing for all public school and college students.

Several different threads supported the majority opinion in favor of drug testing. First, the doctrine of *in loco parentis* reappeared to work hand-in-hand with a notion of a diminished expectation of privacy for school children ("the nature of those rights is what is appropriate for children in school"). Then the Court focused upon the special situation of athletes: like persons who participate in closely regulated industries, "students who voluntarily participate in school athletics have reason to expect intrusions upon normal rights and privileges, including privacy." Then the Court turned its attention to the non-criminal nature of the search, narrow nature of the inquiry, and the limited disclosure of results. Finally, and most importantly,

---

[35]See, e.g., United States v Montoya de Hernandez, 473 US 531, 105 SCt 3304, 87 LEd(2d) 381 (1985).
[36]Veronia School Dist 47J v Acton, 115 SCt 2386, 132 LEd(2d) 564 (1995), affirmed by 66 F(3d) 217 (1995).

the tests are supported, according to Justice Scalia's majority opinion, by the need to "[protect] student athletes from injury, and [deter] drug use in the student population" by testing students who have a limited expectation of privacy because they are subjected to physical exams in school and are often undressed in locker room settings. While the Court undoubtedly concentrated upon the special status of student athletes, the reasoning which ultimately led to upholding the tests could be applied to all students who use or are required to use locker room facilities while in school, which could be the general school-age population.

Finally, the Court pointed out as it has for a quarter of a century that although alternative less intrusive means might have accomplished the same goals, "We have repeatedly refused to declare that only the "least intrusive" search practicable can be reasonable under the Fourth Amendment."[37]

(C) Public employer searches of employee desks and offices

The immediate effect of *T.L.O.* extended far beyond the confines of schools and school children. Although an employee has a legitimate expectation of privacy in his workplace, there are "special needs" associated with public employment that allows searches of public employees' offices, desks, and effects without full compliance with the requirements of the warrant clause. In *O'Connor v Ortega*,[38] the Supreme Court borrowed heavily from *T.L.O.* and curtailed the Fourth Amendment rights of public employees. The Supreme Court could not agree on a bright-line rule, and it is somewhat dangerous to attempt to read too much into *O'Connor*. Justice Scalia was the swing fifth vote in that case, and the rules that emerged are no broader than that to which he agreed.

Justice Scalia and the four dissenters agreed that government employees have a legitimate expectation of privacy in their offices as well as the drawers and files within those offices. Nonetheless, he and the four justices in the plurality agreed that the special needs associated with government employment made compliance with the warrant and probable cause requirements impracticable. Scalia and the plurality were very vulnerable to dissenting Justice Blackmun's charge that they did not prove the existence of special needs in this context.

Justice Scalia, however, would not give a blank check to government employers to search employee offices and effects indiscriminately. He appears to limit the authority only to searches that are for work-related purposes, where the employer seeks to retrieve work-related materials or to investigate violations of work-place rules, or criminal conduct that impacts on fitness for employment.

The Court did not fully resolve the issue whether individualized suspicion and, if so, what degree of suspicion is an essential element of a valid work-related search. A majority agreed that probable cause was not suited

---

[37]Veronia School Dist 47J v Acton, 115 SCt 2386, 132 LEd(2d) 564 (1995), affirmed by 66 F(3d) 217 (1995).

[38]O'Connor v Ortega, 480 US 709, 107 SCt 1492, 94 LEd(2d) 714 (1987).

to the special needs of the government employment. The Court appeared to substitute reasonable suspicion as the standard to justify such searches.

(D) Drug testing

The greatest impact of *O'Connor* has been and will be felt in the area of drug testing of government employees. The primary issues raised by drug testing programs for government employees focus on (1) whether testing is permissible for all government employment; (2) the degree of cause that must exist to justify requiring an employee to submit to a drug test; and (3) whether causeless, random drug testing is ever permissible.

Although government employees are subject to a diminished expectation of privacy within the context of their employment, the constitutionality of a search conducted by a public employer for noninvestigatory, work-related purposes as well as for investigations of work-related misconduct will be judged by the standard of reasonableness under all of the circumstances as to the inception of the search and scope of the intrusion. Compulsory urinalysis is a search and implicates Fourth Amendment interests and is subject to these standards. Even though urine is a waste product, it reveals highly personal information. Urine testing in the presence of a government official is as intrusive as a strip search.

The Supreme Court has held that urinalysis is a search and seizure subject to the dictates of the Fourth Amendment. In two separate cases in which Justice Kennedy wrote both majority opinions, the Court held that drug testing must meet the overall standard of reasonableness within the Fourth Amendment but further held that individualized suspicion is not always an essential requirement.

In *National Treasury Employees Union v Von Raab*,[39] the Customs Service implemented a drug testing program in which a urinalysis was required of each employee who transferred or was promoted to specific positions. The service required that the tests be conducted for those positions in which the employee (1) was directly involved in drug interdiction, (2) carried firearms, or (3) was exposed to classified information. The test itself, while closely monitored, did not involve direct observation of the employee while urinating, nor were the results to be used for any other purpose, including criminal prosecution, without written consent.

The Supreme Court upheld that part of the program requiring suspicionless drug testing of employees applying for promotion to positions involving interdiction of illegal drugs or requiring them to carry firearms. The Court found that there were special needs involved beyond the normal need for law enforcement and held that the interests were to be balanced to determine whether a warrant should be required or indeed any level of individualized suspicion should be required.

This balancing analysis looked at several key factors. The Court held that requiring a warrant would be too burdensome in this context and that it

---

[39]National Treasury Employees Union v Von Raab, 489 US 656, 109 SCt 1384, 103 LEd(2d) 685 (1989), affirmed sub nom National Treasury Employees Union v Bush, 891 F(2d) 99 (1989).

would not effectively afford any further Fourth Amendment protection than was provided under the regulation that (1) limited the testing to the specific positions, (2) notified the prospective employees of the requirements for the positions, and (3) severely limited the use of the results. The Court then focused on the compelling government interest in stopping the flow of drugs and in particular on the critical position that customs officials occupy, noting their daily exposure to large quantities of drugs and their susceptibility to bribery and blackmail. The Court also noted the responsibility of carrying a firearm and being called on to use it instantly in life and death situations. Finally, the Court relied on the diminished expectation of privacy that results both from the notification of the requirements and the general testing involved in determining fitness and probity.

The Court limited its approval to two of the three job categories slated for this testing, remanding the third category, the testing of those handling classified information, to the lower court for further findings. The remand indicates the importance the Court placed on the relationship between the compelling government interest and the critical aspects of the position that further the state interest. It allows for a testing program, without requiring particularized suspicion, for those in ultrasensitive positions while requiring reasonable suspicion for other government employees in less sensitive positions.

In *Skinner v Railway Labor Executives' Assn*,[40] the Federal Railroad Administration imposed a regulation requiring blood and urine testing of employees involved in a major train accident or certain reportable incidents. The Court upheld the regulation, again holding that individualized suspicion was not required. The Court's step-by-step analysis is familiar. The Court found a compelling state interest in the safety of the riding public and the critical position the railroad employees had in ensuring that safety. The Court further found that a warrant would be ineffective, indicating that the delay associated with obtaining a warrant would frustrate the strong governmental purpose. Further, the Court found that the pervasiveness of the regulations diminished the employees' expectation of privacy but found their Fourth Amendment interests sufficiently protected because the regulations limited the scope of the testing. The decision in *Skinner* is not quite as narrow as in *Von Raab*. The Court took an expansive view of the risk associated with railroad employment and appeared to carve out a broader exception for suspicionless testing than it did in the customs case.

(E) Probationer and parolee searches

Perhaps nowhere have the inroads of the special circumstances search been more apparent than in the Supreme Court's upholding of the warrantless search of a probationer's home. In *Griffin v Wisconsin*,[41] the Supreme Court recognized the "special need" of maintaining close supervision of probationers to further the rehabilitative and preventive goals of probation:

---

[40]Skinner v Railway Labor Executives' Assn, 489 US 602, 109 SCt 1402, 103 LEd(2d) 639 (1989).

[41]Griffin v Wisconsin, 483 US 868, 107 SCt 3164 (1987).

> A State's operation of a probation system, like its operation of a school, government office or prison, or its supervision of a regulated industry, likewise presents "special needs" beyond normal law enforcement that may justify departure from the usual warrant and probable cause requirements.

Accordingly, the Court upheld the warrantless search of a probationer's home when a probation officer has reasonable grounds to believe that objects unauthorized in the probation order will be found in the home. The Court stated that requiring a warrant would interfere with the probation system's ability to respond rapidly and would set up a judge "rather than the probation officer as the judge of how close a supervision the probationer requires." Moreover, the Court excused the warrant requirement in this situation because the probation officer, unlike a police officer, is "supposed to have in mind the welfare of the probationer." The Court also found that the more stringent probable cause standard would interfere with a probation officer's ability to respond quickly at the first indication of trouble.

Griffin is highly problematic from several perspectives. While urinalysis is highly intrusive, the search here was of a home which for the first time, in the absence of exigent circumstances, the Court sanctioned a warrantless search on less than probable cause. Moreover, the standard adopted— reasonable cause, did not in this case measure up to reasonable suspicion necessary for a Terry-stop because the Court upheld the probation officer's intrusion on an uncorroborated tip from an unidentified law enforcement officer.

Griffin has been applied in Ohio in several ways. First, the special needs characterization has been applied to parolees as well as probationers.[42] Second, consent to search a probationer's person, home, automobile and possessions has become a standard condition of probation and parole. That condition has been upheld as non-coercive,[43] even where the condition to search the home was added after the initial conditions of probation were set and defendant would have faced a probation revocation proceeding had he not signed the consent form.[44] Moreover, the reasonable cause standard enunciated in *Griffin* was watered-down by the Montgomery County Court of Appeals holding that a parole officer supervising a probationer "had sufficient reasonable cause to conduct the warrantless search [of probationer's home] based on the results" of a prior search conducted three months earlier in which evidence of drug trafficking was found.[45]

One of the justifications utilized by the Supreme Court in *Griffin* to allow probation officers to conduct warrantless searches of homes is that probation officers, unlike police officers, are motivated by the "best interests" of the probationers. However, that distinction is not very significant in practice. It is well accepted for probation and parole officers to seek the cooper-

---

[42]State v Braxton, 102 App(3d) 28, 656 NE(2d) 970 (Cuyahoga 1995).

[43]State v Braxton, 102 App(3d) 28, 656 NE(2d) 970 (Cuyahoga 1995).

[44]State v Pinson, No. 14294, 1994 WL 721582 (2d Dist Ct App, Montgomery, 12-23-94).

[45]State v Pinson, No. 14294, 1994 WL 721582 (2d Dist Ct App, Montgomery, 12-23-94).

ation and assistance of police officers when conducting such searches.[46] Moreover, the distinction between probation officers and police officers was deemed irrelevant where a probation officer requested police assistance but actively conducted the search, rather than police officers using the probationer's status as a pretext to conduct a search.[47]

---

[46]State v Braxton, 102 App(3d) 28, 656 NE(2d) 970 (Cuyahoga 1995).
[47]State v Carter, No. CA-9102, 1993 WL 274293 (5th Dist Ct App, Stark, 6-28-93).

Chapter 17

Consent Searches

17.01   Introduction

Police officers do not need a search warrant when an individual voluntarily consents to a search. Consent is not an exception to the warrant requirement fashioned out of exigent circumstances, but a decision by a citizen not to assert Fourth Amendment rights. At issue are (1) the test of voluntariness, (2) whether the individual consenting may place limitations upon the search, and (3) who is authorized to consent. The burden of proving consent is on the prosecution. Whether a consent to a search is voluntary or the product of duress or coercion is a question of fact to be determined from the totality of the circumstances.[1] The state must show by clear and convincing evidence that the consent was freely and voluntarily given[2] which is more than a mere preponderance but less a certainty than is required to prove guilt beyond a reasonable doubt.[3]

17.02   Voluntariness test

The test governing the voluntariness standard was set forth by the Supreme Court in *Schneckloth v Bustamonte*,[4] where a passenger in a stopped vehicle assented to and aided in the opening of the trunk in response to a police request. The critical issue in *Schneckloth* was whether there can be a valid consent without proof that the person consenting knows he has the right to refuse.

First, the Supreme Court majority rejected the argument that the "strict-waiver" theory of constitutional rights, requiring a knowing, intelligent, and voluntary waiver,[5] be applied to consent searches. The Court reasoned that the "strict-waiver" theory is limited to those trial rights that are guaranteed to ensure a fair ascertainment of truth at trial, and hence a fair trial, while the Fourth Amendment guarantees are of a wholly different order.

In deciding this issue, the Court drew analogy from the voluntariness standard developed in confession cases. Following through on the analogy, the Court determined that whether consent is voluntary or the product of duress is to be taken from the totality of the circumstances. Knowledge of the right is one factor to be considered but is not controlling. Consequently,

---

[1]Schneckloth v Bustamonte, 412 US 218, 93 SCt 2041, 36 LEd(2d) 854 (1973).
[2]Bumper v North Carolina, 391 US 543, 88 SCt 1788, 20 LEd(2d) 797 (1968), affirmed by 275 NC 670, 170 SE(2d) 457 (1969); State v Comen, 50 OS(3d) 206, 553 NE(2d) 640 (1990).
[3]State v Danby, 11 App(3d) 38, 11 OBR 71, 463 NE(2d) 47 (Erie 1983).
[4]Schneckloth v Bustamonte, 412 US 218, 93 SCt 2041, 36 LEd(2d) 854 (1973).
[5]See Johnson v Zerbst, 304 US 458, 58 SCt 1019, 82 LEd 1461 (1938).

police need not advise an individual of his Fourth Amendment right to refuse to consent to a search. The Court distinguished custodial interrogation which must be preceded by *Miranda*[6] warnings as inapplicable since a person consenting to a search is generally not in custody and the atmosphere surrounding the encounter is not inherently coercive. The Court has failed to follow through on the analogy and has not required a warning that an accused has a right to refuse to consent to search even for one in custody.[7] Thus, the fact of arrest does not necessarily render a consent involuntary. The question becomes whether the duress present in a particular case exceeds the normal duress inherent in any arrest.[8] The fact that a defendant is upset at the time of an arrest will not preclude a finding that consent is voluntary if no coercive tactics were used to obtain the consent and the defendant was no more upset than is normal incident to any arrest.[9]

In 1994, the Montgomery County Court of Appeals imposed a new requirement when the request to consent to a search of a car follows upon a traffic stop or arrest, both of which are Fourth Amendment seizures. The court, there, said that an officer must have at least reasonable suspicion to request permission to search the car in the wake of the coercive atmosphere of a traffic stop or arrest.[10]

Consequently, following *Schneckloth*, a court reviewing the legality of a search need only determine whether the abandonment of Fourth Amendment rights and the consent to search was an act of free will, voluntarily given, and not the result of duress or coercion, express or implied. Although the United States Supreme Court has not reviewed the *Schneckloth* policies in the subsequent two decades, important developments in Ohio have altered the doctrine as it applies to requests to search cars following a traffic stop, which was what happened in *Schneckloth*. The Ohio Supreme Court has found that persons do not feel free during the course of a traffic stop to refuse to co-operate with a police officer, whether that officer is asking questions about other offenses or seeking permission to search the vehicle. Moreover, the extension of a traffic stop for the purpose of asking questions about other offenses or seeking permission to search the car, without probable cause to support an extended detention, transforms the legal traffic stop into an illegal detention. Accordingly, the Ohio court has held that consent under those circumstances is *per se* not voluntary unless the officer clearly indicates to the motorist that he is free to leave and free

---

[6]Miranda v Arizona, 384 US 436, 86 SCt 1602, 16 LEd(2d) 694 (1966).

[7]See United States v Watson, 423 US 411, 96 SCt 820, 46 LEd(2d) 598 (1976) (defendant in custody but not at the police station); United States v Gentile, 493 F(2d) 1404 (5th Cir Tex 1974), cert denied 419 US 979, 95 SCt 241, 42 LEd(2d) 191 (1974) (defendant at the police station when consent to search given); see also State v Austin, 52 App(2d) 59, 368 NE(2d) 59 (Franklin 1976) (failure to give *Miranda* warnings to one effectively in custody does not alone invalidate consent to search defendant's home).

[8]State v Simmons, 61 App(3d) 514, 573 NE(2d) 165 (Summit 1989), appeal dismissed by 58 OS(3d) 713, 570 NE(2d) 277 (1991).

[9]State v Hiller, No. 2459, 1989 WL 95013 (9th Dist Ct App, Wayne, 8-9-89).

[10]State v Retherford, No. 13987, 1994 WL 459921 (2d Dist Ct App, Montgomery, 3-16-94); see discussion of this case in Text 14.06(C), Search of an automobile incident to a non-custodial traffic arrest.

not to answer questions about other offenses or consent to a search of his car.[11] If the officer fails to do so, the resulting consent is invalid.[12]

The burden rests on the prosecution to establish that the consent was voluntarily given. It is not voluntarily given when it follows on a police officer's assertion that he has lawful authority, such as a warrant, to conduct a search. A consent following a claim of authority is not voluntarily given but merely an acquiescence and an acknowledgment of authority.[13] This principle appears to have been lost in *State v Danby*,[14] where a court of appeals found a defendant's consent to search his car to be voluntarily given notwithstanding that he was told that "he could sign a waiver for the search or we could get a search warrant drawn up."[15] The *Danby* court did acknowledge that under certain circumstances a statement by police that if consent is not forthcoming a warrant will be obtained may vitiate the voluntariness of any subsequent consent, but in that case concluded that the defendant understood that he had a constitutional right to withhold his consent. One would have expected that change in circumstances to cause a different result in *State v Davis*,[16] where police informed a lessee that her failure to consent would lead to obtaining a search warrant and require her arrest and also lead to removal of her child by a social service agency. Nonetheless, the court found no coercion after the lessee testified that "she didn't mind signing the form." The claim of authority need not even include mention of a search warrant; a police assertion that they have come to search precludes a voluntary consent.[17] Coercion will be determined by all of the circumstances, e.g., time of day, number of officers, show of authority, nature of the request, and the cooperative or uncooperative attitude of the recipient of the request. Any statement by police that leads a person to believe that refusing consent will be fruitless should make any resulting consent involuntary.[18]

Presumably by examining all of the circumstances, the hearing court will be able to distinguish between a voluntary consent and an acquiescence to authority. In *State v Bailey*,[19] the defendant was being questioned by police

---

[11]State v Robinette, 73 OS(3d) 650, 653 NE(2d) 695 (1995).

[12]See discussion of this point in Text Chapter 15, Traffic Stops and Their Aftermath.

[13]Bumper v North Carolina, 391 US 543, 88 SCt 1788, 20 LEd(2d) 797 (1968), affirmed by 275 NC 670, 170 SE(2d) 457 (1969).

[14]State v Danby, 11 App(3d) 38, 11 OBR 71, 463 NE(2d) 47 (Erie 1983).

[15]State v Danby, 11 App(3d) 38, 41, 11 OBR 71, 463 NE(2d) 47 (Erie 1983).

[16]State v Davis, 80 App(3d) 277, 609 NE(2d) 174 (Cuyahoga 1992), appeal dismissed by 65 OS(3d) 1462, 602 NE(2d) 1171 (1992).

[17]Amos v United States, 255 US 313, 41 SCt 266, 65 LEd 654 (1921).

[18]*Compare* State v Foster, 87 App(3d) 32, 621 NE(2d) 843 (Miami 1993) (motorist's consent involuntary where he was told that if he did not consent, his car would be searched anyway after a two hour wait) *with* State v Davis, 80 App(3d) 277, 609 NE(2d) 174 (Cuyahoga 1992), appeal dismissed by 65 OS(3d) 1462, 602 NE(2d) 1171 (1992) (consent voluntary where consenting individual testified that "she didn't mind signing the form," even though police informed her that her failure to consent would lead to obtaining a search warrant and require her arrest and removal of her child by a social service).

[19]State v Bailey, No. 1725, 1989 WL 74861 (4th Dist Ct App, Scioto, 6-27-89).

after coming out of the hotel room of a suspected drug dealer. He was requested to empty his pockets. One of the items, an empty cigarette pack, was found to contain eight individually wrapped packets of cocaine. The state contended that the defendant had consented to the search. The court concluded that the defendant merely acquiesced to the demand of the officers when he emptied his pockets based on the following factors: he had not been advised of his right to refuse to search, nor had he been given *Miranda* warnings; he was not cooperating with the police at the time he was asked to empty his pockets; and "[t]he most significant fact tending to establish that consent was involuntary is [defendant] must have known that by surrendering the cigarette pack discovery of the drugs was inevitable and would result in his arrest."[20] The court considered the failure of the police to advise the defendant that he did not have to consent. *Schneckloth* says that factor is not dispositive but is still one factor to be considered within the totality. The court gave weight to Bailey's surrender of incriminating evidence as proof that his consent was not voluntary. That is a questionable standard to apply. Obviously, a consent may be voluntary, just as a confession may be voluntary, even though it is unwise and results in a defendant's conviction. That fact, alone, does not render a consent involuntary. Here, it was used by the court along with the defendant's uncooperative attitude to show that he was merely acquiescing to the police command.

For over half a century, Ohio courts have recognized that mere failure to resist a search cannot be turned into a valid consent when the claim of authority upon which the search originally rested fails. The strength of that position is illustrated in *Bender v Addams*,[21] when the court of appeals in an action for damages said:

> It is said they did it with the consent of Senator Bender. Well, Senator Bender did not want to create a disturbance by fighting with officers, and so he did what most men would do, made the best of a bad situation, and smilingly, perhaps, permitted them to search the house, but that does not show that they were invited into the house and that he waived any of his rights. It simply shows that he did not obstruct the officers in what they regarded as the performance of their duties.[22]

Since voluntariness is a question of fact to be determined on the totality of the circumstances, similar fact situations may result in different, irreconcilable results. The focus must be on the police behavior and the effect of that behavior on the consenting party. In *Lakewood v Smith*,[23] the Ohio Supreme Court found no consent where police officers appeared at a defendant's door and told him they wanted to come in and ask some questions. The Court held that the consent to enter was granted in submission to authority rather than as an understanding and intentional waiver of the

---

[20]State v Bailey, No. 1725, at 10, 1989 WL 74861 (4th Dist Ct App, Scioto, 6-27-89).

[21]Bender v Addams, 28 App 75, 162 NE 604 (Cuyahoga 1928).

[22]Bender v Addams, 28 App 75, 87, 162 NE 604 (Cuyahoga 1928).

[23]Lakewood v Smith, 1 OS(2d) 128, 205 NE(2d) 388 (1965); see also State v Taylor, 77 App(3d) 223, 601 NE(2d) 541 (Clermont 1991) (officer's statement that he wanted to recover weapon fired by defendant for safekeeping constituted a manifestation of his intent to enter home under color of authority, and mere failure to resist is not a consent).

defendant's constitutional right. In *State v Lett*,[24] however, the Hamilton County Court of Appeals found a valid consent when a defendant, sitting at his kitchen table, was confronted by police officers who had entered his apartment through an open door. The defendant told them to look around and unlocked a closet upon request; the defendant was held to have voluntarily and expressly invited and agreed to a search.

On a motion to suppress, the Franklin County Municipal Court has invalidated a consent given when a large number of officers, some armed with shotguns, appeared at a defendant's door and requested to look around for a fugitive. The defendant's response, "Go ahead. He is not here," under those conditions, was held not to fulfill the prosecution's burden that the consent was "unequivocal, specific, and given freely and intelligently."[25] On the other hand, a defendant, whose car was lawfully stopped on reasonable suspicion that the driver had just burglarized a home, who opened the trunk of his automobile in response to an officer asking what was in the trunk of his car, was held to have voluntarily consented to a search of the automobile.[26] The Ohio Supreme Court had indicated that a motorist stopped only for a traffic offense cannot be questioned about other offenses or asked for consent to search the car until it is clear to the motorist that the traffic stop is over and the motorist is free to leave or refuse consent.[27]

Ordinarily, police may not deceptively gain entry into a home and then claim that the occupant consented to that entry. Where state liquor agents did not identify themselves nor reveal the purpose of their visit but gained entry to the fraternity house through a bogus claim of membership in another chapter of the fraternity, the defendant did not freely and voluntarily consent to the agents' entry and search of the fraternity house.[28] The principle in *State v Pi Kappa Alpha Fraternity* has been limited to situations where the law enforcement officer actively misrepresents his identity or the purpose of his visit.[29] Consequently, where an officer is admitted to premises that he would not be admitted to if he had identified himself as a police officer or law enforcement agent, the consensual admission does not lose its status of being given freely and voluntarily absent express misrepresentation on the part of the officer. Silence is not a misrepresentation for this purpose.[30] *Pi Kappa Alpha* was distinguished in *State v Posey*,[31] where a detec-

---

[24]State v Lett, 114 App 414, 178 NE(2d) 96 (Hamilton 1961).

[25]State v Turkal, 31 Misc 31, 33, 285 NE(2d) 900, 60 OO(2d) 160 (Muni, Franklin 1971).

[26]South Euclid v Di Franco, 4 Misc 148, 206 NE(2d) 432 (Muni, South Euclid 1965).

[27]State v Robinette, 73 OS(3d) 650, 653 NE(2d) 695 (1995).

[28]State v Pi Kappa Alpha Fraternity, 23 OS(3d) 141, 23 OBR 295, 491 NE(2d) 1129 (1986), cert denied 479 US 827, 107 SCt 104, 93 LEd(2d) 54 (1986).

[29]State v Hickson, 69 App(3d) 278, 590 NE(2d) 779 (Cuyahoga 1990) (defendant's consent was invalid where she was led to believe that police officers merely wanted to use her window to look into courtyard, when they in fact wanted entry to search for marijuana plants in defendant's apartment).

[30]State v Taub, 47 App(3d) 5, 547 NE(2d) 360 (Lucas 1988).

[31]State v Posey, 40 OS(3d) 420, 534 NE(2d) 61 (1988), cert denied 492 US 907, 109 SCt 3217, 106 LEd(2d) 567 (1989); see also State v Baker, 87 App(3d) 186, 621

tive, having received information that illegal gambling activity was taking place at an Order of Eagles meeting post, went to the meeting post and observed the illegal activities. The Ohio Supreme Court found that his warrantless entry and search had been consented to even though it would not have been given had the officer identified himself. The Court stressed that the detective in *Posey* did not misrepresent his identity or lie to the doorkeeper about his intentions as did the liquor control agents in *Pi Kappa Alpha*.

A police officer who enters a commercial establishment posing as a customer to make a buy of contraband offered for sale on the premises does not violate the Fourth Amendment.[32] Moreover, where a home is a center of commercial activity, such as a gambling establishment or crack house, no Fourth Amendment violation occurs when an invitation is extended to an undercover police officer to enter the home to engage in the illegal activity even though the invitation would not be forthcoming if the defendant knew that the invitee was a police officer. The officer is lawfully present by virtue of the invitation. However, such invitation does not open the premises to other officers. Similarly, when an informant is allowed into a defendant's home to conduct an illegal transaction, the defendant does not consent to entry by police officers.

17.03 Limits on consent

A search that rests on consent is limited to the extent of that consent. When police rely on a consent to search, they are limited by any conditions, express or implied, attached to the consent. A person consenting can set limits on the time, duration, area and intensity of the search, as well as set conditions governing the search.[33] An intrusion beyond those limitations would not be based on an intentional relinquishment of a right, and the voluntariness standard would not be met.

A citizen who responds affirmatively to an officer's request to enter premises and look around has not seemingly set any limits, and presumably the search can extend to all rooms. A consent search, then, is limited only by its own terms and common sense. Consequently, a defendant's general consent to search his car includes a consent to search closed containers within the car,[34] underneath the front seat,[35] and into all compartments.

NE(2d) 1347 (Hamilton 1993) (where an undercover officer enters a private club with a member of that club and does not misrepresent his identity, there is a voluntary consent to the officer's presence); Columbus v I.O.R.M. Sioux Tribe-Redman Club, 88 App(3d) 215, 623 NE(2d) 679 (Franklin 1993) (members of private club have common authority over admission to club and may consent to officer's entry).

[32]Maryland v Macon, 472 US 463, 105 SCt 2778, 86 LEd(2d) 370 (1985).

[33]State v Perry, Nos. 479, 480, 1985 WL 9481 (4th Dist Ct App, Jackson, 6-7-85).

[34]Florida v Jimeno, 500 US 248, 111 SCt 1801, 114 LEd(2d) 297 (1991). See also State v Whitaker, No. CA78-03-0029 (1st Dist Ct App, Butler, 12-6-78).

[35]State v Patterson, 95 App(3d) 255, 642 NE(2d) 390 (Lake 1993), appeal dismissed by 68 OS(3d) 1470, 628 NE(2d) 1389 (1994).

A court should look at all of the surrounding circumstances to determine the terms of a consent. A home owner's consent for police to come inside should not be deemed a general consent to search the entire house but merely an invitation to enter and look around at what is in plain view in the area where the officer is standing. Where a defendant claims that a consent is limited, the evidence must clearly show what limitations were imposed. Once limitations appear in the record, the burden rests on the state to show that the consent was unconditional or that the search was performed within the conditions.[36] However, courts will not read limitations into a consent that were not clearly on the face of the consent at the time it was given.

In *Lakewood v Smith*,[37] the defendant admitted police officers to his apartment in response to the officers' statement that they wanted to ask him some questions. Once in the apartment, the officers observed a racing form and a "consensus sheet," items which can be lawfully purchased. However, the officers answered defendant's telephone, and the caller attempted to place a bet on a horse. Supporting the principle that a consent search is circumscribed by the nature of the consent, the Ohio Supreme Court said, "One may trespass even after being admitted by the limited consent."[38] Similarly, consent granted for entrance and a search for a specific item is not permission to conduct a general exploratory search of all that is in sight.[39]

Authority to search which is dependant upon consent may be countermanded at any time. In *State v Rojas*,[40] the defendant initially refused permission to search his suitcase but changed his mind after a police dog indicated it contained drugs and officers began speaking with a prosecutor about requesting a warrant. The defendant unlocked the suitcase and indicated verbally and with a gesture that the officers could search it. When one officer picked up two sealed envelopes, the defendant protested that he did not have his consent to search the envelopes. The officers, nonetheless, did open the envelopes after further discussion with the prosecuting attorney. The Cuyahoga County Appellate Court said that the defendant had the right to retract his consent. A concern for the voluntariness of a consent should lead to equal concern for an individual's right to terminate that consent. While that is the prevailing view, there is a split of authority amongst the districts in Ohio.[41]

---

[36]State v Perry, Nos. 479, 480, 1985 WL 9481 (4th Dist Ct App, Jackson, 6-7-85).

[37]Lakewood v Smith, 1 OS(2d) 128, 205 NE(2d) 388 (1965).

[38]Lakewood v Smith, 1 OS(2d) 128, 130, 205 NE(2d) 388 (1965).

[39]State v Glover, 60 App(2d) 283, 396 NE(2d) 1064 (Hamilton 1978); see also State v Smith, 73 App(3d) 471, 597 NE(2d) 1132 (Wood 1991) (cohabitant/victim who summoned police to motel and pointed to specific room consented to police entry but not search of room).

[40]State v Rojas, 92 App(3d) 336, 635 NE(2d) 66 (Cuyahoga 1993), appeal dismissed by 69 OS(3d) 1415, 630 NE(2d) 376 (1994).

[41]See State v Sikora, No. 93-C-42, 1994 WL 149886 (7th Dist Ct App, Columbiana, 4-20-94) (voluntary consent may not be countermanded during the ensuing search); *accord* State v Lett, 114 App 414, 178 NE(2d) 96 (Hamilton 1961).

17.04   Third party consent

A valid consent to search may be given by any person who possesses authority over the area to be inspected. Therefore, police need not seek the consent of a defendant to search if a third person who shares authority with the defendant over the area to be searched grants permission.[42] A problem arises when police bypass a target against whom they are seeking evidence and, instead, seek consent from someone with whom the target lives and shares authority but who, of course, is not a target. The police bypass the target knowing, or at least suspecting, that the target would not grant consent to search, and that the person with whom the target lives is more likely to grant the request in order to disassociate himself from police suspicions. Although this may raise some policy questions about the propriety of purposefully going around a target in order to search his house, the law is clear. A third person may grant consent under these circumstances, even though the complaining party was in police custody at the time consent was sought and, presumably, could have been asked for consent to search.[43] The really critical problem arises when the target has refused consent, and the police seek consent from another with whom the target lives and shares authority. This problem arose in *State v Davis*,[44] where defendant, a suspected burglar, was intercepted in a vehicle. When police requested permission to search the car, the defendant refused. His companion, who was driving the car, which neither owned, gave permission. The court held that the other occupant's permission was sufficient even in the face of the defendant's refusal. A different result was obtained in *State v Williams*,[45] where the court held that a third-person co-tenant could not consent to a search of the defendant's room where the defendant was present and objected to the search.

The issues to be determined following third party consent are (1) whether the third person's consent was freely given; (2) whether the third person had authority to consent;[46] and (3) if the third person does not have authority but did consent, whether police were entitled to reasonably rely on the third person's claim of authority.

To be valid, the consent of the third person must meet the voluntariness standard and must not be procured by coercion. The burden is on the state

---

[42]United States v Matlock, 415 US 164, 94 SCt 988, 39 LEd(2d) 242 (1974).

[43]United States v Matlock, 415 US 164, 94 SCt 988, 39 LEd(2d) 242 (1974) (the defendant was in the police car outside his residence when his girlfriend gave consent to search the bedroom); State v Greer, 39 OS(3d) 236, 530 NE(2d) 382 (1988), cert denied 490 US 1028, 109 SCt 1766, 104 LEd(2d) 201 (1989) (upon request, defendant had accompanied police to station house, when police requested and received permission from defendant's girlfriend to search their residence).

[44]State v Davis, No. CA-720, 1990 WL 79040 (5th Dist Ct App, Morrow, 6-7-90).

[45]State v Williams, 101 App(3d) 340, 655 NE(2d) 764 (Summit 1995).

[46]See, e.g., State v Sanchez, No. 14904, 1995 WL 126667 (2d Dist Ct App, Montgomery, 3-24-95) (neither a motel clerk nor a maid has authority to consent to the search of a motel room that it rented although unoccupied at the time of the search).

to prove that the consent was freely given.[47] Unless the consenter is a family member or has an on-going relationship with the defendant, the consenter, who is likely relieved not to be implicated in the criminal charges, lacks incentive to actively participate in challenging the consent.

Ohio law recognizes the right of a spouse to consent to the search of a vehicle[48] or the couple's common home.[49] Similarly, a parent who owns or controls the premises in which a child resides has the right to consent to a search of the premises even though the search produces incriminating evidence against the child.[50] Courts are reluctant to allow children to consent to a search of their parents' home. The Wayne County Court of Appeals distinguished children consenting to police officers entry of their parents' home from a child consenting to a search of that home.[51]

The authority of a third person to consent is limited to common areas over which co-inhabitants have joint access or control for most purposes.[52] These cases could turn on questions of the consenter's authority, although it was the practice at one time when considering third party consent to decide the question in terms of agency law, looking to see whether the third-person consenter was the agent of the defendant. As a result, the Ohio Supreme Court struck down a search of an automobile based solely on the consent of a casual borrower as unreasonable when the evidence found was to be used against the absent owner.[53] Similarly, where the fifteen-year-old son of a landlord admitted police to the common passageway in the rooming house where he and his parent lived, the court, in dictum, questioned the capacity of a fifteen-year-old to grant consent in the absence of his parent and without the corroboration of a parent.[54]

The issue is not relationship, and courts err when they dwell on it. The question is not whether the consenter had authority to waive the defendant's rights, but whether the consenter had sufficient interest or authority in the place searched to waive his own rights and grant a consent. The problem is clouded when the consenter is a child and the child's consent is sought by the police so that they can search for evidence to be used against the consenting child's parent. There is something suspect in such an operation, and courts look for a solution that may not be readily forthcoming by testing common authority.

---

[47]State v McCarthy, 20 App(2d) 275, 253 NE(2d) 789 (Cuyahoga 1969), affirmed by 26 OS(2d) 87, 269 NE(2d) 424 (1971).

[48]State v Scott, 61 OS(2d) 155, 400 NE(2d) 375 (1980).

[49]State v McCarthy, 26 OS(2d) 87, 269 NE(2d) 424 (1971).

[50]State v Carder, 9 OS(2d) 1, 222 NE(2d) 620 (1966); State v Chapman, 97 App(3d) 687, 647 NE(2d) 504 (Hamilton 1994) (search of defendant's room was legitimate where consent granted by defendant's father who owned the premises).

[51]State v Pamer, 70 App(3d) 540, 591 NE(2d) 801 (Wayne 1990) (upheld children's consent to entry of police officers who were investigating child abuse claims).

[52]United States v Matlock, 415 US 164, 94 SCt 988, 39 LEd(2d) 242 (1974).

[53]State v Bernius, 177 OS 155, 203 NE(2d) 241 (1964).

[54]State v Person, 34 Misc 97, 298 NE(2d) 922 (Muni, Toledo 1973).

That issue was raised in *Columbus v O'Hara*.[55] The court was on the right track when it focused on the quality of the waiver of a twelve-year-old who unexpectedly faces the coercive influence of two police officers requesting admittance but veered off when it said that it was questionable whether a child's invitation when facing such a situation could be a waiver "even assuming the twelve-year-old son had the capacity to waive his mother's rights."[56] The implications of a child admitting police to his home so they could search for evidence to be used against his mother made the court take a wrong direction and discuss waiver of the mother's rights. That is not the issue. The question is whether the child had sufficient authority to invite police to enter his home.

One approach would be to suggest that a child has no authority to permit people into his own home but that probably does not stand up to analysis in light of the fact that children are frequently home alone at all hours of the day and exercise dominion over their homes, which they share with their parents. Alternatively, one could suggest that a twelve-year-old cannot validly waive his constitutional rights without a parent present, but that is a broad proposition that courts are not likely to accept. A third approach would be to say that children do not have authority to admit strangers into their own homes except in an emergency and that a police request to search does not qualify as an emergency.

The inquiry should focus on whether the consenting party has authority to admit police and consent to a search and the rational limits of that authority. Even in a common abode, individuals sharing the premises may hold an expectation of privacy against the other persons in the home, which may not be invaded. Attention, then, must focus on the extent to which parties share common authority over premises, as well as over parts of premises. Where two people share an apartment or a house and each has his own bedroom, the common authority would be confined to those areas that they share. One could not, presumably, grant police authority to search the other's bedroom. However, not all courts subscribe to this analysis. For example, the United States Court of Appeals for the Sixth Circuit has upheld a search of a defendant's bedroom based on the consent of a roommate who did not share the bedroom.[57] The court stressed the defendant's failure to impair the roommate's access to the room through a lock or other obstruction. Such a demand, however, is unrealistic and does not embrace an understanding of how many people live. People who share a house may maintain privacy within parts of that house and exclude the roommates from that part of the house without erecting physical barriers or using locks.

The Tenth District Court of Appeals reached a different conclusion, holding that "ordinarily one co-tenant's separate personal bedroom is not

---

[55]Columbus v O'Hara, No. 85AP-1036, 1986 WL 9530 (10th Dist Ct App, Franklin, 8-28-86).

[56]Columbus v O'Hara, No. 85AP-1036, at 4, 1986 WL 9530 (10th Dist Ct App, Franklin, 8-28-86).

[57]United States v Reeves, 594 F(2d) 536 (6th Cir Ohio 1979), cert denied 442 US 946, 99 SCt 2893, 61 LEd(2d) 317 (1979).

deemed to be in the joint possession of other co-tenants in a home shared by unrelated persons."[58] The Ohio Supreme Court has recognized that persons may maintain a zone of privacy within a shared home even from a spouse. The Court said, "The scope of spousal consent should be limited to a search of areas of the abode under common control, as distinguished from a search directed toward the personal effects of the absent spouse."[59]

In *State v Masten*,[60] police were investigating a complaint that the defendant had sexually abused his daughter with whom he lived along with his wife. The wife was the sole owner of the shared home, and she consented to a search of the house. Police wanted access to the defendant's file cabinet, which was in a den used by all three family members. The wife granted police permission to forcibly open the file cabinet, although she also advised the police that the cabinet was her husband's and that he had the only key. The appellate court reversed the denial of the motion to suppress, holding that the wife did not exercise mutual use or joint control over the file cabinet in view of the defendant's exclusive use and control of the cabinet. Even without locks, married persons may accord to each other areas within their shared home in which each maintains an exclusive privacy interest, which includes the right to exclude the other.

A different result was found in *State v Mignano*,[61] where the consenting party had allowed a friend to store a car in his garage and even to put a lock on the garage door, and where the consenter had no key to the lock. Nonetheless, the appellate court found the consenting party to have retained the right of access to the garage and thus have the authority to consent to its search because he permitted the lock to be installed on the condition that the consenter be allowed to enter the garage at any time.

A different issue arises when a third person holds out to police that he has authority to consent when in fact he either never did or no longer has such authority. The problem arose in *Illinois v Rodriguez*,[62] where police officers gained entry to the defendant's apartment with the help of a woman who claimed to share the apartment with the defendant. She unlocked the door with her key and gave the officers permission to enter. In fact, she had moved out a month earlier and no longer shared common authority over the premises. The Supreme Court held that the warrantless entry is valid, as it was here, when based on the consent of a third party who police erroneously, but reasonably, believe possesses common authority over the premises. The Court said that an objective standard must be used when testing whether facts available at the moment would warrant a reasonably cautious

---

[58]Columbus v Copp, 64 App(3d) 493, 581 NE(2d) 1177 (Franklin 1990); State v Williams, 101 App(3d) 340, 655 NE(2d) 764 (Summit 1995) (related third person could not grant permission to search defendant's bedroom where there was no evidence that such person had access to or used the room).

[59]State v McCarthy, 26 OS(2d) 87, 91, 269 NE(2d) 424 (1971).

[60]State v Masten, No. 5-88-7, 1989 WL 111983 (3d Dist Ct App, Hancock, 9-29-89).

[61]State v Mignano, No. 14223, 1990 WL 18129 (9th Dist Ct App, Summit, 2-28-90).

[62]Illinois v Rodriguez, 497 US 177, 110 SCt 2793, 111 LEd(2d) 148 (1990).

person's believing that the consenting party had authority.[63] In the event that a third person gives consent to enter but where police do not know who gave the consent and under what authority, a court has held that police may only enter and do no more than stand inside the door until additional information about the person giving consent is ascertained.[64]

In *State v Penn*,[65] the Ohio Supreme Court found that police reliance on a pharmacist's authority to consent to a search of a pharmacy was misplaced because the pharmacist was no longer employed at the pharmacy. His actual authority to consent terminated on the date he quit. Moreover, the state could not rely on the pharmacist's apparent authority because he had provided notice to the pharmacy board and the town police that he had quit his employment.

---

[63]See also State v Stoken, No. C-870013, 1987 WL 28162 (1st Dist Ct App, Hamilton, 12-9-87) (police reasonably relied on third person's claim of authority to consent based on assertions in her domestic violence complaint, her possession of a key to the premises, her right to personal clothing in the premises, the arrangement for a visit to recover those items, and her claim that she paid part of the rent); see also State v Paul, 87 App(3d) 309, 622 NE(2d) 349 (Medina 1993) (police could reasonably rely upon a third person's assertion of ownership of a vehicle and consent to search that vehicle when none of other four occupants objected to the search). But see State v Williams, 101 App(3d) 340, 655 NE(2d) 764 (Summit 1995) (officers relying upon erroneous mistake of law rather than a mistake of fact could not reasonably rely upon third person's consent over objection of present defendant; Akron v Harris, 93 App(3d) 378, 638 NE(2d) 633 (Summit 1994) (warrantless entry of house upheld even though officer knew that consenting party did not have authority to do so; court said that consent of a third party to enter should not be held to same standard as consent to search. Editor's note: no basis for this distinction in *Illinois v Rodriguez*).

[64]State v Chapman, 97 App(3d) 687, 647 NE(2d) 504 (Hamilton 1994) (police improperly moved to back of house after obtaining permission to enter from an unknown person).

[65]State v Penn, 61 OS(3d) 720, 576 NE(2d) 790 (1991).

Chapter 18

Motion to Suppress and the Suppression Hearing

18.01   Litigating the suppression motion

All too often lawyers on both sides of a suppression hearing argue the matter entirely on the basis of legal issues. Equally important, however, is forcing the trial judge to decide what actually happened. A prosecuting attorney arguing a *Terry*[1] frisk must persuade the court that the police officer was actually concerned for his or her safety. At the very least, the officer should testify as to that concern and the factual circumstances supporting that concern. Conversely, a defense attorney arguing against a frisk where a "hard object" turned out to be a plastic baggy of vegetable matter should recreate the street scene. The issue should not be argued in the abstract; the plastic bag should be the actual focus of attention. The trial judge should be forced to face the critical issue: whether a reasonable person feeling the baggy, even through heavy clothing, could possibly believe that it might be a hard or sharp object. Similarly, where the state claims that a defendant voluntarily consented to a search which the defense disputes, the defendant should be a witness and testify about the police conduct that produced the alleged consent and the effect of that conduct upon the defendant.

These are all issues where the facts are as critical as the law, and where the judge cannot make an accurate and fair determination unless both attorneys attempt to recreate the scene and force the judge to consider the credibility of the witnesses. Where the motion is to suppress tangible evidence of guilt, police witnesses have a leg up on credibility. But that advantage can disappear if the judge is forced to confront the facts as they existed at the time of the confrontation or search. The issue comes down to credibility, but these issues cannot be properly litigated unless fully developed at the hearing. When lawyers do not confront the hearing judge with the facts and force a determination, the deciding judge may well attempt to finesse this issue in favor of the law enforcement officers. The credibility of witnesses during a motion to suppress is a matter for the trial court and will not be disturbed by the reviewing court.[2]

---

[1]Terry v Ohio, 392 US 1, 88 SCt 1868, 20 LEd(2d) 889 (1968).
[2]State v Fanning, 1 OS(3d) 19, 1 OBR 57, 437 NE(2d) 583 (1982).

18.02   Timely motion

A defendant must initiate inquiry into the admissibility of evidence, a confession, or witness identification through a pretrial motion to suppress.[3] Criminal Rules 12 and 47 should be consulted and closely followed to fulfill the requirements of such motions. The motion is to be filed in the trial court only[4] and is not relevant to the determination of probable cause.[5] It must be filed thirty-five days after arraignment or seven days before trial, whichever is earlier.[6] Failure to file on time may be deemed a waiver of the error.[7] In the interest of justice, a trial court may extend the time for filing a motion to suppress. The decision to extend the time is within the discretion of the trial court.[8] A defendant challenging a trial court's denial of a motion to file late must demonstrate on appeal an abuse of discretion.[9]

The motion must be filed in writing, unless the trial court grants permission for the motion to be filed orally.[10] The motion must give the prosecution notice of specific factual and legal grounds upon which the evidence is challenged.[11] The motion must state with particularity the grounds on which it is made and set forth the relief sought. It must be supported by a memorandum containing citations or authority and may be supported by affidavit.[12]

18.03   Standing to assert Fourth Amendment violations

Suppression of the fruit of a Fourth Amendment violation can be successfully urged only by those whose rights were violated by the search itself. Where the evidence seized was from the person of the defendant, his expectation of privacy is beyond question. Standing is not achieved solely by a person's status as a defendant nor by introduction of damaging evidence.[13] The personal standing requirement applies, as well, to co-conspirators, and the violation of one co-conspirator's Fourth Amendment rights does not confer standing upon another co-conspirator.[14] Consequently,

---

[3]See State v Hamilton, 97 App(3d) 648, 647 NE(2d) 238 (Logan 1994) (trial court erred when it, despite the fact that no motion to suppress was filed, indirectly ruled on the admissibility of a firearm seized in the defendant's vehicle by granting the defendant an acquittal).

[4]State v Clutter, No. 85-CA-5, 1986 WL 9651 (4th Dist Ct App, Washington, 9-4-86).

[5]State v Mitchell, 42 OS(2d) 447, 329 NE(2d) 682 (1975).

[6]Crim R 12(C).

[7]State v Wade, 53 OS(2d) 182, 373 NE(2d) 1244 (1978), vacated in part by 438 US 911, 98 SCt 3138, 57 LEd(2d) 1157 (1978), vacated on death penalty issue by 438 US 911, 98 SCt 3138, 57 LEd(2d) 1157 (1978).

[8]State v Woods, Nos. 3815, 3816, 1985 WL 10760 (9th Dist Ct App, Lorain, 5-15-85); Akron v Milewski, 21 App(3d) 140, 21 OBR 149, 487 NE(2d) 582 (Summit 1985).

[9]State v Kranz, No. C-800486, 1981 WL 9837 (1st Dist Ct App, Hamilton, 6-10-81).

[10]Crim R 47.

[11]Xenia v Wallace, 37 OS(3d) 216, 524 NE(2d) 889 (1988).

[12]State v Forbes, 61 App(3d) 813, 573 NE(2d) 1187 (Coshocton 1991).

[13]Alderman v United States, 394 US 165, 89 SCt 961, 22 LEd(2d) 176 (1969).

[14]United States v Padilla, 508 US 77, 113 SCt 1936, 123 LEd2d 635 (1993).

before a court may review the reasonableness of police behavior, the defendant must be able to demonstrate that his Fourth Amendment right to privacy was violated. A defendant has the burden of proving standing.[15] A defendant was denied standing to object to a search of his grandmother's house in *State v Coleman*,[16] but two persons sharing a motel room and the rental payment for that room had standing to challenge a search of the room.[17]

A dangerous by-product of the personal standing requirement is that police may ignore the Fourth Amendment's commands when attempting to gain evidence against a person who is not the subject of the search. One approach to this issue would be to eliminate the individual standing requirement; a defendant could litigate the validity of a search without proving violation of his personal right.[18] The theory behind this disfavored approach is that if the exclusionary rule solely exists to deter illegal police behavior, it can do so most effectively if all Fourth Amendment violations may be raised without concern for standing.

An alternative approach, devised by the United States District Court for the Northern District of Ohio but rejected by the Supreme Court, is to exclude evidence under the court's supervisory power, in the absence of personal standing, when the government's illegal conduct is egregious. The Supreme Court rejected such supervisory power, holding that violation of a defendant's personal Fourth Amendment rights is an absolute prerequisite to challenging the admission of evidence acquired through an illegal search.[19] Consequently, the standing requirement is firmly entrenched, and there is no indication that Ohio will stray from the mainstream and adopt a more stringent standard under the state Constitution.

The traditional standing requirement is that the defendant must show an interest in the premises searched or the property seized.[20] These requirements created problems in possession cases where possession both convicted and conferred standing. For if the defendant testified that he owned or possessed the item seized, in an effort to establish standing, that admission was used against him at trial. Moreover, requiring the defendant to prove standing in possession prosecutions allowed the government to maintain contradictory positions, subjecting the defendant to the penalties meted out to one in lawless possession while refusing him the remedies designed

---

[15]State v Spencer, No. 11740, 1990 WL 68957 (2d Dist Ct App, Montgomery, 5-18-90).

[16]State v Coleman, 45 OS(3d) 298, 544 NE(2d) 622 (1989), cert denied 493 US 1051, 110 SCt 855, 107 LEd(2d) 849 (1990), affirmed by 70 OS(3d) 1407, 637 NE(2d) 5 (1994).

[17]State v Jones, Nos. 57890, 57891, 1991 WL 8589 (8th Dist Ct App, Cuyahoga, 1-31-91).

[18]See People v Martin, 45 Cal(2d) 755, 290 P(2d) 855 (1955), superseded by constitutional amendment as stated in People v Daan, 161 CalApp(3d) 22, 207 Cal Rptr 228 (1984).

[19]United States v Payner, 447 US 727, 100 SCt 2439, 65 LEd(2d) 468 (1980).

[20]Jones v United States, 362 US 257, 80 SCt 725, 4 LEd(2d) 697 (1960), overruled by United States v Salvucci, 448 US 83, 100 SCt 2547, 65 LEd(2d) 619 (1980).

for one in that situation. The Supreme Court, in *Jones v United States*,[21] alleviated these problems by creating two situations in which standing to assert Fourth Amendment violations was automatic and need not be proven. Automatic standing applied to any person charged with an offense in which possession is an essential element. Secondly, the Court held that any person legitimately on the premises where a search takes place could challenge the lawfulness of the search.

The Court later made the automatic standing for possession offenses somewhat superfluous when it held, in *Simmons v United States*,[22] that testimony given by a defendant to establish standing to object to illegally seized evidence could not thereafter be used against him on the issue of guilt. But the *Simmons* protection has been eroded by analogous cases where confessions inadmissible in the prosecution's case in chief because of *Miranda* violations may be used to impeach a defendant's testimony on cross-examination.[23] Secondly, the *Simmons* Court limited its rule to precluding use of the defendant's suppression hearing testimony "on the issue of guilt," rather than precluding its use at all. The Court has permitted illegally obtained evidence to be used to impeach a defendant's testimony, but that involved a collateral matter.[24] Additionally, the Court has shown itself sensitive to not permitting the *Simmons* shield to be converted into a license to commit perjury.[25] Despite the uncertainty of the breadth of the *Simmons* prophylaxis, what likely doomed automatic standing was the shift in the Fourth Amendment emphasis from protection of property interests to privacy. At that point, the prosecution would no longer be arguing contradictory positions when it asserted that a defendant possessed contraband but was not the victim of a Fourth Amendment violation.

In a series of majority opinions authored by Justice Rehnquist, beginning in 1978 and concluding in 1980, the Supreme Court eliminated automatic standing. The first prong of the *Jones* rule to fall was that anyone lawfully present at the time of a search could raise Fourth Amendment violations. In *Rakas v Illinois*,[26] defendants were passengers in an automobile that had been lawfully stopped on reasonable suspicion but unlawfully searched. The search uncovered a sawed-off rifle under the passenger seat and a box of rifle shells in the locked glove compartment, which helped to link the defendants to the robbery that police were investigating. The defendants never asserted a property interest in the evidence but claimed standing because of their lawful presence as passengers in the vehicle. The Illinois

---

[21]Jones v United States, 362 US 257, 80 SCt 725, 4 LEd(2d) 697 (1960), overruled by United States v Salvucci, 448 US 83, 100 SCt 2547, 65 LEd(2d) 619 (1980).

[22]Simmons v United States, 390 US 377, 88 SCt 967, 19 LEd(2d) 1247 (1968).

[23]See Oregon v Hass, 420 US 714, 95 SCt 1215, 43 LEd(2d) 570 (1975); Harris v New York, 401 US 222, 91 SCt 643, 28 LEd(2d) 1 (1971).

[24]Walder v United States, 347 US 62, 74 SCt 354, 98 LEd 503 (1954).

[25]See United States v Kahan, 415 US 239, 94 SCt 1179, 39 LEd(2d) 297 (1974); see also People v Sturgis, 58 Ill(2d) 211, 317 NE(2d) 545 (1974) (testimony given to establish standing may be used for impeachment purposes if the defendant testifies at trial, finding no valid distinction between Fourth Amendment and *Miranda* violations), cert denied 420 US 936, 95 SCt 1144, 43 LEd(2d) 412 (1975).

[26]Rakas v Illinois, 439 US 128, 99 SCt 421, 58 LEd(2d) 387 (1978).

courts disallowed the claim of standing on the ground that the defendants had neither a privacy nor possessory interest in the vehicle. The issue dealt with in the Supreme Court was whether the *Jones* test conferring standing on one who is "lawfully on the premises" applies to automobiles.

Justice Rehnquist said that standing requires that the defendant suffer an injury in fact and that the claimed injury result from an invasion of a personal right, rather than an invasion suffered by another. Beyond those two considerations, the final determination of standing should rest on the application of substantive Fourth Amendment law rather than on the technical questions of standing. That inquiry, then, requires a determination of whether the disputed search and seizure has infringed on an interest of the defendant, which the Fourth Amendment was designed to protect. Following the Fourth Amendment analysis, Justice Rehnquist contended that the phrase "lawfully on the premises" creates too broad a gauge for measurement of Fourth Amendment rights. He stated that applicability of the protection to a casual visitor to a house does not advance legitimate Fourth Amendment protections. Such a visitor would have no legitimate expectation of privacy, beyond his person, in the invaded place.

The *Rakas* Court held that because defendants were legitimately present in the vehicle did not give them a legitimate expectation of privacy in the searched vehicle. They had neither a property nor a possessory interest in the automobile, nor did they have a "legitimate expectation of privacy" in the glove compartment or the area under the seat of the car in which they were merely passengers. In defining the *Rakas* defendants' "legitimate expectation of privacy," the Court reintroduced property concepts and acknowledged that privacy interests are often defined by property or possessory rights. But property concepts are not conclusive.

Consequently, the Court acknowledged that the defendant in *Jones*, who had the right to be in the apartment that was searched and who held dominion over the apartment from all but the owner, had standing to challenge the legality of the search even though he lacked any property interest in the apartment. Similarly, one who is in lawful possession of a vehicle, though not the title owner, has a legitimate expectation of privacy in the vehicle and standing to assert a Fourth Amendment claim arising out of the unlawful search of the vehicle.[27] On the other hand, as property rights alone will not create standing, an owner of the vehicle who is absent may not have a legitimate expectation of privacy in the car he had loaned out to raise Fourth Amendment violations.

The *Rakas* test properly may be viewed as significantly curtailing the scope of the coverage of the Amendment's protection. A passenger in a vehicle, however, may still be able to establish standing to challenge the admissibility of evidence, but that standing must be based on violation of the passenger's own protected privacy interest. A passenger in a car has

---

[27]State v Carter, 69 OS(3d) 57, 630 NE(2d) 355 (1994) (non-owner driver who demonstrates he has owner's permission to use vehicle has standing to challenge vehicle's search); State v Hines, 92 App(3d) 163, 634 NE(2d) 654 (Franklin 1993), appeal dismissed by 68 OS(3d) 1449, 626 NE(2d) 690 (1994).

standing to challenge the legality of the stop of a car, since that involves a seizure of everyone in the vehicle.[28] Thus, if the passenger is illegally arrested, he will have standing to move to suppress evidence found as a fruit of the unconstitutional arrest.[29]

Rakas was applied in *State v Jones*[30] and *State v Stoddard*,[31] where two co-defendants were riding in a car with a third person who was driving when the car was stopped for speeding. The Third District Court of Appeals denied both defendants standing to challenge the search of the rental vehicle even though one defendant had provided part of the rental fee and the other either paid part or offered to pay part and had the sole key to the trunk of the car in his pocket. Generally, an area must be sufficiently under a defendant's control to successfully assert standing.[32]

The other prong of the *Jones* rule, conferring standing on one charged with a possessory offense, fell in *United States v Salvucci*.[33] Justice Rehnquist, again for the majority, held that automatic standing for persons charged with possessory offenses was premised solely upon the dilemma that would befall a defendant who, charged with a possessory offense, might only be able to establish standing to challenge a search by giving self-incriminating testimony admissible as evidence of guilt. The dilemma, the majority contended, was overcome by *Simmons*, which barred use of a defendant's suppression hearing testimony as evidence of his guilt. The majority refused to consider the fact that the defendant's testimony might be used to impeach the defendant if he takes the witness stand at trial. Further, the Court said that the shift of the Fourth Amendment inquiry from property rights to privacy interests eliminated the second reason for the *Jones* rule in possessory offenses. Since under *Rakas* and *Salvucci* a defendant must have a possessory interest in the items seized *and* also an expectation of privacy in the area searched, for the government to charge a defendant with a possessory crime but assert that he lacks standing to challenge the legality of the search is not contradictory.

An illustration of how the new standing rule works is found in a companion case to *Salvucci* decided the same day. In *Rawlings v Kentucky*,[34] Justice

---

[28]State v Carter, 69 OS(3d) 57, 63, 630 NE(2d) 355 (1994).

[29]State v Carter, 28 App(3d) 61, 28 OBR 101, 501 NE(2d) 1219 (Warren 1985); see also, State v Goodlow, 84 App(3d) 529, 617 NE(2d) 720 (Cuyahoga 1992), appeal dismissed by 66 OS(3d) 1473, 611 NE(2d) 835 (1993) (where car passengers are asked to exit automobile based solely upon fumbling gestures of a back seat passenger, the passengers have been illegally seized and have standing to challenge the subsequent search of the vehicle).

[30]State v Jones, No. 9-89-31, 1990 WL 72394 (3d Dist Ct App, Marion, 5-25-90).

[31]State v Stoddard, No. 9-89-5, 1990 WL 72397 (3d Dist Ct App, Marion, 5-25-90).

[32]State v Sinks, No. 11428, 1990 WL 80582 (2d Dist Ct App, Montgomery, 6-13-90).

[33]United States v Salvucci, 448 US 83, 100 SCt 2547, 65 LEd(2d) 619 (1980).

[34]Rawlings v Kentucky, 448 US 98, 100 SCt 2556, 65 LEd(2d) 633 (1980); see also State v Day, 72 App(3d) 82, 593 NE(2d) 456 (Ross 1991) (defendant has no proprietary or possessory interest in his wife's vehicle, which he abandoned in a public parking lot during a prison escape, and has no standing to challenge inventory search of the vehicle).

Rehnquist held that a defendant had no standing to challenge the legality of the search that uncovered the defendant's drugs, which he had placed in his companion's purse. The Court concluded that while the defendant acknowledged a possessory interest in the drugs, he had no legitimate expectation of privacy in the purse because he could not exclude all others from the purse. However, two Ohio courts considering converse situations where defendants had possessory interests in the places searched but disclaimed ownership of the items seized found, nonetheless, that the defendants had a legitimate expectation of privacy to challenge the legality of the search.[35] Perhaps the key in both cases was that the search was of the defendants' homes.

Clearly the *Rakas-Salvucci-Rawlings* trilogy enabled Justice Rehnquist to erect additional obstacles to block a defendant in a criminal case from litigating Fourth Amendment issues. Rather than create a framework of analytical rules to test subjective and community expectations of privacy, the tests are often counterintuitive and contrary to community expectations. For example, in *Rawlings*, the future Chief Justice relied on the defendant's "casual" relationship with the woman in whose purse he stored his "stash," his powerlessness to exclude her friend from storing her hairbrush in the purse, and the defendant's testimony at the suppression hearing that once the police arrived he expected the purse to be searched as evidence of a lack of expectation of privacy. All of these factors are disingenuous, but the last is outrageous. Because an individual expects police to act illegally should not be turned around and used to bar that person from challenging that behavior.

A rare instance of rationality in this area was demonstrated in *Minnesota v Olson*,[36] where the United States Supreme Court held that an overnight guest in a home has standing to challenge the illegality of a search of that home even though the owner or leaseholder is present. The approach, rather than the result, provides the glimmer of rationality. The Court applied the privacy analysis to determine standing and made it clear that a place need not be a defendant's home in order for there to be a legitimate expectation of privacy. *Olson* is unique because it is a rare instance of the Supreme Court's applying a privacy analysis by relying on the privacy expectations of the general community, based on longstanding social custom. It is

---

[35]State v Masten, No. 5-88-7, 1989 WL 111983 (3d Dist Ct App, Hancock, 9-29-89) (defendant had standing to challenge search even though he disclaimed ownership of locked file cabinet in his home); State v Clark, Nos. C-900245, C-900246, 1991 WL 155213 (1st Dist Ct App, Hamilton, 8-14-91) (defendant who denied ownership of contraband found in her apartment does not lack standing to challenge initial intrusion into her apartment).

[36]Minnesota v Olson, 495 US 91, 110 SCt 1684, 109 LEd(2d) 85 (1990). But see State v Davis, 80 App(3d) 277, 609 NE(2d) 174 (Cuyahoga 1992), appeal dismissed by 65 OS(3d) 1462, 602 NE(2d) 1171 (1992) (defendant has no standing to challenge search of his girlfriend's apartment, even though he has spent the night in the past, where he failed to produce evidence that he was going to stay the night of arrest and had not spent a night in the dwelling over the previous week); State v Day, 72 App(3d) 82, 593 NE(2d) 456 (Ross 1991) (defendant's marital status did not provide him with same possessory and privacy interest in his wife's car which was determined to be her separate property).

a common sense approach to determining the parameters of protected privacy that is not commonly found when the Supreme Court addresses this subject. Chief Justice Rehnquist dissented in *Olson* but did not explain his dissent.

CROSS REFERENCES

Text 1.04, Ch 2

18.04   Burden of proof

(A) In general

Which party must bear the burden of proving the legality or illegality of a search or seizure depends on whether the intrusion was supported by a warrant. Allocation of the burden of proof in Ohio on this issue follows the practice adopted in federal courts and by a majority of the states. If the search was undertaken with a warrant, the burden of proof falls upon the defense. If the evidence is the fruit of a warrantless search, the prosecution must bear the burden of proof.

(B) Where there is a warrant

There is a presumption of regularity when an arrest or a search is authorized by a warrant. A judicial officer has conducted a prior review of the facts and circumstances supporting the request for the warrant and has decided that probable cause exists to justify the intrusion. Generally, any defect in the warrant process or the execution will be readily provable from the affidavits, warrant, and return of the execution on file with the court and is accessible to the defendant. Consequently, the burden of establishing any factual matter proving a defect or error in form falls on the defendant who seeks to exclude the evidence. The defendant must raise any defects in the warrant at the trial court and may not raise those issues for the first time on appeal.[37] Whether probable cause existed to issue the warrant will be ascertainable within the four corners of the supporting affidavits and record of oral testimony taken in support of the request for a warrant. The reviewing court determines whether there was sufficient information presented to the magistrate to justify a finding of probable cause and issuance of a warrant. The reviewing court may not augment the written affidavit with testimony unless such testimony was taken by the magistrate prior to the issuance of the warrant, transcribed and made part of the affidavit.[38]

A defendant is not absolutely entitled to an evidentiary hearing on a motion to suppress evidence secured following a search with a warrant. Where the defendant does not allege falsity in the statements contained in the affidavit, an evidentiary hearing is not required where the trial court finds a search warrant valid on its face.[39]

---

[37]State v Antrican, No. 8976, 1986 WL 3190 (2d Dist Ct App, Montgomery, 3-12-86).

[38]State v Gerace, No. 12177, 1986 WL 2478 (9th Dist Ct App, Summit, 2-19-86).

[39]State v Brewer, No. 84AP-852, 1986 WL 2652 (10th Dist Ct App, Franklin, 2-25-86).

Sometimes in the warrant process the defense will have to establish facts that are not provable from the papers on file in the court, such as when the defense contends that probable cause was established on the basis of perjured statements contained in the affidavits or supplemental testimony. Normally, the issue for review on a suppression motion following a search authorized by warrant is whether the affidavit is sufficient on its face to establish probable cause and justify issuance of the warrant. In *Franks v Delaware*,[40] the Supreme Court held that the Fourth Amendment requires a hearing on a motion to suppress where the defendant makes a substantial preliminary showing that a false statement knowingly and intentionally, or with reckless disregard for the truth, was included by the affiant in the warrant affidavit. At the hearing, the defense must establish by a preponderance of the evidence the allegation of perjury or reckless disregard. Once the falseness of the statement is established, as well as the affiant's requisite mental state, the false material contained in the affidavit must be excised, and the affidavit's remaining content must be scrutinized to determine whether there are sufficient facts and circumstances remaining to establish probable cause. If the remaining content is insufficient to establish probable cause, the search warrant must be voided, just as if probable cause was lacking on the face of the affidavit.

(C) Where there is no warrant

Searches conducted outside the judicial process, without a warrant, are per se unreasonable, subject to a few specifically established and well-delineated exceptions.[41] The burden is on those seeking an exemption from the constitutional process to show the need for it.[42] Statements in *Katz v United States*,[43] *Chimel v California*,[44] and other Supreme Court decisions clearly imply that, where a search is conducted without a warrant, the prosecution bears the burden of proving the facts that justify the search under one of the recognized exceptions. The Supreme Court has held that where a search rests upon consent, the prosecution has the burden of proving that the consent was freely and voluntarily given.[45] Except for consent searches, the Supreme Court has not ruled definitively on the issue of burden of proof in other warrantless search categories. The Ohio Supreme Court has held that the state bears the burden of showing that an officer's warrantless search falls within an exception to the Fourth Amendment warrant requirement.[46] Where there is no warrant, the state is not entitled to the presumption of regularity. Although the Ohio Supreme Court clearly indicated that the prosecution has the burden of proving the legality of a warrantless search, some courts in Ohio distinguished between

---

[40]Franks v Delaware, 438 US 154, 98 SCt 2674, 57 LEd(2d) 667 (1978).
[41]Katz v United States, 389 US 347, 88 SCt 507, 19 LEd(2d) 576 (1967).
[42]Chimel v California, 395 US 752, 89 SCt 2034, 23 LEd(2d) 685 (1969).
[43]Katz v United States, 389 US 347, 88 SCt 507, 19 LEd(2d) 576 (1967).
[44]Chimel v California, 395 US 752, 89 SCt 2034, 23 LEd(2d) 685 (1969).
[45]Bumper v North Carolina, 391 US 543, 88 SCt 1788, 20 LEd(2d) 797 (1968), affirmed by 275 NC 670, 170 SE(2d) 457 (1969); see also State v Nicholl, 9 OO(3d) 285 (App, Cuyahoga 1978); State v Sperry, 47 Misc 1, 351 NE(2d) 807 (CP, Montgomery 1974).
[46]Athens v Wolf, 38 OS(2d) 237, 313 NE(2d) 405 (1974).

the burden of going forward and the burden of persuasion[47] while others held that the state must bear both burdens.[48]

The Ohio Supreme Court, in *Xenia v Wallace*,[49] ended the division among the district courts of appeal. First, the Court in *Wallace* established the obligations of the defendant when challenging a warrantless search. The defendant must (1) establish that a warrantless search took place, and (2) notify the court and prosecution of the factual or legal grounds on which the challenge rests, whether it is based on a failure to adhere to statutory requirement or a constitutional defect such as the absence of probable cause or that the search does not fit within one of the established categories of warrantless searches. To later challenge a notice deficiency, the state must assert the deficiency and preserve it for appeal or the deficiency will be waived.[50] Once the defendant has met this initial burden, the "prosecution bears the burden of proof, including the burden of going forward with the evidence."[51]

Surprisingly, *Wallace* did not end the controversy. The minimal notice requirements imposed on the defendant have been transformed in some instances into major hurdles. This result seems contrary to the Ohio Supreme Court's intention to clarify and simplify the issue. The defendant must provide notice of the specific factual and legal grounds upon which the search or seizure is challenged.[52] A challenge to an intoxilyzer was found defective when the motion in limine contended that "the test equipment was defective and/or unapproved by the Ohio Department of Health."[53] It is unclear what more should have been asserted to satisfy the notice requirement. The defendant's initial burden, enunciated in *Wallace*, was not intended to serve as a land mine to insulate the prosecution from its burden of going forward. For example, the Eighth District Court of Appeals said that the defendant must simply clarify the ground of the challenge.[54]

The Ninth District Court of Appeals has held that the defendant's burden is met by moving to suppress the fruits of a warrantless search; at that point the burden shifts to the state.[55] On the other hand, the Eighth District Court of Appeals held that the "defendant must demonstrate a warrantless

---

[47]See, e.g., State v Kalejs, No. C-85-0272 (1st Dist Ct App, Hamilton, 1-1-86); State v Halko, No. C-850656, 1986 WL 7855 (1st Dist Ct App, Hamilton, 7-16-86).

[48]See, e.g., Xenia v Wallace, 37 OS(3d) 216, 524 NE(2d) 889 (1988); State v Gasser, 5 App(3d) 217, 5 OBR 501, 451 NE(2d) 249 (Paulding 1980).

[49]Xenia v Wallace, 37 OS(3d) 216, 524 NE(2d) 889 (1988).

[50]Xenia v Wallace, 37 OS(3d) 216, 524 NE(2d) 889 (1988); see also State v Lautzenheiser, 77 App(3d) 461, 602 NE(2d) 705 (Van Wert 1991).

[51]Xenia v Wallace, 37 OS(3d) 216, 220, 524 NE(2d) 889 (1988).

[52]State v Lautzenheiser, 77 App(3d) 461, 602 NE(2d) 705 (Van Wert 1991).

[53]State v Buurma, No. H-89-41, 1991 WL 3816 (6th Dist Ct App, Huron, 1-18-91).

[54]Cuyahoga Falls v Cutlip, No. 14884, 1991 WL 43145 (9th Dist Ct App, Summit, 3-27-91).

[55]State v Moon, 74 App(3d) 162, 598 NE(2d) 726 (Lorain 1991); Twinsburg v Lochridge, No. 14906, 1991 WL 81653 (9th Dist Ct App, Summit, 5-15-91); State v Miller, No. 14973, 1991 WL 149582 (9th Dist Ct App, Summit, 7-31-91), cert denied 503 US 998, 112 SCt 1705, 118 LEd(2d) 413 (1992).

search lacking probable cause,"[56] while the Second District Court of Appeals said that all the defendant must do is raise the grounds for the claim of illegality.[57] The First District Court of Appeals cautioned that the requirement that the defendant must affirmatively establish that the search was without a warrant should not "be given a hypertechnical construction."[58] Rather, the court said that the defendant can establish the absence of a warrant (1) by stipulation, (2) through examination or cross-examination, or (3) by inference from the evidence as a whole. Nonetheless, that court also pointed out that, if there is no evidence in the record that the search was without a warrant, the defendant will have failed to properly raise the issue.[59]

In 1994, the Supreme Court reinforced the position it had advanced in *Wallace*. In *State v Shindler*,[60] the Court said that a defendant satisfies the requirement of providing adequate notice by alleging the absence of lawful cause to stop and detain a suspect, or of probable cause to arrest without a warrant. The Court concluded that the defendant's challenges phrased in that manner "set forth a sufficient factual and legal basis ... to warrant a hearing, and gave the prosecutor and court sufficient notice of the basis of her challenge."[61] The particularity standard is satisfied when the prosecutor and court are placed on notice *"of the issues to be decided."*[62]

(D) Standard of proof

Criminal Rule 12(E) requires the trial court to rule on a motion to suppress prior to trial. This requirement serves two valid purposes. The first is to ensure that the jury is not exposed to evidence that is constitutionally inadmissible.[63] Further, an early ruling on a motion to suppress enables the two sides to make a rational choice whether to proceed to trial.

The party bearing the burden must prove by a preponderance of the evidence the legality or illegality of the search.[64] The United States Supreme Court has held that the preponderance standard does not violate due process. The Court distinguished admissibility issues from determinations of guilt, which require proof beyond a reasonable doubt where the higher standard is necessary to ensure against unjust convictions.[65] The

---

[56]State v Long, No. 58793, 1991 WL 118060 (8th Dist Ct App, Cuyahoga, 6-20-91), appeal dismissed by 62 OS(3d) 1445, 579 NE(2d) 490 (1991).

[57]State v Dupree, No. 11907, 1991 WL 60651 (2d Dist Ct App, Montgomery, 4-9-91).

[58]State v Petrosky, Nos. C-900264, C-900265, 1991 WL 40550 (1st Dist Ct App, Hamilton, 3-27-91), appeal dismissed by 61 OS(3d) 1428, 575 NE(2d) 216 (1991); State v Rodriguez, 66 App(3d) 5, 583 NE(2d) 384 (Wood 1990) (where record shows that police entered residence at 7 p.m. and warrant was not issued until 7:45 p.m., record established warrantless search and burden of production shifted to the prosecution).

[59]Cincinnati v Moore, Nos. C-880689 et al., 1989 WL 136387 (1st Dist Ct App, Hamilton, 11-15-89).

[60]State v Shindler, 70 OS(3d) 54, 636 NE(2d) 319 (1994).

[61]State v Shindler, 70 OS(3d) 54, 58, 636 NE(2d) 319 (1994).

[62]State v Shindler, 70 OS(3d) 54, 58, 636 NE(2d) 319 (1994) (emphasis added).

[63]Jackson v Denno, 378 US 368, 84 SCt 1774, 12 LEd(2d) 908 (1964).

[64]Athens v Wolf, 38 OS(2d) 237, 313 NE(2d) 405 (1974).

[65]Lego v Twomey, 404 US 477, 96 SCt 619, 30 LEd(2d) 618 (1972).

same standard of proof, preponderance of the evidence, applies to proving the voluntariness of a confession,[66] compliance with *Miranda* requirements,[67] and exceptions to the derivative evidence rule (independent source,[68] attenuation,[69] and inevitable discovery[70]). However, when attempting to prove that a constitutional error was harmless, the prosecution must establish that fact by a reasonable doubt.[71]

18.05   Rulings on motions to suppress

A pretrial motion to suppress must be determined before trial.[72] This requirement is consistent with the policy of requiring issues whose determination may preclude the need for a trial being decided prior to the commencement of trial. If a motion to suppress is granted, the state may decide not to pursue the prosecution because of the absence of other admissible evidence or, in the alternative, may decide to appeal from the decision. Conversely, if the motion is denied, the defendant may elect to plead guilty or no contest. The requirement serves the policy of economy of resources.

Criminal Rule 12(E) also requires a trial judge to state findings on the record where factual issues are involved in the determination of a motion.[73] A defendant must request findings of fact, or the right to such findings will be deemed waived.[74] Following a request, the failure to make findings is reversible error and will result in a remand directing the judge to enter the factual determinations that led to the decision on the motion.[75] Without these findings the appellate court cannot review the propriety of the trial court's decision on the motion. Because it is the findings of the trial court which may be reviewed by the appellate court; it is not the appellate court's job to reevaluate the evidence or witness credibility.[76] However, where the trial court makes no findings, the record may reflect "implicit findings."[77]

---

[66]Lego v Twomey, 404 US 477, 96 SCt 619, 30 LEd(2d) 618 (1972).

[67]Colorado v Connelly, 479 US 157, 107 SCt 515, 93 LEd(2d) 473 (1986).

[68]Murray v United States, 487 US 533, 108 SCt 2529, 101 LEd(2d) 472 (1988).

[69]Cf. Wong Sun v United States, 371 US 471, 83 SCt 407, 9 LEd(2d) 441 (1963); Brown v Illinois, 422 US 590, 95 SCt 2254, 45 LEd(2d) 416 (1975).

[70]Nix v Williams, 467 US 431, 104 SCt 2501, 81 LEd(2d) 377 (1984), cert denied 471 US 1138, 105 SCt 2681, 86 LEd(2d) 699 (1985).

[71]Chapman v California, 386 US 18, 87 SCt 824, 17 LEd(2d) 705 (1967); see also State v Brown, 65 OS(3d) 483, 605 NE(2d) 46 (1992) (state proved that evidence which may have been erroneously admitted was harmless beyond a reasonable doubt because of "overwhelming evidence of guilt" flowing from other evidence).

[72]Crim R 12(E).

[73]State v Clay, No. 12540, 1991 WL 116643 (2d Dist Ct App, Montgomery, 6-28-91).

[74]Upper Sandusky v Saylor, No. 16-86-6, 1987 WL 12097 (3d Dist Ct App, Wyandot, 6-1-87).

[75]State v Almalik, 31 App(3d) 33, 31 OBR 48, 507 NE(2d) 1168 (Cuyahoga 1986).

[76]City of Toledo v Harris, 99 App(3d) 469, 651 NE(2d) 24 (Lucas 1995).

[77]State v Dupree, No. 11907, 1991 WL 60651 (2d Dist Ct App, Montgomery, 4-9-91).

18.06   Appeals from rulings on motions to suppress

(A) By the state

Criminal Rule 12(J) authorizes the state to appeal from an adverse ruling on a motion to suppress. The provision is an exception to the general rule prohibiting appeals by the state in criminal prosecutions and is to be strictly construed.[78] The purpose of allowing the state to appeal from an interlocutory order is the likelihood that the exclusion of evidence will result in the termination of the prosecution. If the state proceeds to trial without the evidence and the defendant is acquitted, the double jeopardy prohibition of the federal and state constitutions precludes the state from appealing from the acquittal. Further, where the trial court sustains a part of the defendant's motion to suppress and the state fails to appeal that ruling, the state is precluded from contesting that portion of the suppression ruling unfavorable to it in an appeal instituted by the defendant following his conviction on evidence that was not suppressed.[79]

The rule provides for the prosecuting attorney, within seven days of the entry of the order granting the motion to suppress, to file a notice of appeal and certification that the appeal is not for delay purposes and that the granting of the motion has rendered the state's proof on the charge so weak as to destroy the reasonable possibility of effective prosecution. The provision of Criminal Rule 12(J), stating that the appeal may be taken as a matter of right, was struck down as invalid under the state Constitution. The appeal may be taken only upon leave of the appellate court.[80]

While the appeal is pending, the trial court loses jurisdiction and may not dispose of the case.[81] Except in capital cases, a defendant who has not been freed on bail must be released on his own recognizance at the time the prosecuting attorney files the notice of appeal and certification.[82] An appeal taken under the rule is to be diligently prosecuted and takes precedence over all other appeals.[83]

(B) By the defendant

The defendant is not permitted to appeal prior to trial from an adverse ruling on a motion to suppress. Unlike the state's claim, which would die following an acquittal, the defendant will have the opportunity to appeal the trial court's adverse ruling on his motion to suppress following conviction. Moreover, Criminal Rule 12(H) specifically provides that a plea of no contest does not preclude a defendant from asserting upon appeal that the trial court prejudicially erred in ruling on a pretrial motion to suppress evidence.[84] This provision eliminates the necessity of a defendant proceed-

---

[78]State v Caltrider, 43 OS(2d) 157, 331 NE(2d) 710 (1975).
[79]State v Felty, 2 App(3d) 62, 2 OBR 69, 440 NE(2d) 803 (Hamilton 1981).
[80]State v Waller, 47 OS(2d) 52, 351 NE(2d) 195 (1976).
[81]State v Watson, 48 App(2d) 110, 355 NE(2d) 883 (Lucas 1975); State v Newell, 68 App(3d) 623, 589 NE(2d) 412 (Lucas 1990) (court erred in dismissing the case without allowing the state seven days to perfect its appeal).
[82]Crim R 12(J).
[83]State v Caltrider, 43 OS(2d) 157, 331 NE(2d) 710 (1975).
[84]Defiance v Kretz, 60 OS(3d) 1, 573 NE(2d) 32 (1991).

ing to trial when the only issue is the manner in which the prosecution secured the evidence it will use to prove the charges. The rule permits the defendant to preserve the issue only following a plea of no contest; it does not extend this right to cover cases where a guilty plea is entered. However, Criminal Rule 11 permits no contest pleas to be entered in both felony and misdemeanor cases, whereas under prior law the no contest plea was limited to misdemeanors.

CROSS REFERENCES

1 Giannelli & Snyder, Baldwin's Ohio Practice, *Evidence* § 104.8 § 104.05(a)

Chapter 19

Interrogation and Confessions

19.01   Introduction

(A) In general

Despite more than five decades of litigation concerning the admissibility of out-of-court statements given by suspects to police during interrogation, the manner in which confessions are secured remains one of the most controversial subjects in American constitutional law. Additionally, despite the heavy regulation of this subject matter, confessions continue to be an important factor in solving crimes and convicting defendants. No member of the United States Supreme Court has ever advocated making inadmissible all out-of-court statements given to police officers by a defendant. Justice Felix Frankfurter wrote, in *Culombe v Connecticut*,[1] that questioning suspects is indispensable to law enforcement. Some crimes will not be solved without confessions. The *Culombe* case is a good example of this proposition, for the only witness to the double murder in that case was an infant.

The necessity for confessions gives rise to certain problems. The Fifth Amendment to the United States Constitution provides in part, "nor shall [any person] be compelled in any criminal case to be a witness against himself." Consequently, the manner in which a confession is obtained must be reconciled with the Fifth Amendment provision as well as the Sixth Amendment provision guaranteeing the assistance of counsel in criminal prosecutions. Rules governing the admissibility of confessions under the Fifth and Sixth Amendments will be covered separately in this chapter because they differ significantly. A confession that may be admissible under the Fifth Amendment may be barred under the Sixth Amendment guarantee of the assistance of counsel, and a confession that is admissible under the Sixth Amendment may be barred under the Fifth. However, regardless of whether that confession is inadmissible because it is involuntary in violation of *Miranda* or in violation of the Sixth Amendment right to counsel, the erroneous introduction into evidence of any inadmissible confession may be harmless error provided the state can meet the difficult task of proving beyond a reasonable doubt that the confession did not contribute to the

---

[1]Culombe v Connecticut, 367 US 568, 8 SCt 1860, 6 LEd(2d) 1037 (1961).

conviction.[2] The applicability of different constitutional rules, depending on the stage of a criminal prosecution, in large measure is responsible for the confusion that presently exists in this area. Those differences, however, go to the very purposes served by the two constitutional provisions.

Miranda remains the principal framework for analysis of confession cases. Notwithstanding a continuing chipping away at both the core and margins of the *Miranda* protections by the Burger and Rehnquist Courts,[3] some of those core principles embodied in *Miranda* remain viable. Since 1987, the Court has even strengthened the impact of a suspect's invocation of the *Miranda* right to counsel in a manner that is surprisingly consistent with the Warren Court's intent.[4] The Burger-Rehnquist Court, though, has and continues to chip away at the *Miranda* protections. The *Miranda* Court, itself, provided the seeds for such action when it stated that the *Miranda* procedures are not constitutionally mandated but an effort by the Court to protect and further the constitutional privilege against self-incrimination. The current Court has seized on that admission and pursued it to its fullest.[5]

(B) Earliest cases

In 1936, the United States Supreme Court for the first time struck down a state conviction because of the manner in which the confession admitted at the defendants' trial had been obtained. The Fifth and Sixth Amendments were not factors in the Court's decision. The guarantees contained in those amendments were not to be applied to the states through the Fourteenth Amendment for two more decades. Instead, the Court reviewed the convictions in *Brown v Mississippi*,[6] under the fundamental fairness doctrine prescribed by the due process clause of the Fourteenth Amendment, which guarantees that no state shall deprive a citizen of life, liberty, or property without due process of law.

In that case, the confessions of the two defendants, the only substantial evidence against them upon which the verdicts of guilty and the imposition of death sentences rested, were the product of extreme brutality. All of the defendants were uneducated blacks living in rural Mississippi. On the night of the murder, one of the defendants was arrested by a deputy sheriff who was accompanied by a group of white men. They took the defendant to the home of the deceased and accused him of the crime. When the defendant denied the murder, they took him and hanged him twice from the limb of a tree and then lowered him and demanded that he confess to the murder. When he persisted in protesting his innocence, the vigilante group tied him to a tree and whipped him. When he continued to protest his innocence, the defendant was released and permitted to return home, which he did with some difficulty because of the pain suffered from his ordeal. A day or two

---

[2]Arizona v Fulminante, 499 US 279, 111 SCt 1246, 113 LEd(2d) 302 (1991).

[3]Illinois v Perkins, 496 US 292, 110 SCt 2394, 110 LEd(2d) 243 (1990), cert denied 114 SCt 2692, 129 LEd(2d) 823 (1994).

[4]Minnick v Mississippi, 498 US 146, 111 SCt 486, 112 LEd(2d) 489 (1990).

[5]See Oregon v Elstad, 470 US 298, 105 SCt 1285, 84 LEd(2d) 222 (1985); New York v Quarles, 467 US 649, 104 SCt 2626, 81 LEd(2d) 550 (1984).

[6]Brown v Mississippi, 297 US 278, 56 SCt 461, 80 LEd 682 (1936).

later the defendant was rearrested at his home and transported to a jail by a roundabout route that took him into an adjoining state where a deputy sheriff severely whipped the defendant and threatened to continue until the defendant confessed to the crime. The deputy sheriff dictated a statement to which the defendant agreed.

The other two defendants fared no better. They were arrested and taken to the jail by the same deputy sheriff accompanied by a group of white men. There the defendants were forced to strip, were laid over chairs, and their backs were cut to pieces with a leather strap with buckles on it. They too were led to believe that the beating would continue until they confessed in the manner and detail demanded by their assailants. They changed and altered their confessions in every detail to conform to the demands of their torturers. The following day a group of law enforcement officers came to the jail to hear the "free and voluntary confessions" of the defendants. Over the objections of the defense, the confessions were admitted into evidence and the defendants were convicted and sentenced to death. The convictions were affirmed by the Mississippi Supreme Court. The US Supreme Court reversed the convictions in *Brown* and set forth its initial concern in the area of confessions.

The Court said that the trial was a sham based on coerced confessions of doubtful reliability. Doubt upon the reliability of a confession was not confined to statements secured through physical torture. In *Lyons v Oklahoma*,[7] a conviction was reversed because of the unreliability of a confession used at trial that had been secured from a defendant who was forced to hold in his lap a pan of bones that police claimed were the remains of the victim whom he was suspected of murdering.

Brown and other cases that turned on the unreliability of confessions were decided during a period when Supreme Court review of state criminal proceedings was limited in nature. The decision was consistent with another string of decisions in which the Court reviewed state convictions where the reliability of the trial was tainted by the likelihood that the jury verdict was not based on reliable evidence of guilt, such as where the prosecution engaged in "a deliberate deception of court and jury by the presentation of testimony known to be perjured,"[8] or where an accused was "hurried to conviction under the pressure of a mob."[9] During this period, the Supreme Court saw a limited role for itself in the review of state convictions. Its vision of due process was to correct wrongs so fundamental that they "made the whole proceeding a mere pretense of a trial and rendered the conviction and sentence wholly void."

A decade later, the Supreme Court clarified its concern and indicated that the unreliability of a confession was by no means the only ground for its inadmissibility. In *Ashcraft v Tennessee*,[10] the Court said that the due process clause of the Fourteenth Amendment stands as a bar against the

---

[7]Lyons v Oklahoma, 322 US 596, 64 SCt 1208, 88 LEd 1481 (1944).

[8]Mooney v Holohan, 294 US 103, 112, 55 SCt 340, 79 LEd 791 (1935).

[9]Moore v Dempsey, 261 US 86, 87, 43 SCt 265, 67 LEd 543 (1923).

[10]Ashcraft v Tennessee, 322 US 143, 64 SCt 921, 88 LEd 1192 (1944).

conviction of any individual in an American court by means of a coerced confession. Rather than inquiring into the reliability of the confession, the Court emphasized the issue of voluntariness. Justice Black wrote:

> Our conclusion is that if Ashcraft made a confession it was not voluntary but compelled. We reach this conclusion from facts which are not in dispute at all. Ashcraft, a citizen of excellent reputation, was taken into custody by police officers. ... For thirty-six hours after Ashcraft's seizure during which period he was held incommunicado, without sleep or rest, relays of officers, experienced investigators, and highly trained lawyers questioned him without respite. From the beginning of the questioning at 7 o'clock on Saturday evening until 6 o'clock on Monday morning Ashcraft denied that he had anything to do with the murder of his wife.[11]

The Court concluded that the situation was "so inherently coercive that its very existence is irreconcilable with the possession of mental freedom by a lone suspect against whom ... [the state's] full coercive force is brought to bear."[12] Thus the Court set out on a path that developed an exclusionary rule for confessions to deter illegal police behavior.

In *Rogers v Richmond,*[13] the Court was explicit that its inquiry into the voluntariness of confessions was for a purpose other than to determine whether the confession secured as a result of coercive police tactics was likely to be untruthful. In *Rogers,* lower courts had rejected the petitioner's claim because the police behavior "had no tendency to produce a confession that was not in accord with the truth." The Supreme Court rejected this standard. Justice Frankfurter, for the majority, wrote:

> [W]e cannot but conclude that the question whether Roger's confessions were admissible into evidence was answered by reference to a legal standard which took into account the circumstance of probable truth or falsity. And this is not a permissible standard under the Due Process Clause of the Fourteenth Amendment.[14]

Instead of inquiring into the truth or falsity of the confession, the Court said that the trial judge should have focused on the question *whether the behavior of the state's law enforcement officials was such as to overbear petitioner's will to resist and bring about confessions not freely self-determined.* That inquiry was to be answered with complete disregard for whether or not the petitioner spoke the truth.

(C) Voluntariness test

The test that evolved for determining voluntariness was hardly precise, a fact recognized by the justices themselves. The Court saw it as a balancing process, "a weighing of the circumstances of pressure against the power of resistance of the person confessing."[15] Thus the Court looked to the police tactics used in a particular case and the characteristics of the particular defendant to ascertain whether the confession was a product of the defen-

---

[11]Ashcraft v Tennessee, 322 US 143, 153, 64 SCt 921, 88 LEd 1192 (1944).
[12]Ashcraft v Tennessee, 322 US 143, 154, 64 SCt 921, 88 LEd 1192 (1944).
[13]Rogers v Richmond, 365 US 534, 81 SCt 735, 5 LEd(2d) 760 (1961).
[14]Rogers v Richmond, 365 US 534, 543-44, 81 SCt 735, 5 LEd(2d) 760 (1961).
[15]Stein v New York, 346 US 156, 185, 73 SCt 1077, 97 LEd 1522 (1953), overruled by Jackson v Denno, 378 US 368, 84 SCt 1774, 12 LEd(2d) 908 (1964).

dant's "free and rational choice."[16] The test required an examination of "the totality of the circumstances" surrounding an interrogation, and an affirmation of a confession's voluntariness accompanying a confession was deemed meaningless.[17] It must be recognized that voluntariness in the context used in these cases had a rather broad meaning. Even voluntary confessions were secured with pressure, but it was pressure that the Court deemed a defendant capable of handling. Justice Jackson wrote of the test that "of course these confessions were not voluntary in the sense that defendant wanted to make them or that they were completely spontaneous like a confession to a priest, a lawyer, or a psychiatrist. But in this sense no criminal confession is voluntary."[18]

The first element of the inquiry centered around the nature of the police conduct. Through the confession cases, the Court censured unconscionable police activity, relying on "the deep-rooted feeling that the police must obey the law while enforcing the law" because "in the end life and liberty can be as much endangered from illegal methods used to convict those thought to be criminals as from the actual criminals themselves."[19] The Court censured what had previously been considered standard and acceptable police interrogation practices, such as prolonged incommunicado interrogation while a bright light was directed at the suspect's eyes,[20] injecting a heroin addict with a truth serum ostensibly for the purpose of relieving withdrawal symptoms,[21] threatening a woman suspect that the law would take away her children if she did not confess,[22] refusing water to a suspect who had been shot in the liver and lung and who was in pain and gasping for breath,[23] questioning in an out-of-the-way location while the defendant is kept naked,[24] keeping a suspect in a small hot room or in solitary confinement,[25] and telling the suspect that he could expect to be held indefinitely and not be permitted to contact family or counsel until he cooperated and confessed.[26]

Through this process, the Court confronted every aspect of the "third degree" that had been standard procedure, such as depriving the suspect of food[27] and sleep.[28] Some of these interrogation practices were considered so inherently coercive that any confession secured through their use was held to be *violative of the constitutional right of any individual*, no matter his

---

[16]Watts v Indiana, 338 US 49, 69 SCt 1357, 93 LEd 1801 (1949).

[17]Haynes v Washington, 373 US 503, 83 SCt 1336, 10 LEd(2d) 513 (1963).

[18]Stein v New York, 346 US 156, 186, 73 SCt 1077, 97 LEd 1522 (1953), overruled by Jackson v Denno, 378 US 368, 84 SCt 1774, 12 LEd(2d) 908 (1964).

[19]Spano v New York, 360 US 315, 320-21, 79 SCt 1202, 3 LEd(2d) 1265 (1959).

[20]Ashcraft v Tennessee, 322 US 143, 64 SCt 921, 88 LEd 1192 (1944).

[21]Townsend v Sain, 372 US 293, 83 SCt 745, 9 LEd(2d) 770 (1963).

[22]Lynumn v Illinois, 372 US 528, 83 SCt 917, 9 LEd(2d) 922 (1963).

[23]Jackson v Denno, 378 US 368, 84 SCt 1774, 12 LEd(2d) 908 (1964).

[24]Malinski v New York, 324 US 401, 65 SCt 781, 89 LEd 1029 (1945).

[25]Harris v South Carolina, 338 US 68, 69 SCt 1354, 93 LEd 1815 (1949); Watts v Indiana, 338 US 49, 69 SCt 1357, 93 LEd 1801 (1949).

[26]Haynes v Washington, 373 US 503, 83 SCt 1336, 10 LEd(2d) 513 (1963).

[27]Payne v Arkansas, 356 US 560, 78 SCt 844, 2 LEd(2d) 975 (1958).

[28]Chambers v Florida, 309 US 227, 60 SCt 472, 84 LEd 716 (1940) (continuous interrogation for fifteen hours a day each day for six days).

age, education, or other factors that might have allowed him to withstand the psychological pressures associated with interrogation. Where the practice engaged in by the police was not inherently coercive, so that its "very existence [was not] irreconcilable with the possession of mental freedom by a lone suspect,"[29] the likely effect of that practice on the particular suspect was measured by considering the attributes of the suspect.

In reviewing the "totality of the circumstances," the Supreme Court considered the characteristics of the individual suspect, including age, intelligence, education, and racial as well as ethnic background, to determine the effect an interrogation tactic may have had in "breaking the will" of the suspect and producing an "involuntary confession." Some tactics were deemed inherently coercive, creating conditions "calculated to break the strongest nerves and strongest resistance."[30] In *Chambers v Florida*,[31] the defendant was one of forty black males rounded up in a dragnet arrest on mere suspicion and without warrants, held six days and questioned fifteen hours a day under the constant threat of brutality, without rest or sleep. Irrespective of the age, intelligence, or background of the accused, the Court deemed those tactics sufficient to overpower any suspect's mental resistance and produce an involuntary confession.

Other cases turned upon the ability of the suspect to resist pressures where police interrogation tactics were more subtle. When reviewing these cases, the Court recognized that its ability to measure voluntariness turned on probabilities,[32] and the justices recognized that their ability to reach accurate perceptions was severely limited because, as Justice Frankfurter stated, "unhappily we have neither physical nor intellectual weights and measures by which judicial judgments can determine when pressures in securing a confession reach the coercive intensity that calls for the exclusion of a statement so secured."[33] The Court found that the methods used against a fifteen-year-old suspected murderer, which might have left "a man cold and unimpressed [could] overawe and overwhelm a lad in his early teens."[34] Justice Douglas for the majority concluded:

> A 15-year-old lad, questioned through the dead of night by relays of police, is a ready victim of the inquisition. Mature men possibly might stand the ordeal from midnight to 5 a.m. But we cannot believe that a lad of tender years is a match for the police in such a contest. He needs counsel and support if he is not to become the victim first of fear, then of panic. He needs someone on whom to lean lest the overpowering presence of the law, as he knows it, crush him.[35]

---

[29]Ashcraft v Tennessee, 322 US 143, 154, 64 SCt 921, 88 LEd 1192 (1944).

[30]Chambers v Florida, 309 US 227, 239, 60 SCt 472, 84 LEd 716 (1940).

[31]Chambers v Florida, 309 US 227, 239, 60 SCt 472, 84 LEd 716 (1940).

[32]Blackburn v Alabama, 361 US 199, 80 SCt 274, 4 LEd(2d) 242 (1960).

[33]Haley v Ohio, 332 US 596, 606, 68 SCt 302, 92 LEd 224 (1948), cert denied 337 US 945, 69 SCt 1501, 93 LEd 1748 (1949) (Frankfurter, J., concurring).

[34]Haley v Ohio, 332 US 596, 599, 68 SCt 302, 92 LEd 224 (1948), cert denied 337 US 945, 69 SCt 1501, 93 LEd 1748 (1949) (Frankfurter, J., concurring).

[35]Haley v Ohio, 332 US 596, 599-600, 68 SCt 302, 92 LEd 224 (1948), cert denied 337 US 945, 69 SCt 1501, 93 LEd 1748 (1949) (Frankfurter, J., concurring).

Similarly, age was the dominant factor in *Gallegos v Colorado*,[36] where a fourteen-year-old boy signed a confession to a charge of assault and battery after a five-day detention. The police claimed that the boy was advised of his right to counsel but neither requested counsel nor asked to see his parents. Considering the suspect's age, the Court said that the five-day detention, even absent prolonged questioning, gave "the case an ominous cast."[37]

> But a 14-year-old boy, no matter how sophisticated, is unlikely to have any conception of what will confront him when he is made accessible only to the police. That is to say, we deal with a person who is not equal to the police in knowledge or understanding of the consequences of the questions and answers being recorded and who is unable to know how to protect his own interests or how to get the benefits of his constitutional rights.[38]

Race was the critical factor leading to a determination that the defendant's confession was involuntary where a young, illiterate black was questioned while "surrounded by as many as a dozen members of a dominant group [white] in positions of authority."[39] The low mental ability levels or mental illnesses of defendants led to the conclusion that their confessions were not voluntary in several cases.[40] Several of these cases, as evidenced by their repeated reference, involved a combination of factors, such as age and mental ability, that together convinced the Court of the defendant's inability to resist the pressures brought to bear during interrogation.

Another factor considered along with age and mental ability was a defendant's level of education. In *Chambers v Florida*,[41] the defendant was an uneducated tenant farmer who was illiterate. The defendant in *Fikes v Alabama*[42] was uneducated, and the defendant in *Payne v Arkansas*[43] had completed only the fifth grade. On the other hand, one defendant who had graduated from college and completed the first year of law school was deemed capable of resisting the pressures attendant upon interrogation and his statement confessing to the murder of his girlfriend was held to be voluntary.[44] The Court reached this conclusion despite the denial by police

---

[36]Gallegos v Colorado, 370 US 49, 82 SCt 1209, 8 LEd(2d) 325 (1962).

[37]Gallegos v Colorado, 370 US 49, 54, 82 SCt 1209, 8 LEd(2d) 325 (1962).

[38]Gallegos v Colorado, 370 US 49, 54, 82 SCt 1209, 8 LEd(2d) 325 (1962).

[39]Harris v South Carolina, 338 US 68, 70, 69 SCt 1354, 93 LEd 1815 (1949); see also White v Texas, 310 US 530, 60 SCt 1032, 84 LEd 1342 (1940); Ward v Texas, 316 US 547, 62 SCt 1139, 86 LEd 1663 (1942); Fikes v Alabama, 352 US 191, 77 SCt 281, 1 LEd(2d) 246 (1957).

[40]See Fikes v Alabama, 352 US 191, 77 SCt 281, 1 LEd(2d) 246 (1957) (mentally dull, began school at age eight, was in the third grade at age sixteen, and was believed to be schizophrenic and highly suggestible); Payne v Arkansas, 356 US 560, 78 SCt 844, 2 LEd(2d) 975 (1958); Spano v New York, 360 US 315, 79 SCt 1202, 3 LEd(2d) 1265 (1959) (history of emotional instability); Blackburn v Alabama, 361 US 199, 80 SCt 274, 4 LEd(2d) 242 (1960) (legally insane at time of questioning).

[41]Chambers v Florida, 309 US 227, 60 SCt 472, 84 LEd 716 (1940).

[42]Fikes v Alabama, 352 US 191, 77 SCt 281, 1 LEd(2d) 246 (1957).

[43]Payne v Arkansas, 356 US 560, 78 SCt 844, 2 LEd(2d) 975 (1958).

[44]Crooker v California, 357 US 433, 78 SCt 1287, 2 LEd(2d) 1448 (1958), overruled by Escobedo v Illinois, 378 US 478, 84 SCt 1758, 12 LEd(2d) 977 (1964) and Miranda v Arizona, 384 US 436, 86 SCt 1602, 16 LEd(2d) 694 (1966).

of defendant's specific request to see counsel. The Court concluded that the coercion resulting from the denial of a specific request to engage an attorney was negated by the defendant's age, intelligence, education, and the manner in which he refused to answer questions, indicating an awareness of his right to be silent.

The voluntariness test became increasingly difficult to administer. The need to determine voluntariness on the totality of the circumstances deprived Supreme Court decisions of their educational value and provided little guidance to police officers. Since the fact pattern in each case differed, there was little precedential value to the decisions except in those cases where the Court condemned inherently coercive techniques. Perhaps most frustrating to the Court was the fact that the records they relied on to make a determination of voluntariness were made at proceedings that had become "swearing contests" in which the defense contended that the defendant was subjected to abuse that numbers of police witnesses swore had never occurred. Moreover, lower courts invariably resolved the disputed issues in favor of the prosecution. The Court failed to develop a clear definition of voluntariness, and its caseload became burdened with appeals challenging state court findings that confessions were voluntary. It was foreseeable that the Supreme Court would attempt to develop a set of rules making the law concerning confessions predictable and ending the morass in which it found itself imbedded.

(D) Right to counsel

The Court sought to develop concrete rules which would be applicable in all cases, which would avoid the need for case-by-case analysis with results turning on the idiosyncracies of a particular suspect or interrogation technique, and which would provide meaningful guidance for lower courts and law enforcement officers. It is not at all surprising that the Court turned first to the right to counsel rather than the privilege against self-incrimination. In the early 1960s, the Fifth Amendment privilege against self-incrimination had not yet been made applicable to the states through the Fourteenth Amendment. The Sixth Amendment right to counsel had been applicable to the states since 1932,[45] however, and the Court's decisions interpreting the right to counsel were well received and generated less controversy than its confession cases. Moreover, even though the Court had not yet extended the right to counsel to interrogation, reference was made throughout many of the voluntariness cases to the need and beneficial effect of counsel during interrogation. Justice Jackson, for instance, had recognized that to question a suspect without counsel "is a real peril to individual freedom," even though he contended that to bring a lawyer into the interrogation phase of a case would mean a real peril to the solution of the crime.[46] In other cases, the Court recognized that coercion is likely to result from an interrogator's denial of a specific request for counsel,

---

[45]See Powell v Alabama, 287 US 45, 53 SCt 55, 77 LEd 158 (1932).
[46]Watts v Indiana, 338 US 49, 69 SCt 1357, 93 LEd 1801 (1949).

although in *Crooker v California*,[47] such coercion was deemed adequately offset by the defendant's age, maturity, and education.

In 1964, the Supreme Court decided two cases that established the right to counsel during interrogation and paved the way for later developments. In *Massiah v United States*,[48] the defendant was arrested and indicted for various narcotics offenses. He retained a lawyer, pleaded not guilty, and was released on bail. Massiah's co-defendant agreed to cooperate with the prosecution and, unknown to Massiah, permitted police to install a radio transmitter in his car. The co-defendant then arranged to meet with Massiah and discuss the pending charges. During the conversation the co-defendant elicited incriminating statements from the defendant, which were transmitted to a listening federal agent. Those incriminating statements were introduced at the defendant's trial.

The Supreme Court reversed the conviction, holding that the co-defendant's behavior constituted a surreptitious interrogation by police in violation of the defendant's right to counsel, which had attached by virtue of the indictment. *Massiah* turned neither on voluntariness, because the defendant's admissions were certainly made voluntarily even if he did not know that the police were listening, nor on coercion, which was nonexistent in the case. Instead, the decision rested on the absoluteness of the right to counsel that, absent a waiver, attached when the defendant was indicted. For the government to deliberately elicit incriminating statements in the absence of counsel after attachment of the right violated the basic protections of the guarantee. The decision was applied to the states in *McLeod v Ohio*.[49] The fact that the interrogation took place outside the jail after the defendant's release did not, according to the majority, mitigate the violation. The fact that the defendant did not know he was being interrogated was deemed by the Court to make the infringement more invidious.

Six weeks later, *Massiah* was overshadowed when the Court decided *Escobedo v Illinois*,[50] which involved a traditional post-arrest, jailhouse interrogation by police officers. However, *Massiah* has had more lasting effect than the *Escobedo* decision and remains a part of the law of confessions today.

Danny Escobedo was arrested for the murder of his brother-in-law after his alleged co-conspirator confessed and told police that Escobedo had fired the fatal shots. Escobedo had also been arrested earlier on the night of the homicide but was released after interrogation produced no statement. Between his first and second arrests, Escobedo consulted an attorney who told him not to answer any questions if police attempted to interrogate him again. When arrested a second time, and while en route to the police station, Escobedo requested to contact and consult with his attorney. Shortly after the defendant reached the police station, his lawyer arrived

---

[47]Crooker v California, 357 US 433, 78 SCt 1287, 2 LEd(2d) 1448 (1958), overruled by Escobedo v Illinois, 378 US 478, 84 SCt 1758, 12 LEd(2d) 977 (1964) and Miranda v Arizona, 384 US 436, 86 SCt 1602, 16 LEd(2d) 694 (1966).

[48]Massiah v United States, 377 US 201, 84 SCt 1199, 12 LEd(2d) 246 (1964).

[49]McLeod v Ohio, 381 US 356, 85 SCt 1556, 14 LEd(2d) 682 (1965).

[50]Escobedo v Illinois, 378 US 478, 84 SCt 1758, 12 LEd(2d) 977 (1964).

and requested to see Escobedo. The lawyer was refused permission to talk with his client. The two made momentary eye contact when the door to the interrogation room in which Escobedo was being held opened. The lawyer waved to his client, which Escobedo later testified at the suppression hearing he took to be a reminder from his attorney not to say anything. Throughout the interrogation the attorney and Escobedo renewed their requests to see each other. Their requests were denied and they were afforded no opportunity to consult with each other. The police contended that the statement was secured from Escobedo after he was told that his co-defendant had implicated him, and that upon Escobedo's request he was brought face-to-face with his co-defendant and that Escobedo said, "I didn't shoot Manuel, you did it." This was the first time Escobedo admitted any knowledge of the crime, and after this admission he made a full statement.

Escobedo's version of how the statement was ultimately produced differed. He contended that a police officer whom he knew from the neighborhood spoke with him in Spanish and promised that Escobedo and his sister could go home and be involved only as witnesses if Escobedo would make a statement implicating the co-defendant. As a result of that assurance, Escobedo contended that he made the statement. Both sides, however, agreed that Escobedo was not advised by police that he need not say anything, and that he requested and was denied access to his attorney who was present at the police station requesting to see him.

A majority of the Supreme Court held that Escobedo's confession, albeit satisfying the voluntariness tests, was constitutionally inadmissible. Justice Goldberg, for the majority, wrote that where an investigation is no longer a general inquiry into an unsolved crime but has begun to focus on a particular suspect, no statement elicited by police during interrogation may be used against the suspect where he has not been effectively warned of his absolute constitutional right to remain silent and where the suspect has requested and been denied an opportunity to consult with his attorney. Notwithstanding the majority's intention to create a clear rule that would provide guidance to law enforcement officers and would grant the Court a respite from its spate of confession cases, the *Escobedo* rule was opaque because the facts of the case appeared to limit the broad rule set forth by the Court. The fact that Escobedo was in jail when the interrogation took place appeared to limit the "focus on the suspect" standard. Moreover, Escobedo, prior to this arrest, had retained an attorney who was alerted to the arrest and was present at the jailhouse to consult with his client. Would this extended right to counsel be limited to suspects who knew to request an attorney, to those who had already retained counsel, and to those whose attorney was present at the jail when the request was made? The decision was not well received, and lower courts sought to limit the scope of the rule by the facts of the case. Finally, as the dissenters in *Escobedo* pointed out, much of the substance of the rule announced by the majority dealing with the obligation of police to advise a suspect of his right to remain silent depends on interpretation of the Fifth, not the Sixth, Amendment, which was not explored in the opinion.

19.02 *Miranda* rule

Two years after *Escobedo v Illinois*,[51] the United States Supreme Court took the opportunity to reorder the law concerning interrogation and confessions under the Fifth Amendment privilege against self-incrimination, now incorporated into the Fourteenth Amendment due process clause.[52] Decided under the Sixth Amendment right to counsel, *Escobedo* had affirmed the existence of an absolute right to remain silent and the need for police to advise a suspect of that right. The right to remain silent was left dangling within the *Escobedo* rule because of its lack of relationship to the Sixth Amendment. Now, with the Fifth Amendment binding upon the states, the Court, in *Miranda v Arizona*,[53] was free to fashion a set of rules governing interrogation. Historically, the purpose of the Fifth Amendment privilege provided an obstacle. The right was guaranteed to prevent an accused from being compelled to testify in a criminal case; the framers had created a courtroom privilege forever to prevent the establishment of Star Chamber proceedings in the United States. The difficulty facing the *Miranda* Court was to apply the courtroom privilege to post-arrest police interrogation normally occurring before commencement of formal criminal proceedings. The majority overcame that obstacle by co-opting the argument that the privilege had to be applicable to the police station or it would be meaningless at trial because the defendant would, in fact, be compelled to testify through his confession. Once that obstacle was overcome, the Court was free to examine the nature of custodial interrogation.

The majority, in an opinion by Chief Justice Warren, concluded that custodial interrogation must be strictly controlled in order to ensure the elimination of third degree methods—psychological as well as physical brutality—to eliminate "the gap in our knowledge as to what in fact goes on in the interrogation rooms," and to prevent the interrogation environment from being used "to subjugate the individual to the will of his examiner."[54] Therefore, to ensure that statements offered at trial are the product of the voluntary choice of the suspect, the majority felt it necessary to devise and implement a set of prophylactic procedures to mitigate the inherent coerciveness that pervades custodial interrogation.

The *Miranda* requirements govern the admissibility in the prosecution's case-in-chief of any statement made by a defendant following his arrest. These rules are as applicable to exculpatory statements as they are to confessions. An exculpatory statement following arrest would not be offered by the prosecution unless it bolstered the state's case or differed markedly from the evidence that the defense is expected to present. *Miranda* was intended to protect the unknowing arrestee who, more than his experienced

---

[51]Escobedo v Illinois, 378 US 478, 84 SCt 1758, 12 LEd(2d) 977 (1964).
[52]See Malloy v Hogan, 378 US 1, 84 SCt 1489, 12 LEd(2d) 653 (1964).
[53]Miranda v Arizona, 384 US 436, 86 SCt 1602, 16 LEd(2d) 694 (1966).
[54]Miranda v Arizona, 384 US 436, 449, 86 SCt 1602, 16 LEd(2d) 694 (1966).

counterpart, is likely, to believe that he must talk himself out of difficulty following arrest and is likely to offer a statement that is riddled with inconsistencies and that may end up convicting him.

The *Miranda* requirements are applicable whether the offense is a felony or a misdemeanor. In 1984, the Ohio Supreme Court overruled its own 1969 precedent and held that "the classification of the crime being investigated [is] irrelevant to the determination of Miranda's applicability."[55] The court reasoned:

> It is evident that Fifth Amendment protections attach without regard to the severity of the punishment that may be inflicted for the offense. It follows that *Miranda* protections should likewise attach without regard to punishment. ... As long as *Miranda* continues to protect the guarantees of the Fifth Amendment, so should its protection extend to those individuals suspected of minor as well as serious offenses.[56]

The United States Supreme Court concurred with the Ohio Court's ruling and rationale two months later in *Berkemer v McCarty*,[57] involving the arrest of a drunken driver who made incriminating statements at the scene and later at the jail. Justice Marshall, for the majority, wrote that the crucial distinction for purposes of *Miranda* is not between a traffic offense and more serious crimes but between custodial interrogation and less formal police questioning.

CROSS REFERENCES

Text Ch 7

19.03 *Miranda* warnings

(A) The warnings

The Court held that "when an individual is taken into custody or otherwise deprived of his freedom by the authorities in any significant way and is subjected to questioning, the privilege against self-incrimination is jeopardized. Procedural safeguards must be employed to protect the privilege."[58] Those safeguards required that the suspect be advised prior to any questioning as follows:

(1) He has the right to remain silent, that anything he says can be used against him in a court of law;

(2) He has the right to the presence of an attorney;[59] and

---

[55]State v Buchholz, 11 OS(3d) 24, 11 OBR 56, 462 NE(2d) 1222 (1984); Beavercreek v Blue, 16 App(3d) 166, 16 OBR 175, 474 NE(2d) 1235 (Greene 1984) (*State v Buchholtz* does not apply retroactively to offenses committed prior to May 9, 1984).

[56]State v Buchholz, 11 OS(3d) 24, 27, 11 OBR 56, 462 NE(2d) 1222 (1984).

[57]Berkemer v McCarty, 468 US 420, 104 SCt 3138, 82 LEd(2d) 317 (1984).

[58]Miranda v Arizona, 384 US 436, 478 86 SCt 1602, 16 LEd(2d) 694 (1966).

[59]See also RC 120.16(F): Information as to the right to legal representation by the county public defendant or assigned counsel shall be afforded to an accused person immediately upon arrest ... RC 2934.14 and 2935.20 provide for an arrestee to have access, upon request, to a telephone with which to consult an attorney. But see State v Holloway, No. 91AP-365, 1992 WL 82716 (10th Dist Ct App, Franklin, 4-24-92), appeal dismissed by 65 OS(3d) 1416, 598 NE(2d) 1168 (1992) (failure to advise an accused of the availability of the public defender, when the defendant is

(3) If he cannot afford an attorney, one will be appointed for him prior to any questioning if he so desires.

(B) Purpose

The purposes of the warnings were clear on their face. They were to break the atmosphere of coercion that exists immediately after arrest when an uninformed suspect believes that his destiny rests within the total control of his jailers. Therefore, the giving of warnings following an arrest and *prior to interrogation* is an absolute prerequisite to the admissibility of any statement. Failure to give the requisite warnings will foreclose further consideration of the admissibility of the statement. That failure will not be excused no matter who the suspect is, even if he is a police officer who has read the warnings in the past to countless suspects, or a lawyer or judge who presumably has knowledge of these rights. The absoluteness of the requirement provided an indication of the majority's belief as to the inherently coercive nature of custodial interrogation.

Miranda warnings need not be given by someone who is not a law enforcement officer. In *State v Stout*,[60] the defendant dealt with a volunteer of the Middleton Probation Department's Women's Substance Abuse Program. The court in dictum found that the volunteer was not an agent of the state and therefore was not bound by *Miranda* rules. The United States Supreme Court has held that the *Miranda* rules are applicable, however, to a pretrial psychiatric evaluation done by a court-appointed psychiatrist to determine future dangerousness. The death sentence imposed on the accused was tainted by the use, during the penalty phase of the trial, of statements made by the accused without *Miranda* warnings during the psychiatric evaluation.[61]

The warnings were intended to break the spell of coercion that follows on being taken into custody. Moreover, hearing the warnings from a police officer serves an added purpose even for the arrestee who is already familiar with his rights: it serves notice that the police officer, too, is aware that the suspect retains rights and, more importantly, that the officer is prepared to honor these rights. It was only in this way, the *Miranda* majority believed, that a reviewing court could begin to have confidence that a statement secured from a suspect was given voluntarily.

(C) Additional warnings and information

Subsequent Supreme Court decisions have held that these warnings are complete. Yet, it is highly likely that the *Miranda* Court intended to require an additional warning. Several times throughout the majority opinion, Chief Justice Warren warned that a suspect has the right to cut off questioning at any time. However, when specifying the warnings that must be given to a suspect, the Court failed to include that critical one. Following this failure,

---

otherwise Mirandized, is not a constitutional violation and the failure will not lead to suppression of a statement, nor are police obligated to advise an accused about his right to make a phone call).

[60]State v Stout, 42 App(3d) 38, 536 NE(2d) 42 (Butler 1987).

[61]Estelle v Smith, 451 US 454, 101 SCt 1866, 68 LEd(2d) 359 (1981).

an Ohio court has held that there is no affirmative duty to advise a suspect of his right to terminate questioning at any time during the interview.[62]

The right to cut off questioning is as important as the others, especially for the ignorant and the uninitiated who were the suspects the Court sought to protect. Such a person is not likely to intuitively understand that he may assert the right to silence at any time, even after agreeing to answer questions.

The failure of the Warren Court to explicitly require a reading of this right will not be corrected by the Rehnquist Court. Yet, it is probably more important today in light of the later Court's finding that police need not advise a suspect of all the crimes which are the subject of the intended interrogation.[63] In other words, the legitimacy of a waiver of *Miranda* rights is not affected by police trickery in luring a suspect into believing that the interrogation is about one crime when, in reality, the police are most interested in a different crime. The *Miranda* Court warned against deceit and trickery in the obtaining of a waiver; the present Court does not think this trickery goes to the issue of waiver.

Moran v Burbine[64] also provided the context for consideration of police trickery when police questioning a murder suspect in custody failed to advise him that an attorney, contacted by the suspect's sister, had contacted the police on the suspect's behalf. The attorney was promised that the police would not attempt further interrogation until he had an opportunity to see the suspect. The police did not keep that promise and proceeded to administer *Miranda* warnings and interrogate the suspect. No mention was made to the suspect of the attorney's efforts on his behalf.

Although the Court condemned the "ethically objectionable"[65] behavior of the police, the majority held that the police did not have to notify the suspect of the attorney's inquiries, efforts, or availability. The *Miranda* warnings were found complete despite the absence of this information, and the suspect's waiver of his rights was upheld despite the trickery. The warnings are intended to provide a suspect with the knowledge of his constitutional rights to enable him to make a knowing, intelligent, and voluntary decision to invoke or waive those rights. Satisfaction of that standard, the Court held, does not require that the suspect make a wise decision. Consequently, an incomplete warning that did not contain the very relevant information that an attorney stood ready to assist the suspect was deemed adequate provided that it contained the statement of rights required by the *Miranda* decision.

The Supreme Court has held that the warnings are not, themselves, constitutionally protected rights and are only designed to safeguard the privilege against self-incrimination.[66] Therefore, they need not be given in precisely the form prescribed in the *Miranda* decision. In *California v*

---

[62]State v Fort, No. 52929, 1988 WL 11080 (8th Dist Ct App, Cuyahoga, 2-4-88).
[63]Colorado v Spring, 479 US 564, 107 SCt 851, 93 LEd(2d) 954 (1987).
[64]Moran v Burbine, 475 US 412, 106 SCt 1135, 89 LEd(2d) 410 (1986).
[65]Moran v Burbine, 475 US 412, 424, 106 SCt 1135, 89 LEd(2d) 410 (1986).
[66]Michigan v Tucker, 417 US 433, 94 SCt 2357, 41 LEd(2d) 182 (1974).

Prysock,[67] six justices reversed a court of appeals finding that the warnings given a juvenile and his parents were inadequate because they were not told that the services of the free attorney were available *prior to the impending questioning*. Two lower courts had found the warnings about counsel, at best, confusing, and a dialogue between an officer and the suspect's parents at the time warnings were given raises a strong inference that the parents were not at all clear about the availability of appointed counsel prior to questioning. The Supreme Court majority misrepresented the court of appeals position as resting on the order in which the warnings were given rather than on the clarity of the warning pertaining to the critical issue of counsel. The Court stressed that "no talismanic incantation [is] required"[68] to satisfy the *Miranda* standards.

Once the warnings are given, the suspect must be given the opportunity to exercise the rights. Failure to invoke the rights to silence or counsel at the outset of an interrogation does not end the matter. The opportunity "must be afforded ... throughout the interrogation."[69] Consequently, simply giving warnings at the outset of a lengthy interrogation is not likely to satisfy *Miranda* standards. The Court was concerned about the interrogation process wearing an individual down, which would appear to require that a suspect be re-advised of these rights periodically throughout an interrogation and, most certainly, prior to commencement of a second session. Whether the present Supreme Court would enforce this aspect of the *Miranda* decision is still unclear but doubtful.

(D) Failure to give warnings prior to any interrogation

A basic tenet of the *Miranda* decision was that the warnings must be given prior to any custodial interrogation. The failure to advise a suspect of his rights at the outset of an interrogation would render any statement inadmissible even if the suspect is advised of his rights prior to making the admission. The Court sought to impose the proper atmosphere at the outset of an interrogation session and wanted to forestall a situation where a suspect's will is broken down through an interrogation session and then is advised of his rights after he has indicated a willingness to make a confession. To avoid this, the Court indicated that the failure to give the warnings at the outset of the interrogation session creates a coercive atmosphere that is not overcome during that session by giving the warnings.

In *Westover v United States*,[70] one of the cases consolidated and decided as part of the *Miranda* decision, FBI agents advised a suspect of his rights and secured a confession. The confession was ruled inadmissible, notwithstanding that the agents had advised the suspect of his rights, because he had been in custody in the same local jail for over fourteen hours and had been interrogated by local officials at length during that period without having been advised of his rights. The *Miranda* majority obviously concluded that the coercive atmosphere created by the prior lengthy interroga-

---

[67]California v Prysock, 453 US 355, 101 SCt 2806, 69 LEd(2d)696 (1981).
[68]California v Prysock, 453 US 355, 359, 101 SCt 2806, 69 LEd(2d)696 (1981).
[69]Miranda v Arizona, 384 US 436, 86 SCt 1602, 16 LEd(2d)694 (1966).
[70]Westover v United States, 384 US 436, 86 SCt 1602, 16 LEd(2d) 694 (1966).

tion devoid of warnings could not be overcome by the administration of the *Miranda* warnings by the new set of interrogators. The Court indicated that the chain could have been broken if the second authorities had removed the suspect in time and place from the original surroundings and adequately advised him of his rights.

The Burger-Rehnquist Court reads the failure to give *Miranda* warnings as presumptively coercive as distinguished from tactics which are actually coercive. In *Oregon v Elstad*,[71] this Court held admissible a written confession taken at the police station after the giving of the warnings. However, prior to that statement the defendant had given an incriminating response to a police question asked of him in his home, after he had been taken into custody, and before he was given proper warnings. The defendant was then taken to the police station where, after he was given the warnings, he gave a signed confession. The Court held "that a suspect who has once responded to unwarned yet uncoercive questioning is not thereby disabled from waiving his rights and confessing after he has been given the requisite Miranda warning."[72]

In one respect, *Elstad* met the conditions for admissibility set forth in *Westover* for a statement given after proper warnings following interrogation without warnings: the questioning was not continuous, and the locations of the two interrogations were not the same. However, the coercive factors are stronger. The first statement was made at Elstad's house, which is less likely to be a coercive environment than a jail house questioning. He was then removed to a jail, which probably increased, rather than decreased, the coerciveness. More importantly, Elstad's initial statement "let the cat out of the bag." He had admitted complicity in the crime, and the subsequent administration of warnings was not likely to overcome the effect of the earlier admission. When the *Miranda* Court, discussing *Westover*, considered how to overcome the coercion caused by an initial interrogation without warnings, they never considered the effect of an incriminating statement resulting from that first interrogation. It is very unlikely that the *Miranda* Court would have ruled in *Elstad* that the second statement was admissible. That Court did not distinguish between actual and presumptive coercion. Considering that the time elapsed between the two interrogations in *Elstad* was so short, the present Court may find that, in the absence of actual coercion, the giving of *Miranda* warnings is sufficient, even in the same interrogation session, to overcome the presumption of coercion that attached when the session began without warnings.

(E) Warnings prior to each interrogation

The failure to repeat *Miranda* warnings prior to each interrogation session raises a problem the *Miranda* Court anticipated. The initial warnings may be overcome by continuous questioning. Consequently, to offset that effect, warnings should be repeated prior to each interrogation session. Nonetheless, the failure to do so will not necessarily result in the suppres-

---

[71]See Oregon v Elstad, 470 US 298, 105 SCt 1285, 84 LEd(2d) 222 (1985).
[72]See Oregon v Elstad, 470 US 298, 318, 105 SCt 1285, 84 LEd(2d) 222 (1985).

sion of resulting statements. In *State v Cooey*,[73] the Ohio Supreme Court found that under the totality of the circumstances the initial warnings never became too stale so as to fail to protect the defendant from the coerciveness of subsequent custodial interrogation sessions. The Court also held, in *State v Brewer*,[74] that a defendant's statements were admissible notwithstanding the absence of second, fresh *Miranda* warnings because of his apparent willingness to talk and his admitted knowledge of his rights. The Court even held that a reading and waiver of *Miranda* rights less than twenty-four hours prior to the conversation in question, and then a mere restatement that these rights still applied, was sufficient. Even though re-administration of the *Miranda* warnings would have been preferable, the Court said rereading was not mandatory.[75]

Confessions resulting from interrogation following a polygraph examination have been held admissible even though second *Miranda* warnings are not given following the test and prior to the questioning.[76]

19.04   Public safety exception to *Miranda*

Following *Miranda*, commentators wondered whether the failure to give warnings in a life-and-death emergency situation, such as a kidnapping or hostage situation, would or should result in suppression of a resulting statement or evidence. In *New York v Quarles*,[77] decided in the last weeks of the 1984 term, the Supreme Court created a public safety exception to *Miranda*. Justice Rehnquist, writing for the 5-4 majority, acknowledged that the new exception would lessen the desirable clarity of the *Miranda* rules. Justice O'Connor, dissenting in part, attacked the new exception because

> *Miranda* has become reasonably clear and law enforcement practices have adjusted to its strictures … . In my view, a "public safety" exception unnecessarily blurs the edges of the clear line heretofore established and makes *Miranda's* requirements more difficult to understand. … The end result will be a finespun new doctrine on public safety exigencies incident to custodial interrogation, complete with hair-splitting distinctions that currently plague our Fourth Amendment jurisprudence.[78]

---

[73]State v Cooey, 46 OS(3d) 20, 544 NE(2d) 895 (1989), affirmed by 1994 WL 201009 (1994).

[74]State v Brewer, 48 OS(3d) 50, 549 NE(2d) 491 (1990), affirmed by 1994 WL 527740 (1994), cert denied sub nom 116 SCt 101, 133 LEd(2d) 55 (1995); see also State v Dixon, 101 App(3d) 552, 656 NE(2d) 1 (Lucas 1995) (Statements made during second interrogation were admissible despite no new Miranda warnings where court found that defendant was aware of his rights, having evoked them five days prior and where he was advised of his rights during an interrogating four hours earlier).

[75]State v Barnes, 25 OS(3d) 203, 25 OBR 266, 495 NE(2d) 922 (1986), cert denied 480 US 926, 107 SCt 1388, 94 LEd(2d) 701 (1987).

[76]See State v Gordon, No. 1410, 1989 WL 260228 (11th Dist Ct App, Geauga, 3-31-89) (dictum).

[77]New York v Quarles, 467 US 649, 104 SCt 2626, 81 LEd(2d) 550 (1984).

[78]New York v Quarles, 467 US 649, 663-64, 104 SCt 2626, 81 LEd(2d) 550 (1984) (O'Connor, J., dissenting). Justice O'Connor would have reversed as well because "nothing in *Miranda* or the privilege itself requires exclusion of nontestimonial

Quarles arose when a woman approached police and told them she had been raped and that her assailant had entered a nearby supermarket carrying a gun. The officers entered the supermarket and apprehended the defendant. One of the officers frisked the defendant and discovered an empty shoulder holster. Without giving *Miranda* warnings, the officer asked the defendant where the gun was. The defendant responded, directing the officers to the gun. The gun and the defendant's statement were suppressed in the state courts on *Miranda* grounds.

The majority pointed out that the defendant did not claim that his statements were actually compelled by the police, adhering to the Rehnquist distinction between the Fifth Amendment privilege against self-incrimination and the *Miranda* rules. Presumably, if the statement had been secured through practices amounting to actual compulsion, the exception would not have applied.

However, when the failure to give the warnings amounts only to a *Miranda* violation, Justice Rehnquist wrote that "the need for answers to questions in a situation posing a threat to the public safety outweighs the need for the prophylactic rule protecting the Fifth Amendment's privilege against self-incrimination."[79]

The exception carved out by Justice Rehnquist and endorsed by a sharply divided Court is likely to thoroughly confuse this area of the law. First, the majority refused to limit the exception to those situations where the officer testifies that he was concerned for his safety or that of bystanders. Thus, the exception may be applied in situations where the officer was motivated solely by a desire to obtain incriminating evidence, even though a court finds public safety considerations to warrant application of the exception. Second, the New York courts specifically found that the police officers were not acting out of concern for their own physical safety, nor did the lower courts find that the police were motivated by the public's safety. Nonetheless, Justice Rehnquist muddied the waters by holding that "there is a 'public safety' exception to the requirement that *Miranda* warnings be given before a suspect's answers may be admitted into evidence."[80]

Quarles was relied on in *State v Hoyer*,[81] where a drunk driving suspect was permitted to park and lock his car and then, at the police station, was asked where his gun was by the arresting officer after she found cartridges in his pocket. The suspect had already been advised of his *Miranda* rights but had not waived them when the question was asked. He responded that the gun was under the driver's seat in the car. The court held that public safety concerns justified easing of *Miranda* requirements and that the question was thus proper, and the answer admissible, regardless of the subjective motivation behind the question.

---

evidence derived from informal custodial interrogation, and I therefore agree with the Court that admission of the gun in evidence is proper."

[79]New York v Quarles, 467 US 649, 657, 104 SCt 2626, 81 LEd(2d) 550 (1984).
[80]New York v Quarles, 467 US 649, 655, 104 SCt 2626, 81 LEd(2d) 550 (1984).
[81]State v Hoyer, 30 App(3d) 130, 30 OBR 247, 506 NE(2d) 1190 (Wayne 1986).

19.05   Custody

The Supreme Court's attention was riveted on the difficulties of ascertaining what went on in the confines of an interrogation room in a police station. The rules announced in the *Escobedo v Illinois*[82] case were activated when an "investigation is no longer a general inquiry into an unsolved crime but has begun to focus on a particular suspect." The *Miranda v Arizona*[83] decision abandoned this "focus" inquiry and, instead, adopted a narrower test for the attachment of the rights. The Court said that statements *stemming from custodial interrogation* were admissible only on a showing that the procedural safeguards had been followed.

The procedural safeguards adopted in *Miranda* become necessary once a defendant is taken into custody "or otherwise deprived of his freedom of action in any significant way."[84] In a footnote, the Court explained that this was what was meant in *Escobedo* when the Court spoke of an investigation focusing on an accused. The test in the earlier decision was far broader and could have led to the imposition of stricter controls on all police interrogation than the test actually adopted in *Miranda*. But whether the *Escobedo* Court was heading in a different direction was immaterial, for *Miranda* focused on the abuses of custodial interrogation that had preoccupied the Court for several decades. Naturally, the *Miranda* Court did not limit the application of the rules to interrogation taking place in a jail to forestall the likely consequences of such a rule: extended and roundabout trips from the place of arrest to the detention center. Further, the Court added the language pertaining to "otherwise deprived of his freedom of action in any significant way,"[85] rather than limiting the rules to the post-arrest period, to avoid having to rule whether the formal trappings of an arrest had occurred. Consequently, the Court looks to the Fourth Amendment test for determining the applicability of the *Miranda* protections: whether a reasonable person under the circumstances would think that he is under arrest.[86]

The custody must be under the control of the state. Where a suspected shoplifter is detained by a store's security guard, *Miranda* requirements have been held inapplicable even though the custody is authorized by state law.[87]

It is not difficult to determine the applicability of the *Miranda* rules when the interrogation takes place in a police station following an arrest. After all, this was the setting that the Court found to be inherently coercive and sought to control. Moreover, it is the fact of custody, not its purpose, that

[82]Escobedo v Illinois, 378 US 478, 490-91, 84 SCt 1758, 12 LEd(2d) 977 (1964).
[83]Miranda v Arizona, 384 US 436, 86 SCt 1602, 16 LEd(2d) 694 (1966).
[84]Miranda v Arizona, 384 US 436, 444, 86 SCt 1602, 16 LEd(2d) 694 (1966).
[85]Miranda v Arizona, 384 US 436, 444, 86 SCt 1602, 16 LEd(2d) 694 (1966).
[86]Berkemer v McCarty, 468 US 420, 104 SCt 3138, 82 LEd(2d) 317(1984).
[87]State v Giallombardo, 29 App(3d) 279, 29 OBR 343, 504 NE(2d) 1202 (Portage 1986); Columbus v Nickles, 29 App(3d) 281, 29 OBR 345, 504 NE(2d) 1204 (Franklin 1986).

controls. In *Mathis v United States*,[88] Internal Revenue Service agents questioned the defendant about his federal tax liability while he was in prison serving a state sentence. The agents had failed to advise the defendant of his *Miranda* rights, but the government sought to excuse the omission and gain entry of the admissions on the ground that the warnings must be given only where the person "is 'in custody' in connection with the very case under investigation."[89] The Supreme Court rejected the argument which would have permitted law enforcement officers to question an arrestee about every crime but the one for which he was formally arrested.

Presence in a police station or jail, while normally indicative of custody, is not always dispositive of the issue. Statements given by a suspect who appears at a police station on request for questioning but is advised that he is not under arrest and is free to leave are not the product of custodial interrogation and are admissible absent the *Miranda* warnings.[90] *Miranda* warnings are not required simply because the questioning takes place in the police station and the questioned person is a suspect.[91] In *Oregon v Mathiason*, the Supreme Court was convinced that the defendant was not in custody or otherwise deprived of his freedom of action in any significant way since he was not pressed to hold the conversation with the officer at the police station but indicated that he had no preference on the matter, arrived on his own, was advised that he was not under arrest, and left at the conclusion of the interview. The final fact, that the defendant was permitted to leave, was most convincing. The dissenters disagreed, contending that *Miranda* should have applied once the officers told the defendant that his fingerprints were found at the scene of the crime and that they had other independent evidence to link him to the crime. Again, most impressive to the Supreme Court majority was the fact that the defendant was permitted to leave, even after he made incriminating statements, thereby clearly indicating that the police officer did not intend to place him in custody.

Similarly, the Ohio Supreme Court found that *Miranda* warnings were not required where a defendant returned a detective's call and then in response to the detective's request went to the police station but left after a thirty- to forty-five-minute conversation.[92] Moreover, a defendant is not in custody even though he is transported to the police station for questioning

---

[88]Mathis v United States, 391 US 1, 88 SCt 1503, 20 LEd(2d) 381 (1968).

[89]Mathis v United States, 391 US 1, 4, 88 SCt 1503, 20 LEd(2d) 381 (1968); State v Peeples, 94 App(3d) 34, 640 NE(2d) 208 (Pickaway 1994), appeal dismissed by 70 OS(3d) 1445, 639 NE(2d) 113 (1994) (defendant was not interrogated when summoned and interviewed in correctional officer's office where the defendant was not yet the focus of a criminal investigation, was summoned only because he was acting unusual in that he was packing his belongings, and the correctional officer was not even aware at that time that another inmate had been killed; court said, "[i]t is apparent ... [that defendant] did not suffer a 'restriction in his freedom over and above that in his normal prison setting' ").

[90]Oregon v Mathiason, 429 US 492, 97 SCt 711, 50 LEd(2d) 714 (1977).

[91]California v Beheler, 436 US 1121, 103 SCt 3517, 77 LEd(2d) 1275 (1983).

[92]State v Barnes, 25 OS(3d) 203, 25 OBR 266, 495 NE(2d) 922 (1986), cert denied 480 US 926, 107 SCt 1388, 94 LEd(2d) 701 (1987).

in a police car where he called and indicated that he did not have transportation down to the station.[93]

Allowing a suspect to leave at the conclusion of interrogation, while persuasive, is not itself dispositive of the issue of whether the suspect was in custody during the interrogation. The Clermont County Court of Appeals confronted mixed signals in *State v Wilson*[94] and had to decide whether the suspect was in custody while he took a polygraph test. Arguing against a finding of custody were the facts that the suspect voluntarily went in the police cruiser to undergo the test and was permitted to leave the test site upon completion of the test. However, the court found greater significance in the fact that during the test the suspect was told to complete the test after indicating that he wanted to remove the polygraph wires. This fact, coupled with his age and inexperience with the police as an adult, outweighed the indications that he was not in custody and convinced the court of appeals the suspect was in fact deprived of his freedom in a significant way, thereby invoking the *Miranda* rule.

Greater difficulty has been experienced in determining the applicability of *Miranda* when the interrogation takes place out of a police station or jail and on a suspect's familiar grounds. In *Orozco v Texas*,[95] the Court had no difficulty finding that the defendant had been deprived of his freedom of action in a significant way even though police officers had questioned the defendant in his own home. The questioning in *Orozco*, however, took place in the defendant's bedroom at 4 a.m. Additionally, one of the interrogating officers conceded that the defendant was under arrest and would not have been permitted to leave if he had attempted to do so. Rather than hinge its decision on the coercive circumstances surrounding the interrogation in *Orozco*, the majority held that *Miranda* warnings must be given prior to interrogation following an arrest, no matter where the interrogation occurs.[96] *Miranda* will apply even if the formalities surrounding an arrest have not yet occurred. For example, a wounded and hospitalized suspect is actually in custody when being questioned by a police officer who had a warrant in his pocket for the suspect's arrest but who refrained from serving

---

[93]State v Barker, 53 OS(2d) 135, 372 NE(2d) 1324 (1978), cert denied 439 US 913, 99 SCt 285, 58 LEd(2d) 260 (1978); see also State v Gorey, 68 Misc(2d) 44, 646 NE(2d) 1208 (1994); see also State v Yockey, No. 2257, 1987 WL 16914 (9th Dist Ct App, Wayne, 9-9-87) (defendant not in custody where he voluntarily accompanied the officers to the police station for questioning and he was free to leave at any time).

[94]State v Wilson, 31 App(3d) 133, 31 OBR 221, 508 NE(2d) 1002 (Clermont 1986); State v Brown, 91 App(3d) 427, 632 NE(2d) 970 (Wood 1993), appeal dismissed by 68 OS(3d) 1471, 628 NE(2d) 1390 (1994) (even though defendant was told that he was free to leave or not to answer questions, defendant was in custody at Human Services meeting where he was threatened with removal of his child if he did not show up for the meeting, and the interview which was conducted in a small office with the door closed was dominated by a police officer who was 6'5" and 330 pounds and stood "inches away" from the defendant when questioning him).

[95]Orozco v Texas, 394 US 324, 89 SCt 1095, 22 LEd(2d) 311 (1969).

[96]Accord, State v Peters, 12 App(2d) 83, 231 NE(2d) 91 (Franklin 1967) (*Miranda* applicable to interrogation of arrested defendant at his home, absent the egregious circumstances accompanying the interrogation in *Orozco*).

the warrant for the sole reason of avoiding responsibility for hospital costs.[97] However, the custody must be under the control of the state.

The Court found *Miranda* inapplicable to a probationer's interview with his probation officer in *Minnesota v Murphy*.[98] A probation interview, the Court held, is not "custody" even though the probation officer may compel the probationer's attendance.

"Custodial arrest," Justice White wrote, "is said to convey to the suspect a message that he has no choice but to submit to the officer's will and to confess. It is unlikely that a probation interview, arranged by appointment at a mutually convenient time, would give rise to a similar impression."[99] The Court pointed out that the defendant had regular meetings with his probation officer in her office in the past and that his familiarity with her and her office should have insulated him from any psychological intimidation. The fact that the probation officer consciously sought incriminating statements during the interview did not convert the regular appointment into a custodial situation. The probationer's ability to leave the office was considered critical and "not comparable to the pressure on a suspect who is painfully aware that he literally cannot escape a persistent custodial interrogator."[100] The Ohio Supreme Court has held, however, that *Miranda* is applicable to a probation officer's interview with a defendant who is in custody, even though the interview took place not in isolation but in the booking area where the defendant was being processed.[101]

Questioning outside the police station in absence of extraordinary circumstances such as those in *Orozco* is not custodial and therefore does not require issuance of the *Miranda* warnings. In *Orozco*, the Court relied on the officer's testimony that the defendant was under arrest and not free to leave when he was questioned. The Supreme Court would approach the issue differently today. Rather than the officer's perceptions, the present test focuses on how a reasonable person in the defendant's position would perceive the situation. The officer's testimony is only relevant to helping to recreate the factual setting.

---

[97]State v White, No. 1230, 1986 WL 6048 (4th Dist Ct App, Athens, 5-23-86).

[98]Minnesota v Murphy, 465 US 420, 104 SCt 1136, 79 LEd(2d) 409 (1984).

[99]Minnesota v Murphy, 465 US 420, 433, 104 SCt 1136, 79 LEd(2d) 409 (1984).

[100]Minnesota v Murphy, 465 US 420, 433, 104 SCt 1136, 79 LEd(2d) 409 (1984); see also Beckwith v United States, 425 US 341, 96 SCt 1612, 48 LEd(2d) 1 (1976) (*Miranda* inapplicable to questioning by IRS agents from the criminal division at the defendant's home when he was not under arrest).

[101]State v Roberts, 32 OS(3d) 225, 513 NE(2d) 720 (1987). Ohio has generally held that in order for statements made to parole or probation officers to be admissible, the accused must be advised of his right to remain silent. See generally State v Burkholder, 12 OS(3d) 205, 12 OBR 269, 466 NE(2d) 176 (1984), cert denied 469 US 1062, 105 SCt 545, 83 LEd(2d) 432 (1984); State v Gallagher, 38 OS(2d) 291, 313 NE(2d) 396 (1974), vacated by 425 US 257, 96 SCt 1438, 47 LEd(2d) 722 (1976). These cases may be reconsidered after *Murphy* and the emphasis may be repositioned, as in *Roberts*, upon custody, the federal inquiry, although, in addition to custody, *Roberts* focused upon abuse of trust.

The Court's meaning became clear in *Berkemer v McCarty*,[102] arising out of a traffic stop in the Columbus area prompted by the defendant's car weaving in and out of a highway lane. As soon as the defendant stepped out of the car at the highway patrol officer's request and had difficulty standing, the officer decided to arrest him. Nonetheless, that decision was not communicated to the defendant until after he had made some incriminating statements.

Justice Marshall, for the majority, wrote, "[A] policeman's unarticulated plan has no bearing on the question whether a suspect was 'in custody' at a particular time; the only relevant inquiry is how a reasonable man in the suspect's position would have understood his situation."[103] Justice Marshall said that the atmosphere surrounding an ordinary traffic stop, that it is exposed to public view and that a motorist generally faces but one or two officers, is "substantially less 'police dominated' " than the type of situation in which *Miranda* has been found applicable.[104] A single police officer asking a modest number of questions and requesting a suspect to perform a simple balancing test visible to passing motorists was held not "the functional equivalent of formal arrest."[105] *Berkemer* imposed a totally objective test for determining whether a suspect is in custody. An officer's uncommunicated belief that the person interrogated is not a suspect is irrelevant to the custody question. The Supreme Court, in *Stansbury v California*,[106] held that "the initial determination of custody depends on the objective circumstances of the interrogation, not on the subjective views harbored by either the interrogating officers or the person being questioned." The Medina Court of Appeals applied *Berkemer* correctly when it held that "[s]imply requiring defendant to sit in a police car for a short period of time to answer a few questions did not elevate the situation beyond the realm of the ordinary traffic stop."[107] However, while a simple request to be seated in a cruiser may not constitute an arrest, the police questioning that follows may cause a reasonable person in similar circumstances to understand that his freedom of action is limited to a degree associated with a formal arrest.[108]

---

[102]Berkemer v McCarty, 468 US 420, 104 SCt 3138, 82 LEd(2d) 317 (1984).

[103]Berkemer v McCarty, 468 US 420, 442, 104 SCt 3138, 82 LEd(2d) 317 (1984). But see State v Walker, 90 App(3d) 352, 629 NE(2d) 471 (Marion 1993) (defendant was not in custody and not entitled to Miranda warnings where the interrogation took place at his own residence and his movements were not restrained in any way); State v Waibel, 89 App(3d) 522, 625 NE(2d) 637 (Medina 1993), appeal dismissed by 68 OS(3d) 1406, 623 NE(2d) 564 (1993) (defendant was not in custody when interviewed in back of police crusier where he was allowed to call his girlfriend and he was told twice that he was not under arrest).

[104]Berkemer v McCarty, 468 US 420, 439, 104 SCt 3138, 82 LEd(2d) 317 (1984); see also Pennsylvania v Bruder, 488 US 9, 109 SCt 205, 102 LEd(2d) 172 (1988).

[105]Berkemer v McCarty, 468 US 420, 439, 104 SCt 3138, 82 LEd(2d) 317 (1984); see also Pennsylvania v Bruder, 488 US 9, 109 SCt 205, 102 LEd(2d) 172 (1988).

[106]Stansbury v California, 114 SCt 1526, 1529, 128 LEd(2d) 293 (1994), cert denied 116 SCt 320, 133 LEd(2d) 222 (1995).

[107]State v Warrell, 41 App(3d) 286, 287, 534 NE(2d) 1237 (Medina 1987).

[108]State v Rossiter, 88 App(3d) 162, 623 NE(2d) 645 (Ross 1993).

Each situation must be decided on its own facts. The Ohio Supreme Court has held that *Miranda* becomes applicable to an unusually long roadside investigation following a DUI stop.[109] Similarly, the Union County Court of Appeals found that a defendant's freedom of action was significantly affected where the police sent away his ride when the defendant was placed in the back of the police car and transported to the scene of the accident.[110]

Berkemer was improperly relied upon by a trial court that found a defendant not in custody when, along with others at a fraternity party, he was ordered to "freeze" and raise his hands, his ID was confiscated, and he was detained for an hour until individually questioned and a confession of underage drinking was exacted. The Wood County Court of Appeals held that this was "not a temporary, brief, public and non-'police dominated' interview envisioned in the *Berkemer* exception to the *Miranda* rule."[111]

CROSS REFERENCES

Text Ch 4

19.06   Interrogation

In addition to custody, *Miranda* requires interrogation. The two factors must exist together for the rules imposed in the decision to apply. As described in the previous section, questioning outside of a custodial setting, or one in which there are not similar indicia of restraint upon freedom of action, does not activate the need for the warnings. Similarly, the fact of custody alone does not require the warnings unless police intend or do in fact interrogate. The *Miranda* rules are not applicable to a statement volunteered to the police, and police need not stop one who volunteers to incriminate himself while he is advised of his rights. Rather, those rights come into play and the warnings must be given when the two critical factors, custody and questioning, concur. The tone of the *Miranda v Arizona*[112] decision was far different from *Escobedo v Illinois*.[113] The earlier case manifested distrust of all out-of-court statements made by a suspect in the absence of counsel, and the Court almost appeared on the verge of barring all such statements. *Miranda,* on the other hand, sounded a different note, reaffirming that "[c]onfessions remain a proper element of law enforcement."[114] The Court stressed that the fundamental issue was not whether a person in custody could talk to police without benefit of warnings and counsel, but whether he could be interrogated. The absence of *Miranda* warnings will not affect the admissibility of statements made on a suspect's own initiative in the absence of questions or other conduct by the police

[109]State v Henderson, 51 OS(3d) 54, 554 NE(2d) 104 (1990) (probable cause was indisputable; the defendant made no attempt to leave, and the officer testified that he would not have allowed him to leave).
[110]State v Imel, No. 14-86-35, 1989 WL 49485 (3d Dist Ct App, Union, 5-8-89).
[111]State v Wilson, 76 App(3d) 519, 523, 602 NE(2d) 409 (Wood 1991).
[112]Miranda v Arizona, 384 US 436, 86 SCt 1602, 16 LEd(2d) 694 (1966).
[113]Escobedo v Illinois, 378 US 478, 84 SCt 1758, 12 LEd(2d) 977 (1964).
[114]Miranda v Arizona, 384 US 436, 478, 86 SCt 1602, 16 LEd(2d) 694 (1966).

constituting interrogation.[115] Discussions about a crime initiated by an individual who is not a suspect in that crime do not implicate *Miranda* rights even though the individual is in custody and was interrogated on another charge.[116]

The mere fact that police officers ask questions does not always implicate *Miranda* rights. Note, of course, that a defendant must be in custody. Also, police encounter situations where it is perfectly appropriate for them to seek clarification. In *State v Huff*,[117] officers responding to a report of a domestic quarrel found the wife on the porch covered with blood. She told them that her husband, the defendant, had struck her. A subsequent inquiry of the husband was characterized as an attempt to clarify the situation, not interrogation, and therefore held not to implicate *Miranda*. The defendant in *Huff* could also be found not to have been in custody at the time of the inquiry, notwithstanding that custody was likely and forthcoming, although perhaps some answers he could have given might have persuaded the officers not to arrest him.

Answers to questions that are asked as part of the standardized booking process are admissible without prior administration of *Miranda* warnings. Videotaped answers to so-called "pedigree" questions—name, address, height, weight, etc.—are not rendered inadmissible simply because the slurred nature of the defendant's speech is incriminating. The line, which is not altogether clear, is crossed when a defendant's response is incriminating not just because of delivery but because the content of the answer supports an element of the charge. In *Pennsylvania v Muniz*,[118] the Supreme Court held that the line was crossed when the defendant, arrested for DUI, could not provide police with the correct date of his sixth birthday, and the content of his answer supported an inference that his mental state was confused. Statements in response to pedigree questions are admissible even though made after a defendant has exercised *Miranda* rights.[119]

A defendant in custody may be asked to take a breathalyzer test without being advised of *Miranda* rights.[120] And, of course, field sobriety tests, which generally occur before arrest, are not testimonial or communicative and do not implicate *Miranda* rights.[121] Even if the defendant is in custody, nonverbal results of a breathalyzer and field sobriety tests are still not considered testimonial.[122]

---

[115]Akron v Milewski, 21 App(3d) 140, 21 OBR 149, 487 NE(2d) 582 (Summit 1985).

[116]State v Roe, 41 OS(3d) 18, 535 NE(2d) 1351 (1989), affirmed by 1992 WL 246023 (1992), appeal dismissed by 66 OS(3d) 1444, 609 NE(2d) 171 (1993).

[117]State v Huff, No. 17-88-8, 1990 WL 7964 (2d Dist Ct App, Shelby, 1-31-90).

[118]Pennsylvania v Muniz, 496 US 582, 110 SCt 2638, 110 LEd(2d) 528 (1990); see also State v Geasley, 85 App(3d) 360, 619 NE(2d) 1086 (Summit 1993) (asking a DUI arrestee to guess the correct time is not a pedigree question).

[119]State v Geasley, 85 App(3d) 360, 619 NE(2d) 1086 (Summit 1993) (statements made by a suspect in response to instructions on the state's implied consent law are admissible).

[120]State v Feasel, 41 App(3d) 155, 534 NE(2d) 940 (Seneca 1988).

[121]State v Brandenburg, 41 App(3d) 109, 534 NE(2d) 906 (Montgomery 1987).

[122]State v Henderson, 51 OS(3d) 54, 554 NE(2d) 104 (1990).

A helpful understanding of what *Miranda* sought to protect, or at least of how the present Supreme Court views *Miranda's* purpose, was set forth in *Illinois v Perkins*,[123] a quarter century after the *Miranda* decision. *Perkins* involved statements made in custody to a police officer posing as another inmate. *Miranda* focused on the coercion that arises when an arrestee in custody is questioned by a person he knows to be a police officer. The *Miranda* Court was concerned about the unique situation created by a combination of custody and police interrogation that is police-dominated and calculated to impress on the suspect that he must comply with the officer's request for information. To achieve that condition, a suspect would have to know that he is being questioned by a police officer. The Court in *Perkins*, however, pointed out that the compulsion is "not present when an incarcerated person speaks freely to someone whom he believes to be a fellow inmate."[124] Consequently, the defendant did not have to be advised of his *Miranda* rights.

Perkins involved the inapplicability of Fifth Amendment-*Miranda* protections under these circumstances; a different result will obtain later in the life of a case after the defendant is charged and his Sixth Amendment right to counsel comes into play.[125] Justice Brennan concurred, agreeing "that when a suspect does not know that his questioner is a police agent, such questioning does not amount to 'interrogation' "[126] Yet, a troubling aspect of *Perkins* remains unreconciled with *Miranda*. The *Miranda* Court was concerned with deceit and trickery as well as coercion. Justice Brennan indicated in *Perkins* that the police conduct in that case, while not a *Miranda* violation, was probably a due process violation. The author believes that such a claim would be given short shrift by the Supreme Court that remains after the departures of Justices Brennan and Marshall.

The US Supreme Court has also found that it is not custodial interrogation within the meaning of *Miranda* when the police tape record a defendant's answers to his wife's questions during a visit when he is custody.[127] Police were investigating the murder of the couple's child. Certainly, the confrontation between the suspect and his wife was emotionally charged and the subject of their child's death would undoubtedly be the focus of their conversation. The situation met the *Innis* standard, which is now modified, presumably because allowing an accused to consult with family

---

[123]Illinois v Perkins, 496 US 292, 110 SCt 2394, 110 LEd(2d) 243 (1990), cert denied 114 SCt 2692, 129 LEd(2d) 823 (1994).

[124]Illinois v Perkins, 496 US 292, 296, 110 SCt 2394, 110 LEd(2d) 243 (1990), cert denied 114 SCt 2692, 129 LEd(2d) 823 (1994).

[125]See Text Ch 20, Lineups and Pretrial Identification.

[126]Illinois v Perkins, 496 US 292, 110 SCt 2394, , 2399 110 LEd(2d) 243 (1990), cert denied 114 SCt 2692, 129 LEd(2d) 823 (1994) (Brennan, J., concurring).

[127]Arizona v Mauro, 481 US 520, 107 SCt 1931, 95 LEd(2d) 458 (1987); see also State v Brewer, 48 OS(3d) 50, 549 NE(2d) 491 (1990), affirmed by 1994 WL 527740 (1994), cert denied 116 SCt 101, 133 LEd(2d) 55 (1995) (for different but related issue, where defendant's statement while in custody to his wife was observed by police through one-way mirror).

members during a custody situation is not the type of compulsion with which *Miranda* and its progeny are concerned.[128]

Not surprisingly, a quarter of a century after the decision, the courts are still concerned with determining what *Miranda* sought to protect. After all, it was fifteen years after the decision before the United States Supreme Court finally provided a definition of "interrogation." By then the personnel of the Court had changed dramatically, and the interpretations of *Miranda* previously delivered by the Burger Court demonstrated the new Court's antipathy to the Warren Court's views on the need to control custodial interrogation. Nonetheless, in *Rhode Island v Innis*,[129] the Court provided an expansive definition of the operative term.

First, the *Innis* Court looked to the *Miranda* decision for guidance where the Warren Court defined custodial interrogation as "questioning initiated by law enforcement officers."[130] The Burger Court, however, declined to accept the narrow option offered by the language of the *Miranda* decision, which would have limited the necessity for the warnings to instances where there is express questioning. Instead, Justice Stewart for the *Innis* majority acknowledged that "techniques of persuasion, no less than express questioning, were thought, in a custodial setting, to amount to interrogation."[131] Then Justice Stewart stated:

> *Miranda* safeguards come into play whenever a person in custody is subjected to either express questioning or its functional equivalent. That is to say, the term "interrogation" under *Miranda* refers not only to express questioning, but also to any words or actions on the part of the police (other than those normally attendant to arrest and custody) that the police should know are reasonably likely to elicit an incriminating response from the suspect. The latter portion of this definition focuses primarily upon the perceptions of the suspect, rather than the intent of the police. This focus reflects the fact that *Miranda* safeguards were designed to vest a suspect in custody with an added measure of protection against coercive police practices, without regard to objective proof of the underlying intent of the police. A practice that the police should know is reasonably likely to evoke an incriminating response from a suspect thus amounts to interrogation. But since the police surely cannot be held accountable for the unforeseeable results of their words or actions, the definition of interrogation can extend only to words or actions on the part of police officers that they *should have known* were reasonably likely to elicit an incriminating response.[132]

This broad definition should have resolved the issue once and for all. Custodial interrogation, thereby activating the *Miranda* rules governing the admissibility of incriminating statements, is not limited to express questioning but could extend to all words and actions reasonably likely to elicit an

---

[128]State v Rowe, 68 App(3d) 595, 589 NE(2d) 394 (Franklin 1990).

[129]Rhode Island v Innis, 446 US 291, 100 SCt 1682, 64 LEd(2d) 297 (1980), cert denied 456 US 930, 102 SCt 1980, 72 LEd(2d) 447 (1982).

[130]Miranda v Arizona, 384 US 436, 444, 86 SCt 1602, 16 LEd(2d) 694 (1966).

[131]Rhode Island v Innis, 446 US 291, 299, 100 SCt 1682, 64 LEd(2d) 297 (1980), cert denied 456 US 930, 102 SCt 1980, 72 LEd(2d) 447 (1982).

[132]Rhode Island v Innis, 446 US 291, 300-302, 100 SCt 1682, 64 LEd(2d) 297 (1980), cert denied 456 US 930, 102 SCt 1980, 72 LEd(2d) 447 (1982).

incriminating response. However, application of the definition to the *Innis* facts left a substantial measure of uncertainty.

The controversy arose in *Innis* when shortly after the robbery of a taxicab driver, the victim identified a picture of the assailant who had robbed him with a sawed-off shotgun. Innis was spotted on the street by a police officer who arrested him and advised him of his rights. When backup police arrived on the scene, the defendant was advised of his rights two more times. Innis indicated that he understood his rights and wished to speak with an attorney.[133] Three officers were directed to take Innis to the police station, and not to interrogate him along the way.

While enroute to the police station, two of the officers engaged each other in conversation describing their concerns that the shotgun was probably in the vicinity of a school for handicapped girls. One officer expressed his fear that a little girl might find the weapon and accidently cause it to discharge, killing herself. Innis interrupted this conversation and directed the officers to return to the scene of the arrest where he promised to show them the location of the gun. They returned to the scene of the arrest, where officers once again advised Innis of his *Miranda* rights. He told them that he understood his rights but that he wanted to retrieve the gun because of the children at the school. He led police to the spot where the shotgun was hidden.

The Supreme Court reinstated the conviction, concluding that there was no way that the police should have known that their conversation was reasonably likely to elicit an incriminating response from the accused. The majority relied on the absence in the record of any reason to suggest that the police knew or should have known that the accused was unusually upset at the time of his arrest or that he was "peculiarly susceptible to an appeal to his conscience concerning the safety of handicapped children."[134]

The three dissenting justices accepted the majority's definition of interrogation but disagreed with the application of the definition to this case. Justice Stevens argued that the statement made by the police officer was no less interrogation than if he had (1) asked Innis directly where the shotgun was hidden; or (2) told his fellow officer, "If the man sitting in the back seat with me should decide to tell us where the gun is, we can protect handicapped children from danger."[135] According to Stevens, all three forms of the statement, including the one spoken by the police officer, "appear to be designed to elicit a response from anyone who in fact knew where the gun was located."[136] He criticized the majority opinion for making the form of

---

[133]*Innis* was decided before Edwards v Arizona, 451 US 477, 101 SCt 1880, 68 LEd(2d) 378 (1981) Regardless of the officer's subjective or objective intent, the defendant was responding to a statement about the case after indicating a desire to see an attorney which under *Edwards* would require suppression of the statement.

[134]Rhode Island v Innis, 446 US 291, 302, 100 SCt 1682, 64 LEd(2d) 297 (1980), cert denied 456 US 930, 102 SCt 1980, 72 LEd(2d) 447 (1982).

[135]Rhode Island v Innis, 446 US 291, 312, 100 SCt 1682, 64 LEd(2d) 297 (1980), cert denied 456 US 930, 102 SCt 1980, 72 LEd(2d) 447 (1982).

[136]Rhode Island v Innis, 446 US 291, 312, 100 SCt 1682, 64 LEd(2d) 297 (1980), cert denied 456 US 930, 102 SCt 1980, 72 LEd(2d) 447 (1982).

the statement critical, thus turning "Miranda's unequivocal rule against any interrogation at all into a trap in which unwary suspects may be caught by police deception."[137] Note that the Ohio Supreme Court appears less concerned about the form that a police officer's statement takes. In *State v Knuckles*,[138] the Court said that a police officer's statement, "We want to talk to you about Bobby Bennett" (a murder victim), is likely to provoke a response. Although the case dealt with the resumption of interrogation following a request for counsel, it appears to provide a broad test for defining interrogation.

The meaning of the "functional equivalent" of interrogation narrowed somewhat in 1987. With a flair, the Supreme Court stated in *Arizona v Mauro*[139] that police do not interrogate a suspect simply by hoping that he will confess. There, the suspect was arrested for murdering his son. After he was given *Miranda* warnings, he declined to talk with police until he saw a lawyer. The suspect was visited by his wife at her request. The meeting took place with a police officer present and a recorder in plain view. The tape recording of the conversation between the suspect and his wife was played at trial to rebut the defense's insanity claim.

The Court ruled that the police actions following the suspect's decision to exercise his rights did not constitute the functional equivalent of interrogation. The officer who was present during the conversation asked no questions about the crime or about the suspect's conduct. More importantly, the Court said that the police decision to allow the wife to see the suspect was not the kind of psychological ploy that properly could be treated as the functional equivalent of interrogation.

This conclusion is based on three factors. First, the wife was advised that she could see her husband only if an officer was present. Second, the officer who was present produced the recorder and told the couple that their conversation would be recorded. The Court agreed with the trial judge's ruling that the suspect could have chosen not to speak to his wife but, instead, did speak. What the majority failed to focus on was that the suspect was not given advance warning of this meeting, that his wife would be accompanied by a police officer, and that their conversation would be recorded. Moreover, at trial the police acknowledged that they knew that the confrontation was reasonably likely to produce an incriminating statement. Under *Innis* this should be the functional equivalent of interrogation. Third, the Court found legitimate security reasons for not permitting the couple to meet privately. The Court concluded that the police behavior did not *implicate* the purpose of *Miranda*, which was to prevent government officials from using the coercive nature of confinement to extract confessions that would not be given in an unrestrained atmosphere.

---

[137]Rhode Island v Innis, 446 US 291, 314, 100 SCt 1682, 64 LEd(2d) 297 (1980), cert denied 456 US 930, 102 SCt 1980, 72 LEd(2d) 447 (1982).

[138]State v Knuckles, 65 OS(3d) 494, 605 NE(2d) 54 (1992), cert denied ＿＿ US ＿＿, 113 SCt 2986, 125 LEd(2d) 682 (1993).

[139]Arizona v Mauro, 481 US 520, 107 SCt 1931, 95 LEd(2d) 458 (1987).

Nonetheless, the conclusion cannot be avoided that in *Mauro* the Court sanctioned creation of an encounter, which police should know is reasonably likely to elicit an incriminating response, and thus substantially weakened the *Innis* definition of interrogation. The Court said that the actions in this case were far less questionable than the subtle compulsion that was held not to be interrogation in *Innis*. However, that comparison misses the point. The supposedly offhand comment in *Innis* was far less likely to produce incriminating statements than the meeting between the wife in this case and the suspect who had been arrested for murdering their son.[140]

CROSS REFERENCES

　　　　Text 19.01

19.07　Exercising the right to remain silent

(A) In general

The Burger Court filled in the broad outline sketched in *Miranda*. The Court's rulings, however, have distinguished sharply between the exercise of the right to remain silent and the right to counsel. Considering the *Miranda* Court's explicit concern for the unknowing suspect, the Burger Court's greatest impact has been in its development of rules delineating what an accused must do to signify that he is exercising these rights, and the different controls that apply to police interrogators when an accused exercises the right to counsel rather than his right to remain silent. These rules have created a trap for the unwary suspect who does not understand that the rights are different and will be treated differently.

(B) Invoking the right to remain silent

The *Miranda* Court sought to protect unknowing persons who are arrested and have no knowledge of their rights and who are most likely to be coerced by the existing atmosphere during custodial interrogation. Consequently, in addition to inquiring whether the suspect was warned of his rights, the subsequent inquiry focused on whether the suspect wanted to answer the interrogator's questions. The successor Courts, on the other hand, have focused on whether the suspect has invoked his rights, thus marking a significant departure from *Miranda*.

The tone of the *Miranda v Arizona*[141] decision was quite clear. Following administration of the warnings, statements that are the product of interrogation are inadmissible unless the accused explicitly waives the right to remain silent and the right to counsel and consents to the interrogation. The change of tone became clear in *Fare v Michael C.*,[142] where a juvenile taken into custody on suspicion of murder was given *Miranda* warnings and then asked to see his probation officer rather than invoking his right to silence or asking to see a lawyer. The police officer declined to call the

---

[140]See also State v Brewer, 48 OS(3d) 50, 549 NE(2d) 491 (1990), affirmed by 1994 WL 527740 (1994), cert denied 116 SCt 101, 133 LEd(2d) 55 (1995) (same result on a different but related issue).

[141]Miranda v Arizona, 384 US 436, 86 SCt 1602, 16 LEd(2d) 694 (1966).

[142]Fare v Michael C., 442 US 707, 99 SCt 2560, 61 LEd(2d) 197 (1979).

probation officer but, instead, told the juvenile that he could talk to the officers without an attorney present but that he did not have to. The juvenile then agreed to answer the police officers' questions and incriminated himself.

The majority that fashioned the *Miranda* rules likely would have viewed the juvenile's equivocal response as a clear indication of the suspect's unwillingness to undergo questioning. The Burger Court majority, however, refused to interpret the suspect's equivocation as an invocation of either his right to remain silent or to counsel and went on to find a valid waiver of those rights, resulting in the admissibility of the incriminating statements. Consequently, the shift from ascertaining whether the accused waived his rights and was willing to answer questions to whether the suspect had invoked his rights became clear. Hence, the clarity of expression of an accused is critical, which, of course, poses a definite obstacle to the uninitiated who were the class the *Miranda* Court intended to protect.

Cutting off questioning has not been as easy as the *Miranda* opinion has led one to expect. For example, in *State v House*,[143] the Ohio Supreme Court said, "It is well established that the refusal to answer certain questions is not the equivalent of a recession of a previously given waiver of Miranda rights." The Court failed to indicate how many questions the accused refused to answer, whether they were consecutive questions or a series of continuous questions. The Court never explained at what point they would recognize silence as the equivalent of a recession or whether it could never serve that purpose. Clearly, at some point, it should. Ohio was not alone, nor did *House* represent the most strained interpretation. The Idaho Supreme Court held that an accused's statement, "I'd rather not make any other comments at this time," was not sufficient to revoke a waiver and invoke the right to remain silent.[144] The Kansas Supreme Court refused an accused's question, "Well, do I have to say that?", as an expression of his intent that questioning cease.[145]

In all fairness, ascertaining precisely what a suspect intended is not always as easy as the example presented to the Idaho court. A good illustration of how difficult the task can be appears in *State v Wilkerson*,[146] where, during interrogation, the suspect twice said during a response, "I didn't do it and that's all I got to say." The first time he said it, the interrogation continued. The second time, the interrogation stopped. The court could have taken the words at face value and held that this expression constituted an effort by the accused to cut off interrogation. However, after hearing a tape recording of the interrogation, the Franklin County Court of Appeals held differently. The first time the defendant expressed that sentiment, he went on continuing to speak about the alleged crime without prompting before he was asked an additional question. Further, the court said his tone of voice differed. The first time, the court found, his tone of voice was not such that he wished the interview to cease; it confirmed an air of finality,

[143]State v House, 54 OS(2d) 297, 376 NE(2d) 588 (1978).
[144]State v Anspaugh, 97 Idaho 519, 547 P(2d) 1124 (1976).
[145]State v Nichols, 212 Kan 814, 512 P(2d) 329 (1973).
[146]State v Wilkerson, No. 80AP-295 (10th Dist Ct App, Franklin, 12-31-80).

affirming his innocence. The second time that he expressed that sentiment, it followed silence in response to several questions, and the police immediately terminated the interrogation.

Without the tape recording, the statement on its face required suppression and a finding that the accused intended that interrogation cease. The actual rulings by the hearing and appeals courts were clearly based on their ability to discern the accused's intention each time he uttered that sentence. While one can disagree with those conclusions, *Wilkerson* indicates the value of recording or videotaping interrogation sessions. There is no justification for not having such a record of each interrogation. It would likely eliminate disputes about what took place behind closed doors, eliminating some motions to suppress and some briefs in opposition to such motions. Moreover, video recorders are so common today that perhaps a tape recorder is no longer a sufficient substitute. Further, the state should not be permitted to claim that a defendant indicated a willingness to resume questioning or waived rights while the tape was off, although the Ohio Supreme Court clearly disagrees, holding that the alleged inadvertent erasure of a portion of a tape recording, which contained *Miranda* warnings, would not create presumption that such warnings were not given.[147]

(C) Resumption of interrogation

An equally noticeable shift in tone came in the Burger Court's response to the question whether an accused who has asserted his right to silence may be asked subsequently to waive that right and submit to interrogation. The situation arose in *Michigan v Mosley,*[148] where the accused was arrested in connection with a series of robberies. He was taken to the robbery bureau and given *Miranda* warnings. The accused declined to discuss the robberies or submit to questioning; he never requested to see an attorney. After refusing to submit to interrogation, the accused was placed in a cell, and then two hours later he was summoned by a different officer and taken to the homicide bureau. There, the accused was advised again of his *Miranda* rights and questioned about a holdup, other than the one for which the accused had been arrested, which had resulted in the death of the victim. At first the accused denied any involvement in the murder, but after the homicide detective falsely informed him that another suspect had confessed and named the accused as the perpetrator who fired the shot, the accused made an incriminating statement. This second interrogation session, conducted by a different detective in another location within the police headquarters, lasted fifteen minutes. At no time during the fifteen-minute session did Mosley request an attorney or indicate that he did not wish to discuss the murder. The admissibility of the incriminating statement hinged on the permissibility of the police seeking to question the accused after he had exercised his right to remain silent.

---

[147]State v Wiles, 59 OS(3d) 71, 571 NE(2d) 97 (1991), cert denied 506 US 832, 113 SCt 99, 121 LEd(2d) 59 (1992).

[148]Michigan v Mosley, 423 US 96, 96 SCt 321, 46 LEd(2d) 313 (1975), affirmed by 400 Mich 181, 254 NW(2d) 29 (1977), cert denied 434 US 861, 98 SCt 189, 54 LEd(2d) 135 (1977).

Miranda seemed to resolve the issue when Chief Justice Warren wrote:

> Once warnings have been given, the subsequent procedure is clear. If the individual indicates in any manner, at any time prior to or during questioning, that he wishes to remain silent, the interrogation must cease. At this point he has shown that he intends to exercise his Fifth Amendment privilege; any statement taken after the person invokes his privilege cannot be other than the product of compulsion, subtle or otherwise.[149]

Justice Stewart, for the *Mosley* majority, claimed that the above passage could be interpreted literally in three different ways: (1) that the accused could never again at any time or any place be interrogated; (2) that any subsequent statement, even if spontaneously volunteered, must be suppressed as the product of compulsion; or (3) that police could resume interrogation after a momentary respite. But Stewart's three alternatives were strawmen created to avoid recognition of the *Miranda* Court's intent, which viewed the rights to silence and counsel as inextricably linked. Alternatives more closely attuned to the earlier decision would have precluded further interrogation while the suspect remained in custody unless he volunteered to answer questions, or would have precluded the resumption of interrogation and attendant attempts to secure a waiver until after the accused has an opportunity to consult with an attorney. But the *Mosley* majority, intent on limiting the scope and impact of *Miranda*, rejected the strawmen that it created, as well as more appropriate interpretations, and created a new formula governing the resumption of interrogation following an accused's invocation of the right to remain silent.

Justice Stewart found that the police in *Mosley* had "scrupulously honored," as required in *Miranda*, the accused's decision not to submit to questioning or make a statement. He pointed out that the police cut off questioning immediately following invocation of the right to silence and did not attempt to wear the accused down by trying to make him change his mind. Further, the majority found that the police complied with *Miranda* by questioning "only after passage of a significant period of time [two hours]";[150] by issuing complete warnings prior to the unfruitful as well as the second successful interrogation session (which distinguished this case from *Westover*, one of the *Miranda* companion cases); and by restricting interrogation during the second session to a crime that had not been the subject of the earlier interrogation. The majority indicated that its conclusion was buttressed by the facts that the two interrogation sessions took place in different locations (albeit within the same police headquarters) and were conducted by two different detectives. In determining whether police scrupulously honored the accused's right to cut off questioning, the majority stated that the critical issues center on whether the accused is permitted to control the time at which questioning occurs, the subjects discussed, and duration of the questioning. The *Mosley* Court also indicated that its decision was influenced by the fact that Mosley invoked his right to silence but

---

[149]Miranda v Arizona, 384 US 436, 473-74, 86 SCt 1602, 16 LEd(2d) 694 (1966).

[150]Michigan v Mosley, 423 US 96, 106, 96 SCt 321, 46 LEd(2d) 313 (1975), affirmed by 400 Mich 181, 254 NW(2d) 29 (1977), cert denied 434 US 861, 98 SCt 189, 54 LEd(2d) 135 (1977).

never indicated that he wanted to see a lawyer. The procedures required following a request to see a lawyer were spelled out far more specifically in *Miranda*.

The *Mosley* dissenters attacked the majority's factual conclusions, which were critical both to the decision and the formula for testing whether the accused's rights had been "scrupulously honored." The majority found it critical that the second interrogation session concerned an unrelated crime, thereby evidencing the accused's ability to control the subject matter of the interrogation, and not merely a second crack at obtaining a confession on the charge for which Mosley was arrested. But the dissent pointed out that the accused was arrested in connection with a series of robberies, and the murder occurred during a robbery and was the subject of the same anonymous tip that led police to Mosley. Moreover, the dissent was unimpressed with the majority's time and place arguments, since the second session occurred within two hours and on a different floor of the same facility. Some have viewed the ability of police to renew questioning as an intensification of the inherent coercion that the *Miranda* Court automatically associated with custodial interrogation. In that view, the resumption of questioning indicates to the accused that his power to cut off questioning is severely limited and that police are still in total control of the situation, and hence his destiny.[151]

Few courts have interpreted the *Mosley* rule pertaining to the resumption of interrogation. Those fact-specific aspects of the case, which Justice Stewart found so persuasive have generally been ignored, i.e., different crime, different location, different interrogator. Nonetheless, those factors were not merely window dressing. The indication was in that case, that the accused controlled the subject of interrogation. When he did not wish to answer questions about the burglary, the interrogation ceased, and when it resumed the subject matter was different. Absent these differences, the message transmitted to the accused may be that he cannot terminate an interrogation.

Rarely do the same police not attempt to resume interrogation about the same crime. Consequently, it is necessary to isolate those factors in Stewart's opinion in *Mosley* that keep that case from becoming a slight-of-hand revocation of a suspect's right to cut off questioning by exercising the right to silence. Those minimal requirements are, as follows: (1) police must "scrupulously honor"[152] a suspect's attempt to cut off questioning; (2) the interrogation must cease immediately upon exercise of the right, whether at the outset or during an interrogation; (3) substantial time must elapse before police attempt to renew interrogation; and (4) *Miranda* rights must be read again.

---

[151]See People v Pettingill, 21 Cal(3d) 231, 578 P(2d) 108 (1978) (rejecting *Mosley* on state constitutional grounds).

[152]Michigan v Mosley, 423 US 96, 104, 96 SCt 321, 46 LEd(2d) 313 (1975), affirmed by 400 Mich 181, 254 NW(2d) 29 (1977), cert denied 434 US 861, 98 SCt 189, 54 LEd(2d) 135 (1977).

The only Ohio Supreme Court case to actually comment on the essence of *Mosley* is *State v House*,[153] discussed above for its rejection of silence in response to certain questions as indication of an accused's intent to cut off questioning and revoke a waiver. In dictum, Justice Locher wrote of his understanding that an accused's termination of questioning "meant that he desired to cease the interview and therefore necessitate the police officers to repeat the *Miranda* rights and obtain a waiver thereof before continuing the questioning."[154] Clearly the inference from this statement is that repetition of the warnings immediately following invocation of the right to silence satisfies the *Mosley* requirements and would allow the police to resume interrogating an accused about the same crime. The immediate resumption of interrogation makes a mockery of the requirement that police scrupulously honor a suspect's attempt to terminate interrogation at any time. Nonetheless, in *State v Wilkerson*,[155] the court found a fifteen-minute interval, during which time the accused was kept in the interrogation room and may or may not have been permitted to make a phone call, sufficient time before resumption of interrogation.

A more problematic ruling that police conduct complied with *Mosley* requirements is in *State v Lewingdon*,[156] where there were either two or three interrogation sessions depending on how the facts are interpreted. The defendant was interrogated in the evening, and he asked to be left alone. The next afternoon the defendant was brought back to the interrogation room for another round of questions. Before *Miranda* warnings were readministered, the defendant responded positively when police asked him if he would like to see his wife, who was in custody on other charges. While they awaited the wife, the police and the defendant discussed the crime, at which time the defendant told the police that he was not going to say anything. This discussion was not preceded by *Miranda* warnings because police had not intended to initiate it until the defendant had seen his wife. He indicated shortly after 8 p.m. that he was not going to say anything. He then saw his wife alone, and at 8:34 p.m. fresh *Miranda* warnings were given, and the defendant waived his rights and confessed shortly thereafter.

The Hamilton County Court of Appeals considered the issue both ways, that there were two or three interrogations, but in either event found *Mosley* satisfied. The facts of the case seem contrary to *Mosley*'s requirements for validation of the resumption of interrogation. If there were three interrogation sessions, then the defendant was badgered. Twice he told the police that he did not wish to be interrogated, yet less than one-half hour after the second indication, they recommenced interrogation.

If one just focuses on the two sessions held in the afternoon, even the court of appeals recognized difficulty in equating the time between the first discussion and the resumption of questioning less than one-half hour later with the two-hour period that elapsed in *Mosley*. While the court acknowledged the inadequacy of the half hour, it said "it certainly was significant in

---

[153]State v House, 54 OS(2d) 297, 376 NE(2d) 588 (1978).
[154]State v House, 54 OS(2d) 297, 300, 376 NE(2d) 588 (1978).
[155]State v Wilkerson, No. 80AP-295 (10th Dist Ct App, Franklin, 12-31-80).
[156]State v Lewingdon, No. C-790488 (1st Dist Ct App, Hamilton, 12-24-80).

terms of impact." The dramatic change in the defendant's attitude following his visit with his wife when he no longer showed any reluctance to talk was sufficient, according to the court, to demonstrate that his right to cut off questioning had been scrupulously honored, thus paving the way for the admissibility of the statement defendant gave after the visit.

While that may have satisfied the "scrupulously honored" part of the test (although it is not clear how his change of attitude is relevant to that inquiry), it does not satisfy the need to show that he could control the subjects of conversation, which is a prerequisite to resumption of interrogation. Despite the defendant's assertion that he wanted to be left alone, the police made it clear to him that he would be interrogated.

If *Mosley* significantly reduced the effect of the *Miranda* safeguards, these applications of the *Mosley* standards even water down the effect of that rule.

19.08   Exercising the right to counsel

(A) In general

The *Mosley*[157] Court substantially weakened the impact of an accused's invocation of the right to cut off questioning by recognizing limited authority for police to resume interrogation. The *Mosley* Court, however, in dicta, indicated that the result would not have been the same had the accused, instead of exercising his right to silence, invoked his right to counsel. The different result, which on its face may appear to be excessive formalism developed to justify a watering-down of *Miranda* rights, may be traced, in fact, to the language of the *Miranda* decision. Chief Justice Warren's landmark opinion specified only that following an accused's invocation of silence, questioning must cease. There was no clear indication whether the Court intended that to be a permanent cessation, a gap filled by *Mosley*. *Miranda*, however, presented with specificity the conditions for resuming interrogation once an accused requests to consult with an attorney.

Miranda specified that interrogation must cease once an accused requests to see an attorney. Further, the Court stipulated that the interrogation could not resume until the accused had the opportunity to consult with an attorney and have him present during interrogation.[158]

Unlike other issues pertaining to *Miranda*, the Supreme Court has not engaged in undermining the *Miranda* right to counsel. In fact, there has been an on-going strengthening of the right.

(B) Invoking the Miranda *right to counsel*

Any statement made by an accused indicating a desire for an attorney is sufficient to invoke the *Miranda* right and requires cessation of interrogation until the accused has the opportunity to consult with the attorney. In

---

[157]Michigan v Mosley, 423 US 96, 96 SCt 321, 46 LEd(2d) 313 (1975), affirmed by 400 Mich 181, 254 NW(2d) 29 (1977), cert denied 434 US 861, 98 SCt 189, 54 LEd(2d) 135 (1977).

[158]Miranda v Arizona, 384 US 436, 86 SCt 1602, 16 LEd(2d) 694 (1966).

State v Martin,[159] an accused was asked if he would answer questions and responded affirmatively, but answered negatively when asked if he would answer questions without an attorney. The Hamilton County Court of Appeals said the defendant's response was an unambiguous exercise of the right to counsel.

The accused must assert the right to counsel. Failure to indicate that he does not want an attorney is not an invocation of the right to counsel.[160] A request for assistance of counsel at a formal proceeding, such as a preliminary appearance or arraignment, constitutes an invocation of the right to counsel at a police-initiated custodial interrogation as well,[161] provided that the request for counsel at the court proceeding is explicit.[162]

Once an accused makes a clear indication that he wishes to consult with an attorney, police must accept that indication at face value and may not undermine its clarity by asking follow-up questions. An accused's post-request responses to further interrogation may not be used to cast doubt on the clarity of the initial request for counsel. When an accused, in response to being advised of his right to counsel, responded, "Uh yeah, I'd like to do that," the Supreme Court found that initial request clear and unequivocal. The clarity and unequivocality of that response was not affected even though his subsequent statements were ambiguous, cast doubt on the request, and reflected indecision on the accused's part.[163] A simple "Yes" in response to the question, Do you want a lawyer?, is sufficient. Police may not continue at that point. Where, following an affirmative response, police continued and explained the waiver form, the defendant's subsequent confused responses could not be used to undermine her initial "yes" response.[164]

The clarity of a suspect's invocation of the right to counsel has become critical. In a step that substantially weakens the position of a suspect who is fumbling and not sure of himself during custodial interrogation, the U.S. Supreme Court, in *Davis v United States*,[165] said that if a suspect's reference to an attorney is ambiguous or equivocal, police need not cease questioning. Instead, police may continue questioning as though the reference was never made. Only a clear invocation of the right imposes a duty upon the police. Moreover, whether a suspect's reference to an attorney is clear or ambiguous and equivocal is to be determined by a reasonable police officer standard: whether a reasonable police officer under the circumstances would have understood that the suspect was invoking the right to counsel. Police are not obligated, the Court held, to ask any clarifying questions to determine whether the suspect wants an attorney following an ambiguous refer-

---

[159]State v Martin, No. C-860610, 1987 WL 19704 (1st Dist Ct App, Hamilton, 11-10-87).

[160]State v Benner, 40 OS(3d) 301, 533 NE(2d) 701 (1988), cert denied 494 US 1090, 110 SCt 1834, 108 LEd(2d) 962 (1990).

[161]Michigan v Jackson, 475 US 625, 106 SCt 1404, 89 LEd(2d) 631 (1986).

[162]State v Clark, 38 OS(3d) 252, 527 NE(2d) 844 (1988).

[163]Smith v Illinois, 469 US 91, 105 SCt 490, 83 LEd(2d) 488 (1984).

[164]State v Rowe, 68 App(3d) 595, 589 NE(2d) 394 (Franklin 1990).

[165]Davis v United States, ___ US ___, 114 SCt 2350, 126 LEd(2d) 362 (1994).

ence. The message sent by the Supreme Court is clear: a suspect who does not clearly assert his right to counsel will lose it.

However, if the police interpret incorrectly, and a court later determines that a suspect's reference to an attorney was clear and unambiguous, continued interrogation is a violation of *Edwards*. Perhaps, then, *Davis* may turn out to be less of a windfall for police than it seems. Clarifying an ambiguous reference might still be the wisest judgment.

An accused's exact words will be given effect. A clear invocation of the right to counsel, generally, requires cessation of interrogation efforts. But the request is limited by its own terms, even though the language used casts doubt on the accused's ability to understand.

The defendant in *Connecticut v Barrett*,[166] while in custody was given *Miranda* warnings three times. Three times he indicated that he would not make a written statement outside the presence of counsel, and, after being administered the warnings the second and third time, orally admitted his involvement in the crimes under investigation. The Court, however, found that the defendant's actions were unambiguous and his invocation of the right to counsel was limited by its terms to the making of written statements. If the defendant's request for counsel had been ambiguous, the Court said, that request would have to be given broad, all-inclusive effect. But as the Court concluded, the request was not ambiguous but was confined to its terms.

(C) Effect of invoking Miranda right to counsel

Once an accused invokes the *Miranda* right to counsel, questioning must immediately cease and not resume until the accused has an opportunity to consult with an attorney and have him present during interrogation.[167] Moreover, until an accused has an opportunity to consult with an attorney, police may not attempt to interrogate him even about other, unrelated crimes.[168] An accused's invocation of the Sixth Amendment right to counsel at a court appearance also serves to invoke the *Miranda* right to counsel for purposes of custodial interrogation.[169] When an accused invokes the right in court, it is a more limited right. It precludes further interrogation only about the specific charge for which the formal proceeding was held.[170] Obviously the different effect of a request for counsel made to a court from one made to a police interrogator creates confusion and seems hypertechnical. Nonetheless, the confusion results from the different purposes served by the Sixth Amendment and *Miranda* rights to counsel. The former protects an accused's trial rights on the pending charge; the latter asserts the suspect's inability to handle himself during custodial interrogation.

[166]Connecticut v Barrett, 479 US 523, 107 SCt 828, 93 LEd(2d) 920 (1987).

[167]Miranda v Arizona, 384 US 436, 86 SCt 1602, 16 LEd(2d) 694 (1966).

[168]Arizona v Roberson, 486 US 675, 108 SCt 2093, 100 LEd(2d) 704 (1988); State v Knuckles, 65 OS(3d) 494, 605 NE(2d) 54 (1992), cert denied ___ US ___, 113 SCt 2986, 125 LEd(2d) 682 (1993).

[169]Michigan v Jackson, 475 US 625, 106 SCt 1404, 89 LEd(2d) 631 (1986).

[170]McNeil v Wisconsin, 501 US 171, 111 SCt 2204, 115 LEd(2d) 158 (1991).

Following an unfulfilled request for counsel, an accused may waive his Fourth Amendment rights by consenting to a search.[171] A police officer may ask a defendant to consent to a blood test even though the defendant is under arrest for driving under the influence and has exercised the right to counsel.[172] Both propositions are problematic because police are prohibited from initiating any conversation with an accused following a request for counsel.[173] Obviously a police request for a breathalyzer test or for a consent to search involves initiating conversation. While any incriminating statements would be inadmissible, the consents, which are not incriminating, are valid.

(D) Resumption of questioning following an unfulfilled request for counsel

In its first decade, the Burger Court significantly watered down the *Miranda* requirements and appeared heading toward a reversal of the landmark decision. The trend was reversed when the Court strictly enforced the counsel requirement set forth in *Miranda* and for the first time upheld an accused's claim on *Miranda* grounds.[174] In *Edwards v Arizona*,[175] the defendant was arrested for burglary, robbery, and murder. At the police station, after waiving *Miranda* rights, the accused was informed by police that another suspect had implicated him in the crime. Edwards sought to make a deal, but the interrogating officer advised him that he had no authority to make a deal. Then Edwards said, "I want an attorney before making a deal." The interrogator broke off questioning at that point and Edwards was taken to jail. The following morning, a jailer told Edwards that two detectives were there to talk with him. When he replied that he did not want to talk with anyone, the jailer informed him that he had to talk with the detectives and took Edwards out of his cell to meet with them. Edwards was given *Miranda* warnings again, and he informed the officers that he would talk with them after hearing the statement of the accomplice who allegedly had implicated him. After hearing the tape, Edwards told the detectives he would make a statement but that he did not want it on tape. Informed by the detectives that even if the statement was not on tape they could testify in court as to its content, Edwards reiterated his willingness to talk with them about the crime but that he did not want it on tape. He then confessed. On appeal, the Arizona Supreme Court found that Edwards had invoked the rights to silence and counsel at the first interrogation but held that he had waived both rights the following morning when he incriminated himself.

The United States Supreme Court disagreed, applied *Miranda* strictly, and confirmed that different procedural safeguards are triggered when an accused asks to see an attorney rather than refuses to answer questions. Both rights may be waived, but the waiver process differs significantly. *Mosley* held that when an accused indicates that he does not wish to be

[171]State v Childress, 4 OS(3d) 217, 4 OBR 534, 448 NE(2d) 155 (1983), cert denied 464 US 853, 104 SCt 167, 78 LEd(2d) 152 (1983).
[172]State v Wright, 41 App(3d) 80, 534 NE(2d) 872 (Montgomery 1987).
[173]See Text 19.07, Exercising the right to remain silent.
[174]Edwards v Arizona, 451 US 477, 101 SCt 1880, 68 LEd(2d) 378 (1981).
[175]Edwards v Arizona, 451 US 477, 101 SCt 1880, 68 LEd(2d) 378 (1981).

questioned, statements secured from the accused are admissible under certain circumstances even though interrogation is resumed by the police.[176] Statements from an accused who has asked to see an attorney, following a valid waiver of the right, also may be admissible even if he has not consulted with counsel, but *Edwards* held that a strict, two-part waiver test must be met.

First, an accused who has asked to see an attorney "is not subject to interrogation by the authorities until counsel has been made available to him, unless the accused himself initiates further communication, exchanges, or conversations with the police."[177] *Edwards* applies, as well, even when the request for counsel is made at an arraignment in court. Police will be held accountable even if they are not aware of the request for counsel. The Court said, "One set of state actors [the police] may not claim ignorance of defendant's unequivocal request for counsel to another state actor [the court]."[178] A valid waiver cannot be established by showing only that the defendant responded to further police-initiated custodial interrogation. Interrogation must cease immediately upon the request for counsel, and it is irrelevant that the post-request interrogation is in the context of completion of the *Miranda* warnings.[179]

Edwards, however, is not applicable when a suspect indicates a willingness to speak with police at the same time that he invokes the right to counsel for written statements. The police would not be barred from questioning the suspect in that fact situation.[180]

Not only may police not resume interrogating an accused who has requested to see an attorney, but also *Edwards* imposes the additional safeguard that police not initiate any conversation with the accused. The Ohio Supreme Court has determined that *Edwards* creates a bright-line rule which "eliminates the need for *ad hoc* determinations by the courts regarding what communications with a defendant are permissible once counsel is requested."[181] Second, if the accused initiates further conversation, statements which are the product of interrogation are admissible only if there is a finding that the accused knowingly and intelligently waived the right to counsel.

The strict waiver requirement, however, is not applicable to statements volunteered by an accused who has invoked the right to counsel but then initiates conversation and is not interrogated. The Court held that under such circumstances, nothing "would prohibit the police from merely listen-

---

[176]See Text 19.07, Exercising the right to remain silent.

[177]Edwards v Arizona, 451 US 477, 484-85, 101 SCt 1880, 68 LEd(2d) 378 (1981); State v Taylor, 80 App(3d) 601, 609 NE(2d) 1344 (Richland 1992), appeal dismissed by 69 OS(3d) 1408, 629 NE(2d) 1370 (1994) (it is irrelevant that the accused does not know that the person initiating the interrogation following a request for counsel is a police officer).

[178]Michigan v Jackson, 475 US 625, 106 SCt 1404, 1410, 89 LEd(2d) 631 (1986).

[179]Smith v Illinois, 469 US 91, 105 SCt 490, 83 LEd(2d) 488 (1984).

[180]Connecticut v Barrett, 479 US 523, 107 SCt 828, 93 LEd(2d) 920 (1987).

[181]State v Knuckles, 65 OS(3d) 494, 497, 605 NE(2d) 54 (1992), cert denied ___ US ___, 113 SCt 2986, 125 LEd(2d) 682 (1993).

ing to his voluntary, volunteered statements and using them against him at trial ... [for] [a]bsent such interrogation, there would have been no infringement of the right that *Edwards* invoked and there would be no occasion to determine whether there had been a valid waiver."[182] The *Edwards* decision was unanimous, although three justices, Burger, Powell, and Rehnquist, while finding no valid waiver of the right to counsel, rejected the initial prong of the majority's test that police not initiate further conversation with an accused who has invoked the right to counsel.

(E) Initiation of conversation

The first case that the Supreme Court dealt with concerning the issue left over in *Edwards* was *Wyrick v Fields*,[183] which involved a soldier who was suspected of raping an eighty-one-year-old woman. After being released on his own recognizance and discussing the matter with a privately retained civilian attorney and a military attorney, the defendant requested a polygraph test. Prior to undergoing the test, the defendant was advised of his *Miranda* rights and said that he did not want his attorneys present. At the conclusion of the test, which took less than two hours, the defendant was advised by an investigator that there was some deceit and asked why he was uncomfortable with his answers. The defendant admitted having intercourse with the woman. The Supreme Court held that the defendant had initiated the polygraph test and the subsequent interrogation, which followed administration of the test, after consulting with attorneys, and that his waiver of *Miranda* rights prior to the polygraph test applied not only to the test but to the follow-up interrogation as well.

Greater guidance was provided in *Oregon v Bradshaw*,[184] which involved the more serious issue of what constitutes an initiation of conversation by an accused following invocation of the right to counsel. Bradshaw was suspected of responsibility in the death of a minor whose body was found in a wrecked pick-up truck. At the police station, Bradshaw was given *Miranda* warnings. He admitted giving the minor alcoholic beverages but denied involvement in the accident. When an officer suggested that Bradshaw had been behind the wheel, the accused said, "I want an attorney before it goes much further." The officer immediately terminated the conversation, but a few minutes later as Bradshaw was taken from the police station to the jail, he asked the officer, "Well, what is going to happen to me now?" The officer responded that Bradshaw did not have to talk with him, which the accused indicated he understood. General conversation followed as to where Bradshaw would be taken and the charges that would be filed against him. Thereupon, the officer suggested that Bradshaw take a lie detector test, which he did after again receiving *Miranda* warnings. Following administration of the test, the examiner told Bradshaw that he did not believe him, and Bradshaw admitted that he had been driving the vehicle. Following conviction, an Oregon appellate court held that his admissions should

---

[182]Edwards v Arizona, 451 US 477, 485-86, 101 SCt 1880, 68 LEd(2d) 378 (1981).

[183]Wyrick v Fields, 459 US 42, 103 SCt 394, 74 LEd(2d) 214 (1982), cert denied 464 US 1020, 104 SCt 556, 78 LEd(2d) 728 (1983).

[184]Oregon v Bradshaw, 462 US 1039, 103 SCt 2830, 77 LEd(2d) 405 (1983).

have been excluded under *Edwards* because asking what was going to happen to him did not satisfy the two-part waiver test.

Justice Rehnquist, for a plurality of the Court, held that the Oregon court misunderstood the *Edwards* test. He said that the initiation of conversation by an accused need not amount to a waiver, itself, but is merely a requirement instituted to insulate an accused who has requested an attorney from being hounded by the interrogator. Once there is an adequate initiation of conversation evidencing a willingness and a desire for a general discussion about the investigation—as opposed to "a request for a drink of water or a request to use a telephone that are so routine that they cannot be fairly said to represent a desire on the part of an accused to open up a more generalized discussion relating directly or indirectly to the investigation"[185]—then the next inquiry is whether there was a valid waiver of the right to counsel and the right to silence, which is to be determined on the totality of the circumstances. Applying these rules to the facts, Justice Rehnquist found that Bradshaw's inquiry as to what would happen to him, although ambiguous, "evinced a willingness and a desire for a generalized discussion about the investigation."[186] Justice Rehnquist then found that following the initiation of conversation, the accused changed his mind and waived his rights to silence and counsel without any impropriety on the part of the police. The fifth vote was provided by Justice Powell who, again, found it unimportant to determine who initiates the conversation so long as the accused's statements are preceded by a valid waiver of rights.

Bradshaw represents a definite weakening of the *Edwards* standard, and consequently a setback for *Miranda*. Although eight justices, the plurality and the four dissenters, retained the two-part test, the threshold inquiry as applied in *Bradshaw* allows an innocuous comment to open the door to the resumption of interrogation following a request for counsel. While Justice Rehnquist acknowledged that not every comment would satisfy the test, apparently any comment relating at all to the case permits the interpretation that the accused has evinced a willingness to engage in a general discussion about the investigation. The four dissenters, in an opinion by Justice Marshall, agreed with Rehnquist that there must be a two-part analysis but disagreed that Bradshaw's general statement evinced a willingness and desire for a generalized discussion about the investigation. Instead, the dissenters argued, the accused must initiate the communication specifically about the subject matter of the investigation. The dissenters contended that permitting the police to capitalize on Bradshaw's general inquiry as to where he was being taken as though he were reopening the discussion of the suspected crime "is to permit [the police] to capitalize on the custodial setting" contrary to the intent of the *Miranda* and *Edwards* Courts.[187]

Closely adhering to the two-part analysis reconfirmed in *Bradshaw,* a United States District Court reversed a conviction secured by reliance on

[185]Oregon v Bradshaw, 462 US 1039, 1045, 103 SCt 2830, 77 LEd(2d) 405 (1983).

[186]Oregon v Bradshaw, 462 US 1039, 1045-46, 103 SCt 2830, 77 LEd(2d) 405 (1983).

[187]Oregon v Bradshaw, 462 US 1039, 1056, 103 SCt 2830, 77 LEd(2d) 405 (1983) (Marshall, J., dissenting).

defendant's incriminating statements even though there was a knowing and voluntary waiver of the previously invoked right to counsel where the defendant did not initiate the follow-up questioning. The court, convinced by the totality of the circumstances that there was a valid waiver, nonetheless reversed because federal agents violated the per se rule by reinitiating the conversation.[188] In another case, where an accused reopened the interrogation following his request to see an attorney by asking about the charges that were to be filed against him, his incriminating statements were deemed inadmissible when the federal agent failed to readvise the accused of his rights and, without securing a waiver of counsel, elicited those incriminating statements.[189] On the other hand, the Florida Supreme Court has upheld a conviction secured with a defendant's incriminating statements on the basis that there was a valid waiver of counsel without consideration of whether the accused initiated the conversation following invocation of the right to counsel. The court paid no heed to the per se rule.[190]

Ohio appellate courts have been somewhat ambivalent in their enthusiasm to apply *Edwards*. In *State v Fulk*,[191] after the defendant said he wanted a lawyer, he was moved to a second interrogation room and held there alone for an extended period of time. When the interrogating officer returned to the room, the defendant spoke. This was held by the Franklin County Court of Appeals to satisfy the *Edwards-Bradshaw* standards for initiating the conversation leading to waiver. However, the defendant may have been reacting to being left alone for an extended period of time without explanation, but the result was no less comprehensible than that in *Bradshaw* itself. In *State v Simmons*,[192] where the defendant requested a meeting with the interrogating detective after invoking his right to counsel, the Montgomery County Court of Appeals held that *Edwards* was satisfied even though the initial conversation was not one-sided and the detectives had engaged in some questioning. On the other hand, the Huron County Court of Appeals in *State v Scott*[193] held that an expletive cannot be interpreted as indicating a desire to cooperate with the investigation.

The Ohio Supreme Court paid heed to the per se rule but held, in *State v Van Hook*,[194] that an accused may reinitiate the discussion through the agency of a nonattorney third party. The dissent in *Van Hook*, however, pointed out that there was nothing in the record to substantiate the claim that the accused told his mother that he was prepared to talk with the police.

---

[188]United States v Renda, 567 FSupp 487 (ED Va 1983), affirmed by 758 F(2d) 649 (4th Cir Va 1985).

[189]United States v Montgomery, 714 F(2d) 201 (1st Cir Mass 1983).

[190]King v Florida, 436 So(2d) 50 (Fla 1983), cert denied 466 US 909, 104 SCt 1690, 80 LEd(2d) 163 (1984).

[191]State v Fulk, No. 82AP-577, 1983 WL 3489 (10th Dist Ct App, Franklin, 5-3-83).

[192]State v Simmons, No. 7492, 1983 WL 5027 (2d Dist Ct App, Montgomery, 1-25-83).

[193]State v Scott, No. H-86-6, 1986 WL 13174 (6th Dist Ct App, Huron, 11-21-86).

[194]State v Van Hook, 39 OS(3d) 256, 530 NE(2d) 883 (1988), affirmed by 1992 WL 308350 (1992), cert denied 115 SCt 1831, 131 LEd(2d) 751 (1995).

(F) Resumption of questioning after accused has seen an attorney

Following invocation of the *Miranda* right to counsel, police may not reinitiate interrogation without counsel present even though the accused has consulted with the requested attorney. *Minnick v Mississippi*[195] clarified the *Edwards* requirement that counsel be made available to the accused by holding that this requirement refers not to the opportunity to consult with an attorney outside of the interrogation room, but to the right to have counsel present in the interrogation room during custodial interrogation.

Minnick was based on a real understanding of *Miranda* that when an accused requests counsel, he is expressing the thought that he is unable personally to deal with the police interrogation and wishes to do so only through an attorney.

19.09   Waiver of *Miranda* rights

(A) Miranda *waiver*

The United States Supreme Court's approach to waiver of *Miranda* rights was to be skeptical. The burdens were heavy on the state to demonstrate that strict standards were met.

Miranda v Arizona[196] recognized that an accused, properly advised of his rights, may elect to waive those rights and make a statement. The state must demonstrate that the accused knowingly and intelligently waived his privilege against self-incrimination and his right to retained or appointed counsel. A valid waiver may be found even though the accused earlier invoked the right to remain silent or the right to counsel.[197]

The standards delineated for waiver in the *Miranda* decision were intended to be strict and to impose a "heavy burden" on the prosecution to establish a valid waiver when a statement results from interrogation without the presence of an attorney. If the elements of custodial interrogation exist, there can be no waiver absent the giving of warnings. The defendant and the police may differ on whether the warnings were given. The credibility of the witnesses during a motion to suppress is a matter for the trier of fact and will not be disturbed by the reviewing court[198] absent an abuse of discretion.[199] Following the requisite warnings, however, the Court intended that to be valid a waiver must be specific. Chief Justice Warren wrote, "But a valid waiver will not be presumed simply from the silence of

---

[195]Minnick v Mississippi, 498 US 146, 111 SCt 486, 112 LEd(2d) 489 (1990).

[196]Miranda v Arizona, 384 US 436, 86 SCt 1602, 16 LEd(2d) 694 (1966).

[197]See Michigan v Mosley, 423 US 96, 96 SCt 321, 46 LEd(2d) 313 (1975), affirmed by 400 Mich 181, 254 NW(2d) 29 (1977), cert denied 434 US 861, 98 SCt 189, 54 LEd(2d) 135 (1977), discussed in Text 19.07, Exercising the right to remain silent; see also Oregon v Bradshaw, 462 US 1039, 103 SCt 2830, 77 LEd(2d) 405 (1983), discussed in Text 19.08, Exercising the right to counsel.

[198]State v Fanning, 1 OS(3d) 19, 1 OBR 57, 437 NE(2d) 583 (1982).

[199]State v Broom, 40 OS(3d) 277, 533 NE(2d) 682 (1988), cert denied 490 US 1075, 109 SCt 2089, 104 LEd(2d) 653 (1989).

the accused after warnings are given or simply from the fact that a confession was in fact eventually obtained."[200]

The Court specified that waiver was not to be presumed from the silence of an accused following the giving of warnings, nor simply from the fact that he answered some of the questions posed to him. Notwithstanding the *Miranda* discussion of a "heavy burden," the Court has held that the state need prove waiver only by a preponderance of the evidence.[201] Evidence of a waiver is not itself dispositive. For example, notwithstanding that evidence, the Court said that the fact of a lengthy interrogation before a statement is made is strong evidence that the accused did not validly waive his rights. Under those circumstances, the lengthy interrogation is stronger evidence "of the compelling influence of the interrogation," than the waiver is evidence of a voluntary relinquishment of a right. The *Miranda* decision also stated that "any evidence that the accused was threatened, tricked or cajoled into a waiver will, of course, show that the defendant did not voluntarily waive" his rights.[202] This requirement was weakened by the decision in *Michigan v Mosley*,[203] which recognized a waiver after the accused had invoked his right to remain silent, which was provoked by the detective's false assertion that Mosley's accomplice had implicated him in the crime. The *Mosley* Court did not even address the issue.

(B) Shift in waiver standard

While *Miranda* did not say that only an explicit waiver would do, that conclusion may be fairly inferred from the majority opinion. The Ohio Supreme Court in *State v Scott*[204] understood the *Miranda* Court's intent when it said an express waiver is strong proof of its validity but it is not inevitably either necessary or sufficient. The question is not one of form but whether the defendant in fact knowingly and intelligently waived. Moreover, even an explicit waiver is not dispositive;[205] it could be questioned by the events and circumstances surrounding the custodial interrogation, although a successful challenge following an explicit waiver is highly unlikely.

The Supreme Court backtracked from the requirement, allowing a finding of waiver absent an explicit expression. In *North Carolina v Butler*,[206] the accused was advised of his *Miranda* rights and given the FBI's "Advise of Rights" form which he read. In response to an inquiry, the accused stated that he understood his rights. He refused, however, to sign a waiver form. The agents then informed the accused that he need not sign the form or speak, but that the agents would like to talk with him. The accused replied,

---

[200]Miranda v Arizona, 384 US 436, 475, 86 SCt 1602, 16 LEd(2d) 694 (1966).
[201]Colorado v Connelly, 479 US 157, 107 SCt 515, 93 LEd(2d) 473 (1986).
[202]Miranda v Arizona, 384 US 436, 476, 86 SCt 1602, 16 LEd(2d) 694 (1966).
[203]Michigan v Mosley, 423 US 96, 96 SCt 321, 46 LEd(2d) 313 (1975), affirmed by 400 Mich 181, 254 NW(2d) 29 (1977), cert denied 434 US 861, 98 SCt 189, 54 LEd(2d) 135 (1977).
[204]State v Scott, 61 OS(2d) 155, 400 NE(2d) 375 (1980).
[205]State v Stacy, No. 87-CA-23, 1990 WL 71905 (4th Dist Ct App, Pickaway, 5-22-90).
[206]North Carolina v Butler, 441 US 369, 99 SCt 1755, 60 LEd(2d) 286 (1979).

"I will talk to you but I am not signing any form." He neither requested to see an attorney nor indicated that he did not want one. The Supreme Court rejected a per se rule, which would require an explicit waiver, and held that refusal to sign a waiver form is not dispositive of the waiver issue.

> An express written or oral statement of waiver of the right to remain silent or of the right to counsel is usually strong proof of the validity of that waiver, but is not inevitably either necessary or sufficient to establish waiver. The question is not one of form, but rather whether the defendant in fact knowingly and voluntarily waived the rights delineated in the Miranda case. As was unequivocally said in Miranda, mere silence is not enough. That does not mean that the defendant's silence, coupled with an understanding of his rights and a course of conduct indicating waiver, may never support a conclusion that a defendant has waived his rights. The courts must presume that a defendant did not waive his rights; the prosecution's burden is great; but in at least some cases waiver can be clearly inferred from the actions and words of the person interrogated.[207]

The question remains following the *Butler* decision whether a waiver, in fact, could be "clearly inferred" from the defendant's actions and words, or whether the decision represents a weakening of the waiver standard required by *Miranda*. The defendant's words and actions were an ambiguous response to an elliptical statement made by the FBI agent when Butler refused to sign the waiver form. The agent told Butler that he need not speak or sign the form, but that the agent wanted to talk with him. The agent's comment that he wanted to talk with the accused can be read to have undermined the effectiveness of the warnings. Butler reiterated his unwillingness to sign the waiver but agreed to talk. One could infer the defendant's words to mean that he was not going to waive his rights willingly but would acquiesce to the wishes of the agent, which is the inherent compulsion which the Court sought to relieve in *Miranda*. While the *Butler* decision reiterated the *Miranda* principle that there is a presumption against a valid waiver, it made it easier to overcome that presumption.

What is really noteworthy in *Butler* and later cases is that waiver is found despite an explicit refusal to make a complete waiver which at least creates ambiguity and casts doubt on the accused's understanding. Nonetheless, the Court dictates that the issue of waiver is to be resolved on the totality of the circumstances surrounding the interrogation.[208] Following this pattern, the Ohio Supreme Court held that an accused's refusal to sign a waiver form is not conclusive that his waiver was involuntary.[209] Similarly, the United States Supreme Court found an accused's indication that he would not make a written statement without counsel but he was willing to talk about the incident to be unambiguous.[210] He was held to have waived his right to counsel for purposes of oral interrogation. Candidly, the Court said that a suspect's ignorance of the full consequences of his decisions does not vitiate their voluntariness.

---

[207]North Carolina v Butler, 441 US 369, 373, 99 SCt 1755, 60 LEd(2d) 286 (1979).
[208]Fare v Michael C, 442 US 707, 99 SCt 2560, 61 LEd(2d) 197 (1979).
[209]State v Scott, 61 OS(2d) 155, 400 NE(2d) 375 (1980).
[210]Connecticut v Barrett, 479 US 523, 107 SCt 828, 93 LEd(2d) 920 (1987).

(C) Standard of proof for waiver

The burden rests with the prosecution to demonstrate a knowing, intelligent, and voluntary waiver based on the totality of the circumstances surrounding the entire interrogation. Where unanswered facts exist in the record raising questions about the legitimacy and timing of a waiver, the state has not met its burden of proof.[211]

The state must show that the accused understood his rights. There can be no presumption that the defendant understood the rights, nor can the burden be placed on the defendant to show a lack of capacity.[212] The fact that the suspect has informed the police that he understands his rights will not relieve the officers from inquiring further if the suspect's behavior should alert the officers that he may not have understood fully what he was told.[213]

Absent some indication of lack of capacity, police may presumably accept at face value an accused's assertions of understanding. That a defendant understood English and did not seem under the influence of drugs or alcohol was held sufficient to find by a preponderance of the evidence that the defendant understood his rights and knowingly and voluntarily waived his rights following a reading of those rights.[214]

Capacity to understand raises a different issue, but Ohio courts have not delved deeply into the issue. A defendant's claim that he lacked capacity to understand his rights was overcome by the state where the record demonstrated that the defendant was properly advised of his rights prior to each interrogation session, executed a waiver of rights form which was read to him at each session, and stated that he could read and that he understood his rights.[215] Evidence that the accused had a low I.Q. and that he was in a "slow learner class" in school, in *State v Jenkins*,[216] was overcome by the police officer's testimony that they informed the accused of his rights, that he affirmatively responded that he understood and waived those rights, and that his answers to the officer's questions appeared responsive. The officers testified as to their belief that the accused comprehended the rights and the effect of his waiver and that he eventually elected to cut off questioning. Further, a waiver of *Miranda* is not deemed ineffective simply because a defendant is suffering from a minor wound or is under the influence of medication.[217] A Miranda waiver has been found to be valid even though the paranoid schizophrenic defendant was known to police to be unstable

---

[211]State v Paladin, 48 App(3d) 16, 548 NE(2d) 263 (Lake 1988).

[212]Tague v Louisiana, 444 US 469, 100 SCt 652, 62 LEd(2d) 622 (1980) (per curiam).

[213]State v Jones, 37 OS(2d) 21, 306 NE(2d) 409 (1974), cert denied 419 US 860, 95 SCt 109, 42 LEd(2d) 94 (1974).

[214]State v Hill, 37 App(3d) 10, 523 NE(2d) 885 (Wood 1987). See also State v Smith, No. C-880287, 1990 WL 73974 (1st Dist Ct App, Hamilton, 6-6-90).

[215]State v Hall, 48 OS(2d) 325, 358 NE(2d) 590 (1976), vacated in part by 438 US 910, 98 SCt 3134, 57 LEd(2d) 1154 (1978).

[216]State v Jenkins, 15 OS(3d) 164, 15 OBR 311, 473 NE(2d) 264 (1984), cert denied 472 US 1032, 105 SCt 3514, 87 LEd(2d) 643 (1985).

[217]State v Stacy, No. 87-CA-23, 1990 WL 71905 (4th Dist Ct App, Pickaway, 5-22-90)

and despite the bizarre statements he made to police, where he seemed lucid and uninfluenced by drugs or alcohol, he indicated that he understood the rights read to him, and court appointed experts testified that he understood the spoken word.[218]

The knowing and understanding requirements for a voluntary waiver have been explained and limited by the Rehnquist Court. In *Colorado v Spring*,[219] the Court held that a suspect's awareness of all the crimes about which he may be questioned is not relevant to determining the validity of his decision to waive the Fifth Amendment privilege. Defendant was arrested on a weapons violation charge that led to his arrest and then was asked about a murder, which was the principal reason defendant was under investigation. The interrogator's silence about the offense under investigation did not constitute trickery because that silence, once *Miranda* warnings are given, would not cause a suspect to misunderstand his constitutional right to refuse to answer questions. Thus, the "knowingly" requirement is limited to knowledge of the constitutional rights. Ignorance of the full consequences of one's decisions does not vitiate their voluntariness.

In a decision announced before *Spring*, the Clermont County Court of Appeals interpreted similar facts differently.[220] During a polygraph exam following *Miranda* warnings to which the suspect had consented, he was asked about other crimes. The Clermont County court held that the waiver could only have been effective for the crime for which the suspect knew he would be questioned. The court held his waiver could not have been knowing and intelligent with respect to the other crimes because he did not know that he would be asked about those crimes. Even if the Clermont County court's decision is considered inconsistent with *Spring*, there are other factors in the case that indicate the correctness of the decision. When the examiner began to ask about other crimes, the suspect indicated his desire to remove the wires and end the exam. His compliance with the examiner's instruction to complete the exam indicates (1) that the suspect's subsequent answers were involuntary, and (2) that he intended to exercise his *Miranda* right to cut off any further questions.

The same reasoning that decided *Spring* prevailed again in *Connecticut v Barrett*,[221] where the suspect said he would not provide a written statement without an attorney but was willing to talk with police. He was said to have validly waived his *Miranda* rights as to the oral statements even though his ambivalence about having an attorney clearly indicated limited understanding about the significance of orally answering an interrogator's questions.

Moreover, the failure of police to advise a suspect that an attorney has made inquiry on his behalf does not mar an otherwise knowing, intelligent,

---

[218]State v Knotts, No. 10-94-22, 1995 WL 407403 (3d Dist Ct App, Mercer, 7-5-95).

[219]Colorado v Spring, 479 US 564, 107 SCt 851, 93 LEd(2d) 954 (1987); State v Garner, 74 OS(3d) 49, 656 NE(2d) 623 (1995) (validity of waiver is not dependent upon the suspect being aware that he was potentially eligible for a death sentence).

[220]State v Wilson, 31 App(3d) 133, 31 OBR 221, 508 NE(2d) 1002 (Clermont 1986).

[221]Connecticut v Barrett, 479 US 523, 107 SCt 828, 93 LEd(2d) 920 (1987).

and voluntary waiver of *Miranda* rights.[222] In *Moran v Burbine*, the failure to advise a suspect of the attorney's efforts, the Court held, did not prevent the suspect from understanding his rights or the possible consequences of relinquishing them, which is all that is necessary under *Miranda*. The suspect's ability to understand and knowingly give up his rights is unaffected by events of which he is unaware. The determinative factor in these cases, the Ohio Supreme Court has said, is the desire of the accused to consult with counsel, not the desire of counsel to consult with the accused.[223] One can question how the Court can determine that a suspect can "knowingly" waive his rights when he is deprived of critical information bearing upon that knowledge. It obviously offers a very narrow meaning of the term "knowingly." *Moran* does not bear upon a situation where a suspect asks for counsel or otherwise makes police aware of a desire to see an attorney.[224]

The term voluntary has a limited meaning in this context. To be voluntary, a waiver of *Miranda* rights need not be the product of a free will. It simply means that the suspect's decision was free from official coercion.[225] Whether a juvenile's waiver of *Miranda* rights is voluntary has been far more problematic for many states than it has been in Ohio. Ohio rejects the rule adopted in several states that a minor may not waive *Miranda* rights without the assistance of a parent or an attorney.[226] The Ohio Supreme Court in *In re Watson*[227] said that the validity of a minor's waiver of *Miranda* rights is the same as the voluntariness test: the validity of the waiver will be based on the totality of the circumstances, including the age, mentality, and prior criminal experience of the accused, the length, intensity, and frequency of interrogation, as well as the conditions surrounding the interrogation.[228] In *Watson*, the Court found a fourteen-year-old's waiver valid even though his mother was present at the police station but not provided access to her son.

19.10   Voluntariness after *Miranda*

(A) *Voluntariness standard after* Miranda

The voluntariness of a suspect's statements has always been the constitutional test for admissibility. It became submerged, however, within the framework of the *Miranda* rules, which were deemed the best way to ensure that the statements were given voluntarily. But even the *Miranda* Court

---

[222]Moran v Burbine, 475 US 412, 106 SCt 1135, 89 LEd(2d) 410 (1986).

[223]State v DePew, 38 OS(3d) 275, 528 NE(2d) 542 (1988), appeal dismissed by 65 OS(3d) 1475, 604 NE(2d) 167 (1992), affirmed by 70 OS(3d) 1435, 638 NE(2d) 1039 (1994).

[224]State v Luck, 15 OS(3d) 150, 15 OBR 296, 472 NE(2d) 1097 (1984), cert denied 470 US 1084, 105 SCt 1845, 85 LEd(2d) 144 (1985).

[225]Colorado v Connelly, 479 US 157, 107 SCt 515, 93 LEd(2d) 473 (1986).

[226]State v Bell, 48 OS(2d) 270, 358 NE(2d) 556 (1976), reversed on other grounds by 438 US 637, 98 SCt 2977, 57 LEd(2d) 1010 (1978).

[227]In re Watson, 47 OS(3d) 86, 548 NE(2d) 210 (1989), cert denied 495 US 937, 110 SCt 2185, 109 LEd(2d) 513 (1990).

[228]See also State v Edwards, 49 OS(2d) 31, 358 NE(2d) 1051 (1976), vacated in part by 438 US 911, 98 SCt 3147, 57 LEd(2d) 1155 (1978).

recognized that compliance with the warning requirements was not totally dispositive of the admissibility of a statement. For example, in *Miranda*, the Court indicated that a statement, which was forthcoming shortly after a suspect was informed of his rights and indicated his willingness to talk with the police, would satisfy the constitutional requirements. On the other hand, the Court also noted that a statement coming after prolonged interrogation, even if *Miranda* warnings had been given at the outset, might indicate that the suspect's will had been overborne by the interrogation. Therefore, the *Miranda* Court, itself, indicated the continuing need for inquiry into whether the statement was given voluntarily. However, that inquiry has largely been ignored in favor of one focusing solely on waiver of *Miranda* rights. For example, five hours of interrogation over a two-day period has been held not to trigger a consideration of whether it constitutes wearing down.[229] That was largely ignored in the two decades after *Miranda* as lawyers and courts focused only on compliance with *Miranda*.

Voluntariness remains the ultimate issue for determining the admissibility of a statement under Fifth Amendment standards. Compliance with *Miranda* requirements is evidence of voluntariness, but it should not be deemed dispositive of the issue. Police behavior during interrogation following the giving of *Miranda* warnings may be such as to render a suspect's statement involuntary. For example, where an accused's decision to speak is motivated by a police officer's statements constituting "direct or indirect promises" of leniency or benefit and other representations regarding the possibility of probation, which were misstatements of law, his incriminating statements, not being freely self-determined, were improperly induced, involuntary, and inadmissible as a matter of law.[230] On the other hand, in *State v Harvill*,[231] where an investigating officer intentionally misinformed a suspect of the facts, claiming that he had been positively identified, the court held that the suspect's subsequent confession was not involuntary because "his will to remain silent was not so overborne as to vitiate the trustworthiness of his inculpatory statement."[232] Deception is a factor bearing on voluntariness but misrepresentation, standing alone, does not establish coercion and involuntariness.[233]

(B) Re-emergence of the voluntariness standard

As the present Supreme Court chips away at the *Miranda* rules, emphasizing the Court's view that those rules are merely prophylaxes to protect Fifth Amendment rights and not part of the Fifth Amendment right itself, the voluntariness test will assume even greater importance. The Court has said, "The purpose of the *Miranda* warnings instead is to dissipate the

---

[229]State v Wiles, 59 OS(3d) 71, 571 NE(2d) 97 (1991), cert denied 506 US 832, 113 SCt 99, 121 LEd(2d) 59 (1992).

[230]State v Arrington, 14 App(3d) 111, 14 OBR 125, 470 NE(2d) 211 (Erie 1984).

[231]State v Harvill, 15 App(3d) 94, 15 OBR 123, 472 NE(2d) 743 (Hamilton 1984).

[232]State v Harvill, 15 App(3d) 94, 94-95, 15 OBR 123, 472 NE(2d) 743 (Hamilton 1984), citing State v Mandrbah, No. C-810135, 1982 WL 4637 (1st Dist Ct App, Hamilton, 2-10-82).

[233]State v Wiles, 59 OS(3d) 71, 571 NE(2d) 97 (1991), cert denied 506 US 832, 113 SCt 99, 121 LEd(2d) 59 (1992).

compulsion inherent in custodial interrogation and, in so doing, guard against abridgement of the suspect's Fifth Amendment rights."[234]

There has been a significant shift in the Supreme Court's analysis of voluntariness. In *Oregon v Elstad*,[235] where the Supreme Court allowed a second statement following *Miranda* warnings given by a suspect after he had already implicated himself during a first interrogation where he had not received *Miranda* warnings, the Court concluded that the admissibility of the second statement would turn upon the finder of fact's conclusion "that the suspect made a rational and intelligent choice whether to waive or invoke his rights."[236] The issue before the Court was only the admissibility of the second statement; no one contended that the first statement secured without *Miranda* warnings was admissible in the prosecution's case-in-chief.

The emphasis in determining voluntariness has shifted perceptibly from whether the suspect voluntarily chose to answer questions and make a statement to whether he voluntarily waived his rights to silence and counsel. The *Elstad* majority dismissed the effect of the initial unwarned admission on the suspect and, absent actual coercion in the taking of the first statement, did not consider it even a factor in considering the admissibility of the second statement. The Court said:

> There is a vast difference between the direct consequences flowing from coercion of a confession by physical violence or other deliberate means calculated to break the suspect's will and the uncertain consequences of disclosure of a "guilty secret" freely given in response to an unwarned but noncoercive question.[237]

Elstad's initial statement was secured during his arrest while he was still in his home. Dissenting Justice Stevens assumed that the decision was limited to the narrow facts of the case and would not apply when the initial statement is taken in a police car or at the police station where actual coercion, required by the Court, is more apparent. His narrow reading of the majority opinion is wishful thinking and not supported by the broad language of the majority opinion.

It appears that the present Court's analysis represents several backward steps into what is now largely uncharted territory. *Miranda* was predicated on the understanding that *custody plus interrogation without warnings* equals coercion. This Court says there is a difference between presumptive coercion that exists when a statement is obtained without warnings and actual coercion. Moreover, this Court has held more recently that coercive police activity is a necessary predicate to finding that a confession is not voluntary within the meaning of the due process clause.[238] In addition, this Court appears to have a fairly high tolerance for coercion provided that it does not involve "physical violence or other deliberate means calculated to break the suspect's will."[239]

[234]Moran v Burbine, 475 US 412, 106 SCt 1135, 1143, 89 LEd(2d) 410 (1986).
[235]Oregon v Elstad, 470 US 298, 105 SCt 1285, 84 LEd(2d) 222 (1985).
[236]Oregon v Elstad, 470 US 298, 314, 105 SCt 1285, 84 LEd(2d) 222 (1985).
[237]Oregon v Elstad, 470 US 298, 312, 105 SCt 1285, 84 LEd(2d) 222 (1985).
[238]Colorado v Connelly, 479 US 157, 107 SCt 515, 93 LEd(2d) 473 (1986).
[239]Oregon v Elstad, 470 US 298, 312, 105 SCt 1285, 84 LEd(2d) 222 (1985).

(C) Proving voluntariness

Once the admission of a confession is challenged, the state must prove by a preponderance of the evidence that a confession is voluntary.[240] In making that determination, a court should consider the totality of the circumstances.[241] All circumstances surrounding and operative during the taking of a statement are material and must be examined in their totality.[242] The fact that the police and defendant's accounts of the setting in which a confession is given differ does not render the confession inadmissible, but there must be evidence in the record to support a finding of voluntariness.[243] The ultimate question of the voluntariness of a confession is an issue of law, and an appellate court should review the facts to make its own determination of the issue.[244]

Surprisingly, the unreliability of a statement no longer renders it inadmissible under due process concerns absent coercive police activity.[245] A defendant's confession, obtained by coercion—whether physical or mental—is forbidden.[246] Coercive police activity is a necessary predicate to finding that a confession is not voluntary.[247] A confession is not involuntary absent police coercion causally related to the confession.[248] Voluntariness depends on the absence of police overreaching, not on any broader sense of free choice.[249] Absent police coercion, age and low I.Q., standing alone, do not negate the voluntariness of a statement.[250]

Whether a confession is voluntary depends on the totality of the circumstances, including age, mentality, and prior criminal experience of the accused; the length, intensity, and frequency of interrogation; the existence of physical deprivation or mistreatment; and the existence of threat or

---

[240]Lego v Twomey, 404 US 477, 96 SCt 619, 30 LEd(2d) 618 (1972); State v Garcia, 32 App(3d) 38, 513 NE(2d) 1350 (Lorain 1986).

[241]State v Barker, 53 OS(2d) 135, 372 NE(2d) 1324 (1978), cert denied 439 US 913, 99 SCt 285, 58 LEd(2d) 260 (1978).

[242]State v Booher, 54 App(3d) 1, 560 NE(2d) 786 (Defiance 1988), cert denied 493 US 977, 110 SCt 502, 107 LEd(2d) 505 (1989).

[243]State v Cornely, 56 OS(2d) 1, 381 NE(2d) 186 (1978); State v Smith, No. C-880287, 1990 WL 73974 (1st Dist Ct App, Hamilton, 6-6-90).

[244]Arizona v Fulminante, 499 US 279, 111 SCt 1246, 113 LEd(2d) 302 (1991); State v Booher, 54 App(3d) 1, 560 NE(2d) 786 (Defiance 1988), cert denied 493 US 977, 110 SCt 502, 107 LEd(2d) 505 (1989).

[245]Colorado v Connelly, 479 US 157, 107 SCt 515, 93 LEd(2d) 473 (1986).

[246]State v Johnston, 64 App(3d) 238, 580 NE(2d) 1162 (Franklin 1990).

[247]State v Dailey, 53 OS(3d) 88, 559 NE(2d) 459 (1990); State v Todd, 78 App(3d) 454, 605 NE(2d) 411 (Sandusky 1992) (involuntary confession secured by defendant's employer without police involvement does not violate due process).

[248]Colorado v Connelly, 479 US 157, 107 SCt 515, 93 LEd(2d) 473 (1986).

[249]Moran v Burbine, 475 US 412, 106 SCt 1135, 89 LEd(2d) 410 (1986); State v Dailey, 53 OS(3d) 88, 559 NE(2d) 459 (1990).

[250]State v Dailey, 53 OS(3d) 88, 559 NE(2d) 459 (1990).

inducement.[251] Coercion can be mental as well as physical.[252] The test for admissibility is whether the behavior of the police was such as to overbear the accused's will to resist and bring about confessions not freely self-determined.[253] Admonitions to tell the truth or badgering for the truth do not rise to the level of coercive activity.[254] The truth or falsity of the confession is irrelevant to the question of voluntariness.[255]

The US Supreme Court is reconsidering what constitutes voluntariness; this reconsideration is in its earliest stages. A century ago the Court said that to be voluntary a confession must not have been extracted by any sort of threat or violence, nor obtained by any direct or implied promises, however slight.[256] The broad prohibition against promises "does not state [the present] standard for determining the voluntariness of a confession."[257]

The voluntariness of a juvenile's confession is likewise to be considered in the totality of the circumstances.[258] The confession of a minor close to the age of maturity is not treated appreciably differently from one made by an adult.[259]

A suspect's mental handicap must be considered when determining the validity of a waiver. In *State v Rossiter*,[260] the court found that the defendant's mental handicap, which was perceived by the police, precluded an understanding waiver of his *Miranda* rights.

CROSS REFERENCES

Text 19.06, 19.07, 20.03

19.11   Confessions and the Sixth Amendment

(A) Filling in Miranda gaps

There are gaps in the protection of constitutional rights accorded to an accused by *Miranda*,[261] which were widened by its progeny. Those cases,

---

[251]State v Brewer, 48 OS(3d) 50, 549 NE(2d) 491 (1990), affirmed by 1994 WL 527740 (1994), cert denied 116 SCt 101, 133 LEd(2d) 55 (1995); State v Barker, 53 OS(2d) 135, 372 NE(2d) 1324 (1978), cert denied 439 US 913, 99 SCt 285, 58 LEd(2d) 260 (1978); State v Patterson, 95 App(3d) 255, 642 NE(2d) 390 (Lake 1993), appeal dismissed by 68 OS(3d) 1470, 628 NE(2d) 1389 (1994) (defendant's confession found to be voluntary based upon these facts: during the interview, defendant showed no signs of fatigue, was alert, his speech was clear and controlled and he displayed a willingness to confess with great detail).

[252]Blackburn v Alabama, 361 US 199, 80 SCt 274, 4 LEd(2d) 242 (1960).

[253]State v Johnston, 64 App(3d) 238, 580 NE(2d) 1162 (Franklin 1990).

[254]State v Wiles, 59 OS(3d) 71, 571 NE(2d) 97 (1991), cert denied ___ US ___, 113 SCt 99, 121 LEd(2d) 59 (1992).

[255]State v Johnston, 64 App(3d) 238, 580 NE(2d) 1162 (Franklin 1990).

[256]Bram v United States, 168 US 532, 18 SCt 183, 42 LEd 568 (1897).

[257]Arizona v Fulminante, 499 US 279, 111 SCt 1246, 113 LEd(2d) 302 (1991); State v Arrington, 14 App(3d) 111, 14 OBR 125, 470 NE(2d) 211 (Erie 1984).

[258]In re Watson, 47 OS(3d) 86, 548 NE(2d) 210 (1989), cert denied 495 US 937, 110 SCt 2185, 109 LEd(2d) 513 (1990).

[259]Cf. State v Dickens, No. 12967, 1987 WL 17928 (9th Dist Ct App, Summit, 9-23-87).

[260]State v Rossiter, 88 App(3d) 162, 623 NE(2d) 645 (Ross 1993).

[261]Miranda v Arizona, 384 US 436, 86 SCt 1602, 16 LEd(2d) 694 (1966).

decided under the Fifth Amendment privilege against self-incrimination, require both custody and interrogation and seek only to alleviate the inherent coerciveness of custodial interrogation. Absent questioning in a custodial setting by someone who the accused knows is a police officer, the danger of an accused being compelled to incriminate himself is nonexistent. Rightly so, since the *Miranda* decision sought to prevent the compulsion prohibited by the Fifth Amendment; it was not concerned about the propriety of police seeking to obtain admissions from an accused, i.e., to discover the accused, outside of the presence of counsel after commencement of adversary proceedings.

That gap was filled through reliance on the Sixth Amendment right to counsel by the resuscitation of the doctrine announced in *Massiah v United States*.[262] *Massiah* involved the elicitation of incriminating statements following indictment by a co-defendant who had agreed to cooperate with federal prosecutors. There was neither custody nor coercion, and the defendant's statements certainly were made voluntarily to his co-defendant. The Supreme Court reversed, holding the surreptitious interrogation following an indictment to have violated the absolute right of an accused to have the guiding hand of counsel, absent waiver, at every stage of a criminal proceeding. The doctrine was relied and expanded on in *Brewer v Williams*,[263] a case expected by many to be the vehicle used by the Supreme Court to reverse *Miranda*. Instead, it developed a body of rights under the Sixth Amendment which, when applicable, are more comprehensive than *Miranda* rights.

The case involved an escapee from a mental hospital who was wanted for the abduction and murder of a little girl in Des Moines, Iowa. The defendant's car was found the day following the abduction in Davenport, and one day later a Des Moines attorney notified police that he had advised the defendant, who was in Davenport, to surrender to police in that city. The defendant surrendered to Davenport authorities and was given *Miranda* warnings. The defendant spoke with his Des Moines lawyer from the Davenport jail who advised him that police would drive from Des Moines to pick him up and return him to that city, that he would not be mistreated by the police, that they had agreed not to interrogate the defendant, and that the defendant should not discuss the child's disappearance with the police. A preliminary appearance was held in a Davenport court where the defendant was advised, again, of *Miranda* rights, and where he was represented by a local attorney. Following the court appearance, the local attorney requested to accompany the defendant and the police back to Des Moines. That request was refused. The lawyer then advised the defendant of his rights and insisted to the police that they not interrogate the defendant during the trip, to which they agreed.

The detectives who accompanied the defendant to Des Moines knew that the defendant was an escapee from a mental institution and were aware that he was deeply religious. One of the detectives engaged the defendant in

---

[262]*Massiah v United States*, 377 US 201, 84 SCt 1199, 12 LEd(2d) 246 (1964), discussed in Text 19.01, Introduction.

[263]*Brewer v Williams*, 430 US 387, 97 SCt 1232, 51 LEd(2d) 424 (1977), cert denied sub nom *Williams v Iowa*, 446 US 921, 100 SCt 1859, 64 LEd(2d) 277 (1980).

a wide-ranging discussion and referred to the defendant as Reverend Williams. He delivered what was characterized by the Court as the "Christian burial speech":

> I want to give you something to think about while we're traveling down the road. ... Number one, I want you to observe the weather conditions, it's raining, it's sleeting, it's freezing, driving is very treacherous, visibility is poor, it's going to be dark early this evening. They are predicting several inches of snow for tonight, and I feel that you yourself are the only person who knows where this little girl's body is, that yourself have only been there once, and if you get a snow on top of it you yourself may be unable to find it. And, since we will be going right past the area on the way into Des Moines, I feel that we could stop and locate the body, that the parents of this little girl should be entitled to a Christian burial for the little girl who was snatched away from them on Christmas [E]ve and murdered. And I feel we should stop and locate it on the way in rather than waiting until morning and trying to come back out after a snow storm and possibly not being able to find it at all.[264]

Williams, who had responded to the detective's general discussion by promising to tell the police the entire story after meeting with his lawyer in Des Moines, now responded to the burial speech by asking the detective how he knew they would be passing right by the body. After a brief discussion on that subject, the detective told Williams not to answer him but just to think about it. A short while later, Williams renewed the conversation and eventually directed the detectives to the body.

The Supreme Court avoided the *Miranda* issue, which would have required deciding whether the detective's speech was interrogation; the case preceded the *Innis*[265] definition of interrogation. Instead, in a 5-4 decision, the Court revived the *Massiah* rationale and held that the defendant's statements which led the detectives to the body were secured in violation of the Sixth Amendment right to the assistance of counsel. The Court said:

> [T]he right to counsel granted by the Sixth and Fourteenth Amendments means at least that a person is entitled to the help of a lawyer at or after the time that [adversary] judicial proceedings have been initiated against him—"whether by way of formal charge, preliminary hearing, indictment or information, or arraignment."[266]

The Court also recognized that the detective had deliberately elicited information during Williams' isolation from his lawyers, perhaps more effectively than if he had interrogated him. Finally, the Court held that there was no evidence to support the state's claim that by responding to the burial speech Williams had intentionally relinquished or abandoned the right to counsel.

---

[264]Brewer v Williams, 430 US 387, 392-93, 97 SCt 1232, 51 LEd(2d) 424 (1977), cert denied sub nom Williams v Iowa, 446 US 921, 100 SCt 1859, 64 LEd(2d) 277 (1980).

[265]Rhode Island v Innis, 446 US 291, 100 SCt 1682, 64 LEd(2d) 297 (1980), cert denied 456 US 930, 102 SCt 1980, 72 LEd(2d) 447 (1982).

[266]Brewer v Williams, 430 US 387, 398 97 SCt 1232, 51 LEd(2d) 424 (1977), cert denied sub nom Williams v Iowa, 446 US 921, 100 SCt 1859, 64 LEd(2d) 277 (1980).

(B) Attachment of the Sixth Amendment right to counsel

Brewer v Williams moved the Sixth Amendment protections back from the post-indictment stage to the initial court appearance on the arrest warrant, triggering the stricter standards imposed under the Sixth Amendment. The initiation of formal proceedings signals the attachment of the right. Whether or not the defendant has consulted with counsel, any police interrogation following the formal proceeding is a critical stage at which the right to counsel attaches.[267] After the commencement of formal proceedings, any attempt by the authorities to elicit incriminating information from an accused will result in the suppression of such statements unless there is an actual waiver of the right to counsel. It does not matter that the incriminating statements pertaining to the pending charge were secured while police were investigating a different crime. The police's obligation to investigate other crimes may not be used to violate the defendant's right to counsel for pending charges. Police may employ uncounseled interrogation of a formally charged suspect to investigate an uncharged crime, but the evidence secured may not be used at the pending trial.[268]

Michigan v Jackson[269] applied the *Edwards* prohibitions to Sixth Amendment counsel. In *Jackson*, the defendant was advised of his rights and requested counsel at a court arraignment. Later, he was interrogated by police. The Supreme Court held that once the right to counsel has attached and the defendant asserts that right, any waiver of the right in a police-initiated interrogation is invalid. The extent of the *Edwards* protection differs, however, depending on whether a defendant's Fifth or Sixth amendment right to counsel has attached. *Edwards* precludes any interrogation on any charge of an accused who has asserted a *Miranda* right to counsel because, according to the Court, that assertion represents a claim that the defendant is unable to cope with police interrogation except with the assistance of and through a lawyer.[270] The *Edwards* prohibition, when initiated through a request for counsel during a court proceeding under Sixth Amendment rights, is offense-specific, precluding interrogation only on the offense for which counsel has been requested.[271]

(C) Sixth Amendment prohibition against eliciting information

The differences between the Fifth and Sixth Amendment protections were clarified in *United States v Henry*,[272] where the Court relied on the Sixth Amendment right to counsel to invalidate a bank robbery conviction

---

[267]State v Bowshier, No. CA2309, 1987 WL 33784 (2d Dist Ct App, Clark, 12-23-87); but note City of Lakewood v Waselenchuk, 94 App(3d) 684, 641 NE(2d) 767 (Cuyahoga 1994) (court held that while there is no sixth amendment right to counsel prior to taking a breathalyzer, defendant's statutory right to counsel under RC 2935.20 was violated where police did not permit arrestee the opportunity to consult with an attorney after defendant expressed doubt and concern about her ability to make a decision whether or not to take the test without the advice of her lawyer. Breathalyzer test results held inadmissible).

[268]Maine v Moulton, 474 US 159, 106 SCt 477, 88 LEd(2d) 481 (1985).

[269]Michigan v Jackson, 475 US 625, 106 SCt 1404, 89 LEd(2d) 631 (1986).

[270]Arizona v Roberson, 486 US 675, 108 SCt 2093, 100 LEd(2d) 704 (1988).

[271]McNeil v Wisconsin, 501 US 171, 111 SCt 2204, 115 LEd(2d) 158 (1991).

[272]United States v Henry, 447 US 264, 100 SCt 2183, 65 LEd(2d) 115 (1980).

based on incriminating statements made by an indicted defendant to his FBI-informant cellmate. Government agents agreed to pay the informant for any information he obtained about the defendant's offense, instructing him only to be alert to any statements but not to initiate any conversation or question Henry regarding the bank robbery. The informant, nonetheless, acknowledged that he was not a passive listener but had engaged in conversations with Henry, and that the incriminating statements were the product of such conversations. Chief Justice Burger held that the informant deliberately used his position to secure incriminating information from Henry when counsel was not present, conduct which the Court attributed to the government: "Even if the agent's statement that he did not intend that [the informant] would take affirmative steps to secure incriminating information is accepted, he must have known that such propinquity likely would lead to that result."[273]

The Court pointed out that Fifth Amendment considerations were absent in *Henry* because there was no official pressure compelling the accused to incriminate himself. Though in custody, the accused was not interrogated. Furthermore, even if the informant had questioned him, he could not bring to bear the type of coercion inherent to custodial interrogation protected against by the Fifth Amendment and *Miranda*. However, once formal proceedings have commenced, the investigation stage of a case has terminated and the parties are then " 'arms-length' adversaries." The Sixth Amendment requires that the prosecution no longer attempt to build its case by eliciting any information from the accused without first going through his attorney unless the accused knowingly, intelligently, and voluntarily relinquishes the right. An accused who does not know that he is being induced by an agent of the prosecution to make incriminating statements cannot be held to have waived his right to the assistance of counsel.

Finally, *Henry* is most impressive because the informant was instructed not to question the accused, nor was it ever established that he did. Instead, Chief Justice Burger held that it was sufficient that the government intentionally created a situation likely to induce the accused to make incriminating statements without the assistance of counsel. To invoke the sanction of the Sixth Amendment, however, it must be demonstrated that the police informant took some action, beyond merely listening, that was designed deliberately to elicit incriminating remarks. There must be more than the mere demonstration that an informer, either on his own or as a police informant, relayed incriminating information to the police.[274]

A defendant whose Sixth Amendment counsel right has attached may waive that right and be interrogated. Although Sixth Amendment waiver involves the rigorous standard applied to waiver of trial rights, *Miranda*

---

[273]United States v Henry, 447 US 264, 271, 100 SCt 2183, 65 LEd(2d) 115 (1980). But see State v Adkins, 80 App(3d) 211, 608 NE(2d) 1152 (Athens 1992), cert denied 507 US 975, 113 SCt 1423, 122 LEd(2d) 792 (1993) (police have not violated defendant's Sixth Amendment right, where police officer passively sits at a bar with a confidential informant while defendant approaches said informant and makes incriminating statements).
[274]Kuhlmann v Wilson, 477 US 436, 106 SCt 2616, 91 LEd(2d) 364 (1986).

rights are sufficient to appraise a defendant of his Sixth Amendment right to counsel. A defendant may validly waive this right within the context of a *Miranda* waiver.[275]

(D) Differences between Sixth Amendment right to counsel and Miranda *right to counsel*

There are significant differences between *Miranda* and Sixth Amendment counsel rights. *Miranda* attaches earlier and precludes all interrogation; the Sixth Amendment right covers different attempts to elicit information from an accused but is limited to the offense to which the right has attached.

Miranda requires custody and interrogation. The right attaches any time a defendant is interrogated after being taken into custody.[276] Interrogation under *Miranda* requires that the accused be and know that he is being interrogated by a police officer.[277] Police may attempt to re-initiate interrogation of an accused, following safeguards enunciated in *Michigan v Mosley*,[278] after he has exercised his right to remain silent. Police may not interrogate an accused who has asserted his *Miranda* right to counsel unless the accused initiates the discussion and then executes a valid waiver of *Miranda* rights.[279] This prohibition applies to any offense, as well as the offense for which the accused is in custody.[280]

Sixth Amendment protections afforded under *Massiah* and *Williams* require neither custody nor interrogation. No Sixth Amendment rights attach until after a suspect is formally charged.[281] Once proceedings have been initiated, an accused is entitled to the assistance and presence of counsel whenever police deliberately elicit a confession from him regardless of whether he is in custody or even knows he is being interrogated.[282] The prohibition is offense-specific, limited to the offense for which proceedings are pending.[283]

How the rights work is illustrated in *State v McGhee*,[284] where the defendant called his co-defendant at the police station and the co-defendant was permitted to return the call. Police, with the co-defendant's permission, recorded the call. The co-defendant was not in custody and was not interrogated by the police; therefore, no *Miranda* rights attached. No charges had

---

[275]Patterson v Illinois, 487 US 285, 108 SCt 2389, 101 LEd(2d) 261 (1988).
[276]Miranda v Arizona, 384 US 436, 86 SCt 1602, 16 LEd(2d) 694 (1966).
[277]Illinois v Perkins, 496 US 292, 110 SCt 2394, 110 LEd(2d) 243 (1990), cert denied 114 SCt 2692, 129 LEd(2d) 823 (1994).
[278]Michigan v Mosley, 423 US 96, 96 SCt 321, 46 LEd(2d) 313 (1975), affirmed by 400 Mich 181, 254 NW(2d) 29 (1977), cert denied 434 US 861, 98 SCt 189, 54 LEd(2d) 135 (1977).
[279]Edwards v Arizona, 451 US 477, 101 SCt 1880, 68 LEd(2d) 378 (1981).
[280]Arizona v Roberson, 486 US 675, 108 SCt 2093, 100 LEd(2d) 704 (1988).
[281]State v McGhee, 37 App(3d) 54, 523 NE(2d) 864 (Cuyahoga 1987).
[282]Brewer v Williams, 430 US 387, 97 SCt 1232, 51 LEd(2d) 424 (1977), cert denied sub nom Williams v Iowa, 446 US 921, 100 SCt 1859, 64 LEd(2d) 277 (1980); United States v Henry, 447 US 264, 100 SCt 2183, 65 LEd(2d) 115 (1980).
[283]McNeil v Wisconsin, 501 US 171, 111 SCt 2204, 115 LEd(2d) 158 (1991).
[284]State v McGhee, 37 App(3d) 54, 523 NE(2d) 864 (Cuyahoga 1987).

been initiated against the defendant at the time of the call; therefore, there was no Sixth Amendment violation either.

CROSS REFERENCES

Text 19.01, 19.08

19.12   Impeachment exception

Violation of the *Miranda*[285] and *Brewer-Henry*[286] rules precludes the use of any resulting statement in the state's case-in-chief. Similarly, a defendant's silence may not be used in the prosecution's case-in-chief.[287] However, if the defendant takes the witness stand, his statement may be used under certain conditions by the state by way of cross-examination for purposes of impeachment.[288] Statements made in violation of a defendant's *Miranda* and Sixth Amendment rights may be used to impeach his testimony.[289] The evidence may also be used to impeach a particular statement made by the defendant during cross-examination.[290] The impeachment exception to the exclusionary rule may not be used to impeach the testimony of defense witnesses other than the defendant.[291]

Harris v New York[292] involved a narcotics prosecution where the defendant took the stand in his own defense and admitted knowing the undercover police officer, and admitted selling to the officer a glassine bag containing a white substance, but denied that the bag contained heroin. The defendant claimed that the bag contained baking powder and that he sought to defraud the purchaser. On cross-examination, the prosecutor used a statement given by the defendant to the police which contradicted his own testimony, but which did not meet *Miranda* standards and could not have been introduced by the state for proving the charge.

The Supreme Court acknowledged that some statements contained in the *Miranda* decision could be read as indicating a bar to use of an uncounseled statement for any purpose, but since the issue was not essential to the holding in that case, those statements were not deemed controlling. On the other hand, the Court believed that the issue was analogous to its permitting, for impeachment purposes, the use of evidence barred under the Fourth Amendment, although there the impeachment involved a collateral

---

[285]Miranda v Arizona, 384 US 436, 86 SCt 1602, 16 LEd(2d) 694 (1966).

[286]Brewer v Williams, 430 US 387, 97 SCt 1232, 51 LEd(2d) 424 (1977), cert denied sub nom Williams v Iowa, 446 US 921, 100 SCt 1859, 64 LEd(2d) 277 (1980); United States v Henry, 447 US 264, 100 SCt 2183, 65 LEd(2d) 115 (1980).

[287]State v Motley, 21 App(3d) 240, 21 OBR 256, 486 NE(2d) 1259 (Franklin 1985) (where a prosecutor elicited testimony from police officer in state's case-in-chief that defendant chose to remain silent following giving of *Miranda* warnings, conviction must be reversed unless it is clear beyond a reasonable doubt that absent this statement of the officer no juror could have entertained a reasonable doubt as to defendant's guilt).

[288]Harris v New York, 401 US 222, 91 SCt 643, 28 LEd(2d) 1 (1971).

[289]Michigan v Harvey, 494 US 344, 110 SCt 1176, 108 LEd(2d) 293 (1990).

[290]United States v Havens, 446 US 620, 100 SCt 1912, 64 LEd(2d) 559 (1980), cert denied 450 US 995, 101 SCt 1697, 68 LEd(2d) 195 (1981).

[291]James v Illinois, 493 US 307, 110 SCt 648, 107 LEd(2d) 676 (1990).

[292]Harris v New York, 401 US 222, 91 SCt 643, 28 LEd(2d) 1 (1971).

matter rather than testimony bearing directly on the crimes charged.[293] The Court in *Harris* did not believe it necessary to restrict the use of this type of impeachment evidence to collateral matters. Rather, the Court held that statements, inadmissible in the prosecution's case-in-chief, if voluntarily given and not coerced, may be used to impeach the defendant's credibility when he voluntarily takes the witness stand and his testimony is inconsistent from those earlier statements. The majority argued that the "shield provided by *Miranda* cannot be perverted into a license to use perjury by way of a defense, free from the risk of confrontation with prior inconsistent utterances."[294]

The *Harris* Court distinguished between statements that failed to meet *Miranda* standards and those that are coerced or involuntary. The latter are not trustworthy and are not admissible for any purpose. Only those that satisfy the voluntariness standard, judged by the totality of the circumstances, may be used to impeach the defendant's testimony. Statements that are the product of an overborne will "cannot be used in any way against a defendant at his trial."[295] The Court in *Mincey v Arizona* said:

> Statements made by a defendant in circumstances violating the strictures of *Miranda v Arizona* are admissible for impeachment if their "trustworthiness ... satisfies legal standards." But *any* criminal trial use against a defendant of his *involuntary* statement is a denial of due process of law.[296]

The reason for the different treatment of statements that are the product of *Miranda* violations and those that are "coerced or involuntary" stems from the Court's analysis that *Miranda* violations are not Fifth Amendment violations, but "merely" violations of rules intended to protect Fifth Amendment rights. Since the Fifth Amendment contains within its language an exclusionary rule, any statement that is coerced or otherwise involuntary, such as a statement given to a grand jury in return for immunity,[297] is a violation of a Fifth Amendment right and may not be used for any purpose.

The *Harris* opinion, written by Chief Justice Burger, operated on the assumption that *Miranda's* sole purpose was to deter illegal police behavior. He argued that sufficient deterrence flows when the evidence is made unavailable to the prosecution in its case-in-chief. There is, however, a diminution of the deterrent effect of *Miranda* by permitting the use of these statements for any purpose because a statement from an accused becomes a valuable commodity. Either the statement is admissible in the state's case because it meets the *Miranda* test or, if it does not satisfy *Miranda* standards

---

[293]See Walder v United States, 347 US 62, 74 SCt 354, 98 LEd 503 (1954).

[294]Harris v New York, 401 US 222, 226, 91 SCt 643, 28 LEd(2d) 1 (1971).

[295]Mincey v Arizona, 437 US 385, 402, 98 SCt 2408, 57 LEd(2d) 290 (1978), cert denied 469 US 1040, 105 SCt 521, 83 LEd(2d) 409 (1984), modified sub nom Arizona v Hicks, 480 US 321, 107 SCt 1149, 94 LEd(2d) 347 (1987); see also Text 19.01(C), Voluntariness test.

[296]Mincey v Arizona, 437 US 385, 397-98, 98 SCt 2408, 57 LEd(2d) 290 (1978), cert denied 469 US 1040, 105 SCt 521, 83 LEd(2d) 409 (1984), modified sub nom Arizona v Hicks, 480 US 321, 107 SCt 1149, 94 LEd(2d) 347 (1987).

[297]New Jersey v Portash, 440 US 450, 99 SCt 1292, 59 LEd(2d) 501 (1979).

but qualifies under the voluntariness test, it can be used to impeach the defendant's testimony or serve to dissuade him from taking the witness stand.

The Court strengthened the incentive for not complying with *Miranda* in *Oregon v Hass,*[298] where it upheld, for impeachment purposes, statements secured from a defendant who had requested to see an attorney after he received *Miranda* warnings but where the police refused to comply with his request. In *Harris,* the defendant was not given warnings, but in *Hass* there was a total disregard for the defendant's decision to exercise his rights. The rule encourages police to consciously decide to proceed with interrogation and to disregard *Miranda* after assessing the likelihood of securing a statement in compliance with *Miranda* standards. If, however, there is little likelihood of securing such a statement, police may disregard *Miranda* and proceed with the interrogation knowing, at least, that statements may be used to impeach the accused or keep him from testifying in his own behalf. The *Harris-Hass* rule creates an actual incentive, under some circumstances, for police to violate *Miranda.*

Whether a defendant's silence, which may be inconsistent with his in-court explanation, may be used for impeachment purposes depends on when the silence occurs and whether the accused was given *Miranda* warnings. An accused's silence following receipt of the *Miranda* warnings may not be used because of its inherent ambiguity and the impossibility of determining whether that silence is the product of reliance on the *Miranda* warning.[299] Any erroneous reference to a defendant's silence following issuance of *Miranda* warnings requires reversal unless the state can show that the error was harmless.[300] To permit the use of such silence to impeach the defendant would exact a price for the exercise of the right and would make the issuance of *Miranda* warnings a trap for the unwary. Nor may a state use a defendant's post-*Miranda* warnings silence as evidence of the defendant's sanity to refute a defense of insanity. The Supreme Court held in *Wainwright v Greenfield*[301] that

> it is fundamentally unfair to promise an arrested person that his silence will not be used against him and thereafter to breach that promise by using the silence to impeach his trial testimony. It is equally unfair to breach that promise by using silence to overcome a defendant's plea of insanity.

Neither may a prosecutor raise for the first time during closing argument a defendant's post arrest silence.[302]

---

[298]Oregon v Hass, 420 US 714, 95 SCt 1215, 43 LEd(2d) 570 (1975).

[299]Doyle v Ohio, 426 US 610, 96 SCt 2240, 49 LEd(2d) 91 (1976).

[300]State v Moreland, 50 OS(3d) 58, 552 NE(2d) 894 (1990), cert denied 498 US 882, 111 SCt 231, 112 LEd(2d) 185 (1990); State v Motley, 21 App(3d) 240, 21 OBR 256, 486 NE(2d) 1259 (Franklin 1985).

[301]Wainwright v Greenfield, 474 US 284, 106 SCt 634, 639, 88 LEd(2d) 623 (1986). Accord State v Rogers, 32 OS(3d) 70, 512 NE(2d) 581 (1987), cert denied 484 US 958, 108 SCt 358, 98 LEd(2d) 383 (1987).

[302]State v Saunders, 98 App(3d) 355, 648 NE(2d) 587 (Lucas 1994) (prosecutor denied defendant a fair trial by raising silence for first time during closing argument

The Supreme Court, however, distinguished pre-arrest silence, holding that its use for impeachment violates neither the privilege against self-incrimination nor fundamental fairness guaranteed by due process.[303] In *Jenkins v Anderson*,[304] the state was permitted to use the defendant's failure to come forward for two weeks following a homicide to impeach his claim that the killing was in self-defense. Unlike *Doyle v Ohio*,[305] where the defendant's silence following receipt of the *Miranda* warnings may have been induced by the warnings, the Court held that no governmental action induced the defendant to remain silent before arrest. The Court has held post-arrest silence prior to *Miranda* warnings to be analogous to pre-arrest silence because the defendant is not given "the sort of affirmative assurance embodied in the *Miranda* warnings." Thus there is no violation of due process when a defendant is cross-examined as to his post-arrest silence, which has not been induced by police who have not or not yet given *Miranda* warnings.

The ability to use otherwise inadmissible statements and confessions, except those secured through actual coercion, provides a dangerous incentive not to comply with *Miranda* and Sixth Amendment requirements. When an accused asserts his rights, police may proceed and attempt to obtain a statement for several reasons even though it may not be used in the prosecution's case-in-chief. Police may decide they have nothing to lose. If the defendant has asserted his right to silence or counsel, they may assume that no admissible confession will be forthcoming in any event. A statement in violation of *Miranda* or Sixth Amendment rights may be sought at that point in order to impeach the accused if he elects to take the witness stand or may serve to keep the accused off of the witness stand. In either instance it serves to weaken the deterrent effects of *Miranda* and the Sixth Amendment exclusionary rules.

CROSS REFERENCES

1 Giannelli & Snyder, Baldwin's Ohio Practice, *Evidence* § 104.8

---

cutting off defendant's opportunity to call rebuttal witnesses and an opportunity to request the court to remedy any error by limiting instructions).

[303]Jenkins v Anderson, 447 US 231, 100 SCt 2124, 65 LEd(2d) 86 (1980).
[304]Jenkins v Anderson, 447 US 231, 100 SCt 2124, 65 LEd(2d) 86 (1980).
[305]Doyle v Ohio, 426 US 610, 96 SCt 2240, 49 LEd(2d) 91 (1976).

Chapter 20

Lineups and Pretrial Identification

20.01   Introduction

Eyewitness testimony creates a danger zone in the practice of law, for mistaken eyewitness identification has resulted in more miscarriages of justice than any other type of evidence. The Fourth and Fifth Amendment rules pertaining to the admissibility of evidence are in the one case not at all and in the other only partially related to the truth-determining function of a trial. The Fourth Amendment exclusionary rule, for example, operates in derogation of the truth, barring the use of reliable evidence of guilt because of policy reasons inherent in the Amendment. The rules governing the use of eyewitness identification, however, deal directly with the reliability of the guilt-determining process. Second only to confessions, eyewitness identification is the most convincing and damaging evidence; hence reliability is critical. This chapter covers the evidentiary issues raised by the use at trial of prior eyewitness identification and then focuses on the constitutional rules that have been developed to govern the use of eyewitness identification.

20.02   Hearsay

A witness' testimony at trial pertaining to a pretrial identification may serve either of two purposes. If the testimony is used as substantive evidence to prove the identity of the perpetrator, the testimony is hearsay. It is not hearsay if the testimony is used to corroborate the witness' trial identification and to bolster the witness' credibility.

Evidence Rule 801(D)(1)(c) permits an identification witness to testify at trial about a prior identification. The rule declares that the evidence is *not* hearsay if (1) the declarant testifies at trial or (preliminary) hearing and is subject to cross-examination; (2) the out-of-court identification follows "soon after perceiving" the person during the identification procedure; and (3) "the circumstances demonstrate the reliability of the prior identification."[1]

Formerly, state law did not permit the substantive use of prior identifications. RC 2945.55 appears to permit such a use. However, the Ohio Supreme Court interpreted the statute to permit prior identification testimony only for corroborative purposes, to bolster the in-court identification

---

[1] See 2 Giannelli & Snyder, Baldwin's Ohio Pracitce, *Evidence* § 801.15, 801.16.

of the witness, a nonhearsay use.[2] Under that case, once the witness identified the suspect at trial, testimony about prior identification by the witness was admissible only "to corroborate that identification."[3]

With the rule in place, prior identification is admissible for either substantive or corroborative purposes, provided that the prior identification meets constitutional standards.

CROSS REFERENCES

1 Giannelli & Snyder, Baldwin's Ohio Practice, *Evidence* § 607.10
2 Giannelli & Snyder, Baldwin's Ohio Practice, *Evidence* § 801.15, 801.16

20.03   Right to counsel

In a series of companion cases decided in 1967, two of which were decided under the right to counsel, the Supreme Court attempted to exert constitutional controls on pretrial identification procedures.[4] In *United States v Wade* and *Gilbert v California*, the Court held that a post-indictment lineup is a critical stage of a criminal proceeding subject to the right to counsel, and that in-court identification of a suspect may be barred if it is the product of a pretrial lineup where the right to counsel was denied.

The rationale offered by the Court for classifying pretrial identification as a critical stage is that it is "peculiarly riddled with innumerable dangers and variable factors which might seriously, even crucially, derogate from a fair trial."[5] Eyewitness identification was labeled as "untrustworthy" and a major factor contributing to miscarriages of justice because of "the degree of suggestion inherent in the manner in which the prosecution presents the suspect to witnesses for pretrial identification."[6] The Court was concerned because it is generally impossible to reconstruct the lineup at trial, nor are the lineup participants or witnesses likely to be alert for conditions prejudicial to the accused.

The presence of counsel at a lineup, the Court reasoned, could avert prejudice at the pretrial identification and assure a meaningful confrontation and cross-examination at trial. Application of the right to counsel to pretrial identification rested squarely on promoting the determination of truth at trial and insuring the reliability of convictions. These decisions devised a per se exclusionary rule barring all testimony regarding the pretrial identification itself and any in-court identifications that are the product of pretrial identifications in violation of the Sixth Amendment. A Sixth Amendment violation occurs at a lineup when counsel is not provided or notified, if already retained or appointed, unless there is an intelligent waiver of the right by the defendant. The Court refrained from applying the

---

[2]State v Lancaster, 25 OS(2d) 83, 267 NE(2d) 291 (1971).
[3]State v Lancaster, 25 OS(2d) 83, 92, 267 NE(2d) 291 (1971).
[4]United States v Wade, 388 US 218, 87 SCt 1926, 18 LEd(2d) 1149 (1967); Gilbert v California, 388 US 263, 87 SCt 1951, 18 LEd(2d) 1178 (1967); Stovall v Denno, 388 US 293, 87 SCt 1967, 18 LEd(2d) 1199 (1967).
[5]United States v Wade, 388 US 218, 228, 87 SCt 1926, 18 LEd(2d) 1149 (1967).
[6]United States v Wade, 388 US 218, 228, 87 SCt 1926, 18 LEd(2d) 1149 (1967).

rule retroactively, retreating somewhat from the position staked out in *Wade* and *Gilbert* that the rule was devised to assure the integrity and reliability of the guilt-determining process.[7]

Wade and *Gilbert*, however, while creating the per se exclusionary rule, also offered two alternatives for avoidance of application of the rule. The rule does not mandate exclusion of in-court identification testimony, even if counsel was lacking at the pretrial lineup, when the in-court identification is based on observations of the suspect other than the lineup identification. The suppression rule is not applicable when an in-court identification does not amount to an exploitation of the tainted lineup. If the in-court identification had an independent source, separate from the lineup, the identification testimony is admissible. The identification may be premised on observations of the accused at the time of the alleged criminal act, which would be an adequate independent source to overcome the constitutional failure to have counsel present at the time of the lineup. Additionally, the Court held that the constitutional harmless error rule is applicable to pretrial identification violations.[8]

Wade and *Gilbert* held that the right to counsel applies to lineups. The right is equally applicable to show-ups and confrontations where the accused is not in a lineup but presented individually, whether at a pretrial court appearance or out of court.[9] However, the right to counsel is not applicable at photographic displays conducted by police for the purpose of allowing a witness to attempt an identification of an offender.[10] The Court reasoned that a photographic identification differs from a lineup because there are substantially fewer possibilities of suggestion and any unfair influences can be readily reconstructed at trial.[11] Similarly, an identification from a videotape was held not to be a critical stage because it promotes accuracy and protects against abuse.[12]

The lineups in both *Wade* and *Gilbert* occurred after indictment, and the rule emanating from those cases expressly held that a post-indictment lineup is a critical stage, subject to the right to counsel. In both cases, the defendants were already represented by counsel, but no attempt was made prior to the lineup to notify counsel and secure their presence. Most line-

---

[7]Cf. Stovall v Denno, 388 US 293, 299, 87 SCt 1967, 18 LEd(2d) 1199 (1967) (Plurality opinion: "But the certainty and frequency with which we can say in the confrontation cases that no injustice occurred differs greatly enough from the cases involving absence of counsel at trial or on appeal to justify treating the situations as different in kind for the purpose of retroactive application, especially in light of the strong countervailing interests.").

[8]See Chapman v California, 386 US 18, 87 SCt 824, 17 LEd(2d) 705 (1967) (before constitutional error can be deemed harmless, the state must prove beyond a reasonable doubt that the error complained of did not contribute to the verdict obtained).

[9]Moore v Illinois, 434 US 220, 98 SCt 458, 54 LEd(2d) 424 (1977), cert denied 440 US 919, 99 SCt 1242, 59 LEd(2d) 471 (1979).

[10]United States v Ash, 413 US 300, 93 SCt 2568, 37 LEd(2d) 619 (1973).

[11]United States v Ash, 413 US 300, 324, 93 SCt 2568, 37 LEd(2d) 619 (1973) (Stewart, J., concurring).

[12]State v Robertson, No. 11572, 1990 WL 65658 (2d Dist Ct App, Montgomery, 5-18-90), appeal dismissed by 55 OS(3d) 713, 563 NE(2d) 722 (1990).

ups, however, occur prior to indictment, and the rule would have little effect if restricted to the post-indictment phase of a criminal case. It is evident that the Supreme Court, in deciding *Wade* and *Gilbert*, never considered restricting application of the right to the post-indictment stage of a criminal case. In the third companion case, *Stovall v Denno*,[13] a case involving a show-up two days after the crime and one day after the arrest of the defendant, the Court declined to apply the *Wade* and *Gilbert* rules retroactively, but the Court did not consider it significant that the defendant had not been indicted. Indeed, the Court said that "the confrontation is a 'critical stage,' and that counsel is required at *all* confrontations."[14]

The arrest and detention of a suspect does not constitute the initiation of adversary judicial proceedings.[15] The issue was addressed in *Kirby v Illinois*,[16] where the Court was asked to extend the right to counsel to an eyewitness identification that occurred immediately after arrest, one day after the crime was committed, and before any charges were filed. The Court declined, reasoning that the right to counsel attaches only at or after the time that adversary judicial proceedings have been initiated against an accused. In *Moore v Illinois*,[17] the Supreme Court held that the right attached at a preliminary hearing where the accused was identified by the complaining witness. Further insight into how early the right attaches is found in *Brewer v Williams*,[18] a confession case, where the right was held to have attached following the issuance of an arrest warrant and a preliminary appearance.

The *Kirby* Court declined to apply the right prior to the "onset of formal prosecutorial proceedings" or "adversary judicial proceedings," which was further defined as formal charging. It is unlikely that an arrest warrant, alone, is sufficient to activate the right, but the filing of a complaint[19] or any court appearance of an accused following arrest would activate the right. An identification proceeding prior to attachment of the right to counsel will be governed by a straight due process analysis. This distinction between the onset of custody and the initiation of formal proceedings seems calculated to insulate the common police practice of eyewitness identification at the scene of a crime. The right to counsel does not apply to a post-indictment identification that was made from a videotaped lineup held prior to indictment.[20]

---

[13]Stovall v Denno, 388 US 293, 87 SCt 1967, 18 LEd(2d) 1199 (1967).

[14]Stovall v Denno, 388 US 293, 298, 87 SCt 1967, 18 LEd(2d) 1199 (1967) (emphasis added).

[15]State v Wallace, No. CA89-11-027, 1990 WL 70928 (12th Dist Ct App, Madison, 5-29-90).

[16]Kirby v Illinois, 406 US 682, 92 SCt 1877, 32 LEd(2d) 411 (1972).

[17]Moore v Illinois, 434 US 220, 98 SCt 458, 54 LEd(2d) 424 (1977), cert denied 440 US 919, 99 SCt 1242, 59 LEd(2d) 471 (1979).

[18]Brewer v Williams, 430 US 387, 97 SCt 1232, 51 LEd(2d) 424 (1977), cert denied sub nom Williams v Iowa, 446 US 921, 100 SCt 1859, 64 LEd(2d) 277 (1980).

[19]See Crim R 3.

[20]State v Robertson, No. 11572, 1990 WL 65658 (2d Dist Ct App, Montgomery, 5-18-90), appeal dismissed by 55 OS(3d) 713, 563 NE(2d) 722 (1990).

The reference to confession cases for the applicability of the right to counsel makes no sense. The purpose of counsel at lineups is to ensure the fairness of the lineup in order to promote the reliability of the identification. Counsel at a post-arraignment interrogation has nothing to do with ensuring the reliability of any ensuing statement. Counsel may advise his client not to make any statement and to refuse to answer any questions. Counsel at a lineup, of course, cannot advise a suspect to refuse to appear in a lineup. An accused has no right to refuse. The reliability factor applies just as much to identifications made before initiation of formal charges as identifications held after initiation of charges. To attach the right to one and not the other is extremely formalistic and does not further the very purpose of requiring counsel at lineups. Although Ohio does not now impose a stricter requirement than that imposed under the federal Constitution, the Ohio Supreme Court addressed this issue prior to *Kirby* and recognized the critical nature of a confrontation. "The fact that this confrontation occurred prior to indictment in no way lessens the fact that the results might well determine his fate, and that 'counsel's absence might derogate from the accused's right to a fair trial.' "[21]

20.04   Independent basis for in-court identifications

The United States Supreme Court said, "Only a per se exclusionary rule as to ... testimony [concerning an illegal pretrial identification] can be an effective sanction to assure that law enforcement authorities will respect the accused's constitutional right to the presence of his counsel at the critical lineup."[22] The per se rule does not automatically apply to an in-court identification. If the in-court identification is the result of the earlier illegal confrontation or lineup, then it is derivative of that illegality and is barred as the "fruit of the poisonous tree." However, when the in-court identification is based on observations of the defendant other than the tainted lineup, that identification is admissible because it is not the fruit of the poisonous tree. The Court indicated that the prosecution must demonstrate by clear and convincing evidence that the in-court identification is derived from an independent source and not the product of the tainted confrontation.[23] Justice Black predicted that the standard would be practically impossible to meet, and Justice White characterized it as a "heavy burden ... and probably an impossible one."[24] However, it has not been as difficult as the justices predicted to avoid the per se exclusionary rule.

Obviously, the hearing to determine whether to suppress the out-of-court identification and, if so, whether there is an independent basis for an in-court identification takes on critical proportions. The admissibility of the in-court identification will turn on the strength of the witness' testimony about his prior encounter with the accused. Ordinarily, there will only have been

---

[21]State v Lathan, 30 OS(2d) 92, 96, 282 NE(2d) 574 (1972), quoting Stovall v Denno, 388 US 293, 298, 87 SCt 1967, 18 LEd(2d) 1199 (1967).

[22]Gilbert v California, 388 US 263, 273, 87 SCt 1951, 18 LEd(2d) 1178 (1967).

[23]United States v Wade, 388 US 218, 87 SCt 1926, 18 LEd(2d) 1149 (1967).

[24]United States v Wade, 388 US 218, 251, 87 SCt 1926, 18 LEd(2d) 1149 (1967).

one encounter, during the commission of the crime. Among the factors important to the resolution of this issue are the following:

(1) How long the witness had to observe the assailant;

(2) Whether the witness had an opportunity to observe the accused from a position and direction which afforded a full view of the assailant;

(3) Whether lighting conditions were sufficient to allow for a full view; and

(4) The emotional state of the witness at the time of the observation.

Five years after *Wade* and *Gilbert* the Ohio Supreme Court spoke on the issue and applied the independent basis test.

In *State v Tingler*,[25] the appellant was officially charged prior to a face-to-face confrontation held by police without the presence of or notice to his counsel. The Court found the confrontation to be in violation of the accused's right to counsel and hence illegal but refused to overturn the conviction since the state had introduced no evidence of the illegal pretrial identification. There had been no challenge at trial to the in-court identification, which clearly had an independent basis.[26] The *Wade-Gilbert* per se exclusionary rule gives way when there is a factual determination that the in-court identification had a basis independent of the illegal pretrial confrontation/identification.

In *State v Hurt*,[27] a similar fact pattern arose. The appellant had been arrested and charged prior to a confrontation without benefit of counsel. The police wanted to place the defendant in a lineup, but he refused to waive his right to counsel at the lineup. Instead, the police asked the defendant if he was willing to confront the victims of the crimes for which he was being held. The police claimed the defendant consented to the confrontation, a fact which the defense disputed. While the court readily extended the *Wade-Gilbert* rule to this confrontation, which occurred after arrest and charging but before indictment, it still did not overturn the conviction or exclude the in-court identification evidence. The court agreed with the defense that the defendant had not intelligently waived his right to counsel but concluded that the state had met its burden of proving the in-court identifications had an independent basis since no witness expressed any doubt on cross-examination.

State v Lathan[28] also involved an illegal confrontation because of the absence of counsel. The court reversed the conviction and excluded the witness' identification testimony at trial. Reviewing the totality of the circumstances in order to determine the admissibility of the witness' in-court identification, the Ohio Supreme Court found that the witness' opportunity at the time of the crime to observe her attacker was meager. The circumstances surrounding a later improper police confrontation, held without

---

[25]State v Tingler, 31 OS(2d) 100, 285 NE(2d) 710 (1972).
[26]State v Tingler, 31 OS(2d) 100, 285 NE(2d) 710 (1972).
[27]State v Hurt, 30 OS(2d) 86, 282 NE(2d) 578 (1972), cert denied 409 US 991, 93 SCt 337, 34 LEd(2d) 258 (1972).
[28]State v Lathan, 30 OS(2d) 92, 282 NE(2d) 574 (1972).

counsel, between the witness and the suspect were so highly suggestive as to create an opportunity for misidentification. The court concluded that the state had not established clear and convincing evidence that such in-court identification had an independent origin.

In a fourth case later that same year, where police arranged a show-up in jail of the defendant, the Ohio Supreme Court claimed not to condone a substitute confrontation where a lineup could have been arranged but actually did condone the "unsatisfactory" alternative:

> [T]o have required a normal jail line-up in the instant case with numerous 'suspects' would not have aided in avoiding a mistaken identification, since the witnesses had already positively identified the defendant and merely wanted to confirm a feature of this *particular* man.[29]

Such reactions to shortcuts to avoid implementation of *Wade* and *Gilbert* are hardly likely to secure police compliance with those rules.

All of the issues raised by the independent basis test are illustrated in *State v Deal*,[30] a kidnaping and rape case. Shortly after the police were notified, an officer met with the complainant to establish the identity of the witness. She provided a description of her attacker and then viewed slides that were selected according to the description she gave. The complainant selected the defendant and later confirmed this identification by viewing a photo of the appellant. On the day trial began, the police officer and an assistant prosecuting attorney took the witness to the holding cell outside the courtroom where the defendant was being held prior to the commencement of trial proceedings. Here, the witness, again, identified the defendant as the assailant, picking him from a group of four or five black males being held in the cell. This identification took place outside the presence of the defense attorney.

The Cuyahoga County Court of Appeals found that the holding cell identification was a critical stage and should not have been held outside the presence of counsel. Nonetheless, the court affirmed the trial court's denial of the defense motion to suppress, allowing the complainant to identify the defendant in court and holding that her identification was not tainted by the holding cell viewing. The factors considered by the court were the witness' prior opportunity to view the defendant, the detailed description which she gave of her assailant, and her prior identifications of the defendant from the slide and picture. The court concluded that clear and convincing evidence existed in the record that the witness' in-court identification of the defendant was independent of the holding cell identification.

So long as the standard is not beyond a reasonable doubt, the trial and appellate courts in *Deal* could not have decided otherwise. Nonetheless, persistent questions remain. There was no valid reason for the state to have the pretrial identification take place outside the presence of defendant's attorney. It was the day of trial, and counsel was either present in the courtroom or shortly would have been present. The final out-of-court identification took place for either or both of two reasons: a final check to make

---

[29]State v Sheardon, 31 OS(2d) 20, 25, 285 NE(2d) 335 (1972).
[30]State v Deal, No. 57358, 1990 WL 109122 (8th Dist Ct App, Cuyahoga, 8-2-90).

sure that the defendant was the right one or to bolster the witness' testimony and provide the accuser with a live opportunity to see the defendant in order to make her in-court identification more certain. Considering there was no reason whatsoever for excluding the defense attorney from the holding cell identification, the state raised unnecessary uncertainty about its own witness' testimony.

CROSS REFERENCES

Text Ch 2, 20.03

20.05   Due process analysis

Even where the Sixth Amendment right to counsel has not attached, "it remains open to all persons to allege and prove ... that the confrontation resulted in such unfairness that it infringed his right to due process of law."[31] This ground of attack is independent of any right to counsel claim. Since most identifications take place prior to the commencement of formal adversary proceedings, most identification issues will be litigated on due process claims.

To establish a due process violation, a defendant must prove that the out-of-court confrontation was "unnecessarily suggestive and conducive to irreparable mistaken identification," a determination which is to be made on the totality of the circumstances.[32] The defendant in *Stovall v Denno* was suspected of murdering a doctor and stabbing his wife eleven times in the course of a robbery of their home. Two days after the robbery, the suspect was taken to the wife's hospital room in handcuffs by five police officers and two members of the district attorney's staff. The defendant was the only black person in the room at the time of the identification. He was directed to say a few words for voice identification, and then one of the officers asked the critically ill wife if the defendant was the assailant. She identified him from her hospital bed. At trial, the wife made an in-court identification and she and the officers who had been present at the hospital testified to her prior identification.

The Supreme Court plurality acknowledged the danger in showing suspects singly to persons for the purpose of identification, rather than as part of a lineup. However, the Court found no due process violation. Actually, the treatment accorded the due process claim was, at best, cursory and bland. The Court failed to analyze the likelihood of a mistaken identification, although the plurality's account of the facts clearly indicated the presence of all the ingredients for a mistaken identification: a critically injured post-operative witness and a single black suspect manacled to one of a sea of police and officials from the prosecutor's office. Instead, the Court focused on the brutality of the crime and the need for an identification. Reviewing the totality of the circumstances, the Court concluded that an immediate showing of the defendant to the eyewitness was imperative because of the critical nature of her wounds. "[T]he police followed the only

---

[31]Stovall v Denno, 388 US 293, 299, 87 SCt 1967, 18 LEd(2d) 1199 (1967).
[32]Stovall v Denno, 388 US 293, 302, 87 SCt 1967, 18 LEd(2d) 1199 (1967).

feasible procedure and took Stovall to the hospital room. Under these circumstances, the usual police station line-up ... was out of the question."[33]

Stovall indicates the difficulty in establishing a due process violation. The critical factor for the Court, appearing to outweigh the suggestiveness of the procedure, was the necessity for an immediate identification. In *Simmons v United States*,[34] the Court said the identification procedure must be "so impermissibly suggestive as to give rise to a very substantial likelihood of irreparable misidentification." Later, the Court indicated that the due process analysis seeks to strike a balance between the right of a suspect to be protected from prejudicial procedures and the interest of society in a prompt and meaningful investigation and solution of an unsolved crime.[35] The test does not create a per se exclusionary rule based on the procedures used but, instead, focuses on the reliability of the resulting identification.

Identification testimony will be excluded only if the pretrial procedures were so suggestive as to present a very substantial likelihood of irreparable misidentification. "[R]eliability is the linchpin in determining the admissibility of identification testimony."[36] The irreparability of the possible misidentification is the factor to focus on. In determining whether the pretrial identification procedure resulted in a due process violation, the Supreme Court has, in effect, directed that scrutiny be directed to the reliability of the identification and not the reliability of the identification procedures. In *Neil v Biggers*,[37] where a suspect was shown alone to a witness in the absence of exigent circumstances, the Court held that the identification testimony may be admissible if it bears sufficient earmarks of reliability. Those factors which may be considered in evaluating

> the likelihood of misidentification include the opportunity of the witness to view the criminal at the time of the crime, the witness' degree of attention, the accuracy of the witness' prior description of the criminal, the level of certainty demonstrated by the witness at the confrontation, and the length of time between the crime and the confrontation.[38]

The likelihood of misidentification was found to exist where a robbery victim who was unable to identify the defendant in a lineup did identify the defendant at a second lineup. The defendant was the only person who had been in both lineups. The Supreme Court said the suggestive elements in the identification procedure "made it all but inevitable that [the victim]

---

[33]Stovall v Denno, 388 US 293, 302, 87 SCt 1967, 18 LEd(2d) 1199 (1967).

[34]Simmons v United States, 390 US 377, 384, 88 SCt 967, 19 LEd(2d) 1247 (1968) (photo identification).

[35]Kirby v Illinois, 406 US 682, 92 SCt 1877, 32 LEd(2d) 411 (1972).

[36]Manson v Brathwaite, 432 US 98, 114, 97 SCt 2243, 53 LEd(2d) 140 (1977).

[37]Neil v Biggers, 409 US 188, 93 SCt 375, 34 LEd(2d) 401 (1972).

[38]Neil v Biggers, 409 US 188, 199-200, 93 SCt 375, 34 LEd(2d) 401 (1972); Zanesville v Osborne, 73 App(3d) 580, 597 NE(2d) 1200 (Muskingum 1992), appeal dismissed by 64 OS(3d) 1414, 593 NE(2d) 4 (1992) (defendant's due process rights not violated by one-man show-up identification where witness's identification was reliable under five point analysis); State v Battee, 72 App(3d) 660, 595 NE(2d) 977 (Trumbull 1991) (identification was reliable and did not give rise to a substantial likelihood of misidentification, even though undercover officer was shown a single photograph rather than a photographic lineup).

would identify [the defendant] whether or not he was in fact 'the man.' In effect, the police repeatedly said to the witness, '*This* is the man.' "[39] However, even if the pretrial confrontation is so unfair as to make the resulting identification virtually inevitable and thus a violation of due process, the error may be harmless and the conviction may stand. The constitutional harmless error standard will be more difficult to satisfy in the case of a due process violation because the violation itself casts significant doubt upon the reliability of the conviction.

CROSS REFERENCES

Text 20.03, 20.04

20.06   Due process analysis in Ohio courts

Ohio courts have followed the standards set forth in *Neil v Biggers*,[40] concluding that even if the identification procedure is flawed because of suggestibility, the subsequent identification is admissible "so long as the challenged identification itself is reliable."[41] Even unnecessary suggestiveness does not per se require exclusion.[42] The test for determining the admissibility of identification testimony depends on the reliability of the identification under the totality of the circumstances.[43] Where a victim identified the defendant who was the only black male in the police station at the time, the court held it was not likely to create a substantial likelihood of misidentification because the victim had identified the defendant's photograph one week earlier in an untainted procedure.[44]

In *State v Moody*, a witness gave police a description of the person who attempted to rape her. Police told the witness that they had picked up a suspect who fit her description and then showed her five photographs of persons standing in front of a height chart. Only the defendant appeared to fit the height description furnished by the witness, and only the defendant had a moustache, which was one of the elements in the description furnished by the witness. The court set forth the opportunity the witness had to observe her assailant at the time of the attack and concluded that her opportunity to observe and identify her assailant with certainty at trial "[was] not outweighed by the corrupting effect that the challenged identification may have had on [her] in-court identification."[45] Any discrepancies between her initial description and the actual defendant were for the jury to weigh and decide. This standard was applied in *State v Brown*,[46] where the

---

[39]Foster v California, 394 US 440, 443, 89 SCt 1127, 22 LEd(2d) 402 (1969).

[40]Neil v Biggers, 409 US 188, 93 SCt 375, 34 LEd(2d) 401 (1972).

[41]State v Moody, 55 OS(2d) 64, 67, 377 NE(2d) 1008 (1978); State v Garner, 74 OS(3d) 49, 656 NE(2d) 623 (1995).

[42]State v Wallace, No. CA89-11-027, 1990 WL 70928 (12th Dist Ct App, Madison, 5-29-90).

[43]State v Brawley, No. 55796, 1989 WL 95756 (8th Dist Ct App, Cuyahoga, 8-17-89), appeal dismissed by 47 OS(3d) 715, 549 NE(2d) 169 (1989).

[44]State v Scott, 41 App(3d) 313, 535 NE(2d) 379 (Cuyahoga 1987).

[45]State v Moody, 55 OS(2d) 64, 377 NE(2d) 1008 (1978).

[46]State v Brown, 3 App(3d) 131, 3 OBR 148, 443 NE(2d) 1382 (Cuyahoga 1981).

court found "ample evidence of reliability" to overcome the suggestibility of the identification procedure.

The Ohio Supreme Court expanded on *Moody* in *State v Broom*,[47] holding that if the identifications are reliable, they are admissible even though the identification procedures were suggestive. The defendant in *Broom* was the tallest participant in the lineup and the only one wearing an orange, rather than gold, jail uniform. The court stressed that the witnesses focused their attention on the defendant and displayed a high degree of certainty in their identifications, which occurred within twenty-four hours of the crime. Consequently, the court was unwilling to say that the varied physical characteristics and dress affected the reliability of the identifications.

A conviction based on an eyewitness identification at trial following a pretrial identification by photograph will not be set aside unless the photo identification procedure was so impermissibly suggestive as to give rise to a very substantial likelihood of misidentification. Reliability is the linchpin in determining the admissibility of identification testimony. Even though the identification procedure was suggestive, the challenged identification is admissible if it is reliable.[48] The same result was obtained where three witnesses, shown a photo array, first picked out a witness who they were told was in prison at the time of the crime. Two of the three witnesses then picked out the defendant from another array which did not contain a picture of the first man identified. The court held that there was no danger of irreparable misidentification because the two witnesses who ultimately selected the defendant had sufficient opportunity to view the perpetrator and the viewing of the photo arrays occurred "not a substantially long length of time after the crime."[49] While discrepancies existed, the court said that it was for the jury to decide how much weight to give to the identification testimony.

Similarly, a due process challenge based on the use of a one-on-one show-up when a full lineup could have been held at the police station was rejected where the defendant was identified by the robbery victim at the scene of the arrest shortly after the crime. The Ohio Supreme Court rejected this claim on the ground that the only issue is whether there is a very substantial likelihood of misidentification.[50] The Court said:

> In the instant cause, the witness had a clear and lengthy view of the appellant at the time of the crime. In fact, the witness gave police an accurate description of appellant's wearing apparel and characteristics. Furthermore, the witness confronted the appellant within approximately 30 minutes after the robbery.[51]

---

[47]State v Broom, 40 OS(3d) 277, 533 NE(2d) 682 (1988), cert denied 490 US 1075, 109 SCt 2089, 104 LEd(2d) 653 (1989).

[48]State v Kaval, No. 55951, 1989 WL 125139 (8th Dist Ct App, Cuyahoga, 10-19-89), appeal dismissed by 48 OS(3d) 710, 550 NE(2d) 480 (1990).

[49]State v Clement, Nos. 87AP-900, 87AP-1115, at 8, 1988 WL 142115 (10th Dist Ct App, Franklin, 12-30-88).

[50]State v Madison, 64 OS(2d) 322, 415 NE(2d) 272 (1980).

[51]State v Madison, 64 OS(2d) 322, 332, 415 NE(2d) 272 (1980).

The Court found no reason to disapprove of the one-man show-up shortly after the alleged criminal act: "[S]uch a course does not tend to bring about misidentification but rather tends under some circumstances to insure accuracy."[52]

Where a show-up, rather than a lineup, is held some time after the crime, the Court has disapproved, saying:

> We cannot condone the use by police of a pre-trial confrontation to firm up the uncertain memories of potential witnesses where a normal jailhouse lineup could be arranged. The use of a non-lineup confrontation "is, at the least, a practice fraught with perils to a degree suggesting its sparing use as the part of prudence."[53]

A witness' identification of the defendant from six mug shots containing police identification numbers as well as the types of crimes committed by the individuals was held not to indicate an identification procedure so impermissibly suggestive as to give rise to a very substantial likelihood of irreparable misidentification.[54] The use of typical police "mug shots" in a photographic array is not in and of itself improper.[55] Similarly, in *State v Hancock*,[56] a pretrial photographic identification where the defendant's picture was the only one of a man whose hair was in "knots" was held not sufficiently suggestive to violate due process.

In *State v Way*,[57] witnesses, aware that the accused had been injured while attempting to rob a liquor store, picked out the defendant who displayed signs of having been recently injured. There was no evidence that the police told the witnesses that the suspect had been beaten, and although the court found the injuries somewhat suggestive, it held that under the totality of the circumstances, the identification was reliable. The court, however, has disapproved showing a witness a defendant's mug shot immediately prior to a lineup but nonetheless upheld the trial court's judgment that the witness' trial identification was based on prior independent observations of the defendant at the time and scene of the crime.[58]

In *State v Caldwell*,[59] the court condemned the police and the prosecutor where the victim-witness in a rape case, seventeen months after the attack, was asked prior to trial to pick out her assailant in a courtroom where the

---

[52]State v Madison, 64 OS(2d) 322, 332, 415 NE(2d) 272 (1980); State v Boone, No. 53900, 1988 WL 60611(8th Dist Ct App, Cuyahoga, 6-9-88).

[53]State v Hurt, 30 OS(2d) 86, 89-90, 282 NE(2d) 578 (1972), cert denied 409 US 991, 93 SCt 337, 34 LEd(2d) 258 (1972).

[54]State v Perryman, 49 OS(2d) 14, 358 NE(2d) 1040 (1976), vacated in part by 438 US 911, 98 SCt 3136, 57 LEd(2d) 1156 (1978).

[55]State v White, No. C.A. 3057, 1994 WL 43095 (2d Dist Ct App, Clark, 2-2-94).

[56]State v Hancock, 48 OS(2d) 147, 358 NE(2d) 273 (1976), vacated in part by 438 US 911, 98 SCt 3147, 57 LEd(2d) 1155 (1978).

[57]State v Way, No. C-880505, 1990 WL 1295 (1st Dist Ct App, Hamilton, 1-10-90), appeal dismissed sub nom State v Thundercloud Way, 52 OS(3d) 701, 556 NE(2d) 525 (1990).

[58]State v Jackson, 26 OS(2d) 74, 269 NE(2d) 118 (1971); see also State v Way, No. C-880505, 1990 WL 1295 (1st Dist Ct App, Hamilton, 1-10-90), appeal dismissed sub nom State v Thundercloud Way, 52 OS(3d) 701, 556 NE(2d) 525 (1990).

[59]State v Caldwell, 19 App(3d) 104, 19 OBR 191, 483 NE(2d) 187 (Cuyahoga 1984).

defendant was the only black male in the room who was not in uniform. Nonetheless, the reviewing court was persuaded that the victim's identification was based on sufficient independent recollection because she had seen the defendant three days after the rape and was able to reinforce her memory of his features, and she identified him from a newspaper photograph before the show-up in the courtroom.

The suggestive nature of identification procedures may be outweighed by other factors that prove the reliability of the identification. In *State v Barnett*,[60] the complaining witness knew the person who robbed the store. In evaluating the totality of the circumstances, the court held that the identification was not even remotely likely to have created a likelihood of misidentification.

Also, in *State v Hill*,[61] a rape defendant was picked out of a photo array where his photograph was slightly larger in size and had a different border from the others. His photo was picked out by a police officer who had seen the defendant in the car where the rape occurred and by the rape victim who studied her attacker's features because she knew she would have to identify him later. Physical evidence also linked the defendant to the crime. The court held that the photo differences were not impermissibly suggestive and were substantially outweighed by other factors.

On the other hand, some identification procedures are so suggestive as to be unreliable. In *State v Miles*,[62] a complaining witness attacked by three men identified two, who were shown to him alone, only from their clothing, not their personal features. He was then driven to another police precinct where he was told to look through a small window "to pick out the third man."[63] There was only one person in that room, whom the complainant identified as the third assailant. The court found these procedures unduly suggestive and likely to produce irreparable misidentification. Further, the state did not adequately show why the police lacked time or opportunity to employ less suggestive procedures.

Similarly, in *State v Merrill*,[64] a witness picked out an auto theft suspect from a photo array where he was the only curly haired person shown, where all of the others were much older than the defendant, and six of the nine were substantially heavier than the estimate given by the witness. The witness also acknowledged that it was getting dark when she looked out of her kitchen window and allegedly saw the defendant, fifty or sixty feet away, steal an automobile. There were discrepancies in the witness' description and the traits of the suspect. The viewing of the photo array took place ten weeks after the crime occurred, and the witness was allowed to review her original description before viewing the photo array. Consequently, the court of appeals found that the identification failed the *Biggers-Moody* standard, holding that significant indicia of reliability were lacking for the pretrial

---

[60]State v Barnett, 67 App(3d) 760, 588 NE(2d) 887 (Scioto 1990).
[61]State v Hill, 37 App(3d) 10, 523 NE(2d) 885 (Wood 1987).
[62]State v Miles, 55 App(3d) 210, 563 NE(2d) 344 (Cuyahoga 1988).
[63]State v Miles, 55 App(3d) 210, 211, 563 NE(2d) 344 (Cuyahoga 1988).
[64]State v Merrill, 22 App(3d) 119, 489 NE(2d) 1057 (Cuyahoga 1984).

identification and subsequent in-court identification to be based on independent reliable observation.

The rationale for excluding a tainted pretrial identification is to protect the defendant from state misconduct. Two witnesses, who were unable to identify their assailants from a photo array, identified the defendant after one saw him followed around the courthouse by television crews and the other saw his picture in a newspaper. Absent state misconduct, the court held that the alleged suggestiveness goes to the weight of the reliability, a question for the jury, rather than admissibility.[65]

CROSS REFERENCES

Text 20.03 to 20.05

20.07   Right to refuse or to compel a lineup

(A) Refusal to appear in a lineup

An accused has no right to refuse to appear in a lineup. The Fifth Amendment privilege against self-incrimination applies only to testimonial communications.[66] In *United States v Wade*,[67] the Court said:

> We have no doubt that compelling the accused merely to exhibit his person for observation by a prosecution witness prior to trial involves no compulsion of the accused to give evidence having testimonial significance. It is compulsion of the accused to exhibit his physical characteristics, not compulsion to disclose any knowledge he might have.

Wade also held that the privilege did not prohibit police from requiring an accused to speak during a pretrial identification, even if the words are those allegedly uttered by the perpetrator of the crime. Again, the Court held that such utterances are merely to use the voice as an identifying characteristic and are not testimonial in nature. A suspect may be compelled to shave prior to a lineup.[68] Admission of a defendant's refusal to participate in a lineup does not violate the privilege against self-incrimination.[69]

(B) Illegal arrest

Testimony concerning a pretrial identification at a lineup or of a photograph of an accused who has been illegally arrested is excludable as the fruit of a Fourth Amendment violation. In *United States v Crews*,[70] the defendant was arrested without probable cause and detained for one hour so that police could photograph him and show the photograph to robbery victims. The two victims of separate robberies identified the defendant's photograph from the more than 100 that they were shown. The defendant was then

---

[65]State v Brown, 38 OS(3d) 305, 528 NE(2d) 523 (1988), cert denied 489 US 1040, 109 SCt 1177, 103 LEd(2d) 239 (1989).

[66]Schmerber v California, 384 US 757, 86 SCt 1826, 16 LEd(2d) 908 (1966).

[67]United States v Wade, 388 US 218, 222, 87 SCt 1926, 18 LEd(2d) 1149 (1967).

[68]State v Robertson, No. 11572, 1990 WL 65658 (2d Dist Ct App, Montgomery, 5-18-90), appeal dismissed by 55 OS(3d) 713, 563 NE(2d) 722 (1990).

[69]State v Clement, Nos. 87AP-900, 87AP-1115, 1988 WL 142115 (10th Dist Ct App, Franklin, 12-30-88).

[70]United States v Crews, 445 US 463, 100 SCt 1244, 63 LEd(2d) 537 (1980).

taken into custody for a court-ordered lineup where he was positively identified by the same two victims. The defendant contended that testimony concerning the pretrial identification should be excluded as the product of his illegal arrest and argued that the trial identification should be excluded, as well, because he would not have been in court but for the illegal arrest which led directly to his identification and subsequent prosecution.

The Supreme Court agreed that testimony about the photo identification and lineup must be excluded because they were both fruits of the defendant's illegal arrest. This ground, of course, is entirely separate from the Sixth Amendment right to counsel or due process grounds for exclusion. The Court did not accept the defendant's contention concerning the trial identification. A majority of the Court held that the in-court identification fell under the independent source exception to the exclusionary rule based on the victims' voluntary notification of the police, their willingness to testify, and their ability to accurately identify the defendant on the basis of the images formed at the time they were robbed.

But what of the defendant's claim that the witnesses never could have identified him in court if he had not first been illegally arrested, detained, and photographed? Should his physical presence at the time of trial be excluded because of the illegal arrest? Five justices decisively rejected the defense contention out of hand:

> A holding that a defendant's face can be considered evidence suppressible for no reason other than that the defendant's presence in the courtroom is the fruit of an illegal arrest would be tantamount to holding that an illegal arrest effectively insulates one from conviction for any crime where an in-court identification is essential. Such a holding would be inconsistent with the underlying rationale of *Frisbie* [v *Collins*, 342 US 519, 522 (1952) (holding that the power of the court to try a person for crime is not impaired by the fact that he has been brought within the court's jurisdictions unlawfully)] from which we have not retreated.[71]

(C) Right to a lineup

There is no constitutional right to a lineup or other pretrial identification confrontation.[72] Nonetheless, refusal of a defense request to provide such confrontation might, in certain instances, provide the substance for a claim of denial of due process. In *Stovall v Denno*,[73] the Supreme Court approvingly quoted the United States Court of Appeals for the Second Circuit, demonstrating the need for a confrontation in that case between the accused and the critically ill surviving victim:

> [T]he record in the present case reveals that the showing of Stovall to Mrs. Behrendt in an immediate hospital confrontation was imperative.
> ... "Here was the only person in the world who could possibly exonerate

---

[71]United States v Crews, 445 US 463, 478, 100 SCt 1244, 63 LEd(2d) 537 (1980) (White, J., concurring).

[72]State v Taylor, No. 53001, 1987 WL 20197 (8th Dist Ct App, Cuyahoga, 11-19-87); State v Scott, No. 81AP-899, 1982 WL 4066 (10th Dist Ct App, Franklin, 3-30-82).

[73]Stovall v Denno, 388 US 293, 87 SCt 1967, 18 LEd(2d) 1199 (1967).

Stovall. Her words, and only her words, 'He is not the man' could have resulted in freedom for Stovall."[74]

An irretrievably lost opportunity for an exonerating confrontation by a witness who "was the only person in the world who could possibly exonerate" an accused would adequately raise the issue on a showing of a request, a reasonable opportunity to comply with the request, and a denial. Moreover, a request may not be a mandatory prerequisite when the opportunity existed briefly prior to the time that the accused was represented by counsel.

The California Supreme Court has recognized a defendant's constitutional right to a lineup on request. The rationale rests upon the state's due process duty to disclose exculpatory evidence.[75]

---

[74]Stovall v Denno, 388 US 293, 302, 87 SCt 1967, 18 LEd(2d) 1199 (1967).
[75]Evans v Superior Court of Contra Costa County, 11 Cal(3d) 617, 522 P(2d) 681, 114 Cal Rptr 121 (1974) (due process requires in an appropriate case that an accused, upon timely request, be afforded a pretrial lineup in which witnesses to the alleged criminal conduct can participate).

CHECKLISTS

Checklist A
Arrest Provisions

PROBABLE CAUSE FOR ARREST

(A) Probable cause

    (1) Probable cause is information sufficient to justify reasonably prudent person in believing that:

        (a) Offense was committed; and

        (b) Arrestee committed it.

    (2) Probable cause is more than mere suspicion, but less than proof beyond a reasonable doubt.

    (3) Information, in order to support probable cause:

        (a) Must be derived from reasonably trustworthy source(s);

        (b) Must be based on factual information and not just unsupported opinion, hunch, or conclusion;

        (c) May be based on hearsay information or information obtained from other sources, including informants, as long as reliability and lawfulness of source can be shown.

        (d) Will be assessed on the totality of the circumstances.

ENTERING SUSPECT'S HOME TO MAKE WARRANTLESS ARREST

(A) General rule

Officer may not enter suspect's home to effect warrantless arrest unless:

    (1) Emergency situation present; and

    (2) Warrantless arrest otherwise proper, or

    (3) Consent

(B) Emergency situations

Emergency situations justifying entering suspect's home to effect warrantless arrest include:

    (1) Immediate danger to person(s) inside or outside home;

    (2) Officer in hot pursuit of fleeing felon;

    (3) Suspect about to attempt escape; or

    (4) Destruction of evidence about to take place.

        Need to preserve evidence of intoxication re DUI does not justify warrantless home arrest or search (State v Petrosky, Nos. C-900264, C-900265, at 6 n.3 (1st Dist Ct App, Hamilton, 3-27-91)).

417

WARRANTLESS ARREST FOR FELONY

(A) Arrest warrant not required for felony arrest in public.

(B) Arrest warrant should be obtained prior to arrest, unless circumstances do not allow.

(C) Arrest warrant required to enter residence absent consent or exigent circumstances.

(D) Search warrant required to enter residence to arrest nonresident absent consent or exigent circumstances.

(E) Arrest on probable cause

    (1) Under RC 2935.04, officer may arrest without warrant if officer has:

        (a) Reasonable ground to believe felony committed; and

        (b) Reasonable cause to believe suspect committed the offense.

    (2) Reasonable ground and reasonable cause mean probable cause.

WARRANTLESS ARREST FOR MISDEMEANOR OTHER THAN MINOR MISDEMEANOR

(A) In general

Under RC 2935.03, warrantless arrest for misdemeanor permitted if:

    (1) Offense committed in officer's presence; or

    (2) In case of certain offenses enumerated in statute, officer has probable cause.

(B) Offense committed in officer's presence

    (1) Officer may arrest without warrant person "found violating" state law or municipal ordinance within officer's territorial jurisdiction (RC 2935.03(A)).

    (2) "Found violating" requirement means offense must be committed in officer's presence (State v Darrah, 64 OS(2d) 22, 412 NE(2d) 1328 (1980). See Hoover v Garfield Heights Municipal Court, 802 F(2d) 168 (6th Cir Ohio 1986)).

    (3) Presence requirement satisfied if officer:

        (a) Personally witnesses commission of offense (State v Stacy, 9 App(3d) 55, 9 OBR 74, 458 NE(2d) 403 (Lorain 1983));

        (b) Although officer not witness to entire offense, is nevertheless in position to form reasonable belief that misdemeanor committed, based on evidence of his own senses (Columbus v Lenear, 16 App(3d) 466, 16 OBR 548, 476 NE(2d) 1085 (Franklin 1984)).

(4) Presence requirement where officer does not witness DUI

Presence requirement satisfied and warrantless arrest for DUI proper where officer observes defendant's intoxication and also observes sufficient evidence to infer that defendant was driving. Thus, warrantless DUI arrest permitted where:

(a) Officer appears at scene after accident, and vehicle operator admits driving and is visibly under influence of alcohol (Oregon v Szakovits, 32 OS(2d) 271, 291 NE(2d) 742 (1972); State v Allen, 2 App(3d) 441, 2 OBR 536, 442 NE(2d) 784 (Hamilton 1981));

(b) Officer finds damaged car abandoned at accident scene, then finds defendant injured and intoxicated, and defendant admits he was involved in accident but denies driving (Xenia v Manker, 18 App(3d) 9, 18 OBR 33, 480 NE(2d) 94 (Greene 1984));

(c) Officer smells alcohol on driver, and one-car accident otherwise unexplained (State v Bernard, 20 App(3d) 375, 20 OBR 481, 486 NE(2d) 866 (Wayne 1985)).

(C) Warrantless arrest for certain misdemeanors on probable cause

(1) General rule—warrantless arrest on probable cause not permitted

With specific exceptions, warrantless arrest for misdemeanors not committed in officer's presence not permitted, even though officer has probable cause.

(2) Exceptions—warrantless arrest on probable cause permitted

Under RC 2935.03(B) and (C), even though offense not committed in officer's presence, warrantless arrest permitted if officer has reasonable ground (probable cause) to believe one of following offenses committed by suspect in officer's jurisdiction:

(a) Offense of violence as defined in RC 2901.01(I), including:

(i)   Assault (RC 2903.13);

(ii)   Aggravated menacing (RC 2903.21);

(iii) Menacing (RC 2903.22);

(iv)   Arson (RC 2909.03);

(v)   Riot (RC 2917.03);

(vi)   Inducing panic (RC 2917.31); and

(vii) Carrying concealed weapons (RC 2923.12);

(b) Criminal child enticement (RC 2905.05);

(c) Public indecency (RC 2907.09);

(d) Domestic violence (RC 2919.25);

(i)   Written statement of victim or parent of child victim constitutes reasonable ground (RC 2935.03(B));

(ii)   Domestic violence is also an offense of violence. See section 2(a) above;

(e) Theft offense, as defined in RC 2913.01(K);

(f) Felony drug abuse offense, as defined in RC 2925.01(H)(2);

(g) DUI (RC 4511.19(A)), while operating motor vehicle subject to regulation by Public Utilities Commission under RC Title 49; and

(h) Driving commercial vehicle under influence or with detectable level of alcohol or controlled substance (RC 4506.15(A), (B), (C)).

WARRANTLESS ARREST FOR MINOR MISDEMEANOR

(A) In general

Under RC 2935.26, with certain exceptions, officer must issue citation rather than arrest person for minor misdemeanor.

(B) Exceptions

Warrantless arrest for minor misdemeanor permissible when:

(1) Offender requires medical care or is unable to provide for own safety;

(2) Offender cannot or will not offer satisfactory evidence of identity;

(3) Offender refuses to sign citation;

(4) Offender previously issued citation and failed to either appear as directed or dispose of citation by waiver; or

(5) Offense is disorderly conduct (RC 2917.11) in which offender either persists in conduct after reasonable warning or request to desist, or conduct is within 1,000 feet of school premises. In either case, disorderly conduct changes from minor misdemeanor to 4th degree misdemeanor.

WARRANTLESS ARREST OUTSIDE OFFICER'S TERRITORY

(A) Misdemeanor arrests

(1) General rule

Under RC 2935.03, officer's power to make warrantless misdemeanor arrest limited to his territorial jurisdiction.

(2) Exception—hot pursuit (fresh pursuit)

Under RC 2935.03(D), officer in hot pursuit may arrest suspect outside of jurisdiction, if all of following apply:

(a) Offense is felony, first or second degree misdemeanor, or traffic offense for which points chargeable under RC 4507.021(G);

(b) Pursuit begins within officer's territorial jurisdiction; and

(c) Pursuit takes place without unreasonable delay after offense committed.

(3) Exception—arrest for certain motor vehicle offenses

Under RC 2935.03(E), officer may arrest without warrant for following offenses, if observed by officer, and if committed on portion of street or highway immediately adjacent to boundary of officer's jurisdiction:

(a) Failure to file annual application for motor vehicle registration or pay tax (RC 4503.11(A));

(b) Failure to properly display, in plain view, registration number and mark, county identification sticker, validation sticker, or temporary license placard or sticker (RC 4503.21);

(c) Failure to stop motor vehicle and remain stationary until passed when properly signalled to on meeting or overtaking horse-drawn vehicle or person on horseback (RC 4549.01);

(d) Operating motor vehicle without license plates or with unauthorized or improper plates or identification mark (RC 4549.08 to RC 4549.12);

(e) Fraud concerning vehicle identification number (RC 4549.62);

(f) Any violation of traffic laws under RC Chapter 4511;

(g) Any violation of traffic laws under RC Chapter 4513.

(4) Exception—service or mutual aid contract, or legislative authorization

When responding under proper authority to render police services in another political subdivision, officer may make warrantless arrest in other jurisdiction.

(a) Political subdivisions may contract to provide police protection in other political subdivisions (RC 311.29, RC 737.04, RC 505.43).

(b) Legislative authority of municipal corporation or township may authorize police to render aid in another jurisdiction (including adjoining state) without contract (RC 505.431, RC 737.041).

(c) County sheriff may call on peace officers from other jurisdictions to aid in emergency (RC 311.07(B)).

(B) Felony arrests

RC 2935.04 authorizes any person—not merely peace officer—to make warrantless felony arrest on probable cause, without stating any territorial limitations.

   (1) In absence of territorial limitations, authority to make warrantless arrest on probable cause for felony applies anywhere in state.

   (2) As practical matter, because of workers' compensation and related considerations, and also from considerations of professional courtesy, peace officer well-advised to exercise authority outside of territory only when:

      (a) In hot pursuit. See section (A)(2), above;

      (b) Acting under proper authority to render aid under service or mutual aid contract or legislative authorization. See section (A)(4), above; or

      (c) Cooperating with authorities from other political subdivision.

PROCEDURE AFTER WARRANTLESS ARREST

(A) In general

   (1) Under RC 2935.05 and Crim R 4(E)(2):

      (a) Arrestee must be brought before court having jurisdiction over offense without unnecessary delay; and

      (b) Complaint must be filed.

   (2) Under US Supreme Court ruling, arrestee who is detained is entitled to review of probable cause for arrest within forty-eight hours of arrest (County of Riverside v McLaughlin, — US —, 111 SCt 1661, 114 LEd(2d) 49 (1991)).

   (3) Under RC 2935.14 and RC 2935.20, arrestee must be provided with facilities for communicating with attorney or with other person for purpose of obtaining counsel.

(B) Release upon issuance of summons

Under Crim R 4(F), in misdemeanor case:

   (1) Arrestee may be released by issuing summons, when summons appears reasonably calculated to assure person's appearance.

   (2) Summons may be issued by arresting officer, officer in charge of detention facility, or superior of either.

   (3) Issuing officer must note on summons time and place person to appear, and must file complaint describing offense.

ARREST WARRANTS

(A) Requirements for arrest warrant

Arrest warrant must:

  (1) Be based on complaint or affidavit supported by probable cause (Crim R 4(A));

  (2) Contain defendant's name or, if unknown, name or description by which he/she can be identified with reasonable certainty (Crim R 4(C));

  (3) Have copy of complaint or affidavit attached (Crim R 4(C), RC 2935.18);

  (4) Describe offense charged in complaint or affidavit, and state number of statute or ordinance involved (Crim R 4(C));

  (5) Be directed to specific officer or department designated by its chief (Crim R 4(C), RC 2935.18);

  (6) Order that accused be arrested and brought before court issuing warrant (Crim R 4(C), RC 2935.18);

  (7) Be issued by judge, magistrate, or clerk of court. Probate clerk of court or judge not included (Crim R 4, RC 2931.01, RC 2935.10);

  (8) Be dated and signed by issuing judge or clerk (RC 2935.18).

(B) Forms

Forms for affidavit, complaint, and warrant contained in RC 2935.17 to RC 2935.19.

(C) Issuing summons in lieu of warrant

  (1) Under Crim R 4(A)(1), court must issue summons instead of arrest warrant for felony or misdemeanor when:

    (a) Prosecutor requests summons; or

    (b) Summons appears reasonably calculated to assure defendant's appearance.

  (2) Form of summons is same as warrant, except that that summons does not command that defendant be arrested, but rather orders him/her to appear at stated time and place or be arrested for failure to appear (Crim R 4(C)(2)).

EXECUTION OR SERVICE OF WARRANT OR SUMMONS

(A) Execution of arrest warrant

  (1) Execution of warrant by arrest

    Under Crim R 4(D), arrest warrant:

(a) Executed by arresting person named, as commanded by warrant;

(b) May be executed anywhere in state by any officer authorized by law; and

(c) Need not be in officer's possession at time of arrest, so long as defendant is informed of offense charged and fact that warrant issued, and is furnished copy as soon as possible.

(2) Execution of warrant by issuing summons in misdemeanor case

In misdemeanor case, officer holding warrant may issue summons in lieu of arresting defendant, when summons reasonably calculated to assure defendant's appearance (Crim R 4(A)(2)).

(B) Service of summons

Under Crim R 4(D)(3):

(1) Summons issued by court or clerk in lieu of warrant may be served by:

(a) Personal service;

(b) Residence service; or

(c) Service by clerk by certified mail, return receipt requested.

(2) Summons issued by officer holding warrant, in lieu of arresting defendant in misdemeanor case, may be served by:

(a) Personal service; or

(b) Residence service.

(3) Summons issued by arresting officer or officer in charge of detention facility, after arrest for misdemeanor and in order to effect release of arrestee without unnecessary delay, may be served by personal service only.

(C) Return of warrant or summons

Under Crim R 4(D)(4):

(1) In general

(a) Officer executing warrant must report to issuing court before whom arrestee brought;

(b) Person serving summons must endorse fact of service on summons and return to clerk for appropriate docket entry.

(2) Unexecuted warrant; failure of service of summons

(a) Unexecuted warrant must be returned to issuing court and, at prosecutor's request, either cancelled or delivered to authorized officer for execution.

(b) When summons not served within twenty-eight days of issuance, fact must be endorsed on summons and summons returned to clerk for docket entry and, at prosecutor's request, may be delivered to authorized officer for service.

PROCEDURE AFTER ARREST ON WARRANT

(A) Initial appearance

Under Crim R 4(E)(1):

(1) If defendant arrested in county issuing warrant or adjoining county, must be brought before court that issued warrant without unnecessary delay;

(2) If defendant arrested in any other county:

    (a) Must be brought without unnecessary delay before court in that county having jurisdiction over offense;

    (b) Must not be removed from that county unless given opportunity to consult with attorney or other person of his/her choice and to post bail set by judge of that court;

    (c) If not released, defendant must be brought without unnecessary delay before court that issued warrant;

    (d) If released, must be on condition that he/she appear in issuing court at certain time and date.

(B) Pretrial release on summons in misdemeanor case

(1) Bail

If court not in session, defendant in misdemeanor case must be taken before clerk and given opportunity to post bail (RC 2935.13).

(2) Release after service of summons

Under Crim R 4(F), instead of bail, defendant in misdemeanor case may be released on issuance and service of summons, if summons reasonably calculated to assure appearance.

    (a) Release on summons may be by arresting officer, officer in charge of detention facility, or superior of either.

    (b) Summons must note time and place defendant to appear.

    (c) No warrant or alias warrant may issue unless defendant fails to appear in response to summons.

(C) Opportunity to contact lawyer

Arrestee must be provided with facilities for communicating with attorney or other person for purpose of obtaining counsel (RC 2935.14, RC 2935.20).

USE OF FORCE IN MAKING ARREST

(A) Forcible entry

Under RC 2935.12, officer may break door or window to enter building to make arrest or execute warrant only if officer:

(1) Identifies himself/herself;

(2) Announces intention to make arrest or execute warrant; and

(3) Is refused admittance.

(B) General rule on use of force against persons

   (1) Only as much force as is reasonably necessary to make arrest may be used, regardless of whether deadly or nondeadly force involved.

   (2) Test is whether force used was objectively reasonable under facts and circumstances present.

(C) Use of deadly force

   (1) Deadly force may be used only when probable cause to believe suspect:

      (a) Committed crime of violence; or

      (b) Poses threat of serious physical harm to officers or others.

   (2) Violent crime defined as one involving actual or threatened serious physical harm.

   (3) If feasible, warning must be given before deadly force used.

(D) Use of force to suppress riot

   (1) Nondeadly force may be used to disperse or apprehend rioters when and to extent officer has probable cause to believe such force necessary (RC 2917.05(A)).

   (2) Deadly force may be used when and to extent officer has probable cause to believe such force necessary to disperse or apprehend rioters who are creating substantial risk of serious physical harm to persons (RC 2917.05(B)).

Checklist B
Stop and Frisk Provisions

NATURE OF PERMISSIBLE STOP AND FRISK

(A) Permissible stop

Brief investigative stop of person that falls short of arrest is permitted under certain circumstances.

(1) Stop must be supported by reasonable, articulable suspicion that criminal activity underway. Random stop, or stop based on unsupported hunch, not permitted.

(2) Standard is less than probable cause, but officer must still be able to articulate specific facts that provide reason for stop.

(3) Facts observed by officer may be combined with the following to justify stop:

(a) Surrounding circumstances, such as time and location of stop;

(b) Rational inferences drawn from facts, circumstances;

(c) Officer's past experience and prior knowledge; and/or

(d) Information from other sources, including reliable informant.

(4) Fact that suspect traveling in "high crime area" may be used as one reason for stop but may not be only reason for stop.

(B) Permissible frisk

(1) Frisk not automatically justified by valid stop; frisk must be independently authorized.

(2) Frisk justified only by officer's reasonable belief that suspect carrying weapon or is threat to officer's safety.

(3) Suspect's conduct, officer's prior knowledge and experience, surrounding circumstances, and information from other sources may be used to justify frisk.

(4) Frisk must be limited to pat down of suspect's outer clothing.

(a) If pat down reveals object that feels like weapon, item may be retrieved and seized, even if it turns out to be contraband other than weapon.

(b) Object felt that cannot reasonably be weapon may not be seized, unless officer has probable cause that object is contraband.

(c) If officer has information that suspect carrying weapon in specific spot, officer may seize without conducting preliminary pat down.

(C) When stop becomes arrest; use of information obtained

   (1) Lengthy detention, show of authority, or physical seizure or restraint of person or his/her possessions such that person would not feel free to leave may convert stop into arrest, requiring probable cause.

   (2) Information obtained during stop and frisk may give rise to probable cause justifying arrest and search.

AUTOMOBILE STOP

(A) Stop and limited search

   (1) Vehicle may be stopped, and its occupants briefly questioned, in same manner as pedestrian—officer must have reasonable, articulable, factually based suspicion of criminal activity. Random stop, stop based on mere hunch prohibited.

   (2) Limited search of vehicle, or pat down of occupant, permissible only for officer's protection where officer has reasonable belief that accessible weapon present in vehicle or on person.

   (3) Driver, passengers may be ordered from vehicle, but may be searched only if section (C)(2), above, is satisfied.

   (4) If officer's reason for stop is extinguished during investigation or questioning, investigation must be concluded and vehicle allowed to proceed.

(B) When stop becomes arrest; use of information obtained

   (1) Encounter that goes beyond brief, investigative detention for questioning or verification of license information may become arrest requiring probable cause.

   (2) Information obtained during stop may provide probable cause for arrest and search.

(C) During traffic stop, officer may ask about other offenses or request permission to search car, only if

   (1) Reasonable suspicion that other criminal activity is afoot develops during traffic stop, or

   (2) Officer clearly informs motorist that traffic stop is over and motorist is free to leave and not answer questions or consent to search.

Checklist C
Search Warrant Provisions

WHEN SEARCH WARRANT REQUIRED; SCOPE; PROBABLE CAUSE

(A) When required

    (1) Search warrant required for all searches, unless one of recognized exceptions to warrant requirement present, discussed in Checklist D, Provisions for Warrantless Searches.

    (2) Best policy is to obtain warrant, if possible.

(B) Scope of warrant

Under Crim R 41(B), search warrant may be issued to search for and seize:

    (1) Evidence of crime;

    (2) Contraband, fruits of crime, or things otherwise criminally possessed;

    (3) Weapons or other things used, or that reasonably appear about to be used, to commit a crime.

(C) Probable cause requirement

    (1) Search warrant may be issued only on probable cause to believe that evidence of a crime or contraband is now—not was—at place to be searched.

    (2) Probable cause determination is made on totality of circumstances.

    (3) Probable cause may be based on:

        (a) Hearsay;

        (b) Informant's tip, where reliability, trustworthiness of tip shown

            (i) Totality of circumstances surrounding tip used to determine whether tip sufficiently trustworthy to provide probable cause.

            (ii) Relevant factors include corroboration of tip by police, known reliability of informant because of prior dealings.

            (iii) Informant's identity need not be disclosed;

        (c) Anonymous tip, which alone will not give rise to probable cause which police corroborate.

ISSUANCE OF SEARCH WARRANT

(A) Issuance by judge

Search warrant must be issued by judge with territorial jurisdiction over place to be searched (Crim R 41(A)).

(B) Contents

    (1) Under Crim R 41(C) and RC 2933.23, warrant must be accompanied by officer's sworn affidavit, which:

        (a) Names or describes person to be searched, or describes with particularity place to be searched;

        (b) Specifies items to be searched for and seized with as much particularity as possible, not just a general description;

        (c) States substantially the offense to which search related; and

        (d) States factual basis for belief that property located in place described

            (i) Must contain all facts relied on by officers;

            (ii) Generalized or conclusory statement insufficient.

    (2) Warrant must be directed to officer, and must command him/her to search person or place named for property specified (Crim R 41(C), RC 2933.24).

    (3) Description of place and items must appear in command portion of warrant.

    (4) Warrant must be signed by issuing judge.

    (5) Warrant must designate judge to whom it must be returned (Crim R 41(C)).

EXECUTION OF SEARCH WARRANT

(A) Time of execution

Under Crim R 41(C), search warrant must be executed:

    (1) Within three days; and

    (2) In daytime, between 7 a.m. and 8 p.m., unless judge finds and warrant so states that there is reasonable cause for executing warrant at night.

(B) Knock and notify; forcible entry

    (1) Officers must identify themselves, state purpose, and provide copy of warrant to owner of place to be searched.

    (2) If owner not there, police may still enter and search, provided copy of warrant left at premises. If owner returns during search, officers must immediately identify themselves and their purpose.

(3) Officers may use force to enter premises only if they are refused admittance, either actually or constructively, after "knock and notify" (RC 2935.12).

(4) Under RC 2933.231, "knock and notify" requirements may be waived where affidavit for warrant contains request for waiver, which includes:

  (a) Statement that applicant has good cause to believe there is risk of serious physical harm to officers if forced to "knock and notify";

  (b) Statement of facts supporting belief, including names of all known persons believed to pose risk to officers;

  (c) Statement verifying address of place to be searched as correct in relation to offense underlying request for warrant; and

  (d) Request for waiver, plus request for probable cause finding by issuing judge in recorded proceeding, that officers will be exposed to risk of serious physical harm if forced to "knock and notify," and that address is correct.

(C) Seizure; inventory and receipt

  (1) Only items described in warrant may be seized, unless:

    (a) Officer has probable cause to believe additional items closely related to items described or crime being investigated;

    (b) Items are contraband or instrumentalities of crime; or

    (c) Plain view requirements met. See Checklist D, Warrantless Searches.

  (2) Under Crim R 41(D) and RC 2933.241:

    (a) Written inventory of property seized must be made in presence of applicant for warrant and either person from whose possession or premises property taken, or some other person if owner not present;

    (b) Receipt for property must be given to owner or, if not present, left at premises.

(D) Detention and search of people on premises

  (1) Detention during search

    (a) Search warrant gives limited right to detain occupants of premises while search conducted.

    (b) Standards for detention similar to those in stop and frisk situation. See Checklist B, Stop and Frisk.

  (2) Full search must be independently justified

    (a) Search warrant does not give officers automatic right to search persons found on premises searched.

        (b) Officers must have independent probable cause to believe person on premises either involved in criminal activity or armed.

        (c) Officers may conduct limited pat-down search for weapons if there is reasonable cause to believe that persons are armed or dangerous.

(E) Return of warrant

Promptly after execution, search warrant with attached copy of inventory of property seized, must be returned to judge designated in warrant (Crim R 41(C) and (D); RC 2933.241).

Checklist D
Provisions for Warrantless Searches

SEARCH INCIDENT TO ARREST

(A) In general

    (1) Warrantless search permissible if incident to valid arrest.

    (2) Legality of arrest

        (a) Search must be based on valid arrest supported by probable cause.

        (b) Probable cause may not be based on evidence found in search.

        (c) Arrest must not be mere pretext for search.

        (d) Arrest must occur before search; search may precede arrest if arrest immediately follows and officer had probable cause for arrest independent of results of search.

(B) Scope of search—in general

    (1) Search may be for weapons or evidence.

    (2) Complete search of arrestee may be made, as long as arrestee taken into custody.

    (3) Area and possessions within arrestee's immediate control may be searched.

    (4) Delayed search of arrestee and effects associated with person permitted.

(C) Scope of search—arrestee's residence or place of business

    (1) Area within arrestee's immediate control may be searched.

        (a) Area of control may expand or contract during arrest procedure, such as where:

            (i) Necessary for arrestee to go into another room to dress, thus allowing expanded search; or

            (ii) Arrestee is handcuffed, limiting area of control and thus scope of search.

        (b) Arrestee may not be moved around merely to expand area that may be searched.

    (2) Protective sweep of area immediately adjacent to room where arrest takes place (i.e. closet, hallway) permissible without cause.

    (3) Officers may make protective sweep of entire residence where they have reasonable, factually supported belief that substantial danger to officers present, such as presence of accomplice of arrestee on premises. Not to be a search for evidence and should be limited to cursory inspection of places where person may be found and last only so long as time needed to make arrest.

(D) Scope of search—automobile

Passenger compartment, plus all containers in compartment may be searched on arrest of occupant of automobile. But, if offense is traffic offense or non-violent offense and suspect is out of car and secured, search of closed containers impermissible absent probable cause to believe evidence or weapons present in container or valid inventory search conducted.

(E) Scope of search—package, container, purse, briefcase, luggage

    (1) Immediate search of items in arrestee's hands usually upheld, but no clear-cut rule on this.

    (2) Search of arrestee's wallet or purse generally upheld.

    (3) Validity of search of items such as luggage or briefcase depends on circumstances, such as whether item was in area of arrestee's control, whether item was locked, etc.

    (4) If probable cause focused on container prior to its being placed in automobile, only container may be searched, not entire vehicle.

    (5) Delayed warrantless search at stationhouse generally not permissible except as in (E)(6).

    (6) Inventory search of containers as part of routine stationhouse booking procedure permissible.

        (a) Written, standardized policy and procedures must be established and uniformly applied.

        (b) Inventory procedure may not be mere pretext for investigative search. Impoundment must be lawful and serve some legitimate public purpose.

(F) Scope of search—strip search

Strip search permissible where arrestee to be jailed.

    (1) Should be conducted pursuant to standardized, uniform administrative policy and procedures, and, in case of misdemeanor or traffic offenses, requirements of RC 2933.32 must be met. See section (3) below.

    (2) Where arrest for nonviolent, nonserious offense (e.g., DUI), no indication that arrestee combative, armed, or hiding evidence, and arrestee not to be placed in general jail population, strip search may violate civil rights of arrestee. Moreover, requirements of RC 2933.32 must be met. See section (3) below.

    (3) Under RC 2933.32, where person detained or arrested for misdemeanor or traffic offense, strip search may be conducted only if following requirements are met:

(a) Must be probable cause to believe that arrestee concealing evidence of commission of crime, including fruits or tools of crime, contraband, or deadly weapon that could not otherwise be discovered. Nature of offense, circumstances of arrest, and arrestee's prior record, if known, to be considered;

(b) Strip search may be conducted for legitimate medical or hygienic reason;

(c) Officer or employee of law enforcement agency conducting search must obtain written authorization from person in command of law enforcement agency or person designated by person in command, unless there is legitimate medical reason or medical emergency that makes obtaining authorization impracticable; and

(d) Search must be conducted by person of same sex as arrestee and in location that permits only person conducting search to observe.

(4) Limitations upon strip search do not apply to visual observation of arrestee who was given reasonable opportunity to secure bail and failed and who is to be integrated into general population of detention facility while person is changing into clothes required to be worn in facility.

(5) Above requirements do not apply to searches of offenders sentenced to and serving term of imprisonment in detention facility.

(G) Scope of search—body cavities

(1) Requirements for strip search apply to body cavity search. In addition:

(a) Search warrant must be obtained, unless there is legitimate medical reason or medical emergency justifying warrantless search; and

(b) Body cavity search must be conducted under sanitary conditions and only by physician, or registered or licensed practical nurse authorized to practice in Ohio.

(H) Report of strip search or body cavity search

After body cavity or strip search conducted, person who conducted search must prepare written report that includes:

(1) Name of person searched;

(2) Name of person who conducted search, and time, date, and place of search;

(3) List of items recovered in search, if any;

(4) Facts relied on for probable cause determination to conduct search, including without limitation nature of offense, circumstances of arrest, arrestee's prior record;

(5) If search conducted without warrant or strip search without written authorization, legitimate medical reason, or medical emergency must be included.

(6) Copy of report must be kept on file, and copy given to person searched.

(7) Consequences of failure to comply with search requirements:

    (a) Violation of requirements for conducting strip search or body cavity search is 1st degree misdemeanor;

    (b) Failure to prepare report is fourth degree misdemeanor; and

    (c) Civil liability, including punitive damages and attorney's fees, may result.

AUTOMOBILE EXCEPTION TO SEARCH WARRANT REQUIREMENT

(A) Grounds and scope

    (1) Exception applies any time officer stops vehicle, and officer may stop vehicle under exception if probable cause requirement met. See section (3) below.

    (2) Parked vehicle

        (a) Vehicle parked in public area may be seized and searched under exception if probable cause requirement met.

        (b) If vehicle parked on private property, warrantless search may not be proper, particularly where officers had ample time to obtain warrant.

    (3) Probable cause requirement

        (a) Officer must have probable cause, based on objective facts, that vehicle contains specific contraband or evidence of a crime.

        (b) Facts giving rise to probable cause must be such that they would support issuance of search warrant.

    (4) No exigent circumstances need be shown. Fact that item to be searched is vehicle is exigency in itself.

    (5) Vehicle may be searched even if occupants have been arrested and vehicle immobilized.

    (6) Vehicle may be searched on road at time of stop, or searched later at police station.

    (7) All areas of the vehicle where item(s) sought can be hidden may be searched.

(B) Search of containers

Officer may search all containers or receptacles found anywhere in vehicle, including opening closed containers, and even though probable cause focused on container before it was placed in vehicle, provided container could hold the item being searched for.

(C) Inspection of Vehicle Identification Number (VIN)

(1) Need not be justified under automobile exception—flows from traffic violation for which vehicle stopped.

(2) If VIN visible from outside, officer may not enter vehicle to obtain. If VIN not visible from outside, officer may open door to search for, provided search is no more extensive than necessary to locate VIN.

INVENTORY SEARCH OF VEHICLE

(A) Officer may inventory contents of lawfully impounded vehicle

(1) Search is not a permissible inventory search where the alleged inventory purpose is a mere pretext for an investigative search, or where search not conducted in traditional or routine manner of inventory search.

(2) Vehicle is lawfully impounded where:

(a) It is evidence in criminal case, was used to commit crime, or was obtained with funds derived from criminal activities;

(b) Vehicle was unlawfully parked or obstructing traffic, or was abandoned;

(c) Driver was arrested on road; or

(d) Impoundment otherwise authorized by statute or ordinance.

(3) Legally parked vehicle may not be impounded merely because owner or driver has been arrested away from vehicle.

(B) Standard policy

Department should establish written, standardized policy and apply it uniformly, especially with respect to opening closed containers.

CONSENT SEARCHES

(A) In general

Search warrant not required for search made with consent of person whose person or property searched.

(B) Consent must be voluntary

(1) Must be act of free will, not result of duress or coercion, express or implied.

(2) Consent given as result of officer's misrepresentation or in response to show of authority not voluntary.

(3) Whether consent voluntary determined from all facts and surrounding circumstances; that suspect was or was not informed of right to refuse consent is one factor to be considered.

(C) Scope of consent

(1) Scope of consent may be limited by officer's request. Officer has consent to search only what was requested.

(2) Person may set limits on consent and officer may not exceed. May limit time, duration, area, and intensity of search.

(3) Split of authority whether consent may be terminated or retracted during the search.

(4) General consent to search premises or vehicle, without express limitations by owner, authorizes search of entire premises or vehicle (implicit limits might be created by nature of the object sought).

(D) Third party consent

(1) May be relied on where third party has common authority over area to be searched, even though actual suspect was in custody and could have been asked for consent, or in fact refused consent.

(2) Third person's consent must meet same voluntariness standard as above.

(3) Parents who own or control premises where child lives may consent to search for evidence against child.

(4) One spouse may consent to search of common vehicle or residence for evidence against other spouse.

(5) Consent of co-inhabitant of suspect limited to common areas over which co-inhabitants have joint access or control. Thus, one co-inhabitant may not have authority to grant consent to search the other's bedroom or personal effects.

(6) Police may reasonably rely upon apparent authority of person consenting.

PLAIN VIEW EXCEPTION TO SEARCH WARRANT REQUIREMENT

(A) In general

Evidence or contraband in plain view of officer may be seized without warrant, provided requirements listed below are met.

(B) Lawful presence of officer

(1) Officer must be lawfully:

     (a) Present in place where he/she sees item at issue;

     (b) In position that provides him/her with plain view; and

     (c) Present in place where seizure occurs.

(2) If officer is executing valid search warrant:

     (a) Officer may seize unlisted contraband or evidentiary items found during search; but

     (b) Officer may not use plain view to justify extending authorized scope of warrant by searching areas not described in warrant or areas where items listed in warrant could not be found or continuing to search after listed items found.

(3) If officer lawfully present under valid exception to search warrant requirement, he/she may seize items in plain view.

(4) If officer lawfully present for other reasons, such as in public place or in home with owner's permission, evidence in plain view may be seized.

(5) Officer lawfully present when:

     (a) In open field or other open place;

     (b) Enters privately owned land to seize items in plain view, or where property left open to community to view, travel, or use;

     (c) Evidence seized visible from walk leading to house.

(C) Incriminating nature apparent

In order to be subject to seizure under plain view doctrine, incriminating nature of evidence found in plain view must be immediately apparent.

(1) Probable cause to associate item observed with criminal activity is sufficient.

(2) Officer may draw logical inferences from facts observed and draw on his/her knowledge, experience.

(3) Incriminating nature must be apparent from observation without disturbing item.

     (a) Object may not be moved or turned over to determine whether it is criminal evidence; but

     (b) Where item must be moved to search for items listed in warrant, and movement provides different, incidental view of item, this view may be basis of probable cause belief that item is evidence.

(D) Inadvertent discovery rule abrogated

Formerly, plain view doctrine required that discovery of item be inadvertent. This is no longer necessary.

Checklist E
Provisions for Interrogation and Pretrial Identification of Suspect

INTERROGATION

(A) *Miranda* warnings

    (1) Must be given before any custodial interrogation, whether suspect has been charged or not.

    (2) Failure to give warnings means statements, admissions or confession of suspect will not be admissible at trial in prosecution's case-in-chief.

    (3) Contents of warnings:

    Suspect must be advised that:

        (a) He/she has the right to remain silent;

        (b) Anything he/she says can and will be used against him/her in court of law;

        (c) He/she has right to talk to an attorney, and to have attorney present during questioning; and

        (d) If he/she cannot afford attorney, one will be appointed for him/her prior to questioning, if he/she so desires.

(B) Custody

Requirement for *Miranda* warnings applies only to *custodial* interrogations.

    (1) Suspect is in custody when deprived of freedom of action in significant way, regardless of whether formal arrest has taken place. Determination of whether suspect in custody depends on objective circumstances, not subjective understanding of officers or suspect.

    (2) Questioning at police station or jail normally indicates suspect in custody, unless suspect voluntarily appears or agrees to accompany officers to station and is told that he/she is not under arrest and is free to leave.

    (3) Questions at scene where suspect has not been arrested or deprived of freedom of action do not amount to custodial interrogation.

    (4) In DUI cases, *Miranda* does not apply to:

        (a) Questions at scene of traffic stop before arrest made;

        (b) Field sobriety test results;

        (c) Volunteered statements; or

        (d) Requests to submit to alcohol tests.

(C) Interrogation

Miranda warnings must be given when suspect in custody subjected to express questioning or functional equivalent.

(1) Functional equivalent of questioning means any words or actions by officer that officer should know are reasonably likely to cause suspect to give incriminating response.

(2) Statements volunteered by suspect and not in response to questioning are not subject to *Miranda*.

(D) Right to counsel

(1) If suspect indicates in any manner that he/she wishes to see attorney, questioning must stop and cannot begin again until suspect has had opportunity to consult with attorney.

(2) Once request for attorney made, suspect cannot be questioned without attorney present. With respect to DUI cases, see sections (B)(4) above and (D)(3) below.

(3) Right to consult with attorney in DUI case

It has been held that DUI arrestee has right to consult with attorney under RC 2935.20, which goes beyond constitutional right. Thus, where arrestee was denied chance to call father for purpose of obtaining counsel prior to taking breath test, and request well within two-hour time limit for giving test, suppression of breath test results was required (State v Fullan, No. 90-P-2192 (11th Dist Ct App, Portage, 4-5-91). See also State v Scarlett, No. CA 10378 (2d Dist Ct App, Montgomery, 9-3-87) (failure to allow DUI arrestee to consult with an attorney, pursuant to RC 2935.20, provided two-hour time limit not in jeopardy, constitutes due process violation, requiring suppression of breath test results).

(E) Waiver of *Miranda* rights

(1) Waiver of rights to remain silent and to counsel must be made knowingly, intelligently, and voluntarily.

(a) Suspect must be aware of, and understand, rights being waived.

(b) Waiver must not be under duress or coercion, express or implied.

(2) Waiver may not be presumed from silence of suspect following *Miranda* warnings, or fact that suspect has answered some questions.

(3) Form of waiver.

(a) Express, written waiver preferred; but

(b) Oral waiver may be valid if voluntariness requirements met; and

    (c) Waiver may be be inferred if words and actions of suspect show clear and unambiguous intent to waive rights.

  (4) Suspect who initially invokes right to remain silent may still be questioned at future time, provided *Miranda* warnings are given again and valid waiver is made.

  (5) Suspect who invokes right to counsel may waive that right, but first suspect must initiate discussion of case; otherwise attorney must be present for questioning.

  (6) Interrogation of juvenile.

    Special care must be taken.

    (a) Presence of parents may be waived by parents or juvenile, but parents should at least be notified or reasonable attempt made.

    (b) Totality of circumstances determine if waiver valid, including juvenile's age, criminal record, emotional stability, physical condition, mental capacity, and nature and conditions of interrogation.

(F) Public safety exception to *Miranda*

  (1) Warnings not required before questioning where answers needed to deal with immediate and significant threat to safety of officer or public.

  (2) Only questions necessary to safeguard officer or public come under this exception.

PRETRIAL IDENTIFICATION OF SUSPECT; LINEUPS; PHOTOGRAPHIC DISPLAYS

(A) One-on-one showup to identify suspect should be avoided. Lineup or photo display should be used if possible.

(B) Procedure

Procedure used, including comments and instructions by officers, must not be unnecessarily suggestive.

  (1) People in lineup or photos should be similar as to race, height, weight, hair style and color, facial hair.

  (2) Officer should not tell witness that suspect is in lineup or display, but should simply ask if witness sees person at issue.

  (3) If mug shots used in photo display, identification numbers should be covered up.

  (4) Witnesses should be separated, if more than one.

(C) Right to counsel

  (1) Suspect has right to counsel at lineup or individual show-up only if he/she has been indicted or formally charged.

(2) Right to counsel does not apply to photo displays.

(D) Refusal to take part in procedure

Suspect has no right to refuse to appear in lineup or showup.

APPENDICES

Appendix A
Table of Cases

This table is arranged alphabetically letter-by-letter; i.e., each group of words comprising a casename is considered as a continuous series of letters. For example, *Harrison; State v* would precede *Harris; United States v.*

Casename	Text Section(s)
A	
Abkemeier; Broadview Heights v: 83 App(3d) 633, 615 NE(2d) 656 (Cuyahoga 1992), appeal dismissed by 66 OS(3d) 1472, 611 NE(2d) 834 (1993)	14.03(B)
Acevedo; California v: 500 US 565, 111 SCt 1982, 114 LEd(2d) 619 (1991)	1.02, 1.04, 9.03, 9.04(A), 9.04(C), 9.04(E), 12.03, 12.04
Acton; Veronia School Dist 47J v: 115 SCt 2386, 132 LEd(2d) 564 (1995), affirmed by 66 F(3d) 217 (1995)	1.01, 16.05(B)
Adams v New York: 192 US 585, 24 SCt 372, 48 LEd 575 (1904)	2.02
Adamson v People of State California: 332 US 46, 67 SCt 1672, 91 LEd 1903 (1947)	1.02
Adams v Williams: 407 US 143, 92 SCt 1921, 32 LEd(2d) 612 (1972)	14.03(A), 14.04
Addams; Bender v: 28 App 75, 162 NE 604 (Cuyahoga 1928)	17.02
Adkins; State v: 80 App(3d) 211, 608 NE(2d) 1152 (Athens 1992), cert denied 507 US 975, 113 SCt 1423, 122 LEd(2d) 792 (1993)	2.06, 19.11(C)
Agnello v United States: 269 US 20, 46 SCt 4, 70 LEd 145 (1925)	9.02, 10.02
Agosto, In re: 85 App(3d) 188, 619 NE(2d) 475 (Cuyahoga 1993)	14.03(B)
Aguilar v Texas: 378 US 108, 84 SCt 1509, 12 LEd(2d) 723 (1964), overruled by Illinois v Gates, 462 US 213, 103 SCt 2317, 76 LEd(2d) 527 (1983)	1.02, 1.05(B), 3.03(B), 3.05(D), 6.03
Akron Airport Post No. 8975; State v: 19 OS(3d) 49, 482 NE(2d) 606 (1985), cert denied 474 US 1058, 106 SCt 800, 88 LEd(2d) 777 (1986)	16.04
Akron v Harris: 93 App(3d) 378, 638 NE(2d) 633 (Summit 1994)	17.04
Akron v Harris: 36 App(3d) 106, 521 NE(2d) 835 (Cuyahoga 1987)	14.03(B)
Akron v Milewski: 21 App(3d) 140, 21 OBR 149, 487 NE(2d) 582 (Summit 1985)	18.02, 19.06
Akron v Recklaw: No. 14671, 1991 WL 11392 (9th Dist Ct App, Summit, 1-30-91)	5.04(A)
Akron; Wells v: 42 App(3d) 148, 537 NE(2d) 229 (Summit 1987)	14.03(B), 14.05
Akron v Williams: 175 OS 186, 192 NE(2d) 63, 23 OO(2d) 466 (1963)	3.04(A), 8.02
Alabama; Blackburn v: 361 US 199, 80 SCt 274, 4 LEd(2d) 242 (1960)	19.01(C), 19.10(C)
Alabama; Fikes v: 352 US 191, 77 SCt 281, 1 LEd(2d) 246 (1957)	19.01(C)
Alabama; Powell v: 287 US 45, 53 SCt 55, 77 LEd 158 (1932)	19.01(D)
Alabama; Taylor v: 457 US 687, 102 SCt 2664, 73 LEd(2d) 314 (1982)	2.07(H), 4.02
Alabama v White: 496 US 325, 110 SCt 2412, 110 LEd(2d) 301 (1990)	14.03(A)
Alderman v United States: 394 US 165, 89 SCt 961, 22 LEd(2d) 176 (1969)	18.03
Alexander; Cincinnati v: 54 OS(2d) 248, 375 NE(2d) 1241 (1978)	5.02(B)
Alexander; State v: 22 Misc(2d) 34, 22 OBR 342, 489 NE(2d) 1093 (Muni, Hamilton 1985)	14.06(E), 15.08
Allen; State v: 2 App(3d) 441, 2 OBR 536, 442 NE(2d) 784 (Hamilton 1981)	2.03, 5.02(B)
Almalik; State v: 41 App(3d) 101, 534 NE(2d) 898 (Cuyahoga 1987)	14.06(B), 15.04
Almalik; State v: 31 App(3d) 33, 31 OBR 48, 507 NE(2d) 1168 (Cuyahoga 1986)	18.05
Alvis; Cato v: 288 F(2d) 530 (6th Cir Ohio 1961)	5.05
Amador-Gonzalez v United States: 391 F(2d) 308 (5th Cir Tex 1968), overruled on other grounds by United States v Causey, 834 F(2d) 1179 (5th Cir La 1987)	11.10(A)
Amos v United States: 255 US 313, 41 SCt 266, 65 LEd 654 (1921)	17.02
Anchorage; Hinkel v: 618 P(2d) 1069 (Alaska 1980), cert denied 450 US 1032, 101 SCt 1744, 68 LEd(2d) 228 (1981)	11.11(D)
Anderson; Jenkins v: 447 US 231, 100 SCt 2124, 65 LEd(2d) 86 (1980)	19.12
Anderson; State v: 100 App(3d) 688, 654 NE(2d) 1034 (Ross 1995)	15.05, 15.06

Casename	Text Section(s)
Barker; State v: 53 OS(2d) 135, 372 NE(2d) 1324 (1978), cert denied 439 US 913, 99 SCt 285, 58 LEd(2d) 260 (1978)	4.02, 19.05, 19.10(C)
Barlow's Inc; Marshall v: 436 US 307, 98 SCt 1816, 56 LEd(2d) 305 (1978)	16.04
Barnes; State v: 25 OS(3d) 203, 25 OBR 266, 495 NE(2d) 922 (1986), cert denied 480 US 926, 107 SCt 1388, 94 LEd(2d) 701 (1987)	19.03(E), 19.05
Barnett; State v: 67 App(3d) 760, 588 NE(2d) 887 (Scioto 1990)	20.06
Barnwell; State v: 87 App(3d) 637, 622 NE(2d) 1109 (Cuyahoga 1993)	14.02(C)
Barone; United States v: 330 F(2d) 543 (2d Cir NY 1964), cert denied 377 US 1004, 84 SCt 1940, 12 LEd(2d) 1053 (1964)	10.02
Barrett; Connecticut v: 479 US 523, 107 SCt 828, 93 LEd(2d) 920 (1987)	19.08(B), 19.08(D), 19.09(B), 19.09(C)
Barrow; State v: 60 App(2d) 335, 397 NE(2d) 422 (Hamilton 1978)	14.06(A), 15.02
Barshick; State v: No. 1908, 1991 WL 6150 (9th Dist Ct App, Medina, 1-16-91)	2.03, 11.07
Bateson; City of Toledo v: 83 App(3d) 195, 614 NE(2d) 824 (Lucas 1992)	16.04
Battee; State v: 72 App(3d) 660, 595 NE(2d) 977 (Trumbull 1991)	20.05
Bauer; State v: 99 App(3d) 505, 651 NE(2d) 46 (Franklin 1994)	1.02, 15.08
Beachwood v Sims: 98 App(3d) 9, 647 NE(2d) 821 (Cuyahoga 1994)	5.04(A), 14.03(A)
Bean; State v: 13 App(3d) 69, 13 OBR 83, 468 NE(2d) 146 (Lucas 1983)	1.05(A)
Beaton; State v: No. CA94-03-036, 1994 WL 650048 (12th Dist Ct App, Warren, 11-21-94)	15.06
Beavercreek v Blue: 16 App(3d) 166, 16 OBR 175, 474 NE(2d) 1235 (Greene 1984)	19.02
Beck v Ohio: 379 US 89, 85 SCt 223, 13 LEd(2d) 142 (1964)	1.05(A), 2.03, 3.01, 3.02(A), 3.03(A), 9.02
Beckwith v United States: 425 US 341, 96 SCt 1612, 48 LEd(2d) 1 (1976)	19.05
Becvar; Cleveland v: 63 App(3d) 163, 578 NE(2d) 489 (Cuyahoga 1989), appeal dismissed by 45 OS(3d) 716, 545 NE(2d) 701 (1989)	2.06, 8.02
Becvar; Cleveland v: 55 App(3d) 11, 561 NE(2d) 1036 (Cuyahoga 1988)	12.05(B)
Beheler; California v: 436 US 1121, 103 SCt 3517, 77 LEd(2d) 1275 (1983)	19.05
Bell; State v: 48 OS(2d) 270, 358 NE(2d) 556 (1976), reversed on other grounds by 438 US 637, 98 SCt 2977, 57 LEd(2d) 1010 (1978)	19.09(C)
Belton; New York v: 453 US 454, 101 SCt 2860, 69 LEd(2d) 768 (1981)	1.01, 2.04, 9.04(A), 9.04(B), 9.04(D), 10.01, 11.03, 11.08(B), 11.10(A), 11.10(C), 11.11(B), 12.01(B), 12.02, 14.06(D), 15.07
Belton; People v: 55 NY(2d) 49, 447 NYS(2d) 873, 432 NE(2d) 745 (1982)	11.10(D)
Bender v Addams: 28 App 75, 162 NE 604 (Cuyahoga 1928)	17.02
Bendett; State v: No. 93CA005655, 1994 WL 479205 (9th Dist Ct App, Lorain, 9-7-94)	14.04
Benner; State v: 40 OS(3d) 301, 533 NE(2d) 701 (1988), cert denied 494 US 1090, 110 SCt 1834, 108 LEd(2d) 962 (1990)	8.03(C), 13.01, 19.08(B)
Benton v Maryland: 395 US 784, 89 SCt 2056, 23 LEd(2d) 707 (1969)	1.01
Berger v New York: 388 US 41, 87 SCt 1873, 18 LEd(2d) 1040 (1967)	1.03, 3.02(C), 3.02(D)
Berkemer v McCarty: 468 US 420, 104 SCt 3138, 82 LEd(2d) 317 (1984)	19.02, 19.05
Bernius; State v: 177 OS 155, 203 NE(2d) 241 (1964)	17.04
Bertine; Colorado v: 479 US 367, 107 SCt 738, 93 LEd(2d) 739 (1987)	12.05(C)
Bevan; State v: 80 App(3d) 126, 608 NE(2d) 1099 (Lake 1992)	2.07(E), 15.05
Biedenharn; State v: 19 App(2d) 204, 250 NE(2d) 778 (Hamilton 1969)	6.02
Biggers; Neil v: 409 US 188, 93 SCt 375, 34 LEd(2d) 401 (1972)	20.05, 20.06

Casename   **Text Section(s)**

Bird; State v: 49 App(3d) 156, 551 NE(2d) 622 (Lake 1988)   13.02(C),
                                                                                           14.03(B)

Birt; State v: No. 8-86-4, 1987 WL 14998 (3d Dist Ct App, Logan, 7-30-87)   2.07(G)

Bishop; State v: 95 App(3d) 619, 643 NE(2d) 170 (Warren 1994)   11.05(A),
                                                                                           14.03(A)

Biswell; United States v: 406 US 311, 92 SCt 1593, 32 LEd(2d) 87 (1972)   16.04

Bivens v Six Unknown Named Agents of Federal Bureau of Narcotics: 403 US 388, 91   2.01
   SCt 1999, 29 LEd(2d) 619 (1971)

Blackburn v Alabama: 361 US 199, 80 SCt 274, 4 LEd(2d) 242 (1960)   19.01(C),
                                                                                           19.10(C)

Blackburn; Dayton v: No. 11162, 1989 WL 65252 (2d Dist Ct App, Montgomery, 6-8-   14.03(B)
   89)

Blackburn; State v: No. 3084, 1994 WL 95224 (2d Dist Ct App, Clark, 3-23-94)   15.08

Blanchester v Hester: 81 App(3d) 815, 612 NE(2d) 412 (Clinton 1992)   5.04(A)

Blankenship; Village of New Lebanon v: 65 Misc(2d) 1, 640 NE(2d) 271 (Montgomery   15.02
   1993)

Blevins; State v: No. 57231, 1990 WL 118706 (8th Dist Ct App, Cuyahoga, 8-16-90)   10.02

Block; State v: 67 App(3d) 497, 587 NE(2d) 858 (Clermont 1990)   11.02

Blue; Beavercreek v: 16 App(3d) 166, 16 OBR 175, 474 NE(2d) 1235 (Greene 1984)   19.02

Bobo; State v: 65 App(3d) 685, 585 NE(2d) 429 (Cuyahoga 1989), appeal dismissed by   8.05(B)
   50 OS(3d) 714, 553 NE(2d) 1363 (1990)

Bobo; State v: 37 OS(3d) 177, 524 NE(2d) 489 (1988), cert denied 488 US 910, 109   3.05(B), 3.05(C),
   SCt 264, 102 LEd(2d) 252 (1988)   14.03(B)

Bocook; State v: No. CA-9629, 1986 WL 9091 (2d Dist Ct App, Montgomery, 8-19-86)   12.02

Boggs; State v: No. WD-88-73, 1989 WL 61715 (6th Dist Ct App, Wood, 6-9-89)   8.02

Bolan; State v: 27 OS(2d) 15, 271 NE(2d) 839 (1971)   2.08, 5.02(B)

Boll; State v: No. C-810078, 1981 WL 10161 (1st Dist Ct App, Hamilton, 12-16-81)   3.05(D)

Booher; State v: 54 App(3d) 1, 560 NE(2d) 786 (Defiance 1988), cert denied 493 US   19.10(C)
   977, 110 SCt 502, 107 LEd(2d) 505 (1989)

Booker; State v: 63 App(3d) 459, 579 NE(2d) 264 (Montgomery 1989)   3.06

Boone; State v: No. 53900, 1988 WL 60611(8th Dist Ct App, Cuyahoga, 6-9-88)   20.06

Bostick; Florida v: 501 US 429, 111 SCt 2382, 115 LEd(2d) 389 (1991)   4.01, 14.02(C)

Bowe; State v: 52 App(3d) 112, 557 NE(2d) 139 (Summit 1988), cert denied 489 US   5.04(A), 10.02
   1090, 109 SCt 1557, 103 LEd(2d) 860 (1989), appeal dismissed by 53 OS(3d) 703,
   558 NE(2d) 57 (1990)

Bowling; State v: No. CA86-06-038, 1987 WL 6706 (12th Dist Ct App, Warren, 2-17-   14.03(B)
   87)

Bowshier; State v: No. CA2309, 1987 WL 33784 (2d Dist Ct App, Clark, 12-23-87)   19.11(B)

Boya; State v: No. CA 13425 (2d Dist Ct App, Montgomery, 5-21-93)   7.02

Boyd v United States: 116 US 616, 6 SCt 524, 29 LEd 746 (1886)   2.02

Bradley; State v: 101 App(3d) 752, 656 NE(2d) 721 (Cuyahoga 1995)   12.01(A)

Bradley; State v: 26 App(2d) 229, 270 NE(2d) 654 (Scioto 1971)   11.10(B)

Bradshaw; Oregon v: 462 US 1039, 103 SCt 2830, 77 LEd(2d) 405 (1983)   19.08(E),
                                                                                           19.09(A)

Bradshaw; State v: 41 App(2d) 48, 322 NE(2d) 311 (Wood 1974)   12.05(C)

Bragg; State v: No. 58859, 1991 WL 127135 (8th Dist Ct App, Cuyahoga, 6-27-91),   5.04(A), 7.06
   appeal dismissed by 62 OS(3d) 1475, 581 NE(2d) 1097 (1991)

Bram v United States: 168 US 532, 18 SCt 183, 42 LEd 568 (1897)   19.10(C)

Brandenburg; State v: 41 App(3d) 109, 534 NE(2d) 906 (Montgomery 1987)   19.06

Brathwaite; Manson v: 432 US 98, 97 SCt 2243, 53 LEd(2d) 140 (1977)   20.05

Brawley; State v: No. 55796, 1989 WL 95756 (8th Dist Ct App, Cuyahoga, 8-17-89),   20.06
   appeal dismissed by 47 OS(3d) 715, 549 NE(2d) 169 (1989)

Braxton; State v: 102 App(3d) 28, 656 NE(2d) 970 (Cuyahoga 1995)   16.05(E)

Brewer; State v: 48 OS(3d) 50, 549 NE(2d) 491 (1990), affirmed by 1994 WL 527740   19.06, 19.10(C)
   (1994), cert denied 116 SCt 101, 133 LEd(2d) 55 (1995)

Brewer; State v: 48 OS(3d) 50, 549 NE(2d) 491 (1990), affirmed by 1994 WL 527740   19.03(E)
   (1994), cert denied sub nom 116 SCt 101, 133 LEd(2d) 55 (1995)

Brewer; State v: No. 84AP-852, 1986 WL 2652 (10th Dist Ct App, Franklin, 2-25-86)   18.04(B)

Casename	Text Section(s)
Brewer v Williams: 430 US 387, 97 SCt 1232, 51 LEd(2d) 424 (1977), cert denied sub nom Williams v Iowa, 446 US 921, 100 SCt 1859, 64 LEd(2d) 277 (1980)	19.11(A), 19.11(D), 19.12, 20.03
Bridges; State v: No. 55954, 1989 WL 117339 (8th Dist Ct App, Cuyahoga, 10-5-89), appeal dismissed by 51 OS(3d) 703, 555 NE(2d) 315 (1990)	8.05(B)
Brignoni-Ponce; United States v: 422 US 873, 95 SCt 2574, 45 LEd(2d) 607 (1975)	14.06(A), 15.02
Brinegar v United States: 338 US 160, 69 SCt 1302, 93 LEd 1879 (1949)	1.05(A), 3.02(A), 3.03(B)
Broadview Heights v Abkemeier: 83 App(3d) 633, 615 NE(2d) 656 (Cuyahoga 1992), appeal dismissed by 66 OS(3d) 1472, 611 NE(2d) 834 (1993)	14.03(B)
Brock; State v: No. 11449, 1989 WL 109303 (2d Dist Ct App, Montgomery, 9-21-89)	2.06, 8.03(C), 8.05(C)
Brooks; State v: No. 94APA03-386, 1995 WL 390935 (10th Dist Ct App, Franklin, 6-27-95)	10.04, 11.09(B)
Brooks; State v: No. S-87-64, 1988 WL 134181 (6th Dist Ct App, Sandusky 12-16-88)	2.06, 8.02, 8.04
Brooks; State v: No. 50384, 1986 WL 2677 (8th Dist Ct App, Cuyahoga, 2-27-86)	8.03(F)
Brookville v Louthan: 3 Misc(2d) 1, 3 OBR 64, 441 NE(2d) 308 (County Ct, Montgomery 1982)	4.02
Broom; State v: 40 OS(3d) 277, 533 NE(2d) 682 (1988), cert denied 490 US 1075, 109 SCt 2089, 104 LEd(2d) 653 (1989)	19.09(A), 20.06
Brown v Illinois: 422 US 590, 95 SCt 2254, 45 LEd(2d) 416 (1975)	2.05, 2.07(H), 4.02, 18.04(D)
Brown v Mississippi: 297 US 278, 56 SCt 461, 80 LEd 682 (1936)	19.01(B)
Brown; State v: 101 App(3d) 227, 655 NE(2d) 269 (Montgomery 1995)	3.05(D)
Brown; State v: No. 16683, 1994 WL 716234 (9th Dist Ct App, Summit, 12-28-94)	14.02(C)
Brown; State v: 91 App(3d) 427, 632 NE(2d) 970 (Wood 1993), appeal dismissed by 68 OS(3d) 1471, 628 NE(2d) 1390 (1994)	19.05
Brown; State v: 63 OS(3d) 349, 588 NE(2d) 113 (1992), cert denied ___ US ___, 113 SCt 182, 121 LEd(2d) 127 (1992)	1.01, 1.02, 11.10(A), 11.10(D)
Brown; State v: 65 OS(3d) 483, 605 NE(2d) 46 (1992)	18.04(D)
Brown; State v: 83 App(3d) 673, 615 NE(2d) 682 (Cuyahoga 1992), appeal dismissed by 66 OS(3d) 1444, 609 NE(2d) 170 (1993)	14.03(B)
Brown; State v: No. CA-8392, 1991 WL 123714 (5th Dist Ct App, Stark, 6-28-91), reversed by 65 OS(3d) 483, 605 NE(2d) 46 (1992)	12.05(C)
Brown; State v: 38 OS(3d) 305, 528 NE(2d) 523 (1988), cert denied 489 US 1040, 109 SCt 1177, 103 LEd(2d) 239 (1989)	20.06
Brown; State v: 20 App(3d) 36, 20 OBR 38, 484 NE(2d) 215 (Hamilton 1984)	1.05(A), 3.02(A)
Brown; State v: 3 App(3d) 131, 3 OBR 148, 443 NE(2d) 1382 (Cuyahoga 1981)	20.06
Brown v Texas: 443 US 47, 99 SCt 2637, 61 LEd(2d) 357 (1979)	14.02(C), 14.03(B), 14.05
Brown; Texas v: 460 US 730, 103 SCt 1535, 75 LEd(2d) 502 (1983)	1.04, 1.05(A), 3.02(A), 3.03(B), 13.01, 13.03, 13.04
Brown; United States v: 671 F(2d) 585 (DC Cir 1982)	11.11(C)
Bruder; Pennsylvania v: 488 US 9, 109 SCt 205, 102 LEd(2d) 172 (1988)	19.05
Buchholz; State v: 11 OS(3d) 24, 11 OBR 56, 462 NE(2d) 1222 (1984)	19.02
Buie; Maryland v: 494 US 325, 110 SCt 1093, 108 LEd(2d) 276 (1990), cert denied 498 US 1106, 111 SCt 1011, 112 LEd(2d) 1094 (1991)	11.09(A)
Bumper v North Carolina: 391 US 543, 88 SCt 1788, 20 LEd(2d) 797 (1968), affirmed by 275 NC 670, 170 SE(2d) 457 (1969)	17.01, 17.02, 18.04(C)
Burbine; Moran v: 475 US 412, 106 SCt 1135, 89 LEd(2d) 410 (1986)	19.03(C), 19.09(C), 19.10(B), 19.10(C)
Burdeau v McDowell: 256 US 465, 41 SCt 574, 65 LEd 1048 (1921)	2.08

Casename	Text Section(s)
Childress; State v: 4 OS(3d) 217, 4 OBR 534, 448 NE(2d) 155 (1983), cert denied 464 US 853, 104 SCt 167, 78 LEd(2d) 152 (1983)	19.08(C)
Chillicothe v Jobe: No. 1115, 1985 WL 8287 (4th Dist Ct App, Ross, 7-1-85)	7.03
Chimel v California: 395 US 752, 89 SCt 2034, 23 LEd(2d) 685 (1969)	9.02, 9.04(D), 11.03, 11.04(A), 11.08(A), 11.09(B), 11.10(A), 11.11(B), 18.04(C)
Chrisman; Washington v: 455 US 1, 102 SCt 812, 70 LEd(2d) 778 (1982)	9.04(B), 11.08(B), 13.02(C)
Christian; State v: No. 58660, 1991 WL 106041 (8th Dist Ct App, Cuyahoga, 6-13-91)	13.02(C)
Cincinnati v Alexander: 54 OS(2d) 248, 375 NE(2d) 1241 (1978)	5.02(B)
Cincinnati v Moore: Nos. C-880689 et al., 1989 WL 136387 (1st Dist Ct App, Hamilton, 11-15-89)	18.04(C)
Cincinnati v Morris Investment Co, Inc: 6 Misc(2d) 1, 6 OBR 80, 451 NE(2d) 259 (Muni, Hamilton 1982)	16.04
Ciraolo; California v: 476 US 207, 106 SCt 1809, 90 LEd(2d) 210 (1986)	1.02, 1.04
City of Akron v Rowland: 67 OS(3d) 374, 618 NE(2d) 138 (1993)	14.03(B)
City of Cleveland v Stephen: 93 App(3d) 827, 639 NE(2d) 1258 (Cuyahoga 1994)	14.03(B)
City of Garfield Heights v Simpson: 82 App(3d) 286, 611 NE(2d) 892 (Cuyahoga 1992)	7.03
City of Hamilton v Jacobs: 100 App(3d) 724, 654 NE(2d) 1057 (Butler 1995)	14.03(B)
City of Hamilton v Lawson: 94 App(3d) 462, 640 NE(2d) 1206 (1994)	15.02
City of Lakewood v Waselenchuk: 94 App(3d) 684, 641 NE(2d) 767 (Cuyahoga 1994)	2.03, 19.11(B)
City of London v Edley: 75 App(3d) 30, 598 NE(2d) 851 (Madison 1991), appeal dismissed by 62 OS(3d) 1475, 581 NE(2d) 1097 (1991)	14.03(B)
City of Maumee v Johnson: 90 App(3d) 169, 628 NE(2d) 115 (Lucas 1993)	15.02
City of Stow v Riggenbach: 97 App(3d) 661, 647 NE(2d) 246 (Summit 1994)	2.03
City of Toledo v Bateson: 83 App(3d) 195, 614 NE(2d) 824 (Lucas 1992)	16.04
City of Toledo v Harris: 99 App(3d) 469, 651 NE(2d) 24 (Lucas 1995)	14.03(B), 15.02, 18.05
Clark v Carney: 71 App 14, 42 NE(2d) 938 (Hamilton 1942)	4.03(A), 4.03(B)
Clark; State v: Nos. C-900245, C-900246, 1991 WL 155213 (1st Dist Ct App, Hamilton, 8-14-91)	13.02(C), 18.03
Clark; State v: 38 OS(3d) 252, 527 NE(2d) 844 (1988)	19.08(B)
Clark; State v: 40 App(2d) 365, 319 NE(2d) 605 (Cuyahoga 1974)	7.02
Class; New York v: 475 US 106, 106 SCt 960, 89 LEd(2d) 81 (1986)	14.06(B), 15.04
Clay; State v: No. 12540, 1991 WL 116643 (2d Dist Ct App, Montgomery, 6-28-91)	18.05
Clay; State v: 43 Misc(2d) 5, 539 NE(2d) 1168 (Muni, Hamilton 1988)	7.03
Clements v Logan: 455 US 942, 102 SCt 1435, 71 LEd(2d) 653 (1982)	11.07
Clement; State v: Nos. 87AP-900, 87AP-1115, 1988 WL 142115 (10th Dist Ct App, Franklin, 12-30-88)	20.06, 20.07(A)
Cleveland v Becvar: 63 App(3d) 163, 578 NE(2d) 489 (Cuyahoga 1989), appeal dismissed by 45 OS(3d) 716, 545 NE(2d) 901 (1989)	2.06, 8.02
Cleveland v Becvar: 55 App(3d) 11, 561 NE(2d) 1036 (Cuyahoga 1988)	12.05(B)
Cleveland v Corrai: 70 App(3d) 679, 591 NE(2d) 1325 (Cuyahoga 1990)	8.03(G)
Cleveland Heights v Stross: 10 App(3d) 246, 461 NE(2d) 935 (Cuyahoga 1983)	2.08
Cleveland; Nicholas v: 125 OS 474, 182 NE 26 (1932), overruled by State v Lindway, 131 OS 166, 2 NE(2d) 490 (1936), cert denied 299 US 506, 57 SCt 36, 81 LEd 375 (1936)	1.05(A), 3.03(A), 6.03, 8.03(A)
Cleveland v Paltani: No. 60255, 1991 WL 76103 (8th Dist Ct App, Cuyahoga, 5-9-91)	14.06(D), 15.07
Cleveland v Tedar: No. 34622 (8th Dist Ct App, Cuyahoga, 3-4-76)	11.05(A)
Clifford; Michigan v: 464 US 287, 104 SCt 641, 78 LEd(2d) 477 (1984)	10.03, 16.04
Cloud; State v: 91 App(3d) 366, 632 NE(2d) 932 (Cuyahoga 1993)	13.05
Cloud; State v: 61 Misc(2d) 87, 573 NE(2d) 1244 (1991)	5.02(B)
Clutter; State v: No. 85-CA-5, 1986 WL 9651 (4th Dist Ct App, Washington, 9-4-86)	18.02

Casename

Casename	Text Section(s)
Davidson; State v: 82 App(3d) 282, 611 NE(2d) 889 (Darke 1992)	11.10(D)
Davies; State v: Nos. C-850112, et al., 1986 WL 657 (1st Dist Ct App, Hamilton, 1-8-86)	7.02, 8.03(F)
Davie; State v: 86 App(3d) 460, 621 NE(2d) 548 (Cuyahoga 1993)	14.03(B)
Davis v Mississippi: 394 US 721, 89 SCt 1394, 22 LEd(2d) 676 (1969), cert denied 409 US 855, 93 SCt 191, 34 LEd(2d) 99 (1972)	4.02, 14.05
Davis; State v: 80 App(3d) 277, 609 NE(2d) 174 (Cuyahoga 1992), appeal dismissed by 65 OS(3d) 1462, 602 NE(2d) 1171 (1992)	17.02, 18.03
Davis; State v: No. CA-720, 1990 WL 79040 (5th Dist Ct App, Morrow, 6-7-90)	17.04
Davis; State v: No. CA89-03-016, 1989 WL 149413 (12th Dist Ct App, Clermont, 12-11-89), appeal dismissed by 51 OS(3d) 707, 555 NE(2d) 316 (1990)	2.07(F)
Davis v United States: ___ US ___, 114 SCt 2350, 126 LEd(2d) 362 (1994)	19.08(B)
Day; State v: 72 App(3d) 82, 593 NE(2d) 456 (Ross 1991)	18.03
Day; State v: 19 App(3d) 252, 19 OBR 405, 483 NE(2d) 1195 (Tuscarawas 1984)	2.05, 2.06
Day; State v: 50 App(2d) 315, 362 NE(2d) 1253 (Hamilton 1976)	1.04
Dayton v Blackburn: No. 11162, 1989 WL 65252 (2d Dist Ct App, Montgomery, 6-8-89)	14.03(B)
Dayton v Rodgers: 60 OS(2d) 162, 398 NE(2d) 781 (1979)	8.03(G)
Deal; State v: No. 57358, 1990 WL 109122 (8th Dist Ct App, Cuyahoga, 8-2-90)	20.04
Defiance v Kretz: 60 OS(3d) 1, 573 NE(2d) 32 (1991)	2.03, 18.06(B)
DeFiore; State v: 64 App(2d) 115, 411 NE(2d) 837 (Hamilton 1979)	7.02, 8.03(F)
DeForte; Mancusi v: 392 US 364, 88 SCt 2120, 20 LEd(2d) 1154 (1968)	1.04
Delaney; State v: 11 OS(3d) 231, 11 OBR 545, 465 NE(2d) 72 (1984)	4.01
Delaware; Franks v: 438 US 154, 98 SCt 2674, 57 LEd(2d) 667 (1978)	2.05, 3.06, 18.04(B)
Delaware v Prouse: 440 US 648, 99 SCt 1391, 59 LEd(2d) 660 (1979)	2.04, 14.06(A), 14.06(C), 14.06(D), 15.02, 15.06, 15.07
Delgado; Immigration & Naturalization Service v: 466 US 210, 104 SCt 1758, 80 LEd(2d) 247 (1984)	14.02(C)
Dempsey; Moore v: 261 US 86, 43 SCt 265, 67 LEd 543 (1923)	19.01(B)
Denno; Jackson v: 378 US 368, 84 SCt 1774, 12 LEd(2d) 908 (1964)	18.04(D), 19.01(C)
Denno; Stovall v: 388 US 293, 87 SCt 1967, 18 LEd(2d) 1199 (1967)	20.03, 20.05, 20.07(C)
Department of Liquor Control v FOE Aerie 0456: 99 App(3d) 380, 650 NE(2d) 940 (Franklin 1994)	16.04
Dept of Rehabilitation and Correction; Wise v: 97 App(3d) 741, 647 NE(2d) 538 (Franklin 1994)	14.03(A)
DePaso; Columbus v: No. 89AP-268, 1989 WL 111001 (10th Dist Ct App, Franklin, 9-26-89)	7.03
DePew; State v: 38 OS(3d) 275, 528 NE(2d) 542 (1988), appeal dismissed by 65 OS(3d) 1475, 604 NE(2d) 167 (1992), affirmed by 70 OS(3d) 1435, 638 NE(2d) 1039 (1994)	19.09(C)
Dewey; Donovan v: 452 US 594, 101 SCt 2534, 69 LEd(2d) 262 (1981)	16.04
Dickens; State v: No. 12967, 1987 WL 17928 (9th Dist Ct App, Summit, 9-23-87)	19.10(C)
Dickerson; Minnesota v: 508 US 366, 113 SCt 2130, 124 LEd(2d) 334 (1993)	13.05, 14.04
Di Franco; South Euclid v: 4 Misc 148, 206 NE(2d) 432 (Muni, South Euclid 1965)	17.02
Dillon; State v: No. 90-CA-07, 1991 WL 6347 (2d Dist Ct App, Miami, 1-23-91)	2.08
Dixon v Maxwell: 177 OS 20, 201 NE(2d) 592 (1964)	1.05(A), 3.02(C)
Dixon; State v: 101 App(3d) 552, 656 NE(2d) 1 (Lucas 1995)	19.03(E)
Dombrowski; Cady v: 413 US 433, 93 SCt 2523, 37 LEd(2d) 706 (1973)	12.02
Donohue; State v: No. C-860458, 1987 WL 12741 (1st Dist Ct App, Hamilton, 6-17-87)	8.05(B)
Donovan v Dewey: 452 US 594, 101 SCt 2534, 69 LEd(2d) 262 (1981)	16.04
Dorman v United States: 435 F(2d) 385 (DC Cir 1970)	5.04(A)
Dorsey; State v: No. 11657, 1989 WL 150806 (2d Dist Ct App, Montgomery, 12-12-89)	14.03(B)
Dorson; State v: 62 Hawaii 377, 615 P(2d) 740 (1980)	11.09(B)

Casename	Text Section(s)
Fraley; Columbus v: 41 OS(2d) 173, 324 NE(2d) 735 (1975), cert denied 423 US 872, 96 SCt 138, 46 LEd(2d) 102 (1975)	7.03
Franklin; State v: 86 App(3d) 101, 619 NE(2d) 1182 (Hamilton 1993), appeal dismissed by 67 OS(3d) 1421, 616 NE(2d) 504 (1993)	4.02, 14.02(C), 14.03(A), 14.04
Franks v Delaware: 438 US 154, 98 SCt 2674, 57 LEd(2d) 667 (1978)	2.05, 3.06, 18.04(B)
Freeman; State v: 64 OS(2d) 291, 414 NE(2d) 1044 (1980), cert denied 454 US 822, 102 SCt 107, 70 LEd(2d) 94 (1981)	14.03(B)
Fricker v Stokes: 22 OS(3d) 202, 22 OBR 354, 490 NE(2d) 577 (1986)	11.07
Frick; United States v: 490 F(2d) 666 (5th Cir La 1973), cert denied sub nom Petersen v United States, 419 US 831, 95 SCt 55, 42 LEd(2d) 57 (1974)	11.10(B)
Frisbie v Collins: 342 US 519, 72 SCt 509, 96 LEd 541 (1952)	4.01
Frost; State v: 77 App(3d) 644, 603 NE(2d) 270 (Franklin 1991), cert denied ___ US ___, 113 SCt 133, 121 LEd(2d) 87 (1992)	14.02(D)
Fulk; State v: No. 82AP-577, 1983 WL 3489 (10th Dist Ct App, Franklin, 5-3-83)	19.08(E)
Fulminante; Arizona v: 499 US 279, 111 SCt 1246, 113 LEd(2d) 302 (1991)	19.01(A), 19.10(C)
Fultz; State v: 13 OS(2d) 79, 234 NE(2d) 593 (1968), cert denied 393 US 854, 89 SCt 95, 21 LEd(2d) 123 (1968)	3.05(D)
Furry; State v: 31 App(2d) 107, 286 NE(2d) 301 (Wood 1971)	7.02, 8.03(F)

G

Gaddis; State v: 35 App(2d) 15, 299 NE(2d) 304 (Butler 1973)	4.02, 11.02
Gallagher; State v: 38 OS(2d) 291, 313 NE(2d) 396 (1974), vacated by 425 US 257, 96 SCt 1438, 47 LEd(2d) 722 (1976)	19.05
Gallegos v Colorado: 370 US 49, 82 SCt 1209, 8 LEd(2d) 325 (1962)	19.01(C)
Gamble; United States v: 473 F(2d) 1274 (7th Cir Ill 1973)	11.09(A)
Garcia; State v: 32 App(3d) 38, 513 NE(2d) 1350 (Lorain 1986)	19.10(C)
Garcia; United States v: 605 F(2d) 349 (7th Cir Ill 1979), cert denied 446 US 984, 100 SCt 2966, 64 LEd(2d) 841 (1980)	11.11(D)
Gardner; State v: 88 App(3d) 354, 623 NE(2d) 1310 (Hardin 1993)	14.02(D)
Garfield Heights Municipal Court; Hoover v: 802 F(2d) 168 (6th Cir 1986), cert denied 480 US 949, 107 SCt 1610, 94 LEd (2d) 796 (1987)	3.05(B), 7.03
Garner; State v: 74 OS(3d) 49, 656 NE(2d) 623 (1995)	19.09(C), 20.06
Garner; Tennessee v: 471 US 1, 105 SCt 1694, 85 LEd(2d) 1 (1985), cert denied sub nom Memphis Police Dept v Garner, 114 SCt 1219, 127 LEd(2d) 565 (1994)	4.03(B)
Garrett; State v: 76 App(3d) 57, 600 NE(2d) 1130 (Portage 1991)	10.01
Garrison; Maryland v: 480 US 79, 107 SCt 1013, 94 LEd(2d) 72 (1987)	8.03(C), 8.03(F)
Gasser; State v: 5 App(3d) 217, 5 OBR 501, 451 NE(2d) 249 (Paulding 1980)	2.03, 18.04(C)
Gates; Illinois v: 462 US 213, 103 SCt 2317, 76 LEd(2d) 527 (1983)	1.01, 1.02, 1.05(A), 1.05(B), 2.05, 3.02(A), 3.02(D), 3.03(B), 3.04(B), 3.05(A), 3.05(B), 3.05(D), 3.06, 14.03(A)
Geasley; State v: 85 App(3d) 360, 619 NE(2d) 1086 (Summit 1993)	19.06
Gedeon; State v: 81 App(3d) 617, 611 NE(2d) 972 (Lake 1992)	14.03(B)
Gengler; United States ex rel Lujan v: 510 F(2d) 62 (2d Cir NY 1975), cert denied 421 US 1001, 95 SCt 2400, 44 LEd(2d) 668 (1975)	4.01
Gentile; United States v: 493 F(2d) 1404 (5th Cir Tex 1974), cert denied 419 US 979, 95 SCt 241, 42 LEd(2d) 191 (1974)	17.02
George; State v: No. CA-8519, 1991 WL 207941 (5th Dist Ct App, Stark, 9-30-91)	14.03(B)
George; State v: 45 OS(3d) 325, 544 NE(2d) 640 (1989)	2.06, 3.01, 3.02(A), 3.04(B), 3.05(B), 8.02

H

Casename	Text Section(s)
Halczyszak; State v: 25 OS(3d) 301, 25 OBR 360, 496 NE(2d) 925 (1986), cert denied 480 US 919, 107 SCt 1376, 94 LEd(2d) 691 (1987)	13.03, 13.04
Haley v Ohio: 332 US 596, 68 SCt 302, 92 LEd 224 (1948), cert denied 337 US 945, 69 SCt 1501, 93 LEd 1748 (1949)	19.01(C)
Halko; State v: No. C-850656, 1986 WL 7855 (1st Dist Ct App, Hamilton, 7-16-86)	18.04(C)
Hall; State v: No. CA L-85-03, 1995 WL 7373 (6th Dist Ct App, Lucas, 6-30-86)	7.02
Hall; State v: 48 OS(2d) 325, 358 NE(2d) 590 (1976), vacated in part by 438 US 910, 98 SCt 3134, 57 LEd(2d) 1154 (1978)	19.09(C)
Hall; United States v: 525 F(2d) 857 (DC Cir 1976)	14.03(B)
Hamilton v Reasch: 98 App(3d) 814, 649 NE(2d) 922 (Butler 1994)	14.03(A)
Hamilton; State v: 97 App(3d) 648, 647 NE(2d) 238 (Logan 1994)	18.02
Hammett; State v: No. 48675, 1985 WL 6652 (8th Dist Ct App, Cuyahoga, 2-21-85)	2.08
Hancock; State v: 48 OS(2d) 147, 358 NE(2d) 273 (1976), vacated in part by 438 US 911, 98 SCt 3147, 57 LEd(2d) 1155 (1978)	20.06
Harrell; State v: 65 OS(3d) 37, 599 NE(2d) 695 (1992)	2.06, 2.07(G)
Harrell; State v: No. 60888, 1991 WL 95144 (8th Dist Ct App, Cuyahoga, 5-30-91), reversed on other grounds by 65 OS(3d) 37, 599 NE(2d) 695 (1992)	2.06, 3.04(B)
Harrington; State v: No. 14146, 1994 WL 285048 (2d Dist Ct App, Montgomery, 6-1-94)	14.05
Harris; Akron v: 93 App(3d) 378, 638 NE(2d) 633 (Summit 1994)	17.04
Harris; Akron v: 36 App(3d) 106, 521 NE(2d) 835 (Cuyahoga 1987)	14.03(B)
Harris; City of Toledo v: 99 App(3d) 469, 651 NE(2d) 24 (Lucas 1995)	14.03(B), 15.02, 18.05
Harris; Columbus v: No. 86AP-792, 1987 WL 9490 (10th Dist Ct App, Franklin, 3-31-87)	2.03
Harris v New York: 401 US 222, 91 SCt 643, 28 LEd(2d) 1 (1971)	18.03, 19.12
Harris; New York v: 495 US 14, 110 SCt 1640, 109 LEd(2d) 13 (1990)	2.07(C), 2.07(H)
Harris v South Carolina: 338 US 68, 69 SCt 1354, 93 LEd 1815 (1949)	19.01(C)
Harris; State v: 36 App(3d) 106, 521 NE(2d) 835 (Cuyahoga 1987)	14.03(B)
Harris v United States: 390 US 234, 88 SCt 992, 19 LEd(2d) 1067 (1968)	13.01
Harris v United States: 331 US 145, 67 SCt 1098, 91 LEd 1399 (1947), overruled by Chimel v California, 395 US 752, 89 SCt 2034, 23 LEd(2d) 685 (1969)	11.08(A)
Harris; United States v: 403 US 573, 91 SCt 2075, 29 LEd(2d) 723 (1971)	1.05(B), 3.05(D)
Harrison; State v: 20 Misc 282, 251 NE(2d) 521 (CP, Montgomery 1969)	8.03(B)
Hart; State v: 61 App(3d) 37, 572 NE(2d) 141 (Cuyahoga 1988), appeal dismissed by 42 OS(3d) 702, 536 NE(2d) 1172 (1989)	14.05
Harvey; Michigan v: 494 US 344, 110 SCt 1176, 108 LEd(2d) 293 (1990)	19.12
Harvey; State v: No. 14919, 1995 WL 418731 (2d Dist Ct App, Montgomery, 7-12-95)	13.03
Harvill; State v: 15 App(3d) 94, 15 OBR 123, 472 NE(2d) 743 (Hamilton 1984)	19.10(A)
Hass; Oregon v: 420 US 714, 95 SCt 1215, 43 LEd(2d) 570 (1975)	18.03, 19.12
Hathman; State v: 65 OS(3d) 403, 604 NE(2d) 743 (1992)	12.05(C)
Havens; United States v: 446 US 620, 100 SCt 1912, 64 LEd(2d) 559 (1980), cert denied 450 US 995, 101 SCt 1697, 68 LEd(2d) 195 (1981)	19.12
Hayden; Warden, Maryland Penitentiary v: 387 US 294, 87 SCt 1642, 18 LEd(2d) 782 (1967)	8.03(C), 10.04
Hayes v Florida: 470 US 811, 105 SCt 1643, 84 LEd(2d) 705 (1985), cert denied 479 US 831, 107 SCt 119, 93 LEd(2d) 65 (1986)	14.05
Haynes v Washington: 373 US 503, 83 SCt 1336, 10 LEd(2d) 513 (1963)	19.01(C)
Heaton; State v: Nos. 4069, 4070, 1987 WL 6171 (9th Dist Ct App, Lorain, 2-4-87)	8.03(E)
Hegbar; State v: No. 49828, 1985 WL 4219 (8th Dist Ct App, Cuyahoga 12-5-85)	2.08
Heinrichs; State v: 46 App(3d) 63, 545 NE(2d) 1304 (Darke 1988)	14.03(B)
Henderson; State v: 51 OS(3d) 54, 554 NE(2d) 104 (1990)	3.05(D), 4.01, 19.05, 19.06
Henderson; State v: 66 App(3d) 447, 585 NE(2d) 539 (Montgomery 1990), appeal dismissed by 53 OS(3d) 703, 558 NE(2d) 57 (1990)	8.02
Henry; Columbus v: No. 95APC02-159, 1995 WL 507453 (10th Dist Ct App, Franklin, 8-29-95)	7.03
Henry; State v: 1 App(3d) 126, 1 OBR 432, 439 NE(2d) 941 (Franklin 1981)	2.08

Casename	Text Section(s)
Long; Michigan v: 463 US 1032, 103 SCt 3469, 77 LEd(2d) 1201 (1983)	1.01, 1.02, 1.04, 2.03, 12.02, 14.04, 15.06
Long; State v: No. 58793, 1991 WL 118060 (8th Dist Ct App, Cuyahoga, 6-20-91), appeal dismissed by 62 OS(3d) 1445, 579 NE(2d) 490 (1991)	18.04(C)
Louisiana; Duncan v: 391 US 145, 88 SCt 1444, 20 LEd(2d) 491 (1968)	1.01
Louisiana; Tague v: 444 US 469, 100 SCt 652, 62 LEd(2d) 622 (1980)	19.09(C)
Louisiana; Thompson v: 469 US 17, 105 SCt 409, 83 LEd(2d) 246 (1984)	9.04(A), 10.01, 10.03
Louisiana; Vale v: 399 US 30, 90 SCt 1969, 26 LEd(2d) 409 (1970)	10.02, 11.09(B), 13.02(C)
Louthan; Brookville v: 3 Misc(2d) 1, 3 OBR 64, 441 NE(2d) 308 (County Ct, Montgomery 1982)	4.02
Love; State v: 49 App(3d) 88, 550 NE(2d) 951 (Hamilton 1988)	10.02
Lucas; Giacalone v: 445 F(2d) 1238 (6th Cir Mich 1971), cert denied 405 US 922, 92 SCt 960, 30 LEd(2d) 793 (1972)	11.08(B)
Luck; State v: 15 OS(3d) 150, 15 OBR 296, 472 NE(2d) 1097 (1984), cert denied 470 US 1084, 105 SCt 1845, 85 LEd(2d) 144 (1985)	7.01, 19.09(C)
Lynumn v Illinois: 372 US 528, 83 SCt 917, 9 LEd(2d) 922 (1963)	19.01(C)
Lyons v Oklahoma: 322 US 596, 64 SCt 1208, 88 LEd 1481 (1944)	19.01(B)
Lyons; State v: 83 App(3d) 525, 615 NE(2d) 310 (Darke 1992), appeal dismissed by 66 OS(3d) 1455, 610 NE(2d) 420 (1993)	11.09(A)

M

Casename	Text Section(s)
Macon; Maryland v: 472 US 463, 105 SCt 2778, 86 LEd(2d) 370 (1985)	17.02
Madison; State v: 64 OS(2d) 322, 415 NE(2d) 272 (1980)	20.06
Magda; United States v: 547 F(2d) 756 (2d Cir NY 1976), cert denied 434 US 878, 98 SCt 230, 54 LEd(2d) 157 (1977)	14.03(B)
Maine v Moulton: 474 US 159, 106 SCt 477, 88 LEd(2d) 481 (1985)	19.11(B)
Malinski v New York: 324 US 401, 65 SCt 781, 89 LEd 1029 (1945)	19.01(C)
Malloy v Hogan: 378 US 1, 84 SCt 1489, 12 LEd(2d) 653 (1964)	1.01, 19.02
Mancusi v DeForte: 392 US 364, 88 SCt 2120, 20 LEd(2d) 1154 (1968)	1.04
Mandrbah; State v: No. C-810135, 1982 WL 4637 (1st Dist Ct App, Hamilton, 2-10-82)	19.10(A)
Mann; State v: 19 OS(3d) 34, 19 OBR 28, 482 NE(2d) 592 (1985)	7.03
Manson v Brathwaite: 432 US 98, 97 SCt 2243, 53 LEd(2d) 140 (1977)	20.05
Mapp v Ohio: 367 US 643, 81 SCt 1684, 6 LEd(2d) 1081 (1961)	1.01, 1.02, 2.01, 2.02, 2.03, 2.04, 3.04(A)
Marcum; State v: 24 Wash App 441, 601 P(2d) 975 (1979)	12.02
Marini; State v: 78 App(3d) 279, 604 NE(2d) 769 (Cuyahoga 1992), appeal dismissed by 64 OS(3d) 1413, 593 NE(2d) 4 (1992)	14.04
Marko; State v: 36 App(2d) 114, 303 NE(2d) 94 (Franklin 1973)	8.03(E)
Maroney; Chambers v: 399 US 42, 90 SCt 1975, 26 LEd(2d) 419 (1970)	2.04, 12.02
Marron v United States: 275 US 192, 48 SCt 74, 72 LEd 231 (1927)	8.03(C)
Marshall v Barlow's Inc: 436 US 307, 98 SCt 1816, 56 LEd(2d) 305 (1978)	16.04
Martin v Ohio: 480 US 228, 107 SCt 1098, 94 LEd(2d) 267 (1987)	4.03(D)
Martin; People v: 45 Cal(2d) 755, 290 P(2d) 855 (1955), superseded by constitutional amendment as stated in People v Daan, 161 CalApp(3d) 22, 207 Cal Rptr 228 (1984)	18.03
Martins Ferry Eagles; State v: 62 Misc 3, 404 NE(2d) 177 (County Ct, Belmont 1979)	8.03(B)
Martin; State v: No. C-860610, 1987 WL 19704 (1st Dist Ct App, Hamilton, 11-10-87)	19.08(B)
Marts v State: 26 OS 162 (1875)	4.03(D)
Maryland; Andresen v: 427 US 463, 96 SCt 2737, 49 LEd(2d) 627 (1976)	1.05(A), 3.02(D), 8.03(C)
Maryland; Benton v: 395 US 784, 89 SCt 2056, 23 LEd(2d) 707 (1969)	1.01
Maryland v Buie: 494 US 325, 110 SCt 1093, 108 LEd(2d) 276 (1990), cert denied 498 US 1106, 111 SCt 1011, 112 LEd(2d) 1094 (1991)	11.09(A)
Maryland v Garrison: 480 US 79, 107 SCt 1013, 94 LEd(2d) 72 (1987)	8.03(C), 8.03(F)

Casename	Text Section(s)
Maryland v Macon: 472 US 463, 105 SCt 2778, 86 LEd(2d) 370 (1985)	17.02
Maryland; Smith v: 442 US 735, 99 SCt 2577, 61 LEd(2d) 220 (1979)	1.02, 1.04
Massachusetts v Sheppard: 468 US 981, 104 SCt 3424, 82 LEd(2d) 737 (1984)	1.02, 1.05(A), 2.05, 2.06
Massachusetts v Upton: 466 US 727, 104 SCt 2085, 80 LEd(2d) 721 (1984)	1.05(B), 3.05(D)
Massiah v United States: 377 US 201, 84 SCt 1199, 12 LEd(2d) 246 (1964)	19.01(D), 19.11(A)
Masten; State v: No. 5-88-7, 1989 WL 111983 (3d Dist Ct App, Hancock, 9-29-89)	2.06, 2.07(G), 17.04, 18.03
Mathews; State v: 46 OS(2d) 72, 346 NE(2d) 151 (1976)	11.04(C), 11.11(C)
Mathiason; Oregon v: 429 US 492, 97 SCt 711, 50 LEd(2d) 714 (1977)	19.05
Mathis v United States: 391 US 1, 88 SCt 1503, 20 LEd(2d) 381 (1968)	19.05
Matlock; United States v: 415 US 164, 94 SCt 988, 39 LEd(2d) 242 (1974)	17.04
Mattachione; Fairborn v: 72 OS(3d) 345, 650 NE(2d) 426 (1995)	2.03
Maumee v Johnson: 90 App(3d) 169, 628 NE(2d) 115 (Lucas 1993)	15.02
Mauro; Arizona v: 481 US 520, 107 SCt 1931, 95 LEd(2d) 458 (1987)	19.06
Maxwell; Dixon v: 177 OS 20, 201 NE(2d) 592 (1964)	1.05(A), 3.02(C)
Maxwell; Krauter v: 3 OS(2d) 142, 209 NE(2d) 571 (1965)	4.01
Maxwell; Sopko v: 3 OS(2d) 123, 209 NE(2d) 201 (1965)	6.02
Maynard; State v: 1 OS(2d) 57, 203 NE(2d) 332 (1964), cert denied 382 US 871, 86 SCt 105, 15 LEd(2d) 110 (1965)	6.02
Mays; State v: 83 App(3d) 610, 615 NE(2d) 641 (Pike 1992)	2.03
McCarthy; State v: 26 OS(2d) 87, 269 NE(2d) 424 (1971)	1.04, 17.04
McCarthy; State v: 20 App(2d) 275, 253 NE(2d) 789 (Cuyahoga 1969), affirmed by 26 OS(2d) 87, 269 NE(2d) 424 (1971)	17.04
McCarty; Berkemer v: 468 US 420, 104 SCt 3138, 82 LEd(2d) 317 (1984)	19.02, 19.05
McCauley; United States ex rel Guy v: 385 FSupp 193 (ED Wis 1974)	11.04(D)
McClung; State v: No. C-810299, 1982 WL 4678 (1st Dist Ct App, Hamilton, 3-3-82)	1.04
McCoy; Tallmadge v: 96 App(3d) 604, 645 NE(2d) 802 (Summit 1994)	14.03(B), 14.05
McCray v Illinois: 386 US 300, 87 SCt 1056, 18 LEd(2d) 62 (1967)	1.05(B), 3.03(B), 3.05(D)
McCrone; State v: 63 App(3d) 831, 580 NE(2d) 468 (Lorain 1989), appeal dismissed by 48 OS(3d) 704, 549 NE(2d) 1190 (1990)	7.03, 14.05
McDaniel; State v: 91 App(3d) 189, 631 NE(2d) 1140 (Cuyahoga 1993)	14.02(D)
McDaniel; State v: 44 App(2d) 163, 337 NE(2d) 173 (Franklin 1975)	2.08
McDonald; State v: No. 9-87-30, 1988 WL 63955 (3d Dist Ct App, Marion, 6-14-88)	8.02
McDonald v United States: 335 US 451, 69 SCt 191, 93 LEd(2d) 153 (1948)	9.04(C)
McDonald; United States v: 456 US 1, 102 SCt 1497, 71 LEd(2d) 696 (1982), appeal dismissed by 459 US 1103, 103 SCt 726, 74 LEd(2d) 951 (1983)	7.01
McDowell; Burdeau v: 256 US 465, 41 SCt 574, 65 LEd 1048 (1921)	2.08
McFarland; State v: 4 App(3d) 158, 4 OBR 252, 446 NE(2d) 1168 (Cuyahoga 1982)	4.02, 14.05
McGhee; State v: 37 App(3d) 54, 523 NE(2d) 864 (Cuyahoga 1987)	19.11(D)
McGuire; Middleton v: No. CA94-11-202, 1995 WL 591238 (12th Dist Ct App, Butler, 10-9-95	5.02(B)
McHugh; Toledo v: No. CA L-87-008, 1987 WL 19971 (6th Dist Ct App, Lucas, 11-13-87)	2.06
McIntire; State v: No. 94-CA-33, 1995 WL 137025 (2d Dist Ct App, Miami, 3-31-95)	3.05(D)
McLaughlin; County of Riverside v: 500 US 44, 111 SCt 1661, 114 LEd(2d) 49 (1991)	5.05
McLeod v Ohio: 381 US 356, 85 SCt 1556, 14 LEd(2d) 682 (1965)	19.01(D)
McNeil v Wisconsin: 501 US 171, 111 SCt 2204, 115 LEd(2d) 158 (1991)	19.08(C), 19.11(B), 19.11(D)
Medlar; State v: 93 App(3d) 483, 638 NE(2d) 1105 (Cuyahoga 1994)	11.05(C), 15.02
Mendenhall; United States v: 446 US 544, 100 SCt 1870, 64 LEd(2d) 497 (1980)	14.02(A), 14.02(C), 14.05
Merrill; State v: 22 App(3d) 119, 489 NE(2d) 1057 (Cuyahoga 1984)	20.06
Metz; State v: 37 Misc(2d) 3, 523 NE(2d) 363 (Muni, Hamilton 1987)	14.03(B), 14.04

Casename	**Text Section(s)**
Meyers; Florida v: 466 US 380, 104 SCt 1852, 80 LEd(2d) 381 (1984)	12.02
Michael C.; Fare v: 442 US 707, 99 SCt 2560, 61 LEd(2d) 197 (1979)	19.07(B), 19.09(B)
Michel; Columbus v: 55 App(2d) 46, 378 NE(2d) 1077 (Franklin 1978)	14.05
Michigan v Chesternut: 486 US 567, 108 SCt 1975, 100 LEd(2d) 565 (1988)	1.03, 14.02(D), 14.06(A), 15.02
Michigan v Clifford: 464 US 287, 104 SCt 641, 78 LEd(2d) 477 (1984)	10.03, 16.04
Michigan Dept of State Police v Stitz: 496 US 444, 110 SCt 2481, 110 LEd(2d) 412 (1990), affirmed by 443 Mich 744, 506 NW(2d) 209 (1993)	2.04, 14.06(E), 15.08
Michigan v Harvey: 494 US 344, 110 SCt 1176, 108 LEd(2d) 293 (1990)	19.12
Michigan v Jackson: 475 US 625, 106 SCt 1404, 89 LEd(2d) 631 (1986)	19.08(B), 19.08(C), 19.08(D), 19.11(B)
Michigan v Long: 463 US 1032, 103 SCt 3469, 77 LEd(2d) 1201 (1983)	1.01, 1.02, 1.04, 2.03, 12.02, 14.04, 15.06
Michigan v Mosley: 423 US 96, 96 SCt 321, 46 LEd(2d) 313 (1975), affirmed by 400 Mich 181, 254 NW(2d) 29 (1977), cert denied 434 US 861, 98 SCt 189, 54 LEd(2d) 135 (1977)	19.07(C), 19.08(A), 19.09(A), 19.11(D)
Michigan v Summers: 452 US 692, 101 SCt 2587, 69 LEd(2d) 340 (1981)	8.05(B), 8.05(C)
Michigan v Thomas: 458 US 259, 102 SCt 3079, 73 LEd(2d) 750 (1982)	9.04(B), 12.02
Michigan v Tucker: 417 US 433, 94 SCt 2357, 41 LEd(2d) 182 (1974)	2.07(B), 19.03(C)
Michigan v Tyler: 436 US 499, 98 SCt 1942, 56 LEd(2d) 486 (1978)	9.04(A), 9.04(D), 10.03
Middleburg Heights v Theiss: 28 App(3d) 1, 28 OBR 9, 501 NE(2d) 1226 (Cuyahoga 1985)	5.04(A), 7.03, 8.03(F)
Middleton v McGuire: No. CA94-11-202, 1995 WL 591238 (12th Dist Ct App, Butler, 10-9-95	5.02(B)
Mignano; State v: No. 14223, 1990 WL 18129 (9th Dist Ct App, Summit, 2-28-90)	17.04
Milam; State v: 108 App 254, 156 NE(2d) 840 (Cuyahoga 1959)	4.02
Miles; State v: 55 App(3d) 210, 563 NE(2d) 344 (Cuyahoga 1988)	20.06
Milewski; Akron v: 21 App(3d) 140, 21 OBR 149, 487 NE(2d) 582 (Summit 1985)	18.02, 19.06
Miley; State v: No. 56168, 1989 WL 136352 (8th Dist Ct App, Cuyahoga, 11-9-89)	2.07(G), 8.03(C), 8.04
Miller; State v: No. 14973, 1991 WL 149582 (9th Dist Ct App, Summit, 7-31-91), cert denied 503 US 998, 112 SCt 1705, 118 LEd(2d) 413 (1992)	18.04(C)
Miller; State v: 70 App(3d) 727, 591 NE(2d) 1355 (Highland 1990)	5.02(B), 7.03
Miller; State v: No. 8-89-3 et al., 1990 WL 113542 (3d Dist Ct App, Logan, 7-26-90)	6.02
Miller; United States v: 425 US 435, 96 SCt 1619, 48 LEd(2d) 71 (1976)	1.04
Milligan; State v: 40 OS(3d) 341, 533 NE(2d) 724 (1988)	1.04
Mills; State v: No. C-880581, 1990 WL 203563 (1st Dist Ct App, Hamilton, 12-12-90), affirmed by 70 OS(3d) 1407, 637 NE(2d) 5 (1994)	3.04(B)
Mills; State v: No. CA-85-21, 1986 WL 4621 (5th Dist Ct App, Muskingum, 4-14-86), appeal dismissed sub nom State v McHenry, 53 OS(3d) 703, 558 NE(2d) 57 (1990)	3.06
Mimms; Pennsylvania v: 434 US 106, 98 SCt 330, 54 LEd(2d) 331 (1977)	9.04(B), 11.06, 14.06(B), 15.04
Mincey v Arizona: 437 US 385, 98 SCt 2408, 57 LEd(2d) 290 (1978), cert denied 469 US 1040, 105 SCt 521, 83 LEd(2d) 409 (1984), modified sub nom Arizona v Hicks, 480 US 321, 107 SCt 1149, 94 LEd(2d) 347 (1987)	9.04(A), 10.03, 19.12
Minick; United States v: 455 A(2d) 874 (DC Ct App 1983), cert denied 464 US 831, 104 SCt 111, 78 LEd(2d) 112 (1983)	5.04(A)
Minick; United States v: 438 A(2d) 205 (DC Ct App 1981)	5.04(A)
Minjares; California v: 443 US 916, 921, 100 SCt 9, 61 LEd(2d) 892 (1979)	3.04(A)
Minnesota v Dickerson: 508 US 366, 113 SCt 2130, 124 LEd(2d) 334 (1993)	13.05, 14.04
Minnesota v Murphy: 465 US 420, 104 SCt 1136, 79 LEd(2d) 409 (1984)	19.05

Casename   **Text Section(s)**

Minnesota v Olson: 495 US 91, 110 SCt 1684, 109 LEd(2d) 85 (1990)   1.01, 1.04,
                                                                                 2.07(H),
                                                                                 5.04(A),
                                                                                 9.04(A), 10.02,
                                                                                 18.03

Minnick v Mississippi: 498 US 146, 111 SCt 486, 112 LEd(2d) 489 (1990)   19.01(A),
                                                                                 19.08(F)

Miranda v Arizona: 384 US 436, 86 SCt 1602, 16 LEd(2d) 694 (1966)   2.07(B), 17.02,
                                                                                 19.02, 19.03(A),
                                                                                 19.03(C), 19.05,
                                                                                 19.06, 19.07(B),
                                                                                 19.07(C),
                                                                                 19.08(A),
                                                                                 19.08(C),
                                                                                 19.09(A),
                                                                                 19.11(A),
                                                                                 19.11(D), 19.12

Mississippi; Brown v: 297 US 278, 56 SCt 461, 80 LEd 682 (1936)   19.01(B)
Mississippi; Davis v: 394 US 721, 89 SCt 1394, 22 LEd(2d) 676 (1969), cert denied 409   4.02, 14.05
   US 855, 93 SCt 191, 34 LEd(2d) 99 (1972)
Mississippi; Minnick v: 498 US 146, 111 SCt 486, 112 LEd(2d) 489 (1990)   19.01(A),
                                                                                 19.08(F)

Mitchell; State v: No. 1480, 1988 WL 125021 (4th Dist Ct App, Ross, 11-23-88)   13.03
Mitchell; State v: 42 OS(2d) 447, 329 NE(2d) 682 (1975)   18.02
Mobley; State v: No. CA88-08-063, 1989 WL 53604 (12th Dist Ct App, Warren, 5-22-   2.06, 3.06
   89), appeal dismissed by 45 OS(3d) 712, 545 NE(2d) 900 (1989)
Monclavo-Cruz; United States v: 662 F(2d) 1285 (9th Cir Ariz 1981)   11.11(D)
Moncrief; State v: 69 App(2d) 51, 431 NE(2d) 336 (Cuyahoga 1980)   14.06(B), 15.04
Montgomery; United States v: 714 F(2d) 201 (1st Cir Mass 1983)   19.08(E)
Montoya de Hernandez; United States v: 473 US 531, 105 SCt 3304, 87 LEd(2d) 381 14.05, 16.05(B)
   (1985)
Moody; State v: 30 App(3d) 44, 30 OBR 99, 506 NE(2d) 256 (Hamilton 1985)   8.05(C), 16.04
Moody; State v: 55 OS(2d) 64, 377 NE(2d) 1008 (1978)   20.06
Mooney v Holohan: 294 US 103, 55 SCt 340, 79 LEd 791 (1935)   19.01(B)
Moon; State v: 74 App(3d) 162, 598 NE(2d) 726 (Lorain 1991)   18.04(C)
Moore; Cincinnati v: Nos. C-880689 et al., 1989 WL 136387 (1st Dist Ct App,   18.04(C)
   Hamilton, 11-15-89)
Moore v Dempsey: 261 US 86, 43 SCt 265, 67 LEd 543 (1923)   19.01(B)
Moore v Illinois: 434 US 220, 98 SCt 458, 54 LEd(2d) 424 (1977), cert denied 440 US   20.03
   919, 99 SCt 1242, 59 LEd(2d) 471 (1979)
Moore; State v: 28 App(3d) 10, 28 OBR 19, 501 NE(2d) 1209 (Summit 1985)   6.02
Morales; State v: 92 App(3d) 580, 636 NE(2d) 404 (Cuyahoa 1993)   14.03(B)
Moran v Burbine: 475 US 412, 106 SCt 1135, 89 LEd(2d) 410 (1986)   19.03(C),
                                                                                 19.09(C),
                                                                                 19.10(B),
                                                                                 19.10(C)

Moreland; State v: 50 OS(3d) 58, 552 NE(2d) 894 (1990), cert denied 498 US 882, 111   19.12
   SCt 231, 112 LEd(2d) 185 (1990)
Morgan; State v: 55 App(3d) 182, 563 NE(2d) 307 (Mercer 1988)   7.02, 8.03(F)
Morris Investment Co, Inc; Cincinnati v: 6 Misc(2d) 1, 6 OBR 80, 451 NE(2d) 259 16.04
   (Muni, Hamilton 1982)
Morrison; Kimmelman v: 477 US 365, 106 SCt 2574, 91 LEd(2d) 305 (1986)   2.04
Morris; State v: No. 10992, 1989 WL 145175 (2d Dist Ct App, Montgomery, 11-29-89)   10.02
Morris; State v: 48 App(3d) 137, 548 NE(2d) 969 (Cuyahoga 1988)   3.05(B),
                                                                                 14.02(D)

Morris; State v: 42 OS(2d) 307, 329 NE(2d) 85 (1975), cert denied sub nom   2.08
   McSpadden v Ohio, 423 US 1049, 96 SCt 774, 46 LEd(2d) 637 (1976)
Mosher; State v: 37 App(3d) 50, 523 NE(2d) 527 (Summit 1987)   2.07(G)

Casename	Text Section(s)
Ohio; Haley v: 332 US 596, 68 SCt 302, 92 LEd 224 (1948), cert denied 337 US 945, 69 SCt 1501, 93 LEd 1748 (1949)	19.01(C)
Ohio; Mapp v: 367 US 643, 81 SCt 1684, 6 LEd(2d) 1081 (1961)	1.01, 1.02, 2.01, 2.02, 2.03, 2.04, 3.04(A)
Ohio; Martin v: 480 US 228, 107 SCt 1098, 94 LEd(2d) 267 (1987)	4.03(D)
Ohio; McLeod v: 381 US 356, 85 SCt 1556, 14 LEd(2d) 682 (1965)	19.01(D)
Ohio; Smith v: 494 US 541, 110 SCt 1288, 108 LEd(2d) 464 (1990)	1.02, 3.04(A), 11.02, 12.04
Ohio; Terry v: 392 US 1, 88 SCt 1868, 20 LEd(2d) 889 (1968)	1.03, 1.04, 1.06, 2.04, 3.04(B), 3.05(B), 4.02, 8.05(B), 8.05(C), 9.04(B), 11.06, 14.01, 14.02(A), 14.02(B), 14.03(A), 14.04, 14.05, 18.01
Oklahoma; Lyons v: 322 US 596, 64 SCt 1208, 88 LEd 1481 (1944)	19.01(B)
Oliver, In re: No. L-89-118, 1989 WL 155193 (6th Dist Ct App, Lucas, 12-22-89)	14.03(B)
Oliver; State v: 91 App(3d) 607, 632 NE(2d) 1382 (Wayne 1993)	10.02, 10.03
Oliver v United States: 466 US 170, 104 SCt 1735, 80 LEd(2d) 214 (1984)	1.04
Olson; Minnesota v: 495 US 91, 110 SCt 1684, 109 LEd(2d) 85 (1990)	1.01, 1.04, 2.07(H), 5.04(A), 9.04(A), 10.02, 18.03
Opperman; South Dakota v: 428 US 364, 96 SCt 3092, 49 LEd(2d) 1000 (1976)	12.05(A)
Opperman; State v: 247 NW(2d) 673 (SD 1976)	12.05(C)
Order Requiring Fingerprinting of Juvenile, In re: 42 OS(3d) 124, 537 NE(2d) 1286 (1989), cert denied 493 US 857, 110 SCt 165, 107 LEd(2d) 122 (1989)	14.05
Oregon v Bradshaw: 462 US 1039, 103 SCt 2830, 77 LEd(2d) 405 (1983)	19.08(E), 19.09(A)
Oregon v Elstad: 470 US 298, 105 SCt 1285, 84 LEd(2d) 222 (1985)	2.07(B), 19.01(A), 19.03(D), 19.10(B)
Oregon v Hass: 420 US 714, 95 SCt 1215, 43 LEd(2d) 570 (1975)	18.03, 19.12
Oregon v Mathiason: 429 US 492, 97 SCt 711, 50 LEd(2d) 714 (1977)	19.05
Oregon v Szakovits: 32 OS(2d) 271, 291 NE(2d) 742 (1972)	5.02(B)
Orozco v Texas: 394 US 324, 89 SCt 1095, 22 LEd(2d) 311 (1969)	19.05
Orrick; Fairborn v: 49 App(3d) 94, 550 NE(2d) 488 (Greene 1988)	14.05
Ortega; O'Connor v: 50 F(3d) 778, 31 Fed R Serv(3d) 984 (1995)	2.04
Ortega; O'Connor v: 480 US 709, 107 SCt 1492, 94 LEd(2d) 714 (1987)	2.04, 16.01, 16.05(C)
Osborne; Zanesville v: 73 App(3d) 580, 597 NE(2d) 1200 (Muskingum 1992), appeal dismissed by 64 OS(3d) 1414, 593 NE(2d) 4 (1992)	4.02, 20.05

P

Padilla; United States v: 508 US 77, 113 SCt 1936, 123 LEd2d 635 (1993)	18.03
Paladin; State v: 48 App(3d) 16, 548 NE(2d) 263 (Lake 1988)	3.05(D), 19.09(C)
Palicki; State v: 97 App(3d) 175, 646 (2d) 494 (Wood 1994)	1.04
Palider; State v: No. 12557, 1987 WL 6964 (9th Dist Ct App, Summit, 2-18-87)	6.03
Palko v Connecticut: 302 US 319, 58 SCt 149, 82 LEd 288 (1937), superseded by statute as stated in Condemarin v University Hosp, 775 P(2d) 348, 54 ED Law Rptr 669 (Utah 5-1-89)	1.01
Palladino; South Euclid v: 93 Abs 24, 193 NE(2d) 560 (Muni, South Euclid 1963)	11.10(A)

Casename	Text Section(s)
Palmer; Hudson v: 468 US 517, 104 SCt 3194, 82 LEd(2d) 393 (1984)	1.04
Paltani; Cleveland v: No. 60255, 1991 WL 76103 (8th Dist Ct App, Cuyahoga, 5-9-91)	14.06(D), 15.07
Pamer; State v: 70 App(3d) 540, 591 NE(2d) 801 (Wayne 1990)	13.02(C), 17.04
Parma v Jackson: 58 App(3d) 17, 568 NE(2d) 702 (Cuyahoga 1989)	10.02
Parobek; State v: 49 OS(3d) 61, 550 NE(2d) 476 (1990)	2.08
Passaro; United States v: 624 F(2d) 938 (9th Cir Cal 1980) (a wallet is an element of an arrestee's clothing), cert denied 449 US 1113, 101 SCt 925, 66 LEd(2d) 842 (1981)	11.11(D)
Patterson v Illinois: 487 US 285, 108 SCt 2389, 101 LEd(2d) 261 (1988)	19.11(C)
Patterson; State v: 95 App(3d) 255, 642 NE(2d) 390 (Lake 1993), appeal dismissed by 68 OS(3d) 1470, 628 NE(2d) 1389 (1994)	14.03(B), 17.03, 19.10(C)
Paul; State v: 87 App(3d) 309, 622 NE(2d) 349 (Medina 1993)	17.04
Payne v Arkansas: 356 US 560, 78 SCt 844, 2 LEd(2d) 975 (1958)	19.01(C)
Payner; United States v: 447 US 727, 100 SCt 2439, 65 LEd(2d) 468 (1980)	18.03
Payton v New York: 445 US 573, 100 SCt 1371, 63 LEd(2d) 639 (1980)	1.01, 2.03, 2.06, 2.07(C), 5.04(A), 9.04(A), 10.02, 10.04, 11.08(B)
Peay; State v: 62 Misc(2d) 92, 592 NE(2d) 926 (CP, Lucas 1991)	2.03, 5.02(C)
Peeples; State v: 94 App(3d) 34, 640 NE(2d) 208 (Pickaway 1994), appeal dismissed by 70 OS(3d) 1445, 639 NE(2d) 113 (1994)	19.05
Peltier; United States v: 422 US 531, 95 SCt 2313, 45 LEd(2d) 374 (1975)	2.04
Pembaur; State v: 9 OS(3d) 136, 9 OBR 385, 459 NE(2d) 217 (1984), cert denied 467 US 1219, 104 SCt 2668, 81 LEd(2d) 373 (1984)	5.04(B), 7.03
Penn; State v: 61 OS(3d) 720, 576 NE(2d) 790 (1991)	9.04(C), 13.02(C), 16.04, 17.04
Pennsylvania v Bruder: 488 US 9, 109 SCt 205, 102 LEd(2d) 172 (1988)	19.05
Pennsylvania v Mimms: 434 US 106, 98 SCt 330, 54 LEd(2d) 331 (1977)	9.04(B), 11.06, 14.06(B), 15.04
Pennsylvania v Muniz: 496 US 582, 110 SCt 2638, 110 LEd(2d) 528 (1990)	19.06
People v Belton: 55 NY(2d) 49, 447 NYS(2d) 873, 432 NE(2d) 745 (1982)	11.10(D)
People v Collin: 35 Cal App(3d) 416, 110 Cal Rptr 869 (1973)	11.07
People v Floyd: 26 NY(2d) 558, 312 NYS(2d) 193, 260 NE(2d) 815 (1970)	11.03, 11.10(B)
People v Gomez: 632 P(2d) 586 (Colo 1981), cert denied 455 US 943, 102 SCt 1439, 71 LEd(2d) 655 (1982)	11.10(C)
People v Griminger: 71 NY(2d) 635, 529 NYS(2d) 55, 524 NE(2d) 409 (1988)	1.01, 1.02
People v Martin: 45 Cal(2d) 755, 290 P(2d) 855 (1955), superseded by constitutional amendment as stated in People v Daan, 161 CalApp(3d) 22, 207 Cal Rptr 228 (1984)	18.03
People v Oates: 698 P(2d) 811 (Colo 1985)	1.01
People v Ocasio: 85 NY(2d) 982, 629 NYS(2d) 161, 652 NE(2d) 907 (1995)	15.02
People of State California; Adamson v: 332 US 46, 67 SCt 1672, 91 LEd 1903 (1947)	1.02
People v Pettingill: 21 Cal(3d) 231, 578 P(2d) 108 (1978)	19.07(C)
People v Sturgis: 58 Ill(2d) 211, 317 NE(2d) 545 (1974), cert denied 420 US 936, 95 SCt 1144, 43 LEd(2d) 412 (1975)	18.03
People v Superior Court of Yolo County: 3 Cal(3d) 807, 478 P(2d) 449, 91 Cal Rptr 729 (1970)	11.07
Perkins; Illinois v: 496 US 292, 110 SCt 2394, 110 LEd(2d) 243 (1990), cert denied 114 SCt 2692, 129 LEd(2d) 823 (1994)	19.01(A), 19.06, 19.11(D)
Perkins; State v: 18 OS(3d) 193, 18 OBR 259, 480 NE(2d) 763 (1985)	2.07(G)
Perryman; State v: 49 OS(2d) 14, 358 NE(2d) 1040 (1976), vacated in part by 438 US 911, 98 SCt 3136, 57 LEd(2d) 1156 (1978)	20.06
Perry; State v: Nos. 479, 480, 1985 WL 9481 (4th Dist Ct App, Jackson, 6-7-85)	17.03
Person; State v: 34 Misc 97, 298 NE(2d) 922 (Muni, Toledo 1973)	1.04, 17.04
Peters; State v: 12 App(2d) 83, 231 NE(2d) 91 (Franklin 1967)	19.05

Casename   **Text Section(s)**

Petrosky; State v: Nos. C-900264, C-900265, 1991 WL 40550 (1st Dist Ct App,   5.04(A),
   Hamilton, 3-27-91), appeal dismissed by 61 OS(3d) 1428, 575 NE(2d) 216 (1991)   18.04(C)
Pettingill; People v: 21 Cal(3d) 231, 578 P(2d) 108 (1978)   19.07(C)
Pettry; State v: Nos. 617, 618, 1990 WL 119162 (4th Dist Ct App, Jackson, 8-9-90),   7.06
   appeal dismissed by 56 OS(3d) 707, 565 NE(2d) 602 (1990)
Pi Kappa Alpha Fraternity; State v: 23 OS(3d) 141, 23 OBR 295, 491 NE(2d) 1129   1.04, 17.02
   (1986), cert denied 479 US 827, 107 SCt 104, 93 LEd(2d) 54 (1986)
Pinson; State v: No. 14294, 1994 WL 721582 (2d Dist Ct App, Montgomery, 12-23-94)   16.05(E)
Pitts; State v: 31 Misc(2d) 10, 509 NE(2d) 1284 (Muni, Hamilton 1986)   7.03
Place; United States v: 462 US 696, 103 SCt 2637, 77 LEd(2d) 110 (1983)   1.04, 9.04(A)
Plummer; State v: 22 OS(3d) 292, 22 OBR 461, 490 NE(2d) 902 (1986)   2.03
Polansky; State v: No. 45402, 1983 WL 3012 (8th Dist Ct App, Cuyahoga, 5-19-83)   2.08
Ponder; State v: No. 11187, 1989 WL 5803 (2d Dist Ct App, Montgomery, 1-26-89)   14.03(B)
Pope; United States v: 561 F(2d) 663 (6th Cir Ohio 1977)   1.05(C), 3.05(B)
Portash; New Jersey v: 440 US 450, 99 SCt 1292, 59 LEd(2d) 501 (1979)   19.12
Posey; State v: 40 OS(3d) 420, 534 NE(2d) 61 (1988), cert denied 492 US 907, 109 SCt 17.02
   3217, 106 LEd(2d) 567 (1989)
Potts; State v: No. 93 CA 29, 1994 WL 693916 (4th Dist Ct App, Washington, 12-7-94) 15.04
Powell v Alabama: 287 US 45, 53 SCt 55, 77 LEd 158 (1932)   19.01(D)
Powell; Stone v: 428 US 465, 96 SCt 3037, 49 LEd(2d) 1067 (1976)   2.04
Preston v United States: 376 US 364, 84 SCt 881, 11 LEd(2d) 777 (1964)   11.10(A)
Price; State v: 80 App(3d) 108, 608 NE(2d) 1088 (Wayne 1992)   3.05(B)
Prichard; United States v: 645 F(2d) 854 (10th Cir NM 1981), cert denied 454 US 832, 14.06(D), 15.07
   102 SCt 130, 70 LEd(2d) 110 (1981)
Prince; State v: 52 Misc 93, 369 NE(2d) 823 (CP, Fulton 1977)   8.03(B)
Prouse; Delaware v: 440 US 648, 99 SCt 1391, 59 LEd(2d) 660 (1979)   2.04, 14.06(A),
                                                                                 14.06(C),
                                                                                 14.06(D), 15.02,
                                                                                 15.06, 15.07
Pruitt; State v: 97 App(3d) 258, 646 NE(2d) 547 (Trumbull 1994)   8.03(C)
PruneYard Shopping Center v Robins: 447 US 74, 100 SCt 2035, 64 LEd(2d) 741   1.02
   (1980)
Prysock; California v: 453 US 355, 101 SCt 2806, 69 LEd(2d)696 (1981)   19.03(C)
Pugh; Gerstein v: 420 US 103, 95 SCt 854, 43 LEd(2d) 54 (1975)   4.01, 5.05

Q

Quarles; New York v: 467 US 649, 104 SCt 2626, 81 LEd(2d) 550 (1984)   2.07(B),
                                                                                 19.01(A), 19.04
Quintero; Colorado v: 464 US 1014, 104 SCt 543, 78 LEd(2d) 719 (1983)   2.05

R

Rabinowitz; United States v: 339 US 56, 70 SCt 430, 94 LEd(2d) 653 (1950), overruled 9.02, 9.04(C),
   by Chimel v California, 395 US 752, 89 SCt 2034, 23 LEd(2d) 685 (1969)   11.08(A)
Railway Labor Executives' Assn; Skinner v: 489 US 602, 109 SCt 1402, 103 LEd(2d)   16.01, 16.05(D)
   639 (1989)
Raines; State v: No. 1426, 1988 WL 125031 (4th Dist Ct App, Ross, 11-16-88)   11.04(C)
Rainey; State v: No. 11380, 1989 WL 73985 (2d Dist Ct App, Montgomery, 7-6-89)   11.02
Rakas v Illinois: 439 US 128, 99 SCt 421, 58 LEd(2d) 387 (1978)   18.03
Ratcliff; State v: 95 App(3d) 199, 642 NE(2d) 31 (Ashland 1994)   12.02, 15.02
Rawlings v Kentucky: 448 US 98, 100 SCt 2556, 65 LEd(2d) 633 (1980)   11.02, 18.03
Reasch; Hamilton v: 98 App(3d) 814, 649 NE(2d) 922 (Butler 1994)   14.03(A)
Recklaw; Akron v: No. 14671, 1991 WL 11392 (9th Dist Ct App, Summit, 1-30-91)   5.04(A)
Rees; State v: No. 88-CA-17, 1989 WL 145614 (4th Dist Ct App, Gallia, 10-27-89)   2.06
Reeves; United States v: 594 F(2d) 536 (6th Cir Ohio 1979), cert denied 442 US 946, 17.04
   99 SCt 2893, 61 LEd(2d) 317 (1979)
Reid v Georgia: 448 US 438, 100 SCt 2752, 65 LEd(2d) 890 (1980), cert denied 454 US 14.02(C)
   883, 102 SCt 369, 70 LEd(2d) 195 (1981)
Removal of Pickering, In re: 25 App(2d) 58, 266 NE(2d) 248 (Logan 1970)   4.03(C)

Casename	Text Section(s)
Renda; United States v: 567 FSupp 487 (ED Va 1983), affirmed by 758 F(2d) 649 (4th Cir Va 1985)	19.08(E)
Retherford; State v: 93 App(3d) 586, 639 NE(2d) 498 (Montgomery 1994), appeal dismissed by 69 OS(3d) 1488, 635 NE(2d) 43 (1994)	15.02, 15.06
Retherford; State v: No. 13987, 1994 WL 459921 (2d Dist Ct App, Montgomery, 3-16-94)	14.06(C), 17.02
Reymann; State v: 55 App(3d) 222, 563 NE(2d) 749 (Summit 1989), appeal dismissed by 42 OS(3d) 702, 536 NE(2d) 1171 (1989)	2.03, 5.02(B)
Rhode Island v Innis: 446 US 291, 100 SCt 1682, 64 LEd(2d) 297 (1980), cert denied 456 US 930, 102 SCt 1980, 72 LEd(2d) 447 (1982)	19.06, 19.11(A)
Rhude; State v: 91 App(3d) 623, 632 NE(2d) 1391 (Warren 1993)	15.02
Richardson; State v: 94 App(3d) 501, 641 NE(2d) 216 (Hamilton 1994), appeal dismissed by 70 OS(3d) 1446, 639 NE(2d) 114 (1994)	11.05(C)
Richmond; Rogers v: 365 US 534, 81 SCt 735, 5 LEd(2d) 760 (1961)	19.01(B)
Richmond; United States v: 694 FSupp 1310 (SD Ohio 1988)	8.03(F)
Riggenbach; City of Stow v: 97 App(3d) 661, 647 NE(2d) 246 (Summit 1994)	2.03
Riley; Florida v: 488 US 445, 109 SCt 693, 102 LEd(2d) 835 (1989)	1.04
Riley; State v: 88 App(3d) 468, 624 NE(2d) 302 (Wood 1993)	1.04
Roach; State v: 8 App(3d) 42, 8 OBR 44, 455 NE(2d) 1328 (Warren 1982)	10.02
Robbins v California: 453 US 420, 101 SCt 2841, 69 LEd(2d) 744 (1981), overruled by United States v Ross, 456 US 798, 102 SCt 2157, 72 LEd(2d) 572 (1982)	9.03, 12.02, 12.03
Roberson; Arizona v: 486 US 675, 108 SCt 2093, 100 LEd(2d) 704 (1988)	19.08(C), 19.11(B), 19.11(D)
Roberson; United States v: 6 F(3d) 1088 (5th Cir 1993), cert denied 114 SCt 1322, 127 LEd(2d) 671 (1994)	15.06
Robertson; State v: No. 11572, 1990 WL 65658 (2d Dist Ct App, Montgomery, 5-18-90), appeal dismissed by 55 OS(3d) 713, 563 NE(2d) 722 (1990)	20.03, 20.07(A)
Roberts; State v: 32 OS(3d) 225, 513 NE(2d) 720 (1987)	19.05
Roberts; State v: 62 OS(2d) 170, 405 NE(2d) 247 (1980), cert denied 449 US 879, 101 SCt 227, 66 LEd(2d) 102 (1980)	3.06
Robinette; State v: 73 OS(3d) 650, 653 NE(2d) 695 (1995)	1.01, 1.04, 11.05(D), 14.02(D), 15.05, 15.06, 17.02
Robinson; State v: 58 OS(2d) 478, 391 NE(2d) 317 (1979), cert denied 444 US 942, 100 SCt 297, 62 LEd(2d) 309 (1979)	12.05(A), 12.05(C)
Robinson; United States v: 414 US 218, 94 SCt 467, 38 LEd(2d) 427 (1973)	9.04(B), 11.03, 11.04(B), 11.04(C), 11.10(C), 11.11(B), 14.06(D), 15.07
Robins; PruneYard Shopping Center v: 447 US 74, 100 SCt 2035, 64 LEd(2d) 741 (1980)	1.02
Rochin v California: 342 US 165, 72 SCt 205, 96 LEd 183 (1952)	2.02, 11.04(D)
Rodgers; Dayton v: 60 OS(2d) 162, 398 NE(2d) 781 (1979)	8.03(G)
Rodriguez; Florida v: 469 US 1, 105 SCt 308, 83 LEd(2d) 165 (1984)	14.02(C)
Rodriguez; Illinois v: 497 US 177, 110 SCt 2793, 111 LEd(2d) 148 (1990)	2.05, 2.06, 17.04
Rodriguez; State v: 66 App(3d) 5, 583 NE(2d) 384 (Wood 1990)	2.06, 18.04(C)
Rodriguez; State v: 64 App(3d) 183, 580 NE(2d) 1127 (Wood 1989)	2.06
Roe; State v: 41 OS(3d) 18, 535 NE(2d) 1351 (1989), affirmed by 1992 WL 246023 (1992), appeal dismissed by 66 OS(3d) 1444, 609 NE(2d) 171 (1993)	3.02(D), 19.06
Rogers v Richmond: 365 US 534, 81 SCt 735, 5 LEd(2d) 760 (1961)	19.01(B)
Rogers; State v: 32 OS(3d) 70, 512 NE(2d) 581 (1987), cert denied 484 US 958, 108 SCt 358, 98 LEd(2d) 383 (1987)	19.12
Rogers; State v: 43 OS(2d) 28, 330 NE(2d) 674 (1975), cert denied 423 US 1061, 96 SCt 801, 46 LEd(2d) 653 (1976)	5.02(A)

Casename	Text Section(s)
Smith; State v: No. C-880287, 1990 WL 73974 (1st Dist Ct App, Hamilton, 6-6-90)	19.09(C), 19.10(C)
Smith; State v: 45 OS(3d) 255, 544 NE(2d) 239 (1989), reversed by 494 US 541, 110 SCt 1288, 108 LEd(2d) 464 (1990)	11.02, 14.02(D), 14.03(B)
Smith; State v: No. 50700, 1986 WL 5955 (8th Dist Ct App, Cuyahoga, 5-22-86)	2.08
Smith; State v: 56 OS(2d) 405, 384 NE(2d) 280 (1978)	14.04, 15.06
Smotherman; State v: No. 93WD082, 1994 WL 395128 (6th Dist Ct App, Wood, 7-29-94)	15.06
Sniezek; State v: 8 App(3d) 147, 8 OBR 204, 456 NE(2d) 542 (Cuyahoga 1982)	16.04
Snyder v State: 538 NE(2d) 961 (Ind App 1989)	14.06(E), 15.08
Snyder; State v: No. WD-94-098, 1995 WL 504758 (6th Dist Ct App, Wood, 8-25-95)	7.02
Sokolow; United States v: 490 US 1, 109 SCt 1581, 104 LEd(2d) 1 (1989)	14.03(A)
Soldal v Cook County, Illinois: 506 US 56, 113 SCt 538, 121 LEd(2d) 450 (1992)	1.06
Sopko v Maxwell: 3 OS(2d) 123, 209 NE(2d) 201 (1965)	6.02
South Carolina; Harris v: 338 US 68, 69 SCt 1354, 93 LEd 1815 (1949)	19.01(C)
South Dakota v Neville: 459 US 553, 103 SCt 916, 74 LEd(2d) 748 (1983)	11.04(E)
South Dakota v Opperman: 428 US 364, 96 SCt 3092, 49 LEd(2d) 1000 (1976)	12.05(A)
South Euclid v Di Franco: 4 Misc 148, 206 NE(2d) 432 (Muni, South Euclid 1965)	17.02
South Euclid v Palladino: 93 Abs 24, 193 NE(2d) 560 (Muni, South Euclid 1963)	11.10(A)
South Euclid v Samartini: 5 Misc 38, 204 NE(2d) 425 (Muni, South Euclid 1965)	6.02
Spano v New York: 360 US 315, 79 SCt 1202, 3 LEd(2d) 1265 (1959)	19.01(C)
Spaulding; State v: 239 Kan 439, 720 P(2d) 1047 (1986)	2.06
Spaw; State v: 18 App(3d) 77, 480 NE(2d) 1138 (Defiance 1984)	8.03(D)
Spencer; State v: 75 App(3d) 581, 600 NE(2d) 335 (Montgomery 1991)	11.05(C)
Spencer; State v: No. 11740, 1990 WL 68957 (2d Dist Ct App, Montgomery, 5-18-90)	18.03
Sperry; State v: 47 Misc 1, 351 NE(2d) 807 (CP, Montgomery 1974)	18.04(C)
Spinelli v United States: 393 US 410, 89 SCt 584, 21 LEd(2d) 637 (1969), overruled by Illinois v Gates, 462 US 213, 103 SCt 2317, 76 LEd(2d) 527 (1983)	1.05(B), 3.03(B), 3.05(D)
Spitler; State v: 75 App(3d) 341, 599 NE(2d) 408 (Franklin 1991), appeal dismissed by 63 OS(3d) 1409, 585 NE(2d) 834 (1992)	2.06
Sprague; State v: Nos. CA88-05-037, CA88-06-049, 1989 WL 36301 (12th Dist Ct App, Clermont, 4-17-89)	12.04
Spring; Colorado v: 479 US 564, 107 SCt 851, 93 LEd(2d) 954 (1987)	19.03(C), 19.09(C)
Stacy; State v: No. 87-CA-23, 1990 WL 71905 (4th Dist Ct App, Pickaway, 5-22-90)	19.09(B), 19.09(C)
Stacy; State v: 9 App(3d) 55, 9 OBR 74, 458 NE(2d) 403 (Lorain 1983)	5.02(B)
Stanford Daily; Zurcher v: 436 US 547, 98 SCt 1970, 56 LEd(2d) 525 (1978)	1.05(A), 3.02(A), 8.03(C)
Stansbury v California: 114 SCt 1526, 128 LEd(2d) 293 (1994), cert denied 116 SCt 320, 133 LEd(2d) 222 (1995)	19.05
Stargell; State v: No. 14780, 1995 WL 141468 (2d Dist Ct App, Montgomery, 3-29-95)	13.05
State v—See name of defendant.:	
State;—See name of plaintiff.:	
Steagald v United States: 451 US 204, 101 SCt 1642, 68 LEd(2d) 38 (1981)	2.03, 5.04(B), 9.04(A), 10.02, 10.04, 11.08(B)
Stebner; State v: 46 App(3d) 145, 546 NE(2d) 428 (Portage 1988)	8.03(C), 13.03
Steele v United States: 267 US 498, 45 SCt 414, 69 LEd 757 (1925)	8.03(C)
Stein v New York: 346 US 156, 73 SCt 1077, 97 LEd 1522 (1953), overruled by Jackson v Denno, 378 US 368, 84 SCt 1774, 12 LEd(2d) 908 (1964)	19.01(C)
Stephen; City of Cleveland v: 93 App(3d) 827, 639 NE(2d) 1258 (Cuyahoga 1994)	14.03(B)
Steusloff; State v: No. F-85-6, 1986 WL 2956 (6th Dist Ct App, Fulton, 3-7-86)	7.03
Stitz; Michigan Dept of State Police v: 496 US 444, 110 SCt 2481, 110 LEd(2d) 412 (1990), affirmed by 443 Mich 744, 506 NW(2d) 209 (1993)	2.04, 14.06(E), 15.08
Stoddard; State v: No. 9-89-5, 1990 WL 72397 (3d Dist Ct App, Marion, 5-25-90)	18.03
Stoken; State v: No. C-870013, 1987 WL 28162 (1st Dist Ct App, Hamilton, 12-9-87)	17.04
Stokes; Fricker v: 22 OS(3d) 202, 22 OBR 354, 490 NE(2d) 577 (1986)	11.07

Casename	Text Section(s)
Texas v Brown: 460 US 730, 103 SCt 1535, 75 LEd(2d) 502 (1983)	1.04, 1.05(A), 3.02(A), 3.03(B), 13.01, 13.03, 13.04
Texas; Brown v: 443 US 47, 99 SCt 2637, 61 LEd(2d) 357 (1979)	14.02(C), 14.03(B), 14.05
Texas; Orozco v: 394 US 324, 89 SCt 1095, 22 LEd(2d) 311 (1969)	19.05
Texas; Ward v: 316 US 547, 62 SCt 1139, 86 LEd 1663 (1942)	19.01(C)
Texas v White: 423 US 67, 96 SCt 304, 46 LEd(2d) 209 (1975)	12.02, 12.04
Texas; White v: 310 US 530, 60 SCt 1032, 84 LEd 1342 (1940)	19.01(C)
Theiss; Middleburg Heights v: 28 App(3d) 1, 28 OBR 9, 501 NE(2d) 1226 (Cuyahoga 1985)	5.04(A), 7.03, 8.03(F)
Thieman; State v: No. 52803, 1987 WL 10592 (8th Dist Ct App, Cuyahoga, 4-30-87)	14.03(B)
Thierbach; State v: 92 App(3d) 365, 635 NE(2d) 1276 (Hamilton 1993)	1.02
Thomas; Michigan v: 458 US 259, 102 SCt 3079, 73 LEd(2d) 750 (1982)	9.04(B), 12.02
Thompson v Louisiana: 469 US 17, 105 SCt 409, 83 LEd(2d) 246 (1984)	9.04(A), 10.01, 10.03
Thompson; State v: 72 Misc(2d) 39, 655 NE(2d) 835 (CP, Lucas 1995)	2.07(G), 10.04
Thompson; State v: 33 OS(3d) 1, 514 NE(2d) 407 (1987)	2.03, 5.04(A)
Thompson; State v: No. 2161, 1986 WL 9363 (9th Dist Ct App, Wayne, 8-27-86)	14.03(B)
Thornton; State v: 51 App(3d) 97, 554 NE(2d) 955 (Cuyahoga 1989)	13.02(C)
Thurman; State v: No. C-790398 (1st Dist Ct App, Hamilton, 4-30-80)	1.04
Timson; State v: 38 OS(2d) 122, 311 NE(2d) 16 (1974)	3.02(A)
Tincher; State v: 47 App(3d) 188, 548 NE(2d) 251 (Preble 1988)	12.03
Tingler; State v: 31 OS(2d) 100, 285 NE(2d) 710 (1972)	20.04
T.L.O.; New Jersey v: 469 US 325, 105 SCt 733, 83 LEd(2d) 720 (1985)	2.04, 2.08, 9.04(A), 16.01, 16.05(B)
Todd; State v: 78 App(3d) 454, 605 NE(2d) 411 (Sandusky 1992)	19.10(C)
Toledo v McHugh: No. CA L-87-008, 1987 WL 19971 (6th Dist Ct App, Lucas, 11-13-87)	2.06
Torres; State v: No. WD-85-64, 1986 WL 9097 (6th Dist Ct App, Wood 8-22-86)	2.06, 5.03, 6.03
Toscanino; United States v: 500 F(2d) 267 (2d Cir NY 1974)	4.01
Townsend v Sain: 372 US 293, 83 SCt 745, 9 LEd(2d) 770 (1963)	19.01(C)
Townsend; State v: 77 App(3d) 651, 603 NE(2d) 261 (Lake 1991)	11.06
Townsend; State v: No. 1618, 1990 WL 138472 (4th Dist Ct App, Ross, 9-14-90)	6.03
Tress; Elyria v: 73 App(3d) 5, 595 NE(2d) 1031 (Lorain 1991)	7.03
Trupiano v United States: 334 US 699, 68 SCt 1229, 92 LEd 1663 (1948), overruled on other grounds by United States v Rabinowitz, 339 US 56, 70 SCt 430, 94 LEd(2d) 653 (1950)	9.02
Tschudy; State v: No. CA-3187, 1986 WL 7459 (5th Dist Ct App, Licking, 6-24-86)	8.03(E)
Tucker; Michigan v: 417 US 433, 94 SCt 2357, 41 LEd(2d) 182 (1974)	2.07(B), 19.03(C)
Tucker; State v: 98 App(3d) 308, 648 NE(2d) 557 (Sandusky 1994), appeal dismissed by 71 OS(3d) 1499, 646 NE(2d) 1124 (1995)	8.03(C), 8.05(C)
Tuff; State v: No. 10-232, 1985 WL 10227 (11th Dist Ct App, Lake, 6-28-85)	2.06
Turkal; State v: 31 Misc 31, 285 NE(2d) 900, 60 OO(2d) 160 (Muni, Franklin 1971)	17.02
Turner; State v: No. 91-L-029, 1991 WL 274504 (11th Dist Ct App, Lake, 12-20-91)	14.03(B)
Turner; State v: No. CA-7865, 1989 WL 154621 (5th Dist Ct App, Stark, 12-11-89)	8.03(F)
Twinsburg v Lochridge: No. 14906, 1991 WL 81653 (9th Dist Ct App, Summit, 5-15-91)	18.04(C)
Twomey; Lego v: 404 US 477, 96 SCt 619, 30 LEd(2d) 618 (1972)	18.04(D), 19.10(C)
Tyler; Michigan v: 436 US 499, 98 SCt 1942, 56 LEd(2d) 486 (1978)	9.04(A), 9.04(D), 10.03

U

| Ulrich; State v: 41 App(3d) 384, 536 NE(2d) 17 (Franklin 1987) | 2.03 |
| Unger; State v: 67 OS(2d) 65, 423 NE(2d) 1078 (1981) | 2.03 |

Appendix B
Table of Laws and Rules

ABBREVIATIONS

Crim R—Rules of Criminal Procedure
Evid R—Ohio Rules of Evidence
Fed Crim R—Federal Criminal Rule
O Const—Ohio Constitution
RC—Ohio Revised Code
USCA—United States Code Annotated
US Const—United States Constitution

O Const	Text Section(s)
Art I §14	1.02, 3.01

RC	Text Section(s)
120.16(F)	19.03(A)
311.31	15.02
505.67	15.02
737.40	15.02
1905.20	6.03
2901.13(E)	7.01
2917.05	4.03(C)
2921.31	7.03
2921.31(A)	7.03
2921.33	7.03
2921.33(A)	7.03
Ch 2933	8.01
2933.23	8.02, 8.03(A), 11.09(B)
2933.231	8.03(F)
2933.231(B)	8.03(F)
2933.231(C)	8.03(F)
2933.231(D)(1)	8.03(F)
2933.231(D)(2)	8.03(F)
2933.24	8.03(A), 8.03(E)
2933.241	8.04
2933.25	8.03(A)
2933.32	2.03, 11.07
2934.14	19.03(A)
2935.01	4.02
2935.03	2.03, 5.02(B)
2935.03(A)	5.02(B)
2935.03(B)	5.02(B)
2935.03(D)	5.02(B)
2935.03(E)	5.02(B)
2935.04	5.02(A)
2935.041	2.08, 5.02(B)
2935.041(E)	5.02(B)
2935.06	5.02(B)
2935.07	5.02(A)
2935.08	5.05
2935.09	6.02
2935.10	6.03, 6.04
2935.11	6.04
2935.12	7.02, 8.03(F)
2935.13	7.06

RC	Text Section(s)
2935.17	6.02
2935.20	2.03, 19.03(A), 19.11(B)
2935.24	7.01
2935.26	2.03, 5.02(C)
2945.55	20.02
2967.15	2.03
4507.35	14.06(A)

Crim R	Text Section(s)
2	8.03(B)
3	6.02, 20.03
4	5.05, 7.06
4.1(B)	5.02(C)
4(A)(1)	6.02, 6.03, 6.04
4(A)(2)	6.04
4(A)(3)	6.04
4(B)	6.04
4(C)(1)	6.05
4(D)	7.01
4(D)(3)	7.04
4(D)(4)	7.05
4(E)(1)	7.06
4(E)(2)	5.05
4(F)	6.04, 7.06, 11.05
9(A)	6.03
11	18.06(B)
12	18.02
12(C)	18.02
12(E)	18.04(D), 18.05
12(H)	18.06(B)
12(J)	3.04(A), 18.06(A)
41	2.03, 2.06, 5.04(A), 8.01, 8.02, 8.03(E), 11.09(B)
41(A)	6.03, 8.03(A)
41(B)	8.03(C)
41(C)	8.02, 8.03(A), 8.03(F)
41(D)	2.03, 8.04
41(F)	8.03(E)
46	6.04
46(D)	6.04
47	18.02

Evid R	Text Section(s)
801(D)(1)(c)	20.02

US Const	Text Section(s)
Am 1	14.03(B)
Am 4	1.03, 1.04, 2.01, 2.02, 2.03, 2.04, 2.05, 2.07(A), 3.01, 4.01, 4.02, 5.02(C), 5.04(B), 8.03(C), 9.01, 10.02, 10.03, 11.01, 11.03, 11.04(C), 11.07, 12.02, 12.03, 12.05(A), 12.05(C), 13.02(B), 13.03, 14.01, 14.02(A), 14.06(A), 16.01, 16.04, 16.05(B), 17.02, 18.03, 18.04(B), 19.04, 20.01

US Const	Text Section(s)
Am 5	2.02, 2.07(B), 19.01(A), 19.01(D), 19.04, 19.08(D), 19.11(A), 19.12, 20.01, 20.07(A)
Am 6	2.04, 19.01(A), 19.01(D), 19.08(D), 19.11(A), 19.11(C), 20.03, 20.05
Am 14	14.03(B), 19.01(D)

USCA	Text Section(s)
42 USCA 1983	11.07

Fed Crim R	Text Section(s)
41(c)(2)	11.09(B)

Appendix C
Bibliography

ARREST, SEARCH AND SEIZURE

Books

American Law Institute. *Model Code of Pre-Arraignment Procedure* (PO Draft). Philadelphia: American Law Institute, 1975.

Amsterdam, A.G. *Trial Manual for the Defense of Criminal Cases.* 4th ed. 2 vols. Philadelphia: American Law Institute—American Bar Association, 1984.

Carr, J.G. *The Law of Electronic Surveillance.* New York: Clark Boardman Co, 1977.

Choper, J.H., Y. Kamisar, and L.H. Tribe. *The Supreme Court: Trends and Development.* Minneapolis: National Practice Institute, 1981-1982.

Foote, C. "The Fourth Amendment: Obstacle or Necessity in the Law of Arrest?" Sowle, C.R. *Police Power & Individual Freedom.* Chicago: Aldine Publishing (1962).

Forst, B., J. Lucianovic, and S.J. Cox. *What Happens After Arrest? A Court Perspective of Police Operations in the District of Columbia.* Washington DC: Institute for Law and Social Research, 1977.

Harney, M.L., and J.C. Cross. *The Informer in Law Enforcement.* 2d ed. Springfield, IL: C.C. Thomas, 1968.

LaFave, W.R. *Search & Seizure: A Treatise on the Fourth Amendment.* 2d ed. St. Paul, MN: West Publishing Co, 1987.

Schroeder, O., and L. Katz. *Ohio Criminal Law and Practice.* 2 vols. Cleveland: Banks-Baldwin Law Publishing Co, 1974-87.

US Comptroller General. *Impact of the Exclusionary Rule on Federal Criminal Prosecutions.* Washington DC: US General Accounting Office, 1979.

Westin, A.F. *Privacy & Freedom.* New York: Atheneum, 1967.

Articles

Adams, J.A., "Anticipatory Search Warrants: Constitutionality, Requirements, and Scope." 79 *Ky L J* 681 (1990-91).

Alpert, G.P. "Telephonic Search Warrants." *U Miami L Rev* 38 (July 1984): 625-35.

Alschuler, A.W. " 'Close Enough for Government Work': The Exclusionary Rule after Leon." *Sup Ct Rev* (1984): 309-58.

Amsterdam, A.G. "Perspectives on the Fourth Amendment." *Minn L Rev* 58 (January 1974): 349-477.

Barrett, E.L. "Personal Rights, Property Rights & the Fourth Amendment." *Sup Ct Rev* (1960): 46-74.

Bernardi, F. "The Exclusionary Rule: Is a Good Faith Standard Needed to Preserve a Liberal Interpretation of the Fourth Amendment?" *De Paul L Rev* 30 (Fall 1980): 51-108.

Bloom, L.H. "The Law Office Search: An Emerging Problem and Some Suggested Solutions." *Geo LJ* 69 (October 1980): 1-100.

Bloom, R. "The Supreme Court and Its Purported Preference for Search Warrants." *Tenn L Rev* 50 (Winter 1983): 231-70.

Bloom, R. "*United States v Leon* and Its Ramifications." *Colo L Rev* 56 (Winter 1985): 247-63.

Bloom, R. "Warrant Requirements—The Burger Court Approach (Warren Burger's Supreme Court)." *Colo L Rev* 53 (Summer 1982): 691-744.

Bradley, C.M. "The 'Good Faith' Exception Cases: Reasonable Exercises in Futility." *Ind L J* 60 (Spring 1985): 287-304.

Burkoff, J.M. "The Court that Devoured the 4th Amendment: The Triumph of an Inconsistent Exclusionary Doctrine." *Or L Rev* 58 (1979): 151-92.

Burkoff, J.M. "Pretext Searches." *Search & Seizure L Rep* 9 (April 1982): 25-30.

Burkoff, J.M. "Search Warrant Execution: Scope and Intensity." *Search & Seizure L Rep* (April 1986): 25-31.

Butterfoss, Edwin J. "Solving the Pretext Puzzle: The Importance of Ulterior Motives and Fabrications in the Supreme Court's Fourth Amendment Pretext Doctrine." 79 *Ky L J* 1 (1990-91).

Cann, S., and B. Egbert. "The Exclusionary Rule: Its Necessity in Constitutional Democracy." *How L J* 23 (Spring 1980): 299-323.

Canon, B. "The Exclusionary Rule: Have the Critics Proven that it Doesn't Deter Police?" *Judicature* 62 (March-April 1979): 398-409.

Canon, B. "Ideology and Reality in the Debate over the Exclusionary Rule: A Conservative Argument for Its Retention." *S Tex L J* 23 (Midwinter 1982): 558-82.

Cantrell, C.L. "Zurcher: Third Party Searches and Freedom of the Press." *Marq L Rev* 62 (Fall 1978): 35-53.

Chardak, S.R. "Airport Drug Stops: Defining Reasonable Suspicion Based on the Characteristics of the Drug Courier Profile." *BCL Rev* 26 (May 1985): 693-726.

Chevigny, P.G. "Police Abuses in Connection with the Law of Search and Seizure." *Crim L Bull* 5 (1969): 3-33.

Chevigny, P.G. "The Right to Resist an Unlawful Arrest." *Yale L J* 78 (May 1969): 1128-50.

Clarke, D.N., and D. Feldman. "Arrest by Any Other Name." *Crim L Rev* (November 1979): 702-07.

Cloud, M. "Search and Seizure by the Numbers: The Drug Courier and Judicial Review of Investigative Formulas." *BUL Rev* 65 (November 1985): 843-921.

Clymer, S. "Warrantless Vehicle Searches and the Fourth Amendment: The Burger Court Attacks the Exclusionary Rule." *Cornell L Rev* 68 (November 1982): 105-45.

Comment. "Alternative Means of Protection for Fourth Amendment Rights: A Proposal for Ohio." 20 *Capital L Rev* 943 (Fall 1991).

Comment. "Expansion of Individual Liberties Under the Ohio Constitution?" *Ohio St L J* 47 (Winter 1986): 221-33.

Comment. "Firemen and the Fourth Amendment: What are the Requirements of a Post-Fire Search?" *Nor Ky L Rev* 13 (Winter 1986): 153-80.

Comment. "Standing to Challenge Searches and Seizures: A Small Group of States Chart Their Own Course." 63 *Temp L Rev* 559 (Fall 1990).

Comment. "The Use of the Drug Courier Profile in Traffic Stops: Valid Police Practice or Fourth Amendment Violation?" 15 *Ohio North L Rev* 593 (1988).

Cook, J.G. "Probable Cause to Arrest." *Vand L Rev* 24 (March 1971): 317-39.

Cook, R. "Law Office Searches." *Ill Bar J* 70 (November 1981): 170-75.

Cooke, W.C. "Airport Security Searches: A Rationale." *Am J Crim L* 2 (February 1973): 128-45.

Daniel, W. "Stop & Frisk." *Ga St Bar J* 17 (August 1980): 6-11.

Davidow, R.P. "Criminal Procedure Ombudsman as a Substitute for the Exclusionary Rule: A Proposal." *Tex Tech L Rev* 4 (Spring 1973): 317-40.

Davies, T. "A Hard Look at What We Know (and Still Need to Learn) About the 'Costs' of the Exclusionary Rule: The NIJ Study and Other Studies of 'Lost' Arrests." *ABF Res J* (1983): 611-90.

Davis, P. "Records of Arrest and Conviction: A Comparative Study of Institutional Abuse." *Creighton L Rev* 13 (Spring 1980): 863-88.

DeJong, R. "The Emerging Good Faith Exception to the Exclusionary Rule." *Notre Dame Law* 57 (October 1981): 112-36.

Doernberg, D.L. " 'The Right of the People': Reconciling Collective and Individual Interests Under the Fourth Amendment." *NYU L Rev* 58 (May 1983): 259-98.

Donnino, W.C., and A.J. Girese. "Exigent Circumstances for a Warrantless Home Arrest." *Alb L Rev* 45 (Fall 1980): 90-115.

Dutile, F. "Freezing the Status Quo in Criminal Investigations: The Melting Pot of Probable Cause & Warrant Requirements." *BCL Rev* 21 (May 1980): 851-86.

Fennelly, J. "Warrant Searches and the Exclusionary Rule: The Rule in Search of a Reason." *J Natl Dist Atty Assn* 17 (Winter 1983): 32-36.

Folk, T. "Case for Constitutional Constraints upon the Power to Make Full Custody Arrests." *Cin L Rev* 48 (1979): 321-43.

Fyfe, J. "Robbins, Belton & Ross—The Policeman's Lot Becomes a Happier One." *Crim L Bull* 18 (September-October 1982): 461-67.

Gardiner, T. "Consent to Search in Response to Police Threats to Seek or Obtain a Search Warrant." *J Crim L* 71 (Summer 1980): 163-72.

Gardner, M. "Consent as a Bar to Fourth Amendment Scope—A Critique of a Common Theory." *J Crim L* 71 (Winter 1980): 443-65.

Gardner, M. "Searches and Seizures of Automobiles and Their Contents: Fourth Amendment Considerations in a Post-Ross World." *Neb L Rev* 62 (Winter 1983): 1-48.

Gardner, M. "Sniffing for Drugs in the Classroom—Perspectives on Fourth Amendment Scope." *NW L Rev* 74 (February 1980): 803-53.

Giannelli, P.C., and F.A. Gilligan. "Prison Search and Seizure: 'Locking' the Fourth Amendment Out of Correctional Facilities." *Va L Rev* 62 (June 1976): 1045-98.

Gless, A. "Arrest & Citation: Definition & Analysis." *Neb L Rev* 59 (Spring 1980): 279-326.

Goldberger, P. "A Guide to Identifying Fourth Amendment Issues." *Search & Seizure L Rep* 13 (May 1986): 33-40.

Goldsmith, M. "The Supreme Court and Title III: Rewriting the Law of Electronic Surveillance." *J Crim L* 74 (Spring 1983): 1-171.

Goldstein, A. "The Search Warrant, the Magistrate, and Judicial Review." *NYU L Rev* 62 (1987): 1173.

Goodpaster, G. "An Essay on Ending the Exclusionary Rule." *Hastings L J* 33 (May 1982): 1065-1108.

Gormley, Ken and Hartman, Rhonda G. "Privacy and the States." 65 *Temp L Rev* 1279 (Winter 1992).

Grano, J.D. "A Dilemma for Defense Counsel: Spinelli-Harris Search Warrants and the Possibility of Police Perjury." *Ill L F* (1971): 405-57.

Grano, J.D. "Probable Cause and Common Sense: A Reply to the Critics of *Illinois v Gates*." *Mich J L Ref* 17 (Spring 1984): 465-521.

Grano, J. "Rethinking the Fourth Amendment Warrant Requirement." *Am Crim L Rev* 19 (Winter 1982): 603-50.

Grossman, S.P. "Sobriety Checkpoints: Roadblocks to Fourth Amendment Protections." *Am J Crim L* 12 (July 1984): 123-67.

Guzik, J. "The Assumption of Risk Doctrine: Erosion of Fourth Amendment Protection Through Fictitious Consent to Search & Seizure." *Santa Clara L Rev* 23 (Fall 1982): 1051-85.

Haemmerle, Todd M. "Florida v. Bostick: The War on Drugs and Evolving Fourth Amendment Standards." 24 *Tol L Rev* 253 (Fall 1992).

Hancock, C. "State Court Activism & Searches Incident to Arrest." *Va L Rev* 68 (May 1982): 1085-1136.

Hatch, O. "Introduction (to Enforcing the Fourth Amendment by Alternatives to the Exclusionary Rule)." *FRD* 95 (1982): 212-14.

Herz, M. "Forfeiture Seizures and the Warrant Requirement." *Chi L Rev* 48 (Fall 1981): 960-91.

Holtz, Larry E. "The 'Plain Touch' Corollary: A Natural and Foreseeable Consequence of the Plain View Doctrine." 95 *Dick L Rev* 521 (Spring 1991).

Imes, L. "Arresting a Suspect in a Third Party's Home: What is Reasonable?" *J Crim L* 72 (Spring 1981): 293-323.

Jacobs, J.B., and N. Strossen. "Mass Investigations Without Individualized Suspicions: A Constitutional and Policy Critique of Drunk Driving Roadblocks." *UC Davis L Rev* 18 (Spring 1985): 595-680.

Jensen, D.L., and R. Hart. "The Good Faith Restatement of the Exclusionary Rule." *J Crim L* 73 (Fall 1982): 916-38.

Jonas, Daniel S. "Pretext Searches and the Fourth Amendment: Unconstitutional Abuses of Power." 137 *Pa L Rev* 1791 (May 1989).

Kamisar, Y. "Does (Did) (Should) the Exclusionary Rule Rest on a 'Principled Basis' Rather than an 'Empirical Proposition' ?" *Creighton L Rev* 16 (Summer 1982-83): 565-667.

Kamisar, Y. "The Exclusionary Rule in Historical Perspective: The Struggle to Make the Fourteenth Amendment More than 'an Empty Blessing.' " *Judicature* 62 (February 1979): 337-50.

Kamisar, Y. "Gates, 'Probable,' 'Good Faith,' and Beyond." *Iowa L Rev* 69 (March 1984): 551-615.

Kamisar, Y. "Is the Exclusionary Rule an 'Illogical' or 'Unnatural' Interpretation of the Fourth Amendment?" *Judicature* 62 (August 1978): 66-84.

Kaplan, J. "The Limits of the Exclusionary Rule." *Stan L Rev* 26 (1974): 1027-55.

Katz, L.R. "The Automobile Exception Transformed: The Rise of a Public Place Exemption to the Warrant Requirement." *Case WR L Rev* 36 (1985-1986): 375-430.

Katz, L.R. "Automobile Searches and Diminished Exceptions in the Warrant Clause." *Am Crim L Rev* 19 (Winter 1982): 557-602.

Katz. L.R. "In Search of a Fourth Amendment for the Twenty-First Century." *Ind L J* 65 (1990): 549.

Katz, L.R. "Reflections on Searches and Seizures & Illegally Seized Evidence in Canada & the United States." *Canada-US L J* 3 (Summer 1980): 103-38.

Katz, L.R. "United States v Ross: Evolving Standards for Warrantless Searches." *NW L Rev* 74 (Spring 1983): 172-208.

Kelder, G., and A.J. Statmen. "Protective Sweep Doctrine: Recurrent Questions Regarding the Propriety of Searches Conducted Contemporaneously with an Arrest On or Near Private Premises." *Syracuse L Rev* 30 (Fall 1979): 973-1092.

Kitch, E. "Katz v United States: The Limits of the Fourth Amendment." *Sup Ct Rev* (1968): 133-52.

Krancer, M. "Stop & Frisk Based upon Anonymous Telephone Tips." *Wash & Lee L Rev* 39 (Fall 1982): 1437-52.

Kuhns, R.B. "The Concept of Personal Aggrievement in Fourth Amendment Standing Cases." *Iowa L Rev* 65 (March 1980): 493-552.

LaCount S.H., and A.J. Girese. "The 'Inevitable Discovery' Rule: An Evolving Exception to the Constitutional Exclusionary Rule." *Alb L Rev* 40 (1976): 483-512.

LaFave, W.R. "Fourth Amendment Vagaries (of Improbable Cause, Imperceptible Plain View, Notorious Privacy and Balancing Askew)." *J Crim L* 74 (Winter 1983): 1171-1224.

LaFave, W.R. "The Fourth Amendment in an Imperfect World: On Drawing 'Bright Lives' and 'Good Faith.' " *U Pitt L Rev* 43 (Winter 1982): 307-61.

LaFave, W.R. "Improving Police Performance Through the Exclusionary Rule—Part II: Defining the Norms and Training the Police." *Mo L Rev* 30 (Summer 1965): 566-610.

LaFave, W.R. "The Seductive Call of Expediency: *US v Leon*, Its Rationale and Its Ramifications," *Vill L Rev* (Fall 1984): 895-931.

LaFave, W.R., and F.J. Remington. "Controlling the Police: The Judge's Role in Making & Reviewing Law Enforcement Decisions." *Mich L Rev* 63 (April 1965): 987-1012.

Larkin, M. "Exigent Circumstances for Warrantless Home Arrest." *Ariz L Rev* 23 (Summer 1981): 1171-84.

Latzer, B. "Searching Cars and Their Contents: United States v Ross." *Crim L Bull* 18 (September-October 1982): 381-405.

Lederer, F.I., and C.M. Lederer. "Admissibility of Evidence Found by Marijuana Detection Dogs." Pamphlet No. 27-50-4, 1973 *Army Law* (April 1983): 12-16.

Lerman, L. "Expansion of Arrest Power: A Key to Effective Intervention." *Vt L Rev* 7 (Spring 1982): 59-70.

Little, C.D. "The Exclusionary Rule of Evidence as a Means of Enforcing Fourth Amendment Morality on Police." *Ind Legal F* 3 (Spring 1970): 375-412.

Little, R.K. "Protecting Privacy Under the Fourth Amendment." *Yale L J* 91 (December 1981): 313-43.

Loewy, A.H. "Protecting Citizens from Cops and Crooks: An Assessment of the Supreme Court's Interpretation of the Fourth Amendment During the 1982 Term." *NCL Rev* 62 (January 1984): 329-56.

Lowenthal, M.A. "Evaluating the Exclusionary Rule in Search & Seizure." *Mo KC L Rev* 49 (1980): 24-40.

Maki, L.J. "General Principles of Human Rights Law Recognized by All Nations: Freedom from Arbitrary Arrest and Detention." *Cal W L Rev* 10 (Spring 1980): 272-313.

Mascolo, E.G. "Staleness of Probable Cause in Affidavits for Search Warrants: Resolving the Issue of Timeliness." *Conn Bar J* 43 (June 1969): 189-219.

Mendelson, A. "Arrest for Minor Traffic Offenses." *Crim L Bull* 19 (November-December 1983): 501-12.

Mertens, W.J., and S. Wasserstrom. "The Good Faith Exception to the Exclusionary Rule: Deregulating the Police and Derailing the Law." *Geo L J* 70 (December 1981): 365-463.

Miles, J.G. "From Terry to Mimms: The Unacknowledged Erosion of Fourth Amendment Protections Surrounding Police-Citizen Confrontations." *Am Crim L Rev* 16 (Fall 1978): 127-60.

Miller, D.A. "Mandatory Urinalysis Testing and the Primary Rights of Subject Employees: Toward a General Rule of Legality Under the Fourth Amendment." *U Pitt L Rev* 48 (1986): 201.

Moylan, C.E. "Hearsay and Probable Cause: An Aguilar & Spinelli Primer." *Mercer L Rev* 25 (Summer 1974): 741-86.

Moylan, C.E. "*Illinois v Gates*: What It Did and Did Not Do." *Crim L Bull* 20 (March-April 1984): 93-123.

Moylan, C.E. "The Plain View Doctrine: Unexpected Child of the Great 'Search Incident' Geography Battle." *Mercer L Rev 26 (1975): 1047-1101.*

Nestlerode, Jana. "Re-Righting the Right to Privacy: The Supreme Court and the Constitutional Right to Privacy in Criminal Law." 41 *Clev St L Rev* 59 (1993).

Note. "An Analysis of the Preponderance Standard for the Inevitable Discovery Exception." *Iowa L Rev* 70 (July 1985): 1369-83.

Note. "Brown to Payton to Harris: A Fourth Amendment Double Play by the Supreme Court." 43 *Case WR L Rev* 253 (Fall 1992).

Note. "California v. Acevedo and the Shrinking Fourth Amendment." 21 *Capital L Rev* 707 (Spring 1992).

Note. "Criminal Law Search & Seizure: Fourth Amendment Limitations on Warrantless Entries to Arrest." *Mo L Rev* 46 (Spring 1981): 423-39.

Note. "The Fleeing Felon Rule." *St Louis U L J* 30 (October 1986): 1259-77.

Note. "Informants' Tips and Probable Cause: the Demise of *Aguilar-Spinelli.*" *Wash L Rev* 59 (July 1984): 635-51.

Note. *Michigan Department of State Police v. Sitz*: "A Sobering New Development for Fourth Amendment Rights." 20 *Capital L Rev* 279 (Winter 1991).

Note. "The New Warrant Requirements." *U Rich L Rev* 15 (Winter 1981): 407-22.

Note. "Search & Seizure—The Erosion of the Fourth Amendment Under the Terry-Standard, Creating Suspicion in High Crime Areas"—*State v. Andrews*, 57 Ohio St.3d 86, 565 N.E.2d 1271 (1991), *cert denied*, 111 S.Ct. 2833 (interim ed. 1991). 16 *Dayton L Rev* 717 (Spring 1991).

Note. "Search & Seizure—The Exigent Circumstances Exception to the Fourth Amendment Warrant Requirement for Home Arrests: The Key to the Castle." *NM L Rev* 13 (Spring 1983): 511-25.

Note. "Search & Seizure—Home Arrest—A Warrantless Home Arrest in the Absence of Exigent Circumstances Violates the Fourth Amendment." *S Ill LJ* (1981): 101-15.

Note. "Search & Seizure—The Princess and the 'Rock': Minnesota Declines to Extend 'Plain View' to 'Plain Feel.' " 18 *Dayton L Rev* 539 (Winter 1993).

Note. "The Search for the Fourth Amendment Seizure: It Won't Be Found on a Bus:" Florida v. Bostick. 25 *Akron L Rev* 457 (Fall 1991).

Note. "Search of the Newsroom: The Battle for a Reporter's Privilege Moves to New Ground." *Mo L Rev* 44 (Spring 1979): 297-318.

Note. "Supreme Court Reaffirms *Mincey v Arizona*, Rejects Warrantless Murder Scene Searches." *Search & Seizure L Rep* 12 (February 1985): 108.

Note. "The U.S. Supreme Court Adopts 'Apparent Authority' Test to Validate Unauthorized Third Party Consent to Warrantless Search of Private Premises in *Illinois v. Rodriguez*. 20 *Capital L Rev* 301 (Winter 1991).

Note. "United States v. Knox: The Sixth Circuit Expands the Scope of Investigatory Detention." 21 *Tol L Rev* 241 (Fall 1989).

Note. "Walking the Constitutional Beat: Fourth Amendment Implications of Police Use of Saturation Patrols and Roadblocks." 54 *Ohio St L J* 497 (1993).

Peebles, T.H. "The Uninvited Canine Nose and the Right to Privacy: Some Thoughts on Katz and Dogs." *Ga L Rev* 11 (Fall 1976): 75-104.

Poppel, M. "Scope of the Fourth Amendment—Arrest—Search Warrants (12th Annual Review of Criminal Procedure, 1981-1982)." *Geo L J* 71 (December 1982): 342-69.

Pyle, John S. and Gold, Gerald S. "The Fourth Amendment: A Right in Search of a Remedy." 62 *Clev Bar J* 210 (April 1991).

Quintana, M.A. "The Erosion of the Fourth Amendment Exclusionary Rule." *How L J* 17 (1973): 805-22.

Rogers, L.J. "The Drunk-Driving Roadblock: Random Seizure or Minimal Intrusion." *Crim L Bull* 21 (May-June 1985): 197-216.

Rudstein, D.S. "The Search of an Automobile Incident to an Arrest: An Analysis of *New York v Belton*." *Marq L Rev* 67 (Winter 1984): 205-61.

Saltzburg, S. "Standards of Proof and Preliminary Questions of Fact." *Stan L Rev* 27 (1975): 271-305.

Schlag, P.J. "Assaults on the Exclusionary Rule: Good Faith Limitations and Damage Remedies." *J Crim L* 73 (Fall 1982): 875-915.

Schnapper, E. "Unreasonable Searches and Seizures of Papers." *Va L Rev* 71 (September 1985): 869-931.

Schwartz, H. "Stop & Frisk (A Case Study of Judicial Control of the Police)." *J Crim L C & P S* 58 (1967): 433-64.

Sherman, L.W. "Enforcement Workshops: Traffic Stops and Police Officers Authority: A Comment on Pennsylvania v Mimms." *Crim L Bull* 14 (July-August 1978): 343-46.

Sherry, R.J. "Warrantless Entries to Arrest Suspects in the Homes of Third Parties after Payton v NY." *Am J Crim L* 9 (March 1981): 51-87.

Stewart, P. "The Road to Mapp v Ohio and Beyond: The Origin, Development, and Future of the Exclusionary Rule in Search and Seizure Cases." *Colum L Rev* 83 (October 1983): 1365-1404.

Sunderland, L.V. "Liberals, Conservatives, and the Exclusionary Rule." *J Crim L* 71 (Winter 1980): 343-77.

Thomas, G.C. "The Poisoned Fruit of Pretrial Detention." *NYU L Rev* 61 (June 1986): 413-61.

Thompson, G.R. "Unconstitutional Search and Seizure and the Myth of Harmless Error." *Notre Dame Law* 42 (1967): 457-64.

Wald, P.M. "The Unreasonable Reasonableness Test for Fourth Amendment Search." *Crim Just Ethics* 4 (Winter/Spring 1985): 2-6.

Wallack, R. "Belton, Robbins, and Ross: Search and Seizure in Automobiles Revisited." *Wayne L Rev* 29 (Fall 1982): 241-65.

Wasserstrom, S.J. "The Incredible Shrinking Fourth Amendment." *Am Crim L Rev* 21 (Winter 1984): 257-401.

Wasserstrom, S.J., and W.J. Mertens. "The Exclusionary Rule on One Scaffold: But Was It a Fair Trial?" *Am Crim L Rev* 22 (Fall 1984): 85-179.

Watson, G.A. "Fourth Amendment—Balancing the Interests in Third Party Home Arrests." *J Crim L* 72 (Winter 1981): 1263-75.

Waun, T. "Criminal Procedure Search and Seizure—Absent Exigent Circumstances, a Warrantless, Nonconsensual Entry into a Suspect's Home to Make an Arrest Violates the Fourth Amendment." *Det J Urb L* 58 (Spring 1981): 545-59.

Weinreb, L.L. "Generalities of the Fourth Amendment." *Chi L Rev* 42 (1974): 47-85.

White, J.B. "Forgotten Points in the 'Exclusionary Rule' Debate." *Mich L Rev* 87 (April 1983): 1273-84.

Wilkey, M.R. "A Call for Alternatives to the Exclusionary Rule." *Judicature* 62 (February 1979): 351-56.

Wilkey, M.R. "The Exclusionary Rule: Why Suppress Valid Evidence?" *Judicature* 62 (November 1978): 214-32.

Williams, E.B. "The Wiretapping-Eavesdropping Problem: A Defense Counsel's View." *Minn L Rev* 44 (April 1960): 855-940.

Williamson, R.A. "The Dimensions of Seizure: The Concepts of 'Stop' and 'Arrest.' " *Ohio St L J* 43 (Fall 1982): 717-818.

Wilson, J.V., and G.M. Alprin. "Controlling Police Conduct: Alternatives to the Exclusionary Rule." *Law & Contemp Probs* 36 (1971): 488-99.

Wilson, V. "Warrantless Automobile Search: Exception without Justification." *Hastings L J* 32 (September 1980): 127-62.

Wingo, H. "Growing Disillusionment with the Exclusionary Rule." *SW L J* 25 (1973): 573-93.

Wiseman, C.M. "The 'Reasonableness' of the Investigative Detention: An 'Ad Hoc' Constitutional Test." *Marq L Rev* 67 (Summer 1984): 641-72.

Wollin, David A. "Policing the Police: Should Miranda Violations Bear Fruit?" 53 *Ohio St L J* 805 (1992).

Wright, J. "Hijacking Risks and Airport Frisks." *Crim L Bull* 9 (1973): 491-517.

LINEUPS

Books

Sobel, N. *Eye-Witness Identification: Legal and Practical Problems.* New York: Clark Boardman Co., 1972.

Wall, P.M. *Eye-Witness Identification in Criminal Cases.* Springfield, IL: C.C. Thomas, 1965.

Articles

Asselta, M.P. "The Constitutionality of Compulsory Identification Procedures on Less than Probable Cause: Reassessing the Davis Dictum." *Dick L Rev* 89 (Winter 1985): 501-25.

Brigham, J.C. "Accuracy of Eyewitness Evidence: How Do Attorneys See It?" *Fla Bar J* 55 (November 1981): 714-21.

Brigham, J. "Perspectives on the Impact of Lineup Composition, Race & Witness Confidence on Identification Accuracy." *Law & Human Behavior* 4 (Fall 1980): 315-21.

Brigham, J.C., and D. Ready. "Own-race Bias in Lineup Construction." *Law & Human Behavior* 9 (December 1985): 415-24.

Buchanan, D.R. "Enhancing Eyewitness Identification: Applied Psychology for the Law Enforcement Officers." *J Police Sci & Ad* 13 (December 1985): 303-09.

Eisenberg, H.B., and B.G. Feustel. "Pretrial Identification: An Attempt to Articulate Constitutional Criteria." *Marq L Rev* 58 (1975): 659-86.

Grano, J.D. "*Kirby, Biggers,* and *Ash*: Do Any Constitutional Safeguards Remain Against the Dangers of Convicting the Innocent?" *Mich L Rev* 72 (March 1974): 717-98.

Gross, S. "Loss of Innocence: Eyewitness Identification and Proof of Guilt." *J Leg Studies* 16 (1987): 395.

Israel, J.H. "Criminal Procedure, the Burger Court & the Legacy of the Warren Court." *Mich L Rev* 75 (April-May 1977): 1320-1425.

Johnson, S.L. "Cross-racial Identification Errors in Criminal Cases." *Cornell L Rev* 69 (June 1984): 934-87.

Jonakait, R.N. "Reliable Identification: Could the Supreme Court Tell in Manson v Brathwaite?" *Colo L Rev* 52 (Summer 1981): 511-28.

Lefcourt, G.D. "The Blank Lineup: An Aid to the Defense." *Crim L Bull* 14 (1978): 428-32.

Levine, F.J., and J.L. Tapp. "The Psychology of Criminal Identifications: The Gap from Wade to Kirby." *Pa L Rev* 121 (1973): 1079-1131.

Lindsay, R.C.L. "Confidence and Accuracy of Eyewitness Identification from Lineups." *Law & Human Behavior* 10 (September 1986): 229-39.

Lindsay, R.C.L., and G.L. Wells. "What Price Justice? Exploring the Relationship of Lineup Fairness to Identification Accuracy." *Law & Human Behavior* 4 (Fall 1980): 303-13.

Mauet, T.A. "Prior Identification in Criminal Cases: Hearsay & Confrontation Issues." *Ariz L Rev* 24 (Winter 1982): 29-59.

McGowan, C. "Constitutional Interpretation & Criminal Identification." *Wm & Mary L Rev* 12 (Winter 1970): 235-51.

Murray, D.E. "The Criminal Lineup at Home and Abroad." *Utah L Rev* (December 1966): 610-28.

Salisbury, T. "Eyewitness Identifications: A New Perspective on Old Law." *Tulsa L J* 15 (1979): 38-69.

Sanford, R. "Eyewitness Identification in Criminal Cases." *Fla Bar J* 46 (July 1972): 412-14.

Sherwood, W. "The Erosion of Constitutional Safeguards in the Area of Eyewitness Identification." *How L J* 30 (1987): 439.

Starkman, D. "Use of Eyewitness Identification Evidence in Criminal Trials." *Crim L Q* 21 (1979): 361-86.

Steele, W. "Kirby v Illinois: Counsel at Lineups." *Crim L Bull* 9 (1973): 49-58.

Strazzella, J.A. "Ineffective Identification Counsel: Cognizability under the Exclusionary Rule." *Temp L Q* 48 (Winter 1975): 241-80.

Taylor, L.E. "Reliability of Eyewitness Identification." *Trial L Q* 15 (1983): 10-17.

Uviller, R. "The Role of the Defense Lawyer at a Lineup in Light of the Wade, Gilbert & Storall Decisions." *Crim L Bull* 4 (1968): 273-96.

CONFESSIONS AND INTERROGATIONS

Articles

Caminsky, J. "Rebuttal Use of Suppressed Statements: The Limits of Miranda." *Am J Crim L* 13 (Winter 1986): 199-219.

Cline, R.Y. "Equivocal Requests for Counsel: A Balance of Competing Policy Considerations." *Cin L Rev* 55 (Winter 1987): 767-83.

Driver, E.D. "Confessions & the Social Psychology of Coercion." *Harv L Rev* 82 (1968): 42-61.

Gandara, D. "Admissibility of Confessions in Federal Prosecutions." *Geo L J* 63 (November 1974): 305-21.

Graham, K. "What Is 'Custodial Interrogation'?" *UCLA L Rev* 14 (1966): 59-134.

Herman, L. "The Supreme Court, the Attorney General, and the Good Old Days of Policy Interrogation." *Ohio St L J* 48 (1987): 733.

Hottz, L. "Miranda in a Juvenile Setting: A Child's Right to Silence." *J Crim L&C* 78 (1987): 534.

Inbau, F.E. "Common Misconceptions about Interrogations and Confessions: Questions and Answers for Prosecutors and Police." *J Natl Dist Atty Assn* 20 (Spring 1987): 5-8.

Inbau, F.E. "Over-Reaction—The Mischief of Miranda v Arizona." *J Crim L* 73 (Summer 1982): 797-810.

Kamisar, Y. "Brewer v Williams, Massiah and Miranda: What Is 'Interrogation'? When Does It Matter?" *Geo L J* 67 (1978): 1-101.

Leiken, L.S. "Police Interrogation in Colorado: The Implementation of Miranda." *Den L J* 47 (1970): 1-53.

Medalie, R.J., L. Zeitz, and P. Alexander. "Custodial Interrogation in Our Nation's Capital: The Attempt to Implement Miranda." *Mich L Rev* 66 (1968): 1347-1422.

Note. "Leading Cases, US Supreme Court 1985 Term. (Moran v Burbine)." *Harv L Rev* 100 (1986): 125.

Note. "Project, Interrogations in New Haven: the Impact of Miranda." *Yale L J* 76 (July 1967): 1519-1648.

Parry, J. "Involuntary Confessions Based on Mental Impairments." *Mental & Physical Disability L Rep* 11 (January-February 1987): 2-8.

Robinson, C.D. "Police & Prosecutor Practices & Attitudes Relating to Interrogation as Revealed by Pre- and Post-Miranda Questionnaires." *Duke L J* (June 1968): 425-524.

Rothblatt, H.B., and R.M. Pitler. "Police Interrogation: Warnings and Waivers— Where Do We Go from Here?" *Notre Dame Law* 42 (1976): 479-98.

Shapiro, M. "Fair Trial Blow: An End Run Around Miranda." *Trial* 12 (September 1976): 32-35.

Schrock, T.S., R.C. Welsh, and R. Collins. "Interrogational Rights: Reflections on Miranda v Arizona." *S Cal L Rev* 52 (1978): 1-60.

Smith, J.V. "The Threshold Question in Applying Miranda: What Constitutes Custodial Interrogation?" *SCL Rev* 25 (February 1974): 699-735.

Stone, G.R. "The Miranda Doctrine in the Burger Court." *Sup Ct Rev* (1977): 99-169.

Stuntz, W.J. "Self-Incrimination and Excuse." *Colum L Rev* 88 (1988): 1227.

Tomkovicz, J. "Standards for Invocation and Waiver of Counsel in Confession Contexts." *Iowa L Rev* 71 (1986): 975.

White, W.S. "Police Trickery in Inducing Confessions." *Pa L Rev* 127 (January 1979): 581-629.

INDEX

Cross references to another main heading are in CAPITAL LETTERS.

ACCUSED—See DEFENDANTS.

ADMINISTRATIVE SEARCHES, T Ch 16
Administrative board's authority to approve, T 16.04
Arson suspected, traditional warrant must be sought, T 16.04
Building inspections, T 16.01
Businesses, of, T 16.02, T 16.04
Defined, T 16.01
Desk searches by public employers, T 16.05(C)
Dormitory rooms, T 16.05(B)
Drug testing of public employees, T 16.05(D)
Housing inspections, T 16.01
Inspector, requirements, T 16.03, T 16.04
Intrusion on privacy, as, T 16.01
Locker inspections, T 16.05(B)
Notice requirements, T 16.04
Probationer's home, of, T 16.05(E)
Public employer searching employees' desks, T 16.05(C)
Reasonableness standard, T 16.03
   Drug testing of public employees, T 16.05(D)
   Student searches, T 16.05(B)
Regulated businesses, T 16.02, T 16.04
Request for warrant, T 16.03, T 16.04
Schools, T 16.05(B)
Special circumstances searches, T 16.05
State standards of review, T 16.04
Students
   Particular student searched, reasonableness, T 16.05(B)
   Property of, T 16.05(B)
Warrantless searches, T 16.03, T 16.04
Warrants, T 16.03, T 16.04

ADMISSIBILITY OF EVIDENCE—See also particular subject concerned.
Exclusionary rule—See EXCLUSIONARY RULE.
Fruit of the poisonous tree—See FRUIT OF THE POISONOUS TREE.

ADMISSIONS—See CONFESSIONS.

AFFIDAVITS
Arrests, for, T 6.02
Search warrant, for—See SEARCH WARRANTS.

"AGUILAR" TEST, T 3.05(D)

ALCOHOL TESTING STANDARDS
Failure to meet, exclusion of results, T 2.03

APPEALS
Notice
   Suppression motion ruling, T 18.06
Suppression motion ruling, from, T 18.06

APPEARANCE
Arrest, following, T 5.05, T 7.06
Summons—See SUMMONS.

ARRESTS, T Ch 4
Amount of force used as factor distinguishing stop from arrest, T 14.05
Appearance following, T 5.05, T 7.06
Authority to arrest as component of, T 4.02
Behavior of police, effect on determination as "stop" or "arrest", T 4.02
Citation in lieu of, T 5.02(C)
Citizens' arrests—See CITIZENS' ARRESTS.
Components of, T 4.02
Deadly force, use of, T 4.03
   Constitutional limitations, T 4.03(B)
   Reasonableness standard, T 4.03(B)
   Riot dispersion, T 4.03(C)
   Self-defense, T 4.03(D)
Definitions, T 1.03, T 4.02
Detention
   Component of arrest, T 4.02
   Length of as initial factor distinguishing stop from arrest, T 14.05
Exigent circumstances justifying warrantless entry into home to effect arrest, T 5.04(A)
Felonies, deadly force used in prevention or apprehension, T 4.03(A)
Forced entry, T 7.02
"Hot pursuit," police chasing suspect into private residence; warrant unnecessary, T 5.04(A), T 10.04
Illegal—See ILLEGAL ARRESTS.
Intent to arrest, T 4.02
"Knock and announce" rule, T 7.02
Length of time of detention, effect on determination as "stop" or "arrest", T 4.02
Location of arrest to determine necessity for warrant, T 5.01
Misdemeanors
   Citation in lieu of arrest, T 5.02(C)
   Entry into home without warrant to effect, T 5.04(A)
   Release, T 7.06
   Strip search following, T 11.07

BRIEFCASES
Searching, T 11.11(D)

"BRIGHT-LINE" RULES, T 9.04(B)
"Chimel" standard diminished by, T 11.03
Motor vehicle searches, T 11.10(C)

"BUGGING"—See ELECTRONIC SURVEIL-LANCE.

BUILDING INSPECTIONS
Administrative search, as, T 16.01

BUSINESS PREMISES
Resisting unlawful entry into, privilege limited, T 7.03
Warrantless entry, T 5.04(B)
Warrantless inspection, T 16.02, T 16.04

CAPITAL OFFENSES—See FELONIES, generally.

"CHADWICK" RULE, T 11.11

"CHIMEL" CONTROL TEST
Containers, applicability, T 11.11
Limitations on search incident to arrest, T 11.03
Motor vehicle searches, applicability, T 11.10

"CHRISTIAN BURIAL SPEECH"
Right to counsel, effect, T 19.11(A)

CITATIONS
Misdemeanor, T 5.02(C)
Previous disregard of citation for same offense, arrest for minor misdemeanor permissible, T 5.02(C)
Refusal to sign, arrest for minor misdemeanor permissible, T 5.02(C)

CITIZENS' ARRESTS
Felony, requirements, T 5.02(A)
Notice to arrestee of intent to arrest and cause of arrest, prerequisite, T 5.02(A)
Resisting unlawful arrest by, standard of resistance, T 7.03

CIVIL PROCEEDINGS
Evidence illegally seized by state officials, use in federal civil proceedings, T 2.05

CLERKS OF COURTS
Arrest warrants, issuance by, T 6.03
Search warrants not to be issued by, T 8.03(A)

COLLEGES
Administrative searches, T 16.05(B)

COMPLAINTS
Answers—See DEFENSES.
Arrest warrant issued upon, T 6.02

CONFESSIONS, T Ch 19
See also SELF-INCRIMINATION.
Age of accused, factor in determining voluntariness, T 19.01(C)
Brutality to obtain, inadmissible, T 19.01(B)
Clothing withheld to obtain, inadmissible, T 19.01(C)
Coercion to obtain, inadmissible, T 19.01(B)
Education of accused, factor in determining voluntariness, T 19.01(C)
"Escobedo," effect, T 19.01(D)
Ethnic background of accused, factor in determining voluntariness, T 19.01(C)
"Focus on the suspect" standard, T 19.01(D)
Food withheld to obtain, inadmissible, T 19.01(C)
"Inherently coercive" tactics, confession rendered inadmissible, T 19.01(B)
Intelligence of accused, factor in determining voluntariness, T 19.01(C)
Interrogation after defendant's release, applicability of right to counsel, T 19.01(D)
Mental torture to obtain, inadmissible, T 19.01(B)
Miranda rule, T 19.02
Prolonged incommunicado interrogation with bright lights, inadmissible, T 19.01(C)
Racial background of accused, factor in determining voluntariness, T 19.01(C)
Reliability questionable, inadmissible, T 19.01(B)
Right to counsel, T 19.01(D)
Security guard, extracted by; Miranda warnings not required, T 2.08
Sleep withheld to obtain, inadmissible, T 19.01(C)
"Third degree" tactics censured, T 19.01(C), T 19.02
Threats to obtain, inadmissible, T 19.01(C)
Torture to obtain, inadmissible, T 19.01(B)
"Totality of the circumstances" test, T 19.01(C)
Truth serum to obtain, inadmissible, T 19.01(C)
Voluntariness test, T 19.01(C)
Water withheld to obtain, inadmissible, T 19.01(C)

CONFIDENTIAL INFORMATION—See PRIVILEGED INFORMATION.

CONSENT SEARCHES, T Ch 17
Authority claimed by police officer, consent not voluntary, T 17.02
Burden of proof, T 17.01
Consent voluntarily given, prosecution to show, T 18.04(C)
Child's consent to search of parent's property, T 13.02(C), T 17.04
Coercion, determination, T 17.02
Conditions of search can be set by individual, T 17.03
Consent to enter for questioning not consent to search, T 17.02
Countermanding of consent during search, T 17.03
Deceptively gaining entry, T 17.02
Failure to resist not valid consent, T 17.02

MIRANDA RIGHTS—*continued*
Standard booking questions, answers to; warnings
    not required, T 19.06
Time to give, T 19.03(C) to T 19.03(E)
"Totality of the circumstances" test, waiver of
    rights, T 19.09(B)
  Confessions, voluntariness of, T 19.10(C)
Traffic offenses, applicability, T 19.02
Trickery resulting in waiver of rights prohibited, T
    19.09(A)
Videotaping or recording interrogation, value, T
    19.07(B)
Voluntariness of statements, T 19.09(C), T 19.10
Voluntary statements to police, applicability, T
    19.05, T 19.06
Waiver of rights, T 19.09
  Initiation of conversation by defendant after
      right to counsel invoked, statements
      admissible only if waiver of right found,
      T 19.08(D), T 19.08(E)
  Silence, T 19.07
  Suspect's age, mental state; consideration of in
      determining voluntariness, T 19.10(C)

MISDEMEANORS
Arrests
  Citation in lieu of arrest, T 5.02(C)
  Entry into home to effect, without warrant, T
      5.04(A)
  Exigent circumstances justifying warrantless
      entry into home to effect arrest, T
      5.04(A)
  Extraterritorial warrantless arrests, T 5.02(B)
  Release after, T 7.06
  Strip search following, T 11.07
  Summons in lieu of warrant, T 6.04
  Warrantless, T 5.02(B)
Citation for minor misdemeanor, T 5.02(C)
Definitions, T 5.02(C)
Domestic violence, exception to "in presence"
    requirement for warrantless arrest, T
    5.02(B)
Drunk driving, warrantless arrest permitted
    although officer did not observe driving
    of vehicle, T 5.02(B)
Exigent circumstances justifying warrantless entry
    into home to effect arrest, T 5.04(A)
Extraterritorial warrantless arrests, T 5.02(B)
Identity, evidence of not offered; arrest for minor
    misdemeanor permissible, T 5.02(C)
"In presence" of officer requirement for arrest, T
    5.02(B)
Medical aid required, arrest for minor misde-
    meanor permissible, T 5.02(C)
Minor misdemeanors, T 5.02(C)
Miranda warnings, applicability, T 19.02
Refusal to sign citation, arrest for minor misde-
    meanor permissible, T 5.02(C)
Strip search following arrest, T 11.07
Theft offense, exception to "in presence" require-
    ment for warrantless arrest, T 5.02(B)
Traffic offenses—See TRAFFIC OFFENSES.

MISDEMEANORS—*continued*
Unable to provide for own safety, arrest for
    minor misdemeanor permissible, T
    5.02(C)
Warrantless arrests, T 5.02(B)
  Entry into home to effect, T 5.04(A)
  Exigent circumstances justifying warrantless
      entry into home to effect arrest, T
      5.04(A)
  Extraterritorial arrests, T 5.02(B)

MOTEL ROOM
Eavesdropping on, T 1.04
Privacy expectation in, T 1.04

MOTIONS
Suppression—See SUPPRESSION OF EVI-
    DENCE.

MOTOR VEHICLE SEARCHES
Automobile exception, T Ch 12
  "Belton" rule, applicability, T 12.02
  Containers and receptacles, T 12.02, T 12.03, T
      12.04
    Placed in vehicle after probable cause
        focused on container, T 12.03, T 12.04
  "Coolidge" restriction, T 12.04
  Development, T 12.02
  Diminished expectation of privacy in motor
      vehicle, T 12.02
  Exigent circumstances requirement eliminated,
      T 12.02
  Field sobriety testing, search during, T 12.04
  Government regulation of motor vehicles as
      justification of warrantless searches, T
      12.02
  Impounded cars, T 12.05, T 12.05(B)
    Delayed search, T 12.02
    Owner or driver arrested while away from
        car, impoundment illegal, T 12.05(B)
  Inventory searches, T 12.05, T 12.05(B)
    Plain view limitation, T 12.05(C)
    Standardized policy, pursuant to, T 12.05(C)
  Limitations, T 12.04
  Parked vehicles, T 12.04
  Police custody, vehicle in; warrantless search
      permitted, T 12.02
  Private property, vehicle parked on, T 12.04
  Probable cause to believe evidence of crime
      within vehicle, T 12.01(B)
  Search incident to arrest differentiated from, T
      12.01(B)
  Warrantless search scope as broad as search
      with warrant, T 9.04(D), T 12.03
Consent to search, T 17.02
  Borrower's consent, T 17.04
  Spousal consent, T 17.04
  Voluntariness after traffic stop, T 14.06(B), T
      14.06(C)